(312)

ex. 207

Harris

Criminal Justice

Criminal Justice

James A. Fagin

East Stroudsburg University of Pennsylvania

Boston ■ New York ■ San Francisco
Mexico City ■ Montreal ■ Toronto ■ London ■ Madrid ■ Munich ■ Paris
Hong Kong ■ Singapore ■ Tokyo ■ Cape Town ■ Sydney

Series Editor: Jennifer Jacobson
Senior Development Editor: Mary Ellen Lepionka
Editorial Assistant: Elizabeth Lee
Marketing Manager: Krista Groshong
Editorial-Production Administrator: Annette Joseph
Editorial-Production Service: Colophon
Text Designer: Carol Somberg
Electronic Composition: Publishers' Design and Production Services, Inc.
Composition and Prepress Buyer: Linda Cox
Manufacturing Buyer: Megan Cochran
Cover Administrator: Linda Knowles
Cover Designer: Susan Paradise

For related titles and support materials, visit our online catalog at *www.ablongman.com.*

Library of Congress Cataloging-in-Publication Data

Fagin, James A. (James Arlie)
Criminal justice / James A. Fagin.
p. cm.
Includes bibliographical references and index.
ISBN 0-321-04950-0 (alk. paper)
1. Criminal justice, Administration of—United States. I. Title.

HV9950 .F345 2002
364—dc21 2002026120

Printed in the United States of America

10 9 8 7 6 5 4 3 2 VHP 07 06 05 04 03

Photo credits:

Credits continue on page 566, which constitutes a continuation of the copyright page.

Page 1: TL & TR, AP/Wide World Photos; 1 ML, © Rhoda Sidney/The Image Works; 1 MR, © 2001 Dennis Brack/Stockphoto.com; 1 BL, © David Young-Wolff/Photo Edit; 1 BR, © A. Ramey/PhotoEdit; 3, AP/Wide World Photos; 7, © Wally McName/Corbis; 10, © Corbis Sygma; 13, AP/Wide World Photos; 18, AP/Wide World Photos; 22, AP/Wide World Photos; 24, 33, AP/Wide World Photos; 39, © Rhoda Sidney/The Image Works; 45, © 2001 Dennis Brack/Stockphoto.com; 47, AP/Wide World Photos; 51, Reuters NewMedia Inc./Corbis; 55, © David Young-Wolff/PhotoEdit; 62, © A. Ramey/PhotoEdit; 68 TL, North Wind Picture Archives; 68 TR, © Underwood & Underwood/Corbis; 68 ML, © B.W. Hoffmann/Unicorn Stock Photos; 68 MR, ©1995 Raymond/Contact Press Images; 68 BL, AP/Wide World Photos; 68 BR, Photo by POOL/Philip Kamrass/Getty Images; 71, © Corbis Sygma;

Brief Contents

Contents

chapter 8

part four

chapter 9

chapter 10

Courtroom Participants and the Trial 296

"A criminal trial is a complex event involving many participants. Many participants in a criminal trial are invisible to the public as they do their work behind the scenes. The public's perception of a criminal trial is strongly influenced by the media, as few people outside of the system have the interest and patience to observe a criminal trial."

chapter 11

Sentencing and Sanctions 332

"What happens once the defendant is convicted of a crime? What is the appropriate punishment for that crime? What is the purpose of punishment? Should perpetrators of crime suffer pain similar to what they inflicted on their victims? Are there crimes for which the death of the criminal is justified?"

List of Tables and Figures

Tables

Figures

Preface for Instructors

I believe we all agree that the criminal justice system is undergoing tremendous change, and that it is critically important that your students understand these changes. These changes will make a difference in the civil liberties they have, in their legal rights and responsibilities, in their quality of life, and in their feelings of safety and security. The dynamic, value-driven nature of the criminal justice system is a major theme of this textbook.

The criminal justice system is one of the most dynamic, powerful, and ubiquitous powers of government, touching the lives of everyone in society, not just criminals and not just those who work in the system. The idea underlying this textbook is that the criminal justice system is a complex set of relationships between citizens and government. The nation's founding principles of democracy, justice, and equality are played out in the everyday interactions of citizens and police, in the Supreme Court's power to declare certain laws and behaviors unconstitutional, and in society's responses to crime and problems such as illegal drug use, juvenile murderers, or overcrowded prisons. The criminal justice system is complex and can be difficult to understand, but also it is exciting, changing, and very important to all our lives. Every individual will have some contact with the criminal justice system during his or her lifetime.

I believe students will find this textbook informative, accessible, accurate, and interesting, and instructors will find it a great resource from which to teach. *Criminal Justice* represents a balanced viewpoint that is both critical and admiring of the American criminal justice system, its roots, and its transformations. This textbook is student oriented but provides comprehensive in-depth coverage of the criminal justice system. It discusses the impacts of historical and philosophical issues on the criminal justice system today and connects the criminal justice system with other political systems and social values. It emphasizes practical application, problem solving, and change.

Criminal Justice provides students with a complete and comprehensive overview of the criminal justice system. It describes the responsibilities of the agencies, the roles of the personnel, and the interrelationships of criminal justice to political agencies and other factors that influence the criminal justice system. It also focuses on change. Since the terrorist attacks on the World Trade Center and the Pentagon on September 11, 2001, there have been many changes in the criminal justice system and heightened interest in how and why the criminal justice system works. There is renewed interest in how the criminal justice system fits into the big picture of security and justice. This textbook emphasizes the criminal justice system as part of a complex, interrelated, and dynamic social system based on checks and balances. It does not attempt to be all-inclusive, however, recognizing that many topics—such as criminology, criminal law, juvenile justice, and corrections—are whole separate courses in the criminal justice curriculum. It also recognizes that instructors have individual preferences for the specific issues and trends in criminal justice that they wish to emphasize in their courses.

Goals of this textbook are to explain the criminal justice system to undergraduate students, to provide sufficient background knowledge for students to understand important concepts, and to prepare students for success in other criminal justice classes as well as for careers in public service. It introduces the history, influences, and related fields of knowledge that are connected to the criminal justice system. It strives to present a comprehensive, balanced, concrete description of how the criminal justice system works, why it works that way, why it is different from past systems and from systems of other cultures, and how it is influenced by scientific knowledge, social norms, and prevailing beliefs about justice. Thus, it enlightens students on the reasons behind the development and evolution of contemporary situations in the criminal justice system. For instance, it explains why the United States has a decentralized law enforcement model, why local police have difficulty responding to terrorism and international drug trafficking, why jurisdictional conflicts exist among criminal justice agencies, and why prisons are overcrowded.

Criminal Justice presents an honest look at the criminal justice system, warts and all, as opposed to superficial or uncritical presentations that gloss over the deficiencies, weaknesses, and injustices of the system. This textbook is intended to provoke critical thinking and debate. Students will want to know why certain practices are not changed, why the criminal justice system at times seems to ignore common sense, and why at times it appears to act opposite to its goal of providing "justice." At times they will question the effectiveness of a system that on one hand upholds law, and on the other hand is capable of abusing constitutional rights, ignoring scientific knowledge, and imprisoning the innocent. Thus, another purpose is to provide students with opportunities to develop critical communication skills. You will find that this textbook encourages students to dig deeper into the workings of the criminal justice system, to examine their beliefs about justice, and to assess the efficiency and effectiveness of the criminal justice system.

While comprehensive, this textbook is not an encyclopedia. It does not attempt to summarize and compartmentalize topics and provide all the information on a topic in a single place. Some topics are very complex and influence many aspects of the criminal justice system; therefore, specific aspects of these topics may be discussed in different chapters. For example, there is no separate chapter for juvenile justice as in many other textbooks; however, juvenile justice is described in several chapters. Following the discussion of the adult criminal justice system, there is a discussion and a diagram of the juvenile justice system. When adult drug courts are described, a discussion of juvenile drug courts is included. Juvenile violence and on-campus spree killings by juveniles are discussed, and juvenile boot camps are presented in the discussion on corrections. Likewise, "insanity" is a topic in the chapters on law, prosecution and defense, and sentencing. First is the question of what insanity is and whether the insane person should be held accountable for his or her actions. Second is the question of how the insanity plea should be handled during a criminal trial. Third is the question of what to do with insane defendants after conviction or acquittal. For example, public opinion polls reported that many people were convinced that Andrea Yates, the Houston woman convicted of capital murder on March 15, 2002, was mentally ill when she drowned her five children, but there was sharp disagreement as to the appropriate response of the criminal justice system. Thus, discussions of topics such as these are placed in the context of the larger criminal justice system so that the student will appreciate how they are interconnected and interdependent.

Organization

This textbook is organized into fifteen chapters in six parts. Part I has two foundational chapters on the criminal justice system and the criminal justice process, with a special focus on terrorism. Part II has two foundational chapters with historical perspectives on criminology and criminal law, plus a chapter on due process and procedural law in law enforcement. Part III has three chapters on the police. This is followed by three chapters on the court system in Part IV, and three chapters on the correctional system in Part V. These last three parts also include historical and comparative perspectives on law enforcement, the courts, and criminal sanctions. A concluding chapter in Part VI contains a survey and analysis of selected issues and trends in criminal justice.

Pedagogy

A number of pedagogical features help students comprehend and evaluate the criminal justice system. Each chapter opens with an outline, a list of learning objectives, and a relevant real-life example from today's headlines of an event in the criminal justice system. Some of the illustrated chapter-opening stories are humorous, others are serious, but all are real. It is true that a judge really did sentence a young man to listen to polka music for disturbing the peace by playing loud rock music on his car radio. While there is a certain humor to this situation, there is an underlying serious question: What is the appropriate punishment for violation of a criminal law?

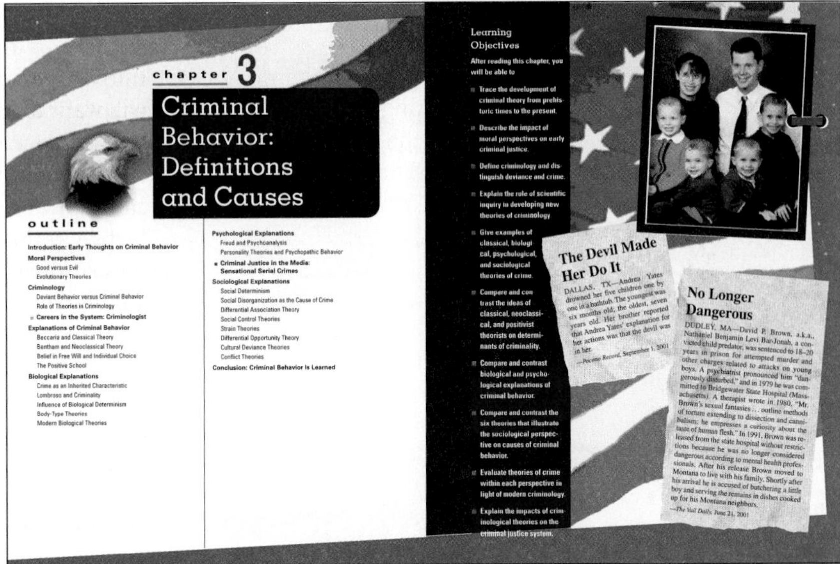

chapter 3

Criminal Behavior: Definitions and Causes

outline

Introduction: Early Thoughts on Criminal Behavior

Moral Perspectives
- Good versus Evil
- Evolutionary Theories

Criminology
- Deviant Behavior versus Criminal Behavior
- Role of Theories in Criminology

■ **Careers in the System: Criminologist**

Explanations of Criminal Behavior
- Beccaria and Classical Theory
- Bentham and Neoclassical Theory
- Belief in Free Will and Individual Choice
- The Positive School

Biological Explanations
- Crime as an Inherited Characteristic
- Lombroso and Criminality
- Influence of Biological Determinism
- Body-Type Theories
- Modern Biological Theories

Psychological Explanations
- Freud and Psychoanalysis
- Personality Theories and Psychopathic Behavior

■ **Criminal Justice in the Media: Sensational Serial Crimes**

Sociological Explanations
- Social Determinism
- Social Disorganization as the Cause of Crime
- Differential Association Theory
- Social Control Theories
- Strain Theories
- Differential Opportunity Theory
- Cultural Deviance Theories
- Conflict Theories

Conclusion: Criminal Behavior Is Learned

Learning Objectives

After reading this chapter, you will be able to

- Trace the development of criminal theory from prehistoric times to the present.
- Describe the impact of moral perspectives on early criminal justice.
- Define criminology and distinguish deviance and crime.
- Explain the role of scientific inquiry in developing new theories of criminology.
- Give examples of classical, biological, psychological, and sociological theories of crime.
- Compare and contrast the ideas of classical, neoclassical, and positivist theorists on determinants of criminality.
- Compare and contrast biological and psychological explanations of criminal behavior.
- Compare and contrast the six theories that illustrate the sociological perspective on causes of criminal behavior.
- Evaluate theories of crime within each perspective in light of modern criminology.
- Explain the impacts of criminological theories on the criminal justice system.

The Devil Made Her Do It

DALLAS, TX—Andrea Yates drowned her five children one by one in a bathtub. The youngest was six months old; the oldest, seven years old. Her brother reported that Andrea Yates' explanation for her actions was that the devil was in her.

—*Pocono Record*, September 1, 2001

No Longer Dangerous

DUDLEY, MA—David P. Brown, a.k.a., Nathaniel Benjamin Levi Bar-Jonah, a convicted child predator, was sentenced to 18–20 years in prison for attempted murder and other charges related to attacks on young boys. A psychiatrist pronounced him "dangerously disturbed," and in 1979 he was committed to Bridgewater State Hospital (Massachusetts). A therapist wrote in 1980, "Mr. Brown's sexual fantasies . . . outline methods of torture extending to dissection and cannibalism; he empresses a curiosity about the taste of human flesh." In 1991, Brown was released from the state hospital without restrictions because he was no longer considered dangerous according to mental health professionals. After his release Brown moved to Montana to live with his family. Shortly after his arrival he is accused of butchering a little boy and serving the remains in dishes cooked up for his Montana neighbors.

—*The Vail Daily*, June 21, 2001

Chapters systematically give students the opportunity to check their retention and comprehension of the material. At the beginning of each main section of text, "The Main Idea" briefly summarizes what is important to remember about that section. Then, at the end of each main section of text, "Just the Facts" (borrowed from a line made famous in Jack Webb's television show *Dragnet*) asks the student to answer interim review questions about the section of text they just read. Key terms and names to remember are bolded in the chapter narrative, defined in the margins and in a Glossary, and listed at the end of the chapter with page cross-references. Margins also contain useful stable URLs that students can access for more practical or in-depth information about the criminal justice system. These Internet sites put students in contact with local, state, federal, and international criminal justice agencies and reference materials.

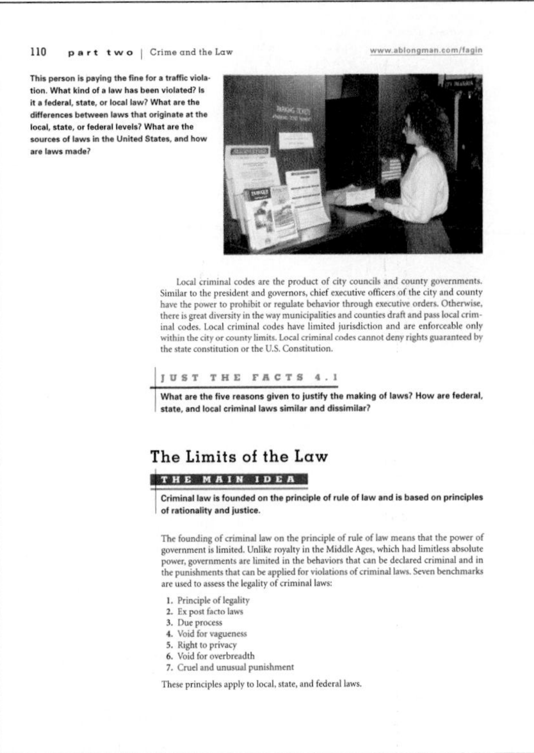

110 part two | Crime and the Law www.ablongman.com/fagin

This person is paying the fine for a traffic violation. What kind of a law has been violated? Is it a federal, state, or local law? What are the differences between laws that originate at the local, state, or federal levels? What are the sources of laws in the United States, and how are laws made?

Local criminal codes are the product of city councils and county governments. Similar to the president and governors, chief executive officers of the city and county have the power to prohibit or regulate behavior through executive orders. Otherwise, there is great diversity in the way municipalities and counties draft and pass local criminal codes. Local criminal codes have limited jurisdiction and are enforceable only within the city or county limits. Local criminal codes cannot deny rights guaranteed by the state constitution or the U.S. Constitution.

JUST THE FACTS 4.1

What are the five reasons given to justify the making of laws? How are federal, state, and local criminal laws similar and dissimilar?

The Limits of the Law

THE MAIN IDEA

Criminal law is founded on the principle of rule of law and is based on principles of rationality and justice.

The founding of criminal law on the principle of rule of law means that the power of government is limited. Unlike royalty in the Middle Ages, which had limitless absolute power, governments are limited in the behaviors that can be declared criminal and in the punishments that can be applied for violations of criminal laws. Seven benchmarks are used to assess the legality of criminal laws:

1. Principle of legality
2. Ex post facto laws
3. Due process
4. Void for vagueness
5. Right to privacy
6. Void for overbreadth
7. Cruel and unusual punishment

These principles apply to local, state, and federal laws.

Chapters close with a summary, vocabulary review, list of names and events to remember, and "Think about This" questions. "Think about This" presents provocative questions designed to stimulate critical thinking about the application of chapter concepts to real-world situations. These questions do not have "right" and "wrong" answers but are designed to generate discussion and debate about the practical outcomes or implications of important concepts in the chapter. Chapters also close with a comprehensive ContentSelect activity in which students answer specific questions based on a chapter-related journal article.

Students access and read these articles online through the online ContentSelect Research Database. The Supplements section below has more information about this valuable student research tool.

Features

In addition, boxed features in each chapter focus on providing an inside look into how the criminal justice system actually works. The five types of features are Criminal Justice in the Media, Criminal Justice in the World, Ethics in the System, Diversity in the System, and Careers in the System. Every box closes with critical thinking questions for students to answer and link to chapter content. Criminal Justice in the Media examines the influence of the mass media and entertainment media on crime, public responses to crime, and people's assumptions about the criminal justice system. Criminal Justice in the World gives interesting information about the criminal justice systems of other countries, providing a basis for comparison and contrast with the American criminal justice system. Ethics in the System raises important questions about ethical behavior in all aspects of the criminal justice system. Diversity in the System highlights how the criminal justice system both reflects and responds to American diversity in race, ethnicity, age, gender, and social class, and how sometimes the criminal justice system itself becomes a source of injustice. These features also illustrate how the criminal justice system changes in response to changing values and laws and how the criminal justice system is used as a tool to bring about equality. Careers in the System gives students an inside look at what people who work in the system do and how they feel about it, as well as practical information and advice about salaries, academic requirements, and career strategies. For example, students need to know that the FBI does not hire people without experience, that deputy sheriffs may be required to work in the jail before they can get other assignments, and that jails and prisons need many other professionals besides correctional officers.

ethics in the system

Racial Profiling in Automobile Stops

Racial profiling has created a firestorm of controversy related to the Carroll Doctrine. Before the terrorist attack on the World Trade Center, the term *ground-zero* was used to identify racial profiling in New Jersey.[18] *Racial profiling* is the term used to describe the stopping of minority motorists by police officers for alleged minor offenses or suspicion, when in reality the primary reason that motorists have been singled out is that they are persons of color. The practice is also known as "driving while black" or in the case of Hispanics, "driving while brown."[19] New Jersey became known as ground-zero because of the alleged egregious conduct of New Jersey State Police troopers.

The problem of racial profiling has been elevated to crisis level by recent public safety campaigns to encourage seat belt use and the war on drugs. In the 1990s, many states passed mandatory seat belt laws. In 1998, the National Highway Traffic Safety Administration promoted a "Buckle Up America" drive to make failure to wear seat belts a primary traffic offense in all 50 states. A *primary offense* is a violation for which the police have justification to stop a motorist. Civil rights groups quickly protested, citing widespread fears among blacks that police would use primary enforcement seat belt laws for arbitrary stops and searches.[20] The war on drugs also has contributed to charges of abuses of racial profiling. The American Civil Liberties Union claims that police officers unfairly target blacks in deciding which cars to search for drugs.[21] Critics claim that "U.S. highways have become like minefields for motorists of color, as authorities comb the roads in search of 'mules,' those smuggling narcotics—and often guns. . . ."[22]

In 1998, New Jersey state troopers became the focus of an intense investigation into abusive traffic stops based on racial profiling when state troopers John Hogan and James Kenna pulled over three black men and one Hispanic and opened fire on the unarmed men. It is alleged that the men were singled out simply because of their race and/or ethnicity. The troopers claim that the vehicle was speeding[23] and that they began shooting at the occupants of the van when the driver tried to back up over them with the vehicle. The minority community was angered when a judge dismissed the case against the two troopers.

Despite numerous long-standing complaints of racial profiling, former New Jersey Attorney General Peter

careers in the system

Qualifications for Police Work

While local, state, and federal police agencies have similar standards for employment and frequently recruit from the same pool of applicants, there are some major differences in the conditions of employment among the various agencies. While municipal police, county sheriff, and state agencies will hire people as young as 21 years old and may require only a high school diploma, many of the federal agencies have a higher age limit and require a bachelor's degree.

One of the biggest differences between federal employment and local or state employment is related to the jurisdiction of the agency. Municipal and county police officers can expect that their job will always be located within the geographical limits of the city or county. A municipal or county police officer will not be transferred from one city to another or from one county to another. In federal agencies, especially the ATF, DEA, FBI, and Secret Service, agents can expect to be transferred several times in their careers.

Most federal police agents must complete their initial training either at the FBI Training Center in Quantico, Virginia, or the Federal Training Center in Glenyco, Georgia. After completion of the training academy, the federal agent is assigned to an office according to the need of the agency. Because of the nature of the work, ATF, DEA, and FBI agents may be transferred every several years. Secret Service agents can expect frequent and sometimes extended travel, including foreign travel. If the president or other protected person travels overseas, Secret Service agents travel in advance to check the security arrangements and travel with the president or protected member during the entire trip. If staying in one place is an important consideration for the type of job one wants, the choice between a federal or local police agency is critical.

Persons interested in and qualified for law enforcement employment may also possess similar characteristics that make them desirable to the CIA or NSA. While recruitment by both agencies is by competitive examination of job-related abilities, skills, and knowledge, these agencies tend to be secretive about the actual job duties of their employees. Both agencies actively recruit from the ranks of military personnel. Other desirable characteristics for those seeking employment in the CIA or NSA are a high IQ, a good memory, foreign travel, and fluency in a foreign language.

■ **How might qualifications for employment in local, state, and federal law enforcement agencies differ?**

Supplements

We carefully designed a supplement package that supports the aims of *Criminal Justice* in order to provide both students and instructors with a wealth of support materials to ensure success in teaching and in learning. Most student supplements are available for FREE when packaged with the textbook so that students can benefit from them without incurring additional cost.

Student Resources

CASEBOOK PLUS: The *Casebook Plus* contains cases that are based either on actual events or hypothetical situations tied to each chapter of the textbook. They provide students with opportunities to apply what they are learning throughout the semester. The "Plus" in *Casebook Plus* refers to the Practice Tests and the PowerPoint Lecture Notebook that are also included in this supplement, making it a complete learning tool to help students achieve success in the course. The *Casebook Plus* is available in a ValuePack with the textbook.

ISEARCH: CRIMINAL JUSTICE: This helpful booklet explains how to do high-quality online research and how to document it properly. It also contains weblinks and activities specific to criminal justice. This booklet also contains an access code to Research Navigator™ and the ContentSelect Research Database (see below). Available FREE when packaged with the text.

RESEARCH NAVIGATOR AND CONTENTSELECT: Allyn & Bacon's new Research Navigator™ is the easiest way for students to start a research assignment or research paper. Complete with extensive help on the research process and three exclusive databases of credible and reliable source material, Research Navigator™ helps students make the most of their research time.

Research Navigator™ includes:

1. ***EBSCO's ContentSelect Academic Journal Database*** organized by subject. Each subject contains up to 100 of the leading academic journals for that discipline. Instructors and students can search the online journals by keyword, topic, or multiple topics. Articles include abstract and citation information and can be cut, pasted, emailed or saved for later use.
2. **The New York Times Search by Subject One Year Archive,** organized by subject and searchable by keyword, or multiple keywords. Instructors and students can view full-text articles written by the world's leading journalists from the *New York Times.*
3. ***Link Library,*** organized by subject, offers editorially selected "Best of the Web" sites. Link Libraries are continually scanned and kept up to date, providing the most relevant and accurate links for research assignments.

In addition, Research Navigator™ includes extensive online content that carefully walks students through the steps in the research process including: **Starting the Research Process; Evaluating Sources; Citing Sources; Internet Research;** and **Using Your Library for Research** with library guides covering 31 core subjects. Each Library Guide includes an overview of major databases and online journals, key associations and newsgroups, and suggestions for further research.

An Access Code to Research Navigator™ is *FREE* when packaged with Fagin, *Criminal Justice.* Use ISBN 0-205-38478-1 to order this package. Contact your local representative for more information. A free trial subscription is available to instructors. Visit www.ablongman.com/researchnavigator today!

CAREERS IN CRIMINAL JUSTICE, SECOND EDITION: This set of biographies of criminal justice professionals helps students and professors answer the often-asked question, "What can I do with a degree in criminal justice?" The text provides meaningful answers to a specific, targeted audience—typical students who are taking their first criminal justice course. The biographies are organized by various subfields and include discussions of what can be done with a B.A., M.A., Ph.D., or a combination of degrees. Available FREE when packaged with the text.

COMPANION WEBSITE PLUS: This dedicated website, located at www.ablongman.com/fagin, gives students the opportunity to quiz themselves on key chapter content online and to explore additional activities and resources. The CW Plus contains an online study guide, features an Interactive Timeline of terrorism and counterterrorism events of the last several decades, offers online versions of many cases from the *Casebook Plus*, and includes links to the wealth of student and instructor resources available at Criminal Justice Online, located at www.ablongman.com/criminaljustice.

STATE SUPPLEMENTS: Allyn and Bacon currently offers 11 state supplements, each a 48-page booklet with state-specific information on each state's criminal justice system. These can be packaged for FREE with *Criminal Justice*. The following states are currently available: CA, FL, IL, KY, MI, NC, NY, OH, PA, TX, and WV.

Instructor Resources

ANNOTATED INSTRUCTOR'S EDITION (AIE): The AIE contains a complete Instructor's Section featuring Chapter-at-a-Glance grids and annotations throughout the text with teaching tips and guidance on integrating supplementary materials into the course.

INSTRUCTOR'S MANUAL AND TEST BANK: This ancillary contains the complete Instructor's Section from the AIE for ease of transport as well as a complete Test Bank with over 75 questions per chapter in four different question types.

TESTGEN EQ COMPUTERIZED TESTING PROGRAM: This computerized version of the Test Bank is available with Tamarack's easy-to-use TestGen software, which lets you prepare tests for printing as well as for network and online testing. It provides full editing capability for Windows and Macintosh.

CALL-IN AND FAX TESTING: One toll-free call to our testing center will have a finished, ready-to-duplicate test on its way to you within 48 hours, via mail or fax.

DIGITAL MEDIA ARCHIVE FOR CRIMINAL JUSTICE, VERSION 2.0: Newly updated for adopters of *Criminal Justice*, this CD-ROM contains electronic images of charts, graphs, maps, tables, and figures; media elements such as video and audio clips, and related weblinks; and introductory criminal justice PowerPoint (PPT) lecture presentations. Instructors can customize pre-formatted PPT lectures or import the media assets into their own.

POWERPOINT LECTURE PRESENTATIONS: A complete set of chapter-by-chapter PowerPoint lecture presentations, containing approximately 20 slides per chapter specific to Fagin, *Criminal Justice*, is also available to qualified adopters.

TRANSPARENCIES: A set of color acetate transparencies featuring graphics from the textbook is also available for the traditional overhead projector.

VIDEOS: Qualified adopters receive one or more videos, including the Allyn and Bacon Interactive Video for Criminal Justice 2002 or "Prime Time Crime," and can also choose from a complete Video Library. Additional up-to-date news footage on hot topics is also available. Contact your Publisher's Representative for more information.

THE BLOCKBUSTER APPROACH: ***Teaching Criminal Justice and Criminology with Video,*** **Second Edition:** This supplement effectively guides the instructor on how to successfully integrate feature films into the introductory course and offers hundreds of film suggestions for the general topics covered in the course.

COURSECOMPASS: Instructors can focus on teaching the course—not on the technology—and easily create an online presence. CourseCompass combines the strength of Allyn and Bacon content with state-of-the-art technology that simplifies course management. This easy-to-use and customizable program enables instructors to tailor the content and functionality to meet their individual needs. Visit www.ablongman.com/coursecompass/ for more information.

BLACKBOARD AND WEBCT: Both of these popular online learning platforms are available for use with Fagin, *Criminal Justice*. Visit www.ablongman.com/techsolutions for more information.

CUSTOM PUBLISHING OPPORTUNITIES: Create your own customized reader with content and organization that matches your course syllabus. Select from hundreds of readings available through *Boundaries*—the Pearson Custom Publishing database in deviance, crime, and criminal justice. The anthology includes readings on the hottest topics, such as terrorism and white-collar crime, and news articles from the latest headlines, and also includes a wealth of state-specific information. You may also include your own writing, course-related information, or readings from outside sources. Contact your Publisher's Representative for more information on how easy and inexpensive it is to go Custom!

To the Student

As you read through this textbook you will notice how dynamic and ever-changing the discipline of criminal justice is. As we enter the twenty-first century, the criminal justice system and the world are characterized by rapid and far-reaching change. For example, at the turn of the twenty-first century new laws, new governmental agencies, and new powers for law enforcement and courts have changed the traditional concepts of justice and civil rights. Existing agencies such as the Federal Bureau of Investigation (FBI) have assumed new roles, and newly created agencies such as the Office of Homeland Security are evolving as government and society struggle to define their role and power.

New ways of doing things often have results, some unintended, that extend far beyond those expected. Public concern for the safety of aviation has resulted in federalization of airport security, airline pilots wanting to carry firearms, more intrusive scanning and searching of passengers and baggage, and debate regarding the merits of a national identification card. Although these actions and discussions focus on airline security, they also spill over into issues such as the infringement of civil rights, the right of privacy, and the conflict between public safety and the rights of individuals.

Criminal Justice contains examples of horrific crimes, outrageous behaviors, new technologies, new criminal justice programs, and shocking examples of innocent people caught up in the criminal justice system. However, today's news story will soon be replaced by another news story. Often the criminal justice system is confronted with new situations that require innovation and change. As a result of new policing strategies, new correctional philosophies, new drug rehabilitation programs, and new threats from domestic and international terrorism, the criminal justice system has and will continue to undergo tremendous change in your lifetime. It is important that you understand these changes, because they will affect you. They will make a difference in the civil liberties you have, in your legal rights and responsibilities, in your quality of life, and in your feelings of safety and security.

Our criminal justice system has changed over time. Did you know that at one time the prevailing scientific belief was that criminals were congenitally subhuman and should be incarcerated for life, eliminated, or sterilized? Also, our criminal justice system is very different from that used in other countries. For example, during a criminal trial in France, jurors and judges sit together to hear a case and both vote on the innocence or guilt of the defendant. Japan, however, has abandoned the routine use of the jury trial, arguing that criminal law is too complicated for a layperson to understand. The reason for these differences is that criminal justice systems reflect the values, technologies, scientific beliefs, politics, and other characteristics of a society. The dynamic, value-driven nature of the criminal justice system is a major theme of this textbook.

The purpose of this textbook is to describe the American criminal justice system as you experience it and as it operates in interrelationship with other social, governmental, and civil agencies. I want you to understand not only what happens in the criminal justice system but also why it happens, why it is different from other times and countries, why it changes, and how it affects you. This textbook does not assume that everyone in a criminal justice class wants to work in the criminal justice system.

It does assume that you need to know about it, whatever your academic major or intended career.

And you do need to know about the criminal justice system, because it is one of the most dynamic, powerful, and ubiquitous powers of government. The criminal justice system touches the lives of everyone in society, not just criminals and not just those who work in the system. The idea underlying this textbook is that the criminal justice system is a complex set of relationships between citizens and government. The nation's founding principles of democracy, justice, and equality are played out in the everyday interactions of citizens and police, in the Supreme Court's power to declare certain laws and behaviors unconstitutional, and in society's responses to crime and problems such as drug abuse, juvenile violence, and overcrowded prisons. The criminal justice system is complex and can be difficult to understand, but it is also exciting, changing, and very important to your life. I can guarantee that you—everyone—will have some contact with the criminal justice system during your lifetime.

Acknowledgments

It is said that it takes a village to raise a child and without a doubt it takes a team to bring a book like this to publication. Dozens of people have worked to make this book possible. Allyn and Bacon, a Pearson Education Company, has provided a number of very talented and dedicated people to help me, including Mark Palmer, who contributed to chapter pedagogy, and Mary Ellen Lepionka, Senior Development Editor. Mary Ellen has been a pillar of support, encouragement, and inspiration. Her editorial talent has helped me to stay focused and to keep the text consistent from chapter to chapter and interesting. On the one hand, Mary Ellen encouraged me during the long task of drafting manuscript, and on the other she challenged me. She edited the manuscript mercilessly and insisted that data be current and concepts cutting-edge. Many words, paragraphs, and pages were changed or deleted as her sage advice helped me sharpen the focus of discussions to say what I meant and mean what I said. There is no doubt that she went above and beyond the call of duty, and I am deeply indebted to her for her assistance.

This book would not have been possible without the support of Jennifer Jacobson, and I extend my gratitude to her for her assistance, support, and encouragement. Also, I would like to thank Tom Jefferies and Janice Wiggins-Clarke for their roles in bringing this book to print. I am especially thankful for Janice for her work and guidance in getting this project started.

Many reviewers took the time to make invaluable suggestions that led to the finished product you have before you now. They are

Laura Bedard, Florida State University
Charles Chastain, University of Arkansas–Little Rock
Tere Chipman, Fayetteville Technical Community College
Joel Powell Dahlquist, Moorhead University
L. Edward Day, Pennsylvania State University, Altoona
Richard H. De Lung, Wayland Baptist University
C. Randall Eastep, Brevard Community College
Richard Finn, Western Nevada Community College
Robert M. Freeman, Shippensburg University
Pamela Hart, Iowa Western Community College
G.G. Hunt, Wharton County Junior College
Michael Kane, Coastal Bend College
Charles S. Kocher, Cumberland Community College
Robert L. Marsh, Boise State University
Donna Massey, University of Tennessee, Martin
William J. Mathias, University of South Carolina
Kenneth Mentor, New Mexico State University
Bernie Meyer, University of Pittsburgh–Bradford
Robert P. Morin, California State University, Chico
Angela M. Nickoli, Ball State University
Victor Ortloff, Troy State University
Steve Owen, Radford University

Scott R. Senjo, Weber State University
Jeanette M. Sereno, California State University, Stanislaus
Gregory B. Talley, Broome Community College
Ronald Walker, Trinity Valley Community College
David Wedlick, Westchester Community College.

I extend my heartfelt thanks to the numerous colleagues who have assisted me in the preparation of this textbook. I would like to give special thanks to Dr. Dae H. Chang, a fine scholar, gentleman, and friend. I also thank the thousands of students who for more than two decades enrolled in the criminal justice classes that I taught. Their probing questions, requests for additional explanations, and interest in understanding the complexities of the criminal justice system have helped me hone my skills in explaining the criminal justice system in this textbook. My students' enthusiasm for understanding the criminal justice system is at the heart of my effort in developing this textbook. I hope it will be of fundamental value to them as they pursue their careers in criminal justice or related fields.

Finally I extend my deepest thanks and gratitude to my wife Gretchen and my children, James-Jason, Elizabeth, and Émilie to whom I have turned often for support and assistance. Their sacrifices during the many evenings that I was working on this book were remarkable, and I dedicate this book to them.

About the Author

James Fagin's diverse background lends itself beautifully to introductory textbook authorship.

Experience

HANDS-ON BACKGROUND AND EXPERIENCE IN LAW ENFORCEMENT

Jim Fagin began his law enforcement career as a police academy student and became a commissioned police officer. He has worked with numerous local, state, and federal criminal justice agencies. He was special assistant to the Carbondale Police Department (Illinois); police reserve officer for the Kansas City Police Department (Kansas); academy training officer for the Wyandotte County Sheriff's Department (Kansas); and training academy lecturer for the Leavenworth Police Department (Kansas) and the State of Hawaii Sheriff's Department. His direct real-life experience in law enforcement gives *Criminal Justice* a special relevance, authenticity, and passion.

Expertise

AN EXPERT IN AREAS OF CRIMINAL JUSTICE OF GREATEST CONTEMPORARY CONCERN

Jim Fagin is an expert and consultant on transnational terrorism, computer crime, and computer technologies in criminal justice. His other special areas of expertise include effective community policing, police recruitment, and police performance, including stress management. He has published and conducted seminars internationally in these areas. In its currency, examples, comparative insights, and practical applications, *Criminal Justice* reflects these areas of expertise.

Educator

A RECOGNIZED EDUCATOR IN THE ADMINISTRATION OF JUSTICE

Jim Fagin received his B.A. degree from the University of Nevada, Las Vegas, and his M.S. and Ph.D. from Southern Illinois University. He has taught criminal justice courses for almost 30 years and has been involved in ground-breaking off-campus criminal justice education programs for Wichita State University. The American Society of Public Administration named him "Outstanding Educator" in 1996. His interest in higher education in criminal justice began when he served as a curriculum developer for the U.S. Department of Justice Law Enforcement Assistance Administration, an organization with whom Dr. Fagin also worked to upgrade the knowledge and skills of criminal justice managers and to train police officers in computer crime and hostage negotiations. Today he is the Dean of Graduate Studies and Research at East Stroudsburg University of Pennsylvania and remains an active member of the John Howard Society and the Academy of Criminal Justice Sciences. Fagin's commitment to teaching is reflected in his new text, which features an applied and practical, student-centered framework.

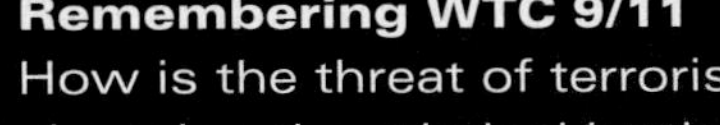

Remembering WTC 9/11
How is the threat of terrorism changing the criminal justice system?

Providing Public Service
How are careers and opportunities in criminal justice expanding?

Gathering Data on Crime
What do we really know about crime and crime prevention?

Holding Justice in the Balance
How does the criminal justice system balance crime control with due process?

Booking at Arrest
What steps in law enforcement precede a criminal court trial?

Sentencing at Trial
How does the criminal justice system screen and funnel offenders?

part one

ntroduction to Criminal Justice

Criminal justice is a social institution and a system. As a social institution, the system attempts to meet society's needs for law and order. In the United States, law and order must be won without unwarranted violations of civil liberties and civil rights. As a system, criminal justice depends on due process involving the police, the courts, and corrections at the federal, state, and local levels. Due process is provided through procedural laws with the goal of obtaining justice that is accurate, timely, fair, and humane. Criminal justice also is an academic discipline with a history, a future, and career paths for people who wish to provide public service. This service is built on definitions of crime, the gathering of crime data, and the development of criminal justice agencies and programs.

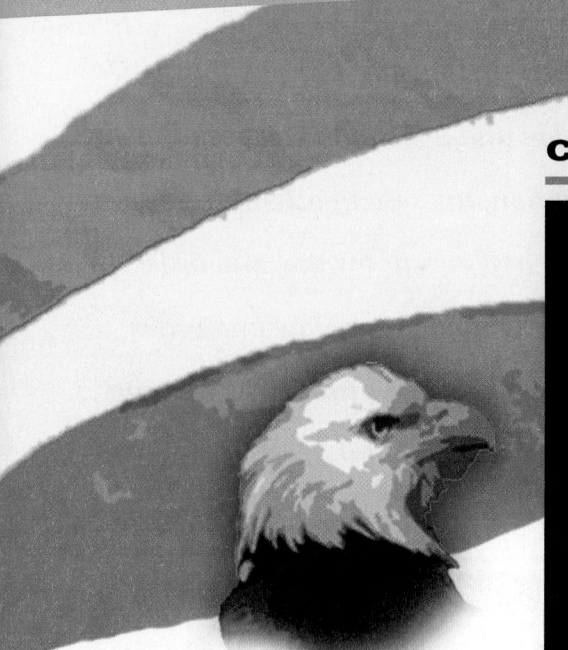

chapter 1

Criminal Justice

outline

Learning Objectives

After reading this chapter, you will know

- The three phenomena of the 1960s and 1970s that stirred interest and led to changes in the criminal justice system.
- The challenges brought on by the War on Terrorism, including challenges of safety versus freedom and how to prepare for and respond to terrorism.
- The key issues surrounding the need to balance the maintenance of order and individual rights.
- The problems in trying to define the concept of terrorism.
- The role the criminal justice system will play in the ongoing War on Terrorism.
- How the study of criminal justice became a major academic pursuit.

Turning John Jay into Terrorism U

When college recruitment fairs resumed after the September 11 attack, Alan Weidenfeld, an admissions counselor for John Jay College of Criminal Justice in New York City, found that they weren't attracting the usual handful of prospective students. Instead, they were drawing a crowd. "Students who might have looked at chemistry or biology at another college three months ago are checking out our forensic-science program," says Weidenfeld, who estimates inquiries have tripled. Those prospective students, Weidenfeld says, are influenced by patriotism, but they're also thinking about their futures. "Many of them want to know, 'Will John Jay prepare me for the FBI, Secret Service and INS?' "

"It's a new day in criminal-justice education," says college president Gerald Lynch. . . . Some ongoing classes have already undergone a mid-semester transformation. Before the attacks [on the World Trade Center in New York City and the Pentagon in Washington, DC], students taking security design discussed threats to Manhattan landmarks. Following September 11, says student Peter Linken, "We needed to have an entirely new discussion on how to prevent the unexpected." At John Jay, that discussion is hardly academic. The school counts a staggering 110 current and former students killed in the World Trade Center. Those losses, says president Lynch, fuel their determination to better equip the crime fighters of the future.

—From "Turning John Jay into Terrorism U" by Peg Tyre from *Newsweek*, November 12, 2001, p. 52.

introduction:

Fear, Terror, and the Criminal Justice System

The American criminal justice system receives the most public attention during times of crisis. A crisis can be precipitated by an unsolved horrific murder, an outrageous police scandal, a rise in the crime rate, the conviction of a person for a crime that person did not commit, rioting in the streets, or terrorist attacks. Thus, the **September 11, 2001 (WTC 9/11)** terrorist attacks on the World Trade Center and the Pentagon caused people to question the ability of the criminal justice system to defend public safety. When people fear that the informal social system cannot maintain order and security and the common good, they make greater demands on the criminal justice system to provide law and order. More than that, the September 11 terrorist attacks caused people to question the principles and practices on which the criminal justice system is based.

Fear of violence is a primary reason for crises of confidence in the criminal justice system. Justice Roscoe Pound said the cornerstone of civilization is the belief that "our fellowman will abide by the Law." He said that without the fulfillment of and belief in this presupposition, it would be impossible to maintain our society because of the "excessive energies that would be spent in preparations for self-defense, in the effort to compel obedience to the laws by force, and in the resolution of conflicts through force."[1] However, there are times when people do not abide by the law and it becomes necessary for the criminal justice system to intervene to ensure order and justice. There were two major periods in the contemporary history of the criminal justice system when fear of violence brought the criminal justice system to the forefront of public attention: the civil rights and war protests of the 1960s and 1970s and the crisis following the September 11 (2001) destruction of the World Trade Center (WTC) in New York City.

Rioting and Crime in the 1960s and 1970s

THE MAIN IDEA

Public awareness of safety issues in the 1960s made crime a government priority and led to legislation to improve the criminal justice system.

Prior to September 11, the height of crisis in public confidence in the criminal justice system to provide a safe environment occurred during the late 1960s and early 1970s. In 1968, 31 percent of Gallup survey respondents said they were afraid to walk in their own neighborhoods at night, and by the end of 1972, the number had risen to 42 percent. In 1972, according to a Gallup poll, one person in six said they did not feel safe in their own home at night.

A decade of prosperity followed the end of World War II, and crime and the criminal justice system were of little concern to the average citizen. For the most part, there were no academic departments of criminal justice at colleges and universities, because there was little interest or reward in studying the subject. Three phenomena stirred interest in the criminal justice system and led to its prominence as one of the most examined and criticized aspects of the government: (1) the civil rights movement, (2) the Vietnam War, and (3) the rising crime rate and the public's increased awareness of the pervasiveness of crime. In many respects, these three influences were interrelated and cumulative in their effect on the criminal justice system.

See http://www.crime.org for crime statistics, crime rates, information on the origin of crime data, and discussions of the accuracy of crime data. ■

Civil Rights and War Protests

Protests against institutional racism and the United States' involvement in the Vietnam War posed significant challenges to the criminal justice system. Prior to the Civil Rights Act of 1964, if citizens of color in the United States suffered racial discrimination they had no legal recourse. Businesses, hotels, restaurants, and public transportation could and did refuse service with impunity to citizens of color. For example, in 1956, the University of Alabama expelled its first black student, Autherine Lucy, on the grounds that her presence was a threat to public order. In the South, blacks were frequently the victims of lynching, violence, and denial of public and private services. In Cicero, Illinois, when Harvey Clark, a black war veteran, tried to take up residence in the all-white town, a riot ensued. The building in which Clark had intended to live was plundered while the Cicero police looked on. The rioting lasted four days; when it was over, the only persons charged with a violation of the law were an NAACP attorney, the owner of the apartment building, her lawyer, and her rental agent. They were charged with conspiracy to injure property by causing depreciation in the market selling price.[2]

When citizens, both black and white, protested racial discrimination, they were often opposed by violence—even death. In 1961, when civil rights workers attempted to desegregate the bus stations and waiting rooms, the bus in which they were traveling was fire-bombed and the demonstrators were beaten. NAACP leader Medgar Evers was murdered, and, due to the complicity of the police in the crime, it took decades to bring his killer to justice. Civil rights protesters often feared not only the violence of the mob but also that of local law enforcement. Local law enforcement defended segregation as a way of life and often brutally attacked civil rights protesters without cause.

Civil rights leader Martin Luther King, Jr. promoted the tactic of civil disobedience, which also challenged the criminal justice system. King said, "I submit that an individual who breaks a law that conscience tells him is unjust and willingly accepts the penalty by staying in jail to arouse the conscience of the community over its injustice, is in reality expressing the very highest respect for law." One of the most well-known examples of civil disobedience occurred when Rosa Parks refused to move to the rear of the bus, as required by the law, and was arrested. Although King advocated nonviolence, there were many who rioted. Rioting during the 1960s caused millions of dollars in property damage, the injury of thousands of people, and the deaths of dozens.

Political protests against U.S. involvement in the Vietnam War also generated acrimonious conflict in which the police defended the status quo and often were captured on film engaged in brutality against the protesters. On the Kent State University campus, National Guard troops opened fire on unarmed student demonstrators, killing four and injuring many more.

During this period, the crime rate continued to climb, to the point that, according to a 1965 Gallup poll, Americans viewed crime as the most serious problem in the country.[3] The ability of the police to maintain law and order was called into question, and many citizens thought the police were part of the cause, not the solution, to the rising crime rate. In one survey, citizens described the average police officer as "tense, suspicious, and overbearing" in his relationship with the public, as being likely to disregard constitutional rights, as using convenient methods without conscience, and as a man selected on the bases of political considerations or physical qualities.[4] In response to a survey of Newark citizens, black respondents selected the word *brutal* as best fitting the average police officer.[5] The **President's Commission on Law Enforcement and Administration of Justice** concluded that most people had lost confidence in the ability of the police to maintain law and order: "Many persons stayed home after dark, put iron bars on their windows, left the lights on at night, and kept a dog on the premises. Many others attended judo and karate classes, bought mace cans and tear-gas pens, carried knives or handguns, and took other drastic steps to protect themselves."[6]

The War on Crime

The criminal justice system appeared to be failing. To counter the attack of crime and social disorder, on July 25, 1965, President Lyndon Johnson declared a **War on Crime.** He authorized a series of federal presidential commissions to study crime and justice in the United States and to recommend suggested reforms to restore public confidence. A study of the criminal justice system, with an eye on reform, was a great challenge, and many people thought the task impossible. The American Bar Association declared that the criminal justice system in America was, in reality, a "nonsystem."[7]

The findings of the President's Crime Commission reported that crime was not committed by a handful of people and that the riots were not the result of a few criminal types. The Commission concluded that fear of crime had eroded the basic quality of life for many Americans. It also recognized the importance of crime prevention, as opposed to crime fighting, and the necessity of eliminating injustices in the criminal justice system. To win the war on crime, the Commission called for the development of a broad range of services in response to the crime problem, strategies to attract better quality personnel at all levels of the criminal justice system, research into the problems of crime and criminal administration, greater resources at all levels of the system, and much greater community and civil involvement.[8]

Omnibus Crime Control and Safe Streets Act of 1968

In response to recommendations of the President's Commission and demands from the public, substantial resources were added to the criminal justice system. For example, to attract better qualified personnel, the police had to increase salaries; as a result, policing costs skyrocketed in major cities.[9] To help defray these costs, local and state governments sought assistance from the federal government, whose response was to pass the Omnibus Crime Control and Safe Streets Act of 1968. This act is a watershed in criminal justice history in the United States, as it is the point of origin from which major changes in the criminal justice system were derived.

The **Omnibus Crime Control and Safe Streets Act of 1968** attempted to counter restrictions imposed on law enforcement by the United States Supreme Court by declaring that (1) confessions could be admitted in federal trials even if the accused had not been advised of their legal rights, and (2) local and state law enforcement agencies could tap telephones for brief periods without a court order. The Omnibus Act also created the **Law Enforcement Assistance Administration (LEAA)** and the Law Enforcement Educational Program (LEEP). LEAA acted as a conduit for transfer of federal funds to state and local law enforcement agencies. However, these funds were not without "strings."

The LEAA appointed the **National Commission on Criminal Justice Standards and Goals,** which had the purpose of formulating specific standards and goals for police, courts, corrections, juvenile justice, and crime prevention. To receive the generous funds available from the federal government that were dispersed by the LEAA, local and state agencies had to show that they had implemented the Commission's standards

The civil rights movement, desegregation of schools, and the antipoverty and antiwar protest era led to widespread public disorder in the late 1950s through the 1970s. How did that disorder impact the American criminal justice system? How did crime rates, law enforcement, and the courts change? What is the difference between dissent or protest and terrorism?

and goals. For example, police departments with more than 75 sworn officers could not receive federal funds unless they had an internal affairs department and an office of research. Many of the advances made within law enforcement agencies were a result of compliance with standards and goals necessary to qualify for federal funds.

The **Law Enforcement Educational Program (LEEP)** was a branch of the LEEA. The goal of LEEP was to promote education among criminal justice personnel. LEEP was directly responsible for the drastic increase in education for police officers. LEEP grants and loans paid the tuitions of criminal justice personnel (other than attorneys) and students who promised to enter criminal justice after graduation (other than as an attorney). Students could obtain any degree or take college classes at any college or university for any major other than law. The impact of this funding was significant. In 1966, there were 184 programs offering criminology or criminal justice courses. By 1978, that figure rose to over 1,000 colleges and universities offering degrees ranging from associate to doctorate levels.[10] At its peak in 1975, LEEP funded the education of 100,000 students and spent $40 million on criminal justice education.[11]

After massive amounts of federal assistance, numerous reform efforts, and the adoption of new and innovative strategies by the police, courts, and corrections, public confidence in the criminal justice system was restored and the crime rate dropped. People felt it was safe to go out in public again. Residents of large cities reported that they felt safe using public transportation. Violent crime rates for nearly all categories dropped. Local and state governments found equilibrium in funding the criminal justice system and the other needs of government. Things were looking up for public confidence in the criminal justice system until September 11, 2001 (or WTC 9/11, as the event came to be known).

JUST THE FACTS 1.1

What three phenomena of the 1960s and 1970s led to greater interest in the criminal justice system? What was the purpose of the Omnibus Crime Control and Safe Streets Act? What effect did LEAA funding have on standards and education in the criminal justice system?

The New Challenge: WTC 9/11

THE MAIN IDEA

The September 11, 2001, terrorist attacks against the United States led the federal government to expand antiterrorism policies and programs and stimulated new debates on how to balance the ideals of public safety and civil liberty.

In his address to the nation on September 20, 2001, following the September 11 attack on the World Trade Center in New York City and other acts of terror against the United States, President George Bush declared, "Freedom itself is under attack. . . . Freedom and fear are at war. . . . Whether we bring our enemies to justice or justice to our enemies, justice will be done. . . . Terror unanswered cannot only bring down buildings, it can threaten the stability of legitimate governments. . . . The only way to eliminate terrorism is to stop it, eliminate it, and destroy it where it grows."

The crisis of confidence in the 1960s and 1970s was caused by domestic strife, but the crisis in the twenty-first century was caused by a foreign attack on the United States. Just as President Johnson declared a war on crime, President Bush declared **War on Terrorism.** The loss of life in the WTC attack alone exceeded the loss of life in the attack on Pearl Harbor that precipitated the U.S. entry into World War II. However, in the case of WTC 9/11, there was no one government, no single identifiable foreign enemy on which to wage war.

In the first crisis of confidence, as you have read, President Johnson appointed a series of presidential commissions to study crime, and Congress created the LEAA and passed the Omnibus Crime Control and Safe Streets Acts of 1968. In the second crisis, President Bush appointed a new Cabinet position—Office of Homeland Defense, headed by former Pennsylvania Governor Tom Ridge, to coordinate the antiterrorism activities among federal law enforcement and intelligence agencies. As in the first crisis, the attack on the WTC led to a call for greater police powers, including expanded authorization for wiretaps, expanded powers of search and seizure, and expanded powers to detain foreign nationals. Millions, perhaps billions, of dollars will be added to the budgets of criminal justice agencies in the effort to restore public confidence, including confidence in the ability of the government to protect its citizens.

When people lose confidence, the news media demand answers: What went wrong? How can it be fixed? Will it happen again? Whose fault was it? Why did it happen? When people fear that the criminal justice system can no longer protect them, they cry for new powers to be given to the police. The war on terrorism raises new questions: (1) What shall be the balance between individual rights and the powers of the government? (2) How shall terrorism be defined and understood? (3) What shall be the role of the criminal justice system, particularly the police, and how will we know when we are winning that war?

Safety versus Freedom

Legitimate government depends on the effective operation of the criminal justice system. Citizens have granted the criminal justice system great powers, including the power of life and death. Thus, criminal justice is a much more complex endeavor than simply enforcing the law or waging a war on crime, drugs, or terrorism. When challenged with a choice between safety and liberty, people often choose safety over liberty. The war on terrorism poses one of the most serious threats since the 1960s to the balance between safety and liberty.

In the past, the United States chose to suspend civil liberties when faced with challenges to safety. Abraham Lincoln suspended the right of habeas corpus (i.e., right to a trial) during the Civil War. During World War II, 120,000 American men, women, and

criminal justice 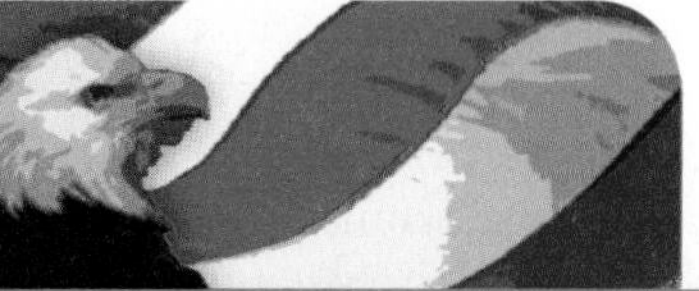 in the world

Many Choose Safety over Civil Rights

Other countries that have had to choose between safety and liberty in the fight against terrorism have chosen safety. In 1998, the Real Irish Republican Army (IRA) exploded a bomb in Omagh, Ireland, that killed 28 civilians and wounded more than 300. In response to this attack, the Dublin parliament proposed several extreme abridgements of civil liberties to enable the police and criminal justice system to counter future terrorist attacks. The new laws would (1) permit the seizure of property, including land that has been used for stockpiling bombs and other weapons; (2) allow the police to detain terrorist suspects for questioning for 72 hours, as opposed to the former limit of 48 hours; (3) deprive terrorist suspects of the right to avoid self-incrimination (under this provision, the police and courts could infer guilt when a terrorist suspect refused to answer questions); and (4) make directing an unlawful organization, training persons in the use of firearms or explosives, and withholding information concerning terrorist actions criminal offenses.[12]

As another example, when the Peruvian government faced a serious terrorist assault in the late 1990s, President Alberto K. Fujimori abandoned recently instituted democratic practices to wage war on terrorism. In April 1992, he suspended democratic institutions and ordered mass arrests of union and opposition leaders. In response to attacks by the Maoist Shining Path and other terrorist groups, President Fujimori reduced the power of the judiciary. In April 1997, when the Tupac Amaru rebels took 71 hostages at the Japanese Ambassador's residence, President Fujimori ordered commandos to storm the residence. All 14 rebels were killed, and it is reported that some were executed after they surrendered.[13]

For his actions in the war against terrorism, United States officials called President Fujimori a tyrant, and U.S. foreign aid to Peru was cut. However, the citizens of Peru supported the abridgment of civil liberties. The popular view was that human rights mandates helped the terrorists, not the victims of terrorism. Each time President Fujimori took decisive but undemocratic action against the terrorists, his public popularity rose. When he arrested union and opposition leaders, the public's approval rating rose from 53 percent to 81 percent. When he ordered the execution of the Tupac Amaru rebels, his approval rating jumped from 52 percent to 67 percent.[14] Apparently, Peruvians were not particularly upset over their president's strategy to defeat terrorists by suspending civil rights.

■ **Do you think the powers given to police in Ireland can be successful against terrorism there? Which civil liberties were suspended? Why did Peruvians think that human rights favored terrorists rather than victims? Why is public approval important in a democracy? How can police power endanger a democracy?**

children of Japanese descent were forcibly moved to detention centers because the United States was at war with Japan. Other countries also have had to choose between safety and individual freedom.

Terrorism impacts day-to-day activities that are taken for granted, such as freedom of travel. In 1997, when terrorists slaughtered 67 foreign visitors in Egypt, the U.S. State Department issued a travel warning for Egypt. Travel warnings are issued for a number of foreign countries because of threats of terrorist attacks against Americans. Terrorist threats also lead to restrictions on public access to places and things. In 1999, for instance, public tours of the U.S. missile-tracking headquarters in Colorado Springs were suspended due to fear of terrorist attacks, and public tours of the White House were suspended following WTC 9/11.[15] Waging war on terrorism also can have a chilling effect on the freedom of speech. While opinion polls report that in the wake of terrorist attacks Americans overwhelmingly support the idea of the First Amendment, these polls also report that 49 percent of Americans would support a ban on flag burning.[16] Thus, terrorism leads to a loss of freedoms.

See http://travel.state.gov for a current listing of travel warnings and security information. ■

Responses to terrorism can have a net-widening effect. If certain measures are effective in protecting against terrorism, should the public also consider adopting protective measures against other violent acts? In 1998, Delaware Governor Thomas Carper signed into law a measure requiring sex offenders to be identified as such on their driver's licenses. The driver's license of sex offenders is marked with the letter Y.[17] While this measure can be justified in the name of promoting public safety, such actions can lead us down a slippery slope. If it is okay to identify sex offenders, perhaps it could be justified that other criminals be identified in a similar fashion. Murderers, burglars, thieves, and juvenile offenders could all receive a special mark on their driver's licenses to help protect the public from harm. But where would such labeling stop?

After the September 11 attack on the WTC and the Pentagon, there were several calls to curtail civil liberties and expand police powers to prevent further terrorist attacks. Larry Ellison, the chief executive officer of Oracle, called for the adoption of a national identification card for every individual, with digitized photograph and thumbprint tied to a central database. His proposal was called a "communal necessity." Ellison argued that the only freedom that would be lost was the freedom to falsify one's legal identity. Donald Hamilton, the former adviser to the **National Commission on Terrorism,** endorsed the idea of a national identification card and added that it would be useful in other areas of law enforcement besides terrorism.[18]

After September 11, several web sites pulled information from their web pages that they thought might aid terrorists in planning attacks. The Federation of American Scientists' web site removed diagrams and photos of U.S. intelligence facilities. Maps of military installations also were removed. Details on nuclear sites abroad were deleted, and some sites stopped selling high-resolution maps of U.S. locations. The Environmental Protection Agency removed information on chemical plants and their emergency response plans.[19]

Office of Homeland Security

Taking the reigns of the newly created cabinet-level post of **Office of Homeland Security,** Director Tom Ridge, according to reporter Jerry Schwartz, "expects to take on multifaceted responsibilities in his new job, including preparing a strategic plan to defend the United States against terrorist activities, coordinating the antiterrorism work of agencies ranging from the FBI to the Coast Guard, helping states and local governments beef up emergency response networks, and finding the right balance between making Americans safe and protecting their liberties."[20] Stepping down from his job as gover-

In 2001, President George W. Bush appointed Tom Ridge to head the Office of Homeland Security, a new cabinet-level post created in the aftermath of the September 11 terrorist attacks on the United States. How is this office different from the post of National Coordinator for Security, created by President William Clinton? What other changes in government have international terrorist attacks brought about? What new counterterrorism measures have been put into place as a result of the September 11 terrorist attacks on the United States? How do these decisions reflect the importance of the changing political contexts in which the criminal justice system operates?

nor of Pennsylvania, in his farewell remarks to the Pennsylvania General Assembly, Ridge quoted Benjamin Franklin: "Those that can give up essential liberty to purchase a little temporary safety deserve neither liberty nor safety." Ridge pointed out that the definition of *essential liberties* could be found in the Bill of Rights.[21]

Accepting the position of director of the new agency, Ridge assumed responsibility for protecting almost 600,000 bridges, 170,000 water systems, more than 2,800 power plants, 190,000 miles of interstate pipelines for natural gas, 463 skyscrapers more than 500 feet tall, 20,000 miles of borders, innumerable airports and stadiums, train tracks, the food supply, schools, and industry.[22] Prior to the creation of the Office of Homeland Security, President Clinton had created the post of **National Coordinator for Security**—the first formal centralization of federal counterterrorism efforts. Richard Clarke was appointed as the first director and was named the government's first "terrorism czar."[23] Like Ridge, Clarke was charged with coordinating the more than 40 federal agencies involved in some aspect of counterterrorism. The post of National Coordinator for Security was in response to the rise in acts of domestic terrorism, such as the 1995 Oklahoma City bombing, the 1996 Olympics bombing in Atlanta, and various attacks on abortion clinics and personnel.

http://www.ciao.gov/News/EOonOfficeofHomelandSecurity.html presents the executive order establishing the Office of Homeland Security, including a complete description of its duties. ■

JUST THE FACTS 1.2

Which initiatives did President Bush take to fight the war on terrorism? Which issues of civil liberties and civil rights are involved in counterterrorism efforts? What is the job of the Office of Homeland Security?

Law and Order versus Individual Rights

THE MAIN IDEA

The rights of individuals in the United States are limited by the need to maintain social order, while the powers of government are limited by the principles stated in the U.S. Constitution.

Democratic governments promote the value of freedom but must place limits on individual freedoms. One person cannot harm another in the name of individual freedom. Actions that would cause alarm or harm are prohibited for the common good. Thus, one has freedom of speech, but the Supreme Court has ruled that this does not give one the freedom to shout "Fire" in a crowded theater, where such a false alarm could result in the harm of others.

This concept of limiting freedom for the common good is very old. For example, the Greek philosopher Aristotle argued that it was necessary that people be governed by law due to their inability to govern themselves (1) because of a tendency to react to fear and emotion rather than reason[24] and (2) because people are subject to corruption.[25] Many would argue that these are still valid reasons to justify government's right to limit individual freedom to promote the common good.

In the United States, it is argued that individual freedom is limited (1) to ensure order within society, (2) to protect citizens from one another, and (3) to promote the common welfare. Society uses several means to achieve these goals, including informal and formal sanctions. **Informal sanctions** include social norms that are enforced through the social forces of the family, school, government, and religion. These social institutions teach people what is expected for normative behavior. In addition to

informal sanctions Social norms that are enforced through the social forces of the family, school, government, and religion.

teaching normative behavior, these primary social institutions also provide punishment when people violate **social norms.** In the informal system, parents punish children for disobedience, bosses reprimand employees, teachers discipline students, and religious groups call on offenders to repent their sins.

Social order and the common welfare also are promoted through use of **formal sanctions** (such as laws) found within the criminal justice system. Frequently, the informal and formal systems of order maintenance overlap. For example, it is immoral, according to some people, to be naked in public. Also, in most places, it is *illegal* to be naked in public. According to certain religious beliefs, it is a sin for a person to be married to more than one person. The criminal justice system considers it *illegal* to be married to more than one spouse. It is considered wrong to steal or to hurt other people, and it is also *illegal* to do these things.

For the most part, people conform to the rules of society, including both formal and informal rules. However, when someone breaks the rules of society, the system responds. Formal sanctions are carried out by the criminal justice system. In the United States, the **criminal justice system** is based on the enforcement of obedience to laws by the police, the courts, and correctional institutions. When group and society norms are codified into law, government has the power to compel obedience to the rule on pain of punishment, including death.

The more homogeneous and stable the people and their belief systems, the fewer the violations of social norms. In a homogeneous, stable society with a common belief system, there is less need for reliance on a formal **system of social control** to maintain order and regulate interactions. Social control systems operate most effectively and efficiently where there is constant and unified, overt and covert, cultural and social support from all control agencies.[26] When this support is consistently reflected in all social control agencies and value systems of a society, people tend to conform, and they regulate their interactions rather than depend on external force and threats of punishment to abide by the social contract. However, contemporary American society is not characterized by a homogeneous and stable group of people with a common belief system. Rather, the United States is characterized by great diversity in race, religion, ethnicity, and values.

The criminal justice system has assumed an important central role in **order maintenance.** For the most part, people would prefer to go about their everyday business without giving much thought to the criminal justice system. When stopped by a police officer for a traffic violation, it is not uncommon for motorists to question why the officer is not spending his or her time doing serious police work instead of writing traffic tickets to "undeserving" drivers. Citizens seem to prefer an invisible criminal justice system—a criminal justice system that does not intrude into day-to-day life but devotes its time to chasing "bad guys" and leaves "ordinary" citizens alone. Nevertheless, the criminal justice system is an important part of conflict resolution, crime prevention, order maintenance, and the preservation of individual liberties.

social norms The expected normative behavior in a society.

formal sanctions Social norms enforced through the laws of the criminal justice system.

criminal justice system The enforcement, by the police, the courts, and correctional institutions, of obedience to laws.

system of social control A social system designed to maintain order and regulate interactions.

order maintenance A system of maintaining the day-to-day life of ordinary citizens, a primary goal of the criminal justice system.

The Balance between Individual Rights and the Power of Government

In *Two Treaties of Government* (1690), philosopher John Locke argued that all human beings are endowed with what he called "natural rights." These rights are given to people by a power higher than government, and people cannot be deprived of them. People give up some rights when they enter into communities and form governments. Governments exist, according to Locke, to serve individuals. People surrender certain rights with the understanding that they will receive as much, or more, in other benefits, such as safety, order, and preservation of property rights. Locke said that the purpose of government is to regulate and preserve property and to employ the force of the community in the execution of laws and in the defense of the commonwealth from foreign injury—and all of this only for the public good.[27] Locke conceded that the government must have the power of physical force to protect people and their property from the physical violations of others.[28] However, this power was to be balanced against the need to preserve individual liberty. In the nineteenth century, John Stuart Mill (1806–1873) defined liberty as "doing what one desires.... So long as we do not harm others we should be free to think, speak, act, and live as we see fit, without molestation from individuals, law, or government."

Civil Liberties and Civil Rights

John Locke's philosophies had a great influence on Thomas Jefferson when he drafted the Declaration of Independence.[29] This document declares that people have unalienable rights given to them by their Creator. These rights include life, liberty, and the pursuit of happiness. It states that government derives its power from the consent of the governed and that "whenever any form of government becomes destructive of these ends, it is the right of the people to alter or to abolish it, and to institute a new government, laying its foundation on such principles, and organizing its powers in such form, as to them shall seem most likely to effect their safety and happiness."

The Constitution of the United States of America reflected a distrust of a strong centralized government. The new government defined in the Constitution consisted of three independent branches: the executive, the legislative, and the judicial. The Constitution divided power among these three branches of government and provided checks and balances. It set up a federal court system and gave power to the states to set up court systems as they deemed appropriate. The original ten amendments, called the Bill of Rights, were added to the Constitution in 1791. The **Bill of Rights** delineated certain guaranteed freedoms of citizens, such as trial by jury, freedom of speech, and the right to be secure in one's home from unreasonable search and seizure (Figure 1.1 on page 14). Originally, the Bill of Rights applied only to actions of the federal government. However, the U.S. Supreme Court has used the due process clause of the Fourteenth Amendment to extend many of the rights to protect individuals against action by the states.[30]

Compared with today's government, the state and federal government of the late 1700s intruded only minimally into the day-to-day life of its citizens. There were no full-time municipal police, no federal or state income taxes, only two federal law enforcement agencies (U.S. Marshall's Office and Office of Postal Inspector), and few federal and state crimes defined by law. By comparison, today's government has grown in complexity and intrusiveness into the day-to-day affairs of its citizens.

In response to all of the proposals and changes resulting from the WTC and Pentagon attacks, *Chicago Tribune* columnist Clarence Page asked the question, "Do we have

These Muslim students were given police protection following the terrorist attacks of September 11, 2001. Law enforcement officials were afraid that law-abiding Muslim Americans would be blamed for terrorist acts. Many Muslim foreign nationals left the country because they were afraid that the principles on which the United States was founded—as expressed by Aristotle, John Locke, Thomas Jefferson, and John Stuart Mill—would be cast aside, and they would become victims of terror. What are those principles, and how are they reflected in the American system of criminal justice? To what extent were these students' fears justified?

to destroy civil liberties in order to save them?"[31] He argued that while many proposals emerging as a result of 9/11 were wise amendments to update the powers of the police in the face of changing technology, the important question is "How do we give our anti-espionage and counterterrorism agencies the tools they need while preserving civil liberties?"[32] For example, the government is asking for more powers in regard to detaining both legal and illegal immigrants. How will the government use this new power if it is

Figure 1.1

The Bill of Rights

Amendment I

Congress shall make no law respecting an establishment of religion, or prohibiting the free exercise thereof; or abridging the freedom of speech, or of the press; or the right of the people peaceably to assemble, and to petition the Government for a redress of grievances.

Amendment II

A well regulated Militia, being necessary to the security of a free State, the right of the people to keep and bear Arms, shall not be infringed.

Amendment III

No soldier shall, in time of peace be quartered in any house, without the consent of the Owner, nor in time of war, but in a manner to be prescribed by law.

Amendment IV

The right of the people to be secure in their persons, houses, papers, and effects, against unreasonable searches and seizures, shall not be violated, and no warrants shall issue, but upon probable cause, supported by Oath or affirmation, and particularly describing the place to be searched, and the persons or things to be seized.

Amendment V

No person shall be held to answer for a capital, or otherwise infamous crime, unless on a presentment or indictment of a Grand Jury, except in cases arising in the land or naval forces, or in the Militia, when in actual service in time of War or public danger; nor shall any person be subject for the same offence to be twice put in jeopardy of life or limb; nor shall be compelled in any criminal case to be a witness against himself, nor be deprived of life, liberty, or property, without due process of law; nor shall private property be taken for public use, without just compensation.

Amendment VI

In all criminal prosecutions, the accused shall enjoy the right to a speedy and public trial, by an impartial jury of the State and district wherein the crime shall have been committed, which district shall have been previously ascertained by law, and to be informed of the nature and cause of the accusation; to be confronted with the witnesses against him; to have compulsory process for obtaining witnesses in his favor, and to have the assistance of counsel for his defence.

Amendment VII

In Suits at common law, where the value in controversy shall exceed twenty dollars, the right of trial by jury shall be preserved, and no fact tried by a jury, shall be otherwise re-examined in any Court of the United States, than according to the rules of the common law.

Amendment VIII

Excessive bail shall not be required, nor excessive fines imposed, nor cruel and unusual punishments inflicted.

Amendment IX

The enumeration in the Constitution, of certain rights, shall not be construed to deny or disparage others retained by the people.

Amendment X

The powers not delegated to the United States by the Constitution, nor prohibited by it to the States, are reserved to the States respectively, or to the people.

The first ten amendments were passed by Congress on September 25, 1789, and were ratified on December 15, 1791.

granted? The case of Mazen Al-Najjar, former faculty member at the University of South Florida, is interesting to review in light of this request by government. Al-Najjar was detained, based on secret government evidence, and suspected of being affiliated with the terrorist group Islamic Jihad. He was jailed and held without bail from May 1997 to December 2000 without being formally charged.[33] Should the government be permitted to hold persons for more than 3 years without charging them with a crime, offering bail, or providing an opportunity to refute the evidence?

See "Criminal Justice" at www.aclu.org, the American Civil Liberties Union web site. ■

JUST THE FACTS 1.3

Why and in what ways is individual freedom limited in the United States? How do formal and informal sanctions help maintain order? What is the role of the criminal justice system in order maintenance? What rights were provided in the Constitution and in the Bill of Rights?

What Is Terrorism?

THE MAIN IDEA

Defining terrorism has been difficult, because domestic and international terrorists use acts of violence to promote political or social change, and political ideology is judged relative to one's political beliefs and desires. Different countries and different government agencies within the United States do not define *terrorism* in the same way.

The Greek philosopher Aristotle declared, "Justice is not the will of the majority or of the wealthier, but the course of action which the moral aim of the state requires."[34] Aristotle goes on to say that a citizen is someone who possesses political power. By this criterion, some United States citizens would say they are not really citizens at all. People who are deemed powerless are targeted by terrorists. A strategy of terrorism is to convince the citizens of a legitimate government that their government has rendered them powerless and that they are oppressed. **Social injustice** thus is an ally of forces of terrorism.

The history of the United States is, in part, one of social injustice. Like the criminal justice system, it reflects changing social values. The making and enforcement of laws involves a complex interaction between social institutions and social values. Prior to the Civil War, for instance, the U.S. Supreme Court ruled that slavery was a legal practice and that slaves were to be treated as property, not as persons, by the justice system. In 1954, the same institution ruled against racial segregation in public schools, despite widespread opposition to desegregation. Social values had changed during the intervening years. The Court required states to provide indigent defendants with free legal counsel and restricted the power of the police in interrogating suspects. As another example, in the 1960s, police officers denied civil rights protesters their constitutional rights, but in the 1990s, Los Angeles police officers gathered evidence to prosecute four of their own for violating the civil rights of Rodney King, a victim of police brutality.

■ Criminal Justice and Social Justice

social injustice The state in which citizens of a legitimate government are powerless and oppressed.

Ideally, criminal justice and social justice are the same, and what is legal is right. However, this is not always the case. The police, the courts, and the prisons operate in the

ethics

in the system

Foreigners on Death Row

Washington, DC (AP)—Only four of 123 foreigners who have been on America's death row in the past quarter-century were promptly told they could seek help from their consulates, death penalty watchdog groups say. Such failures violate a treaty that also helps U.S. citizens abroad.

In the latest case, Oklahoma has delayed the execution of Gerardo Valdez, a Mexican-born murderer who sat on death row for more than a decade before his consulate learned of his fate.

"We believe Mr. Valdez has to pay for what he did," said Miguel Monterubio, a Mexican Embassy spokesman. But he added: "Had we known about this, we would have had a better defense for him and we are sure that he would not have been sentenced to death."

Foreigners detained by U.S. authorities must be told "without delay" that they can seek consulate help, according to the 1963 Vienna Convention on Consular Relations. Death penalty groups say authorities often fail to tell defendants for months, even years.

At least 97 foreigners currently await execution in the United Sates, according to the Death Penalty Information Center. (See Figure 1.2)

Since 1976, at least 15 have been executed; 3 were freed after appeals or retrials and 8 had their death sentences overturned on appeal, said Amnesty International's Mark Warren, who compiles the statistics.

The treaty also protects the roughly 2,500 Americans detained abroad each year.

The United States signed the Vienna agreement mainly to protect its citizens in Eastern Europe, said international law professor John Quigley of Ohio State University.

"The United States was fairly aggressive about getting strong protections written into it," he said. "Now it's being used mostly against the United States because many other countries have implemented it to a much greater degree."

When a U.S. spy plane made an emergency landing on a Chinese island earlier this year, President Bush cited the Vienna treaty when demanding U.S. consular visits to the plane's crew.

Five months earlier, when Bush was still governor of Texas, Swedish, French, and European Union diplomats asked him to stop the execution of Miguel Flores. They argued that the Mexican-born convicted murderer, who died by injection last November, was not granted consular rights until he appealed his death sentence.

Last month, the International Court of Justice ruled that the United States violated the Vienna treaty in the case of Karl and Walter LaGrand, two German brothers executed in 1999.

The LaGrands were convicted of murdering a bank manager during a botched 1982 robbery in Arizona. A decade passed before the German consulate learned of the case.

The United States has promised better compliance. During the past three and one-half years, the State Department has overseen training programs in 34 cities and mailed more than 93,000 brochures and 400,000 pocket cards to educate police forces about the treaty and help avoid future violations.

Source: Associated Press, "Foreigners on Death Row Rarely Advised of All Rights." *Pocono Record,* July 10, 2001, p. A6.

■ **Should foreign nationals suspected of violating American laws have the same protections as U.S. citizens? Will American compliance with the Vienna Treaty increase or decrease in the aftermath of September 11? Should international terrorists be tried in an international court of justice instead of in American courts?**

terrorists People who use violence and fear in an effort to panic or punish groups, institutions, or countries that they perceive as perpetrating social injustice.

name of justice but are sometimes found wanting in the balance. Terrorist groups take advantage of the social injustice that exists within a society or between societies to justify the violent overthrow of government. Terrorism, however, is not the same as dissent. Not every group that reveals the social injustice of laws is a terrorist group. Often in the name of social justice, people violate the law or protest through civil disobedience, but nonviolent civil disobedience is not terrorism. **Terrorists** use violence and fear in an effort to panic or punish groups, institutions, or countries that they perceive as perpetrating social injustice.

Figure 1.2

Reported Foreign Nationals on Death Row

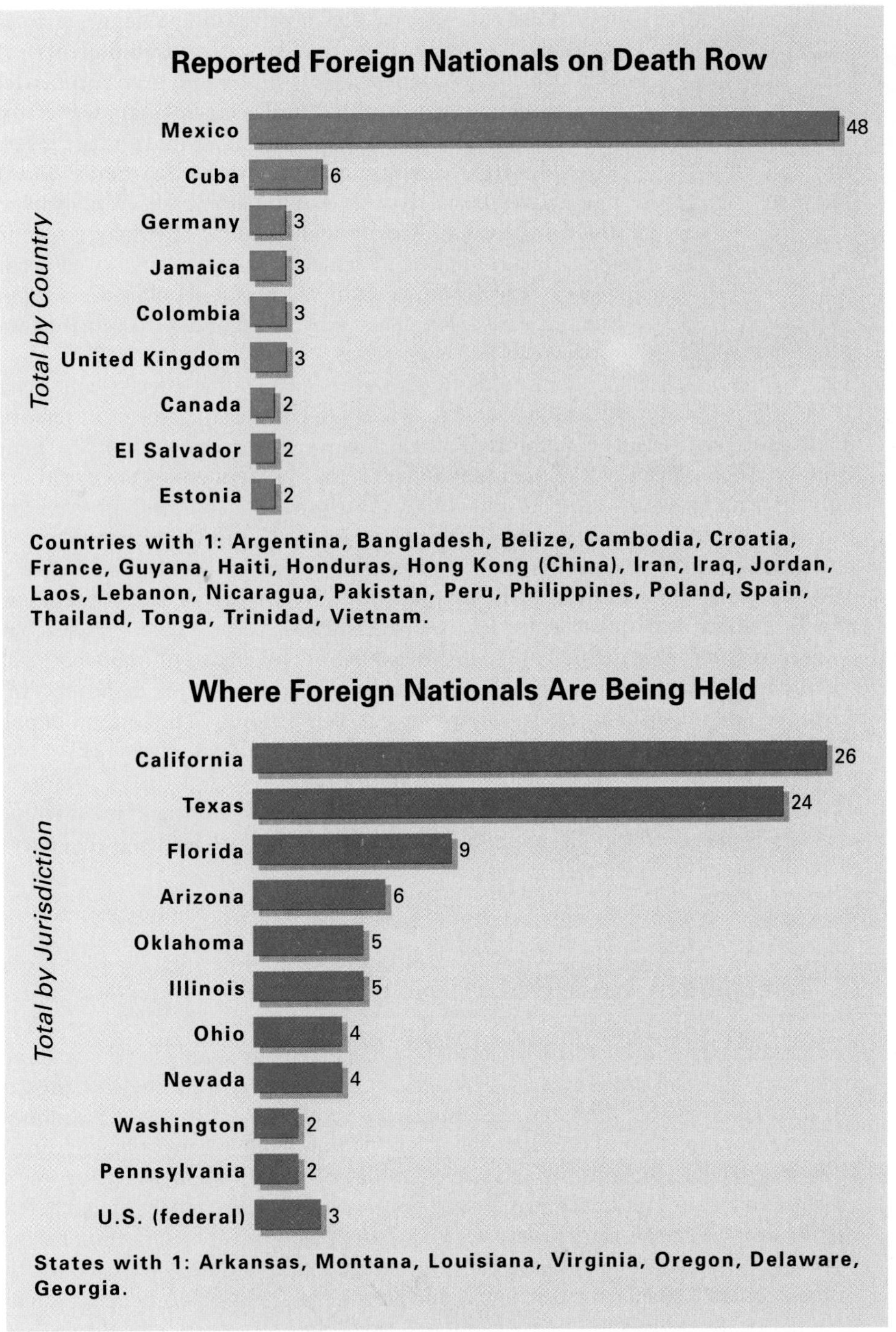

Source: "Foreigners on Death Row Rarely Advised of All Rights" reprinted with permission of The Associated Press.

The use of terror and violence by groups and individuals in pursuit of political ideology or social change is commonplace. Charles O. Jones, a presidential historian from Wisconsin, said after the September 11 attack on the WTC and the Pentagon, "People are scared.... Never before, at least not since we killed each other in the Civil War, have we had to face the possibility that military engagement will lead directly to domestic causalities."[35] White House press secretary Ari Fleischer reinforced Jones's point, referring to the fact that civilians in the United States may suffer injuries, saying that Americans need to "prepare for casualties in this war."[36]

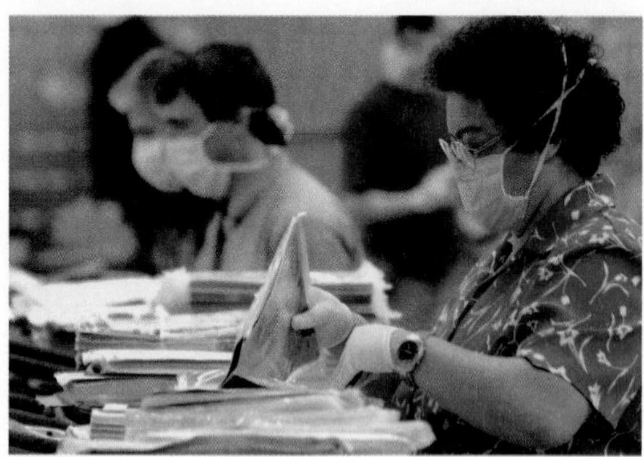

These postal inspectors hoped they were protected against anthrax spores contained in letters of unknown origin sent through the mail. Anthrax delivered through the mail or through contaminated postal centers to unsuspecting citizens caused several deaths in late 2001. This and other forms of bioterrorism are the latest threats against safety and security in the United States and other countries. Why is it difficult to treat this kind of terrorism as merely a crime? What changes and sacrifices are being made in the United States in the interest of safety and security?

Industrial nations are highly vulnerable to terrorism, including the threat of biochemical warfare, or **bioterrorism.** By October 2001, Americans were in a panic over anthrax-laced mail, initiating a costly public health crisis. Unknown terrorists had attempted to spread the disease as a white powder in letters to newspapers, television networks, and U.S. senators and representatives. Postal workers, studio staffers, and even a baby were among those exposed, though medical technology solutions were quickly applied. Pharmaceutical plants increased production of anthrax and smallpox vaccines, and public water supplies and nuclear power plants were placed under close guard against further acts of bioterrorism.

Technology has always been a double-edged sword. As new technology enables society to counter the attacks of terrorists, it also gives terrorists new methods of attack and even greater powers of destruction. Until the September 11 attacks on the WTC and the Pentagon, most terrorism in the industrial nations had occurred outside of the United States. Although Americans traveling abroad, U.S. government and military personnel, and U.S. property were frequently targets of violence, citizens within the borders of the United States had remained relatively unafraid of being victimized by terrorists. The September 11 attacks changed Americans' attitudes toward terrorism.

Terrorism can be defined as the organized use of violence to promote political or social change. It is characterized by the ruthlessness and desperate dedication of its advocates and the brutality or destructiveness of their actions.[37] The concept of political terrorism is rooted in the Reign of Terror of the French Revolution (1793–1794).[38] Maximilien Robespierre created an organization that tried to systematize murder and other lawlessness into a set of rules and political ideology.[39] Robespierre's attempt to translate violence into a political philosophy through a "Rein of Terror" is the source of the terms *terror, terrorist,* and *terrorism.*

Terrorism and Relativism

The dilemma in defining terrorism is that political ideology is judged relative to one's own political beliefs and desires. The American revolution against England, the Russian revolution against the Czar, the Hungarian revolt against the Soviet Union, the Iranian revolution against the Shah, the Solidarity union movement of Poland, and the Palestine struggle for a homeland are examples of situations in which people use violence in an attempt to achieve desired political and social change. Thus, the judgment of whether the actors were terrorists or freedom fighters cannot be made absolutely. Whether the conflict is called urban guerrilla warfare, a war of liberation, or the People's Struggle, the fact is that one person's terrorist is another person's freedom fighter. As early as 1974, Yassir Arafat, head of the Palestinian Liberation Organization (PLO), told the United Nations Assembly that the efforts of the PLO to liberate Palestinian Arabs from the Israelis are just like the efforts of American colonists to liberate themselves from the British. Arab leaders such as Muammar Qaddafi of Libya and the infamous Osama bin Laden of Saudi Arabia and Afghanistan have even accused the United States of the "highest degree of terrorism in the world." What, then, is terrorism?

Lack of consensus about what constitutes terrorism dates back to the 1937 **Geneva Convention for the Prevention and Suppression of Terrorism,** one of the first international antiterrorism efforts. The Geneva Convention, sparked by the 1934 assassination of King Alexander I of Yugoslavia in France, drafted an agreement that required the signing nations "to abstain from all action encouraging terrorist activity directed against

bioterrorism Use of biological or biochemical weapons in terrorist acts.

terrorism The organized use of violence, the aim of which is the promotion of political or social change.

diversity in the system

Freedom Fighters or Terrorists?

An example of how relative is the definition of terrorism is seen in President William Clinton's 1999 offer of clemency to 12 jailed members of a Puerto Rican nationalist group known as FALN, the Spanish-language initials for Armed Forces of National Liberation. The Puerto Rican nationalists were serving sentences for offenses related to 130 bombings in the 1970s and 1980s that killed 6 people and maimed dozens of others. Nearly all United States law enforcement agencies opposed the president's offer of clemency. The terrorist attack had targeted New York City, and the offer of clemency was strongly opposed by New York Mayor Rudolph Giuliani and Senator Daniel Patrick Moynihan. Mayor Giuliani said that Clinton had undercut his own government's efforts to combat terrorism.[40]

On the other hand, Jan Susler, the lawyer who represented the 12 members of the group, said she was "elated by the prisoners' release" and that "it was a tremendous victory and accomplishment for the Puerto Rican people and people who love justice."[41] One of the group, Edwin Cortes, told the Associated Press before he boarded a plane to San Juan, Puerto Rico, "I'm sure that we'll be received as patriots in our country, not the criminals we've been labeled as in the United States."[42] He was correct. When the members of the group arrived in San Juan, they were greeted by crowds of people waving flags and chanting nationalist hymns. One bystander remarked, "These people are not terrorists. They are heroes, and we support them 100 percent." Another said, "I'm very happy for these guys. They are a symbol of Puerto Rico."[43] Hilton Fernandez, a former member of the Macheteros guerrilla group, was critical of the parole conditions that forbade the released members from associating with convicted felons, including one another, saying the parole conditions "are for criminals."[44]

■ **What is the relationship between criminal justice and social justice? What role, if any, do you think cultural relativism or historical relativism should play in defining terrorism? Do you think there are contexts in which acts of terrorism might be justified? Do the ends ever justify the means?**

another country and to prevent the acts such activity engenders." The agreement was not ratified by the participating nations. The failure of the 1937 Geneva Convention was basically due to the same reasons that the international community today cannot come to a unanimous condemnation of terrorism, although international support for antiterrorism efforts has greatly increased since the events of September 11.

See http://www.historyplace.com/speeches/mandela.html for the speech that Nobel Peace Prize winner Nelson Mandela gave at the opening of his trial in 1964. Mandela had been accused of plotting terrorism. ■

The major obstacle to successful international antiterrorism efforts has been the difficulty of defining *terrorism*. One interpretation points to so-called economic terrorism, in which wealthier nations oppress poorer ones through economic policies and practices. In another interpretation, less developed nations typically regard international terrorism as the exclusive problem of Western industrial giants. Those nations often seek to exclude from the definition of terrorism all activities of national freedom movements and violent actions against any form of foreign rule. Less developed nations also seek to include in the definition of terrorism actions by colonialist, racist, or foreign regimes against oppressed peoples within their own countries.

Figure 1.3 on page 20 shows how the FBI's **Office of Domestic Terrorism and Counterterrorism Planning** defines *terrorism*. Domestic perpetrators of terrorism include lone offenders and extremist elements of right-wing groups. Lone offenders often are seeking revenge for individual grievances or vendettas against other citizens. Many are mentally unstable or belong to countercultures that believe in the violent overthrow of the government. Some acts of domestic terrorism are pranks designed to spread panic or force the government into an emergency response. International terrorist threats come from **state-sponsored terrorism** on the part of certain nations, such as the

state-sponsored terrorism
International terrorist threats instigated and sponsored by certain nations, such as Afghanistan under the Taliban-led government.

Figure 1.3

FBI Classification of Terrorists

Domestic Perpetrators of Terrorism

1. Lone offenders
   - Personal revenge
   - Mentally unstable
   - Government overflow
   - Prank threats
2. Extremist elements of right-wing groups

Foreign Perpetrators of Terrorism

1. State-sponsored terrorism
2. Terrorist organizations
3. Loosely affiliated extremist groups

Source: Federal Bureau of Investigation Office of Domestic Terrorism and Counterterrorism Planning.

Taliban-led government of Afghanistan; terrorist organizations, such as al Qaeda; and extremists in loosely affiliated groups.

Terrorists tend to organize into groups no larger than cells. A cell generally is composed of four to twelve highly dedicated terrorists. Members of the cells that hijacked the passenger jets that were flown into the WTC and Pentagon, for instance, were prepared to sacrifice their lives in suicide missions. Each cell was organized and managed on a need-to-know basis, and members had only the minimum necessary knowledge about other members, advance planning, or other cells. This organizational structure minimizes risks to security from infiltration or betrayal. It also makes it very difficult for government to target those responsible for terrorism.

Both domestic and international terrorists use certain tactics to achieve their goal of causing general disruption and widespread fear, though they typically do not expect this destructiveness to topple the legitimate government. On the contrary, terrorists achieve their goals through the response of the government to their acts. They count on overreaction of the government and the media. The ability to create widespread fear does not depend on military strength or strength in numbers but on the ability of the mass media to magnify terrorist actions and to broadcast this magnified image internationally. The widespread fear of anthrax exposure, which brought some businesses and mail distribution systems to a standstill in the wake of 9/11, is a prime example. As early as 1976, the National Advisory Commission on Criminal Justice Standards and Goals *Report of the Task Force on Disorders and Terrorism* concluded, "The spectacular nature of terrorist activities assures comprehensive news coverage; modern communications make each incident an international event."[45]

JUST THE FACTS 1.4

Why has terrorism been difficult to define? How do terrorists use fear to achieve their aims? How does the FBI define *terrorism*? What were the major obstacles to defining terrorism at the 1937 Geneva Convention?

Roles of the Criminal Justice System in the War on Terrorism

THE MAIN IDEA

The United States and other countries clearly are vulnerable to terrorist attacks. The criminal justice system must put improved systems into place to combat both domestic and international terrorism.

In 1998, President Clinton declared before the United Nations that terrorism is a "clear and present danger to tolerant and open societies and innocent people everywhere."[46] A study of America's ability to respond to terrorism at that time concluded that the United States has three weaknesses in responding to terrorism: (1) lack of information about terrorism, particularly domestic terrorism; (2) vulnerability of the nation's infrastructure to high-tech attacks; and (3) lack of a formal system of cooperation among the numerous federal, state, and local police departments and related agencies, particularly the inability to relay intelligence information from one agency to another.[47,48] Subsequent events confirmed these weaknesses, which the criminal justice system has a role in correcting.

Following the September 11 attack on the WTC and the Pentagon, the criminal justice system assumed new roles in the war on terrorism. Prior to the attack, the system, especially law enforcement, saw its role primarily as one of crime fighting. Politically motivated acts of violence were viewed as crimes. The police and courts responded to them as crimes. The police did not consider airline hijackers as possible freedom fighters or right-wing militant attacks as political statements. When abortion clinics were bombed or abortion clinic personnel murdered, the police investigated the incident as they would any other crime. The perpetrator was not called a domestic terrorist but a criminal. When responding to the four types of domestic terrorism defined by the Federal Bureau of Investigation, this crime-fighting approach worked pretty well on both lone offenders and extremist elements of right-wing groups. Thus, operating under the philosophy that violent acts are crimes, the police and criminal justice system effectively countered hijacking in the 1960s and 1970s and numerous assaults on society by bombers, murderers, and arsonists operating under the banner of political ideology. International terrorism, however, is more than just a crime.

Domestic Terrorism

Except in cases of aircraft hijacking, local and state police are most often the first responders when violent acts are committed. Three acts of **domestic terrorism** most often encountered by local and state police are (1) acts of violence committed by militias and extremist groups or individuals, (2) violence against abortion clinics and personnel, and (3) **ecoterrorism**—violent destruction of the environment or natural resources on which we depend, such as the water we drink or the air we breathe, including the release of disease organisms into the environment.

Numerous militia and extremist groups have adopted violence as a tactic. The Ku Klux Klan is one of the oldest domestic groups that endorses the use of violence to achieve its goals. Other extremist groups are committed to racial and ethnic segregation, such as the skinheads, neo-Nazis, the John Birch Society, and the Order of Thule. Militia movements that advocate the use of violence also include right-wing patriot groups, such as Family Farm Preservation, Posse Comitatus, and the Constitutional Party, which disagree with various practices of the legitimate government. The FBI estimates that there are about 194 militia and extreme right-wing groups. Timothy McVeigh, who was responsible for the bombing of the Alfred P. Murrah Federal Building in Oklahoma City, is the most well known individual in this category of domestic terrorism.

Violent acts against abortion clinics and their personnel have included harassment, arson, bombing, and murder. Persons who commit these acts of violence are frequently lone individuals rather than extremist groups. Eric Robert Rudolph, wanted for the 1998 bombing of an Alabama abortion clinic, is an example of a domestic terrorist in this category.

Ecoterrorist groups use tactics such as arson, mail bombs, and destructive raids on research facilities to advance their political agenda. The two most well known groups are the Earth Liberation Front (ELF) and the Animal Liberation Front (ALF). The FBI has labeled ELF as one of this country's greatest domestic terrorism threats. ELF claims to have destroyed property worth more than $37 million in its attacks.[49] ELF claimed credit for a fire at the University of Washington Horticultural Center that caused more than $2 million of damage, destroying more than 20 years of work and records.[50] ELF also claimed credit for destroying genetically altered crops at the University of Minnesota and for causing, through arson, $500,000 in damage to Agricultural Hall at Michigan State University and the destruction of all records and equipment used by the

domestic terrorism Acts of terrorism committed by citizens of the country being terrorized.

ecoterrorism Violent destruction of the environment or natural resources on which people depend.

university's Agricultural Biotechnology Support Project.[51,52] ELF's most expensive single act of terrorism was the 1998 arson of several buildings and ski lifts in Vail, Colorado, resulting in an estimated $12 million in damage.[53] ALF focuses its actions on "liberating" animals used in scientific experiments.[54]

International Terrorism

Militant groups, antiabortion extremists, and ecoterrorists have caused extensive property damage and deaths, but they have not seriously challenged the ability of the criminal justice system to respond or the confidence of the public to conduct day-to-day business in relative safety. However, international terrorism has caused an extensive examination of the role and capacity of the criminal justice system. Normally, local and state criminal justice agencies provide the lead in crime fighting, but in **international terrorism,** federal agencies assume the leadership role. For example, it was the FBI, and not state or local police, who raided homes and arrested five U.S. citizens of Yemeni descent on charges of providing material support to al Qaeda in the Buffalo, New York, area in September 2002. This shift has caused the public to reexamine the value of the decentralization deliberately built into the criminal justice system to promote the preservation of civil rights. As you have read, the new international threat of terrorism has also challenged the balance between freedom and security.

international terrorism
Acts of terrorism committed by citizens of another nation.

In October 1998, *U.S. News and World Report* described Osama bin Laden's terrorist group al Qaeda as penetrated by spies, its foot soldiers as amateurs, and an organization lacking in sophistication. Furthermore, bin Laden was said to be running out of money. A Central Intelligence Agency (CIA) official said, "Al Qaeda is not all it's cracked up to be.... Al Qaeda is not as disciplined or sophisticated as the state-sponsored terrorists that attacked America in the past, such as the Libyan-backed Palestinian organization Abu Nidal.... He [bin Laden] can't be characterized as the guy pulling the lever blowing things up everyplace."[55] In June 1999, bin Laden called for *jihad,* a holy war, against his number-one enemy, the United States. The news article announcing the call for this holy war did not make front-page news. The United States responded by offering a $5 million reward for information leading to bin Laden's arrest, and the FBI put

The U.S. invasion of Afghanistan in October 2001 after the attack on the WTC and Pentagon was followed by the search for international terrorist cells in the United States. The six suspected al Qaeda terrorists from Lackawanna, N.Y., are depicted in this artist's rendering from October 8, 2002, as they await the judge's decision in their bail hearing. It is the various law enforcement and investigative agencies of the criminal justice system, not the military, which are responsible for searching out terrorism on U.S. soil. Often the criminal justice system is not well adapted to the fight against international terrorism within the U.S. What are some of the problems of using law enforcement agencies and criminal courts to fight international terrorism? Should international terrorists in the United States have the same rights and protections as U.S. citizens?

him on its "Ten Most Wanted" list.[56] On October 7, 2001, the United States found it necessary to mount a full-scale military assault—a war—against Afghanistan, the Taliban and its allies, al Qaeda, and Osama bin Laden. Mug shots of international terrorists on the television show *America's Most Wanted* generated thousands of leads from the viewing public around the world, leading to new arrests.

The vulnerability of the United States to international terrorism dates to November 5, 1990, when New York City engineer El Sayyid Nosair walked into a room full of witnesses at the New York Marriott Hotel and shot and killed Rabbi Meir Kahane.[57] The state of New York was able to convict Nosair only for possession of an illegal firearm because of errors in evidence handling by the New York Police Department. Furthermore, no one took notice of items that turned up in a search of Nosair's apartment: instructions for building bombs; photographs of targets, including the Empire State Building and the World Trade Center; and numerous documents, which were not translated. The message to terrorists was that "back home in Egypt, suspected terrorists are dragged in and tortured. In America, they can hire a good lawyer and beat the system."[58] Since 1990, thousands of international terrorist events have been recorded.[59] Among the more serious events is the February 26, 1993, attempt to blow up the WTC by using a 1,500-pound bomb, which terrorists drove into the basement of the building. Omar Abdel-Rahman, who ran a mosque in Jersey City, New Jersey, was linked to this plot. In 1998, terrorists suspected of being directed by bin Laden bombed U.S. embassies in Kenya and Tanzania, killing 247 people. In October 2000, suicide bombers pulled alongside the destroyer *USS Cole* in the Yemeni port of Aden and blew up their small boat, which was filled with explosives, taking lives. Table 1.1 provides statistics on terrorist attacks against the United States between 1994 and 2000.

table 1.1 **Terrorism[a] in the United States and against Americans, 1994–2001**

	1994	1995	1996	1997	1998	1999	2000
Total attacks against the United States (State Dept.)	66	99	73	123	111	169	200
Total bombing attacks[b]	43	65	55	108	96	111	179
Total casualties in attacks against U.S. citizens	11	70	535[c]	27	23	11	62
Terrorist events reported by FBI	1	1	3	4[d]	5	10	—

[a]The U.S. State Department defines *terrorism* as "premeditated politically-motivated violence perpetrated against noncombatant targets by subnational groups or clandestine agents, usually intended to influence an audience. International terrorism is terrorism involving citizens or territory of more than one country" (Source: 2000, p. vi). The U.S. Department of Justice defines *terrorism* as "a violent act, or an act dangerous to human life, in violation of the criminal laws of the United States or of any State, to intimidate or coerce a government, the civilian population, or any segment thereof, in furtherance of political or social objectives" (Source: 1999, p. ii). See *Sources* (below) for full source information.

[b]Includes detonated and undetonated devices, tear gas, pipe bombs, letter bombs, and fire bombs.

[c]The bombing of the Al Khubar U.S. military housing complex near Dhahran, Saudi Arabia, on June 25, 1996, accounts for this increase. Previously, the bombing of the World Trade Center in New York City on Feb. 26, 1993, had caused 1,011 casualties. Prior to that the most deadly attack against Americans was the downing of Pan Am flight 103 in 1988, in which 189 Americans were killed.

[d]In 1997, the FBI also investigated 73 cases involving suspected use of weapons of mass destruction.

Sources: U.S. Department of State, *Patterns of Global Terrorism: 1994,* p. 67; *1995,* pp. 73–74; *1995,* pp. 73–74; *1996,* p. 74; *1997,* p. 88; *1998,* p. 96; *1999,* p. 106; *2000,* pp. 87–88 (Washington, DC: U.S. Department of State); U.S. Department of Justice, Federal Bureau of Investigation, *Terrorism in the United States, 1999;* available online at http://www.fbi.gov/publications/terror/terror99.pdf. Adapted from *Sourcebook of Criminal Justice Statistics Online;* available online at http://www.albany.edu/sourcebook/1995/pdf/t3198.pdf:_t3197.pdf:_t3195.pdf

See www.fbi.gov (the official FBI web site) for news updates, links to FBI agencies, Top Ten Most Wanted lists, and employment information. ■

In 1998, authorities questioned whether the United States was facing a new upsurge in terrorism,[60] some expressing the belief that the American law enforcement–based approach to counterterrorism is one reason groups seem to get away with terrorism.[61] In February 1999, with a change to military tactics in response to terrorism, President Clinton asserted the right to bomb government facilities in nations that provide sanctuary to international terrorists. After the September 11 attacks on the WTC and the Pentagon, the Bush government responded by declaring war on the terrorists in Afghanistan. Bush vowed that they would be "brought to justice or justice will be brought to them." But if a law enforcement approach won't work for international terrorism as it does for domestic terrorism, what will?

Counterterrorism Measures

The criminal justice system is unprepared for international terrorism on U.S. soil. American police lack the resources, training, and coordinated programs necessary to counter terrorism. The police are prepared primarily for responding after a terrorist event, as if it were a regular crime. However, local law enforcement agencies are grossly unprepared to respond adequately to terrorism or to mount a **counterterrorism** campaign. Only a few police departments have units trained to respond to terrorist attacks, and most of these focus on hostage taking. Furthermore, legislation during the 1970s and 1980s sharply restricted law enforcement's authority to gather and maintain intelligence files, one of the most effective counterterrorism measures.

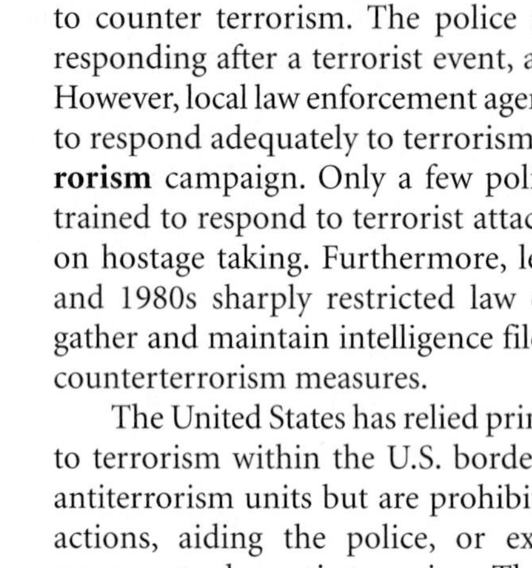

Among the many outcomes of the September 11 attack and the war on terror are new careers, such as airport security guards, who are now under the employ of the federal government. What are other outcomes affecting the law, law enforcement, the courts, and corrections? How is the war on terror affecting the field of criminal justice as an academic discipline? Trends in criminal justice as a career also include many more opportunities for women in government, law, law enforcement, protective services, the courts, juvenile justice, corrections, and criminology. When and how did criminal justice emerge as a field of study? How is the field of criminal justice changing today?

The United States has relied primarily on the FBI to respond to terrorism within the U.S. borders. The military has special antiterrorism units but are prohibited from performing police actions, aiding the police, or exercising police powers in response to domestic terrorism. The FBI has attempted to continuously upgrade its response capacity to terrorism. An International Training Section was added to the FBI training program. In 1998, the FBI opened a high-tech $20-million **Strategic Information and Operations Center (SIOC)** staffed with specially trained agents to increase its capacity to deal with multiple crises simultaneously. In 1999, Director Louis Freeh restructured the FBI to put a greater emphasis on preventing terrorism and espionage. He strengthened the predictive intelligence of the agency and tripled the budget to enhance predictive and antiterrorism capacities. In April 2000, the FBI requested $75 million in budget appropriations to expand their information technology, which would enable them to perform more sophisticated data surveillance. One request was for the power to gather information for a greater number of databases. Civil liberties activists responded by challenging that this power would erode constitutional protections of individual rights.[62]

A major flaw of counterterrorism measures in the United States is a lack of interagency cooperation and data sharing. The FBI must depend on the cooperation and effectiveness of over 40 other federal agencies involved in counterterrorism but has no authority over these agencies. Critics have identified the Immigration and Naturalization Service (INS) as a source of major deficiencies in effective intelligence gathering and preventive action. Following the September 11 attack on the WTC and the Pentagon, critics argued that if the INS had been more efficient in tracking visa holders

counterterrorism The response to terrorism and efforts to stop it.

whose names were flagged by law enforcement and intelligence agencies or whose visas had expired, they would have detained several of the people involved in the incidents.[63] A goal of the newly created cabinet-level Office of Homeland Security is to provide oversight and promote cooperation and data sharing among the various federal agencies with counterterrorism responsibilities. If successful, this effort may increase FBI effectiveness as the lead antiterrorist law enforcement agency. On October 26, 2001, President Bush signed into law the USA Patriot Act (USAPA). This legislation provides for extensive new powers to both domestic law enforcement and international intelligence agencies and eliminates checks and balances that previously enabled courts to prevent abuses of such powers. It is expected that many of the provisions of the USAPA will be challenged in the Supreme Court as they are implemented. The impacts of 9/11 on all aspects of the criminal justice system, such as law, the courts, and corrections, are discussed in other chapters.

JUST THE FACTS 1.5

What are some examples of domestic and international terrorism, and what counterterrorism measures are in place? What flaws in the current system of gathering intelligence were exposed by the 9/11 attacks?

Criminal Justice as an Academic Discipline

THE MAIN IDEA

The field of criminal justice has evolved into a major academic discipline, which has benefited law enforcement and related fields by having better-trained people for careers in criminal justice.

The War on Terror has led to a resurgence of interest in careers in criminal justice. The War on Terror has even created new kinds of careers in criminal justice and in protective services (such as sky marshal). Increased airport security, intelligence work, and Internet surveillance, it is hoped, will help prevent the events that made the disasters of September 11 possible.

The presence of academic departments dedicated to the study of criminal justice is a relatively new phenomenon. The study of criminal behavior can be traced to the earliest origins of civilization, but it was not until the mid-nineteenth century that a word was coined to describe this endeavor. In 1855, Italian law professor Raffaele Garofalo coined the term *criminologia*—the study of crime. In 1887, French anthropologist Paul Topinard used *criminologie* to refer to any scientific concern with the phenomenon of crime.

The American sociologist Edwin Sutherland provided a definition of criminology that is widely used when referring to the study of crime by the various academic disciplines. He described **criminology** as "the body of knowledge regarding crime as a social phenomenon. It includes within its scope the process of making laws, of breaking laws, and of reacting toward the breaking of laws.... The objective of criminology is the development of a body of general and verified principles and of other types of knowledge regarding this process of law, crime, and treatment or prevention."

Criminology is different from the study of the criminal justice system. **Criminal justice** usually refers to the study of the processes involved in a system of justice, the people who perform these tasks, the scope and nature of the system, and public policy, laws, and regulations that shape the administration and outcomes of a criminal justice system. Criminology often includes the study of the criminal justice system, but the criminologist may focus more on theoretical investigations, such as who breaks the law,

criminology The body of knowledge regarding crime as a social phenomenon and as a behavior.

criminal justice The study of the processes and people involved in a system of justice and the public policies, laws, and procedures that shape the administration and outcomes of those processes.

See http://www.acjs.org/ (the Academy of Criminal Justice Sciences web site) for a section on scholarships and awards. ■

why do people break the law, why do people not break the law, what motivates law breaking, and what discourages law breaking.

Criminology can be included in the study of criminal justice. Because the academic discipline of sociology preceded that of criminal justice, the sociology departments of many colleges and universities offer criminology classes, even when the institution has a criminal justice major. It is not uncommon for sociology departments to distinguish between the study of criminology and the study of criminal justice. These two fields of study have separate professional organizations. Sociology professors often prefer membership in the **American Society of Criminology (ASC),** whereas, many criminal justice professors prefer membership in the **Academy of Criminal Justice Sciences (ACJS).** However, many different scientific, professional, and academic disciplines contribute to the study of criminal justice, and these include biology, chemistry, criminology, forensics, law, medical science, neurology, political science, psychiatry, psychology, public administration, and sociology.

Criminology tends to focus on the development of principles, concepts, and theories, while criminal justice tends to focus on the processes of the criminal justice system. Criminology tends to focus on research, while criminal justice tends to focus on real-life application, public policy, decision making, and career development. The fields of both criminology and criminal justice are eclectic disciplines that borrow research and theories from many related disciplines. Some of the earliest criminologists were medical doctors and psychiatrists, while many influential criminologists of the twentieth century were sociologists.

Criminal Justice and Higher Education

While courses in criminology have existed in sociology departments since the beginning of the twentieth century, few colleges and universities had a criminal justice department until the demand created by LEEP funding in the 1970s. The first academic departments of criminal justice drew on the contributions of fields, such as sociology, political science, psychology, public administration, the sciences (for forensic science classes), communications, and math (for research classes). During the first 10 to 15 years following the advent of LEEP funding, criminal justice programs reflected great diversity in both content and academic quality. Departments had diverse names: Administration of Justice, Justice Studies, Crime Studies, Law Enforcement, and Center for Study of Crime. Widespread use of *criminal justice* as the field of study did not emerge until the late 1980s.

The academic curriculum of early criminal justice programs was strongly oriented toward applied knowledge rather than research and theoretical inquiry. Some college curriculums included courses such as report writing, self-defense, firearms, and first aid. These types of courses were clearly aimed at professional development for students expecting to enter the criminal justice field. Early programs focused primarily on law enforcement, and were sometimes derogatorily referred to by other academic disciplines as "cop schools." Criminal justice majors were considered less academically qualified than majors in related fields such as political science, criminology, sociology, and psychology. This perception was not helped by the fact that colleges and universities frequently used part-time instructors to teach in the criminal justice program. These instructors were often police or corrections personnel or attorneys and lacked advanced degrees, which was expected of instructors in other academic disciplines.

Currently, however, the study of criminal justice has a legitimate place in the academic and professional environment. The focus of this discipline is an examination of criminal justice agencies, personnel, and mission for the purposes of training, education, and research. In this role, criminal justice contributes to society, government, social order, and public service. Important contributions include the study of topics

criminal justice in the world

Cross-Cultural Perspectives on Criminal Justice

The comparative study of criminal justice systems offers the possibility of gaining new insights and new solutions. Nations have adopted different formal and informal systems for crime control and justice. Japan, for example, does not use the jury system; instead, cases are heard by three judges. In Japan, if a defendant apologizes and writes a letter of apology to the victim, the prosecutor can drop the charges. In France, jurors and judges collaborate to determine the guilt of the defendant, and both judge and juror vote on a verdict. France has two national police forces, and their duties are based on the population of a city.

The study of such criminal justice systems worldwide offers a great opportunity to consider the adoption of different policies and procedures, ones that might lead to improvements in the American criminal justice system. In addition, the globalization of both crime and law enforcement requires, more than ever before, greater understanding of the criminal justice systems of other countries. The increasing role of the United Nations in criminal justice matters; the need to deal effectively with international terrorism; an ever-shrinking world, enabling criminals to flee from one country to another with ease; and the international cooperation necessary for the extradition of fugitives make it essential to know more abut the criminal justice systems of other nations.

Americans traveling abroad sometimes become victims of crime or suspects or perpetrators of crimes and thus become involved in the criminal justice systems of other countries. Other countries' systems can be quite different, and Americans often find themselves challenged to cope with them. For instance, many countries do not have laws guaranteeing civil rights or due process, or even human rights. Concepts of justice and appropriate punishment for crimes vary widely. In 1996 Lori Berenson, a New Yorker accused of planning terrorist acts in Peru, was convicted and sentenced to life imprisonment by a hooded military judge without the benefit of a trial.[64] Not all encounters with foreign criminal justice systems are so dramatic, however, but many more Americans are more likely to have to deal with the criminal justice system of another country.

International cooperation in law enforcement is needed for public safety as well as for crime control. For example, pirates are still a major threat in many parts of the world, with hundreds of attacks on ships and crew members each year. Today, ships that are worth millions, even billions, of dollars have small unarmed crews that are easy targets for pirates.[65] International challenges in law and order are one reason that American law enforcement officers are recruited for overseas peacekeeping duties. In the 1990s, $15 million was spent recruiting thousands of American civilian law enforcement officers to serve with the International Police Task Force in Bosnia. Some recruits were offered as much as $100,000 to do so.[66]

■ **What are at least five reasons that the comparative study of criminal justice systems is so important? How can the American criminal justice system benefit from knowledge of the criminal justice systems of other countries? Why is a cross-cultural perspective on criminal justice systems especially important in today's world?**

such as youth violence, drug crimes, organized crime, terrorism, victimization, law enforcement, corrections, and social policy aimed at crime prevention. Criminal justice research employs sophisticated statistical modeling to predict crime, and advances in science are applied to criminal justice practices. Criminal justice instructors now have doctoral degrees in criminal justice, and even most part-time instructors have master's degrees. Significant changes in the criminal justice discipline in the past four decades mirror changes in the criminal justice system (discussed in greater detail in subsequent chapters).

Careers in Criminal Justice

A purpose of criminal justice departments in colleges and universities is to prepare students for public service through employment in the criminal justice system. In the late 1960s, Jerry Wilson, Chief of Police of Washington, DC, and member of the President's Crime Commission, recommended that police officers model themselves on carpenters, bricklayers, plumbers, and the other so-called master craftsmen.[67] He cautioned that police work would probably bore many college graduates and recommended against college education for police officers. Today, however, many police departments require that new employees have a bachelor's degree, and most require the completion of some college coursework. The FBI will not accept applications from anyone with less than a bachelor's degree and prefers applicants to have advanced degrees in fields such as law, economics, and computer science. The ranks of probation officers are comprised primarily of college graduates, and the norm for federal probation and parole officers is the master's degree.

Criminal justice has become a much more open, complex, and technically sophisticated occupation than it was just 40 years ago. Affirmative action legislation opened the field to all qualified applicants of both sexes and all racial and ethic backgrounds. In today's criminal justice environment, formal education plays a vital role in job performance, promotions, and rewards. There are many diverse, rewarding, and challenging careers in criminal justice, and opportunities for employment can be found within local, county, state, federal, private, military, civilian, and international agencies. Careers span a wide range—from enforcement to courts to corrections. Teaching careers in criminal justice also are available in colleges and universities, law enforcement academies, and correctional institutions. Most state prisons and federal penitentiaries have educational programs for inmates, including high school equivalency diploma programs, advanced academic degrees, and professional career-development programs.

Criminal justice remains distinct from the study of law, including criminal law. A student anticipating a career as an attorney or judge may use the undergraduate degree in criminal justice to satisfy the baccalaureate admission requirements for entry into law school. Table 1.2 lists some of the many employment opportunities in criminal justice. In addition, all branches of the criminal justice system hire civilian employees in the areas of human resources, training, administration, departmental support, and technical support.

table 1.2 **Employment Opportunities in the Criminal Justice System**

Law Enforcement	Courts	Corrections
Patrol officer	Prosecuting attorney	Probation officer
Sheriff	Defense attorney	Parole officer
Detective	Judge or magistrate	Correctional officer
FBI agent	Bailiff	Warden
Game warden	Court clerk	Counselor
Juvenile officer	Court stenographer	Caseworker
Airport security	Court reporter	Recreation specialist
Crime laboratory technician	Victim advocate	Mental health worker
Dispatcher		Educator

An exciting development in the field of criminal justice is the growing interest in criminal justice systems of other countries, accompanied by greater interest in transnational crime and international criminal justice. At one time, obstacles such as language barriers, transportation expenses, and conflicting political ideologies made the study of foreign criminal justice systems difficult or impossible. Now, however, the criminal justice systems of countries such as China, Japan, and Russia can be studied. The United States has student, professional, and academic exchanges with other countries, and most criminal justice departments offer travel-abroad programs to those who wish to study the criminal justice system of another country.

JUST THE FACTS 1.6

What is criminology? What is the academic focus of the study of criminal justice? What are the educational requirements for a career in law enforcement?

conclusion:

A New Future for Criminal Justice

The criminal justice system touches the lives of every one of us. At times, it is relatively invisible to the average citizen going about his or her day-to-day business. However, the criminal justice system plays an important role in safeguarding the freedoms and rights guaranteed by the government. In homogeneous and stable societies, behavior is often effectively controlled by informal institutions such as family, religion, and group norms. However, in large societies with diverse populations and conflicting values, formal institutions such as the police, courts, and corrections take on more importance in order maintenance.

Loss of confidence in the criminal justice system by the public can cause a crisis that may even threaten the survival of the government. An effective, efficient, and just criminal justice system is essential to the well-being of government, especially in a democracy. Because it is closely tied to social justice and fairness, an effective criminal justice system is much more than securing the absence of crime. The criminal justice system of the United States has had some ignoble moments in its history; however, one of its strengths is the ability to correct past mistakes and build a better system for the future. Ignorance of the criminal justice system is dangerous in that such allows the repetition of past mistakes and the perpetuation of serious problems.

Following the September 11 terrorist attacks on the United States, public safety became a primary concern. Strict security procedures were immediately instituted at airports, government buildings, cultural centers, and many other facilities. The FBI advised state and local law enforcement agencies to move to their highest level of alert and be prepared to respond to any further acts of terrorism.[68] Armed National Guard troops supplemented airport security officers. Military aircraft flew protective patrol over U.S. cities, and the Coast Guard patrolled coastlines and ports. The ability of local and state police to provide for the safety of citizens within their jurisdictions was called into question.

These challenges will change the criminal justice system. During the twentieth century, the system faced a similar challenge when civil unrest, rioting, and a runaway crime rate caused the public to doubt the capacity of the system to provide law and order. Now, as then, the criminal justice system will be forced to redefine itself, to evaluate its capacity and role, and to assess the adequacy of its personnel and resources. The criminal justice system of the twenty-first century will differ in that police departments in particular will have new roles and capacities and will operate in a different environment. Thus, this book begins with basic questions: What is the criminal justice system, and how is that system changing?

Chapter Summary

- Social order is maintained by both formal and informal means. The criminal justice system—the police, the courts, and corrections—is society's way of formally dealing with order maintenance.
- Challenges that have redefined the American criminal justice system are (1) the social unrest, rioting, and out-of-control crime rate of the 1960s and 1970s and (2) the threat of international terrorism following the September 11 attacks on the World Trade Center and the Pentagon and the subsequent bioterrorism launched against American seats of government.
- The challenge of the criminal justice system is to provide the maximum individual liberty for people while ensuring law and order.
- When crime and disorder threaten public safety, public opinion often favors restricting individual liberties and expanding the powers of police and government.
- The threat of international terrorism has caused a serious reexamination of the criminal justice system. New agencies, new laws, and new police powers have been proposed.
- The threat of international terrorism has placed great responsibility on the newly created cabinet-level position of Office of Homeland Security and on the Federal Bureau of Investigation as the lead agency in responding to such terrorism.
- Criminal justice is a new academic discipline in higher education that developed in the 1960s and borrows from many related fields, including sociology and criminology.
- The study of the criminal justice systems of other countries is more important now than ever before.
- The criminal justice system is an increasingly significant source of employment for individuals with college credits and college degrees.

Vocabulary Review

bioterrorism, 18
counterterrorism, 24
criminal justice, 25
criminal justice system, 12
criminology, 25
domestic terrorism, 21
ecoterrorism, 21
formal sanctions, 12
informal sanctions, 11
international terrorism, 22
order maintenance, 12
social injustice, 15
social norms, 12
state-sponsored terrorism, 19
system of social control, 12
terrorism, 18
terrorists, 16

Names and Events to Remember

Academy of Criminal Justice Sciences (ACJS), 26
American Society of Criminology (ASC), 26
Bill of Rights, 13
Geneva Convention for the Prevention and Suppression of Terrorism, 18
Law Enforcement Assistance Administration (LEAA), 6
Law Enforcement Educational Program (LEEP), 7
National Commission on Criminal Justice Standards and Goals, 6
National Commission on Terrorism, 10
National Coordinator for Security, 11
Office of Domestic Terrorism and Counterterrorism Planning, 19
Office of Homeland Security, 10
Omnibus Crime Control and Safe Streets Act of 1968, 6
President's Commission on Law Enforcement and Administration of Justice, 6
September 11, 2001 (WTC 9/11), 4
Strategic Information and Operations Center (SIOC), 24
War on Crime, 6
War on Terrorism, 8

Think about This

1. What are some significant similarities and differences between the 1970s' War on Crime and 2001's War on Terrorism?
2. Why is it so important to balance public safety and security with individual freedoms and civil rights? Why is it important to balance citizens' rights and government's powers?
3. How has the September 11 attack and its aftermath affected the American people and the American criminal justice system? What challenges do the American and international criminal justice systems face in their war on terrorism?
4. What do you think should be the role of the criminal justice system in preventing terrorism?

ContentSelect

Go to the ContentSelect web site and type in the keyword *terrorism*. Read "Fighting Terrorism in the 21st Century" from the March 1999 issue of the *FBI Law Enforcement Bulletin*. This article provides an interesting perspective of law enforcement's views and preparations for terrorist attacks in the years preceding the September 11 World Trade Center and Pentagon attacks. Sample the article to answer the following questions.

1. According to the article, what were the FBI's "current terrorist threats" as of 1999? How have those threats changed?
2. According to your text, what has been the major flaw in counterterrorism measures in the United States? Do you think that flaw is now being addressed?
3. What role does the Office of Homeland Security play in counterterrorism? How does this agency assist the FBI in dealing with counterterrorism?
4. In the time since your text was published, what advances have been made in the war on terrorism?

chapter 2

An Overview of the Criminal Justice Process

outline

arning
ojectives

er reading this chapter,
 will know

- How crime is counted and the strengths and weaknesses of different methods of counting crime.
- The difference between the due process model and the crime control model and understand how the American criminal justice system is a balance of these two models.
- The due process rights that the criminal justice system provides for the defendant.
- The major agencies involved in processing a person through the criminal justice system and their roles.
- The differences among the adult, juvenile, state, and federal criminal justice systems.
- The major steps involved in moving a person from arrest to conviction.
- How the defendant is transitioned from the police to the courts to corrections.

Killer of Ten-Year-Old Gets Justice

CHICAGO, ILLINOIS—Rolando Cruz looked like the kind of person who could have killed and raped 10-year-old Jeanine Nicarico. The victim was kidnapped from her home, raped, beaten, killed, and left in a wooded area. Cruz was arrested and convicted of the brutal murder. Cruz, a Hispanic street tough, tried to pass himself off as an informant in hopes of obtaining a $10,000 reward for the capture of the killer. His undoing was telling the detectives that he had a vision of the murder. Cruz supplied police with details of the ghastly murder that only the killer could know. The prosecution was able to obtain a death penalty verdict against Cruz based to a large degree on Cruz's vision statement.

The public slept a little better after the arrest and conviction of Rolando Cruz. His execution would add closure to an unspeakable crime. Then Northwestern University law professor Lawrence Marshall did the unthinkable: He appealed Cruz's case. The police had little evidence linking Cruz to the crime other than his vision statement. Marshall admitted that Cruz was wrong in seeking to obtain the reward when he knew nothing about the case but said that playing a game with the police does not deserve the death penalty.

Cruz's guilt was called into question when a similar crime was committed by Brian Dugan while Cruz was on death row. Dugan confessed to that crime and also to being the killer of Jeanine Nicarico. One problem with this turn of events is that it was discovered that Dugan had confessed to the murder and rape of the 10-year-old prior to Cruz's conviction. Police and prosecutors had chosen to ignore Dugan's confession.

After Dugan's confession came to light, Cruz's attorney was able to collect DNA evidence that cleared Cruz as the killer. Further investigation uncovered that the police had neither tape-recorded nor taken notes about Cruz's vision statement, which had been so instrumental in his conviction. Investigation by special prosecutor William Kunkle revealed that the police had fabricated the vision statement and prosecutors had suppressed evidence to frame Cruz. Cruz was set free, and charges were filed against three former Du Page, Illinois, prosecutors and four sheriff's deputies for their part in framing Cruz. All of the defendants protested their guilt, denying that they framed Cruz.

—From "The Frame Game" by Adam Cohen from *Time,* March 29, 1999.

introduction:

People and Processes in Criminal Justice

People are horrified when a terrible crime is committed and want swift justice and stern punishment. The arrest, conviction, and death sentence of Rolando Cruz appeared to demonstrate the effectiveness of the criminal justice system in dealing quickly and decisively with crime. The appeal of Cruz's case caused alarm because it was interpreted as a guilty person trying to escape his just punishment. The revelation that the police and prosecutors might have framed Cruz causes one to pause and consider the workings of the criminal justice system.

If the police arrest you for a crime, what happens next? How do you prove your innocence? How does a person end up in prison? What are the safeguards that prevent the conviction—and perhaps wrongful execution—of an innocent person? The American criminal justice process is a complex interaction of numerous agencies. The process from arrest to trial to incarceration can take years. This chapter examines the American criminal justice process, the agencies that make up this system, and the decisions that are made as the accused is processed through the system.

As you will see, the criminal justice system can be viewed as an input-process-output model. Basically, the criminal justice system detects and selects people to be processed by the system, processes them through the system, and then provides a means for their exit from the system. The agencies, people, and resources used by the criminal justice system are all focused on moving people through the system from arrest to an exit portal. A major background step in that process is counting and gathering data on crime.

Counting Crime

THE MAIN IDEA

Statistics on crime and research on the operation of police, the courts, and corrections drive public policy and underlie development and change in the agencies that make up the criminal justice system.

The number of crimes committed is a measure of the effectiveness and efficiency of the criminal justice system. However, counting crime can be an inexact science. Josiah Stamp, an early American critic of government statistics, said, "The government is very keen at amassing statistics. They collect them, add them, refer them to the *n*th power, take the cube root, to prepare wonderful diagrams. But you must never forget that every one of these figures comes in the first instance from the [village watchman], who just puts down what he damn pleases."[1]

Crime statistics and measures of the criminal justice system are subject to error, and the further one goes back, the more prominent the error appears. Today, various official agencies, such as the Federal Bureau of Investigation, the **Bureau of Justice Statistics,** and the National Criminal Justice Reference Service, gather and disseminate data about nearly every aspect of the criminal justice system. The gathering of criminal justice statistics is a recent phenomenon. Quantitative data older than the 1970s is untrustworthy. For instance, the New York City coroner's office recorded 323 homicides in 1913, but the police filed only 261 homicides. Likewise, in 1915, the San Francisco Police Department reported only 50 homicides, but the coroner reported 71.[2]

As you read in Chapter 1, public fears about crime control and order maintenance arose during social upheavals dating to the 1950s, but the roots of those fears began in the 1920s, when crime was perceived mainly as a big-city problem. After World War I, more people migrated to the cities. As urban populations swelled, the public became more concerned with crime. In the 1920s, Cleveland, Ohio, and Chicago, Illinois, were among the first major cities to perform crime surveys.[3,4] These surveys were motivated by the desire to correct what were perceived as major deficiencies in the criminal justice system. The basic premise was that the absence of crime is the best measure of police effectiveness. If reforms to the criminal justice system were effective, it was believed that the results would be reflected in decreasing crime rates.[5]

The public perception that the Great Depression of the 1930s brought a crime wave heightened interest in counting crime. The news media exaggerated the crime wave with colorful stories of organized crime figures and infamous public enemies such as John Dillinger, Charles "Pretty Boy" Floyd, George "Baby Face" Nelson, and Bonnie Parker and Clyde Barrow. Stories of bank robberies were front-page news. The public was entertained with stories of shoot-outs with the police.

Passage of the Eighteenth Amendment, which prohibited the manufacture, sale, and possession of alcoholic beverages, added fuel to the fire. The Prohibition Amendment, or the Volstead Act, as it was called, increased rather than decreased crime as gangs warred for control of the lucrative illegal sale of alcoholic beverages. Crime bosses such as Al Capone appeared to be immune to arrest because of pervasive corruption within the criminal justice system. The average citizen was left with the impression that crime was everywhere and no one could do much about it. Without a way to determine objectively whether crime was increasing or decreasing, the public had no idea which side—the criminal justice system or the criminals—was winning. Without crime statistics, it was not possible to determine the impact of money spent, resources invested, reform efforts, and new laws on the problem of crime.

Visit the Bureau of Justice Statistics at http://www.ojp.usdoj.gov/bjs/ and follow links to explore statistics on crime, victims and perpetrators of crimes, and the criminal justice system. ■

The *Uniform Crime Report*

The problem with determining crime rates was that there existed no single standard for collecting and counting crime data. Based on the efforts of the International Association of Chiefs of Police Committee on Uniform Crime Reports, on June 11, 1930, Congress passed the first federal legislation mandating the collecting of crime data. The Federal Bureau of Investigation (FBI) was charged with the responsibility of collecting crime data from police departments and disseminating the data to the nation. While these efforts served a public purpose, law enforcement officials also saw crime data as a way to exploit the fear of crime to justify their requests for additional personnel and increased resources.[6] As a result, crime data were collected and used in a manner that tended to emphasize the pervasiveness and seriousness of crime.

THE CRIME CLOCK One of the data presentation strategies used by the FBI during this period, and still in use today, is the **Crime Clock,** which reported how often a crime occurred (Figure 2.1 on page 36). The Crime Clock was used frequently to emphasize that crime occurred nearly all of the time. For example, according to the Crime Clock, larceny–theft occurred every 4 seconds, burglary was committed every 11 seconds, and aggravated assault every 28 seconds. It was easy for citizens to conclude that they could hardly walk outside without becoming a crime statistic. These data are terribly distorted, however. While it may be accurate to say that a murder occurs every 33.9 minutes, it does not mean that every 33.9 minutes, a murder occurs in every community. It means that every 33.9 minutes, a murder occurs somewhere in the United States.

Crime Clock Data presentation strategy used by the FBI to report crime rates in terms of how often a crime occurs.

Furthermore, murders are not randomly distributed among cities but tend to be concentrated in urban areas. Rural communities may go years or even decades without a murder. Even in large cities such as New York, Los Angeles, Chicago, and Atlanta, murder does not happen every 33.9 minutes. If that were the case, there would be about 2 homicides every hour and 48 murders in a single day! Despite the inflationary statistics the Crime Clock generates, it continues to be used as a method of presenting crime data.

USES OF UCR DATA Over the years, crime data collected by the FBI and published under the title ***Uniform Crime Report*** **(UCR)** have become useful as databases for examining crime trends. These data are used for numerous purposes: a measure of crime rates, a factor in indexes calculating quality of life in U.S. cities, and a factor in policy decisions. Based on UCR trend data, municipalities may decide to add more police officers to their force. Grants aimed at crime prevention and curbing drug crime use UCR data to measure effectiveness. The release of new UCR data is often anxiously awaited by many agencies, because they want to know if recent changes such as com-

Figure 2.1

Crime Clock

The Crime Clock should be viewed with care. The most aggregate representation of UCR data, it conveys the annual reported crime experience by showing a relative frequency of occurrence of index offenses. It should not be taken to imply a regularity in the commission of crime. The Crime Clock represents the annual ratio of crime to fixed-time intervals.

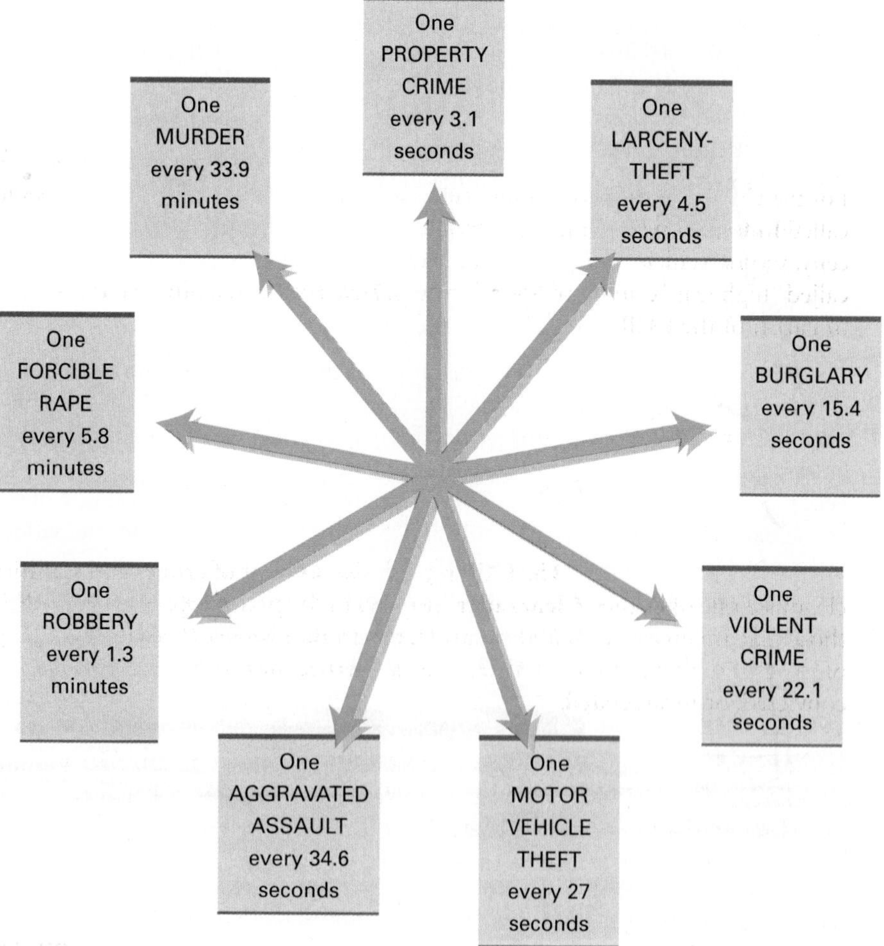

Source: The 2000 FBI *Uniform Crime Report.*

munity policing, neighborhood watches, or "get-tough" sentencing policies have had an impact on the crime rate.

UCR DATA COLLECTION The UCR had its origins at a time when there were no computers, no computerized databases, and no statistics and graphics software. Crime data were collected, stored, and transmitted manually. Collecting and reporting crime data was a labor-intensive process. Most police departments kept file cabinets filled with cards detailing each crime. The cards were arranged by case number and offense and were filed under the various crime categories (murder, rape, burglary, etc.). Anyone wanting to know the number of burglaries committed during a particular period had to go to the file cabinet, pull the cards for burglary, and count the number of cards one by one. Under the circumstances, the FBI had to adopt rules for counting crime that were consistent with the limitations imposed by the system.

THE HIERARCHY RULE Each crime card contained the information for one case or incident based only on the most serious charge. In a single incident, several crimes might have been committed. A person might have been both robbed and assaulted, and both crimes would be noted in one police report, recorded on one card, and filed under "robbery." This method of counting only the most serious crime in incidents involving multiple crimes is called the **hierarchy rule.** Also, if more than one victim were involved in the incident (e.g., a group of people was robbed), the UCR reported only the most serious offense for the incident as a whole and not for individual victims. As you can imagine, use of the hierarchy rule results in an undercounting of crime.

In addition, the UCR does not report data for all crimes. Only a few crimes have been selected for inclusion in the UCR database. Again, the decision to limit the number of crimes tracked was based initially on the limitation that all crime data were paper-based and manually counted. It was simply not feasible to count all crimes. In all, the UCR provides data for 27 criminal violations, which are divided into two categories: serious crimes and less serious crimes.[7] The serious crimes are reported in Part I of the UCR, and the less serious crimes are reported in Part II. The 8 crimes in Part I, called **Index Crimes** are murder, forcible rape, robbery, aggravated assault, burglary, larceny, motor vehicle theft, and arson. All of these crimes except arson are sometimes called "high fear" crimes or "street" crimes. Data for the remaining crimes are reported in Part II of the UCR (Table 2.1 on page 38).

At the time the FBI started gathering UCR data, arson was not included in Part I crimes. The intention of Part I crimes was to gather data about those crimes that appeared to have the greatest impact on quality of life and of which people had the greatest fear of victimization. Arson was not added to the Part I UCR until 1979. Arson is a crime against habitation and buildings, whereas the other Part I crimes are those against people.

CLEARANCE RATES The UCR reports the number of crimes and statistics on the clearance rate of crimes. **Clearance rate** refers to the percentage of crimes solved versus those that are unsolved. *Solved* means that the police believe they know the perpetrator of the crime. *Solved* does not mean that the perpetrator has been arrested, prosecuted, convicted, or incarcerated. It merely means that the police are reasonably certain they know who committed the crime. In most cases, a crime is "cleared" by the arrest of the suspect, but police consider the crime cleared if they *believe* the suspect committed the crime, regardless of whether there is a conviction. Other cases in which a crime is cleared even though the suspect is not charged or tried include the suspect's death, immunity from arrest, or flight beyond the reach of American law enforcement.

WHY UCR DATA ARE INADEQUATE There are several major shortcomings of UCR data that encourage the collection of crime data by other means. One shortcoming is that UCR data represent only crimes that are *known* to the police; unreported

hierarchy rule Practice in data collection for the FBI's *Uniform Crime Reports* of counting only the most serious crime in incidents involving multiple crimes or with multiple victims of the same crime.

Index Crimes The eight crimes in Part I of the *Uniform Crime Reports:* murder, forcible rape, robbery, aggravated assault, burglary, larceny, motor vehicle theft, and arson.

clearance rate Percentage of reported crimes determined to be solved.

table 2.1 FBI's *Uniform Crime Report* Part I and Part II Offenses, 2000–2001

Part I Offenses (Crime Index)	Part II Offenses (*Continued*)
Criminal Homicide Murder, nonnegligent manslaughter, and nonjustifiable homicide. Manslaughter by negligence is a Part I crime but is not included in the Crime Index.	**Stolen Property** Buying, selling, receiving
	Weapons Carrying, possessing
Forcible Rape "Carnal knowledge"; includes sexual assault; does not include statutory offenses	**Prostitution and Commercialized Vice**
	Sex Offenses Statutory rape and offenses against morality
Robbery "Taking" or attempting to take anything of value from a person by force, threat, or fear	**Drug Abuse Violations** State or local laws against unlawful possession, sale, use, growing, or manufacturing of opium, cocaine, morphine, heroin, codeine, marijuana, and other narcotic and dangerous nonnarcotic drugs
Aggravated Assault Attack on a person for the purpose of inflicting bodily harm, usually through use of a weapon	
Burglary Breaking or entering a structure to commit a felony or theft, including attempt	**Gambling**
Larceny Includes theft of property that does not involve force, violence, or fraud	**Offenses against Family and Children** Nonsupport, neglect, desertion, abuse
Motor Vehicle Theft Does not include motorboats, construction equipment, airplanes, or farming equipment	**Driving under the Influence** Of alcohol or drugs
	Liquor Laws State or local laws
Arson Willful or malicious burning or attempt to burn any property for any reason	**Drunkenness**
	Disorderly Conduct
Part II Offenses	**Vagrancy**
Simple Assault No weapon or serious injury	**All Other Violations** Of state or local laws
Forgery and Counterfeiting	**Suspicion** Suspect released without charge
Fraud	**Curfew and Loitering Laws** Persons under age 18
Embezzlement	**Runaways** Persons under age 18 in protective custody

crimes are not included. The lack of this type of information is particularly significant: People often do not report crimes because they have lost confidence in the police, which includes both confidence in the ability of police to do something about the crime and confidence that the police are not corrupt and that no harm will come to innocent people if they report a crime.

In addition, the UCR (1) includes data only about local and state crimes, not federal offenses; and (2) depends on the voluntary cooperation of local and state police agencies for data collection. When the UCR began, federal law enforcement agencies did not play as prominent a role in crime fighting as they do today. Today, nearly all local and state police agencies report crime data to the FBI, but this was not always the case. In the early years, many local police departments did not report crime data, because they lacked adequate record keeping or personnel to gather the facts or because they feared embarrassment or simply did not want to report the data. To this day, there is no official sanction of local and state police for failing to report crime data to the FBI.

Finally, UCR data are about local and state crimes, and definitions of crimes are not the same from place to place. In one jurisdiction, a felony theft may require the taking of property valued at $100, whereas in another jurisdiction, the limit for felony theft may be $1,000. One of the most bothersome problems is the definition of *rape*. The UCR uses a definition that is not as inclusive as that used by states that have adopted progressive sexual assault criminal codes. The UCR defines *forcible rape* as "the carnal knowledge of a female forcibly and against her will." This definition excludes many offenses that are counted as sexual assault by many states.

The National Incident-Based Report System

The FBI recognized the shortcomings of the old UCR crime data survey methods and instituted a plan to address many of these problems. Taking advantage of the computer technology that is now possible in crime reporting, the new system, called the **National Incident-Based Reporting System (NIBRS),** is now not a simple frequency count of crime. Under NIBRS, additional data about crimes will be reported, including information on place-of occurrence, weapon used, type and value of property damaged or stolen, personal characteristics of the offender and the victim and the nature of any relationship between the two, the disposition of the complaint, and so on. Implementing the NIBRS has been complicated by the complexity of the task of changing from a fairly simple data-gathering and -reporting system to a complex methodology. The new NIBRS data will provide much more insight into the crime picture, and researchers will have greater success in correlating crime data with other factors suspected of contributing to the incidence of crime and effective crime prevention.

The National Crime Victim Survey

In addition to the NIBRS, another major data collection effort to address the shortcomings of the UCR data is the **National Crime Victim Survey (NCVS).** NCVS dates back only to 1972 when it was recognized that a significant number of crimes go unreported to the police. Unreported crime was called the "dark figure" of crime, and many authorities believed that knowledge about unreported crime could significantly change the conclusions that were being based only on UCR data. The NCVS gathers data about crime incidents such as the relationship between victim and offender, the use of drugs or alcohol, bystander behavior, suspected offender gang involvement, and self-protection measures taken by the victims.

The NCVS provides important data not gathered by the UCR, but it also has deficiencies. The NCVS depends on self-reported data by the victim, which may be inaccurate. Victims may forget when the crime occurred, for instance, and include crimes that occurred outside the requested time frame. The NCVS is sent to households, so the survey does not reliably pinpoint where the crime occurred, as do the UCR data. Also, household members who have previously withheld information about victimization from family members are not likely to report their victimization in the NCVS.

Find interesting data from diverse sources at the Criminal Justice Sourcebook, http://www.albany.edu/sourcebook. ■

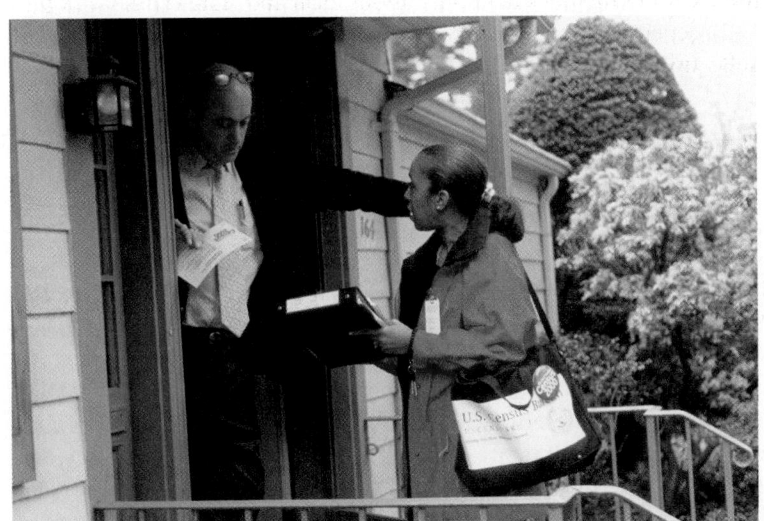

National Crime Victim Survey data are gathered by the Bureau of Justice Statistics (BJS) with assistance from the U.S. Census Bureau. The BJS mails over 40,000 surveys to households—not to individuals—(similar to the procedure used in gathering census data) and asks that all members 12 years of age and older living in that household report their experience with victimization. Data from the NCVS have provided tremendous insight into the crime picture and have altered thinking about effective crime prevention strategies.

Other Sources of Criminal Justice Data

State-sponsored research includes surveys of crime similar to the UCR, conducted by the individual states, and surveys of crime in public schools, including colleges and universities. These crime surveys are useful in that the crimes reported match the criminal codes used by a state. Statistics on crimes such as sexual assault and larceny are much more likely to be accurate. Schools and colleges and universities are not required to report their crime data to the FBI for inclusion in the UCR data, however. If a crime occurs on school property or a college or university campus, unless that crime is also reported to the police, it is not included in the UCR data, although public disclosure is required.

CAMPUS CRIMES As of 1992, the **Crime Awareness and Campus Security Act** has required colleges and universities to report crime data. Every institution must make a public disclosure of the crimes occurring on its campus whether or not these crimes were reported to the police. Some school districts have begun to report crimes that occur on school property. For example, in the past at a K–12 school when a student's lunch money was taken by force, such incidents often were unreported or were handled by the school administration outside of the criminal justice system. Now these incidents are being reported as robberies, which has caused an apparent increase in crime. As a result of this act, students and parents can obtain specific crime data about any college or university campus of their choice.

HATE CRIMES Unique challenges to counting crime are raised by the **Hate Crime Statistics Act** of 1990 and the Violent Crime Control and Law Enforcement Act of 1994. These acts require that crimes motivated by hatred, bias, or prejudice, and based on the actual or perceived race, color, religion, national origin, ethnicity, gender, or sexual orientation of another individual or group of individuals, be reported separately.[8] The criminal justice system has struggled to report such crimes accurately. Often it is difficult to determine or agree on the motivation of the offender. The purpose of the legislation is to help determine the extent of crimes committed by extremist and racially biased groups such as the Ku Klux Klan, neo-Nazis, tax protesters, skinheads, antigay groups, and anti-Semitic groups.

SELF-REPORTS Crime data gathered from self-reports (surveys of perpetrators' and potential perpetrators' reports of their offenses) concerning crimes such as drug use, driving while intoxicated (DUI), and consensual crimes such as prostitution and gambling indicate that the UCR seriously underreports the incidence of such crimes. For example, self-reported crime data indicate that many drug users started using drugs as juveniles and that heroin addicts are most likely to commit crimes.[9] As another example, 60 percent of a sample of adult men between the ages of 20 and 30 admitted to driving while intoxicated.[10]

Comparing and Contrasting Crime Data

Comparing the various criminal data often provides illuminating insights into a crime. For example, when criminal victimization is compared with other harmful life events, the life chances of being a victim of theft ranks third behind the two top events—accidental injury (242 per 1,000) and accidental injury at home (70 per 1,000).[11] The risk of death due to homicide is less than 1 per 1,000 persons, whereas the risk of death from heart disease is 4 per 1,000 and death from cancer is 2 per 1,000.[12] A comparison of the reported incidents of sexual assault by the NCVS and the UCR indicates that the UCR significantly underreports sex crimes. In 1996, the UCR reported 95,769 forcible rapes, whereas the NCVS reported 307,000 rapes. Robbery, aggravated assault, burglary, and larceny were all reported by the NCVS at rates two or three times greater than rates given in UCR data (Table 2.2).

table 2.2 Comparison of UCR and NCVS Crime Data, 2000–2001

	UCR	NCVS
Date and reason for origin	Authorized by Congress in 1930 in response to public fear of "crime wave"	Began in 1972 to discover "dark figures" of crime (i.e., unreported crime)
Data gathered by	FBI	Bureau of Justice Statistics and U.S. Census Bureau
How data are gathered	Crime reported to the police, who in turn report it to the FBI	Random biannual survey of 42,000 households; excludes crime victims less than 12 years of age
Level of analysis	Reports individual crimes	Surveys all members in a household
Publications	*Uniform Crime Report:* Crime in the United States (quarterly and annual reports)	*Crime and the Nation's Households* *Criminal Victimization* *Annual Report on Criminal Victimization in the United States*
Crimes included in report	Part I—murder, rape, robbery, aggravated assault, burglary, larceny-theft, motor vehicle theft, and arson. Part II—simple assault, forgery and counterfeiting, fraud, embezzlement, stolen property, vandalism, weapons, prostitution, sex offenses, drug law violations, gambling, offenses against the family, DUI, liquor law violations, public drunkenness, disorderly conduct, vagrancy, curfew/loitering, and runaways	Rape, robbery, assault, burglary, personal and household larceny, and motor vehicle theft; does not collect crime data concerning murder, kidnapping, victimless crimes, commercial robbery, and burglary of businesses
Major weaknesses	Underreports crime because crimes not reported to the police are not counted; simple frequency count of crime	Crime data error due to false or exaggerated crime reports not known; does not have crime data beyond 1972
Major strengths	Historical data back to 1930; official data of crime reported to police	Captures data on crime not reported to the police; captures data on completed and attempted offenses; provides victimization data about the relationship of victim–offender, location of crime, and other data related to the crime
Major contribution to criminology	Provides standardized data on crime, crime rates, and comparative data for states and cities. The Crime Index is used in many measures of quality of life and effect of crime prevention and drug-use prevention programs.	Revealed a significantly higher rate of crime than that reported by the UCR. Data about crime victimization allows criminologists to build explanations as to the causes of crime.
Improvements being made	Inclusion of sexual assault crimes rather than just rape, data about crime victimization, hierarchy rule modified, more comprehensive data on dollar loss, persons involved, and weapons data	Better methods to ensure accurate reporting of data, more comprehensive data on domestic violence, data regarding alcohol and drug use by offenders, data on gang-related crime

The picture that emerges is that statistics fail to capture the extent of criminal behavior. Two of the most accurate crime statistics are homicide and automobile theft. Homicide rates are accurate because there is a body. Data regarding automobile theft is consistent from survey to survey because most people report the theft of their automobile to the police as a requirement to collect insurance on loss of the vehicle. Other than for these two crimes, it is difficult to get an accurate picture of just how much crime is committed and who commits it.

One final note regarding counting crime is the warning that crime statistics are only a snapshot of the past. Crime statistics indicate what crime has occurred, not what crime will occur. There is a delay between the gathering and reporting of crime statistics, and it is possible that an alarming report of rising crime rates is inaccurate. Crime rates might already have dropped by the time a report is issued and might continue dropping, making drastic action unnecessary. Thus, looking at crime statistics is like looking into the rearview mirror of an automobile, which shows you where you have been but not where you are going. Crime trends may take some time to establish with any certainty.

JUST THE FACTS 2.1

How is crime counted in federal and state data collection? What are the problems with the UCR, NCVS, and other methods of reporting as sources of data on crime? Why are accurate data on crime so important, yet so difficult to achieve?

The Search to Define the Criminal Justice System

THE MAIN IDEA

The criminal justice system is a dynamic model of interrelated, independent agencies that operate under numerous checks and balances. These agencies process criminal offenders through a complex system of decision points.

When examining the criminal justice system, there are two perspectives: (1) the agencies and people involved in the criminal justice system and (2) the processes and flow of the criminal justice system. This book discusses various agencies and the people who work in them, but the criminal justice system is much more than the sum of its components. To understand the criminal justice system, it is necessary to examine the interactions, checks and balances, and decisions that are made. Each person and agency in the criminal justice system has a certain amount of autonomy, but each is also controlled by the criminal justice system. By exploring the balance between autonomy and control, you can appreciate the ever-changing, flexible, and responsive nature of the criminal justice system. Thus, the criminal justice system is not a static model, but a dynamic model that is constantly evolving, changing, and redefining itself. This dynamic nature has always been a characteristic of the American criminal justice system, and the description of it in this book is only a portrait of one place and time.

Agencies and People

The criminal justice system is divided into three categories of agencies: police, courts, and corrections. Each of the agencies in the criminal justice system is independent. There is no single agency that has oversight control of all of the criminal justice agencies. This decentralization and autonomy is an intentional characteristic of the American criminal justice system. One of the values of the early founders of the United States was a mistrust of a strong, centralized government and as a result, the U.S. government was created with numerous checks and balances. This philosophy is mirrored in the criminal justice system.

See www.policeemployment.com for links to federal agencies, state police, and city police; employment opportunities; and tips for getting police jobs. ■

The most significant agencies in the criminal justice system are (1) the police, (2) the courts, (3) the probation and parole agencies, and (4) the jails, prisons, and other correctional agencies. These agencies exist in the local, state, and federal levels of government. Each jurisdiction has its own distinctive criminal justice agencies that provide services to the local, state, or federal government. For example, there are local police, state police, and federal police. Likewise, there are local, state, and federal courts and correctional institutions.

One of the difficulties of capturing the dynamics of this multilevel system is understanding that the local, state, and federal political agencies, while independent, are at the same time united and interdependent. For example, a defendant arrested by the municipal police for loitering can end up pleading his or her case before the U.S. Supreme Court. While the criminal justice system has been described as an input–output model, it is also appropriate to describe the courts as the hub of the criminal justice system. In a sense, the activities of the criminal justice system are arranged around the mission of the courts.

Over 2 million people are employed by the criminal justice system.[13] However, each of the thousands of criminal justice agencies hires its own employees. There is no central employment agency for the criminal justice system. Each agency sets standards of employment, defines job responsibilities and duties, and pays its employees independently of central control. As a result, there is great diversity in the educational achievement, skills, knowledge, and abilities of the people who work in the criminal justice system. One community may require police officers to have only a high school diploma, whereas another community may require a bachelor's degree. One city may have no requirements of legal training for its municipal judges, whereas another city may require that municipal judges meet strict standards for education and other qualifications.

One may be tempted to think of the criminal justice system as a wedding cake with three layers: local, state, and federal. However, the analogy of a wedding cake implies that each political entity is separate and that there is a hierarchy with local political entities at the bottom and the federal government at the top. This is not accurate; however, a better analogy is to think of the criminal justice system as a picket fence. In the **picket fence model,** the horizontal boards in the fence represent the local, state, and federal governments, and the vertical boards represent the various functions within the criminal justice system, such as law enforcement, courts, and corrections (Figure 2.2 on page 44). For example, local municipal courts have their own mission, personnel, and resources. However, a case can be appealed from a local municipal court to a state court, and from a state court to a federal court. Thus, each court system is separate, but each is linked by a vertical picket.

Process and Flow

The process and flow of the criminal justice system refers to the means by which people accused of a crime enter the criminal justice system, their guilt or innocence is determined, and they are punished or exit the system. This process, from being accused of a crime to final disposition or exit from the criminal justice system, can take years or even decades to complete. There is no standard time limit for processing a case through the system. Different defendants with similar charges and circumstances can take significantly different amounts of time for their cases to go through the system.

picket fence model Model of the criminal justice system, with the local, state, and federal criminal justice systems depicted as three horizontal levels connected vertically by the roles, functions, and activities of the agencies that comprise them.

The flow of a person through the criminal justice system is not a one-way process. People can enter the system, be processed up to a certain point, and exit the system, only to be brought back into the system at a later time. A good example of this is the case of the four Los Angeles police officers accused of using excessive force in the traffic stop

Figure 2.2

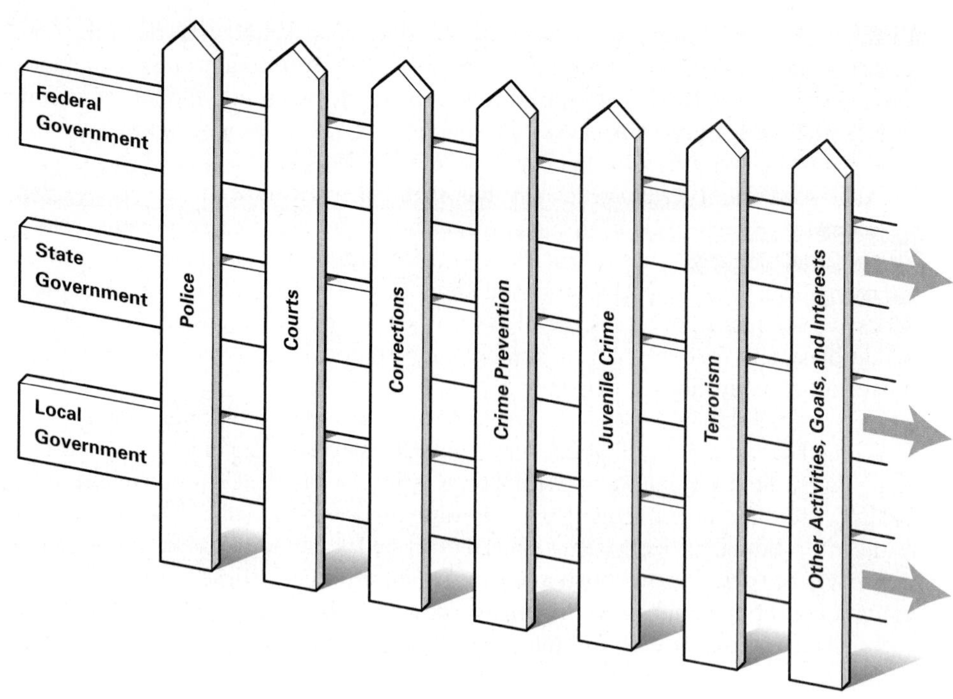

The Picket Fence Model of the Criminal Justice System

Local, state, and federal governments are separate but are linked by common activities, goals, and interests. In this model, the horizontal "boards" represent the various levels of government. Each is separate, but vertical "pickets" join them. (Note that the horizontal boards are not equal in size; local government performs the majority of criminal justice activities.) Examples of the links joining levels of government include federal funding, which may link local and state programs to the federal government; combined efforts to combat terrorism or other special tasks; the system of appeals by which a municipal court case could be appealed all the way to the U.S. Supreme Court; and projects such as prison reform, community policing, delinquency and gang outreach, and drugs and organized crime.

of motorist Rodney King. These officers were arrested, tried in state court, found innocent of the charges against them, and freed. However, they were brought back into the system at the federal level. Federal charges of civil rights violations were filed against these officers, and they were arrested, tried, and convicted of these federal charges.

No agency or person oversees the status of an offender's process through the criminal justice system. Rather, each agency processes people through their part of the system independently, which often results in bottlenecks. Aggressive police strategies resulting in a significant increase in arrest for drunk driving can overwhelm the court's ability to process the increased number of cases. A get-tough sentencing philosophy can result in many more inmates than the prisons can house. There is no "traffic cop" to direct the flow and process of people through the criminal justice system.

JUST THE FACTS 2.2

Why is the model of the criminal justice system more like a picket fence than a wedding cake? What agencies and processes do the vertical and horizontal boards in the picket fence model represent?

Criminal Justice Models

THE MAIN IDEA

The criminal justice system has the goals of both crime control and due process. These goals sometimes conflict with each other.

The criminal justice system has more than one purpose. One of the primary purposes is to provide for the orderly interaction of citizens in a complex society. The criminal

During the years that Earl Warren was chief justice of the U.S. Supreme Court, there was a great emphasis on due process, even at the expense of crime control. During this era, court decisions such as *Mapp v. Ohio, Gideon v. Wainwright,* and *Miranda v. Arizona* ushered in a new era of due process rights. Similar decisions extended this protection of individual rights to juveniles, prisoners, probationers, and parolees. How do the crime control and due process models of criminal justice differ?

justice system also has the goal of promoting socially approved behaviors, morals, and values. Another goal is to provide an environment that promotes commerce by encouraging honesty and trust in commercial transactions. There are various means to achieve each of these goals, but there is no single best criminal justice system.

The criminal justice system of a society reflects its values as well as its desire to be safe from crime. This reflection of values is one of the reasons that countries have adopted different criminal justice systems. In countries with little or no separation between state and religion, the criminal justice system strongly reflects religious laws and values. In totalitarian governments, the criminal justice system reflects the values of preserving state power and the status quo. In the United States, the criminal justice system reflects a balance between crime control and due process; both goals are esteemed, and the balance between them changes from time to time. More than other criminal justice agencies, the U.S. Supreme Court monitors the balance between individual rights and community safety. Through its power of judicial review, the Court can declare when laws violate constitutionally protected liberties and can rule against certain practices of the criminal justice system.

Crime Control versus Due Process

As you read in Chapter 1, the preservation of citizens' individual rights must be balanced against the necessity to enforce laws and maintain social order. Law without order is anarchy, but order without law is tyranny. The balance between law and order resembles a pendulum that swings back and forth between the two values. For example, in the western frontier in the late 1800s, there was minimum concern for due process: Justice was quick, simple, and often violent. At times, justice was carried out by the courts, but at other times citizens took justice into their own hands. Concern for due process swung to its most liberal extent in the 1960s and then back to the right again with the "law and order" platform on which Richard Nixon based his campaign for the presidency. In that period of social unrest, many people were receptive to the promise of crime control, community safety, and swift—preferably harsh—justice for the offender. This emphasis on efficient and effective justice is known as the **crime control model.**

crime control model
Model of the criminal justice system in which emphasis is placed on fighting crime and protecting potential victims.

The United States is a representative form of democracy and as such, the values of individual liberty and pursuit of happiness are considered as important as crime control. Crime control cannot be achieved at the expense of constitutionally protected liberties. The emphasis on ensuring that individuals are protected from arbitrary and excessive abuse of power by the government is known as **due process.** Due process means that in the quest for crime control, the government is bound to follow certain rules and procedures. Even if a person is guilty, if the government does not follow the rules and procedures in obtaining a conviction, the courts can void the conviction.

The basic source of due process rights is the U.S. Constitution and the Bill of Rights, which guarantee protections against unreasonable searches, forced and self-incriminating testimony, excessive bail and fines, and cruel or unusual punishment, as well as rights to a speedy public trial by jury. Other due process rights have been crafted by court rulings and rules of evidence, including the right to an attorney to represent a defendant in a serious criminal case, the right to be treated equally before the court, and the right to be informed of one's rights.

The combined emphasis on crime control and due process results in a criminal justice process that is slow, contradictory, and oriented toward protecting the rights of the accused as opposed to securing justice for the victim. This orientation guards against abuse of power by police, prosecutors, courts, and corrections at the expense of swift and sure justice for the victim. This decision is a deliberate choice, not an accidental characteristic of the criminal justice system. By insisting that the government operate within certain limitations in securing the conviction of the accused, citizens are protected against the misuse of the enormous power of the government, which could be brought to bear in prosecuting the individual. Thus, justice may be delayed—or even denied—in favor of protecting the due process rights of the accused. Better that a guilty person should escape the punishment of justice than that an innocent person should be wrongfully accused. As mentioned earlier, this value stems from the mistrust of a strong, centralized government held by early leaders of this country.

due process Rules and procedures for protecting individuals accused of crimes from arbitrary and excessive abuse of power by the government.

presumption of innocence Most important principle of the due process model, requiring that all accused persons are treated as innocent until proven guilty in a court of law.

adjudicated A court case is decided without determination of guilt or innocence, especially in juvenile court, when a judge places a juvenile in the custody of the state for treatment or confinement.

status offenses Offenses committed by a juvenile that are prohibited (declared illegal) only because of the offender's age.

parens patriae Philosophy of the juvenile court that the court is acting in the best interests of a juvenile, as if it were the juvenile's parent.

The central premise of the criminal justice due process model is the **presumption of innocence.** Regardless of overwhelming evidence against the accused, the court proceeds on the presumption that until the guilt of the accused is proven beyond a reasonable doubt in a court of law, the defendant will be treated as if he or she were innocent of the charges. The crime control model, on the other hand, has the opposite presumption: If common sense and evidence clearly indicate guilt, the accused awaiting trial should be treated as such for the protection of the community. In the crime control perspective, community safety and quality of life are threatened by pretending that a career burglar, serial rapist, or pedophile is innocent until proven guilty when the evidence clearly suggests otherwise.

Because the criminal justice system is subject to political influence, it is not surprising that political party labels have been applied to these two models. The due process model is frequently associated with liberals, and the crime control model is identified with conservatives. Attitudes toward crime can take on political significance, especially during election campaigns. In addition, as in our two-party system, the criminal justice system shifts back and forth between the two models. Factors such as prosperity, low crime rates, and the absence of media coverage of horrific and frightening crimes promote more concern over due process issues such as equality, justice, and human dignity. However, rising crime rates, an economic downturn, or sensational media coverage of a ghastly crime can cause the public to demand quicker police response, tougher sentencing, and less concern for the rights of the accused.

Adult versus Juvenile Criminal Justice Process

The criminal justice system has separated the processing of adults and juveniles. At the beginning of the twentieth century, the American criminal justice system crafted a separate and unique system for juvenile justice. While utilizing many of the same criminal justice agencies and concepts as the adult criminal justice system, the juvenile justice system, represented in Figure 2.3 on page 48, is significantly different.

Juveniles who are less than 18 years old are processed by the juvenile criminal justice system. Juveniles who commit particularly appalling violent crimes or whose repetitive involvement in serious crime suggests that they and community safety are no longer served by the juvenile justice system can be waived to the adult criminal justice system.

The mission of the juvenile justice system emphasizes rehabilitation and restorative justice rather than punishment and retribution. The juvenile justice system avoids the use of terms such as *arrest, trial, guilt,* and *sentencing.* Juveniles are not arrested but are processed into the system by "intake" officers. Juveniles have hearings without juries. Juvenile hearings are closed to the public and the media. Until recently, juveniles were not even permitted to be represented by an attorney. Juveniles are not found guilty by a jury; their cases are **adjudicated** (i.e., their cases are decided by a judge). Juveniles do not serve time for offenses they commit; they are remanded to the custody of the state for rehabilitation. The operating premise of the juvenile justice system is that the juvenile can be rehabilitated and reintegrated into society.

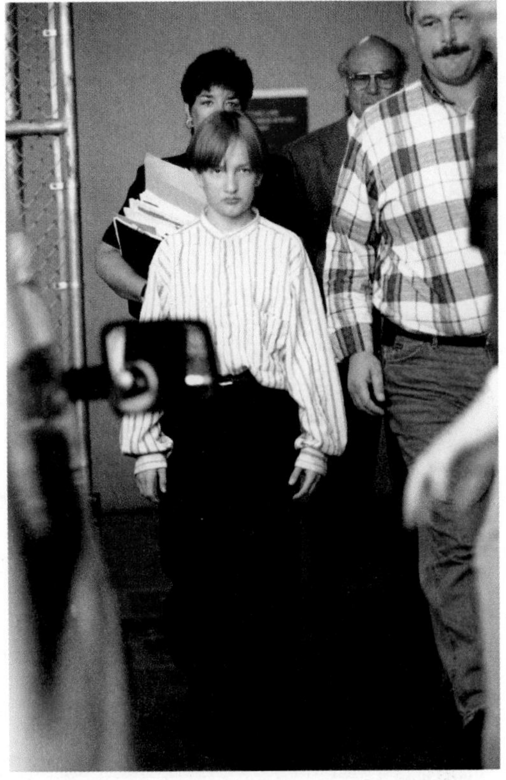

Ray DeFord, 12, arrested in 1996 for setting a fire that killed eight people, will remain in custody of the Oregon Youth Authority until he is 25 years old. The juvenile justice system is broader in its mission than is the adult justice system. The juvenile justice system aims to protect the welfare of juveniles and regulates their behaviors that would be legal if they were adults. In addition to crimes like DeFord's, juvenile courts handle cases of alleged child abuse, runaway juveniles, undisciplined behavior, neglected juveniles, and dependent children. How exactly do the juvenile and adult criminal justice systems differ, and how do they interact?

The juvenile justice system has its own court system and criminal justice agencies dedicated to processing juveniles through the justice system. There is no separate police for juveniles, but many police departments have identified police officers who specialize in juvenile crime and offenders and work closely with the juvenile courts. Juveniles are not permitted to be incarcerated with adult offenders at any time during the criminal justice process. Thus, there are separate correctional and rehabilitation agencies for juveniles.

A unique role of the juvenile justice system, which has no corresponding model in the adult criminal justice system, is the juvenile court's responsibility toward the status offender. Certain acts, such as smoking, drinking, and sexual activity, are legal for adults but are prohibited for juveniles. These are called **status offenses.** Juveniles, for example, are required to attend school. It is an offense for a child not to attend school, whether it is because of his or her own choice or due to the behavior of the child's parent. Juveniles who do not attend school are status offenders and can be processed by the juvenile court. In this role, the court frequently acts as if it is the child's parent, concerned about the welfare of the child, rather than as a judge determining criminal liability. This responsibility of the court is called ***parens patriae.***

The recent increase in violent juvenile crime has raised the concern that the juvenile justice system needs serious review as to its mission and effectiveness. When juvenile offenses include such crimes as murder, rape, and robbery, the premise that the focus of the juvenile justice system should be rehabilitation and not punishment is seriously questioned.

State versus Federal Criminal Justice Systems

There are two distinct criminal justice systems in the United States: the federal system and the state system. Each state has the autonomy to design its own criminal justice system. From state to state there are differences in each of the criminal justice systems. These differences are discussed in more detail in later chapters that focus on the

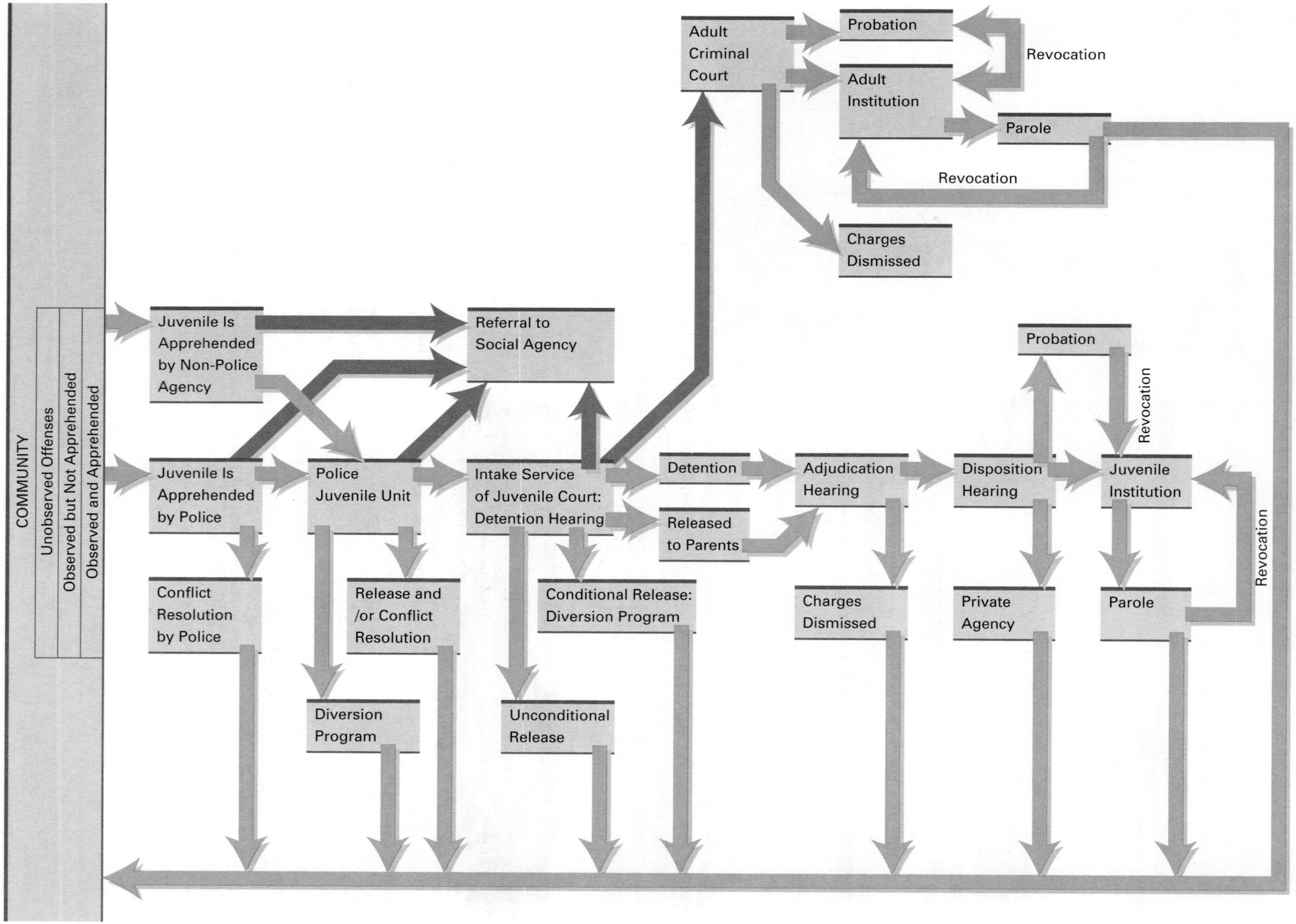

Source: Galan M. Janeksela, "Juvenile Delinquency and the Criminal Justice System," in Dae H. Chang (ed.), *Introduction to Criminal Justice: Theory and Application* (Dubuque, IA: Kendall/Hunt, 1979).

diversity  in the system

Who Is a Child?

Juveniles were not always separated from adults in the criminal justice system. In fact, the separation of juveniles and adults is a relatively new requirement, dating back only to 1899. The purpose of the juvenile court is to protect the young offender from the criminal justice system's ability to impose sanctions and is based on the premise that the young offender does not have the same criminal intent as an adult offender. Also, the juvenile justice system is based on the premise that the young offender can be rehabilitated and that society would be better served by rehabilitating the offender than punishing the offender.

The legal end of childhood was originally set at age 18 in 1899. This age was actually quite old when compared with the life expectancy of a person at that time. In 1899, it was not uncommon for 17-year-olds to marry, to have gainful employment, and to live separately from their parents. This marker was also quite a significant increase in the common law age of youth. The practice in British common law, in the American colonies, and in the United States before 1899 was to set the age of innocence at age 7. Older offenders could and did suffer the same punishment as adults. For example, in 1786, the state of Connecticut executed a 12-year-old girl for the killing of a playmate.[14]

At what age should an offender be treated differently by the criminal justice system? The criminal justice system does not appear to use scientific evidence to determine the answer to this question. Nor is there universal agreement as to what constitutes the age of accountability. While 17 years of age is the norm for state and federal courts, each state has established a lower age at which the juvenile offender can be transferred to the adult court. This age differs significantly from state to state.

Some members of the public have expressed their concern that 17 years of age is too old. They argue that children are more mature today, have access to and use guns in the crimes they commit, and use the protection of the criminal justice system to avoid punishment for serious crimes such as murder, rape, drug trafficking, robbery, and burglary.

The criminal justice system has numerous examples of youthful offenders who have committed serious crimes. Shannon Franklin Kane, age 17, committed more than 22 various felonies, including kidnapping, sexual assault, sodomy, robbery, and terroristic threatening, as well as stabbing another 17-year-old with a screwdriver. Kip Kinkel, age 17, was sentenced to 112 years in prison for the murder of his parents and two students and the wounding of 25 others at his Oregon high school. Andrew Wurst, age 14, killed his eighth-grade teacher and was sentenced to 30 to 60 years in prison. Nathaniel Brazill, age 13, rode his bike home, took a pistol from his grandfather's dresser drawer, returned to school, and shot his teacher, Barry Grunow, in the head. Victor Cordova, Jr., age 12, shot Araceli Tena, age 13, in the head and killed her. Nathaniel Abraham, age 11, was tried as an adult for the murder of Ronnie Greene, Jr., age 18.

■ **Can 11-, 12-, or 13-year-old offenders appreciate the criminal nature of their actions? Should the criminal justice system be more concerned with rehabilitating juvenile offenders or protecting society? At what age should the focus turn from rehabilitation to punishment? At what age should juveniles be held accountable for their crimes?**

various criminal justice agencies. The federal government has its own separate criminal justice system that is distinct from the state system. Thus, there is a system of federal police, courts, and correctional agencies that operates separately from state agencies. Both criminal justice systems are subject to the overview of the U.S. Supreme Court and resemble each other in the processes and agencies that define the system. However, it is important to note that the two systems are not interchangeable.

Figure 2.3

Operations of the Juvenile Justice System

A defendant is processed into one or the other of these systems, depending on certain criteria regarding the offense committed, where it was committed, and by whom it was committed. For example, if a husband and a wife were to get into a domestic dispute and harm one another, normally this would be a matter for the local police and the state criminal justice system. However, if this event were to occur in a national park or on a federal reservation, federal police and federal courts would handle it. Military personnel and aircraft passengers who commit offenses are subject to federal jurisdiction. Native Americans living on reservation lands are subject to the jurisdiction of the Tribal Indian Police or the federal government. The criminal justice process for the federal and the state criminal justice systems is very similar in terms of processing of the offender through the particular system. The significant difference is that each system has its own personnel and agencies for processing defendants through the system.

See http://ojjdp.ncjrs.org, the official web site of the federal Office of Juvenile Justice and Delinquency Prevention. ■

There are some offenses in which the defendant may be processed by both the federal and the state criminal justice systems. Some offenses are both federal and state offenses, and each system retains the right to prosecute the accused. In such cases, it is possible that the accused can be charged and processed through both systems. For example, Timothy McVeigh's offense against his victims in the Oklahoma City federal building was both a federal and a state offense. Because the offense was committed on federal property, the federal criminal justice system could claim responsibility for prosecuting him. His actions resulted in the murder of citizens of Oklahoma and, thus, the state of Oklahoma could claim responsibility for prosecuting him. In the end, the execution of Timothy McVeigh by the federal criminal justice system provided a final resolve as to any responsibility of the state of Oklahoma in prosecuting McVeigh.

International Criminal Justice

Each country has its own criminal justice system, but it is obvious that there must be some means by which countries may collaborate in the prosecuting of offenders. Certain offenses and offenders threaten more than community safety within their country. Also, in today's highly mobile environment, the offender may commit offenses in several countries or may commit an offense in one country and escape to another. There is no international criminal justice system, but there are two primary cooperative efforts among nations to deal with the problem of international crime: the United Nations (UN) and the International Police Association (INTERPOL).

The UN is involved in numerous international missions, including criminal justice, but does not have legitimate authority within the borders of a nation without the invitation and cooperation of the host nation. The criminal justice mission of the UN involves four primary goals. The first goal of the UN is to conduct surveys to gather data about international and comparative crime. The United Nations World Crime Surveys gather data from member states for the purpose of providing a snapshot of comparative criminal activity. The second goal of the UN is to provide peacekeeping efforts in countries in which the domestic police are no longer able to perform their duties or in which domestic police do not exist.

The third mission is to promote crime prevention. The UN encourages member nations to focus on the problems of crime, links governments for innovative and cooperative solutions, and promotes regional and international agreements to strengthen international cooperation in crime prevention. The UN plays an important role in preventing crimes involving transnational terrorism and drug trafficking.

Finally, the UN seeks to promote a common standard of justice and fair treatment of defendants and convicted persons. Through resolutions such as the **International Bill of Human Rights** and the Standard Minimum Rules for the Treatment of Prisoners, the UN has worked to secure fair and just treatment of the accused by the criminal justice systems of the world.

Go to United Nations information on world crime at http://www.uncjin.org/. ■

The **International Police Association (INTERPOL)** depends on the cooperative effort of participating nations. First formed in 1914, INTERPOL had no significant

United Nations peacekeeping efforts require the insertion of armed forces within a nation, which is one of the most sensitive operations relating to criminal justice that the UN performs. The insertion of multinational UN peacekeepers into a country to replace its domestic police force—like these British UN soldiers in war-ravaged Albania—is usually done only as a last resort. When UN forces are placed in a country to enforce law and order, their job is complicated by the fact that to many in the host nation, they resemble a foreign army rather than a domestic police force.

presence in international criminal justice until after World War II, when it became a clearinghouse for information on offenses and suspects believed to operate across national boundaries, especially in cases of international terrorism and drug trafficking.

In the United States, the contact point for INTERPOL is the U.S. Department of Justice. Under the authority of the Justice Department, a cooperative unit called the National Central Bureau draws on personnel from a dozen federal law enforcement agencies. INTERPOL–U.S. National Central Bureau does not have original jurisdiction but performs crime scene investigations and initiates investigations of criminal activity. Its focus is centered more on identifying and apprehending criminal offenders who have fled the jurisdiction of the countries in which they committed their crimes.

JUST THE FACTS 2.3

How does the adult criminal justice system differ from the juvenile justice system? What are the differences between the state and federal criminal justice systems? How do national and international criminal justice systems differ, and how do they cooperate?

The Due Process Model

THE MAIN IDEA

As the defendant is processed by the police, prosecution, courts, and corrections, he or she is entitled to the protection of certain rights to guarantee fair and equitable treatment.

criminal justice

in the world

The Globalization of Due Process

Professor David H. Bayley examined the experience with foreign assistance to police abroad and submitted a report to the U.S. Department of Justice, which was published in 2001 under the title *Democratizing the Police Abroad: What to Do and How to Do It.* Bayley concluded that the "reforms considered most important in developing a police force that supports democracy are creation of a responsible public-service orientation, adherence to the rule of law, protection of human rights, and transparency with respect to the activities of the agency and the people within it."[15] His study delineates the following lessons that have been learned from the study of foreign police departments.

1. Foreign assistance cannot produce democratic reform against the opposition of the host government.
2. All police reform is political in the sense that it affects the position and interests of different groups of people both inside and outside of the police.
3. The norms of democratic policing may be achieved by different institutional mechanisms in different countries.
4. To produce democratic reform abroad, programs of police foreign assistance must be adapted to local conditions. This requires the collection and analysis of information about the traditions and practices of the police as well as about society in general.
5. No amount of external inducement or pressure can produce democratic reform against the hostility or indifference of the indigenous police. Unless a foreign police force is seriously committed to reform, it will not occur.
6. Foreign assistance personnel operating abroad must guard against condescension in their relations with local police. The fact that a country might profit from assistance does not mean that its practitioners are unsophisticated.
7. Democratic police reform requires the separation of police from the military.
8. The growth of violence, crime, and civil strife will subordinate police reform to the enhancement of police capacity.
9. The impulse for democratic reform may be weakened by the public's belief that reform will make it more vulnerable to crime and disorder.
10. Nongovernmental organizations dedicated to protecting human rights must learn to work with, as well as against, the police.
11. Creating effective disciplinary systems within the police should be a first-order priority in democratic reform.
12. The concern of foreign advisers and donors with their own problems of international crime and law enforcement decreases their enthusiasm for democratic reform abroad.
13. In order for police reform to be effective, whether for capacity building or democracy, it must be accompanied by reform throughout the criminal justice system.
14. Technical assistance should not be the centerpiece of foreign assistance if democratic reform of policing is the objective.
15. Foreigners assigned to produce change abroad must reside in the country for substantial periods of time to provide programmatic continuity, expeditious advice, and informed midcourse corrections.
16. Institutional reform cannot be produced simply by increasing knowledge about policies and practices elsewhere.
17. People engaged in police reform abroad, both public and private, should construct ways to share lessons learned and to coordinate activities.

These "lessons learned" suggest that democratic reform of a foreign criminal justice system is a slow and difficult process.

■ **What are the advantages to the United States of having foreign police departments respect due process? Are there countries whose police cannot be democratized? What lessons learned from democratizing police abroad can be applied to the police in the United States?**

A general overview of the American criminal justice **due process model** provides an understanding of the interaction—both cooperation and conflict—within the system. There is no specific reference in the Constitution nor is there a federal law defining the American criminal justice process. Rather, it is a complex system, represented in Figure 2.4 on page 54, that has emerged over time.

As mentioned previously, the criminal justice system has three major components: police, courts, and corrections. Within these three major components are criminal justice agencies that have various roles to play in making this system work. Each of the agencies is independent, but they must work together. Each has a limited role in processing the defendant, and the system has a built-in process for moving offenders from the police to the courts to corrections. Six major processes in the criminal justice system are (1) deciding what is a crime, (2) detecting a crime and arresting a suspect, (3) determining whether the accused is to go to trial, (4) determining guilt or innocence in a trial, (5) deciding on a punishment for the convicted, and (6) administering the prescribed punishment (carrying out the sentence).

Deciding What Is a Crime

Boundaries are set for determining who and what behaviors are subject to the criminal justice system. In the United States, these boundaries are determined by criminal laws that define illegal behaviors. People suspected of performing these behaviors are subject to arrest and possible punishment if found guilty of committing them. Local, state, and federal legislative bodies define criminal laws. Criminal laws are fluid and change from time to time. New behaviors are criminalized, and old behaviors are decriminalized. (Criminal law is the subject of Chapter 4.)

Deciding to Arrest

The police are the primary agency responsible for detecting crime violators and bringing these individuals into the criminal justice system. Law enforcement agencies at the local, state, and federal levels are charged with the specific responsibility of discovering and apprehending crime violators. Investigating crime and apprehending suspects is the primary job function of police detectives. Another job function of the police is exercising their power of arrest.

The power of arrest means that police can forcibly restrain persons for the purpose of entering them into the criminal justice process. The police are highly regulated in the exercise of this power. In the due process model, whether the police followed the criteria authorizing them to make an arrest is often a point of serious debate. If the defendant can prove that the police did not follow these criteria, the court may dismiss all of the charges against the defendant, even if it is obvious that the defendant is guilty.[16]

LIMITS ON THE POWER OF ARREST Guidelines that the police must observe in making an arrest are (1) to ensure that persons arrested understand their constitutional rights, (2) to arrest only when police have **probable cause** that a crime has been committed or are acting under the power of the court through an arrest warrant, and (3) to document the circumstances of the arrest and take all evidence into custody.[17] Police typically recite to arrestees their constitutional rights. *Probable cause* means that the police cannot arrest a person unless there is evidence, more than a suspicion or "feeling," that the person has committed a crime. The police are the first persons of authority to arrive at the scene of a crime, and, as mentioned, it is their responsibility to document the circumstances that existed at the time of arrest and to take all evidence into custody. The reports that the police fill out when they arrest a person become one

due process model Model of the criminal justice system in which emphasis is placed on protecting the rights of the accused.

probable cause Determination from evidence and arguments that there are valid reasons for believing that the accused has committed a crime.

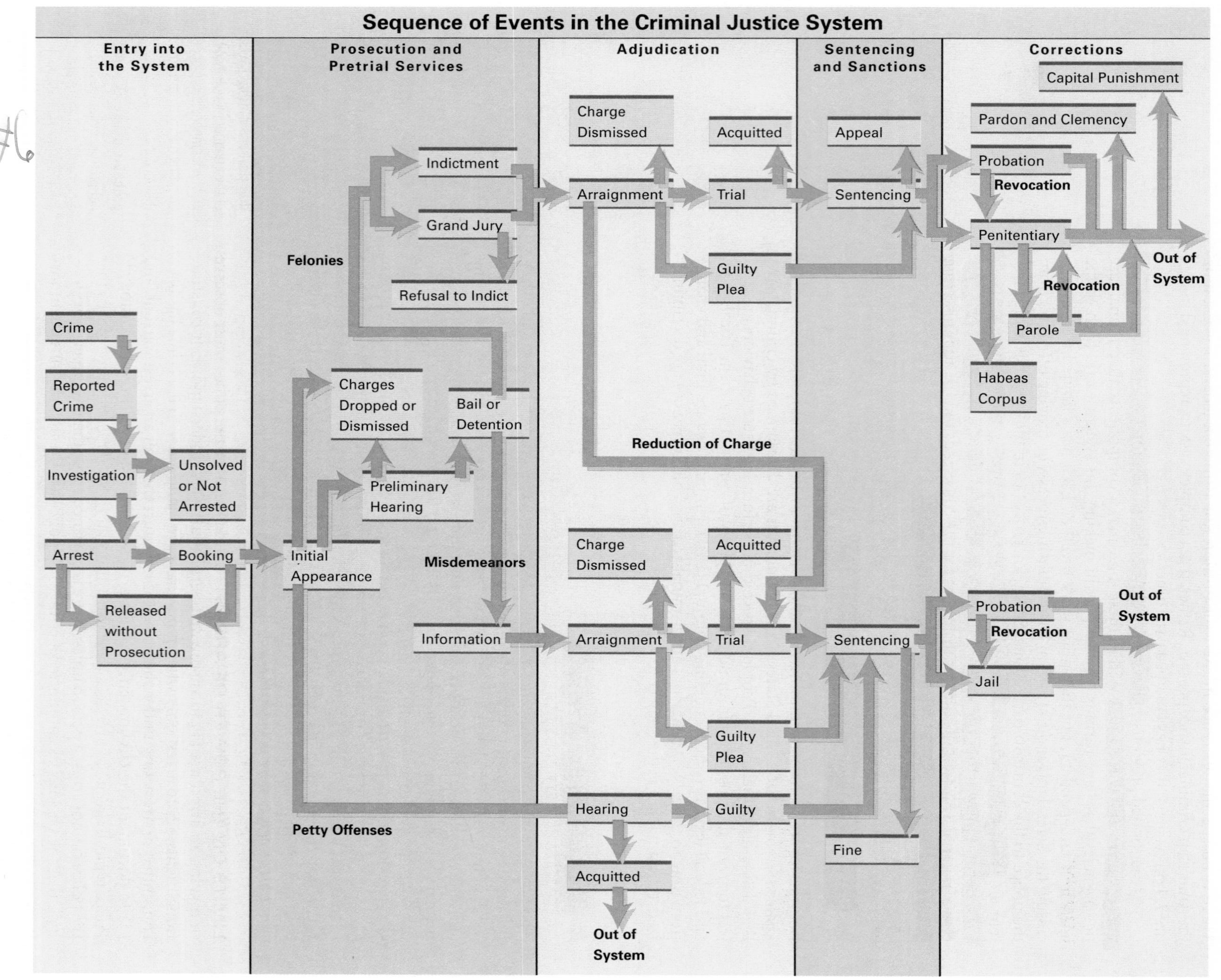

Sequence of Events in the Criminal Justice System
Entry into the System
Prosecution and Pretrial Services
Adjudication
Sentencing and Sanctions
Corrections
Crime
Reported Crime
Investigation
Unsolved or Not Arrested
Arrest
Booking
Released without Prosecution
Initial Appearance
Felonies
Indictment
Grand Jury
Refusal to Indict
Charges Dropped or Dismissed
Bail or Detention
Preliminary Hearing
Misdemeanors
Information
Petty Offenses
Charge Dismissed
Arraignment
Acquitted
Trial
Guilty Plea
Reduction of Charge
Hearing
Guilty
Out of System
Appeal
Sentencing
Fine
Capital Punishment
Pardon and Clemency
Probation
Revocation
Penitentiary
Parole
Habeas Corpus
Jail

of the primary pieces of evidence at the trial used to determine the guilt of the accused. If the police cannot produce evidence gathered at the scene of the crime at the trial or if there is doubt regarding whether the evidence has been securely stored to prevent tampering, the court may dismiss charges against the accused. (Due process and police procedure are discussed in more detail in Chapter 5.)

BOOKING Once the police determine that they have probable cause to make an arrest or arrest a person through the power of an arrest warrant, they must process that person so that he or she may be forwarded on to the next step in the criminal justice system—determining if the accused will stand trial. The way they do this is to complete formal paperwork that (1) establishes the identity of the person and (2) charges the person with a specific violation of the criminal law. **Booking** is the procedure that acts as the transition point for moving the arrested person from the police department into the jurisdiction of the court.

Police transport the arrested person to a booking facility, where the arrestee may be detained for up to two days. At the booking facility, the police establish positive identification of the person arrested, cross-checking social security number, driver's license number, and date of birth with the physical appearance of the person to determine that the arrestee is properly identified. Photographs and fingerprints are taken of the arrested person, and these fingerprints may be checked against those stored in law enforcement databases. Once identity is established, other local, state, federal, and international law enforcement agencies are contacted to check to see if there are any outstanding warrants for the arrest of the person booked.

While the booking facility is establishing the identity of the arrestee, the arresting officer consults with supervisors, detectives, and perhaps the prosecuting attorney regarding the charges to be filed against the person. In making an arrest report, it is common for the police to charge the person with multiple offenses, beginning with the most serious offense. An example of an arrest report is presented in Figure 2.5 on page 56.

After the allowed 48 hours of detention have elapsed, police must formally charge the person with a crime or release him or her. If the police release the person without filing charges, they may rearrest that person at a later time for the same offense when they feel they have more substantial evidence. If police formally charge a suspect with a crime, the person is moved to the next step in the criminal justice process.

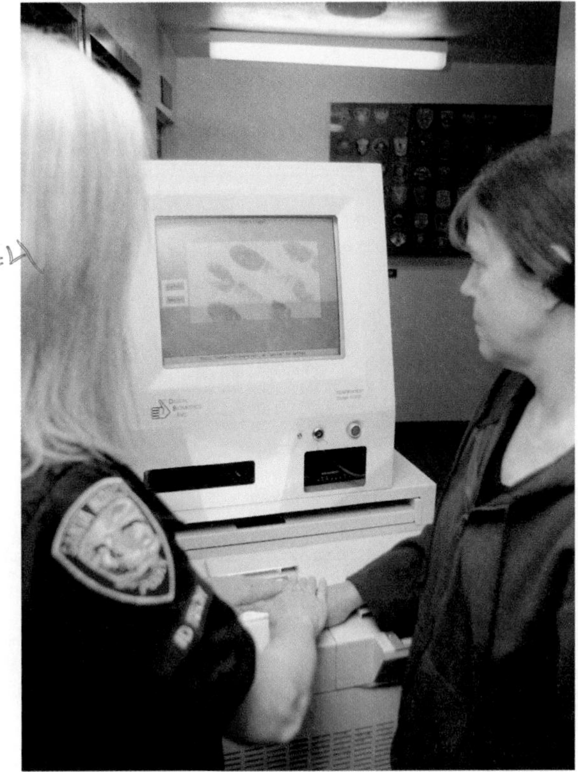

If the identity of arrestees cannot reliably be established, the police are empowered to hold them in booking until their identities can be established. People who refuse to identify themselves are booked as "John Doe" or "Jane Doe," and the police attempt to establish their identities by fingerprint match. Identification is a critical factor in law enforcement. Fingerprint databases frequently match persons booked for minor offenses with outstanding warrants on more serious charges, and they often match persons booked in one state with crimes committed in other states. What are the other steps in bringing a suspect to trial?

booking Police activity that establishes the identification of an arrested person and formally charges that person with a crime.

Figure 2.4

The Criminal Justice System

COMMONWEALTH OF PENNSYLVANIA
COUNTY OF: ______

POLICE CRIMINAL COMPLAINT

Magisterial District Number:
District Justice Name:
Address:

Telephone:

COMMONWEALTH OF PENNSYLVANIA
VS.
DEFENDANT: NAME and ADDRESS

Docket No.:
Date Filed:
OTN:

Defendant's Race Ethnicity ☐ White ☐ Asian ☐ Black ☐ Hispanic ☐ Native American ☐ Unknown	Defendant's Sex ☐ Female ☐ Male	Defendant's D.O.B.	Defendant's Social Security Number	Defendant's SIO (State Identification Number)
Defendant's A.K.A. (Also known as)	Defendant's Vehicle Information Plate Number / State / Registration Sticker (MM/YY)			Defendant's Driver's License Number State
Complaint/Incident Number	Complaint/Incident Number if other Participants			UCR/NIBRS Code

District Attorney's Office ☐ Approved ☐ Disapproved because: ______

(The district attorney may require that the complaint, arrest warrant affidavit, or both be approved by the attorney for the Commonwealth prior to filing Pa.R.Cr.P. 107.)

______ (Name of Attorney for Commonwealth - Please Print or Type) ______ (Signature of Attorney for Commonwealth) ______ (Date)

I, ______ (Name of Affiant - Please Print or Type) ______ (Officer Badge Number / I.D.)

of ______ (Identify Department or Agency Represented and Political Subdivision) ______ (Police Agency ORI Number) ______ (Orginating Agency Case Number (OCA))

do hereby state: (check appropriate box)

1. ☐ I accuse the above named defendant, who lives at the address set forth above
   ☐ I accuse the defendant whose name is unknown to me but who is described as ______

   ☐ I accuse the defendant whose name and popular designation or nickname is unknown to me and whom I have therefore designated as John Doe

   with violating the penal laws of the Commonwealth of Pennsylvania at ______ (Place-Political Subdivision)

   in ______ County on or about ______

   Participants were: (if there were participants, place their names here, repeating the name of above defendant)

2. The acts committed by the accused were:
   (Set forth a summary of the facts sufficient to advise the defendant of the nature of the offense charged. A citation to the statute allegedly violated, without more, is not sufficient. In a summary case, you must cite the specific section and subsection of the statute or ordinance allegedly violated.

(continued)

(Continuation of No. 2)

POLICE CRIMINAL COMPLAINT

Defendant's Name:
Docket Number:

all of which were against the peace and dignity of the Commonwealth of Pennsylvania and contrary to the Act of Assembly, or in violation of

1. ________ (Section) ________ (Subsection) of the ________ (PA Statute) ________ (counts)

2. ________ (Section) ________ (Subsection) of the ________ (PA Statute) ________ (counts)

3. ________ (Section) ________ (Subsection) of the ________ (PA Statute) ________ (counts)

4. ________ (Section) ________ (Subsection) of the ________ (PA Statute) ________ (counts)

3. I ask that a warrant of arrest or a summons be issued and that the defendant be required to answer the charges I have made. **(In order for a warrant of arrest to issue, the attached affidavit of probable cause must be completed and sworn to before the issuing authority.)**

4. I verify that the facts set forth in this complaint are true and correct to the best of my knowledge or information and belief. This verification is made subject to the penalties of Section 4904 of the Crimes Code (18 PA. C.S. § 4904) relating to unsworn falsification to authorities.

________________, ____ ________________ (Signature of Affiant)

AND NOW, on this date ________________, ____, I certify that the complaint has been properly completed and verified. An affidavit of probable cause must be completed in order for a warrant to issue.

(continued)

Figure 2.5

Police Arrest Report

Each police agency has its own type of arrest report, but all such forms are similar in that on the arrest report, the police officer must clearly identify the defendant and accuse him or her of a specific crime. In the arrest report, the officer must explain what the defendant did that caused the arrest. The district attorney's office will review the arrest report and either approve or deny it. The district attorney's office may choose to dismiss all charges, to accept some of the charges, or to charge the defendant with other crimes. The police officer must have knowledge of the law to properly identify the various elements of the crime.

Defendant's Name:
Docket Number:

POLICE CRIMINAL COMPLAINT

AFFIDAVIT of PROBABLE CAUSE

I, ______________________________, BEING DULY SWORN ACCORDING TO LAW, DEPOSE AND SAY THAT THE FACTS SET FORTH IN THE FOREGOING AFFIDAVIT ARE TRUE AND CORRECT TO THE BEST OF MY KNOWLEDGE, INFORMATION, AND BELIEF.

____
(Signature of Affiant)

Sworn to me and subscribed before me this ________ day of ________________, ____.

__________ Date __________________________, District Justice

Figure 2.5

Police Arrest Report (*Continued*)

Deciding to Prosecute

In this next step of the due process model, the prosecuting attorney reviews the charges filed by the police and the supporting evidence collected. If the prosecutor does not believe there is sufficient evidence to justify the charges, he or she can refuse to accept the case from the police, in which case the police may be liable for a civil law suit for false arrest. If the prosecutor accepts the case, the defendant is processed further in a preliminary hearing and arraignment, beginning with the first appearance.

first appearance Judicial hearing before a magistrate, following booking. The magistrate judge reviews the charges, advises defendants of their rights, and sets bail.

FIRST APPEARANCE After the paperwork is forwarded to the prosecuting attorney, the accused is brought before a magistrate judge for a **first appearance.** Magistrate judges are judicial officers with authority to evaluate charges filed by police against the accused and determine if the charges are legitimate according to state statutes and federal laws. Magistrates also advise the accused of his or her legal rights and determine if the person has legal representation. When charges are filed that may result in a prison sentence of 6 months or more, the magistrate determines if the person has sufficient funds to obtain legal counsel. If it is determined that the accused cannot afford a lawyer, the court appoints an attorney to represent him or her at no charge.

BAIL Finally, the magistrate decides if the person should be released on bail or held in a correctional facility until a later time. **Bail** is a promise, sometimes backed by a monetary guarantee, that the accused will return for further proceedings in the criminal justice system. Bail cannot be set before the first appearance because until that point, the actual charges against the person are not known. For minor charges, the amount of bail may be set by a schedule of established fees. Fees are usually based on the fine that typically is levied against the person if found guilty. The higher the fine for guilt, the greater the bail set by the magistrate. At the first appearance, the accused is not asked how he or she intends to plead (e.g., guilty or not guilty). Guilt or innocence is not yet an issue. The first appearance is concerned with due process and securing the rights of the accused, and it may take only a few minutes to complete the entire process.

PRELIMINARY HEARING After charges are filed against the person in the first appearance, he or she moves to the next step in the criminal justice system. The **preliminary hearing** is sometimes referred to as a "probable cause" hearing, reflecting its purpose. At the preliminary hearing, the judge takes an active role in asking questions of the prosecution and the defendant.

In this hearing, it is the responsibility of the prosecution to convince the judge that there is probable cause to believe that (1) an offense as defined by the criminal laws of the jurisdiction has been committed within that jurisdiction and (2) the defendant accused of the offense committed it. The charges against the defendant may be changed from those charged at the first appearance. New charges can be added, and old charges can be dropped. The prosecution must specify the offense, the law it violated, and the date the offense was committed.

Defense counsel can challenge the evidence of the prosecution. If the prosecution cannot convince the judge that the evidence presented would cause a reasonable person to believe that the defendant committed the specific crime alleged, the judge has the authority to dismiss the charges against the defendant. If charges are dismissed, the prosecution may gather additional evidence and/or modify the charges and bring the defendant before the court again. If, on the other hand, the judge is convinced that a reasonable person would believe that the defendant committed the offense, the defendant proceeds to the next step in the criminal justice system: the arraignment. The issue of bail for the defendant can be raised again at the preliminary hearing. Bail can be raised, lowered, or revoked.

INFORMATION OR INDICTMENT An alternative method of bringing a person to trial is the grand jury system, the only secret judicial process in the criminal justice system. A **grand jury**, as the name implies, is a panel of citizens who are selected to hear evidence against an accused person. In many ways, a grand jury proceeding has the characteristics of a trial. It is held in a courtroom; a judge presides over the trial, and the prosecutor presents witnesses and evidence to convince the members of the grand jury that the defendant has committed an offense. The major difference is that defendants are not present at the sitting of the grand jury, cannot have an attorney represent them at the grand jury proceedings, and are not even informed that they are the subjects of the grand jury's attention. Defendants in a grand jury session do not know what charges have been filed against them and are not given a chance to rebut the evidence or deny the charges. After the grand jury session is over, the members of the grand jury are not allowed to discuss in public the cases and evidence they heard. The grand jury does not

bail Release of a defendant from custody on the promise, often secured with a monetary bond, that the defendant will return to court at the necessary times to address the charges.

preliminary hearing Hearing before a magistrate judge in which the prosecution presents evidence to convince the judge that there is probable cause to bring the defendant to trial.

grand jury Panel of citizens similar to a trial jury that decides whether there is probable cause to indict a defendant on the charges alleged.

determine guilt or innocence. Rather, it fulfills the same purpose as the preliminary hearing: to determine if there is probable cause that the defendant committed the crime that the prosecution alleges.

If, after hearing the evidence of the prosecution, the grand jury believes there is probable cause that the defendant committed the crime, it returns an indictment against the defendant. An **indictment** is a formal, written legal document forwarded to the court, asserting that there is probable cause that the defendant committed an offense. This indictment authorizes the court to issue an arrest warrant for the defendant. The court delivers the arrest warrant to the prosecution, which delivers it to the police. Armed with this arrest warrant, the police have the authority to arrest the defendant. If the grand jury does not find probable cause that the defendant committed the crime, the prosecution cannot process the defendant into the criminal justice system. If the prosecution cannot obtain an indictment through the grand jury, it can use the preliminary hearing to bring the defendant to trial.

A grand jury indictment offers certain advantages because it can be sealed. The decision of the grand jury remains secret and is not disclosed to the public or to the defendant. The arrest warrant that the court authorizes does not have to be served immediately. In cases in which there are multiple defendants, such as in drug trafficking or organized crime cases, the grand jury allows the prosecution and police to obtain indictments and arrest warrants against all of the defendants without tipping them off that they have been targeted for arrest and prosecution.

ARRAIGNMENT An indictment by a grand jury does not establish the guilt of the defendant. It only provides the prosecution with the authority to process the defendant to the next step in the criminal justice system: the arraignment. The **arraignment** is the last step in determining if the defendant will go to trial. At the arraignment, the defendant appears before the court with his or her attorney to hear the formal charges that the prosecution alleges. These charges may differ substantially from the charges initially filed by the police. A charge of first-degree murder may be reduced to homicide. Burglary may be reduced to trespass. Multiple counts and multiple charges against the defendant may be reduced to a single charge. A defendant accused of a dozen burglaries may be charged with only one. A defendant accused of killing four people may be charged with the murder of only one.

The reason for reducing charges to the one for which there is the best evidence is to reduce the likelihood of having to change charges later in the process. After arraignment, the prosecution cannot change the charges before the trial. If the prosecution wants to change the charges at that point, the current charges must be dropped and the whole process must begin again with a probable cause hearing or new indictment. Thus, once charges are filed, the prosecution is committed to proving those charges. Even if new evidence emerges, changing the charges is not undertaken lightly. This procedure ensures that the defendant will have a fair opportunity to prepare his or her defense. If the charges against the defendant could be changed after the arraignment and before the trial, the defense would not know what evidence to prepare for the trial or what evidence it should prepare to refute the new charges.

MOTIONS AND PLEAS At the arraignment, after charges are read, the judge asks the defendant for a **plea.** The defendant or the defendant's attorney is expected to answer in one of three ways: (1) not guilty, (2) guilty, or (3) no contest (*nolo contendere*). If the defendant does not respond to the question of guilt, the judge enters a plea of not guilty for the defendant and sets a trial date.

A number of motions may be made at the arraignment. A **motion** is a formal request of the court by the prosecution or the defense for a ruling on a particular matter. Motions about pleas may concern such matters as the competency of the defendant to stand trial, the location of the trial, the jurisdiction of the court, and objections to evidence gathered by the police.

indictment The formal verdict of the grand jury that there is sufficient evidence to bring a person to trial.

arraignment Short hearing before a judge in which the charges against the defendant are announced and the defendant is asked if he or she is guilty or not guilty.

plea Defendant's statement that he or she is guilty, not guilty, or offers "no contest."

motion Formal request by the prosecution or defense for the court to rule on any relevant matter in a case, such as the competency of the defendant to stand trial, the location of the trial, the jurisdiction of the court, or objections to evidence gathered by police.

SETTING A TRIAL OR SENTENCING DATE As mentioned earlier, the arraignment process may take only a few minutes. If the defendant pleads not guilty or "stands mute before the court" (refuses to enter a plea), a trial date is set. If the defendant pleads guilty or no contest, there is no need for a trial. In this case, the judge sets a sentencing date. No evidence is presented, no witnesses are called, and the defendant does not have the opportunity to deny guilt. When the defendant is returned to the court, it will be to hear the sentence for the offense. Because of the serious consequences of a guilty plea, a judge is not obligated to accept the defendant's guilty plea at the arraignment. The judge may enter a not guilty plea on behalf of the defendant if the judge believes the defendant is not competent to plead guilty or does not understand the charges. If the judge does this, a trial date is set for the defendant. (The pretrial and trial processes are discussed in more detail in Chapter 9.)

See www.courttv.com, the web site of Court TV, for a wealth of information on the courts, as well as specific information on dozens of trials, current and past. ■

Determining Guilt or Innocence

The trial is the judicial process that determines the guilt or innocence of the defendant. Only the trial court can make this determination. The judge or the jury makes the actual decision as to whether the defendant committed the crime. Some states allow defendants to waive their right to a jury trial and leave the decision as to guilt or innocence to the judge. This type of trial is called a bench trial. In a **bench trial,** the judge acts as both referee and jury. In a **jury trial,** the judge has the authority to determine the sentence if the defendant is found guilty, but the jury, not the judge, determines guilt.

THE TRIAL In a jury trial, after hearing the evidence, the jury is asked if the defendant is guilty or not guilty as charged. The jury is instructed to use only the evidence presented at the trial to make this decision. If the jury cannot come to a unanimous verdict as to the guilt or innocence of the defendant, the judge may request that the jury go back and achieve a verdict. If the jury still cannot decide on a verdict, the judge will declare a mistrial due to a deadlocked jury, or hung jury. In the case of a mistrial, the prosecution has the option of requesting a new trial. A new trial as a result of a mistrial does not violate the defendant's protection against being tried twice for the same crime. If, however, the jury returns a verdict of not guilty, the defendant is acquitted and set free.

PLEA BARGAINING Trials are expensive, involve considerable criminal justice personnel, require public civil service (i.e., jury duty), and are unpredictable. Both prosecutors and defense attorneys have legitimate reasons for wanting to avoid a trial. In fact, most cases do not go to trial. In more than 80 percent of the criminal cases filed against defendants, the defendant pleads guilty.[18] This high percentage of guilty pleas is attributable to plea bargaining. Sometime during the criminal justice process, even after the trial has started, the defendant may contact the prosecution and request that a deal be made. The prosecutor also may initiate the request for a plea bargain. In **plea bargaining,** the defendant agrees to plead guilty if the prosecution will change the charge to a crime carrying a lighter sentence, to one with fewer counts, or in return for a promise of reduced sentence. Prosecutors do not have the resources to take every good case to court, so they depend on plea bargaining to deliver justice efficiently. (The pros and cons of plea bargaining and the details of the trial are discussed in Chapter 10.) Another means of settling a case while avoiding a trial is **diversion.**

bench trial Judicial process to determine the guilt or innocence of a defendant in which the determination is made by a judge, not a jury.

jury trial Judicial process to determine the guilt or innocence of a defendant in which the determination is made by a jury, not a judge.

plea bargaining Negotiations between the prosecution and the defense for a plea of guilty in exchange for reduced charges or a lighter sentence.

diversion Sentencing option in which the defendant is diverted from the correctional system through alternatives such as community service.

Deciding on a Punishment

After the trial, the defendant is released if found not guilty. If the defendant is found guilty, a punishment must be imposed. It is the responsibility of the judge to determine the punishment. However, the judge does not administer the punishment. He or she

Defendants have a constitutional guarantee of a fair public trial by a jury of their peers for all serious offenses. An offense is serious if a defendant with a guilty verdict could receive a sentence of six months or more in jail or prison. A *fair trial* means that no substantial mistakes were made that could have affected the fairness of the court's decision as to the guilt of the defendant. A *public trial* means that the press, media, and public cannot be barred from attending the trial. However, the court does not need to accommodate everyone who wants to attend, and some states do not allow the media to air broadcasts of trials to the public.

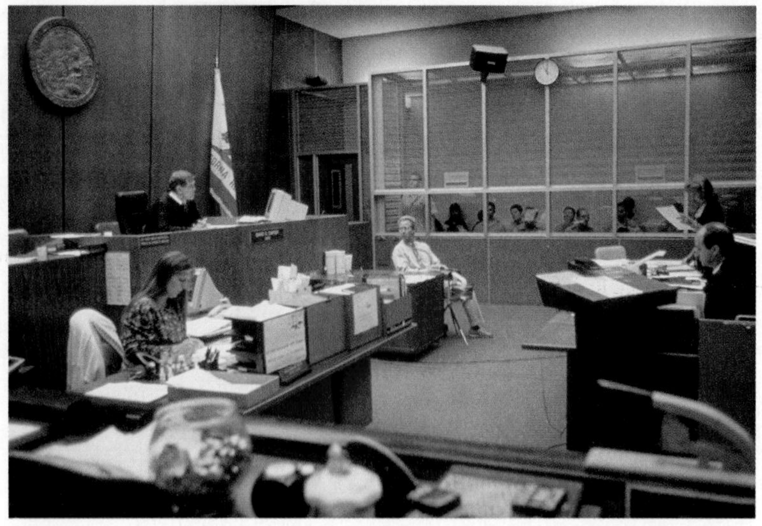

only decides what punishment is legal and appropriate. Each offense has a specified punishment, but often the range of punishment is broad; for example, the punishment for homicide may range from 1 to 20 years in prison. In addition to imprisonment, the judge may impose a fine, sentence the defendant to community service, require the defendant to seek drug or mental health counseling, or suspend the sentence.

SENTENCING To determine which **sentence,** or punishment, the defendant is to receive the judge is guided by the law and input received from the presentence investigation report. The law provides such guidelines as the minimum and maximum length of imprisonment and the maximum fine that can be assessed against the defendant. The law may restrict sentencing options or give judges great latitude in sentencing. Federal criminal codes tend to be more restrictive in specifying the term of imprisonment than are state criminal codes.

Both federal and state judges depend on information provided in a **presentence investigation report,** an investigation by a probation and parole officer or presentence investigator. This report includes evidence other than that presented during the trial. During the trial, the evidence that can be considered by the jury to determine guilt or innocence is restricted to only that which relates to the specific offense of which the defendant is accused. Other information not permitted as evidence includes, for example, previous crimes the defendant committed and the defendant's employment status. The presentence investigation, however, gathers information about the defendant's employment record, family relationships, financial responsibilities, contributions to the community, and prior convictions. Prior convictions and any lack of cooperation on the part of the defendant can result in a harsher sentence. This information, the defendant's entire life, can help a judge to determine an appropriate sentence. Once sentenced, the defendant is convicted, and there is no longer a presumption of innocence. At this point, the convicted defendant is considered guilty and loses many of the due process rights that were guaranteed before conviction.

sentence Disposition of a case by determining the punishment for a defendant convicted of a crime.

presentence investigation report Report on the background of the convicted defendant and any other information relevant for determining the most appropriate sentence.

During the time that the presentence investigation is being conducted, the convicted defendant is held in a correctional institution or is released on bail until the sentencing report is complete. Those convicted of state crimes are held in a state or county correctional institution, and those convicted of federal crimes are held in a federal correctional institution. Convicted defendants released on bail are required to appear before the court at their sentencing hearing.

APPEAL Sentences may be appealed. The prosecution can protest that the sentence is too lenient and does not protect the community. The defendant can argue that the

ethics in the system

Diversion Options

Judges have been given great latitude in the sentences they can impose on offenders and have used this authority to craft creative and innovative ones. In both the juvenile and adult criminal justice systems, judges, guided by the philosophy that overburdened and often brutal prisons do not promote rehabilitation and, in fact, may promote the criminality of the defendant, have sought to avoid processing the defendant further into the system.

Juveniles are the prime targets for diversion sentencing. Juveniles who commit "minor" crimes, such as shoplifting, are often offered the opportunity to avoid entering the juvenile justice system if they will attend classes designed to extinguish the unlawful behavior. Men who have been arrested for domestic violence may be offered the opportunity to avoid prison if they attend anger-management classes. Drug addicts can have the charges against them dropped if they seek treatment. First offenders who are employed and have a family to support may be offered the chance to avoid prison if they agree to abide by such conditions as alcohol or drug counseling, regular payment of child support, and no further negative contact with the police.

Some jurisdictions may offer offenders a "deferred agreement of guilty" plea, or DAG. With a DAG, the judge sets the sentencing aside for a period of time, usually 1 year. If during that period of time defendants comply with the orders of the court to receive appropriate assistance from alcohol treatment, drug treatment, or anger-management agencies and do not have any negative contact with the police, the charges against them will be dismissed. In a sense, their records will be wiped clean, as the official record will show they were found not guilty and they will not suffer any of the consequences of a guilty verdict on their records. A DAG plea is often used in domestic violence cases. Abusive spouses who get help and are able to maintain healthy relationships with their mates can have the charges dismissed.

Diversion sentencing is done with good intentions, but, as mentioned, it is also in response to an overburdened correctional system. There are simply not enough beds in prisons to accommodate the increasing number of inmates.[19]

■ **What are the advantages and disadvantages of diversion for the correctional system? For communities? For offenders? For alcohol or drug abusers? For juveniles? How can "deferred agreement of guilty" pleas be criticized as unfair?**

sentence is beyond that required for rehabilitation and community protection, is cruel and unusual, or does not confirm to sentencing guidelines. At a **sentencing hearing,** the judge listens to the arguments of the two sides and determines the final sentence to be imposed. (Sentencing and sanctions are discussed in more detail in Chapter 11.)

The defendant retains the right to appeal to a higher court both the sentence and the conviction. A defendant convicted in a state court can appeal to the state supreme court and then to the U.S. Supreme Court. A federal defendant can appeal to the U.S. Supreme Court. Appeals courts can choose to hear or reject the appeal. An appeal must be made on a claim that the defendant was denied a fair trial, but the defendant cannot appeal on the grounds that he or she is innocent; the philosophy of the court is that the decision regarding guilt has been settled. The purpose of the appeal is to correct judicial errors that might have occurred.

sentencing hearing
A gathering before a judge that hears appeals, in which the prosecution and the defense argue the accuracy of the presentence report and the appropriateness of the sentence.

■ Carrying Out the Sentence

Once the court determines the appropriate punishment for the defendant, he or she is transferred to the custody of a correctional agency. Three main categories of agencies in corrections are (1) institutional corrections, (2) probation and parole, and

(3) community corrections. Institutional corrections include jails, state prisons, and federal penitentiaries. Probation is a sentence served outside of a correctional institution, and parole is a form of early release from prison. Community corrections (the subject of Chapter 14) are intermediate sanctions administered in a community setting.

CORRECTIONS Once transferred to a correctional institution, the convicted defendant is referred to as an inmate. The presumption of innocence and many of the due process rights to which the defendant was entitled up to this point are gone. The criminal justice system now focuses on the role of punishment and rehabilitation. One of the most acrimonious debates in corrections is the purpose of confinement in a correctional institution. Is the purpose to punish inmates while in prison by the use of harsh conditions and physical discomfort, or is the purpose to rehabilitate inmates so that, when released, they will be able to integrate into society as productive citizens? (This debate and other issues in corrections are explored in Chapters 12 and 13.)

PROBATION AND PAROLE Most sentences do not require that the defendant serve time in a prison or penitentiary.[20] When the defendant is sentenced to serve time in a prison or penitentiary, however, he or she may not serve the full term of the sentence. The court may impose a sentence and suspend it if the convicted defendant abides by certain conditions, or the sentence may be cut short due to the good behavior of the inmate while in prison.

The Office of Federal Probation and Parole supervises defendants convicted of federal crimes. Each state has its own probation and parole agency that supervises those convicted of state crimes. Probation and parole are distinctly different but are often handled by the same agency and personnel. **Probation** provides the convicted defendant the opportunity to avoid serving time in prison by fulfilling certain conditions imposed by the court. **Parole** allows the defendant to serve less than the maximum sentence imposed by the court, based on his or her behavior and progress toward rehabilitation while in prison. Community corrections include various intermediate sanctions, such as house arrest, community service, drug rehabilitation, and restitution. (Probation and parole are the subjects of Chapter 13.)

probation Disposition in which a convicted defendant is offered an opportunity to avoid serving any time in prison by agreeing to fulfill conditions set forth by the court.

parole Early release from prison before the maximum sentence is served, based on evidence of rehabilitation and the good behavior of the inmate.

JUST THE FACTS 2.4

What is required before police can arrest a suspect? Before the prosecution can bring the defendant to trial for a crime? Before a defendant can be convicted of a crime? How is a punishment determined and carried out? Do convicted criminals lose their due process rights?

conclusion:

Goals of Due Process

As you can see, the criminal justice system operates like a funnel that channels cases through various agencies in ever-narrowing outlets (Figure 2.6). In this funneling operation, due process is the driving force.

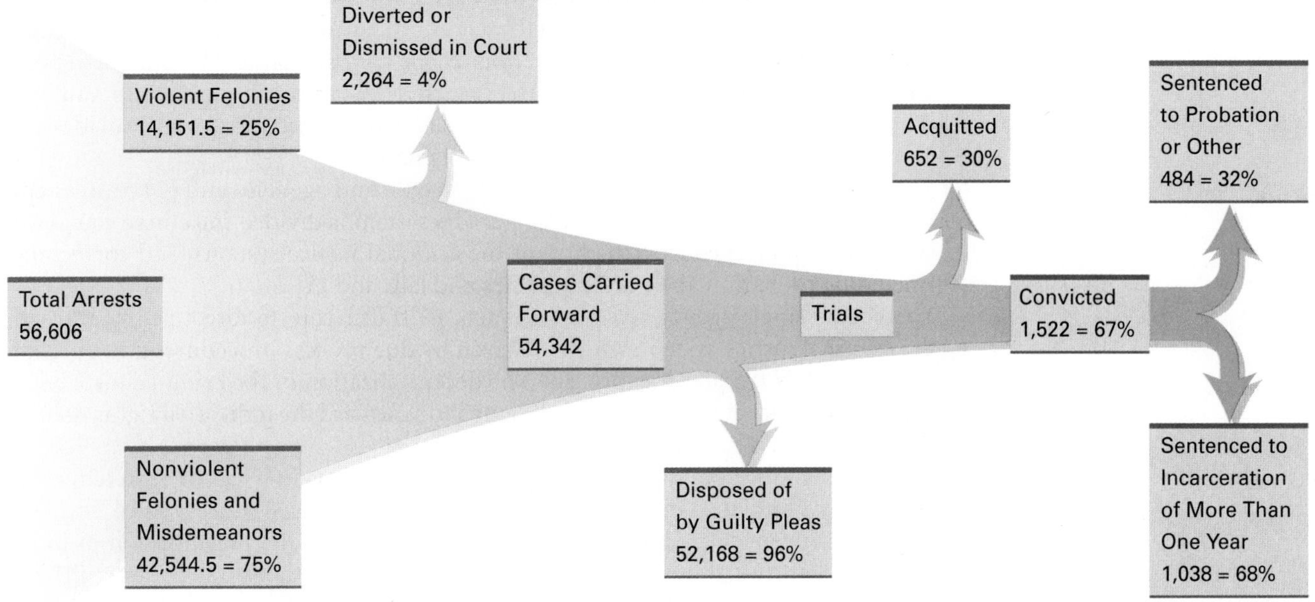

Source: Bureau of Justice Statistics, *Criminal Case Processing Statistics,* filed in state courts for the nation's 75 largest counties during May 1998 (Washington, DC: 2000).

Figure 2.6

The Criminal Justice Funnel

Due process does not protect the rights of the innocent. It protects the rights of the accused, whether innocent or guilty. Therefore, at times when the guilty appear to be advantaged by due process rights, some persons protest the ineffectiveness of the criminal justice system. The criminal justice system is ineffective, but it is ineffective on purpose. The American criminal justice system has its origins in a revolt against tyranny and a strong, centralized government that usurped the rights of its citizens. A decentralized system with many checks and balances on the various semi-autonomous agencies and their personnel ensures maximum preservation of constitutionally guaranteed liberties and rights. It takes a long time and great resources to process a person through the criminal justice system from arrest to conviction, but this is the way it is supposed to be. The criminal justice system is not designed for efficiency. A popular saying is that the "wheels of justice grind exceeding slow but fine." There may be argument as to whether it grinds fine, but it is assuredly true that it grinds slowly.

Chapter Summary

- Counting crime is important because these statistics drive public policies and budgets. The FBI's *Uniform Crime Report* and the Census Bureau's National Crime Victim Survey are two major indexes of crime. Other crime data are gathered from self-reports and state-sponsored and special sources, such as data on campus crimes and hate crimes. Comparison and contrast of crime data from different sources provides significant insight into patterns and trends in crime.
- The criminal justice system consists of (1) people and agencies and (2) process and flow and is undergoing constant change. The system is divided into three categories of agencies: police, courts (the hub of the criminal justice system), and corrections (including probation and parole agencies and jails and prisons).
- There is no single agency or office that acts as "traffic cop" to direct people through the criminal justice system, which is driven by due process procedures and decision points and is not a one-way process. The decentralization of the criminal justice system, as in the picket fence model, is designed to safeguard the individual rights defined in the U.S. Constitution.
- The criminal justice system reflects the values of society. The values reflected in the American criminal justice system are a balance between crime control and due process. The central premise of the due process model is the presumption of innocence. Due process protects the rights of the accused, whether innocent or guilty.
- The criminal justice system has separate processes for dealing with adults and juveniles. The mission of the juvenile justice system, in which the court acts as *parens patriae,* is rehabilitation and restorative justice. There also are separate state, federal, and international criminal justice systems. The United Nations and INTERPOL are the two primary agencies that deal with transnational crime.
- Six major processes in the criminal justice system are (1) deciding what is a crime, (2) detecting crime violation and making an arrest, (3) determining if the accused is to go to trial, (4) deciding guilt or innocence in the trial, (5) determining punishment, and (6) administering the punishment. Overall, these processes act like a funnel for moving people through the criminal justice system.
- The police are responsible for investigation, arrest, and booking, which establishes the identity of the person and charges the person with a specific violation of criminal law. A magistrate judge reviews the charges to determine if they are legitimate, advises the person of his or her legal rights, and determines bail.
- A case moves from the police to the prosecutor via the preliminary hearing, in which probable cause is established for believing that the defendant has committed the charged offense. In some cases, prosecutors use the grand jury system to obtain a secret indictment and arrest warrant for a suspect.
- At the arraignment, the defendant pleads not guilty, guilty, or no contest to the charges. Guilt or innocence is determined by the judge in a bench trial or by the jury in a jury trial. Most cases do not go to trial but are settled by plea bargaining or by diversion.
- The judge determines the appropriate sentence for a convicted defendant, based in part on data in a presentence investigation report. Convicted defendants lose many due process rights, starting with the right to a presumption of innocence. The sentence is announced at a sentencing hearing, at which time the prosecution and defense can debate the sentence. Appeals of a verdict are based on alleged judicial errors, not innocence.
- The convicted defendant may become an inmate in a correctional facility, but most sentences do not require the serving of time in a prison. Probation calls for fulfilling certain conditions imposed by the court to avoid incarceration. Parole permits, under certain conditions, early release from a correctional facility.

Vocabulary Review

adjudicated, 46
arraignment, 60
bail, 59
bench trial, 61
booking, 55
clearance rate, 37
Crime Clock, 35
crime control model, 45
diversion, 61
due process, 46
due process model, 53
first appearance, 58
grand jury, 59
hierarchy rule, 37
Index Crimes, 37
indictment, 60
jury trial, 61
motion, 60
parens patriae, 46
parole, 64
picket fence model, 43
plea, 60
plea bargaining, 61
preliminary hearing, 59
presentence investigation report, 62
presumption of innocence, 46
probable cause, 53
probation, 64
sentence, 62
sentencing hearing, 63
status offenses, 46

Names and Events to Remember

Bureau of Justice Statistics, 34
Crime Awareness and Campus Security Act, 40
Hate Crime Statistics Act, 40
International Bill of Human Rights, 50
International Police Association (INTERPOL), 50
National Crime Victim Survey (NCVS), 39
National Incident-Based Reporting System (NIBRS), 39
Uniform Crime Report (UCR), 36

Think about This

1. What are the best ways to improve the reliability, validity, and comparability of the local, state, and federal criminal justice statistics on which so much public policy is based?
2. Both the due process model and the crime control model focus on the offender and not the victim or the crime. Should more concern be given to the victim and the crime? If so, how should this be done?
3. Each state has its own criminal justice process, agencies, and personnel. What would be the advantages and disadvantages of requiring the states to adopt a common standard for its criminal justice system? What are some arguments for and against this idea?
4. The police are the primary agency with the responsibility of deciding if someone should be arrested, and the prosecutor (also called district attorney in some states) is the primary agency with the responsibility of deciding if an arrested person should go to trial. What is the potential for abuse in arrest and prosecution when such powers reside primarily in one criminal justice agency?
5. Given the international mobility of criminals and the threat of terrorism, should the United States be thinking about more ways to empower international criminal justice agencies?

ContentSelect

Go to the ContentSelect web site and type in the keyword phrase "Due Process." Read "Miranda Revisited" from the August 2001 issue of *FBI Law Enforcement Bulletin*. Sample the article to answer the following questions.

1. Prior to the Miranda decision, what rule had governed the admissibility of confessions in court for 180 years?
2. Explain the Miranda decision, including the four specific warnings that police are required to provide to a suspect.
3. What is meant by the "potential civil liability of individual law enforcement officers and their departments" that resulted from the Dickerson decision?
4. What practical guidelines can be used to reduce exposure to civil liability that could result from a failure to comply with Miranda?
5. According to your text, how does the Miranda decision apply to due process?

Colonial Witches
What philosophies and theories guide explanations of deviant behavior?

Future Criminals?
How can society, socialization, and social forces be causes of crime?

Law Library
What does it mean to have a criminal justice system with rule by law?

Robbery in Progress
How does the law define types and degrees of crime?

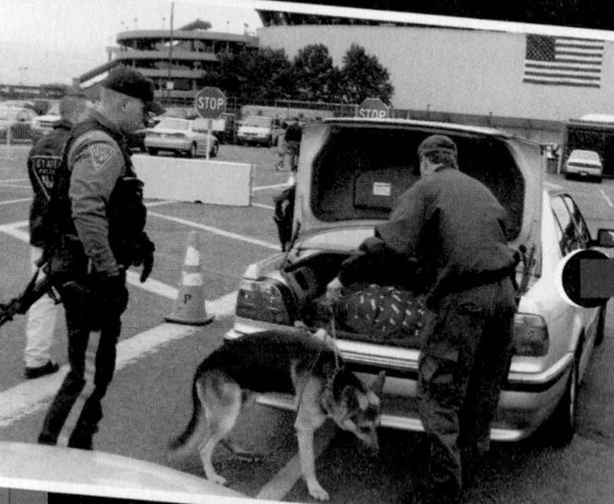

Search and Seizure
How does procedural law define legal law enforcement?

Police Corruption
What happens when police break the law, and how can this be stopped?

part two

Crime and the Law

Societies define and distinguish deviance and crime. Moral, philosophical, biological, psychological, and sociological perspectives offer diverse explanations of the causes of criminal behavior. Criminologists tell us that criminal behavior is learned. Laws define criminal behavior and the boundaries between individual liberty and government control. Laws define specific crimes, the elements that determine if a crime has occurred, and the defenses people charged with crimes can use in court. Procedural laws, based ultimately on the U.S. Constitution, govern due process. For example, police practices in search and seizure, interrogation, and arrest are governed by rules of evidence. Oversight bodies—internal, local, state, federal, and public—seek to ensure police compliance with procedural laws. Oversight bodies also deal with police and other public servants who violate criminal laws.

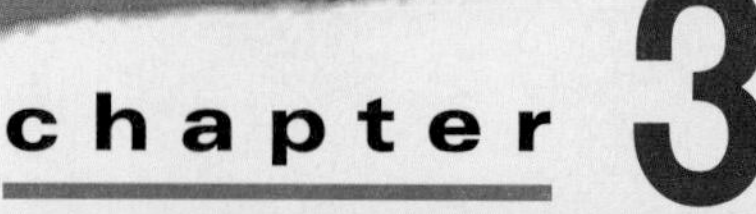

chapter 3 Criminal Behavior: Definitions and Causes

outline

Learning Objectives

After reading this chapter, you will be able to

- Trace the development of criminal theory from prehistoric times to the present.
- Describe the impact of moral perspectives on early criminal justice.
- Define criminology and distinguish deviance and crime.
- Explain the role of scientific inquiry in developing new theories of criminology.
- Give examples of classical, biological, psychological, and sociological theories of crime.
- Compare and contrast the ideas of classical, neoclassical, and positivist theorists on determinants of criminality.
- Compare and contrast biological and psychological explanations of criminal behavior.
- Compare and contrast the six theories that illustrate the sociological perspective on causes of criminal behavior.
- Evaluate theories of crime within each perspective in light of modern criminology.
- Explain the impacts of criminological theories on the criminal justice system.

The Devil Made Her Do It

DALLAS, TX—Andrea Yates drowned her five children one by one in a bathtub. The youngest was six months old; the oldest, seven years old. Her brother reported that Andrea Yates' explanation for her actions was that the devil was in her.

—*Pocono Record*, September 1, 2001

No Longer Dangerous

DUDLEY, MA—David P. Brown, a.k.a., Nathaniel Benjamin Levi Bar-Jonah, a convicted child predator, was sentenced to 18–20 years in prison for attempted murder and other charges related to attacks on young boys. A psychiatrist pronounced him "dangerously disturbed," and in 1979 he was committed to Bridgewater State Hospital (Massachusetts). A therapist wrote in 1980, "Mr. Brown's sexual fantasies . . . outline methods of torture extending to dissection and cannibalism; he empresses a curiosity about the taste of human flesh." In 1991, Brown was released from the state hospital without restrictions because he was no longer considered dangerous according to mental health professionals. After his release Brown moved to Montana to live with his family. Shortly after his arrival he is accused of butchering a little boy and serving the remains in dishes cooked up for his Montana neighbors.

—*The Vail Daily*, June 21, 2001

introduction:

Early Thoughts on Criminal Behavior

While few modern criminologists take seriously Andrea Yates' claim that the devil is in her, it appears that in the prehistoric and ancient worlds serious consideration was given to the explanation that bad behavior happened because the person was possessed by an evil or bad spirit. In some societies, experts of the time were convinced that this bad spirit resided within one's skull. The cure was to use a sharp tool to cut a 1- to 2-inch-diameter hole in the afflicted person's skull, a practice called trepanning. It was believed that once a hole was made in the skull, the bad spirit could escape and the person would be cured. The discovery of hundreds of skulls with evidence of trepanning suggests that the practice was widespread. In Western Europe trepanning continued as a common medical procedure from the Middle Ages well into the eighteenth century. Medical experts of that time continued to believe that people who exhibited certain symptoms of what is known today as mental illness would be cured if these presumed bad spirits could just be released from within the brain.

This chapter examines the history and theories related to the study of crime from the viewpoint of scholars from various academic and professional disciplines. There has never been a lack of opinion as to why people are bad. Even as far back as the Neolithic period there is evidence that deviant and antisocial behaviors, especially those that were harmful to society and others, were a major concern for the "experts" of that prehistoric time. Deviant and antisocial behaviors were defined in ancient laws based on religious scriptures, like the laws of Moses.

Moral Perspectives

THE MAIN IDEA

Theories about the causes of criminal behavior began with nonscientific beliefs about good and evil and the moral order.

The study of human behavior can be approached from two major perspectives: the scientific method and the nonscientific method. Early explanations of deviant and criminal behavior were derived primarily from nonscientific methodologies. Most of these nonscientific investigations searched for principles underlying human conduct and thought based on logic or beliefs assumed to be true. These principles often were based on social and religious morals instead of empirical observations and facts. It was believed that people are, or can be, inherently evil, that people like Andrea Yates and cannibal David Brown are born "bad to the bone."

Later theories explaining criminal behavior are based on scientific inquiry, which involves observation and isolation of variables relating to cause and effect. As you read in Chapter 2, *criminology,* which focuses on the causes and consequences of crime, uses methodologies developed in emerging sciences such as sociology, psychology, and genetics.

Good versus Evil

A common starting point in examining human behavior from the nonscientific viewpoint is the debate over the underlying nature of humans: Are humans predisposed to good or bad behavior? The question as to whether humans are naturally bad or good has been debated in virtually every society. On the one hand, it is argued that humans are naturally selfish, evil, and violent. For example, the medieval political philosopher Niccolo Machiavelli (1469–1527) argued that humans, if left to their own nature, would naturally tend toward bad behaviors. He believed that humans must be controlled by rules and by threat of punishment and that behavior is determined by one's social status. The philosopher Thomas Hobbes (1588–1679) also presumed that all humans are fundamentally mean-spirited and brutish animals.

On the other hand, there are those who argue that humans are naturally good. Thus, external control of people through law and authority is not necessary or is only minimally required. The fewer laws, the better. Laws are only necessary as a guide, for it is believed that, for the most part, if left to their own instincts, humans would coexist in peace. The debate as to whether humans are born good or bad is still not settled. Classic contemporary literature, such as William Golding's *Lord of the Flies,* continues to reflect on this question.

Basic assumptions about human nature underlie the various contemporary theories that explain criminal behavior. In Western civilization, the foundation for the explanation of criminal behavior is rooted in the religious beliefs of the European Middle Ages and the Renaissance. During this time, the Catholic Church and, later, the Protestant church were influential in defining morality and ethics in society.[1] As a result of the strong influence of religious values on society, there was little differentiation between sin and crime. The Catholic Church was the major source of criminal law during Europe's Middle Ages, and the Church was an active agent in determining the guilt and innocence of individuals accused of breaking the law.

The common belief of people from the Middle Ages to the Age of Enlightenment was that bad behavior and thoughts were caused by sin. If asked why someone was bad, the most common answer given by people at that time would be that the person was morally weak or had succumbed to temptations of the world, such as greed or lust, or temptations of Satan. It could be said of this period that many people thought the reason that people committed crimes was, as Andrea Yates said, the influence of the devil.

In the American colonies, the infamous **Salem witch trials** of 1692 are a testament to the extent that people believed in evil spirits, supernatural explanations, and a cosmic battle of good against evil. During this time, any unusual event in one of the colonies was attributed to mystical powers, including coincidences, unusual diseases, and misfortunes.[2] In their sermons, prominent preachers regularly warned parishioners of the dangers of witchcraft, satanic possession, and the Devil. In an effort to rid colonial Massachusetts of the Devil's presence, citizens used the judicial process as a protection against satanic influences, and this led to the witchcraft trials. Between 1672 and 1692, there were 40 cases filed involving the Devil in the Massachusetts Bay Colony. During the height of the witchcraft trials in 1692, over 150 people were arrested, 19 people were hung for practicing witchcraft, 1 was pressed to death, and 4 died while in prison awaiting trial.[3]

Evolutionary Theories

A significant landmark in criminological theories was the publication of naturalist Charles Darwin's (1809–1882) theory of evolution. Darwin's theory of natural selection shifted the focus from nonscientific explanations to scientific explanations of human behavior. And efforts to explain criminal behavior scientifically moved criminological

In the Salem witch trials, villagers were put to death for acts performed when allegedly possessed by the devil. What is a general name for the ancient view of crime causation based on concepts of spirit possession and inherent evil or sinfulness?

theories outside the Church. At the same time, however, people in Darwin's day ascribed moral values to evolutionary stages. Good and evil still applied but in the form of adaptive behavior versus maladaptive behavior.

Darwin's theory, which specifically addressed evolution and adaptation in lower order plants and animals, was quickly applied to humans. Darwin's premise was that species evolve through survival of the fittest, and that not all organisms evolve equally. This idea revolutionized criminological thought, because the argument was advanced that people who committed criminal acts did so because they had failed to evolve properly or at all. Thus, criminals were not only different, they were subhuman, and the fact that they were either misfit or not fully human was the reason for their bad behavior.[4] Modern theories have abandoned this belief.

JUST THE FACTS 3.1

What were some reasons given for criminal behavior historically? How did Darwin influence the concept of criminal behavior? What perspective replaced the moral and social evolution explanations?

Criminology

THE MAIN IDEA

Criminology is the scientific study of criminal behavior, which is related to the concept of deviance. Theories in criminology contribute to explaining, predicting, and preventing crime.

The twentieth century ushered in a new era of scientific inquiry. Many of the scientific fields that emerged at the turn of the twentieth century, such as sociology, psychology, and psychiatry, offered innovative theories to explain human behavior. Scholars quickly adopted this new knowledge to explain criminal behavior, and, often, the validity of these new explanations was tested through the criminal justice system. The study of crime became a popular scientific pursuit, and criminology was studied as a discipline in colleges and universities.

The goal of the criminologist is to discover verifiable principles, concepts, and theories "regarding the process of law, crime, and treatment or prevention."[5] Modern criminologists have abandoned the concept that crime is caused by evil or the Devil. Instead, they seek to find relationships between criminal behavior and the principal determinants or causes of that behavior. As determinants and causes, criminologists study the role of variables such as the environment, genetics, social relationships, poverty, unemployment, education, population, intelligence, parenting, and personality. What specific variables cause or contribute to which criminal acts? Because of ethical standards—for instance, the ability to conduct scientific experiments with humans is very limited—criminologists often must use indirect or secondary evidence to test their theories. Much of the data gathered by criminologists are in the form of observations and surveys expressed as statistical frequencies and correlations.

Deviant Behavior versus Criminal Behavior

Deviance is the breaching of a social norm. In examining the relationship between principal determinants and criminal behavior, criminologists distinguish among vices, abnormal behavior, mental illness, deviant behavior, and criminal behavior. While all of these behaviors may deviate from the accepted norms of society, not all deviant behavior is criminal behavior. For example, it would be considered deviant by most standards to wear a swimsuit to a formal dinner party; however, doing so is not a crime. Likewise, while it is the social norm to face front in an elevator, remaining facing the rear is not a criminal act. A crime is committed when deviant behavior is in violation of a social norm that has been required or prohibited by law.

Criminologists recognize that there is no universal standard for judging deviant behavior. For example, certain religions may prohibit their followers from eating specific foods, may require fasting at certain times, or may require followers to stop daily activities to pray at specified times. The members of those religions, whether a minority or a majority of the society, would regard failure to observe these rules as sinful or deviant. However, they would not view such failures as criminal. Nonmembers would not even view them as deviant. In fact, nonmembers might define the behavior of members of a religious minority as deviant.

At the same time, some behaviors prohibited by religious beliefs also are prohibited by law. For example, many religions prohibit stealing, giving false witness against another, assault, and murder, which are also against the law. However, behaviors such as drug use, smoking, use of alcoholic beverages, and abortion represent complex patterns of social rules and interactions. Whether these behaviors are considered personal choices, deviant acts, vices, or crimes depends on the laws in particular times and places and the values of the groups with which individuals identify.

It appears, then, that not all criminal behavior is deviant behavior; that is, some acts, such as speeding, are well within social norms in terms of their common occurrence but are nevertheless against the law. However commonplace, exceeding the posted speed limit is illegal. Ironically, a motorist lawfully observing the speed limit might be angrily scorned as deviant by impatient drivers who feel adversely affected.

Another interesting phenomenon investigated by the criminologist is who possesses the power and authority to label behavior deviant.[6] People typically do not regard themselves as criminals when they violate a law they and others regard as unjust or unnecessary. For example, during the Prohibition Era, many Americans who otherwise regarded themselves as law-abiding citizens openly and routinely violated the Volstead Act, which prohibited the consumption of alcoholic beverages. In society, there is often conflict over issues such as recreational drug use, reproductive choices, and free speech,

deviance Behavior that violates social norms; deviance becomes crime when the behavior violates social norms that are expressed as criminal laws.

Defining criminal behavior and its causes can be difficult. Why? Is the behavior in this photograph a crime? What standards should be applied to determine if it is a crime? What do you think is the cause of this behavior? How might a present-day criminologist attempt to explain it?

wherein opponents on each side of an issue view those with differing viewpoints as deviant or criminal.

Finally, is it desirable to have absolute conformity within a society? A society without deviant views and acts is a society without change. Without violations of norms, there would be no change in the way that things are done—no new inventions, no new music or art, no new fashions, and no new philosophies.[7] Students of criminology focus on the causes and consequences of deviant behaviors that are harmful to society.

Role of Theories in Criminology

In his or her studies, the criminologist studies both the formal systems for the control of behavior, such as the legal system, and the informal systems of control, such as the family, school, social group, and religious affiliation. The criminologist is interested in observing what happens when there are conflicts among these various control systems. For example, what happens when a teenager is encouraged by peers to consume alcoholic beverages when he or she is aware of the legal prohibitions against it and his or her parents have indicated their disapproval? Does the teen drink, as encouraged by peers, or abstain, as encouraged by their parents and the law? Which factors are most influential in determining behavior? Do all people react the same in similar circumstances, or is one's behavior also influenced by other qualities, such as self-control and personality? By studying such behaviors and gathering reliable data about individuals and their social environment, the criminologist seeks to construct theories that can be used to predict behavior.

theories Statements of relationship or of cause and effect that attempt to explain or predict behavior or events; theories are macro, middle range, or micro depending on the number of cases and level of generalization.

The purpose of a theory is not to predict what a specific individual will do in a specific case. **Theories** attempt to define general principles that will apply in a number of similar cases, but not necessarily all cases. Thus, if 95 of 100 people would act a certain way under certain conditions, the claim could be made confidently that the variables correlate significantly with the behavior, despite the fact that for 5 people, the variables did not cause them to commit a crime. Theories attempt to define and explain the factors that influence or determine behavior and how these factors interrelate.

General theories, or *macro theories,* attempt to explain most people's behavior over a broad range of situations. *Middle-range theories,* on the other hand, may focus only

careers in the system

Criminologist

A number of people earn their living studying crime and criminals. Many people whose jobs are the study of crime and criminals are employed as teachers or researchers in colleges and universities, in government agencies, or in firms devoted to social science research. Most criminologists have a background in sociology, and criminology also is an avenue to careers in criminal justice and law. Criminology was a field of academic study long before criminal justice departments emerged in colleges and universities in the 1960s. Employment as a criminology or criminal justice professor or researcher at a college or university usually requires a terminal graduate degree, such as a doctoral degree or a law degree. Two-year colleges often prefer to hire teachers who have experience in the criminal justice field and have at least a Master's degree. Criminologists also work in public safety, corrections, government, law, health and human services, and business.

People with training in criminology may be involved in analyzing data collected by the FBI and other agencies and may also work in crime mapping or crime profiling. Criminologists who do psychological profiling of criminals often have a graduate degree in psychology or psychiatry rather than sociology, and also have extensive experience working in the mental health profession. Profiling is a specialized field and does not employ many people. Psychological profilers typically have full-time mental health positions and do psychological profiling of criminals on an as-needed basis. There simply is not enough demand for psychological profiling to create a large job market. The FBI has a unit devoted to psychological profiling. However, only senior agents with extensive experience and mental health professionals are appointed to this unit. Unlike some portrayals in the entertainment media, newly appointed FBI agents are not assigned to the special detective units that do psychological profiling.

The future of criminology looks promising, especially in the study of crimes of the twenty-first century and their victims and perpetrators. These studies are focusing, for example, on violent crimes, crimes involving domestic and international terrorism, high-tech fraud and computer crimes, and trafficking in humans.

■ **What might be some advantages of having an advanced degree in criminology? If you decided to become a criminologist, what type of crime or criminal do you think you would like to study and try to explain or predict?**

on certain types of offenders in certain situations. For example, research by Meda Chesney-Lind focuses on delinquent behaviors of female juveniles living in Hawaii.[8] It is difficult to make generalizations about all female juvenile delinquency on the basis of such a study, but through similar research in other places, a middle-range theory could be built up to a more general explanation.

Some criminologists conduct case studies. A *case study* is a detailed examination of a specific person or crime. The most common case studies focus on sensational crimes, such as mass and serial murders. To use the case study methodology to study a mass or serial murder, the criminologist conducts an extensive in-depth study of the murderer's life. Case studies, while interesting, have limited value, because the information does not transfer easily to other cases. A great many case studies have to be done before patterns begin to emerge in the data; in fact, this is how crime profiling is done.

Many criminologists today aim to develop *micro theories* that focus on the way social interaction creates and transmits meaning. These studies emphasize the social process by which people and events become criminal. Micro theories can be built up into middle-range theories that will explain or predict the behavior not only of the subjects studied, but also of other subjects in a similar situation. For example, a criminologist may study thousands of school-age children in the state of California. However, the goal is to craft a theory that will explain the behavior of children in general, not just those in the school district under study.

JUST THE FACTS 3.2

What is the goal of criminology? What is deviance, and how is it different from crime? What kinds of theories are there in criminology, and what are their powers and limitations?

Explanations of Criminal Behavior

THE MAIN IDEA

Theories of the causes and consequences of criminal behavior can be grouped into four perspectives, based on their assumptions about what determines criminal behavior.

As you can imagine, there are numerous theories that have been put forth to explain criminal behavior. This chapter does not attempt to review all the criminological theories, because such a review is beyond the scope of this book. Instead, this chapter focuses on theories that have had significant impact on the criminal justice system.

There are hundreds of theories that attempt to explain crime, and these are grouped together in terms of their common elements. These groups of theories are called schools of thought. A common element used to define schools of thought is the body of assumptions on which the theories are based. These assumptions state what is most important in explaining criminal behavior.

Using this methodology to group theories produces four main perspectives or paradigms for the determinants of criminal behavior: (1) the classical perspective, (2) the biological perspective, (3) the psychological perspective, and (4) the perspective of social determinism. This chapter examines major theories in each of these four schools of thought. Keep in mind, however, that in reality, theories influence one another, share common elements, undergo changes, are discarded, and often are reinvented.

In classical and neoclassical theories, the explanation for crime is based on the assumption that criminal behavior is a matter of choice. The individual has free will to choose to commit or refrain from criminal behavior. The individual's choice of behavior is influenced by a rational analysis of the gain to be achieved from committing the criminal act versus the punishment or penalty that could be suffered if sanctioned by society for the criminal behavior. Theories that share this assumption of free will and rational choice are commonly called **classical school** theories or **neoclassical school** theories.

classical school Theories of crime causation based on Cesare Beccaria's assumption that criminal behavior is a matter of free-will choice.

neoclassical school A later version of classical theory in which children under the age of seven and offenders suffering mental disease should be exempt from criminal liability because their conditions interfere with the exercise of free will.

Two theorists representing the classical and neoclassical theories are Cesare Beccaria (1738–1794) and Jeremy Bentham (1748–1832), considered the founders of classical and neoclassical criminology, respectively. Their theories were a radical departure from the contemporary thought of their time. When published, these theories were not labeled "classical" but were the cutting edge of criminological thought. It is only in historical hindsight that they are called classical.

Beccaria and Classical Theory

Cesare Beccaria, known as the founder of classical criminology, is extremely important in criminological theory because his theories on crime marked the beginning of a new approach to criminological thought. Beccaria's ideas actually preceded the development of criminology as an academic discipline. Beccaria was an Italian nobleman and jurist who was dissatisfied with the justice system of his time and attempted to bring about change. During the 1700s, the Italian criminal justice system was a barbaric system that leaned toward extreme punishments and questionable justice. Laws were unwritten, arbitrary, and unfairly applied. The situation was made worse by unschooled judges whose decisions were often arbitrary and based to a large degree on the social class of the accused. The punishments handed out by the court consisted of corporal and capital punishments that were considered a source of public entertainment. Defendants had no rights, there was no due process, and torture was regarded as an effective interrogation method.

Beccaria's was a marchese, a member of the nobility (like a marquis in France), an important social distinction during his time. As a marchese and magistrate, Beccaria was in a unique position to criticize his country's judicial system. However, Beccaria did not do any statistical or scientific studies of the criminal justice system. His methodology was more similar to what would today be called "philosophy." He based his criticisms and recommendations for improvement on logic and appeal to reason.

The ideas of Cesare Beccaria had a major influence on the development of criminology. According to Beccaria, what are the causes of criminal behavior, and how can it be prevented? What school of thought did Beccaria promote? How did his views differ from those of Jeremy Bentham?

ON CRIMES AND PUNISHMENT Beccaria composed only a single volume addressing his concerns about the criminal justice system of Italy, *Dei delitti e Delle Pene,* published in 1764 and translated into English in 1768 under the title *On Crimes and Punishment.*[9] In 1771 he was appointed Counselor of State and a magistrate. Beccaria probably had no idea that his short text would become the single work responsible for a revolution in the philosophy of criminal justice. Even today, Beccaria's ideas (Figure 3.1 on page 80) seem completely contemporary and can be clearly identified as the foundation underlying the contemporary American criminal justice system.

Beccaria was not the first person or the only person during his time to advocate the principles found in *On Crimes and Punishment.* However, his essay clearly summarized the concept of the criminal justice system as a social contract based on logic, goal orientation, and humanistic principles. The concepts in his books—innocent until proven guilty, trial by a jury of one's peers, the right of appeal, the classification of crimes, and equal treatment of all people before the court, and so on—reflect the principles of American jurisprudence.

THE PAIN-PLEASURE PRINCIPLE Beccaria was influenced by the Age of Enlightenment. His ideas on the cause of criminal behavior were based on the philosophical axiom that people are rational. He reasoned that people seek to do that which brings them pleasure and to avoid that which causes pain. He further assumed that members of society are responsible for their actions. There were no mitigating circumstances or excuses for one's criminal behavior. The same standard of justice and punishment was applied to people of all ages and mental abilities. He advocated certain, swift punishment of appropriate intensity and duration for the offense committed, for the purpose of deterring people from committing crimes. According to Beccaria, the reasons for the continued presence of crime in eighteenth-century Italian society was that the criminal justice system did not provide for swift, certain, and appropriate punishment.

The Italian system of justice instead depended heavily on the threat of severe punishment, especially death, for even the most minor crimes, based on the belief that the threat of such severe sanctions would act as a deterrent against crime. Beccaria opposed the death penalty but argued that the uncertainty of punishment—for few judges even then were willing to send a man to the gallows for the theft of a loaf of bread—diluted the effectiveness of the threat of punishment. Basically, Beccaria argued that even minor punishments would be more effective if they were swift and certain. If one stole a loaf of bread and it was virtually certain that he or she would immediately receive a punishment appropriate to the crime, he argued, such punishment would be more effective than the threat of death, which was rarely carried out for minor theft. This concept—that criminal behavior is a matter of free-will choice and that certain, swift, and appropriate pain would detour people from criminal behavior—is the basic premise of the classical theory of criminology.

Figure 3.1

Beccaria's Principles

From *Of Crimes and Punishments:* Nine principles to follow to effectively prevent crime.

1. A society must make sure laws are clear and simple.
2. A society must make sure that the entire nation is united in defense.
3. A society must make laws not against classes of people.
4. People must fear laws and nothing else.
5. There should be a certainty of outcome of crime.
6. Members of society must have knowledge, because enlightenment accompanies liberty.
7. A society must reward virtue.
8. A society must perfect education.
9. A society should direct the interest of the justice system as a whole to observance rather than corruption of the laws.

Other ideas that Beccaria advocated:

- Laws should clearly define crimes so that judges do not interpret the law, but only decide if a law has been broken.
- Criminal laws should be rational.
- Punishments should be in degree to the severity of the crime.
- Obtaining confessions by torture violates the principles of justice.
- A person is innocent until proven guilty.
- Long imprisonment is a more powerful deterrent than capital punishment.
- Offenders must be judged by their peers.
- There should be no secret accusation by government.
- Judges should be impartial searchers after truth.
- Women should not be excluded as witnesses.
- It is better to prevent crimes than to punish them.
- There should be a set term of incarceration for each crime.
- Individuals should be punished equally for the same crime.
- Law should apply equally to all people.

Bentham and Neoclassical Theory

The English philosopher and scholar **Jeremy Bentham** is credited with the formation of the neoclassical school of criminology,[10] which is similar to the classical school in that the basic foundation is the concept that criminal behavior is a free-will choice and the choice to commit criminal behavior can be deterred by pain and punishment. The major difference between Beccaria's classical criminology and Bentham's neoclassical school is that Bentham believed that Beccaria's unwavering accountability of all offenders was too harsh. Bentham believed in mitigating circumstances. Whereas Beccaria would hold a child of 5 or 6 just as responsible for a law violation as an adult, Bentham argued that children under the age of 7 and offenders suffering mental disease should be exempt from criminal liability. Although he was trained in the law, Bentham chose to write about the criminal justice system rather than participate in it as a lawyer or jurist. Like Beccaria, he was opposed to the use of the death penalty. His most significant contribution to criminological thought was his work *An Introduction to the Principles of Morals and Legislation,* written in 1780 and published in 1789.

Like Beccaria, Bentham reasoned that people are human calculators who logically evaluate the pleasure to be gained by the commission of an act versus the punishment to be suffered for it. When the pain of punishments outweighs the pleasure to be derived, individuals refrain from criminal behavior. Thus, the goal of the criminal justice system was to craft laws and punishments such that the pleasure from engaging in criminal behavior was less than the pains of punishment. Harsher prohibitions and punishments were both unnecessary and inefficient. If one were deterred from theft by the threat of 3 strokes of the cane, then a threat of 20 strokes or of hanging made the judicial system seem ignorant and inappropriate.

Bentham's theorems regarding the balancing of pain and pleasure as a means to discourage criminal behavior is known as the ***felicitic calculus***—the pain versus pleasure principle. Bentham's philosophy is called "utilitarianism," and states that a rational system of jurisprudence provides for the greatest happiness for the greatest number of people. Based on the principles that people act rationally and that the punishment should fit the crime, Bentham's neoclassical philosophy became the foundation of the English jurisprudence system, and hence the American jurisprudence system. His concepts are easily recognized in principles set forth in the Declaration of Independence and the Bill of Rights. Bentham's influence on the English criminal justice system was enormous, starting with the philosophy that youthful offenders and mentally defective offenders are not fully responsible for their behavior. Also, the views of both Bentham and Beccaria are frequently found in the arguments of contemporary opponents of the death penalty.

In a cabinet in the foyer of University College, London, sits the preserved body of Jeremy Bentham on view to the public and linked to the Internet via video cameras. Bentham's philosophy of utilitarianism emphasized education, democratic reform, and rational decision making. He assumed that criminals were rational persons who did not differ substantially from noncriminals, an uncommon view in his time. More popular was Lombroso's theory that criminality was a defect in human evolution.

Belief in Free Will and Individual Choice

When Beccaria's and Bentham's ideas on criminal behavior were published, they competed primarily with irrational arguments of demon possession, class-based justice, and harshly exaggerated punishments. Today the idea remains popular that crime is a free-will choice based on the weighing of potential pleasure and pain. The contemporary criminal justice system appears to be based ultimately on the principles of classical and neoclassical criminology. Proponents of harsh punishments, abolishment of parole, and trying juveniles as adults often phrase their arguments in logic similar to that found in classical and neoclassical thought.

The other three schools of thought—the biological, psychological, and sociological theories of criminal behavior—differ from the classical and neoclassical models in that they reject the concept that crime is a matter of free choice. According to these theories, criminal behavior is caused by various social, psychological, biological, economic, and environmental factors—a position referred to as positivism. Positivists emphasize the importance of the scientific method to determine the factors that cause or contribute to criminal behavior.

The Positive School

The scientific method emphasizes that knowledge about criminal behavior should be gathered using tools such as observation, surveys, case studies, statistics, and experimentation. The **positive school** includes most modern theories of criminology. Sociology and psychology are the two academic disciplines that have made significant contributions to the understanding of crime causation. Biology, chemistry, and medical science (including genetics) have also made important contributions to the scientific understanding of crime and criminals.

The explanation that crime is a matter of free will choice was the predominant criminological theory from about the mid-1700s to the mid-1800s. The scientific revolution of the late 1800s challenged free-will theories, however. Scholars and scientists suggested that, contrary to the free-will premise, perhaps people commit crimes because of uncontrollable internal or external factors that can be observed and measured. Some

felicitic calculus In classical and neoclassical theory, such as Jeremy Bentham's, the pain-pleasure principle by which people decide whether or not to commit a crime.

positive school School of thought that emphasizes the importance of the scientific method to determine the factors that contribute to criminal behavior.

of the factors thought to predetermine behavior were heredity, physical appearance, physiological factors, poverty, and even the shape of the bumps on one's head! These positivist scholars and scientists were also known as determinists.

One of the early proponents of determinism was **Franz Joseph Gall** (1758–1828). While Gall's theories appear ludicrous to today's student of criminology, they were widely accepted by his contemporaries. Gall's theory of human behavior was based on the mistaken notion that the brain is similar to a muscle; if parts of it are exercised, it will enlarge, and parts not exercised shrink. While this assumption is recognized as completely baseless today, it was considered a scientific fact during Gall's time. What is accepted today as common knowledge about the function of the brain was unknown at the time. Knowledge of the role of the brain in controlling various bodily functions was just beginning to emerge.

Gall combined his theory that the various parts of the brain expanded and contracted with use with another erroneous assumption—that the skull will contract or expand to accommodate the size of the brain.[11] Thus, if a part of the brain expanded, Gall reasoned, the skull would expand outward to accommodate the growth. Conversely, if a part of the brain shrank, the skull would contract to conform to the reduction in mass. Mapping the bumps and indentations of the skull could correlate with characteristics of the brain and perhaps predict criminality and other character traits. Gall's theory was known as **phrenology.**

Gall's theory, by the standards of his day, offered a scientific explanation of behavior that was independent of morality, ethics, religion, and free-will choice. Gall's theory was discarded when further scientific discoveries revealed that the brain is an organ, not a muscle, and that it does not change in size or shape through use or disuse.

The importance of Gall's work was that it was a scientific inquiry into the causes of human behavior, based on observation and testing rather than logic and philosophy. Another important contribution was that Gall's work was based on the belief that criminals have distinctive, innate, identifiable physical traits that they cannot change. Criminals were thought to be different from noncriminals in their appearance, which led to theories based on the assumption that it is possible to identify potential criminals by some aspect of their physiognomy.

JUST THE FACTS 3.3

What are the four basic perspectives on the determinants of criminal behavior? On what assumptions are classical, neoclassical, and positivist theories based, and who are their proponents? How did these theories influence the American criminal justice system?

Biological Explanations

THE MAIN IDEA

Biological explanations focus on inherited predispositions toward criminal behavior.

phrenology Franz Joseph Gall's science of reading bumps on the skull to identify character traits such as criminality.

Darwin's *Origin of Species* (1859) provided an important portal for the development of new criminological theories. One of the dilemmas in the advancement of criminological theories was the belief commonly held in Christian theologies that humankind was created by God in God's image and therefore is inherently good. This foundational belief, while consistent with the free-will school of thought, posed great difficulties for any theory asserting that some people are not created good but are bad from birth. To say that one was born bad seems to place the fault with God or to deny the goodness of God's creation. If people are good from birth, on the other hand, then it becomes necessary to explain how one becomes bad. The theory of evolution and adaptation of the species provided an answer to this question.

Darwin proposed what was then a radical and, according to some people, heretical view—that evolved to the argument "humans are fundamentally animals, developed from a common biological ancestry along with all animals and other living things." Darwin proposed that animals are controlled by certain factors of heredity and environment that are beyond the realm of self-control or free will. Animals adapt to their environment through deterministic biochemical and physical forces. Species are influenced by their past heredity because they are in a constant state of evolution, though some, like birds, appear to diversify greatly and others, like sharks, hardly at all.

Crime as an Inherited Characteristic

Two studies attempting to apply a heredity model to the analysis of criminal behavior were the **Richard Dugdale** (1841–1883) study of the Jukes family and the study of Martin Kallikak's family tree by Henry Goddard (1866–1957). These studies, while flawed in their conclusion, suggested that criminality is an inherited trait. Dugdale traced the family tree of **Ada Jukes,** showing how this one person was responsible for hundreds of criminals and imbeciles.[12] Dugdale was so impressed by the criminal lineage of Ada Jukes that he called her the "mother of criminals" (Table 3.1). Goddard compared the biological offspring from Martin Kallikak's wife, "a woman of his own quality," and his illegitimate son from a servant girl. Goddard noted a significant difference in the two lineages and concluded that criminality is a degenerative trait transmitted through biology.[13]

Needless to say, these studies were not scientific. For one thing, they failed to identify and account for all the variables that might be involved in the outcomes. Despite this

table 3.1 The Jukes Family Legacy*

Ada Jukes' (1st gen.) Descendants	Total Persons	Illegitimate	Prostitutes	Paupers	Criminals
2nd Generation	10	0	0	0	0
3rd Generation	50	9	14	30	3
4th Generation	176	5	35	77	29
5th Generation	308	42	76	99	40
6th Generation	157	33	3	10	4
7th Generation	8	1	0	0	0
TOTALS	709	90	128	206	76

*"Over a million and a quarter dollars of loss in 75 years, caused by a single family 1,200 strong, without reckoning the cash paid for whiskey, or taking into account the entailment of pauperism and crime of the survivors in succeeding generations, and the incurable disease, idiocy and insanity growing out of this debauchery, and reach further than we can calculate. It is getting to be time to ask, do our courts, our laws, our alms-houses and our jails deal with the question presented?"

What school of thought in the history of criminology used "statistics" of this sort to back their theories? What was the impact of these theories on the development of the criminal justice system in the United States? In particular, what practice might account for the precipitous decline of the Jukes family line?

Source: From Richard Louis Dugdale, *The Jukes: A Study in Crime, Pauperism, Disease and Heredity,* 4th ed. (New York: G.P. Putnam's Sons, 1884), p. 69.

See http://sociology.about.com; enter "Lombroso" in the search window for more information on Lombroso and the positive school of criminology.

and other defects in scholarship, studies like these set the stage for developments in the positive school of criminology. Cesare Lombroso's theory of the "criminal man" was the first important theory to emerge.

Lombroso and Criminality

Cesare Lombroso (1835–1909) was an Italian medial doctor who took an interest in the causes of criminal behavior. He was particularly influenced by previous scholars whose writings suggested that criminality was inherited. He was influenced by Darwin's theory of adaptation and non-adaptation, Gall's theory of phrenology, and other applications of evolutionary theory. For example, it was believed that criminal types are throwbacks to an earlier stage of evolution.

For his theory explaining criminal behavior, Lombroso collected extensive data from Italian prisoners and Italian military personnel. Lombroso believed that criminal behavior was a characteristic of humans who had failed to fully develop from their primitive origins, such that criminals are closer to apes than to contemporary humans. He described criminals as a retarded species and as "individual mutations or natural accidents living among civilized humans." Criminals could be differentiated clearly from noncriminals on the basis of distinctive physical features, such as protruding jaws, sloping foreheads, left-handedness, and red hair. Lombroso concluded that criminals were a case of "atavism"—a throwback to primitive times.[14]

Criminals were born inferior, prehuman, according to Lombroso. Thus, little could be done to prevent such a person from becoming a criminal or to rehabilitate them. Criminality was not a result of choice or rational thought but a result of flawed human development—or lack of development. Lombroso made extensive physical measurements to define what he called the "criminal man."[15] The study of the physical traits of criminals was called **atavistic stigmata.**

Lombroso concluded that there are three types of criminals, each accounting for approximately one-third of all criminals. The first type is the "born criminal." This person has failed to evolve physically and intellectually and is more apelike. The second type of criminal is the "insane criminal." These persons are not born criminals, but due to some trauma to the brain or other cause of insanity, they become criminals after birth. The last type of criminal is the "occasional criminal," which includes pseudo-criminals, "criminoloids," and habitual criminals. These persons are criminal because of uncontrolled passions or weak natures or because they pursue a life of crime as a trade or occupation. He placed women in a special category. He was of the opinion that "women have many traits in common with children." He said that women were by nature "revengeful, jealous, and inclined to vengeance of a refined cruelty" but that this nature was controlled by "maternity, piety, and weakness." Thus, when "a woman commits a crime," he said, "we may conclude that her wickedness must have been enormous."

Lombroso's theories were further developed by **Raffaele Garofalo** (1852–1934) and Enrico Ferri (1856–1929). While the theories of Garofalo and Ferri contained significant deviations from those of Lombroso, the central theme was that criminals should not be held morally responsible for crimes because they did not choose to commit crimes. The positive school of criminology, led by Lombroso, Garofalo, and Ferri, argued that the concept of free will is a fiction. Lombroso suggested that preventive actions would have little or no impact on the prevention of criminal behavior. Ferri was more hopeful that preventive measures could overcome congenital tendencies. He favored obliging criminals to work, believing that a strong work ethic could help a criminal overcome defects of character. Garofalo focused more on psychic anomalies and the reform of the judicial system of Italy. For example, he argued that juries were ill equipped to make judgments regarding the fate of criminals because criminality was more a medical condition than a moral defect. This "medicalization of crime" had an enduring impact on the criminal justice system.

atavistic stigmata Physical characteristics, representing earlier or prehuman stages of evolution, that were believed to distinguish criminals from others.

How did Cesare Lombroso, William Sheldon (page 86), and Sigmund Freud (page 88) contribute to biological and psychological explanations of criminal behavior? What are some other theories that suggested biological or psychological causes of crime rather than cases based on morality and free will?

During the late 1800s Lombroso and his contemporaries' theories on criminality were immensely popular both in Europe and America. Lombroso's influence was so pervasive that he is referred to as the "father of modern criminology." Although his theories have all been rejected as scientifically invalid, he is honored for the way he attempted to formulate them. Rather than rely on logic or philosophy or morality, he emphasized the role of empirical observations and careful collection of data to test one's theory.

Influence of Biological Determinism

Despite the fact that Lombroso's theory was later invalidated, it was and continues to be influential in the study of criminology. For example, his theory influenced the way convicted persons were treated in prison. Emphasis on corporal punishment and moral correction through religious instruction was replaced by an emphasis on identification, isolation, and extermination. For example, castration was a common correctional treatment based on the belief that criminality is an inherited characteristic. For example, in his opinion supporting castration as a valid treatment for criminals, U.S. Supreme Court Justice Oliver Wendell Holmes Jr. declared, "It is better for all the world, if instead of waiting to execute degenerate offspring for crime, or to let them starve for their imbecility, society can prevent those who are manifestly unfit from continuing their kind."

Body-Type Theories

An idea that has persisted is Lombroso's premise that criminal behavior can be identified by physical appearance. Various theories continue to be based on the assumption that body physique is a reliable indicator of personality and hence, criminality. Methods for detecting a relationship between some physical attribute and personality include Chinese face reading, handwriting analysis, and palm reading. In the mid-twentieth century, criminologists were influenced by the research of **Ernest Kretschmer** (1888–1964), **William Sheldon** (1889–1977), and **Sheldon** and **Eleanor Glueck.** The writings of these criminologists formed the basic tenets of the **somatotype school** of criminology. The somatotype, or body-build, theory is based on the assumption that there is a link between the mind and the body and that this link is expressed in the body type of the person.

Sheldon was influenced by the theories of Darwin and built on the work of German psychiatrist Ernest Kretschmer. Kretschmer concluded that there are three types of physiques: asthenic (lean), athletic (muscular), and pyknic (round). Sheldon linked personality to body type by an extensive study of 40,000 male subjects in which he correlated body types with the results of personality tests. Similar to Kretschmer, he concluded that there are three body types: ectomorph (lean), mesomorph (athletic), and endomorph (round). Sheldon claimed to have found a positive correlation between criminality and the mesomorphic (athletic) body type. Somatotype theories have largely been replaced by modern biological explanations.

Modern Biological Explanations

Lombroso proposed his theory of criminality without benefit of the knowledge provided by modern genetic science. As the contribution of genetics to various human conditions was recognized, several studies revisited Lombroso's basic axiom that criminality is inherited. Studies of identical twins performed by Karl O. Christiansen[16] and others all concluded that, for identical twins, if one twin engaged in criminal behavior, the probability that his or her identical twin would be a criminal was statistically significantly higher. Another study indicated that in the case of adopted children, the criminality of the biological parent appears to have greater influence on the adopted child than the criminality of the adoptive parents.

Proponents of the biological perspective on criminal behavior argue that some people are born with a biological predisposition to be antisocial—to behave in ways that run counter to social values and norms. Unlike early biological determinists, modern biocriminologists concede that environmental factors can inhibit or stimulate hereditary predispositions for criminality. **Biocriminology** focuses on research into the roles played by genetic and neurophysiological variables in criminal behavior, how important they are, and what can be done to modify them.

Modern biology-based theories identify a diverse number of variables suspected of contributing to criminal behavior. Often these theories have emerged after scientific discoveries have revealed new knowledge about how the brain works and the contribution of genetics to behavior. For example, as the role of chromosomes became clear in influencing certain human characteristics, the XYY chromosome theory of violent behavior emerged. The **XYY chromosome theory** stems from genetic research on the characteristics of DNA chromosomes.[17] The normal male has an X and a Y chromosome in the cells that determine the sex of a person. It was discovered that some males have an extra Y chromosome, and studies of prisoners convicted of violent crimes have found a high correlation between conviction for a violent crime (as opposed to a property crime) and the presence of an extra Y chromosome in the male. Multiple sex chromosomes in both males and females contribute to various abnormalities.

somatotype school Theories of crime causation based on the assumption that there is a link between the mind and the body and that this link is expressed in body types, and based on Cesare Lombroso's theory that a criminal can be identified by physical appearance.

biocriminology A new field in criminology encompassing modern biological approaches (such as neurochemistry and neuroendocrinology) to explaining criminal behavior.

XYY chromosome theory Biological theory of crime causation that an extra Y chromosome may lead to criminal behavior in males.

THEORIES OF AGGRESSION In modern biological theories, ideas about causes of crime are expressed in research about causes of human aggression. In an application of neuroendocrinology, for instance, a glandular theory of crime argues that an imbalance of the body's chemicals is the cause of violent behavior. **Katherine Dalton**'s study of female crimes concluded that 49 percent of all crimes of 156 female subjects were committed either just before or during a menstrual period. Her argument is that hormones released during those times are responsible for aggressive behavior. However, this finding (basically 50-50) is what one would expect, given the law of averages![18]

Neurochemistry posits that the cause of violent behavior is the effect of nutrition on humans. This theory is based on the observation that chemicals, food additives, preservatives, and certain foods can stimulate aggressive behavior. A popular related theory is that refined sugar causes hyperactivity and aggression in children.[19] The effect of sugar actually was used as a defense in the murder trial of Dan White. White killed San Francisco mayor George Moscone and city supervisor Harvey Milk, but claimed that the murders occurred after he binged on Twinkies and soda pop as a result of depression. The defense was billed in the news media as the **Twinkie defense.** Interestingly, White received a reduced sentence.

The causes of aggression and violent behavior have been studied by numerous scholars, and some studies suggest that these causes are biological. Studies of animal behavior have suggested that many animals have a natural instinct to defend their territory and attack space violators. Theorists proposed that aspects of human behavior such as territoriality have a genetic basis in the form of instincts. With its overcrowding and competitive orientation, modern society brings out innate aggressive behaviors that in the past served to ensure survival of the fittest. Thus, aggression as a human trait was instrumental in assuring survival of the species but is dysfunctional in modern society.

Some aggression theorists attribute gender differences in aggression to biological programming related to survival of the species. Nearly all violent crimes are committed by males, and males account for approximately 90 percent of all convicted criminals. These data suggest that sex-linked aggression that helped ensure the survival of the species in prehistoric times may be a contributing factor in modern criminality.

Theories of aggression rooted in biology and evolution often overlap with theories of aggression rooted in learned social behavior. For example, the competitive desire for material possessions, which is learned rather than inherited, may cause some people to try to obtain these possessions through illegitimate means if other means are blocked. Thus, property crimes such as robbery and larceny are motivated by a desire to obtain cash-value items. There is no intent to harm anyone, but if someone interferes with the goal, the perpetrator may attack or harm that person as a means to an end.

Another example is the link aggression theorists see between population density and violence. The hypothesis that overcrowding causes crime is consistent with data showing that violent crime is predominately an urban phenomenon. Generally there is more violent crime per unit of population in larger cities than in smaller cities or rural areas. However, data from comparative international studies of crime fail to support this hypothesis. If overcrowding and population density is a prime cause of violence behavior, then Tokyo and Singapore should have much more violence than major American cities, but they do not.

CRIMINALITY AND THE BRAIN Other biological theories of crime causation come from studies of **minimal brain dysfunction (MBD),** autonomic nervous system studies, and brain pathology. Minimum brain dysfunction studies show that violent behavior is caused by small disruptions of normal brain functioning, detectable only through electroencephalogram (EEG) measurements of electrical impulses emitted by the brain. This theory suggests that MBD may be responsible for a variety of behavioral problems including attention deficit hyperactivity disorder. Autonomic nervous system studies have found that the autonomic nervous system (ANS) is the primary control center for the fear response. Children with a quick ANS response learn to react to stimuli with fear, and generally that fear inhibits any desire to engage in criminal activities. Individuals a slow ANS response are not so inhibited. A number of research studies indicate that people who exhibit criminal behavior tend to have slower ANS responses. ANS studies may offer insight in efforts to understand sociopathic or psychopathic

minimal brain dysfunction (MBD) A biological explanation of crime, suggesting that small disruptions of normal brain functioning are responsible for violent behavior.

behavior. Finally, brain pathology studies have focused on the impact of disease, trauma, and central nervous system disorders on the brain as causes of violent behavior.

JUST THE FACTS 3.4

What are the contributions of Lombroso and his followers to criminology? How did the biological explanations of the positivists and determinists influence the criminal justice system? How do studies of twins, human aggression, and the brain contribute to our understanding of criminal behavior?

Psychological Explanations

THE MAIN IDEA

The psychoanalytical theory that criminal behavior is driven by unconscious forces and personality theory have received limited acceptance in the criminal justice system.

Freud and Psychoanalysis

See http://sociology.about.com/cs/analy/ for further information on Freud and psychoanalysis.

At the end of the 1800s **Sigmund Freud** introduced the new **psychoanalytic theory.** In the twentieth century, the science of psychoanalysis became universally accepted as a way of understanding previously unexplainable human behavior.[20] Freud based his theory on the underlying assumption that behavior is not a free-will choice but is controlled by subconscious desires. Furthermore, not all behavior is rational. Some behaviors are not only irrational, but also destructive. Yet despite the self-destructive nature of some behaviors, Freud said that frequently people are unable to control them. At the root of Freud's theory is the concept of the id, the ego, and the superego. Freud hypothesized that human thoughts and actions are controlled by these three components of the unconscious mind. The ego can be considered the logical, thinking part of our consciousness. The superego controls moral and value choices. It is what allows a person to distinguish right from wrong. The id is the subconscious impulses and chaos that, if allowed to influence behavior and thought, result in dysfunctional and harmful behaviors. The id, ego, and superego are not physical structures found in the brain but psychological forces. While these psychological forces are not biological in nature, they exert powerful control over human behavior and actions.

Freud did not focus on the study of criminal behavior. However, his theory of psychoanalysis has been extensively applied to the study of criminals. Freud's theory provides a completely different perspective on criminal behavior. To simplify a fairly complex theory, it could be said that in Freudian theory, crime is a symptom of unresolved psychological conflict.[21] This conflict is caused by free-floating feelings of guilt and anxiety. *Free-floating* means there is no specific cause that the person can identify for the guilt. He or she just feels guilty but does not know why. Freudian theory attributes this guilt to traumatic psychological events that happened in childhood. These events have been repressed and the person is not aware of their influence on his or her emotions and behaviors.

psychoanalytic theory
Sigmund Freud's theory that behavior is not a free-will choice but is controlled by subconscious desires.

To alleviate the feelings of guilt, the person commits a crime so that he or she will be punished. The punishment brings temporary relief. However, because the punishment is not truly related to the source of the feelings of guilt, the guilt returns and it is necessary for the person to commit another crime so that he or she will once again receive

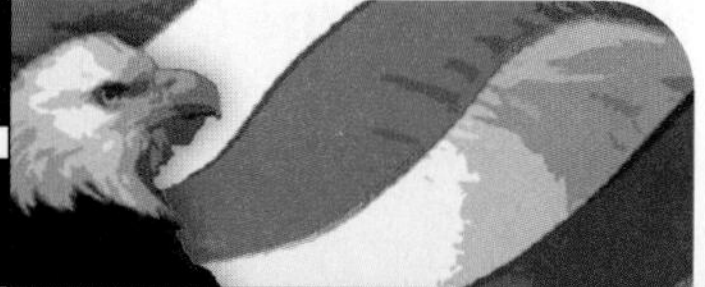

criminal justice in the media

Sensational Serial Crimes

Murders, especially mass murders and serial murders, fascinate the public and criminologists. Murder is the least committed crime but receives the most attention. Murder trials often capture the attention of the entire nation. The O.J. Simpson murder trial was one of the most watched television programs in the history of network Neilson ratings. The names of serial and mass murderers and the numbers of their victims are common knowledge to many, and people are able to recall the statistics of murderers as if they were the performance statistics of sports figures. In fact, one company even published cards similar to baseball cards but with the picture of infamous murderers on one side and facts about them and their crimes on the back. Figure 3.2 on page 90 identifies some of them.

People are fascinated by individuals capable of committing monstrous crimes. Media coverage of sensational, violent crimes contributes to the public perception that they are in constant danger of becoming victims of this type of crime. During the 1990s, occurrences of school homicides perpetrated by students against their classmates contributed to this perception, and in the twenty-first century, terrorist acts against large numbers of innocent civilians increased concerns about mass murder. Yet, serial homicides actually are among the rarest of crimes. Despite all of the publicity, psychological studies of mass and serial murderers have not contributed as much to the understanding of crime causation as other more mundane studies that focus on juveniles and the various social and psychological variables affecting delinquency.

■ What is the impact of media coverage of sensational mass murders and serial crimes? How might Freudian theory explain why people commit mass or serial murders? How would biological theories explain this? What would classical theorists say?

the relief of punishment. This dysfunctional cycle of guilt and criminal behavior continues because, in reality, the punishment received cannot alleviate the feeling of guilt.

The perspective that crime is rooted in dysfunctional, psychologically induced behaviors has received limited acceptance by the criminal justice system. This explanation of criminal behavior does not lend itself to crime prevention and rehabilitation programs, which may require extensive treatment by mental health professionals over an extended period. The criminal justice system recognizes the need for defendants to be mentally competent to stand trial, for offenders to have access to the defense of insanity, for youths to have drug counseling, and for prison inmates to have psychological counseling, but there are no large-scale government programs whose purpose is to improve the mental health of a large number of potential delinquents or offenders. Psychological examination of the mental health of the offender has not been a significant perspective of crime prevention programs.

■ Personality Theories and Psychopathic Behavior

criminal personality Theories from psychology that identify personality traits and habits of mind believed to be associated with criminality.

One of the psychology-based theories that has gained some acceptance and use in the criminal justice system is Samenow and Yochelson's theory of the **criminal personality.**[22] Their theory hypothesizes that criminals have a different way of thinking than noncriminals. The criminal sees and responds to the world differently, and Yochelson and Samenow identified as many as 52 patterns of thinking common to the criminals they

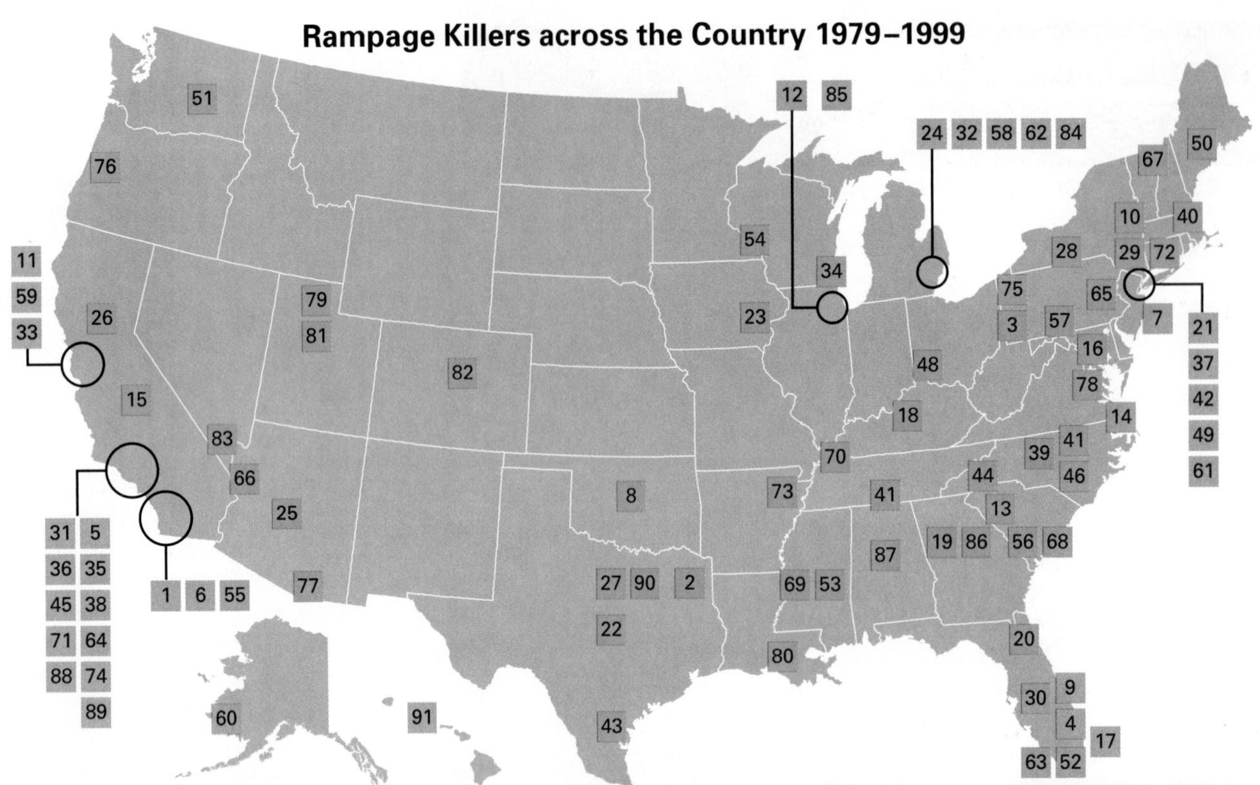

	Year	Name	Age	Number of Persons Killed	Number of Persons Hurt
1	1979	Brenda Spencer	16	2	9
2	1980	Alvin Lee King III	46	5	10
3	1980	Victor Belmonte	23	4	1
4	1982	Carl Brown	51	8	3
5	1984	Tyrone Mitchel	28	1	12
6	1984	James O. Huberty	41	21	19
7	1985	Sylvia Seegrist	25	3	7
8	1986	Patrick H Sherrill	44	14	6
9	1987	William Cruse	59	6	12
10	1987	Robert L. Beebe	55	3	2
11	1988	Richard W. Farley	39	7	5
12	1988	Laurie Dann	30	1	6
13	1988	James W. Wilson	19	2	9
14	1988	Nicholas Elliott	15	1	1
15	1989	Patrick E. Purdy	24	5	31
16	1989	Emmanuel Tsegaye	33	3	1
17	1989	Joseph Besaraba Jr.	44	2	1
18	1989	Joseph t. Wesbecker	47	8	12
19	1990	James C. Brady	31	1	4
20	1990	James E. Pough	42	10	4
21	1991	Joseph M. Harris	35	4	0
22	1991	George Hennard	35	23	23
23	1991	Gang Lu	28	5	1
24	1991	Thomas McIlvane	31	4	4
25	1992	Pete C. Rogovich	2	4	0
26	1992	Eric Houston	20	4	10
27	1992	George Lott	45	2	3
28	1992	John T. Miller	50	4	0
29	1992	Wayne Lo	18	2	4
30	1993	Paul Calden	33	3	2
31	1993	Mark R. Hilbun	45	1	2
32	1993	Larry Jasion	45	3	0
33	1993	Gian L. Ferri	55	8	6
34	1993	Dion Terres	25	2	1
35	1993	Sergio Nelson	19	2	0
36	1993	Alan Winterbourn	33	4	4
37	1993	Colin Ferguson	35	6	9
38	1994	Tuan Nguyen	29	3	2
39	1994	Ladislav Antalik	38	2	2
40	1994	John C. Salvi	22	2	5
41	1995	Wendell Williamson	26	2	2
42	1995	Christopher Green	29	4	1
43	1995	James Simpson	28	5	0
44	1995	James F. Davis	41	3	4
45	1995	Willie Woods	42	4	0
46	1995	William J. Kreutzer Jr.	26	1	18
47	1995	Jaime Rouse	17	2	1

	Year	Name	Age	Number of Persons Killed	Number of Persons Hurt
48	1995	Gerald Clemons	53	3	0
49	1995	Michael Vernon	22	5	3
50	1996	Mark Bechard	37	2	2
51	1996	Barry Loukaitis	14	3	1
52	1996	Clifton McCree	41	5	1
53	1996	Kenneth Tornes	42	5	2
54	1996	Dan Copeman	40	2	2
55	1996	Frederick M. Davidson	36	3	0
56	1996	David M. Hill	36	3	0
57	1996	Jillian Robbins	19	1	1
58	1996	Gerald M. Atkins	29	1	3
59	1995	Jody T. Gordon	24	1	2
60	1997	Evan Ramsey	16	2	2
61	1997	Ali Hassan Abu Kamal	69	1	6
62	1997	Allen Griffin Jr.	21	3	2
63	1997	Jeffrey Wallace	36	1	3
64	1997	Daniel S. Marsden	38	2	4
65	1997	Drue Cade	69	1	2
66	1997	Katsuyuki Nishi	53	2	3
67	1997	Carl Drega	67	4	4
68	1997	Arthur H. Wise	43	4	3
69	1997	Luke T. Woodham	16	3	7
70	1997	Michael Carneal	14	3	5
71	1997	Arturo Reyes Torres	41	4	2
72	1998	Matthew Beck	35	4	0
73	1998	Mitchell Johnson	13	5	10
		Andrew Goldstein	11	5	10
74	1998	David Rothman	51	2	0
75	1998	Andrew Wurst	14	1	3
76	1998	Kipland Kinkel	15	4	22
77	1998	Gracie Verduzco	35	1	4
78	1998	Russell Weston Jr.	41	2	1
79	1999	Lisa Duy	24	1	1
80	1999	Shon Miller	22	4	4
81	1999	Sergei S. Babarin	70	2	5
82	1999	Eric Harris	18	13	23
		Dylan Klebold	17	13	23
83	1999	Zane Floyd	23	4	1
84	1999	Joseph Brooks Jr.	28	2	4
85	1999	Benjamin N. Smith	21	2	9
86	1999	Mark Barton	44	12	13
87	1999	Alan E. Miller	34	3	0
88	1999	Buford O. Furrow Jr.	37	1	5
89	1999	Dung Trinh	43	3	0
90	1999	Larry G. Ashbrook	47	7	7
91	1999	Byran K. Uyesugi	40	7	0

Source: "Rampage Killers across Country 1979–1999" from The *New York Times,* January 1, 2000.

studied in their research. Criminals, they said, are angry people who feel a sense of superiority, have a highly inflated self-image, and do not expect to be held accountable for their acts. Other personality researchers described criminals as lacking self-control, responsibility, and respect for others. However, criminologists have remained skeptical of the relationship of personality to criminality. Nevertheless, it is clear that some criminals exhibit psychopathic behavior and that possible relationships between mental illness and criminality cannot be denied.

JUST THE FACTS 3.5

On what assumptions are psychological theories based? How was Freud's psychoanalytical theory applied to criminal behavior? Why has this theory been rejected in the criminal justice system? Are there links between personality and criminality?

Sociological Explanations

THE MAIN IDEA

Sociological theories of criminal behavior consider environment, social class, social disorganization, social learning, social interaction, cultural deviance, and social conflict.

In the twentieth century, the belief that criminal behavior is strongly influenced by the environment, social processes, and social structure gained in popularity until it became the predominately accepted explanation for criminal behavior. These sociological theories of crime causation reflected the changing American environment, scientific knowledge, social norms, and values of the time. From 1900 to approximately 1950, American society underwent tremendous social, environmental, scientific, and cultural change. The United States became a world industrial leader, relatively lax immigration laws admitted waves of immigrants from Europe, and the introduction of numerous new inventions, such as the telephone, automobile, and television, caused profound change. Not surprisingly, many social scientists concluded that these variables had great impact on social behavior, especially criminal behavior.

Social Determinism

Theories based on the idea that society—social forces and social groups and institutions—is the cause of crime reflect a philosophy of **social determinism.** Society—not free will, biology, or psychology—determines criminal behavior. The earliest sociological theories to emerge focused on the poverty and dysfunctional social environments of communities with higher than normal crime rates. Later theories postulated that criminal behavior is influenced by social relations and social interactions.

social determinism The assumption that criminal behavior is caused by social factors and social forces rather than by moral, environmental, psychological, or biological causes.

Figure 3.2

Serial and Mass Murderers

In the 1920s, vast urban slums developed around Maxwell Street and other commercial areas in Chicago. What developments in early twentieth-century criminology were responses to conditions in urban environments such as those seen in this photograph? What sociological explanations of crime emerged from studies of social forces such as urbanization?

Social Disorganization as the Cause of Crime

Early sociologists found crime and the criminal convenient and interesting subjects for study. The University of Chicago had one of the earliest sociology departments in the United States. **Robert Ezra Park** (1864–1944) was one of the founders of this department, and he focused on explaining and understanding social disorder. Park believed that human behavior is influenced by the environment and that an overcrowded and disordered environment leading to social isolation contributes to deviant and criminal behavior.[23] Gathering data from the surrounding Chicago area, Park and his students engaged in a comprehensive study of the relationship between urbanization and social isolation, based on **Emile Durkheim**'s theory of *anomie.* **Anomie** is a feeling of "normlessness" and lack of belonging that people feel when they become socially isolated. According to Durkheim, people with anomie lack the ties to society that would inhibit them from committing crimes against society.

anomie Emile Durkheim's concept of normlessness and social isolation as symptoms of a dysfunctional society and causes of deviant behavior.

social disorganization theory Theories of crime causation based on the assumption that social conditions such as poverty, unemployment, poor schools, and substandard housing are significant factors contributing to delinquency and crime.

zone theory Environmental theory of crime causation based on the belief that structural elements of society such as poverty, illiteracy, lack of schooling, unemployment, and illegitimacy are powerful forces that influence human interaction.

SOCIAL DISORGANIZATION THEORY In the early 1900s, Chicago grew rapidly due to industrialization and immigration. Park's research demonstrated that criminal behavior was independent of individual characteristics and much more dependent on disruptive social forces. This is called **social disorganization theory.**[24] Subsequent studies by Clifford Shaw and others demonstrated that Chicago was divided into territorial patterns with distinct populations.[25] Each population had a distinct ecological niche and a life of its own that was more or less conducive to crime. This environment-based theory of criminal behavior became known as zone theory.

ZONE THEORY According to the **zone theory,** social environments based on status differences—poverty, illiteracy, lack of schooling, unemployment, and illegitimacy—are powerful forces that influence human interaction. For example, large groups of immigrants who entered Chicago as part of the urbanization and industrialization process tended to concentrate near the industrial section of the city. Because of their limited financial resources, limited language abilities, differences in cultural values, and the general poverty of their social environment, these groups of immigrants tended to become socially isolated and their youth had higher rates of juvenile delinquency. Studies by Shaw and McKay showed that from 1900 to 1933 the highest rates of delinquency persisted in the same neighborhoods of Chicago, even though the ethnic composition changed.[26] Thus, the basic cause of delinquency was not the ethnicity of the juveniles, but the social structures, institutions, and environmental variables in that zone. As one moved away from the industrial heart of the city, the rates of delinquency dropped.

See http://www.geocities.com/CollegePark/Library/8419/wbpthfnd.html (the SocioWorld Sociology web site) for links to sociology sites, including criminology. ■

Since the 1930s social disorganization theory and especially zone theory have had a strong influence on crime prevention efforts. Based on the assumption that social conditions such as unemployment, poor schools, and substandard housing are significant factors contributing to delinquency and crime, many government-sponsored programs have attempted to fight crime by improving employment opportunities, social services, schools, and housing. **Crime prevention through environmental design** (CPTED) was founded on the theory that crime prevention is related to environmental design, particularly housing design. Using CPTED principles, many housing projects have been planned in hopes that attention to environmental details such as public space, lighting, and population density will reduce the higher than normal crime rate associated with public housing projects.[27] Another crime prevention program rooted in social disorganization theory is the "broken window theory," discussed further in Chapter 8. This crime prevention program is based on the idea that signs of neighborhood neglect, community deterioration, and tolerance of petty crime all contribute to more crime and crime-inducing environments.[28]

Differential Association Theory

Other theories of causes of criminal behavior focused on the actors rather than on their environment. Implicit in these theories is the idea that behavior is learned and socialized through observation and interaction in groups. Learning theory and the concept of socialization, concepts shared by both sociology and psychology, were the basis for Sutherland's **differential association theory,** which proposes that criminal behavior is learned entirely through group interaction. This theory, proposed by **Edwin Sutherland** (1883–1950), argues that criminal behavior is learned in intimate peer groups that reward or reinforce antisocial or delinquent behaviors.[29] Thus, a life of crime is culturally transmitted through peer groups. The more a youth associates with deviant peers than with others, the more "socialized" the youth becomes to a life of crime. One reason that this theory is popular is because it offers an explanation of delinquency that does not depend on other sociological factors that may be involved in crime causation, such as social disorganization.

Sutherland's explanation did not refer to environmental or class factors or to economic motivation, poverty, or opportunity. Criminal behavior was not explained as an expression of economic needs or moral-cultural values, and criminals were not necessarily mentally defective, morally bankrupt, or economically deprived. Rather, Sutherland emphasized that criminal or deviant behavior is simply learned behavior. He believed that criminal behavior does not originate in the social status of the person, poverty, inadequate housing, or substandard schools. Rather, criminality is learned in the same manner as other learned behaviors in the normal course of socialization.

crime prevention through environmental design (CPTED) Theory that crime can be prevented through environmental design, particularly urban housing design.

differential association theory Edwin Sutherland's theory that criminal behavior is learned through association with a peer group that engages in criminal behavior.

Because of its basis in learning theory, differential association theory can explain white-collar crime and crime by upper-class adolescents. Why do children of respectable, middle-class parents choose to engage in criminal behavior? How is it that some people, such as correctional officers, do not adopt the values of the criminals they interact with on a daily basis? Differential association theory answers these questions by emphasizing that criminal behavior is the result of learning through normal social interactions. If a "good kid" from a middle-or upper-class family has criminal friends whom he esteems, then during the normal course of social interaction with them the "good kid" will learn criminal behavior.

Extensions of Sutherland's theory have identified other agents of socialization, especially the mass media, that may contribute to the learning of delinquent behavior and aggressive behavior. Other theories focus on the mechanisms by which learned criminal behavior persists.[30] Whether a behavior persists depends on behavioral principles such as reinforcement; that is, behavior persists when it is rewarded or reinforced in some way, while behavior that is punished or ignored may be extinguished. A teenager may learn how to shoplift from his or her peers, for instance, but getting caught stealing a candy bar may be so unpleasant that the teen never again engages in that behavior.

While learning theories continue to dominate criminological thought and social programming, they have several significant shortcomings. They do not adequately explain how and why a person chooses to learn criminal behavior. Why is it that one correctional officer spends a lifetime career in close association with criminal inmates without esteeming their criminal values, while another correctional officer begins to accept those values and engages in criminal behavior soon after employment? Learning theory does not explain why a person who has two friends, one law-abiding and one criminal, chooses to emulate and learn from one and not the other.

Social Control Theories

Theories of crime causation that emphasized the role of social disorganization gave rise to others, such as social control theories, strain theories, and cultural deviance theories. These theories start with the assumption that because the majority of people, including members of the lower classes, are not criminal, there must be some social factors that operate against deviant and criminal behavior.[31]

Social control theory emphasizes that social and cultural values exert control over individuals' behavior and that social institutions enforce those values. Social institutions that contribute to the formation of social values are the family, school, neighborhood, religion, and government. These institutions exert control both informally (e.g., parental disapproval or social rejection) and formally (e.g., school suspension or arrest). The influence of informal and formal systems of social control makes people basically law-abiding to the extent that they identify with and conform to social expectations.[32]

Data from comparative criminology studies support the premise of social control theory. International surveys of crime indicate that countries with very strong informal social control systems have the lowest crime rates. Social control theories posit that when social institutions are intact and have strong influence, deviant behavior is minimized, and when social institutions begin to deteriorate, crime increases.[33]

Social control studies focus on the reasons that people conform to norms. People of all socioeconomic backgrounds are subject to the temptation of crime and desire what they do not have. People also have impulses that they do not act on and desires that they do not fulfill. So what causes some people to turn to crime and others not? Social control theories emphasize that both environmental variables and individual self-control are influential in preventing or suppressing criminal behavior.[34]

social control theory Theories of crime causation based on the assumptions that people's belief in and identification with the values of their society and culture influence their behavior.

containment theory Walter Reckless's theory that people are deterred from deviant behavior because of the influence on individuals of both internal and external social control factors.

CONTAINMENT THEORY Walter Reckless's (1899–1988) **containment theory,** for example, proposes that there is a dual defense system against deviant behavior. He believed that there are "outer containments" and "inner containments" that suppress criminal behavior.[35] Outer containments are variables such as positive role models, opportunity for individual achievement, cohesion among members of a group, sense of belongingness, and identification with the group. However, if outer containments fail to prevent deviant behavior, a second defense is the influence of inner containment. Inner containment variables include a good self-concept, self-control, a strong ego, and a well-developed conscience.

Reckless proposed that in addition to the forces that keep one from criminal behavior, there are forces that tend to push one toward criminal behavior. Acting against inner and outer containment are internal pushes, such as the need for immediate gratification, restlessness, and hostility, as well as external pressures, such as poverty, unemployment, and blocked opportunities. Reckless believed that the dynamic interaction of these factors determines the outcomes of one's behavior. The most conducive situation for criminal behavior is one in which there is weak inner and outer containment and strong internal pushes and external pressures. Under such conditions, the likelihood of criminality is high.

NEUTRALIZATION THEORY **Gresham Sykes** and **David Matza's neutralization theory** is based on the assumption that one cannot completely resist criminal behavior and that most people have committed some criminal or deviant act at one time or another. These researchers focused on variables similar to those of Reckless's inner containment. They argue that deviant and criminal behavior produces a sense of guilt and that the pains of conscience are sufficient to keep most people from engaging in extended and extensive criminality. How, then, do people overcome their guilt so as to be able to carry on a continued career of crime. Sykes and Matza's explanation is that criminals learn neutralization techniques—for example, rationalizing their behavior and denying responsibility for harm they cause—that allows them to avoid being guilt-ridden.[36]

The shortcoming of neutralization theory is that it does not explain the prime motivation. Why would some people learn neutralization techniques to continue to engage in criminal behavior, while others are detoured and cease criminal activity? Because neutralization techniques appear to be basic psychological defenses, such as rationalization, denial, and appeal to higher loyalties, anyone could employ these techniques to avoid guilt, but only a few choose to do so.

BOND THEORY A third offshoot of social control theory is **Travis Hirschi's social bond theory,** which explains behavior as an interaction of four variables: attachment, commitment, involvement, and belief.[37] According to social bond theory, these variables lead to strong social and emotional ties to social values and norms and to the community, which have the effect of lessening deviant behavior. Proponents of the social bond theory focus on evidence that the bonds that help prevent delinquency appear to be weakening in contemporary society. They point to breakdowns in school discipline and oversight, widespread erosion of the authority of teachers, and less effective parenting as evidence that the bond of attachment is weakening. They see evidence of less commitment, involvement, and belief in declining civic participation and civility in general, further weakening the social bonds that inhibit criminal behavior.

A criticism of social control theories is that important variables, such as attachment, are abstract concepts that are difficult to operationalize, measure, and test scientifically. This also makes it difficult to compare the levels or strengths of the different variables as determinants of criminal behavior.

LABELING THEORY Explanations emphasizing society's control over individual behavior through symbolic interaction include labeling theory. **Labeling theory** focuses on crime from the perspective of society's reactions to and expectations of delinquents and criminal offenders. **Frank Tannenbaum**[38] and **Howard Becker**[39] contributed significantly to the development of labeling theory. Labeling theory does not focus on the person or the crime or even the circumstances of the crime but on people's social reactions to behavior. Becker's perspective is that deviance is created by society, because society defines norms and norm violations. Everyone violates some criminal laws in his or her lifetime. A youth may engage in illegal behavior, but it is society that makes the juvenile a delinquent, not the behavior itself.[40] The belief in labeling theory underlies the practice of withholding from the public the names of juveniles alleged to have committed criminal acts. According to labeling theory, the public would

neutralization theory Gresham Sykes and David Matza's theory that criminals learn techniques that allow them to rationalize their behavior, deny responsibility for harm, and avoid being guilt ridden.

social bond theory Travis Hirschi's theory that strong social and emotional ties to social values and norms lessen the likelihood of deviant behavior.

labeling theory Frank Tannenbaum and Howard Becker's theory that people are strongly influenced by society's expectations of them, such that juveniles labeled as criminals are more likely to become criminals.

treat the youths as delinquents, possibly trapping them into a lifetime of deviant behavior. Essentially, the label that society attaches to them becomes true, like a self-fulfilling prophecy.

Strain Theory

Some sociologists focus on impacts of class differences on behavior. Strain theories, for example, have as their starting point the belief that all members of society subscribe to a set of cultural values defined by the middle class. The most important value, economic success, was assumed to be universal in society, especially in the early twentieth century before government safety nets existed to help citizens in need. Sociologist **Robert Merton** formulated a popular **strain theory** based on the assumption that people are law-abiding but will resort to crime when they are frustrated in finding legitimate means to economic success.[41] His theory assumed that people are motivated to achieve the comforts and security of a middle-class lifestyle, but that some people find they cannot achieve this goal through traditional, socially acceptable means. Unable to adapt, these individuals might then resort to illegal means.

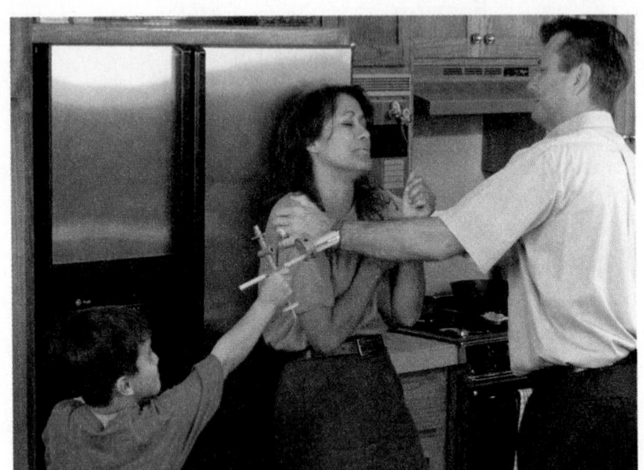

Sociological explanations of crime focus on criminal acts as learned behavior. Dysfunctional societies, disordered neighborhoods, law-breaking street gangs, and abusive families create criminals. What are the names and principal ideas of these theories based on social determinism?

strain theory Robert Merton's theory that people are naturally law-abiding but resort to crime when frustrated in finding legitimate means to economic success.

differential opportunity theory Richard Cloward and Lloyd Ohlin's theory that criminality stems from blocked opportunities based on where one lives, who one knows, and what skills, talents, and resources one has.

According to Merton, people attempt to adapt means to goals in five basic ways: conformity, innovation, ritualism, retreatism, and rebellion.[42] Innovators, retreatists, and rebels often reject the goals or choose illegitimate means, becoming delinquents or criminals. Innovators, for instance, accept society's goals but have few legitimate means of achieving them. Thus, they design their own means of getting ahead, which might include cheating, bad-check passing, vandalism, burglary, robbery, embezzlement, fraud, or other crimes. Retreatists, on the other hand, reject the goals; that is, they give up on achieving a middle-class lifestyle. Instead, retreatists withdraw from society through acts such as drug use and addiction, vagrancy, and other "victimless" crimes. Rebels, meanwhile, often reject both the goals and the means, pursuing values of their own in their own way. Merton's category of ritualism describes people who abandon the goals and just "go through the paces" or "play the game," while conformists are content with both the legitimate goals of society and the legitimate means of achieving them (Figure 3.3).

Merton believed that social conditions, especially poverty and ethnicity, are powerful factors in determining the adaptations individuals make to socially prescribed goals and the lifestyles that develop as a result. It was predicted that the greatest proportion of crime would be found in the lower classes because, Merton believed, lower-class people have the least opportunity to reach middle-class goals legitimately. However, in its emphasis on crime as a product of economic frustration, Merton's theory has limited value in explaining crimes of passion and white-collar crimes by members of the middle and upper classes. Also, in such a diverse society as the United States, it may be presumptuous to assume that everyone shares the same value system and common goals. Nevertheless, strain theory has had a major impact on the government's response to crime. Programs such as Head Start, Job Corps, and others aimed at providing economic opportunities to the poor and disadvantaged are justified by the belief that economic opportunity deters crime.

Differential Opportunity Theory

Richard Cloward and **Lloyd Ohlin**'s **differential opportunity theory** pointed out that in high-crime neighborhoods with youth gangs, as in the wider society, opportunities

Adaptation to Norms	Acceptance of Goals	Acceptance of Means
Conformity	Positive	Positive
Innovation	Positive	Negative*
Ritualism	Negative	Positive
Retreatism	Negative	Negative*
Rebellion	Rejection and Substitution	Rejection and Substitution*

*Greater likelihood of engaging in criminal behavior

Source: Based on Robert K. Merton, *Social Theory and Social Structure* (New York: Free Press, 1957).

Figure 3.3

Merton's Strain Theory

for legitimate success and illegitimate success are not equally distributed.[43] Neighborhoods characterized by transience and instability offer few opportunities to get ahead in criminal activities. Thus, opportunities to reach one's goals may be blocked within the criminal world as well. Gangs unsuccessful in illegitimate goals may substitute violence as a means to gain status. Gangs unsuccessful in both legitimate and illegitimate goals may retreat into a world of panhandling, pimping, or searching for the next high. According to Cloward and Ohlin, individual success as a criminal depends on where one lives, who one knows, and the skills and talents one has. An adolescent may associate with peers who are successful in shoplifting, for example, and may be taught how to shoplift; however, this learning does not guarantee that he or she necessarily has the ability to learn the skills well enough to be a successful shoplifter. As you can see, Cloward and Ohlin's work combines elements of strain theory, differential association theory, and social disorganization theory.

Cultural Deviance Theories

While strain theories are based on the core values of the wider society, **cultural deviance theories** are based on the idea that the values of subcultural groups within the society have even more power over individual behavior. Subcultures have different, sometimes conflicting, values.[44] Organized crime families, juvenile gangs, and hate groups can be described as deviant subcultures, for example. Within these groups, behaviors defined as deviant by outsiders actually are expected among insiders and are seen as normal.[45] Cultural deviance theorists focused on differences in values and norms between mainstream society and subcultural groups, including immigrant groups who entered the United States during the first half of the twentieth century.

cultural deviance theories Theories of crime causation based on the assumption that criminal behavior is learned through participation in deviant subcultures or countercultures within a society.

reaction formation Albert Cohen's term for his cultural deviance theory in which lower-class youths reject middle-class values that they cannot attain and instead join countercultures that express the opposite values.

Cultural deviance theories begin with the assumption that subgroups or subcultures within a society have different value systems. **Albert Cohen** defines distinct subcultures in terms of variables such as parental aspirations, child-rearing practices, and classroom standards. Cohen uses the term **reaction formation** to describe how lower-class youths reject middle-class values, which they perceive they cannot achieve, embrace new countervalues that are the opposite of middle-class values, and create unique countercultures.[46] Members see the new values as obtainable and accept them as measuring rod of normative behavior, and the counterculture reinforces these values.

For example, **Walter Miller** pointed out that while middle-class values include patience, sharing, honesty, and politeness in adolescents, delinquents reject these values and substitute values such as toughness, risk taking, group loyalty, spontaneity,

See http://faculty.ncwc.edu/toconnor/criminology.htm, the Criminology Mega-Site, for information on all the perspectives on causes of crime, including radical criminology. ■

intensity, danger and excitement, smartness, luck, and group autonomy. According to Miller, members of delinquent subcultures are not impressed by and do not attempt to achieve middle-class benchmarks of success, such as succeeding in school and getting a good job. Striking out against society, delinquents embrace antisocial values, often including random acts of violence against property or persons.[47]

Conflict Theories

Another perspective on crime causation emphasizes that crime has less to do with deviant behavior than with competition and conflict between social classes and institutional discrimination. Conflict theorists do not focus on individual motivation or learning or on group interaction. Rather, they focus on how a society's system of social stratification (division of society into social classes) and social inequality influence behavior.[48] **Conflict theories** are based on the assumption that powerful ruling political and social elites—persons, groups, or institutions—exploit the less powerful and use the criminal justice system to their own advantage to maintain their power and privilege.[49] In this view, criminology is the study of crime in relation to society's haves and have-nots.

Theories of crime based on social inequality have their roots in the social criticisms of Karl Marx and Friedrich Engels in nineteenth-century Europe. Marxism assumes a division between the poor (workers) and the rich (property owners, capitalists) in which the rich control the various social, political, and economic institutions of society. The rich use their power and position to control the poor.[50] The criminological theories associated with Marxism, referred to as "radical criminology" or "new criminology," however, do not advocate Marx's solution, which was the violent overthrow of the ruling class. Instead present-day conflict theorists suggest that reducing social inequality is the only or best way to reduce criminal behavior.[51]

Because of international communism, the "red scare," and the McCarthyism of the 1940s and 1950s, Marxism-based criminological theories were not popular in the United States. Beginning in the 1960s, however, there was greater social and academic acceptance of the idea that class conflict might have a role in explaining crime. **Richard Quinney** argued, for example, that the criminal justice system is a state-initiated and state-supported effort to rationalize mechanisms of social control, which are based on class structure. The state is organized to serve the interests of the dominant economic class. Criminal law was seen as an instrument that the state and the ruling class use to maintain and perpetuate the social and economic order.[52] Some conflict theorists went so far as to claim there is a deliberate conspiracy to suppress the lower classes, especially the "dangerous poor."[53]

Feminist criminology, which is based on the conflict model, focuses on gender inequality as well as class inequality as a basis of crime. **Feminist criminology** assumes that the underlying cause of criminal behavior by females is the inequality of power between men and women. Advocates such as **Freda Adler,**[54] **Meda Chesney-Lind** and Kathleen Daly,[55] and Rita J. Simon[56] argue that inequality of political, economic, and social power and wealth is the root cause of female criminal behavior.

conflict theories Theories of crime causation based on Marxian theory or the assumption that the sources of criminal behavior are class conflict and social inequality.

feminist criminology Field based on the assumption that gender inequality lies at the heart of crimes in which women are the victims or the perpetrators.

Conflict theorists have strongly criticized mainstream criminology and the criminal justice system. Research data began to support claims that inequality of opportunity contributes to crime, and inequalities were found to exist in the operation of the criminal justice system. It was found, for example, that disproportionate numbers of poor and minority citizens were being stopped, arrested, and incarcerated than were other groups.[57] Radical criminologists such as **William Chambliss** saw the law and the system as a means of institutional discrimination rather than as a means of providing fairness in justice.[58] While efforts have been made to address these criticisms of the criminal justice system, conflict-based theories of crime causation have not had a role in crime prevention or rehabilitation programs. For one thing, conflict theorists have depended more on philosophical and political arguments than on data from quantitative studies, necessary for an objective examination of the hypotheses regarding crime causation.

Conflict theories do not explain why the ruling elite is so prejudiced against the poor or why it is impossible for the poor to benefit under capitalism in a democratic society. Nevertheless, it would be a mistake to dismiss them as entirely without merit. Conflict theorists point out that the primary focus of mainstream criminology and the criminal justice system is property crimes and crimes against persons. Disproportionate attention to these crimes often obscures the greater social harm done by white-collar crimes, corruption, political crimes, and other abuses of power. Conflict theorists also point to flaws in the criminal justice system that appear to be based on class distinctions, although critics argue the system often is self-correcting. For example, old laws that provided for imprisonment for the crime of failing to be gainfully employed were struck down as unconstitutional, and numerous rulings have extended the due process protections of the Constitution to the poor and indigent.

JUST THE FACTS 3.6

On what assumptions are sociological explanations of criminal behavior based? What are the original sociological theories of criminality? How do theories based on social disorganization, association, social control, strain, opportunity, cultural deviance, and social conflict compare?

conclusion:

Criminal Behavior Is Learned?

As you can see, there is no single theory that explains crime. Various theories, summarized in Table 3.2 on page 100, have appeared to explain crime throughout history based on the scientific knowledge and social values of the era in which they were developed. Often advances in scientific knowledge reveal the flaws in a crime theory. It is not easy to explain crime because of the very complex nature of crime and the many variables that influence criminal behavior. Combinations of variables coming from several different bodies of knowledge may apply, including biology, psychology, and sociology.

Despite their flaws and shortcomings, sociological theories of crime causation are the most popular for use by criminologists and the criminal justice system. Sociological explanations offer solutions for building programs and attempting to prevent crime. At the same time, it is unreasonable to expect a single theory to emerge in the near future that will explain the cause of all crime and provide a blueprint for the rehabilitation of all criminals. Yet without an underlying theoretical foundation, the various attempts to reduce crime and rehabilitate offenders is nothing more than a guess. Most modern criminologists have abandoned the belief that criminals are completely different from other citizens. The focus of criminology is on isolating those variables that appear to have the greatest influence on human behavior.

table 3.2 Explanations of Criminal Behavior

Type of Explanation	School of Thought	Theory	Proponent	Cause of Crime	Solution to Crime
Moralism				Evil; sin Spirit possession	Elimination of offenders from society
Positivism	Classical	Pain-pleasure principle	Cesare Beccaria	Rational free choice	Deterrence through pain of punishment over pleasure of crime
	Neoclassical	Utilitarianism	Jeremy Bentham	Rational free will except for the young and insane	Deterrence through laws fitting the punishment to the crime
Biological Determinism	Evolutionary	Darwinism; concept of atavism	Cesare Lombroso Richard Dugdale (Ada Jukes)	Heredity; no free will and thus no moral accountability	Prevention impossible; give medical treatment (and castrate or sterilize criminals)
		Somatotype	Willliam Sheldon	Inherited predispositions revealed through body type	Prevention through identification
	Biocriminology	XYY chromosome hormones; nutrition MBD (minimal brain dysfunction)		Physiological disorders or chemically induced aggression	Medical treatment and control
Psychological Determinism		Psychoanalytical theory	Sigmund Freud	Psychopathology; irrational, unresolved, unconscious conflict from guilt/anxiety from childhood trauma	Counseling and rehabilitation
		Criminal personality		Antisocial attitudes and lack of self-control	Early childhood intervention
Social Determinism	Environmentalism	Zone theory	Robert Ezra Park	Society; dysfunctional social environments	Reduce anomie through environmental design and urban renewal; reduce poverty
	Interactionism	Differential association theory	Edwin Sutherland	Socialization in delinquent peer groups	Diversion and reeducation
		Cultural deviance	Albert Cohen	Socialization in deviant subculture or counterculture	Distinguish cultural diversity and dissent from deviance

table 3.2 Explanations of Criminal Behavior (*Continued*)

Type of Explanation	School of Thought	Theory	Proponent	Cause of Crime	Solution to Crime
Social Determinism (*Cont.*)	Social control			Breakdown of social institutions; lack of conformity	Enforcement of social values and norms; strengthening of institutions, such as the family; strengthening of social and emotional bonds to others and to society.
		Containment theory	Walter Reckless	Loss of self-control and social control	
		Neutralization theory	Gresham Sykes/ David Matza	Rationalization of yantisocial acts	
		Social bond theory	Travis Hirschi	Loss of sense of attachment	
		Labeling theory	Howard Becker	Society's reactions to deviance	
	Structuralism			Social structure; structure of opportunity	Level the playing field; provide equal opportunity
		Strain theory	Robert Merton	Frustration in achieving middle-class goals legitimately because of poverty or ethnicity	Eliminate frustrations and disadvantages or help people overcome them
		Differential opportunity	Richard Cloward and Lloyd Ohlin	Blocked opportunities to reach goals	
		Conflict theory		Social inequality; class conflict; institutional discrimination	Social and political equality; redistribution of wealth and power in society
			Richard Quinney	Criminal justice system as a weapon of the ruling class; racial discrimination	Equal rights; equal protection
			Freda Adler	Gender inequality	Equal rights; equal protection

Chapter Summary

- Prior to Beccaria, the cause of crime was thought to be evil spirits or yielding to the temptations of sin.
- Criminology is the scientific study of verifiable principles, concepts, and theories regarding the process of law, crime, and treatment or prevention.
- Criminal behavior is not the same deviant behavior, sin, vice, or mental illness. Deviance is behavior that violates a social norm.
- Criminology uses theories to develop hypotheses about the causes of crime. Theories can be macro, middle-range, or micro, but all good theories have explanatory power that can be generalized to the population under study.

- The major perspectives concerning crime causation are the classical perspective, the biological perspective, the psychological perspective, and the sociological perspective.
- Classical and neoclassical theories of crime, such as Beccaria's and Bentham's, assume that crime is a rational free-will choice based on the pleasure-pain principle.
- Biological theories of crime, such as Lombroso's, assume that crime is an inherent or innate predisposition, not an act of free will. Biology-based theories have focused on body types, twin studies, body chemistry, and genetics.
- Psychology-based theories such as Freud's assume that criminal behavior is the expression of repressed feelings, personality maladjustment, or mental illness.
- Sociological theories assume that crime is caused not by body, mind, or individual motivation, but by society. Social groups and institutions create the conditions that lead to criminal behavior. The belief that society is at the root of crime is called social determinism.
- The belief that crime is caused by social disorganization—poverty, unemployment, inadequate housing, breakdown in family values, violence in the media, failure of the schools—is the theoretical basis for many crime prevention and treatment programs. Social disorganization theory and zone theory are based on the role of environment in causing crime.
- The theory that is best accepted in the criminal justice system is Sutherland's theory of differential association and other learning theories. These theories say that crime is a learned behavior. Thus, crime can be unlearned.
- Theories based on the dynamics of social control and the role of interpersonal interaction say that behavior, including conformity and deviance, is shaped by individuals' responses to others' expectations. Examples are containment theory, neutralization theory, social bond theory, and labeling theory.
- Merton's strain theory identifies strain between societal goals and the means for achieving these goals as a source of criminal behavior. Individuals who cannot achieve the goals legitimately tend to reject or substitute for the goals or turn to illegitimate means.
- Cohen's theory of deviant subcultures identifies reaction formation as a cause of delinquency and criminal behavior in youth gangs. Cloward and Ohlin's theory of differential opportunity states that delinquent subcultures of diverse types flourish in lower-class areas because opportunities for illegitimate success are just as unequally distributed as opportunities for legitimate success.
- Conflict theories are based on the assumption that social inequality is the cause of crime through imbalances of power in the system. Some conflict theorists believe that the rich and powerful use the criminal justice system to oppress the poor and maintain their own positions. Feminist theories focus on the role of gender inequality in criminal behavior.
- No single theory explains crime, but theory is important in developing crime prevention and treatment programs.

Vocabulary Review

anomie, 92
atavistic stigmata, 84
biocriminology, 86
classical school, 78
conflict theories, 98
containment theory, 94
crime prevention through environmental design (CPTED), 93
criminal personality, 89
cultural deviance theories, 97
deviance, 75
differential association theory, 93
differential opportunity theory, 96
felicitic calculus, 81
feminist criminology, 98
labeling theory, 95
minimal brain dysfunction (MBD), 87
neoclassical school, 78
neutralization theory, 95
phrenology, 82
positive school, 81
psychoanalytic theory, 88
reaction formation, 97
social bond theory, 95
social control theory, 94
social determinism, 91
social disorganization theory, 92
somatotype school, 86
strain theory, 96
theories, 76
XYY chromosome theory, 86
zone theory, 92

Names and Events to Remember

Freda Adler, 98
Cesare Beccaria, 78
Howard Becker, 95
Jeremy Bentham, 80
William Chambliss, 98
Meda Chesney-Lind, 98
Richard Cloward and Lloyd Ohlin, 96
Albert Cohen, 97
Katherine Dalton, 86
Richard Dugdale, 83
Emile Durkheim, 92
Sigmund Freud, 88
Franz Joseph Gall, 82
Raffaele Garofalo, 84
Eleanor Glueck, 86
Sheldon Glueck, 86
Travis Hirschi, 95
Ada Jukes, 83
Ernest Kretschmer, 86
Cesare Lombroso, 84
Robert Merton, 96
Walter Miller, 97
Robert Ezra Park, 92
Richard Quinney, 98
Walter Reckless, 94
Salem witch trials, 73
William Sheldon, 86
Edwin Sutherland, 93
Gresham Sykes and David Matza, 95
Frank Tannenbaum, 95
Twinkie defense, 87

Think about This

1. While there are numerous theories and much debate on crime causation, often the criminal justice system must adopt basic principles on which to base prevention programs. Why? How do theories relate to practice? Consider a crime prevention or rehabilitation program such as DARE, Crime Watch, Project Exile (a get tough on crime program involving firearms), or community policing. On what theoretical perspectives are these programs based? How successful are they in addressing the primary factors associated with criminal behavior?
2. One of the most important concepts in crime causation is whether one believes that crime is a matter of free-will choice, biology-based programming, or psychologically motivated behavior, or is caused by social interaction and variables in the environment. For example, if crime is an inherent predisposition over which the offender has minimal control, then incarceration and prison time would not be a deterrent to crime. What do you believe is the primary cause of criminal behavior? What are the implications of your belief for the treatment of criminals?
3. Most people who study crime and criminals accept that violent crimes against persons and property—murder, rape, robbery, burglary—are the most serious crimes. However, others who study crime and criminals believe that white-collar crime, corruption, and Internet crime are more harmful to society. Do you agree? Why or why not? Do you think the government and the criminal justice system uses violent crimes to distract people from possible threats to their freedom from government, big business, and the ruling class? Why or why not?

ContentSelect

Go to the ContentSelect web site and type in the keyword phrase "social control theory." Read "Race, Crime, and the American Dream" from the May 2000 issue of the *Journal of Research in Crime and Delinquency*. The article discusses social control and strain theories. Sample the article to answer the following questions.

1. What does the article say about the role of the "American dream" on behavior and crime?
2. According to the article, is the American dream alive and well among African Americans? How does the American dream orientation affect the outlook of lower socioeconomic status African Americans?
3. Compare and contrast the findings of the study on views of the future held by the "Hallway Hangers" (white teenagers) and "Brothers" (African American teenagers).
4. According to your text, how do social control and strain theories explain crime, and how can those explanations help prevent crime? Did the findings of the article support this view?
5. According to your text, what government programs have been initiated as a result of strain theory beliefs?

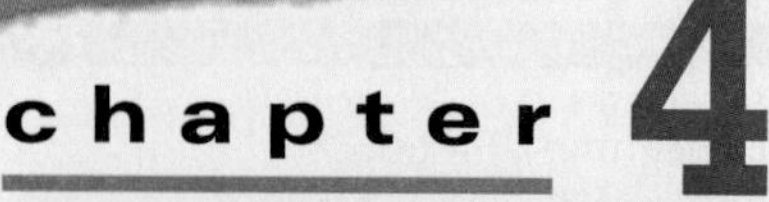

chapter 4

Criminal Law: Control versus Liberty

outline

Learning Objectives

After reading this chapter, you will know

- How federal, state, and local criminal laws are created and changed.
- Why limits are imposed on criminal laws and how those limits are defined.
- The major elements of a crime that must be present to prosecute offenders for their actions.
- The major defenses against charges of criminal conduct and how those defenses are defined.
- How crimes are categorized and defined according to the Model Penal Code.
- How criminal liability for crimes and the seriousness of crimes are determined.

It's Against the Law—or Was at One Time

Horses of more than 1 year old are prohibited in a place of worship. (Virginia)

State law forbids any establishment from charging admission to see a one-armed piano player. (Iowa)

It is against the law to sleep in your refrigerator. (Pennsylvania)

It is against the law for a lady to lift her skirt more than 6 inches while walking through a mud puddle. (Michigan)

Married couples must live together or be imprisoned. (Michigan)

It is illegal for anyone to give lighted cigars to dogs, cats, and other domesticated animals kept as pets. (Zion, Illinois)

It's illegal for men to be seen publicly in any kind of strapless gown. (Miami)

Corrupt practices or bribery are prohibited by any person other than political candidates. (Virginia Code of 1930)

A woman cannot dance on a saloon table unless her clothing weighs more than 3 pounds 2 ounces. (Helena, Montana)

If a police officer in Coeur d'Alene, Idaho, suspects a couple is having sex inside a vehicle, the officer must honk his horn three times, and wait 2 minutes before being allowed to approach the scene.

Boogers may not be flicked into the wind. (Alabama)

You may not have an ice cream cone in your back pocket at any time. (Alabama)

introduction:

The Rule of Law

In 1198, Pope Innocent III wrote to the Emperor of France that the pope was like the sun and the emperor was like the moon. The sun was greater than the moon, and the moon derived its light from the sun. In other words, the pope was greater and more powerful than the emperor. For the next three centuries, the royal rulers of England and France engaged in a continuous power struggle as to who was the supreme authority. King Henry VIII appeared to tip the balance of power to royalty when in 1534 he proclaimed himself the head of the Church of England and the king of the land.[1] He claimed to be both the moon and the sun.

After breaking away from England, the American colonies rejected the authority of both the Church and the king as the supreme authority and declared that the United States is founded on the superiority of the rule of law. The **rule of law** declares that the standards of behavior and privilege are established not by kings or religious leaders but by rules and procedures that define and prohibit certain behaviors as illegal or criminal and prescribe punishments for those behaviors. All people, regardless of rank, title, position, status, or wealth, are accorded the same rights and privileges under the law. Three major categories of law are civil law, administrative law, and criminal law. The differences among these kinds of law are discussed in Chapter 9, while this chapter focuses on an examination of criminal law.

The Making of Law

THE MAIN IDEA

Federal, state, and local government bodies pass criminal laws to protect citizens.

As you might conclude from the examples provided at the beginning of this chapter, laws have history. Laws also are made in social and political contexts, though one might wonder why anyone would want to bring a horse of any age to church! Why do governments—local, state, and federal—create criminal laws? The **American Law Institute,** a private, voluntary association of distinguished judges, lawyers, and law teachers, gives five reasons for laws[2]:

1. To forbid and prevent conduct that unjustifiably and inexcusably inflicts or threatens substantial harm to individual or public interests
2. To subject to public control persons whose conduct indicates that they are disposed to commit crimes
3. To safeguard conduct that is without fault from condemnation as criminal
4. To give fair warning of the nature of the conduct declared to constitute an offense
5. To differentiate on reasonable grounds between serious and minor offenses

rule of law Principle that standards of behavior and privilege are established by laws and not by monarchs or religious leaders.

Specific laws may be passed because it is thought that they prohibit actions that are harmful to society. For example, prohibitions against murder, rape, robbery, and arson are seen as serving all people in society. Such conduct is prohibited because it is considered harmful in itself, or ***mala in se.*** Other laws may be passed because it is felt by some that there is a need to regulate certain actions—for example, parking regulations, minimum drinking-age limits, and various licensing regulations. This conduct is ***mal prohibita***—prohibited only because of the law and not because it is necessarily harmful or inherently evil.

Much debate is generated about what laws should be passed and what purposes the law actually serves. Some laws are based on the morals and values of the community. Laws against abortion, obscenity, and drug use often are based on moral and ethical beliefs not shared by all members of society. Some laws are passed based on public fear. Kidnapping was made a federal crime after the kidnapping and murder of Charles Lindbergh's child, for example. And Megan's Law, which requires the registration of sexual offenders, was passed after a sexual offender unknown to the community abducted and murdered a small child.

Ideally, laws serve the public good (the consensus model), but sometimes laws benefit a small group or special interests (the conflict model). The actual laws of the land are derived from (1) federal criminal laws, (2) state criminal laws, and (3) local criminal laws. Each level of government has the authority to enact laws within its jurisdiction.

At http://www.ali.org/, the official web site of the American Law Institute, learn more about the institute and its programs.

Federal Criminal Laws

Federal criminal laws are found in (1) the U.S. Constitution, (2) *U.S. Criminal Codes,* (3) judicial decisions interpreting codes, and (4) executive orders. The only crimes defined in the U.S. Constitution are treason and sedition, but the Constitution provides for the establishment of the court system and the process by which laws may be enacted. The Constitution also provides the reference for judging the validity of laws. Laws that are contrary to the freedoms and rights provided by the Constitution and its amendments may be declared null and void by the U.S. Supreme Court.

The ***U.S. Criminal Codes*** is the publication that contains all of the federal laws. Federal criminal laws must originate in the House of Representatives or the U.S. Senate. A senator or representative introduces a proposal (known as a bill) to create a new law or modify an existing law. The merits of the bill are debated in the House or Senate and a vote is taken. If the bill receives a majority vote, it is passed on to the other house of Congress where it is again debated and put to a vote. If any changes are made, the amended bill must be returned to the house of Congress where it originated and voted on again. This process continues until the House and Senate agree on a single version of the bill. The bill is then forwarded to the president, who can sign the bill into law, veto it, or take no action, in which case the bill dies automatically when Congress adjourns. If the president vetoes a bill, Congress can pass the law over the president's veto by a two-thirds vote of both Houses. Whether approved by the president and the Congress or by the Congress alone, a bill becomes law when it is published in the *U.S. Criminal Codes.*

Federal criminal laws can be modified or influenced by judicial decisions. Federal judges cannot make law, but their influence can be so great that the end result is nearly the same.[3] Rules governing the use of evidence in a trial, for instance, come from the courts rather than the legislative bodies, but the impact is the same as if they were laws. Finally, while not in a strict sense a criminal law, the president can issue executive orders that have the weight of law in prohibiting and regulating certain conduct.

State Criminal Laws

The sources of state criminal laws are the state constitution, state criminal codes, common law, and judicial decisions interpreting codes and the common law. Each state has the right to enact criminal laws seen as appropriate for its citizens. This autonomy leads to great variety in laws, but most states have similar criminal laws. Some reasons for the

mala in se Acts that are crimes because they are inherently evil or harmful to society.

mala prohibita Acts that are prohibited because they are defined as crimes by law.

similarity of state criminal codes are that (1) all state criminals laws must preserve the rights guaranteed in the U.S. Constitution, (2) many states (approximately 22) have adopted substantial proportions of their criminal codes from the Model Penal Code published by the American Law Institute in 1962, (3) state criminal laws had as their common origin early English common law, and (4) if one accepts the consensus model, then laws will serve similar public benefit in each of the states.

State constitutions cannot negate any right guaranteed in the U.S. Constitution, but a state's constitution can add to rights not covered by the U.S. Constitution. For example, Alaska and Hawaii have added the right of privacy as a guaranteed freedom for the citizens of their states, whereas privacy is only an implied right in the U.S. Constitution. Most state criminal codes are passed by state governments in a similar manner as the federal criminal codes. A bill must originate in one of the state legislative bodies, be passed by both bodies, and then be endorsed by the governor of the state. Like the president, state governors have veto power and the power to create rules and regulations through executive orders.

In their particulars, state criminal codes differ significantly among states. For example, some states prohibit consensual sex among persons of the same sex, whereas, other states permit such conduct. Some states allow citizens to carry concealed weapons, whereas other states have strict prohibitions against this practice. Any person within a state is under the jurisdiction of the laws of that state regardless of the person's state of residence or citizenship. Thus, a person from a state that permits carrying a concealed weapon who travels to a state that prohibits such behavior must conform to the laws of the state he or she is in. Likewise, a state's criminal laws are not applicable outside that state's boundaries. Thus, while Utah prohibits gambling, its bordering state, Nevada, has legalized gambling. If a Utah resident travels to Nevada, Utah's prohibition against gambling does not prevent the Utah resident from gambling while in Nevada.

One of the distinctions between federal criminal laws and state criminal laws is the area of law known as **common law,** or unwritten law. Criminal law in the United States was greatly influenced by early English common law. English criminal law was based on the assumption that the vast majority of citizens was illiterate and thus would not understand written law. Written laws were stated simply, leaving it to judges to interpret and apply laws to specific situations. For example, as written, the law simply declared that murder is prohibited or that it is against the law to disturb the peace. The law offered no guidance as to what behaviors constituted disturbing the peace or the grounds for determining that a person had committed murder. This judge-mediated common law became the basis for criminal law in the American colonies.

This pattern of law can be seen in today's small claims courts and traffic courts. Also, television shows in which the parties to a dispute appear before a "television judge" who hears and resolves their dispute mimic the principles of common law in that the "judge" is empowered to resolve specific disputes based on general principles or guidelines. Federal courts and federal judges are specifically prohibited from operating under the rules of common law.

common law Unwritten, simply stated laws from the English common laws, based on traditions and common understandings in a time when most people were illiterate.

felony Serious criminal conduct punishable by incarceration for more than one year.

misdemeanor Less serious criminal conduct punishable by incarceration for less than a year.

violation An illegal action that is less serious than a misdemeanor and may carry the punishment of only a fine or suspension of privilege.

Local Criminal Laws

The sources of local criminal laws are city or county charters, municipal or county ordinances or violations, common law, and judicial decisions of municipal judges interpreting codes and common law. Nearly all local criminal laws are misdemeanors or violations. Serious criminal conduct is called a **felony,** and less serious criminal conduct is called a **misdemeanor.** The difference between a felony and a misdemeanor is usually defined by the amount of time in prison or jail one can receive as punishment for violation of the statute. Felonies commonly are crimes for which one can receive a punishment of 1 year or more in a state prison, while misdemeanors are crimes for which one can receive a punishment of 1 year or less in a state prison or county jail.

ethics in the system

Blue Laws

There are laws on the books, some which are enforced, that prohibit certain behaviors on moral grounds, based on standards of morality from colonial times. For example, some states have laws prohibiting certain types of commercial transactions, the operation of entertainment establishments, or the selling of tobacco or alcohol on Sunday. These laws restricting Sunday sales and entertainment have their roots in colonial government. In 1732 a colony of Puritan settlers in New Haven, Connecticut, adopted a set of laws for the governance of their settlement. These laws reflected the deeply held religious beliefs of the people and had harsh punishments for offenses such as Sabbath breaking, drunkenness, and immodest dress.

The privilege of voting and holding official office was contingent on good standing in a church of the colony and loyalty to religious values. For example, in Protestant New Haven, the law provided that a Catholic priest found within the colony could be seized by anyone and without a warrant. The punishment for the first offense of trespass by a priest was banishment, and the second offense was punishable by death. It was also forbidden to give food or lodging to a Quaker, Adamite, or other "heretic." Persons who converted to the Quaker religion were banished from the colony and could be put to death if they returned.

New Haven's laws also forbade the wearing of "clothes trimmed with gold, silver, or bone lace, above two shillings by the yard." Adultery was punishable by death. Persons found to engage in fornication were required to be married or punished "as the court may think proper." Married persons were required to live together upon punishment of imprisonment for failure to do so. The punishment for theft, which included picking an ear of corn growing in a neighbor's garden, was death. Celebrations and festive entertainment on Christmas or saints' days were prohibited.

These laws based on colonial codes of morality are called **blue laws,** but the origin of the name is obscure. The term first appeared in 1791 in the writings of Reverend Samuel Peters' book *General History of Connecticut*. Peters said the laws were written on blue paper and were so named for the color of the paper, but whether this is the exact origin of the term cannot be determined.

Other settlements in the American colonies adopted similar blue laws requiring obedience to the religious values of their communities. Today the influence of these old laws remains in state statues prohibiting certain businesses, especially movie theaters, from operating on Sundays and the Sunday sale of alcoholic beverages and cigarettes. Also, some states make fornication a felony, prohibit sodomy, or have laws that reflect colonial values against obscenity and nudity.

The federal courts have upheld the constitutionality of state and local blue laws because they do not violate federal laws. However, commercial competition has forced many communities to abandon their prohibitions against Sunday commerce and entertainment. In a competitive free market where beliefs about morality are no longer universal, shoppers flock to neighboring communities without blue laws. Some businesses will not locate in communities that restrict Sunday sales. When Orlando, Florida, repealed its law against Sunday sales of alcoholic beverages in 1999, sales for beer and wine jumped 10 to 15 percent and new businesses moved into the city.[4]

■ **On what were the blue laws based? Do you think laws should be continually updated to reflect changes in morality? Why have blue laws persisted, and in what circumstances should they be changed? Are repeal of blue laws on economic grounds in the common interest of all citizens of a community?**

Violations, a relative new classification of prohibited behaviors, commonly regulate traffic offenses.[5] A **violation** is less than a misdemeanor and may carry the punishment of only a fine or suspension of privilege, such as losing one's driver's license temporarily. Many states have redefined traffic offenses as violations that use to be classified as misdemeanors. The advantage is that violations free up the resources of the criminal courts for more serious cases and allow for speedier processing of cases through the system.

This person is paying the fine for a traffic violation. What kind of a law has been violated? Is it a federal, state, or local law? What are the differences between laws that originate at the local, state, or federal levels? What are the sources of laws in the United States, and how are laws made?

Local criminal codes are the product of city councils and county governments. Similar to the president and governors, chief executive officers of the city and county have the power to prohibit or regulate behavior through executive orders. Otherwise, there is great diversity in the way municipalities and counties draft and pass local criminal codes. Local criminal codes have limited jurisdiction and are enforceable only within the city or county limits. Local criminal codes cannot deny rights guaranteed by the state constitution or the U.S. Constitution.

JUST THE FACTS 4.1

What are the five reasons given to justify the making of laws? How are federal, state, and local criminal laws similar and dissimilar?

The Limits of the Law

THE MAIN IDEA

Criminal law is founded on the principle of rule of law and is based on principles of rationality and justice.

The founding of criminal law on the principle of rule of law means that the power of government is limited. Unlike royalty in the Middle Ages, which had limitless absolute power, governments are limited in the behaviors that can be declared criminal and in the punishments that can be applied for violations of criminal laws. Seven benchmarks are used to assess the legality of criminal laws:

1. Principle of legality
2. Ex post facto laws
3. Due process
4. Void for vagueness
5. Right to privacy
6. Void for overbreadth
7. Cruel and unusual punishment

These principles apply to local, state, and federal laws.

Principle of Legality

Government cannot punish citizens for specific conduct if no specific laws exist forewarning them that the conduct is prohibited or required. This **principle of legality,** which has its roots in the Roman Empire, requires that laws must be made public before they can be enforced. When a law is passed, it must be published in an official government publication to become valid. Until the law is published, even though it is passed, it is not binding on behavior. Thus, it is possible that there will be a gap between the time that a behavior is prohibited and the time that the prohibition can be enforced by the police. Regardless, the principle of legality also declares that any behavior that has no law against it is legal. Thus, prostitution is legal in some counties of Nevada, not because there is a law allowing it but because there is no law prohibiting it.

Ex Post Facto Laws

Ex post facto ("not after the fact") laws are related to the principle of legality. This **ex post facto law** principle declares that persons cannot be punished for actions committed before the law prohibiting the behavior was passed.[6] For example, Timothy Leary, a university psychology professor, experimented with and advocated the use of LSD prior to the time that laws were passed making possession or use of LSD illegal. Despite public knowledge and his acknowledgment that he used LSD prior to the passing of laws prohibiting its use, charges could not be brought against him. When he continued to use LSD after the law was passed, however, he was arrested, although the charges against him had to be limited to offenses he committed after the drug law was published.

The principle of ex post facto law also prohibits government from increasing the punishment for a specific crime after the crime was committed. Assume, for instance, that a person is convicted of mass murder in a state that does not have the death penalty. The public, upset by the brutality of the crime, may support a successful campaign to change the law and adopt a death penalty for mass murder. Even with the new law, however, the convicted person's sentence cannot then be changed from life in prison to death.

The government also cannot reduce the amount of evidence or alter the kind of evidence required for conviction when the offense was committed. If a person committed a crime on January 1, was arrested for the crime on January 30, and was scheduled for trial on July 1, a change in the law any time after January 1 regarding the kind of evidence required for conviction when an offense is committed could not be applied in court to the detriment of the defendant (although a change could be applied to the defendant's benefit).[7] Generally, the defendant has to be tried under the rules of evidence and laws that were in effect at the time the alleged crime was committed.

principle of legality The belief that specific laws defining crimes and penalties for crimes must exist and be made public before the government can punish citizens for violating them.

ex post facto law A law related to the principle that persons cannot be punished for actions committed before the law prohibiting the behavior was passed.

substantive due process Limits on the power of governments to create crimes unless there is compelling, substantial public interest in regulating or prohibiting the conduct.

Due Process

As you read in Chapter 2, the principles of due process are extrapolated from the U.S. Constitution and Bill of Rights. The principle of due process states simply that government must treat people fairly and equally before the law. There are two types of due process rights: substantive and procedural. **Substantive due process** limits the power of governments to create crimes unless there is compelling, substantial, public interest in regulating or prohibiting the conduct. The government, in a sense, is limited in what can be declared illegal. Conduct deemed illegal for which there is no rational justification for the law violates the principle of due process. Governments, in other words, cannot make arbitrary and capricious criminal laws.

Recent examination of the law for gender bias has resulted in a number of laws being declared unconstitutional because of violation of due process. Laws that apply to

What does it mean to live in a social system with rule by law? What are the alternatives? What does it mean that the legality and limits of laws in the United States are decided on the basis of a system of *stare decisis*? Generally what document is the ultimate authority on the legality of laws?

only one sex are violations of due process. Thus, a New York law that prohibited females from sunbathing on public beaches topless was struck down as unconstitutional because it applied only to females. The court ruled that the law had to apply equally to both sexes.

Procedural due process requires the government to follow established procedures and to treat defendants equally. Procedural laws, explained further in Chapter 5, regulate the conduct of the police and the courts and the criminal justice system in general. These laws, called "rules of evidence," define, for example, what is fair treatment, what order of events must be followed, what types of evidence can be admitted at a trial, and the rights of defendants.

Because of procedural due process, case law precedents play a big role in adjudication in the American system of justice. Attorneys can argue that the court must allow similar evidence or testimony as was admitted in the past in similar cases. This case law system, called ***stare decisis,*** is not common to all criminal justice systems, however. For example, France uses the Continental system, in which each case is compared with the elements of the written law rather than with past cases.

In the United States, although *stare decisis* guides their actions, the courts can interpret cases and decide to what extent a case is like or unlike any previous cases. To change the basis on which precedents are judged, a court must explain why it is changing its interpretation and what the new criteria for judgment are. A case in which such a change of opinion is declared by the court is called a "landmark case." Since the 1960s, for example, the U.S. Supreme Court has issued numerous landmark decisions affecting the criminal justice system in matters such as search and seizure, confessions, cruel and unusual punishment, and prisoner rights. Because of the practice and importance of *stare decisis,* criminal attorneys must have excellent research abilities and access to records of previous court cases.

procedural due process The requirement that the government must follow established procedures and treat defendants equally.

stare decisis The American system of developing and applying case law on the basis of precedents established in previous cases.

void for vagueness Laws that are illegal because they do not provide clear and reasonable definitions of the specific behaviors that are prohibited.

Void for Vagueness

The law must say what it means and mean what it says. Laws that do not provide reasonable guidelines that define the specific prohibited behaviors are **void for vagueness.** For instance, a New Jersey statute that made it a crime to be a member of a gang was struck down because the Court declared that the word *gang* was too vague.[8] In another example, in the municipal court of Lincoln, Nebraska, a man was convicted of violating Section 9.52.100 of the Lincoln Municipal Code declaring, "It shall be unlawful for any person within the City of Lincoln . . . to commit any indecent, immodest or filthy act in the presence of any person, or in such a situation that persons passing might ordinarily see the same." On appeal, the Supreme Court of Nebraska reversed the conviction on the grounds that "The dividing line between what is lawful and what is unlawful in terms of 'indecent,' 'immodest,' or 'filthy' is simply too broad to satisfy the constitutional requirements of due process."[9]

Laws must use wording that clearly specifies what behavior or act is unlawful. Vague wording subject to different interpretations, such as "immoral," "indecent," "too close," or "interfere with," does not provide the average person with sufficient information to determine if their behavior is in violation of the law. If a law is so vague that members of a Boy Scout troop may be considered to be in violation of a prohibition against belonging to a "gang," the law is vague.

Right to Privacy

Laws that violate reasonable personal privacy may be declared void. The right to privacy is not clearly delineated in the U.S. Constitution but is a constructed right, inferred from the provisions of the First, Third, Fourth, and Ninth amendments. Some state constitutions, such as those of Alaska, Florida, and Hawaii, have explicit rights to privacy that can be far-reaching. For example, under the protection of Alaska's right to privacy, the possession of small amounts of marijuana in the privacy of one's home is insufficient grounds for an arrest warrant or search.[10]

Right to privacy claims have resulted in several well-known U.S. Supreme Court decisions. The Court has struck down laws that made it a crime for married couples to use contraceptives[11] or for a person to possess pornography within the privacy of one's home.[12] However, the Court has upheld state statutes making it a crime to possess child pornography or to commit sodomy in the privacy of one's home.[13] Thus, privacy is not an overarching right that permits otherwise harmful or prohibited behaviors merely because they are performed in one's home.

Void for Overbreadth

Laws that have been declared **void for overbreadth** are laws that go too far; that is, in an attempt to prevent a specific conduct, the law not only makes that conduct illegal, but also prohibits other behaviors that are legally protected. Void for overbreadth laws frequently are connected with free speech and expressive conduct. Cases challenged for overbreadth that have made their way to the U.S. Supreme Court involve laws prohibiting activities such as public protest, nude dancing, panhandling, erotic art, and flag burning.[14]

A law that is void for overbreadth is not vague in what it prohibits (like a law that is void for vagueness); rather, it simply prohibits legal activities as well as illegal activities. For example, in an attempt to provide a better quality of life, the city of New York prohibited panhandling or begging in the New York subways, because panhandlers and beggars frightened passengers. The law was not vague in what it prohibited, but it could also be applied to prohibit free speech activities, which are protected under the U.S. Constitution.[15] Not all activities can be justified under the claim of free speech, however. The Court upheld an Indiana statute banning nude dancing in public, for instance, on the grounds that the statute did not prohibit dancers from expressing themselves but only from expressing themselves while nude.[16]

void for overbreadth Laws that are illegal because they are stated so broadly as to prohibit legal activities as well as illegal activities.

cruel and unusual punishment Punishment that violates the principle of proportionality and is considered too harsh for the crime committed; prohibited by the Eighth Amendment.

Cruel and Unusual Punishment

To be valid, a law must specify the punishment to be applied for violation of the law. If that punishment is in violation of the Eighth Amendment prohibiting **cruel and unusual punishment,** it may be declared unconstitutional. This legal philosophy appears to be based on the premise of classical criminology that punishment should be

Figure 4.1

Limits of the Law

Rule of Law			
Rationality		Justice	
Legality	Laws must be made public before they can be enforced.	**Due Process**	Government must treat people equally and fairly before the law.
Ex post facto	Actions prior to enactment of laws cannot be punished after the fact.	**Right to Privacy**	Laws must not violate reasonable personal privacy of citizens.
Void for Vagueness	Laws must take care to define crimes clearly.	**Cruel and Unusual Punishment**	Laws must state the punishment for crimes, which must be proportional to the seriousness of the crime.
Void for Overbreadth	Laws must not prohibit behaviors that are legally protected.		

To read a thought-provoking essay that discusses issues in Canada on cruel and unusual punishment, follow links at http://www.nacdl.org/. ■

appropriate to the crime. While the argument of cruel and unusual punishment has frequently been applied to cases involving the death sentence, the focus of the prohibition is on applying the **principle of proportionality** for the appropriate punishment for a crime.[17] This focus involves much more than just appeals about the merits of the death penalty. The roots of this principle extend all the way back to the Magna Carta, which prohibited excessive fines.

Numerous cases have been appealed on the claim that the punishment was cruel and unusual. ***Weems v. United States*** (1910) has been used as a criterion for judging the limits of proportionality. Weems was convicted of falsifying a public document, was sentenced to 15 years at hard labor in chains, and was permanently deprived of his civil rights. The U.S. Supreme Court overturned the conviction on the grounds that the punishment was not proportional to the harm done by the crime.[18] However, the Court has not overturned a death penalty sentence on the grounds that the death penalty is cruel and unusual. The Court has ruled only that the death penalty must be fairly and equally applied.[19]

The Court also has decided that sentencing a seriously ill person to prison does not constitute cruel and unusual punishment if adequate medical treatment for the condition is available.[20] Sentencing a person to prison for drug addiction is cruel and unusual, as drug addiction is deemed an illness rather than a criminal behavior. However, sentencing a person for possessing or using drugs is not cruel and unusual.[21] The Court has ruled that the use of corporal punishment in prison is cruel and unusual punishment and has prohibited such punishment.

principle of proportionality The belief that less serious harms should carry lesser punishments than more serious harms.

JUST THE FACTS 4.2

How does a bill become a law? What are the seven benchmarks used to assess the legality of a criminal law, and in what circumstances is each benchmark applied?

Criminal laws must specify the punishment for a crime, and the punishment must meet the principle of proportionality; that is, it must be appropriate to the seriousness of the offense. The United States Constitution makes it illegal to exact "cruel and unusual" punishment, which in an earlier age could be used on any offender for any kind of offense. What are the six other benchmarks used to assess the legality of a criminal law?

Elements of a Crime

THE MAIN IDEA

The actions and intent of the criminal, as well as the seriousness of the crime, all carry weight in determining punishment.

Punishments specified by law are based on the principle of proportionality. Less serious harms such as misdemeanors carry lesser punishment than more serious harms, which are classified as felonies. However, even within felonies there are various degrees of punishment. Even the same act, such as the killing of a human being, may be punished by a sentence ranging from 1 year in prison to the death penalty. Determining what punishment should be attached to a crime depends on the conduct and the intention of the actor or perpetrator.

The actions of the person are referred to as the ***actus reus*** of the crime. The intent of the person is referred to as the ***mens rea.*** In assessing whether a crime has been committed and the seriousness of the crime, the law examines what the person did, the person's state of mind or intentions, whether the person's actions were the cause of the outcome, and the specific harm that resulted from the actions.

elements of a crime The illegal actions (*actus reus*) and criminal intentions (*mens rea*) of the actor along with the circumstances that link the two, especially causation.

actus reus The actions of the person committing a crime as defined by law, one of the key elements of a crime.

mens rea The state of mind and intent of the person committing the *actus reus*, one of the key elements of a crime.

Actus Reus

American law is firmly rooted in the classical criminological principle that crime is a voluntary action; that is, a person chooses to commit a crime. As a result, one of the first elements necessary to assert that a crime has been committed is that the actions of the person must be voluntary. An old British case of ***King v. Cogdon*** is cited as the benchmark for determining the voluntariness of an action. In that case, Mrs. Cogdon, who suffered from delusions, was found not guilty of the axe murder of her daughter. During her sleep, Mrs. Cogdon had a delusion and while "sleep walking" struck and killed her daughter. The British Court ruled the act was involuntary. Involuntary actions do not extend to conduct that is foreseeable, however. For example, a person who has an epileptic seizure while driving a car and as a result causes someone's death can be held accountable for the death. For a person with epilepsy, losing control of a motor vehicle is a foreseeable possibility.[22]

People have an obligation to conduct themselves in such a manner so as not to create a harm to others. Thus, "accidental" injuries may be deemed voluntary even if the people deny that they intended to inflict harm. For example, a person whose thumb slips while holding back the hammer of a pistol, causing the wounding or death of another, is considered to have voluntarily committed the act even though the defendant denies the intention to fire the weapon.[23] The *actus reus* of some crimes does not require a bodily or physical action and can consist of verbal actions. Crimes such as conspiracy, solicitation, terroristic threats, and inciting to riot are examples of crimes whose *actus reus* consists of verbal acts.

FAILURE TO ACT There are some crimes in which the *actus reus* is the failure to act or a lack of action. These are called **crimes of omission.** The criminal intent of a crime may be the failure to act when there is a legal duty to act. A lifeguard employed by the government is under a legal obligation and may be considered guilty of a crime if while on duty he or she fails to act to save a swimmer in distress. However, if that same lifeguard, while on vacation in another state, observes a swimmer in distress and fails to act to offer assistance, he or she may be criticized for failing a moral duty but has committed no crime.

In crimes of omission, hospitals, caregivers, and even bystanders can come under the requirement of a legal duty to help another. For example, if you help someone when you are under no duty to do so but fail to exercise reasonable care for the safety and security of the person you are attempting to help, then you may be regarded as having criminal liability.[24] It is fear of criminal (or civil) liability that causes some people to refuse to act when they could render life-saving care to a victim. As a result, a number of states have passed "Good Samaritan" laws that extend legal protection against civil or criminal action against a person who renders aid to someone in distress. Some states even require that motorists stop and render reasonable aid for persons they observe who appear to be in distress. For example, Alaska requires that motorists render assistance to stranded motorists, and failure to do so is considered criminal. Given Alaska's climate and vast stretches of wilderness, failure to render aid to a stranded motorist could result in the death of the person.

Parents are considered to have a legal duty to aid and assist their children. Failure to fulfill this duty can be criminal. The Court has ruled that even if the danger is from another parent, as in the case of child abuse, the parent has a legal duty to assist the children when under attack or at risk of physical danger.[25] This means that the spouse of an abusive parent could be charged with a crime even though the spouse did not cause harm to the child. The failure to prevent harm is criminal. Thus, a parent who fails to seek medical attention for his or her child could be held criminally liable in the event of the child's death. The same legal duty does not extend to the marital relationship, however. If a spouse fails to seek medical attention for his or her partner, who dies as a result of the lack of care, there is no legal duty that would make this action criminal.[26]

crimes of omission Crimes resulting from the failure to act or the lack of action rather than the commission of illegal acts.

possession Knowingly having, holding, carrying, or knowing the location of an illegal or prohibited item; can constitute the *mens rea* of a crime.

POSSESSION AS *ACTUS REUS* Possession of an illegal or prohibited item can constitute the *actus reus* of a crime. In a case in which a person has an illegal firearm in the trunk of his or her automobile, possession of the weapon is considered the *actus reus* of the crime. Three types of **possession** are recognized by the Model Penal Code: constructive possession, knowing possession, and mere possession.[27]

It is deemed *constructive possession* when a person does not have physical or actual possession of the illegal item but the defendant exercised, either singularly or jointly, care, custody, control, and management over the contraband, and the defendant knew that what he or she possessed was contraband. A drug dealer who mails a package of drugs or gives it to another to deliver is considered to have constructive possession of the drugs even though he or she does not have actual possession.

It is deemed *knowing possession* when a person has actual possession and knows that what he or she possesses is contraband, whereas it is considered *mere possession* when a person has actual possession of an item but does not know that it is contraband. However, mere possession may not be sufficient *actus reus* to constitute a crime. Assume that a person rents a car from a reputable rental agency and is stopped by the police for an equipment defect. During the course of the stop, the police discover that cocaine has been concealed in a secret compartment in the trunk of the vehicle. If the person who rented the vehicle had no knowledge of the contraband, this is mere possession and may not be criminal. Also, if the person has possession of the contraband but is unaware of the nature of the item, this is mere possession and may not be criminal. Thus, a delivery driver who, in the course of normal business, transports illegal contraband from point A to point B has mere possession of the contraband, and that is insufficient *actus reus* to constitute a crime.[28]

Mens Rea

The second critical element in determining the criminality and seriousness of an act is the *mens rea,* or criminal intent, of the actor, sometimes referred to as "guilty mind." A person who extends the arm and hand in the gesture of a yawn may strike and harm a person nearby. The blow may cause great physical pain but was not struck with the intent to cause harm. In such a case, in which the action is voluntary but the harm is unintentional, the person is said to lack *mens rea,* and no crime has been committed. (The injured party may seek damages under civil suit wherein *mens rea* is not a requirement.) The general principle of law is that an act is not bad without a guilty mind.

INTENT The only direct evidence of *mens rea* is the defendant's confession. Otherwise, in criminal law *mens rea* is determined primarily by circumstantial or indirect evidence. In examining the criminal **intent** of a person, there are four different states of guilty mind that can be applied to an action: (1) general intent, (2) specific intent, (3) transferred intent, and (4) constructive intent.[29]

General intent refers to the logical outcomes associated with a criminal act—the *actus reus*. A person who intentionally strikes someone on the head with a heavy instrument is assumed to have intended to harm the person. *Specific intent* refers to the legal requirement of the elements of a crime. For example, burglary requires the commission of a trespass with the intent to commit a crime, and larceny requires the taking of property with the intent to carry it away and permanently deprive the owner of the property. Without the specific intent to commit a crime, trespass cannot be elevated to burglary, and without the specific intent of permanently depriving the owner of the property, the taking of property may be nothing more than "borrowing."

Transferred intent covers incidences in which a person injures another but did not intend to harm the party. An interesting application of this *mens rea* is the principle of felony murder. This principle says that if, during a bank robbery, a police officer responding to the bank alarm shoots at the robber but misses and hits an innocent bystander, the bank robber may be charged with the bystander's murder. The police officer had no criminal intent to harm the bystander, and the robber did not intend for the officer to shoot the bystander. However, under the principle of transferred intent, the criminal intent of the bank robber is applied to the *actus reus* of the death of the bystander. A more common application of the principle of transferred intent is when two persons are arguing and one commits an act intended to harm the other but instead harms an innocent third party. The criminal intent to harm the other person in the argument is transferred to the harm suffered by the third party.

It is considered **constructive intent** when an actor did not intend to harm anyone but should have known that his or her behavior created a high risk of injury. A common situation for the application of constructive intent is injury or death caused by a

intent Criminal intentions or the state of "guilty mind" in *mens rea,* including general, specific, transferred, and constructive intent.

constructive intent When an actor did not intend to harm anyone but should have known that his or her behavior created a high risk of injury.

Figure 4.2

Elements of a Crime

	1. *Actus reus*	2. *Mens rea*	3. Concurrence
Necessary and Sufficient Characteristics	• Voluntary behavior • A physical or verbal act or failure to act • Possession of an illegal item	• Confession of criminal intent • Assumption of general intent • Evidence of specific intent • Transferred intent in a felony crime • Presence of constructive intent • Strict liability crime	• Completeness of the crime • Direct connection between *actus reus* and *mens rea* • Evidence of crime causation from the union of *actus reus* and *mens rea* • Inchoate offenses
Examples	• Breaking into a car • Taking disks from work for personal use • Failing to perform a legal duty • Making terrorist threats	• Acting purposefully to cause injury • Knowing that an act or failure to act will cause injury • Causing injury by recklessness or negligence	• Acting on intent to deprive a car owner of his/her CD player • Carrying out a plan to murder a spouse • Soliciting, conspiring to commit, or attempting crimes

person who fires a gun into the air in an act of celebration, such as on New Year's Eve. The person who fired the gun had no intent to harm anyone, but constructive intent assigns *mens rea* on the principle that the person should have known that this behavior created a high risk of injury.

In assigning *mens rea* to a crime, the Model Penal Code distinguishes four types of intent: purposely, knowingly, recklessly, and negligently.[30] Each has a lesser degree of criminal intent, and as a result, the punishment assigned to each differs according to the degree of criminal intent. A person who causes the death of another purposely is guilty of murder and can be punished by death or extended imprisonment, whereas a person who causes the death of another recklessly is guilty of manslaughter and will receive a lesser punishment.

STRICT LIABILITY Some actions are considered criminal without the necessity of any criminal intent, and these actions are called **strict liability crimes.** Parking violations are an example of a strict liability law. The registered owner of the illegally parked vehicle is held liable for the fine regardless of whether he or she parked the car, was operating the car, or even had knowledge of the parking violation. Consider the case of a son who borrows the family car and receives a parking violation but throws the citation away and does not inform anyone. The son who committed the act is not held liable for the parking violation. However, the parent, the registered owner of the vehicle, is held accountable even though he or she had no knowledge of the citation.

strict liability crimes
Actions that do not require criminal intent to be defined as crimes, such as parking violations.

Most strict liability laws cover minor actions, such as illegal parking, but some concern felony crimes. For some states, escape from prison is a strict liability crime. In ***State v. Marks,*** a prisoner fell out of a truck returning from a work detail, and fellow prisoner, Marks, jumped out, he claimed, to assist the inmate who fell. When the driver noticed the missing prisoners, he returned and found the two waiting beside the road. Marks was charged with the crime of escape.[31] The conviction was upheld on appeal on the grounds that the statute did not spell out a requirement for any specific intent to be formed by the prisoner to commit the crime of escape. In some states, statutory rape or sexual relations with a person under the age of consent is a strict liability crime. The state considers the welfare of children an important issue and places an affirmative burden on the defendant to positively establish the age of the sexual partner even in cases in which the sex is claimed to be consensual.[32]

As an example, see a list of Texas criminal laws regarding inchoate offenses at http://www.bakers-legal-pages.com/pc/pct04.htm. ■

Incomplete Crimes or Inchoate Offenses

Concurrence is the legal requirement that there is a union of *actus reus* and *mens rea;* that is, a perpetrator had criminal intent at the time the perpetrator's act caused harm. **Causation** means that the resulting harm is the direct outcome of this union of *actus reus* and *mens rea*. Consider the case of an employee who harbors ill will toward a supervisor. Assume that the employee is in danger of losing his or her job and a performance review is imminent. The employee strikes the supervisor in the parking lot with his or her automobile and causes harm. Is the action a crime or an accident? If the employee had no criminal intent at the time he or she hit the supervisor, then it is an accident. The principle of concurrence requires that criminal intent is present at the time of the act, such that having criminal intent prior to or following the act does not satisfy the requirement. The requirement of concurrence raises questions about **incomplete crimes,** in which the *actus reus* and *mens rea* do not coincide but would have if the person had completed all they planned or if circumstances had been different.

concurrence The legal requirement for a crime that there is a union of *actus reus* and *mens rea.*

causation The legal requirement for a crime that the harm is the result of the union of *actus reus* and *mens rea.*

incomplete crimes Crimes that go beyond thought, but the *actus reus* and *mens rea* do not coincide because the plans were not carried out for any reason.

inchoate offenses Incomplete crimes such as solicitation, conspiracy, and attempt.

One cannot be convicted of a crime for thinking about murder, rape, robbery, larceny, burglary, or any other crime. The law punishes people only for what they do, not what they think. Crimes that go beyond mere thought but do not result in completed crimes are called incomplete crimes or inchoate offenses. The three common **inchoate offenses** are (1) solicitation, (2) conspiracy, and (3) attempt. Attempt, conspiracy, and solicitation stand on a continuum, with attempt closest to and solicitation farthest from actual commission of the crime.

This is a drug bust in a private home. But has a crime by law been committed? What are the elements of a crime that will determine if a crime has occurred? How must those elements interrelate to meet the definition of a crime? How is the seriousness of the crime determined? What will determine the suspect's criminal liability?

SOLICITATION **Solicitation** is the urging, requesting, or commanding of another to commit a crime. The other person does not have to have *mens rea* or any intent whatsoever of complying with the solicitation to commit the crime. Thus, a person who solicits an undercover police officer to commit murder, to engage in illegal sexual behavior, or to commit any crime may be charged with solicitation.[33] Solicitation is a criminal charge against the person making the offer, command, or encouragement, not against the person to whom the offer is made. The crime of solicitation requires specific criminal intent. A person who makes a remark such as, "Wouldn't it be neat to steal that car and take it for a ride," to a general group of people has not satisfied the specific intent required for solicitation.

CONSPIRACY Conspiracy requires no *actus reus* other than communication. A plot to commit a bank robbery is not conspiracy if it is not shared or if no steps are taken in preparation for the planned robbery. **Conspiracy** by definition requires two or more people to plan a crime. Actions that require two people, such as fornication, bigamy, bribery, and gambling, are not considered examples of conspiracy. Thus, if a correctional officer accepts money to help an inmate escape, the two could not be charged with conspiracy. The appropriate criminal charge would be bribery, which requires at least two persons—one to make the offer and the other to accept the offer.

Conspiracy requires that two or more people take steps in preparation for the commission of a crime. Any step or steps taken may constitute conspiracy. In the case of a bank robbery that is anticipated to take months to plan and hundreds of steps to execute, the first meeting of the parties involved to discuss how to proceed constitutes a conspiracy. Furthermore, the parties to a conspiracy do not have to meet face to face. They may satisfy the requirements of conspiracy by any form of collaboration, including verbal, written, or electronic. As another example, if two or more persons plan to commit forgery and take steps to obtain a certain type of paper required to commit forgery, this is sufficient *actus reus* to constitute conspiracy. The supplier of the items needed for the commission of a crime is not guilty of conspiracy unless the supplier is aware of the illegal use planned for the materials.[34]

ATTEMPT What happens when things do not go as the criminal planned and he or she is not able to complete the intended criminal activity? Has a crime been committed? Yes, he or she has committed the crime of **attempt.** For every crime that can be committed there is a corresponding crime of attempt, that is, attempted murder, attempted kidnapping, attempted rape, attempted burglary, and so forth. Attempt is the closest act to the completion of the crime and therefore carries a greater punishment than conspiracy or solicitation but a lesser punishment than if the crime had been completed.

Consider the case of ***State v. Wagner*** in which Wagner approached a woman in a laundromat from behind.[35] He had a gun and forced her into the laundromat's bathroom and demanded that she remove her clothes. The victim was able to escape before Wagner could commit any further crime. Wagner was convicted of attempted kidnapping and sentenced to 72 years in prison despite the fact that he was unable to complete the full intent of his criminal activity or restrain his victim.

RENUNCIATION OF CRIMINAL INTENT It is possible that a person may have criminal intent and may take steps toward completing a crime but then change his or her mind before the crime is fully executed. Does renunciation of criminal intent absolve one of punishment? No, it does not.[36] If a person approaches a bank with a mask, a gun, and a demand note for the teller and then changes his or her mind and goes home, the person nevertheless has satisfied the criminal intent requirement to be charged with attempted bank robbery. If a person intends to commit burglary but is frightened away by a noise after committing trespass, the person has satisfied the criminal intent requirement to be charged with attempted burglary. And, a person who demands sex under threat of force but is "talked out of it" by the victim has satisfied the

solicitation The incomplete crime of urging, requesting, or commanding another person to commit a crime.

conspiracy Criminal act requiring no *actus rea* other than communication.

attempt An incomplete criminal act, the closest act to the completion of the crime.

criminal intent requirement to be charged with attempted rape.[37] The law does not take the view that a stroke of luck or a retreat from criminal activity based on fear of getting caught makes one immune from criminal prosecution.

JUST THE FACTS 4.3

What are the elements of a crime? How are offenses differentiated between minor and serious crimes? Is a person who commits the *actus reus* of a crime liable for the offense under all circumstances? If not, what determines criminal liability? What are some examples of liability for incomplete crimes?

Defenses against Charges of Criminal Conduct

THE MAIN IDEA

Several defenses, defined by law, can be used in court to excuse an accused offender or to lessen his or her criminal liability.

The fact that a person has committed the act required by law to constitute a crime does not mean that the person will be held criminally liable for that crime in a court of law. There are numerous defenses that a person can offer at trial as defense. Two types of **defenses** to criminal charges are a perfect defense, in which the person is excused from all criminal liability and punishment, and an imperfect defense, in which the person's liability or punishment is reduced. The most common defenses are:

- Alibi
- Consent or condoning by the victim
- Entrapment, frame-up, and outrageous government conduct
- Immunity, privilege, or acting under the authority of another
- Involuntary actions
- Mistake or ignorance of fact or law
- Necessity
- Self-defense
- Youth
- Insanity

Alibi

The use of an **alibi** as a defense requires that the defendant present witnesses who will give testimony in court or other evidence establishing the fact that he or she could not have committed the offense. The most common alibi strategy is for defendants to claim that they could not have been at the scene of the crime at the time the crime was committed and to offer witnesses who will testify to that fact. The jury is the ultimate judge of an alibi. The jury may choose to believe or to not believe the testimony of alibi witnesses or the evidence presented.

defenses Justifications or excuses defined by law by which a defendant may be released from prosecution or punishment for a crime.

alibi A witness or evidence in court establishing that the defendant could not have committed the crime.

Consent or Condoning by the Victim

Boxing, wrestling, hockey, and other sports can often result in injury or even death. If the injury occurs during the normal course of the rules of engagement, the player causing the injury can offer **consent** as a defense. However, if the injury is outside the accepted standards of conduct for the sport, the defense of consent is not valid. For sports like boxing, in which the object of the sport is to inflict injury on the other contestant, consent can be a defense even if the opponent dies. For other sports, like basketball, in which fighting among the players is prohibited by the rules of the game, the defense of consent cannot be used in cases of deliberate physical assault on another player.

The defense that the victim said it was okay—condoned the act—is not a valid defense for criminal actions.[38] For example, consent is not a valid defense in mercy killing or assisted suicide. Dr. Jack Kevorkian constructed a "suicide machine" to help terminal patients end their life. Despite the "victims'" consent—even plea—for his assistance to commit suicide, the Michigan Court did not recognize the defense of consent. Likewise, consent is not a defense in murder-suicide pacts, and in those cases, any surviving member can be charged with murder.

Entrapment, Frame-up, and Outrageous Government Conduct

Entrapment and outrageous government conduct are related to the principle that the defendant's criminal actions must be voluntary. If the defendant did not have the *mens rea* or the means necessary to commit a crime, he or she would not have acted. However, if agents of the government provided both the *mens rea* and the means to commit the crime, the courts have ruled that the defendant may be defended on the grounds of **entrapment** or outrageous government conduct. Entrapment is an *affirmative defense,* which means that the defendant must admit that he or she committed the crime as alleged. The person is not innocent but claims that if it had not been for the actions of the government agents, he or she would not have committed the crime.

Entrapment is different from *encouragement,* in which law enforcement officers may pretend they are victims or co-conspirators in crime, for example, or may promise the suspect benefits from committing the crime, or may offer to supply materials or help the suspect obtain contraband. Encouragement becomes entrapment when the government agents actually provide the motivation and the means to commit the crime.[39] The concern of the court is that otherwise innocent persons should not be induced to commit crime by the government. This concern also affects undercover sting operations.[40] For example, in sting operations involving prostitution or drugs, the police must be aware of the street price of sex and drugs, because if the undercover agent offers illegal goods or services at too low a price, the defendant may claim entrapment.

consent A defense in criminal law in which the defendant claims the action that caused the injury or death occurred during normal, acceptable standards of conduct.

entrapment A legal defense that agents of the government provided both the *mens rea* and the means necessary to commit the crime.

immunity A legal defense that the accused is exempt from prosecution because of diplomatic immunity, legislative immunity, witness immunity, or professional privilege.

Immunity or Privilege

In the defense of **immunity,** the accused has special protection against being prosecuted. Four forms of this defense are diplomatic immunity, legislative immunity, witness immunity, and privilege. The U.S. government extends diplomatic immunity to certain government officials of foreign countries while they are in the United States. *Diplomatic immunity* grants the foreign diplomat complete immunity from any criminal prosecution, including murder and traffic violations. There are disadvantages to diplomatic immunity, especially in an age of international terrorism. However, there has been no serious movement to remove this protection. In return for extending immunity to foreign diplomats, U.S. diplomats in foreign countries receive the same protection. If a foreign diplomat commits a serious felony crime in the United States, the only recourse is to ask for the diplomat's recall to his or her country or to request that the country voluntarily waive the diplomat's immunity.

A lesser form of immunity extended to lawmakers in the United States is *legislative immunity*. Based on abuse by government agents, dating back to the English rule of the

American colonies, most representatives and senators receive limited immunity from arrest while the legislature is in session. Unlike diplomatic immunity, legislative immunity only postpones the time that the legislator can be arrested until after the legislative session is adjourned. Also, legislative immunity does not protect the legislator from arrest for felonies and treason.

See http://www.ediplomat.com/main/immunity.htm for a discussion of diplomatic immunity. ■

An interesting affirmative defense, normally afforded only to the guilty, is *witness immunity*. The defendant admits to the criminal acts as charged but in exchange for his or her cooperation with a government investigation is granted immunity from further prosecution based on the offered testimony. Essentially, in hopes of catching more culpable criminals, the government promises the defendant that any information he or she gives that could incriminate other criminals will not be used against the defendant in a court of law.

Immunity is not a defense in cases in which defendants claim they were acting only under the orders or advice of a superior authority—unless that authority is authorized by law to interpret the law. Relying on illegal advice or acting on the advice of someone who does not have the legal authority to give such advice does not negate criminal liability. For example, in the 1980s John Ehrlichman, one of the Watergate break-in defendants, claimed that he was acting under the authority of Richard Nixon, then president of the United States. The Court refused to grant immunity from prosecution, however, because even the president does not have the power to authorize burglary. In another famous case, Lieutenant William Calley, tried for committing atrocities against civilians during the Vietnam War, offered as a defense that he was only following the orders of his superiors.[41] Even if such orders had been given—even in wartime—they would have constituted illegal advice, and Calley's criminal liability would not have been reduced.

The defense of *privilege* is the claim that the defendant committed a violation of the law but was immune from punishment because of his or her official office or duty. For example, the courts have recognized as a privilege the right of operators of emergency vehicles to violate traffic regulations when responding to a call. As another example, a correctional officer who shoots an escaping prisoner may not be liable for murder. Even if the escaping prisoner is unarmed and no immediate threat to the correctional officer, the officer's actions may be justified if he or she is acting within the scope of duty.

Involuntary Actions

The American criminal justice system is based on the assumption that the actions of the defendant were voluntary. If defendants can establish that their actions were not of their own free will but were the result of a third person or involuntary condition, this can be a defense against criminal liability. A simple example of this defense is when a bank teller gives the bank's money to an armed robber. It could be argued that the bank teller does not have the authority to give away the bank's money, but the teller has not committed a crime because the actions are not voluntary. The teller is operating under **duress.**

In this defense, the cause of the acts, as well as the acts that constitute the crime, must be involuntary. A person who voluntarily consumes alcohol, achieves a drunken stupor, and commits a crime while in that state cannot claim a defense of involuntary action, even with no memory of ever having acted. Getting drunk is voluntary behavior, and a similar test is held for crimes committed during drug conditions.[42] If a person is unknowingly drugged by someone and then engages in criminal behavior, the defense of involuntary actions is valid. However, a person who chooses to take a hallucinogenic drug and commits a crime while under its influence cannot use the defense of involuntary actions during a drug condition.

duress A legal defense in which the accused acted involuntarily under threat of immediate and serious harm by another person.

Case law has established that under certain conditions defendants must accept responsibility for knowing when they are consuming drugs or alcohol. In one case, the defendant claimed involuntary action as his defense to the charge of driving while intoxicated. He claimed that he attended a party and drank "punch" that he was told falsely did not contain alcohol. The defendant consumed enough punch to be legally drunk and was arrested for DUI as he drove home from the party. The court ruled that the defendant should have been able to recognize the signs of intoxication as he continued to consume the beverage. Thus, despite the misinformation he received, he should have been able to determine his condition and remained liable for his offense.

Duress cannot be used as a defense against the charge of murder, however. If a person murders another but claims that he or she did so only because of coercion or duress through threats made against family members or personal friends, this is not a defense. The Court has ruled that even in such a dire situation, with awful potential consequences, a person does not have the right to take the life of another.

Mistake or Ignorance of Fact or Law

The presumption of the law can be contrary to common sense. In Charles Dickens's novel *Oliver Twist,* Bumble and his wife are arrested for the manner in which they operated the orphanage in their charge. Bumble appeals to the authorities that it was his wife's scheme and that he is an innocent party. He is told that the law presumes the husband to be the head of the wife and therefore his defense falls on deaf ears. Bumble replies if the law presumes the man to be in command of his wife, "then the law is an ass." In this case, his **mistake or ignorance of fact or law** did not constitute a legal defense.

The American criminal justice system places an affirmative burden on citizens to be aware of the laws of the land and proceeds as if this is the case. As mentioned previously, laws are published as a matter of public record, partly so offenders cannot claim ignorance of the law as an excuse for their behavior. The assumption that people know the law imposes a twofold burden. First, the government must make the law known, and, second, citizens must be held accountable, however complex the law and whatever the difficulty in knowing it. Most citizens know very little of the many volumes of law that govern their lives, but the law usually does not recognize *ignorance of the law* as a valid defense. Ignorance of the law may be considered a defense if the law in question is so unusual or obscure that the court finds that a reasonable person would not have knowledge of it. However, simple ignorance of the law is not a defense against prosecution or punishment for crimes.

Mistake or ignorance of fact, on the other hand, is a valid defense. If at the end of class you pick up a backpack that you think is yours and walk out of the class, have you stolen the backpack if it in fact belongs to another student? What if the backpack contains a large amount of money or valuable property? Does that change the situation? *Mistake or ignorance of fact* is a defense that claims to negate the requirement of *mens rea,* or criminal intent. Thus, there is a great difference between the standard used to distinguish ignorance of the law and mistake of fact.

If a person has a reasonable belief that the action they are doing is legal, mistake of fact may be a valid defense. If your backpack resembled the backpack that you mistakenly picked up and if you do not take steps to permanently deprive the owner of his or her property, whatever its value, then you have not committed theft, and mistake of fact is a reasonable defense. However, a restaurant patron who walks away with another customer's leather coat instead of his or her cloth coat would have difficulty convincing the court that he or she had made a mistake of fact.

mistake or ignorance of fact or law An affirmative legal defense claiming that the defendant made a mistake or acted out of ignorance and therefore did not meet the requirement for *mens rea.*

necessity An affirmative legal defense claiming the defendant committed the act as a result of forces of nature and therefore did not meet the requirement for *mens rea.*

Necessity

The defense of necessity is sometimes known as the defense of the "lesser of two evils." **Necessity** is an affirmative defense in which the defendant must admit that he or she committed the act but claim that it was done because of necessity or need and not because of *mens rea.* This defense is commonly used against charges of property crime, such as trespass, theft, or burglary.[43] In the classic case in which this defense is successful, defendants are faced with life-threatening situations and choose to commit illegal acts to save their lives. For example, a cross-country skier caught in an unexpected blizzard may break into a mountain home, start a fire, and consume food found there. Under normal circumstances, these actions constitute the crime of burglary, but because of the threat of death from exposure to the elements, the court may recognize the defense of necessity as a perfect defense.

Can necessity be used as a defense against murder? This is a grim question that has come before the court. If a group of people is stranded without food, can they kill and eat one of their numbers to preserve their lives? The British Court has refused to recognize this defense, but the American Court has allowed it as a perfect or an imperfect defense.[44] To be an acceptable defense, the necessity must be immediate and specific and the person must be chosen by lot. All members of the party must have an equal opportunity of being killed and eaten.

Self-Defense

The claim of **self-defense** is a complex defense usually associated with murder and physical assault. Again, this is an affirmative defense: The defendant admits to the murder or assault but claims he or she lacked criminal intent. The lack of criminal intent is based on the claim that the defendant was protecting him- or herself from deadly attack or serious bodily injury.[45] The courts have also recognized self-defense when applied to (1) protecting another from deadly attack or serious bodily injury and (2) defending one's home from invasion. The self-defense used by the defendant must be appropriate and proportional to the force used by the attacker. Before deadly force is justified as self-defense, the attacker must create a situation in which the defendant fears death or great bodily harm. Timing is a controversial issue in capital cases involving the claim of self-defense. Is a routinely abused spouse or child justified in killing an attacker when not under immediate threat of deadly attack or serious bodily injury?[46] The courts have decided differently on different occasions, leading to stronger legislation designed to prevent or combat domestic violence. Generally, however, the standard courts use to judge whether the force the defendant used in self-defense was justifiable is whether a reasonable person would feel they were in immediate danger of death or great bodily injury.[47]

The use of self-defense in protecting one's home against invasion also varies significantly in different states. Some states require that, when reasonable, the occupant of the house must first attempt to flee from the home to escape attack. Other states do not have such a requirement but follow the "castle doctrine," which means that occupants have the unqualified right to protect their home against trespass.[48] Most states do not permit the claim of self-defense in resisting arrest—whether lawful or unlawful—by a police officer.[49]

Youth

A 14-year-old boy steals a car, refuses to stop when pursued by the police, and ends up destroying the vehicle in a high-speed crash. Is he just a kid and therefore held to a different standard of culpability than an adult? Since 1899, the answer for the American criminal justice system has been "yes." Prior to 1899, age was a defense based on the British principle that children under 7 years of age, and possibly even under 14 years of age, could not form *mens rea*. Children over 14 were considered capable of forming *mens rea*, but youth could be offered as an affirmative defense if the defendant could demonstrate lack of *mens rea*. Operating under the British standard, defendants as young as 11 and 12 were hung for the crime of murder in the American colonies.

self-defense An affirmative legal defense in which a defendant claims he or she committed the crime in defense of self and lacked criminal intent.

Figure 4.3

Criminal Defenses

Alibi Defense
Burden of proof is on the defense, which must present evidence that the defendant was not at or near the scene of the crime at the time the crime was committed.

Affirmative Defense
Burden of proof is on the defense, which must present additional evidence that the defendant, though he or she committed the crime, should not be found guilty because of extenuating circumstances.

Justifications	Excuses	Exemptions
• Involuntary actions • Duress • Self-defense • Necessity • Entrapment	• Youth • Insanity or diminished capacity • Mistake or ignorance of law or fact	• Consent • Immunity or privilege

In 1899, Cook County (Chicago) adopted the use of the juvenile court. This separate court system operated under significantly different rules and standards of proof to adjudicate the crimes of youthful offenders under the age of 18 separately from adult offenders. The use of the juvenile court quickly caught on and is now practiced in all 50 states.[50]

The states and the federal government have set the age of *mens rea* at 18. Each state has provisions allowing younger offenders to be held accountable for their actions in adult court under certain circumstances. Controversy over the accountability of juvenile offenders occurs most often in cases of murder. Juveniles as young as 14 have been stripped of the protection offered by the juvenile court and had their trial transferred to adult court.

insanity A legal claim by a defendant that he or she did not understand the difference between right and wrong or was suffering from a disease or mental defect that made the defendant unable to appreciate the criminality of his or her action.

Insanity

The **insanity** defense has an interesting connection to Sir Robert Peel, father of modern policing. In 1843, Daniel M'Naghten suffered the paranoid delusion that Sir Robert Peel, then prime minister of England, intended to kill him. Based on this belief, M'Naghten undertook to kill Peel first in what he perceived as a form of self-defense. M'Naghten obtained a pistol and lay in wait for Peel to pass by. Fortunately for Peel but unfortunately for his secretary, Edward Drummond, M'Naghten shot, missed Peel, and struck and killed Drummond.[51]

This security video reveals a robbery in progress. What kind of crime is this in the basic system by which crimes are classified in the United States? What legal defenses are available to the offender for possible use at trial to reduce criminal liability or lessen punishment? Based on the evidence of the security video, which defenses probably wouldn't work?

M'Naghten was tried for murder but was acquitted based on his successful insanity defense.[52] M'Naghten's acquittal was the fifth acquittal based on the insanity plea of a commoner who had attacked a person of nobility. The Queen expressed alarm over the frequent successful use of the insanity defense and called for a commission to develop legal guidelines for the use of the insanity defense. The House of Lords, England's highest court, formulated a new—and much more stringent—standard for the insanity defense. Under the new standard, a defendant was not to be considered insane unless he or she met two conditions: (1) He or she must suffer from a disease or defect of the mind, and (2) the disease or defect must cause the defendant either to not know the nature and quality of the criminal act or to not know that the act was wrong. This standard for insanity was commonly called the M'Naghten standard, rule, or test, and became the primary standard for the insanity defense in Great Britain and the United States for over a century.

The M'Naghten rule requires that the defendant does not understand that his or her actions are illegal, wrong, or punishable. A defendant who flees after committing a crime, who attempts to conceal his or her crime, or denies his or her guilt may not meet the standard for the M'Naghten rule for judging insanity based on these actions, which indicate that he or she knew the crime was wrong. The M'Naghten rule requires that the defendant be like a very young child who is unable to form a concept of right and wrong and therefore does not fear punishment because he or she does not appreciate the criminality of the action. Because of this requirement, the M'Naghten standard is also known as the Right-Wrong test of insanity. Interestingly, if M'Naghten had been tried using this standard, he would not have been successful in avoiding conviction.

Other Criminal Defenses

Defendants have claimed that it was their victims' fault that they committed a crime, that they were motivated by patriotism, or that there was no personal gain for them. These defenses have not received serious recognition by the court as legitimate defenses against criminal prosecution. Rapists have argued that provocative clothes worn by their victims contributed to their *mens rea*. Lieutenant Colonel Oliver North argued that any crime he committed in the Iran-Contra scandal was motivated by his desire to protect democracy and America. Defendants who have stolen from large business only to give the profits of their crime to the poor have used the "Robin Hood" defense to claim that they did not personally gain from the fruits of their crime. These defenses have not been readily accepted by the court.

JUST THE FACTS 4.4

What are 10 common defenses by which defendants accused of crimes can seek to escape prosecution or punishment? What conditions are necessary for each defense to succeed in court? How is homicide divided into serious and less serious offenses? How has the law against rape changed over time? What are some examples of defenses that are likely to fail?

Crimes by Law

THE MAIN IDEA

The Model Penal Code classifies crimes into categories by victims as well as defines specific offenses of crimes.

Crimes are defined by laws, and the laws governing society are numerous, complex, and diverse. The federal, state, and local governments have specific, different, and overlapping criminal codes. It would be impossible to discuss here the criminal laws of each of the 50 states, the federal government, and the thousands of county and municipal governments, and it would be a useless exercise to pick a single state and use it as an example. What could be true of larceny in Louisiana may not be true of larceny in California. To simplify the teaching of the law and propose guidelines for effective legislation, in 1962 the American Law Institute published a code of criminal laws. These guidelines, called the **Model Penal Code,** have been adopted by law schools as the bases for their curriculum and are used by most textbooks on criminal law.

The Model Penal Code classifies crime according to the victim of the crime. Crimes are classified in the following ways:

- Crimes against the state
- Crimes against persons
- Crimes against habitation
- Crimes against property
- Crimes against public order
- Crimes against public morals

A discussion of the numerous laws governing all of these criminal behaviors is beyond the scope of this chapter, which presents a brief summary of only the more serious offenses, using the definitions and principles of the Model Penal Code. The criminal laws proposed by the Model Penal Code are based on logic and reflect the history of criminal law. Each crime has a definition that includes a description of the actions that constitute criminal behavior and the criminal intent that must accompany the actions. The Model Penal Code is based on the principle that laws should reflect the continuum of harm that is possible. Generally, the more harm to a person or society done or intended, the more serious the crime.

Model Penal Code Guidelines for U.S. criminal codes published in 1962 by the American Law Institute that define and classify crimes into categories according to victim, including crimes against the state, persons, habitations, property, public order, and public morals.

Crimes against Persons

In the Model Penal Code, crimes against persons include murder, rape, sexual assault, kidnapping, robbery, and assault and battery. These specific offenses are discussed to illustrate important points about criminal law: the elements required for an offense, the grading of the offense, and how the offense and the punishment reflect social values.

HOMICIDE The defining of **homicide**—the killing of one human being by another—takes into account the harm done to the victim and the different degrees of criminal intent. Based on the degree of harm intended, homicides are divided into murder and manslaughter. **Murder** is divided into *first-degree murder*—the premeditated and deliberate killing of another—and second-degree murder. *Second-degree murder* includes the killing of another without premeditation, with the intent to inflict serious bodily injury but not death, as the result of extreme recklessness, and during the commission of a felony in which there was no intent to kill or injure another. **Manslaughter** is the killing of another without malice, that is, without the specific intent to kill. The Model Penal Code divides manslaughter into three categories: voluntary, involuntary, and vehicular.

ELEMENTS REQUIRED FOR MURDER Before a defendant can be charged with murder or manslaughter, the state must establish four facts: (1) that a crime occurred (*corpus delicti*), (2) that a person was killed, (3) that the defendant's actions were the cause of the death, and (4) that the defendant had criminal intent.

The state first must present ***corpus delicti***—reasonable evidence that a crime has actually occurred in which someone was murdered. Circumstantial evidence, such as the fact that the person is missing, is not normally considered reasonable proof. The state can establish death through a coroner's inquest or medical examiner's report, but in some cases it is not possible to produce the body. It may have been destroyed or hidden by the murderer and cannot be recovered. In these cases, courts have allowed the charge of murder where other non-circumstantial evidence can establish that a person was killed.

Second, the state must establish that the person was killed and did not die of natural causes. While this requirement seems commonsensical, it is fraught with legal complexities. For example, murder cases have hinged on the debate as to whether an aborted fetus is a "person" who has been murdered, as opposed to a miscarried fetus that has died of natural causes.[53] Given the legality of abortion alongside laws against feticide—the willful killing of a fetus—murder has to be defined in precise terms to include acts involving criminal intent and to exclude acts that are within women's legally protected rights. In a homicide case, even "death" has to be defined in precise terms.[54] Death traditionally has been defined as the cessation of the heart and the respiratory system. Scientific advances have made this definition obsolete, however, and the American Medical Association now defines death as the cessation of brain function. The legal system has adopted "brain death" as the new definition of death, but there are still debates in court as to which definition to apply.

Third, the state must establish that the defendant's actions were the cause of the person's death.[55] Causation can be difficult to interpret and to prove. If an elderly woman suffers a heart attack and dies during a burglary, is the burglar liable for her death? If a person who can't swim drowns while escaping someone's murderous verbal threats, is the threatener liable? If an attack victim survives the attack but dies during surgery, is the attacker a murderer? According to case law, the answer to these questions is "yes." A critical factor in causation is the time lapse between the defendant's attack on the victim and the death of the victim. Because everyone will die sometime, is it murder if the defendant attacks a person and the person dies of pneumonia 18 months after the attack? No. Many states have a rule that the time between the attack and the death of the victim cannot be longer than a year and a day. However, California has extended the time limit to 3 years, and Michigan has abolished any preestablished time.

Finally, the most difficult element of the crime to establish is the criminal intent of the accused. Did the defendant kill the victim accidentally, with malice aforethought, knowingly, purposely, intentionally? Was the defendant provoked by the victim? Was the victim killed recklessly, with gross criminal negligence or while the defendant was committing another crime? Criminal intent cannot be established with direct evidence other than the testimony of the defendant. Thus, the state must depend on circumstantial evidence to establish the intent. Intent is very important, as the killing

homicide Murder and manslaughter.

murder All intentional killings and deaths that occur in the course of aggravated felonies.

manslaughter The killing of another without malice, without the specific intent to kill.

corpus delicti Reasonable evidence that a crime has actually occurred.

of a human being with reckless criminal intent may result in a light sentence of imprisonment, whereas the intentional killing of a human being with malice aforethought can be punished by death.

For first-degree murder, the state must prove malice aforethought; the perpetrator killed knowingly, purposely, and intentionally. Second-degree murder requires the state to prove that the killer intended to cause serious bodily injury, which can also include killings that result from resisting lawful arrest or that take place during the commission of a crime (the felony murder rule). For voluntary manslaughter, the state must prove that the defendant intentionally killed under provocation, such as the heat of passion or the defendant's unreasonable belief that he or she was acting in self-defense. If the killing was done recklessly, with gross criminal negligence or while committing a misdemeanor, the crime is involuntary manslaughter. Finally, if the state can show that the killing was the result of negligence but not gross negligence, the appropriate charge is negligent homicide. It is common to use negligent homicide as the charge in fatal car accidents.

Homicide laws also must take into account the nature of the crime and deal with a great number of different possibilities, such as serial murders, murder by arson, mercy killings, prison murders, hate-crime murders, murder for hire, drug overdose, product-tampering murder, and killing by collapse of a structure. Factors such as the pain and suffering of the victim, the use of a weapon, or the amount of time between the provocation and the actual killing all contribute to the determining of the appropriate charge for homicide.

RAPE OR SEXUAL ASSAULT Rape, or the more contemporary term *sexual assault,* is a crime that shows how criminal codes reflect changing social values. Rape is also one of the few behaviors in which criminal liability is determined by the intent rather than the act, because consensual sex, unlike nonconsensual sex, is not a crime. The lack of consent makes **rape** a crime.

Historically, rape was rooted in the concept of carnal knowledge, sexual intercourse by a man with a woman not his wife, forcibly and without her consent.[56] In the Middle Ages, rape was a crime against property. The "victim" was the husband or the father of the woman, as she was considered the property of her husband or, if unmarried, her father. From the 1600s to the early 1970s, the crime of rape focused on the element of consent. Women had to show by physical resistance that they did not consent. The law required that women must use all the power at their command to resist the attack. If at any time they did not resist, the sex was considered consensual. Even consent obtained by fraud did not constitute rape.[57] Sexual intercourse with women incapacitated by intoxication or mental deficiency and with minors was regarded as rape whether the victim was forced or gave consent.

NEW STANDARDS FOR DETERMINING CONSENT Starting in the 1950s, many state courts adopted a new standard for determining consent, called "measured resistance." In Virginia, for example, the law according to the new standard does not require a woman to resist to the utmost of her physical strength if she reasonably believes that resistance would be useless or would result in serious bodily injury.[58] Since the 1950s, states that required proof that the victim resisted the assault have dropped this element of proof.

Starting in the 1970s, numerous other changes have been made to the elements necessary to prove rape. Many states have changed the classification from rape to sexual assault to more clearly identify the crime as an assault as opposed to a sexual act. *Sexual assault* has been defined to include all sexual penetration with the penis or any other object. States also have enacted statutes recognizing that men also can be raped, by women or by men. The martial rape exception has been eliminated in many states. Finally, some states have enacted rape shield laws that prohibit the defense from questioning the victim about past sexual experiences.[59]

rape (sexual assault)
Non-consensual sexual relations.

DETERMINING THE SERIOUSNESS OF THE OFFENSE The Model Penal Code provides for the classification of sexual assault into categories based on the amount of force used by the defendant to effect penetration. The least crime is offensive touching, and first-degree sexual assault is defined as sexual penetration against the victim's will and through the use or threat of force or fear. Threats of imminent death, serious bodily injury, extreme pain, or kidnapping, and the infliction of serious bodily harm aggravate the offense to first-degree rape. The Model Penal Code also recognizes that constructive force (such as threats to kill, seriously injure, or kidnap either the victim or another) substitutes for the actual use of force. In cases in which the perpetrator obtains consent fraudulently (as with a consenting minor or a person with mental retardation), the act of penetration itself suffices as the element of *actus reus*.

This woman, a victim of sexual assault, is giving a statement about the crime and her assailant. How is sexual assault defined by law? What is statutory rape, and what role does consent play? This victim was beaten, and she did not resist her attacker out of fear of graver harm. Does her lack of resistance lessen his criminal liability or the seriousness of his offense? How does the Model Penal Code help to answer these questions?

Although different states have adopted various provisions of the Model Penal Code's definition of sexual assault, the national crime statistics kept by the FBI still reflect the definition of rape as defined by carnal knowledge. Also, some state statutes still declare that obtaining consent under fraud is not illegal. As stated in the opinion of a New York court, "It is still not illegal to feed a girl a line, to continue the attempt, not to take no for a final answer, at least not the first time.... It is not criminal conduct for a male to make promises that will not be kept, to indulge in exaggeration and hyperbole, or to assure any trusting female that, as in the ancient fairy tale, the ugly frog is really the handsome prince."

ROBBERY In common speech, robbery is frequently confused with burglary. **Robbery** is the taking and carrying away of property from a person by force or threat of immediate use of force. A couple might declare that while they were out for the evening someone broke into their house and robbed them. This is burglary. Houses are burgled, but only people can be robbed. The mistake is understandable because robbery actually involves the elements of two crimes: theft from crimes against property, and assault from crimes against persons.

The *actus reus* of robbery requires that property be taken from a person by force or threat of force, and that the threat of force has to be immediate. It is not robbery if the perpetrator forces a victim to hand over money by threatening to come back the next day and destroy property or cause physical harm. Rather, because the threat of force is not immediate, this is the crime of extortion. *Extortion* differs from robbery in that it is based on the threat of future harm, whereas robbery involves the threat of immediate harm. In extortion, the threat may include harm to reputation and property as well as physical harm to the person. In robbery, threats of harm apply to the person. The use of a weapon and serious bodily injury can lead to classification as the more serious crime of aggravated robbery. The *mens rea* of robbery requires that the actor intends to permanently derive the owner of his or her property. Someone who takes property from another, even if by the use of force, but does not intend to permanently deprive the owner of the proper has committed the crime of assault.

robbery The taking and carrying away of property from a person by force or threat of immediate use of force.

assault The crime of willfully inflicting injury on another.

ASSAULT AND BATTERY **Assault** is defined as inflicting injury on another, while *battery* is the unlawful striking of another. The actual state codes governing assault and battery vary significantly. Some states use the terms interchangeably or have defined the crime as "assault and battery" instead of one crime called "assault" and another crime called "battery." The elements of the crime that have to be proven do not require great physical harm or injury. In *United States v. Masel*, for example, spitting was considered sufficient injury to satisfy the element of inflicting harm for the crime of assault. *Mayhem* is an offense similar to battery, but the elements of mayhem require unlawfully and violently depriving the victim of full use of any part of body, such as a hand, foot, or eye.

If a firearm or other dangerous weapon is used in the crime, it becomes the more serious offense of aggravated assault/battery. Simple assault is considered a less serious crime, but aggravated assault/battery is considered a more serious crime and is reported by the Federal Bureau of Investigation as a Part I crime.

Because contact with other people—including contact that can result in physical injury—is common, the criminal code has to carefully distinguish the criminal intent of the perpetrator. Fighting is a crime, but striking a child for the purposes of reasonable discipline is legal. Causing physical injury in contact sports is legal. However, giving a dog an order to attack a person is assault. A police officer striking a person resisting lawful arrest or a correction officer injuring a person attempting to escape from lawful detainment is legal. Striking a person who first struck you may be legal if the initial attack was unprovoked.

ASSAULT AGAINST AN AIRLINE CREW MEMBER Federal law has made the inflicting of harm or striking of an airline crew member a serious federal offense. Unlike local or state laws, in which simple assault usually is punishable by small fines or only a few days of imprisonment, assault on an airline crew member can result in a substantial fine or years in prison. The reason for this difference in punishment is that federal lawmakers have determined that the harm that could result from assaulting an airline crew member is much more serious than the harm that could result from assaulting someone else.

ASSAULT AGAINST A FAMILY MEMBER OR SPOUSE States have moved to classify assault and battery among family members and persons living together as a separate crime under the category of *domestic violence.* Some states have special criminal intent elements that allow police officers to treat domestic violence differently from simple assault. For example, a number of states have allowed police officers to arrest persons accused of assault and battery against a domestic partner or family member based on probable cause, even over the objection of the injured party. Allegations of domestic violence may be heard in a special court, sometimes called Family Court, in which the presiding judges are trained to deal with family violence and disturbances.

Crimes against Habitation

Burglary and arson are crimes committed against places where people live. Both offenses require specific criminal intent. **Burglary** requires the person to commit the crime of trespass with the specific criminal intent to commit a crime thereafter. **Arson** requires the specific criminal intent to commit a malicious burning. Both offenses have a long history dating back to English common law, which reflects the values placed on the importance of securing a safe place for persons to live.

BURGLARY Burglary has its roots in the English common law of breaking and entering. Originally, burglary was an offense that applied only to invasion of the home at night. *Breaking and entering,* as it was known then, meant the actor committed an illegal trespass during the night against a place where people lived, with the intent to commit another crime once the trespass was accomplished. The purpose of English common law was to protect the people in their home while the occupants were present and in a relatively defenseless state (i.e., sleeping). Thus, a person who committed the same act of breaking and entering during the day committed theft or *trespass,* a minor crime, not burglary.

burglary A combination of tresspass and the intent to perform a crime.

arson The malicious burning of a structure.

In a time when modern police patrol of neighborhoods was unknown, society primarily relied on civil behavior and the threat of severe sanctions for violations that threatened the safety of the community. Burglary was a capital offense. Furthermore, the burglar, if caught, was at the mercy of the homeowner, because the law allowed the homeowner to use any force necessary to defeat the burglar. Today most jurisdictions do not allow the victim to use deadly force against a burglar unless there is threat of death or serious bodily harm.

MODERN BURGLARY STATUTES The modern offense of burglary combines two less serious crimes—trespass and intent to commit a crime—into a serious felony crime. The Model Penal Code and most state codes define several degrees of burglary, do not limit burglary to a nighttime offense, and expand burglary to include property other than homes, such as cars, campers, airplanes, tents, and vacation cabins. Burglary does not require breaking and entering or the intent to steal.[60] A person who remains in a habitation when not authorized to do so satisfies the criminal intent in burglary. For example, someone who enters a public building during authorized hours and hides until after-hours is considered to have committed the specific intent of trespass required in burglary. The modern offense of burglary does not require the burglar to actually "break" anything, and entering a marked, restricted space is burglary even if there is no door, lock, or obstacle to open or cross.

It is common to think of burglary as a crime involving the intent to steal something. Modern burglary statutes require only that once the person commits the trespass, he or she intends to commit another crime, whether a felony such as theft or a misdemeanor such as vandalism. A person who commits only trespass with no specific intent to commit another crime has not satisfied the specific criminal intent required for the crime of burglary. Modern burglary statutes also cover a multitude of structures where people live and sleep, in addition to abandoned homes and partly constructed houses. Again, the offense requires the offender to commit a trespass. Thus, a person who pulls up the stakes of a camper's tent and drags off the tent and all its contents has committed theft. But a person who enters the tent and takes property from it has committed burglary.

OFFENSES RELATED TO BURGLARY Modern burglary codes include a number of related offenses. If the burglar has a weapon, the offense is aggravated burglary, even if the burglar does not display or use the weapon. Attempted burglary is any action taken by the actor with the specific criminal intent to commit a trespass and a crime thereafter. A person who approaches a house with the intent to enter it and take property has committed attempted burglary even if he or she retreats before entering the house. The law also extends to prohibitions against the possession of burglary tools. A person who has the criminal intent to commit burglary and possesses any tool that would facilitate the offense, even a common tool such as a pry bar or screwdriver, may be charged with the offense of possession of burglary tools.

ARSON English common law did not consider it a crime for a person to burn or destroys his or her own property. The intentional or accidental burning of one's home or even the property of another was not arson. Arson was a crime only if the burning was malicious. The Modern Penal Code reflects changes in community concerns regarding safety and defines as arson the willful and malicious burning or attempted burning of any structure, including one's own. Because of the many motivations a person may have for burning a structure and the serious harm that can come to innocent parties, nearly all malicious burnings constitute arson.[61]

Modern arson codes also include destroying a structure by the use of explosives. Arson includes the burning of homes, factories, personal property, and vehicles. If the structure is occupied, even if the arsonist is unaware of this fact, the crime is more serious. A person who destroys property by malicious burning for the purposes of defrauding an insurance company commits arson even if there is no danger or harm to others.

criminal justice in the world

Japan's Criminal Code

It is instructive to compare the modern penal codes of other countries with those of the United States. The Penal Code of Japan, for instance, is interesting to examine because of its unique history. The criminal laws of Japan were based on thousands of years of history and social values that were significantly different from Western values. However, at the end of World War II, Japan adopted a constitution and a penal code—largely under mandate by the American military occupying Japan—based on the American criminal justice system. The Japanese Constitution reflects American legal and moral principles. For example, the preamble to the Constitution of Japan declares, "We, the Japanese people, acting through our duly elected representatives in the National Diet, determined that we shall secure for ourselves and our posterity the fruits of peaceful cooperation with all nations and the blessings of liberty throughout this land, and resolved that never again shall we be visited with the horrors of war through the action of government, do proclaim that sovereign power resides with the people and do firmly establish this Constitution."

The previous government had been established on the principle that the emperor was the absolute and divine ruler of the people. The new Constitution declared, "This Constitution shall be the supreme law of the nation and no law, ordinance, imperial prescript or other act of government, or part thereof, contrary to the provisions hereof, shall have legal force or validity." The emperor, once considered a deity, was redefined as "the symbol of the State and of the unity of the people, deriving his position from the will of the people with whom resides sovereign power."

The Constitution of Japan provides familiar rights to the accused, such as the following:

- No person shall be apprehended except upon warrant . . . (Article 33)
- No person shall be arrested or detained without being at once informed of the charges against him or without the immediate privilege of counsel . . . (Article 34)
- The right of all persons to be secure in their homes, papers and effects against entries, searches and

Crimes against Property

Numerous statutes define offenses against property, including theft, larceny, embezzlement, receiving stolen property, false pretenses, forgery, and uttering. These various modern offenses originated in the ancient felony of larceny, which covered only the wrongful taking of the property of others. Originally, having property taken through fraud, dishonesty, or false statements was not considered an offense.[62] Early English common law considered it the responsibility of the property owner to see to it that they were not cheated or defrauded. If someone were foolish enough to fall victim to lies or con games, the law would not assist the owner in attempting to recover the property or punish the taker. Changing social values, increasing complexity in the business world, and disregard for the old principle of *caveat emptor* ("let the buyer beware") has resulted in numerous new crimes. Modern criminal codes concerning crimes against property make it illegal to take stocks, bonds, checks, negotiable paper, services and labor, minerals, crops, utilities, and even trees. Virtually all property falls within the scope of modern larceny statutes.

larceny Wrongfully taking and carrying away of another's property with the intent to permanently deprive the property's owner of its possession.

LARCENY Larceny is the most commonly committed crime in the United States. The Modern Penal Code defines **larceny** as the wrongfully taking and carrying away of another's property with the intent to permanently deprive the property's owner of its possession. The temporary taking of property, even if unlawful, is not larceny. The

seizures shall not be impaired except upon warrant... (Article 35)

- In all criminal cases the accused shall enjoy the right to a speedy and public trial by an impartial tribunal. (Article 37)

The crimes defined in the **Penal Code of Japan** reflect the American criminal justice system. For example, homicide is defined by Article 199 as "A person, who kills another, shall be punished with death or penal servitude for life or not less than three years." The crimes of attempt and conspiracy are likewise similar. Ignorance of law is not considered as lack of intent to commit a crime, but acts by youths under 14 years of age are not punishable (Chapter VII, Article 38).

The Penal Code of Japan is an amazingly compact document of only 61 pages, compared to the volumes of statutes of the United States. Because of Japan's centralized government, there is only one penal code rather than diverse local, state, and federal criminal codes, as in the United States. Japan's code also reflects Japanese social values and priorities. For example, it regulates water utilization and crimes relating to places of worship and graves. The crime of homicide includes specific provisions prohibiting the killing of a lineal relative or the lineal relative of one's spouse.

A sampling of the categories of criminal laws of Japan include the following:

- Crimes Related to Civil War
- Crimes Related to External War
- Crimes of Obstructing the Performance of Official Duties
- Crimes of Escape
- Crimes of Riot
- Crimes of Arson and Fire Caused by Negligence
- Crimes of Traffic Obstruction
- Crimes of Trespass
- Crimes Relating to Smoking Opium
- Crimes Relating to Drinking Water
- Crimes of Obscenity, Rape, and Bigamy
- Crimes against Reputation
- Crimes Relating to Stolen Property

Despite the fact that this penal code was to a large degree forced on Japan as a consequence of being defeated by allied countries in World War II, Japan has retained the penal code fairly intact from its original. The Penal Code reflects traditional Japanese culture as well and has been revised but not rescinded.

■ How does Japan's penal code reflect both American and Japanese values? What are the advantages and disadvantages of having a single, unified, nationwide penal code? Do you think the United States would benefit from such a code? Do you think "justice" would be served by instituting an international penal code on which each nation's penal code could be built?

theft of motor vehicles is defined by separate criminal codes, but the same criteria apply. Thus, taking a car to use it temporarily is not theft; it is defined as the crime of joy-riding.

The punishment prescribed for larceny depends on (1) the market value of the property taken, (2) the method of taking, and (3) the intrinsic value assessed by society. The punishment for larceny can range from a minor fine or a few days in jail to the consequences of a serious felony crime. The application of punishment often is inconsistent, however. A person may receive a less severe sentence for embezzling $3 million than for bouncing three checks. Nor is the standard consistent from state to state. In one state, the theft of property worth less than $100 may be considered a felony, and in another state, the value of the property may have to exceed $1,000 before it is considered a felony. Because of the difficulty of establishing specific criminal intents for property offenses, some states have adopted consolidated theft statutes. A *consolidated theft statute* removes the requirement of establishing specific criminal intent to misappropriate property by stealth, conversion, or deception.

OFFENSES RELATED TO LARCENY Receiving stolen property is a criminal offense. The offense requires that an individual has knowledge (or should have knowledge) that the property is stolen. A different standard often is applied to businesses such as pawn shops. Pawn shop owners may commit the offense of receiving stolen property if the criminal intent is recklessness or negligence rather than knowledge alone. Even

Examples of crimes against:

The State	Persons	Habitation	Property	Public Order	Public Morals
• Treason • Sedition	• Murder • Rape • Sexual assault • Kidnapping • Robbery • Assault	• Burglary • Arson	• Theft • Larceny • Embezzlement • Fraud • Receiving stolen property • Forgery	• Disturbing the peace • Inciting to riot	• Prostitution • Gambling

Figure 4.4

Classification of Crimes in the Model Penal Code

lost property can be stolen, so it is not true that you have a right to keep any lost property that you find. Modern statutes consider the taking of lost property larceny.

As society has created different means of wealth other than precious metals or money, the law has enacted criminal codes to protect wealth. For example, it is a crime (forgery) to sign a painting with an artist's name in an effort to increase the painting's value. It is also illegal (fraud) to sign an unsigned painting with the artist's name even if it is known that the artist created it. The laws protecting property continue to evolve. Today the cutting edge of property law concerns the protection of intellectual property, property exchanged on the Internet, and property such as genetically engineered foods, frozen eggs and sperm, and cloned living organisms.

INTERNATIONAL CONFLICT OVER DEFINING PROPERTY OFFENSES As countries are becoming more interdependent and trading and business is becoming more global, there often is dispute over the property laws of nations. Russia, for example, at the close of the twentieth century, provided only minimum protection of intellectual property. Based on communist ideology, Russian law considered intellectual property the property of all citizens. Large software companies doing business with Russia and other countries of the former Soviet Union did not have such a radical attitude toward the protection of their software. One of the challenges of the Economic Union in Europe has been to agree on a common standard of statutes to be applied to the protection of various kinds of property, the specific criminal intent required to prove an offense, and the punishment for crimes against property. As you can imagine, winning international support for a common criminal code for property crimes is a major challenge.

JUST THE FACTS 4.5

How are the crimes of homicide, rape, robbery, assault, burglary, arson, and larceny defined and evaluated in terms of acts, seriousness, and intent? How have laws against persons, habitations, and property changed to reflect societal changes? Why is it difficult to write laws prohibiting the illegal taking of property?

conclusion:

Criminal Law Is a Pillar of Social Order

Thousands of other offenses are defined by local, state, and federal criminal codes. While precision is required in establishing criminal intent for crimes such as murder, robbery, and rape, there is general agreement that these offenses should be crimes. For other offenses, there is not only debate as to the criminal intent necessary to prove an offense, but also disagreement as to whether any intent is sufficient to make the offense a crime. Citizens and the courts disagree sharply, for example, on the criminal intent necessary to prove offenses such as profanity, obscenity, unlawful assembly, and restricted speech. Many citizens claim that the Second Amendment gives them the right to possess and use firearms, while others argue that no such right exists in the Constitution.

Often the debate as to what is a crime and what is legal behavior defines the limits of personal freedom. Many argue that laws prohibiting fornication, illicit cohabitation, prostitution, homosexuality, and sodomy are rooted in religious values and should not be crimes. Laws that give the police the right to restrict public protest gatherings or to limit political messages are criticized as infringements on First Amendment freedoms. Others argue that greater harm would be done without the ability to regulate possible conflict among groups, to provide order for public meetings, and to prevent interference with the normal work of others.

As new values are embraced by society, new laws are created. Concern over harm to members of minority groups has resulted in the demand for hate-crime legislation. Concern over gun deaths has increased the demand for prohibitions against the ownership and use of firearms. And concern about the separation of religion and the state is at the root of many debates about the law. The criminal law code is constantly changing.

It can be difficult to define the *actus reus* and criminal intent that constitute the dividing line between criminal behavior and protected personal rights. Frequent violation of laws by citizens causes general disrespect for the law and for all aspects of the criminal justice system. Likewise, laws that give police too much discretion or do not clearly identify the harm to society erode citizens' respect for the law. Laws that reflect the religious values of only some of the citizens of society or that treat the poor with fear and suspicion do not strengthen the bonds of civilized behavior. A critical question in assessing the constitutionality of laws is the balance between the need for conformity and public safety versus privacy rights and individualism. The principle of the law is the most important part of the criminal code. Even laws with minor punishments may be appealed all the way to the U.S. Supreme Court, based on the principle of the law alone.

Chapter Summary

- The U.S. criminal justice system is founded on the rule of law.
- Separate criminal codes define offenses for local, state, and federal governments.
- Laws must meet certain standards to be considered constitutional: principle of legality, ex post facto laws, due process, void for vagueness, right to privacy, void for overbreadth, and cruel and unusual punishment.
- An offense is defined as an act (*actus reus*) committed with criminal intent (*mens rea*) and a resulting harm (concurrence).
- The punishment for an offense must be specified in the law or the law is void.
- Sometimes the *actus reus* of a crime may be words, the failure to act, or the possession of contraband.
- There are two types of criminal intent: general and specific. Some crimes require proof of specific intent. Strict liability laws do not require the proof of criminal intent.
- Actions that do not result in completed crimes are punishable as conspiracy, solicitation, or attempt.
- Common defenses to the charges of criminal conduct include alibi, consent, entrapment, immunity, involuntary actions (such as duress), mistake or ignorance, necessity, self-defense, youth, and insanity.
- Most law schools and law textbooks use the Model Penal Code to teach law. While state criminal codes may be similar, there may be significant differences.
- The Model Penal Code classifies crimes according to the categories of crimes against the state, crimes against persons, crimes against habitation, crimes against property, crimes against public order, and crimes against public morals.
- Punishments for crimes are graded by the harm and criminal intent of the actor.
- Often a crime is a complex matter of determining the intent of the actor. Homicide can be classified along a continuum from first-degree murder to negligent homicide, depending on the *mens rea*.

Crimes reflect social values. The offense of rape has been significantly redefined over the years as society has redefined the role and rights of women. Laws against breaking and entering originally protected homes from trespass and theft at night, but modern burglary laws protect many types of property and under numerous circumstances, not only at night. Larceny, the most common crime committed, is difficult to legislate against because of the numerous ways things can be taken, the difficulty of defining intentional versus unintentional taking, and the numerous ways in which property changes hands in the normal course of business and social interaction.

Vocabulary Review

actus reus, 115
alibi, 121
arson, 132
assault, 131
attempt, 120
burglary, 132
causation, 119
common law, 108
concurrence, 119
consent, 122
conspiracy, 120
constructive intent, 117
corpus delicti, 129
crimes of omission, 116
cruel and unusual punishment, 113
defenses, 121
duress, 123
elements of a crime, 115
entrapment, 122
ex post facto law, 111
felony, 108
homicide, 129
immunity, 122
inchoate offenses, 119
incomplete crimes, 119
insanity, 126
intent, 117
larceny, 134
mala in se, 107
mala prohibita, 107
manslaughter, 129
mens rea, 115
misdemeanor, 108
mistake or ignorance of fact or law, 124
Model Penal Code, 128
murder, 129
necessity, 124
possession, 116
principle of legality, 111
principle of proportionality, 114
procedural due process, 112

Names and Events to Remember

Think about This

1. What are the advantages of a system that operates by the rule of law? Whom do the laws protect? In the United States, as a result of the rule of law, people who commit a crime may go unpunished if the criminal justice system fails to protect the rights of the criminal. In most states, the victim has no such rights. Does the rule of law harm society through excessive safeguards on the rights of the accused?
2. The laws of the criminal justice system are based on the principles of classical criminology. What are these principles? Are they compatible with modern psychological, scientific, and medical knowledge? Is there a need to seriously examine the underlying principles of the criminal codes? How might those principles be changed and to what end?
3. The United States has a complex system of numerous local, state, and federal criminal codes. Some argue that there are too many laws and not enough law enforcement. One single criminal code for all states would greatly reduce the complexity—even the conflict—of the criminal codes. What would be the advantages and disadvantages of a single criminal code for the United States?

ContentSelect

Go to the ContentSelect web site and type in the natural language search phrase "cruel and unusual punishment." Read "Mental Abuse as Cruel and Unusual Punishment" from the April 1999 issue of *Crime and Delinquency*. The article discusses whether boot camps violate the Eighth Amendment to the U.S. Constitution. Sample the article to answer the following questions.

1. Why does the article maintain that correctional boot camps may be considered "cruel and unusual punishment"?
2. How might the correctional boot camp violate the Eighth Amendment or otherwise deprive juvenile offenders of due process? Does "mental suffering" constitute an Eighth Amendment violation?
3. If participation in a boot camp is voluntary and results in a shorter jail term, how is it possible to consider a boot camp "cruel and unusual punishment"?
4. According to your text, a rule of proportionality applies in setting punishments for crimes. In your opinion, what types of criminal offenses would warrant the use of a correctional boot camp?

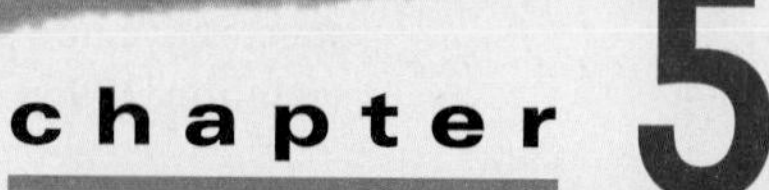

Due Process and Police Procedure

outline

Learning Objectives

After reading this chapter you will be able to:

- Define due process and identify procedural laws that guarantee due process.
- Explain how the rules of evidence influence police behavior.
- Describe how police procedure reflects case law relating to the Fourth and Fifth Amendments.
- List exceptions to the exclusionary rule regarding search and seizure.
- Identify situations that can make evidence from interrogations, confessions, and arrests inadmissible in court.
- Compare and evaluate the roles of the branches of government, government agencies, police departments, mass media, and the public in oversight of the police.
- Discuss sources and consequences of police brutality and corruption.
- Assess the effectiveness of criminal prosecutions and civil suits against the police.

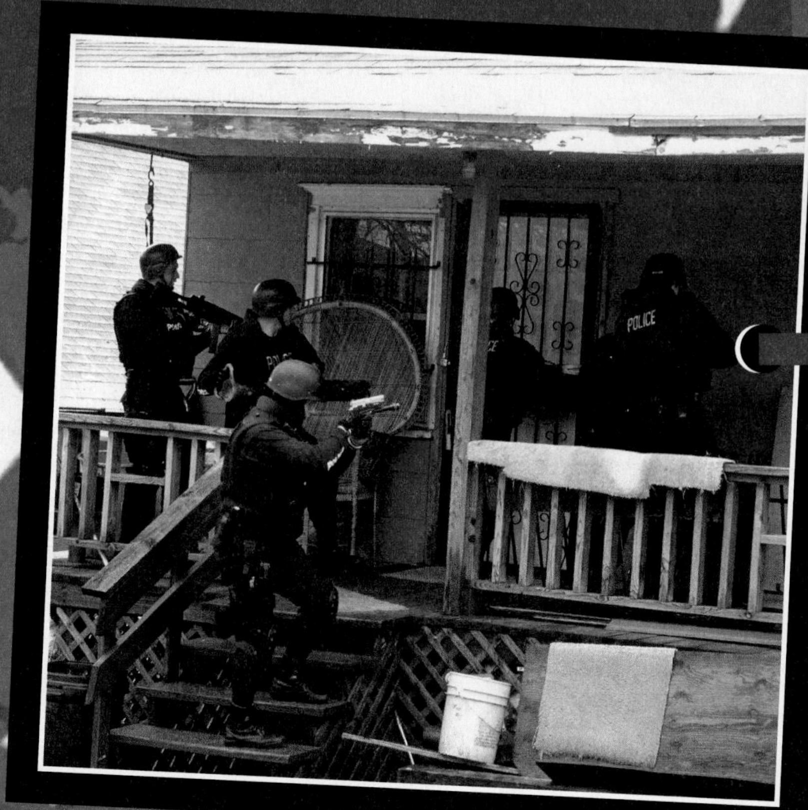

Drug Raid Goes Wrong

Associated Press

KENT, WASH—King County officers in Washington state invited the television show *COPS* to film their drug raid. It was an exciting operation as police kicked in the door of the suspected crack dealer's duplex and confronted the suspected drug-dealing couple with drawn guns. This demonstration of dangerous police work was all caught on film and would have made great TV viewing except for the fact that the police had written the wrong address on an affidavit used to obtain a search warrant and as a result raided the wrong side of the duplex.

—From *Honolulu Advertiser*, May 25, 1992.

introduction:

Procedural Law and Oversight of the Police

The criminal justice system is governed by **procedural law**—a body of laws for how things should be done at each stage of the criminal justice process. This includes court procedures, such as rules of evidence, and police procedures, such as search and seizure, arrest, and interrogation.

The criminal justice system, other branches of government, local communities, and the media all have roles in exercising oversight over the police to ensure that all legal procedures are carried out. This oversight of police conduct also extends to responding to unprofessional behavior and incidents of police incompetence, brutality, and corruption. This chapter discusses the difficult problem of police professionalism and accountability. How can police officers avoid making mistakes in practice, like the police who raided the wrong address, and what happens if they deliberately abuse their power?

Procedural laws are developed through legislative and judicial oversight. Police practices are affected by city and county councils, state legislatures, and the federal Congress. These legislative bodies can pass laws that limit or expand police jurisdiction, create standards, and provide remedies for police practices not acceptable to the community. For example, some states, such as the Commonwealth of Pennsylvania, have in recent years passed legislation restricting the use of radar speed traps by municipal police in response to allegations of abuse.[1]

Police conduct also is influenced by the judiciary, especially the U.S. Supreme Court, as in the well-known ruling that a suspect being placed under arrest must be read his or her rights prior to questioning. The tremendous influence that the Supreme Court exerts is indirect, however, and may take years, sometimes decades, to correct police malpractice. Because of the separation of powers and checks and balances in U.S. government, the Supreme Court cannot issue a direct order to a police department or state or federal law enforcement agency dictating how they should act. Similarly, according to the separation of powers, police officers have the power to arrest people, but not the power to prosecute people for the charges on which they have been arrested. The power to file a criminal complaint against a defendant—even to decide who will be brought to court to face charges and who will not—rests with the judicial branch of government in the hands of the district attorney or attorney general of the state.

Go to http://www.ablongman.com/criminaljustice for audio and activities relating law enforcement procedures to the U.S. Constitution. ■

procedural law Body of laws for how things should be done at each stage of the criminal justice process.

Rules of Evidence

THE MAIN IDEA

Police procedure is guided by rules defining what is legal evidence admissible in a court of law.

The Supreme Court has the power to establish the rules by which lower courts operate. Each court is governed by rules concerning everyday practices, such as how judges will be assigned cases, the qualification of attorneys to practice before the court, the order of presentation of the case, and the rules regarding proper conduct of attorneys and observers in the courtroom. Rules that relate to the presentation of evidence in a trial are called the rules of evidence.

Rules of evidence stipulate the requirements for introducing evidence and define the qualifications of an expert witness and the nature of the testimony he or she may give. According to the rules of evidence, for example, the prosecutor must show the defense the evidence he or she has gathered against the defendant. Rules define when evidence is relevant to the case and material (relevant to a particular issue in the case). Through its power to decide what evidence can be introduced at a trial, the Supreme Court influences police practices.

Rules of evidence affect police officers' conduct, because collecting evidence is part of their job. If evidence is not collected properly, it can be declared inadmissible, in which case it cannot be used against a defendant. For example, if a defendant is on trial for the illegal possession of drugs and the drugs he or she is accused of possessing are declared inadmissible as evidence, the prosecutor cannot present this evidence to the jury. Thus, the prosecutor has no case. He or she cannot tell the jury that the defendant is accused of possessing something if the object cannot be presented in court. The rules also state that evidence gathered through immoral, illegal, or unconstitutional means should not be used as evidence in a trial. Evidence gathered by such means is not admissible in court, and to avoid this, it is assumed, police officers will follow the rules of evidence.

The Exclusionary Rule

Evidence is declared inadmissible under the **exclusionary rule,** which prohibits the use of evidence or testimony obtained in violation of the U.S. Constitution. The Constitution protects civil liberties and civil rights, which may not be violated by agents of the criminal justice system.

The origins of the exclusionary rule can be traced back to a case heard by the Supreme Court in 1914, ***Weeks v. United States.***[2] In the *Weeks* case, the U.S. Supreme Court ruled that evidence against Weeks had been obtained in violation of his protections under the Constitution. Evidence was obtained through a search without a warrant in violation of the Fourth Amendment.

Initially, the exclusion rule applied only to federal courts. The rights guaranteed by the First Amendment (freedom of speech and freedom of association), Fourth Amendment (privacy and search and seizure), and Fifth Amendment (self-incrimination and double jeopardy) to the Constitution did not apply to the actions of local police or state courts. Until 1949 state courts were free to write their own rules of evidence.[3]

rules of evidence Requirements for introducing evidence and testimony in court.

exclusionary rule Prohibits the use of evidence or testimony obtained in violation of the Fourth and Fifth Amendments of the U.S. Constitution, established in *Weeks v. United States* (1914) and extended to the states in *Mapp v. Ohio* (1961).

Fruit of the Poisoned Tree Doctrine

At first, the exclusionary rule established in the *Weeks* case applied only to primary (directly obtained) evidence, but not to secondary evidence. For example, if federal agents obtained the business books of a company by unconstitutional means, those books could not be used as evidence to incriminate the defendant, but a copy of the information could. Also, inadmissible evidence could lead to other evidence, which then could be introduced in court. Thus, if an unconstitutional search produced a map indicating where the defendant had buried the body of the person he or she was accused of murdering, the map could not be introduced as evidence. However, using the knowledge obtained from the map, the police officers could go to the gravesite, uncover the body, and introduce it as evidence.

Four years after the *Weeks* decision, the Supreme Court reconsidered the exclusionary rule and added another rule of evidence, known as the **Fruit of the Poisoned Tree Doctrine.** The name of the doctrine comes from the analogy that if the tree is "poisoned," then the "fruit" of the tree also will be poisoned. In ***Silverthorne Lumber Co. v. United States*** (1918), the Supreme Court declared that the rules of evidence applied not only to evidence directly obtained by illegal means, but also to any other evidence obtained indirectly.[4] Under this rule, the copy of the business books and the body found through the aid of the map are not admissible as evidence.

The U.S. Supreme Court required the federal courts to follow this rule but still did not interfere in the procedures of state courts. Only 17 states chose to adopt similar rules of evidence. However, In ***Wolf v. Colorado*** (1949), the U.S. Supreme Court declared that state courts had to enact procedures to protect the rights of citizens against police abuses of search and seizure.[5] *Wolf v. Colorado* gave the states wide latitude in developing rules of evidence such as the exclusionary rule and the Fruit of the Poisoned Tree Doctrine to discourage such abuses. Twelve years later, in 1961, the Supreme Court decided that the states had failed to act to protect the constitutional rights of the defendant.

Application to State Courts: *Mapp v. Ohio*

Without any "punishment" for gathering evidence and obtaining confessions contrary to constitutional protections, local and state law enforcement officers paid little attention to the federal constitutional rights of citizens. They knew that any evidence they obtained would be admissible at trial in state court. It was common practice for police to search without a warrant or probable cause, obtain confessions by the use of force, and in general ignore the constitutional rights of suspects. Then, in 1961 in ***Mapp v. Ohio,*** the U.S. Supreme Court reversed itself and required state courts to use the exclusionary rule.[6]

The facts of *Mapp v. Ohio* are that Cleveland, Ohio, police officers received a tip from an informant that a bombing suspect was at the home of Dolree Mapp and that there was evidence at her house to connect her to the numbers racket. When police officers went to the home of Dolree Mapp and asked permission to search her house, she refused. The police officers returned and announced that they had obtained a search warrant. When she asked to see the search warrant, they showed her a piece of paper, which she grabbed and stuffed into her dress. The police officers forcibly retrieved their "search warrant," which actually was a blank piece of paper.

At that point, the police proceeded to search Mapp's house without the benefit of search warrant, probable cause, or consent. They did not find the bombing suspect or the numbers evidence, but they did find a bag of obscene books and arrested her for possession of obscene materials. Mapp was convicted in state court for possession of obscene materials. Mapp felt that her Fourth Amendment rights had been violated, but when she appealed, the Ohio Supreme Court upheld the conviction. Mapp appealed to the U.S. Supreme Court, which ruled that local police officers were accountable to the same standard as in *Weeks v. United States*. Therefore, the evidence obtained illegally was inadmissible. Mapp's conviction was reversed.

Fruit of the Poisoned Tree Doctrine Extends the exclusionary rule to secondary evidence obtained indirectly in an unconstitutional search, established in *Silverthorne Lumber Co. v. United States* (1918) and in *Wolf v. Colorado* (1949).

Mapp v. Ohio was the first case in which the U.S. Supreme Court applied the exclusionary rule to state courts. All state courts were required to adopt rules of evidence, which declared that evidence would be inadmissible in criminal court if it was gathered without benefit of warrant, probable cause, or consent. Other decisions affecting the admissibility of evidence in state courts followed quickly and had sweeping effects on state criminal court procedures.

Today the rules of evidence in state and federal criminal courts are shaped by numerous U.S. Supreme Court decisions. Furthermore, these rules continue to change as the Court modifies and sometimes even reverses the standard of what is admissible evidence. Police officers in all jurisdictions must adhere to these standards in gathering evidence and obtaining confessions or they will find that the evidence and confessions that they have gathered will be declared inadmissible at trial. The major actions regulated by the exclusionary rule include searches, confessions, and arrest.

JUST THE FACTS 5.1

What are the rules of evidence? What landmark cases were involved in establishing the exclusionary rule at both the federal and state levels? How does the exclusionary rule influence police conduct? What three basic standards must be met for evidence to be admissible in court?

Search and Seizure

THE MAIN IDEA

The rules of evidence define legal search and seizure of places, automobiles, and persons and also define exceptions to the exclusionary rule.

warrant Legal permission to conduct a search, signed by a judge.

probable cause Strong likelihood of a direct link between a suspect and a crime.

The **Fourth Amendment** states that "The right of the people to be secure in their persons, houses, papers, and effects, against unreasonable searches and seizures, shall not be violated, and no warrants shall issue, but upon probable cause ...." Thus, evidence obtained by police with the use of a valid **warrant** issued by a judge is admissible as evidence at a criminal trial, and searches based on **probable cause**—the likelihood of a direct link between a suspect and a crime—are legal. However, there are other circumstances under which the police can gather evidence without a warrant.

Why do these officers have to be mindful of the exclusionary rule? Are they conducting a legal search and seizure? What constitutional rights does the exclusionary rule protect? What is the difference between reasonable suspicion and probable cause as standards of proof in police action? Why does the exclusionary rule have the power to influence police conduct? What are some major exceptions to the exclusionary rule, and why were these exceptions made?

Search Incident to Lawful Arrest

The Supreme Court has granted that when the police make a lawful arrest, they are entitled to make a search of the person arrested without a search warrant. This is called **search incident to lawful arrest.** The question that arose was how extensive a search police can make under this justification. When police officers extended their search to rooms not occupied by the person arrested and to areas beyond the person's reach, a search incident to a lawful arrest is limited to the area within the immediate control of the person.[7] Otherwise, the evidence obtained is not admissible in criminal court.

Plain-View Searches

Evidence in the plain view of the police officer is admissible in criminal court (***Harris v. United States***).[8] This assumes that the police officer had the legal right to be where he or she was. If a police officer is invited into someone's home and that person was thoughtless enough to leave a pile of marijuana on the table that they were in the process of cleaning and sorting, the Court has ruled that such evidence obtained in a plain-view search is admissible. However, the police officer cannot move objects to get a view of the evidence.[9] For example, if the marijuana on the table had been completely covered with a cloth, the police officer could not remove the cloth (without permission, a search warrant, or probable cause) to see what was there. Likewise, if a police officer were to enter a room and move electronic equipment to see the serial numbers to check against a list of stolen merchandise and found a match, such evidence would be inadmissible without permission, a search warrant, or probable cause.[10] However, the police do not have to act blind or stupid. In the language of the Court, "inadvertence is not necessary."[11] That is, the police are not required to be heedless or inattentive to their environment. A police officer who sees a cloth covering something on the table and smells marijuana may have probable cause to look under the cloth.

Whether evidence from a **plain-view search** is admissible can depend on even minor variations. For example, if a 6-foot-tall police officer is walking by a 5-foot-high fence and sees a marijuana plant growing on the other side on private property, the evidence is in plain view. If a 5′8″ police officer is walking by a 6-foot-high fence and stands on a ladder and sees a marijuana plant growing on the other side, the evidence is not in plain view. Similarly, if a police officer uses a flashlight to look into an automobile at night, the Court has ruled that the use of a flashlight does not violate the plain-view doctrine. However, if a police officer uses binoculars to view evidence, that may violate the plain-view doctrine.

search incident to lawful arrest Right to search an arrestee without a warrant, established in *Chimel v. California* (1969).

plain-view search Right to gather evidence in plain sight without a warrant, established in *Harris v. United States* (1968) and redefined in *United States v. Irizarry* (1982), *Arizona v. Hicks* (1987), and *Horton v. California* (1990).

Consent to Search

If a person gives permission for a search, any evidence discovered is admissible (***Florida v. Jimeno,*** 1973).[12] The person who gives the permission must have the authority to do so. For example, a landlord cannot give valid permission to search an apartment currently occupied by a tenant but can give permission once the tenant vacates the apartment. A motel owner cannot give permission to search a motel room rented to a guest but can give permission to search the room after the guest checks out. A parent can give permission to search the room of a legal dependant living in the same house but cannot give permission to search the room of a boarder living in a room rented in the house. The complexity of society has resulted in numerous rulings by the Court defining who has the authority to grant permission to search.

Search of Automobiles

As early as 1925, the Supreme Court addressed the question of the constitutionality of searches of automobiles without a search warrant. Recognizing that the mobility of automobiles adds a new dimension to searches, the Court established the Carroll Doctrine, based on ***Carroll v. United States*** (1925).[13] In the **Carroll Doctrine,** evidence obtained in the search of an automobile without a warrant is admissible in criminal court if the police officer (1) has probable cause to believe that a crime has occurred and (2) the circumstances are such that delay in searching the automobile would result in loss of the evidence. This rule requires that an officer must have probable cause to stop the car in the first place.[14] If an officer does not have the authority to stop the car in the first place, any evidence obtained in a search is not admissible.

Closely related to the Carroll Doctrine is the search of a vehicle that has been lawfully impounded by the police. Any evidence obtained during an inventory of the contents of a lawfully impounded vehicle is admissible in criminal court.[15] For example, if the police arrest a driver for DUI (driving while under the influence of alcohol) and impound the vehicle, they can perform a thorough search of the vehicle, including any locked glove compartments or trunks. They also can remove any boxes, suitcases, or other items and search those items. The police may even force locks for the purpose of inventorying the contents of an automobile. The philosophy is that the police assume liability for the loss of anything of value in the vehicle when they impound it and, therefore, are authorized to inventory the entire vehicle and its contents to establish the presence and value of any contents. Also, locked containers in a vehicle might hide things that pose a danger to police or the public, such as a bomb hidden in a suitcase in the vehicle, in which case the police have a right and duty to determine such danger.

Read about the history, current news, and debate on the issue of racial profiling at http://www.aclu.org/profiling/. ■

Search of Persons: The Pat-Down

The U.S. Supreme Court has appreciated the fact that the police operate in an environment that can be life threatening. Thus, the police are allowed to take certain reasonable precautions in dealing with the public. In the course of taking reasonable precautions, such as frisking or patting-down a detainee suspected of carrying a weapon, if the police find incriminating evidence, such evidence is admissible in criminal court. The doctrine governing the search of persons without probable cause but with reasonable suspicion is called the pat-down doctrine and has its origins in ***Terry v. Ohio.***[16]

Police officers frequently approach or are approached by citizens to interact. At close range, a citizen's possession of a weapon could be deadly to the officer. In some contexts, the police may be able to determine by simple visual inspection if a citizen is carrying a concealed weapon, but outer clothing often makes it impossible to tell. In such cases, officers are authorized to pat down or frisk the citizen, even when there is no probable cause.

The **pat-down search** may be conducted solely to ensure the safety of the officer.[17] If in the course of a pat down, the police officer feels an object that may be a weapon, the officer legally can reach into the pocket or clothing to further explore the nature of the object. If the officer still believes that the object may be a weapon, he or she may remove the object and examine it. If it is a weapon, and the person is not authorized to carry it, the weapon is admissible as evidence. However, if the officer feels an object that clearly is not a weapon but may be illegal, such as a bag of narcotics, the officer may not reach into the pocket to explore the nature of the object or remove it for inspection. An object acquired in an illegal pat-down search is not admissible as evidence in a court of law.

Carroll Doctrine Terms defining the admissibility of evidence obtained in a warrantless search of an automobile, established in *Carroll v. United States* (1925).

pat-down search Right to search a person for a concealed weapon on the basis of reasonable suspicion, established in *Terry v. Ohio* (1968).

ethics in the system

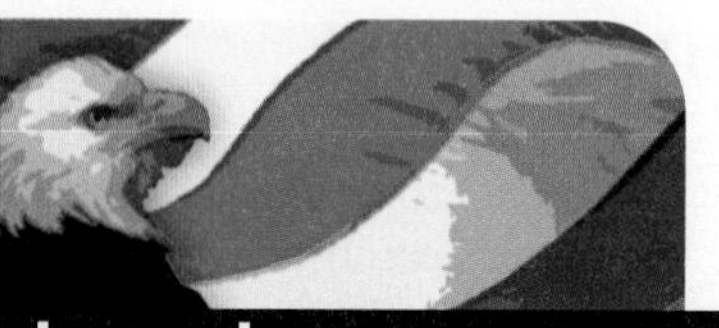

Racial Profiling in Automobile Stops

Racial profiling has created a firestorm of controversy related to the Carroll Doctrine. Before the terrorist attack on the World Trade Center, the term *ground-zero* was used to identify racial profiling in New Jersey.[18] *Racial profiling* is the term used to describe the stopping of minority motorists by police officers for alleged minor offenses or suspicion, when in reality the primary reason that motorists have been singled out is that they are persons of color. The practice is also known as "driving while black" or in the case of Hispanics, "driving while brown."[19] New Jersey became known as ground-zero because of the alleged egregious conduct of New Jersey State Police troopers.

The problem of racial profiling has been elevated to crisis level by recent public safety campaigns to encourage seat belt use and the war on drugs. In the 1990s, many states passed mandatory seat belt laws. In 1998, the National Highway Traffic Safety Administration promoted a "Buckle Up America" drive to make failure to wear seat belts a primary traffic offense in all 50 states. A *primary offense* is a violation for which the police have justification to stop a motorist. Civil rights groups quickly protested, citing widespread fears among blacks that police would use primary enforcement seat belt laws for arbitrary stops and searches.[20] The war on drugs also has contributed to charges of abuses of racial profiling. The American Civil Liberties Union claims that police officers unfairly target blacks in deciding which cars to search for drugs.[21] Critics claim that "U.S. highways have become like minefields for motorists of color, as authorities comb the roads in search of 'mules,' those smuggling narcotics—and often guns. . . ."[22]

In 1998, New Jersey state troopers became the focus of an intense investigation into abusive traffic stops based on racial profiling when state troopers John Hogan and James Kenna pulled over three black men and one Hispanic and opened fire on the unarmed men. It is alleged that the men were singled out simply because of their race and/or ethnicity. The troopers claim that the vehicle was speeding[23] and that they began shooting at the occupants of the van when the driver tried to back up over them with the vehicle. The minority community was angered when a judge dismissed the case against the two troopers.

Despite numerous long-standing complaints of racial profiling, former New Jersey Attorney General Peter

Drug smuggling and other drug laws have resulted in the interesting situation in which people swallow drugs wrapped in some type of protective covering or conceal drugs in personal body cavities in an effort to prevent their detection by the police. Even if the police have probable cause to believe that someone has swallowed illegal drugs in an effort to conceal them, the Court has been fairly consistent in requiring a search warrant to retrieve drugs by medical procedures such as pumping the stomach or conducting invasive searches of the body.[24]

JUST THE FACTS 5.2

What does the Fourth Amendment to the Constitution say about search and seizure? In what circumstances can a legal search be conducted, and in what ways are those circumstances open to interpretation? When do searches violate civil rights?

Verniero, who oversaw the state police during from 1996 to 1999, issued a denial that the New Jersey State Police used discriminatory law enforcement or a policy of racial profiling. However, a federal investigation revealed that not only was racial profiling tolerated, but troopers were instructed "to look for Colombian males, Hispanic males, Hispanic and black males together, Hispanic male and female posing as a couple." Troopers also were instructed "to focus on minorities when scanning the roadways as possible drug traffickers."[25] The data suggested that Verniero knew of and encouraged this practice as a drug-control policy.[26] He and the New Jersey State Police were accused of covering up institutionalized racism.

According to investigation data, black and Hispanic motorists were nearly 5 times more likely to be stopped than whites, suggesting that racially motivated stops were commonplace. In one case, a 42-year-old African American dentist reported that between 1991 and 1999 he had been pulled over by state troopers on the New Jersey Turnpike more than 50 times but was never issued a ticket.[27] State troopers were accused of attempting to cover up the extent of their racial profiling by recording the race of some stopped motorists as white rather than black of Hispanic.[28]

John Farmer, the new attorney general of New Jersey, appealed the dismissal of the charges against troopers Kenna and Hogan on the grounds that the grand jury was misled by prosecutors who withheld key portions of the evidence.[29] The statistics showed that 77.2 percent of searches by the state police were of blacks or Hispanics.[30] In 1999, State Police Superintendent Colonel Carl Williams issued a statement blaming minorities for most of the state's cocaine and marijuana traffic.[31]

The firestorm caused by the bitter charges and countercharges of racial profiling affected the criminal justice system. In April 1999, North Carolina passed a law requiring the police to record the race, age, and gender of every motorist stopped. Similar bills were introduced in other states. In June 1999, President Clinton ordered federal police agencies to gather racial statistics on people they target for traffic stops, border inspections, and other routine searches. In 1999, the American Civil Liberties Union set up a national DWB (Driving while Black) hotline (1-877-6-PROFILE) and filed their first lawsuit claiming racially motivated abuse by the police in May of that year.[32] In 2000, nearly every state undertook a study to determine the extent, if any, of racial profiling by police, and many states adopted laws to curb race-based traffic stops.[33]

■ If race is a factor in stopping motorists, what might be the role of race in juvenile justice and in serious offenses leading to arrest? How do policies and practices of racial profiling skew crime statistics, and with what consequences? Should people ever be detained on the basis of their race or ethnicity alone? Do you think racial profiling should be used to suspend people's civil rights in the war on terrorism?

Other Exceptions to the Exclusionary Rule

THE MAIN IDEA

Search and seizure without probable cause, a warrant, or consent is permitted in some circumstances, especially when there is clear and present danger or when public safety is at stake.

Since the 1960s, the U.S. Supreme Court has restricted the situations in which the police may conduct a search without a warrant. However, the Court has continued to recognize that there are certain circumstances that may justify a warrantless search. The two most common exceptions to the requirements for a search warrant are public safety and good faith.

ethics in the system

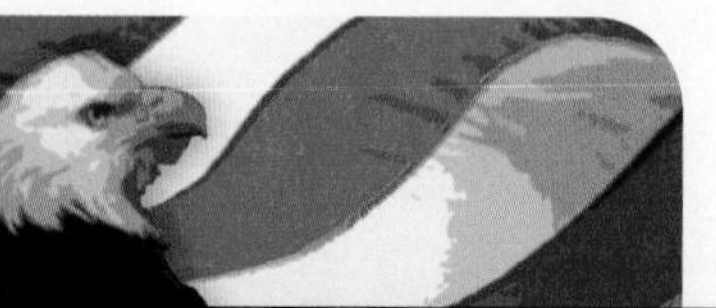

Anonymous Tips and Probable Cause

Imagine a situation in which an on-duty police officer observes a person known to police enter a bar and suspects that the person might be engaging in criminal behavior. The officer goes to a public telephone and calls 9-1-1 and, disguising his voice, gives an "anonymous tip" to the dispatcher that he wants to report a man with a gun in a bar. The information is based on deception, not probable cause. The officer fails to reveal to the police dispatcher that he is the beat officer for that district.

The dispatcher notifies the officer by police radio of an anonymous tip about a man with a gun in a nearby bar. The officer responds to the call, quickly locates the suspect who fits the description he himself provided, and performs a search of the person. In this case, the false anonymous tip is used to establish a basis of probable cause. If the officer does find a gun or illegal drugs, should that evidence be admissible in court?

The Supreme Court has recognized the potential for abuse by the police if probable cause for a search without a warrant can be justified by an anonymous tip. Recall the *Mapp v. Ohio* case as an example of such abuse. The Court has mandated that before information from an informant can be used as probable cause to justify a search or obtain a search warrant, the informant must pass certain tests establishing his or her credibility. Only after an informant's credibility has been established can a search be conducted or a search warrant issued.[34]

What do you think has been the effect of this ruling on the use of anonymous tips as justification for a search? Whose rights and interests are in the balance in rulings on probable cause?

The Public Safety Exception

Certain situations require immediate action by the police. If the police are chasing a person who has just committed a crime using a firearm and catch the person but fail to find the firearm on him or her, the Court has ruled that the police have the right to perform a search without a warrant in places where the person may have discarded the firearm. The justification for this exception is the argument that if the search is not performed immediately, the presence of the weapon in the community may pose a serious threat to public safety.[35] For example, if a person committed armed robbery and fled from the police into a mall, but did not have the firearm when caught, the police would be justified in immediately searching the stores in the mall for the weapon. There is the danger that a citizen, especially a juvenile, might find the weapon and accidentally harm someone by discharging it. The firearm, if found by police in a warrantless search, would be admissible as evidence.

public safety exception
Right to search without probable cause for the public good.

Another example of the **public safety exception** is the acceptance of searches without probable cause of airline passengers for the public good. The justification for this kind of search is that it is necessary for public safety and that passengers implicitly consent to be searched in exchange for the right to board an airplane. Law enforcement officers extended this philosophy to bus passengers. In an effort to detect drug smugglers who use public transportation to move illegal drugs from Florida to the Northeast, law enforcement officers obtained permission from bus companies to search the possessions and baggage of bus passengers. Arguing that they had the permission of the operating company, similar to permission given by the airline industry to search air passengers, officers began routine searches of bus passengers, a practice known as "working the busses." Evidence seized in these searches could legally justify an arrest and be used as evidence in court.[36]

Warrantless searches by U.S. Customs officials also have been granted greater leeway by the Court. Like airline security personnel, U.S. Customs agents can conduct strip searches and body cavity searches and can use sophisticated x-ray machines that can see through a person's clothing. Such searches do not require probable cause or a search warrant, and evidence found of illegal activity is admissible in criminal court.[37]

Fleeing Felon and Deadly Force

Public safety is also at the crux of rulings on deadly force used at the discretion of police. Have you seen old movies in which the police shout to a fleeing criminal, "Stop or I'll shoot!"? When the criminal fails to stop, the police either fire warning shots or take aim at the felon. Prior to 1985, shooting at fleeing suspects who refused to stop as commanded was a common and legal police practice involving the use of **deadly force.**

Many police departments had standard operating procedures detailing the circumstances under which an officer was justified in firing warning shots or using deadly force. Some departments allowed officers to use deadly force against fleeing people who were only "suspected" of committing crimes, and some jurisdictions did not differentiate between misdemeanors or felonies when using deadly force against a fleeing suspect. This practice was known as the fleeing suspect or **fleeing felon doctrine.** The police justified this practice on the basis of public safety. They argued that a suspect allowed to escape could be a potential danger to the community. If the person were suspected of having committed murder, they reasoned, a failure to apprehend might create an undue risk for the public—a justification for use of deadly force.

In ***Tennessee v. Garner*** (1985), the Court disagreed with that reasoning.[38] Attorneys representing Garner, who had been slain by a police officer in pursuit when Garner refused to stop, made the argument that the officer's use of deadly force was a form of search and seizure for which the officer lacked probable cause or a warrant. The Court accepted the validity of the argument and ruled that the search and seizure by deadly force against a fleeing suspect was a violation of the person's constitutional rights. The ruling in *Tennessee v. Garner* immediately superceded the rules of all police departments and the laws of the states that had permitted the practice. All law enforcement officers (local, state, and federal) were immediately prohibited from using deadly force as a means to stop a fleeing suspect. If the ruling was ignored, the officer and department could be held liable in a lawsuit for violation of the person's constitutional rights.

This ruling caused great confusion for a period of time as law enforcement officials and state legislators tried to determine the limits of the prohibition.[39] For example, if a person committed murders in the presence of a police officer and then threw down his or her weapon and fled from the scene, and if there were no other way to stop the person from escaping, could the officer use deadly force? The argument for the use of deadly force would be based on the potential threat an escaped murderer poses to a community. The argument against the use of deadly force would be based on the fact that after the person threw down his or her weapon, that person was no longer an immediate threat to the officer or the public, such that the use of deadly force was an unreasonable violation of his or her constitutional rights. If deadly force were used and the person died, he or she would be deprived the right to a trial by jury for the alleged criminal conduct.

While there are legitimate arguments to support both the prohibition and sanction of the use of deadly force in this case, the present legal position is that when there is a **clear and present danger** to the public posed by the escape of the person, deadly force may be justifiable.[40] In the lack of a clear and present danger, the use of deadly force to apprehend a fleeing suspect or criminal is a violation of the person's constitutional rights.

Read an article advising law enforcement officers on how to conduct effective search and seizure at http://www.fsu.edu/~crimdo/fagan.html. ■

deadly force Police power to incapacitate or kill in the line of duty.

fleeing felon doctrine Police practice of using deadly force against a fleeing suspect, made illegal in *Tennessee v. Garner* (1985), except when there is clear and present danger to the public.

clear and present danger Condition relating to public safety that may justify police use of deadly force against a fleeing suspect.

The Good Faith Exception

good faith exception Admissibility of evidence obtained in an illegal search when the police are found to have acted in good faith on the belief that their search was legal, established in *United States v. Leon* (1984) and *Massachusetts v. Sheppard* (1984) in contradiction to an earlier ruling in *Illinois v. Gates* (1982).

wiretapping A form of search and seizure in which citizens' rights to privacy on the telephone are protected by the Fourth Amendment, first established in *Olmstead v. United States* (1928) and extended to e-mail in *Katz v. United States* (1967).

Another common exception to the requirement of having a warrant or probable cause to conduct a legal search is when the police act in good faith. In the news story that begins this chapter, it could be argued that the King County, Washington, Sheriff's Department acted in good faith when it mistakenly raided the wrong side of a duplex due to a clerical error in the search warrant. However, whether evidence of any illegal activity seized in the wrongful search would be admissible in court is not certain. What if someone who is not the intended target of a search warrant is found to be in violation of a criminal law? Initially, the Court did not support the **good faith exception,** taking the position that good faith by the police does not override the violation of the valid search warrant requirement.[41] However, the Court later reversed itself and allowed evidence obtained in good faith but without a valid search warrant to be admitted in evidence.[42]

Wiretaps and the Issue of Privacy

Another area affected by the Fourth Amendment in which the Court has reversed itself is the issue of obtaining evidence by **wiretapping.** At the time the U.S. Constitution was drafted and the rights of citizens were enumerated in the Bill or Rights, there obviously was no mention of the right of privacy of one's telephone communications or messages sent by computer or e-mail. A hundred years after the drafting of the Constitution, the telephone was invented and law enforcement officers begin listening in on private telephone conversations between bootleggers. Using the information obtained by listening to these conversations, the police were able to make arrests and win convictions. In one case, the bootleggers appealed their conviction, and in 1928 the Supreme Court heard its first case in the area of electronic communications (***Olmstead v. United States,*** 1928).[43]

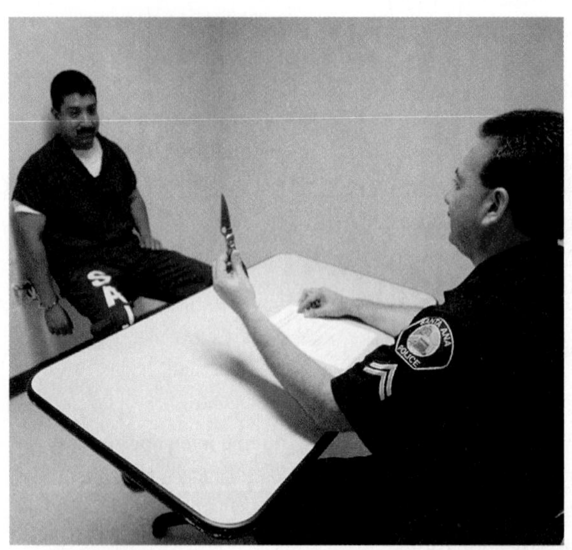

If this suspect were in England's Star Chamber in medieval times, his interrogator would torture him to force him to confess. The confession would then be used to convict him in court. Why did Americans reject the Star Chamber model? What procedural laws were established in the U.S. Constitution to guarantee due process? In addition to torture, what other practices in interrogation and arrest are illegal?

Initially, the Court ruled that the telephone lines and public telephone booths were not an extension of the defendant's home and were therefore not protected by the constitutional guarantee of privacy. Thirty-nine years later, the ruling in *Olmstead* was reversed, and it was declared that electronic communication was indeed private communication and protected as a constitutional right (***Katz v. United States,*** 1967).[44] Violating this privacy without consent, probable cause, or a warrant constituted illegal search and seizure.

The issue of privacy in relation to electronic communications has gone beyond court-mandated rules of evidence, requiring new legislation. Major pieces of legislation addressing electronic communications privacy are the **Electronic Communications Privacy Act of 1986,** the **Communications Assistance for Law Enforcement Act of 1994,** and the **Telecommunications Act of 1996.** These laws provide specific details governing the collection of evidence by wiretaps and other means and the definition of what electronically transmitted information is protected by the expectation of privacy.

Except in cases of suspected terrorism, law enforcement officers generally must satisfy stringent requirements before they can obtain information transmitted electronically or stored in computer databanks, such as stored e-mail messages. If law enforcement officers fail to follow the provision of the law, not only is the evidence not admissible in court, but for some violations, the officer may be subject to fines or incarceration.

JUST THE FACTS 5.3

In what specific circumstances can the exclusionary rule be ignored? How do exceptions to the exclusionary rule impact police pursuits and wiretapping? How do these exceptions highlight conflicts between privacy and security in law enforcement?

Interrogations and Confessions

THE MAIN IDEA

In defining admissible testimony, rules of evidence also reflect case law relating to the Fifth Amendment.

In addition to obtaining evidence through search and seizure, procedural laws affecting police conduct also govern obtaining testimony through interrogations and confessions. The confession is an effective method of convincing a jury that the defendant has committed the crime of which he or she has been accused. In medieval England, confessions were routinely obtained by torture. The **Star Chamber** was an English court interrogation room where confessions were forced through the use of pain. Contemporary British and American courts do not allow the use of torture or pain to obtain a confession. In the United States, the **Fifth Amendment** in the Bill or Rights guarantees citizens the right to avoid **self-incrimination.**

Use of Physical Punishment and Pain

Law enforcement practices traditionally have not been conducive to protecting citizens' Fifth Amendment rights. The U.S. Supreme Court first addressed the admissibility of confessions obtained by the use of force in ***Brown v. Mississippi*** (1936).[45] The case illustrates the need for Court intervention in that the deputy sheriff's officer accused of obtaining a confession from Brown by whipping him did not deny the charge. His defense was that the whipping was "not too much for a Negro; not as much as I would have done it if it were left to me."[46] In *Brown v. Mississippi,* the Court ruled that confessions obtained by force were tainted.

The Court has addressed various other abuses of the Fifth Amendment in landmark cases. In ***Ashcraft v. Tennessee,*** it was ruled that confessions obtained by the use of around-the-clock interrogation were inadmissible.[47] While Ashcraft was not physically beaten, he was interrogated for 36 hours by police officers, an ordeal known as receiving "the third degree." The Court ruled that under the circumstances, the confession given by Ashcraft was not voluntary and violated his Fifth Amendment rights.

self-incrimination Involuntary confession or forced testimony of the accused, prohibited by the Fifth Amendment, as in the inadmissibility of evidence obtained by force in *Brown v. Mississippi* (1936) and extended in *Ashcraft v. Tennessee* (1944) and *Leyra v. Denno* (1954).

Lying to the Suspect

Court rulings have not clearly prohibited police from obtaining a confession by lying to the suspect.[48] For example, confessions have been admitted even when obtained by police falsely telling one suspect that his partner in crime had confessed and named him as the "trigger man." And confessions have been admitted when obtained by placing a police officer dressed in prisoner clothing in the same cell as the suspect. On the other hand, a confession was prohibited as evidence when the police knowingly lied to

Figure 5.1

The Fourth and Fifth Amendments

Amendment IV

The right of the people to be secure in their persons, houses, papers, and effects, against unreasonable searches and seizures, shall not be violated, and no warrants shall issue, but upon probable cause, supported by Oath of affirmation, and particularly describing the place to be searched, and the persons or things to be seized.

Amendment V

No person shall be held to answer for a capital, or otherwise infamous crime, unless on a presentment or indictment of a Grand Jury, except in cases arising in the land or naval forces, or in the Militia, when in actual service in time of War or public danger; nor shall any person be subject for the same offence to be twice put in jeopardy of life or limb; nor shall be compelled in any criminal case to be a witness against himself, nor be deprived of life, liberty, or property, without due process of law; nor shall private property be taken for public use, without just compensation.

a suspect by telling him that an attorney was not available when the suspect attempted to exercise his right to talk with an attorney. Confessions also have been prohibited when obtained through the use of psychiatrists pretending to be medical doctors supposedly helping the accused. In ***Leyra v. Denno*** in 1954, the police used a psychiatrist to obtain a confession from the suspect, who thought he was receiving treatment for a medical condition. The psychiatrist persuaded the suspect that he would feel better if he confessed to his crime. The Court ruled that such deception was beyond the accept-

Figure 5.2

Standards for an Admissible Confession

- The confession must be given knowingly and not as a consequence of lies or deception.
- The suspect must be informed of his or her rights.
- The confession must be voluntary.
- Confessions may not be obtained through threats, such as
  - threatening to turn an illegal foreign alien over to Immigration authorities for deportation;
  - threatening to report a mother to child protective services for child abuse to have her children taken away from her;
  - threatening to report suspects to a welfare agency for the purpose of having their welfare benefits suspended.
- Confessions may not be obtained through use of pain or through constructive force, such as beating up one suspect in front of another and telling the second suspect that he or she is next if a confession is not forthcoming.

able limits of professional police conduct and that the confession obtained was inadmissible.[49]

For example, an embarrassing moment for the Federal Bureau of Investigation clearly illustrates the concept that a confession must be given knowingly. During the 1996 Olympic Games in Atlanta, Georgia, the FBI attempted to obtain a confession by deception from Centennial Park bombing suspect, Richard Jewell. Agents contacted Jewell and asked him to participate in a training video they were making in which Jewell was to play the part of the suspect. The agent would play the part of the interrogating officer and would advise him of his rights, which Jewell would waive. On the training video he would consent to the questioning.

The intent of the FBI was to use this consent obtained in the training video as a real waiver and interrogate Jewell on camera. While it could be argued that Jewell voluntarily waived his right against self-incrimination, and while he was indeed informed of his rights, because of the trickery any confession he gave could not be said to have been given knowingly. The suspect thought he was only pretending to waive his rights for the purpose of making a training video. Jewell was acquitted for lack of evidence that he had anything to do with the bombing.[50]

In 1996, the FBI attempted to trick Richard Jewell into falsely confessing to a crime he did not commit. Because the rules for lawful interrogation had not been observed, Jewell's confession would not have been admissible. Why are there rules governing police procedures in interrogations and confessions? What constitutional rights do these rules protect?

Police Lineups

A question related to the Fifth Amendment rights of suspects concerns **police lineups,** in which a victim is given an opportunity to identify a criminal from among a number of suspects. What are a suspect's rights in a lineup? Landmark cases have addressed the following questions:

- Can the police compel a suspect to appear in a lineup?
- Can the police compel a suspect to submit handwriting samples or voice samples?
- What constitutes a "fair" lineup?
- At the scene of a crime, can the police drive a witness by a suspect to see if the witness can identify the person as someone who participated in the crime?
- Does the suspect have the right to have his or her attorney present during a lineup?

Rulings have suggested that suspects' guarantees against self-incrimination apply in police lineups, but not to the degree that they apply in police interrogations. Law enforcement officers need to perform certain investigative tasks essential to gathering information about a crime. As long as police act in a professional and fair manner, they have greater latitude than in interrogations.[51] For example, police can drive a witness by a suspect to see if the witness can identify the person as someone who participated in the crime, and this can be done without informing the suspect or obtaining the suspect's consent. Suspects can be required to participate in a lineup without their consent and can be required to give a handwriting or voice sample.[52]

Lineups must be fair, however, and suspects have the right to have an attorney present. A fair lineup is defined as one that contains suspects who are similar and match the description given by the witness. Fair lineups contain actual suspects and not police personnel masquerading as suspects.[53]

The Right to an Attorney

Because of concern that the rights of the suspect are protected against self-incrimination, the Court has required that a suspect is entitled to have an attorney present when he or she is interrogated by the police, as well as in court. The right to have the benefit of an attorney when accused of criminal charges was established in the landmark case of ***Gideon v. Wainwright*** (1963).[54] The details of the case are striking as they illustrate

police lineups Opportunities for victims to identify a criminal from among a number of suspects.

Read an essay on interrogations and confessions from the perspective of law enforcement at http://www.courttv.com/confessions/bratton_essay.html. ■

the influence that a single case concerning a relatively obscure defendant can have on the entire criminal justice system.

Gideon was convicted of burglary and sentenced to an extended prison term under the habitual offender act. Gideon did not have the funds to hire an attorney to represent him in court, and the state refused to grant him one free of charge. Left to defend himself, Gideon apparently did not do very well against the trained and experienced state prosecutors, and he was convicted of the crime. While in prison, Gideon sent a handwritten letter to the Supreme Count in which he protested the unfairness of his conviction. He argued it was unfair for him to have to defend himself, without the benefit of counsel, in a court of law against the resources of the state.

After due consideration, the Court agreed with Gideon's position and issued an opinion that he was entitled to a new trial and that at this trial he was entitled to be represented by an attorney. If he could not afford an attorney, the state would have to provide him one free of charge. Gideon was found not guilty in his retrial. Gideon's case established the practice of **indigent defense.** If a person cannot afford an attorney, it is the duty of the state to provide legal counsel.

Once this right was established, it was extended beyond the courtroom. In ***Argersinger v. Hamlin*** (1972), the right to an attorney was extended to include anyone facing a potential sentence of imprisonment, not just felony charges.[55] It was extended to juveniles accused of crimes in ***In re Gault*** (1967).[56] In ***Escobedo v. Illinois*** (1964), the right to an attorney was extended to include the right to have an attorney present during police interrogation.[57]

JUST THE FACTS 5.4

What does the Fifth Amendment to the Constitution say about interrogations and confessions? What are the standards for an admissible confession and a fair lineup? What landmark case established the right to an attorney?

indigent defense Right to have an attorney provided free of charge by the state if a defendant cannot afford one, established in *Gideon v. Wainwright* (1963) and extended in *Argersinger v. Hamlin* (1972), *In re Gault* (1967), and *Escobedo v. Illinois* (1964).

arrest Official taking into police custody of a lawbreaker or suspect with a warrant or probable cause.

Miranda rights Five rights protecting, for example, the right to avoid self-incrimination and the right to an attorney, of which citizens are informed during police arrest and interrogation, established in *Miranda v. Arizona* (1966).

Arrest

THE MAIN IDEA

Procedural laws also govern arrests made by police and define false arrest.

Limitations on police powers of arrest stem from abuses by the English government during the colonial period in the American colonies and in England. As a result of historical suspicion against the government's power to incarcerate citizens on questionable charges or without due process, the powers of the police to make an **arrest** are limited. Law enforcement officers can initiate an arrest only (1) with an arrest warrant issued by the court, (2) when they observe a violation of the law, (3) under exigent circumstances, or (4) when they have probable cause to believe that someone has committed a crime. In many states, the police are limited to arresting people justified by probable cause that someone has committed a crime only when the crime is a felony.

Miranda

In the famous case of ***Miranda v. Arizona*** (1966), the Court issued an opinion in which it summarized all of the rights of a citizen during police arrest and interrogation.[58] Initially, the Court was very strict in requiring that these rights, known as the **Miranda rights,** were read word-for-word to all suspects during arrests and interrogations. Grad-

Figure 5.3

The Miranda Rights

- You have the right to remain silent.
- Anything you say can be used against you in a court of law.
- You have the right to talk to a lawyer and to have a lawyer present when you are being questioned.
- If you want a lawyer before or during questioning but cannot afford to hire a lawyer, one will be appointed to represent you at no cost before any questioning.
- If you answer questions now without a lawyer here, you still have the right to stop answering questions at any time.

✔ Do you understand each of these rights I have explained to you?
✔ Having these rights in mind, do you now wish to answer questions?
✔ Do you now wish to answer questions without a lawyer present?

ually, however, the Miranda protections have been weakened by exceptions. Courts decided that not all Miranda rights had to be read or that they did not have to be read immediately at the beginning of questioning. Controversies surrounding *Miranda* have included concerns of law enforcement that the requirement to read people their rights impedes efficient police work.

Entrapment and Police Intelligence Activities

The U.S. Supreme Court has required that arrest cannot be contingent on **entrapment,** in which the police provide the motivation and means for committing the crime (***Jacobsen v. United States,*** 1992).[59] Entrapment is a defense against criminal charges in court.

Police intelligence activities in the past have sometimes involved entrapment. During the 1950s, 1960s, and early 1970s, many police departments, especially large departments, engaged in active intelligence gathering. Intelligence gathering occurs when the police gather information about people who are not currently under suspicion or investigation for any specific crime. The primary targets for police intelligence units during these decades were (1) suspected members of the Communist Party, defined as a danger to the United States; (2) people engaged in or suspected of engaging in protest against the United States involvement in the Vietnam War; and (3) people engaged in civil rights protests. The federal law enforcement agency most actively engaged in the gathering of intelligence information was the FBI under the directorship of J. Edgar Hoover.

The justification for intelligence gathering was that if a crime occurred, law enforcement already would have sufficient information about citizens to quickly identify suspects and make arrests, thereby protecting the public from subversives and terrorists. However, abuses by the FBI and state and municipal police departments led to public concern, legislative initiatives prohibiting intelligence gathering activities, and Supreme Court cases condemning the targeting of citizens for intelligence operations who were not under suspicion of committing a crime. The full extent of FBI abuses finally became known through the Freedom of Information Act, and police intelligence activities came to be seen as an unjustifiable intrusion on the constitutionally protected privacy of

entrapment Illegal arrest based on criminal behavior for which the police provided both the motivation and the means, tested in *Jacobson v. United States* (1992).

citizens. However, attitudes toward police intelligence changed again dramatically on September 11, 2001. Horrifying terrorist attacks on the World Trade Center in New York City and the Pentagon in Washington, DC, changed the balance between privacy and security, with far-reaching consequences.[60]

JUST THE FACTS 5.5

In what circumstances can an arrest legally be made? What issues surround the "mirandizing" of arrestees and arrests based on police intelligence work and entrapment?

Oversight of Police Practice and Procedure

THE MAIN IDEA

Police accountability is assured through many layers of oversight, both external and internal and both official and public.

Who polices the police? In the United States, oversight of law enforcement operates at all levels of government, throughout the criminal justice system, internally in police departments, in communities by citizens, and by the media. In legislative oversight, for example, bodies such as city councils, state legislatures, and the U.S. Congress pass laws that limit or expand police jurisdiction, create standards, or provide remedies for police practices not acceptable to the community.

The Courts and Prosecutors

In judicial oversight, as you have seen, the courts have great power to influence police behavior and professionalism through rules of evidence and rulings on constitutionality. The prosecuting attorney or district attorney in particular has special power to demand competent, legal behavior from police officers. This power is based on the prosecutor's discretion in whether or not to press charges.

While serving as district attorney of Alameda County, California, **Earl Warren** noted that "[The] district attorney has become the most powerful officer in local government... who declares and determines the law enforcement standards of his county, and, through the exercise of quasi-judicial functions, determines, in the main, who shall be prosecuted and who shall not be subjected to our criminal procedures."[61] Warren, later appointed as chief justice of the United States Supreme Court, refused to prosecute cases in which law enforcement officers had failed to act within the limitations of the law and good practice in the gathering of evidence and conducting of interrogations. Today, all county prosecutors and state attorney generals have the power to correct unprofessional police practices by refusing to file charges when they suspect that the police did not act properly.

Role of the FBI

The FBI is not a national police agency and does not have oversight powers over local and state police. Nevertheless, the FBI performs several valuable services in helping to promote police professionalism and to curb police corruption. The FBI aggressively

criminal justice  in the media

Oversight on the Evening News

The news media is one of the most public, aggressive watchdogs of police abuse of power or unprofessional conduct. The news media in the United States enjoy the freedom to investigate and report on abuses by government agencies. The police, including state and federal law enforcement agencies, are a prominent target of the news media.

The freedom of the United States' news media to report stories critical of law enforcement agents and agencies is not enjoyed by all nations. Prohibitions against news stories critical of the government are not limited to dictatorships. In Egypt, for example, it is a crime for a reporter to publish a news story that is critical of the government or its agents. A journalist who accuses a government agency such as the police of abuse of power can be arrested for "embarrassment of the nation." The punishment for this offense is the loss of one's journalism occupational license. Kenya has many of the characteristics of a democratic government, including the election of its president, yet in Kenya it is a crime to publish news reports that are critical of the president. Reporters, even private citizens, can be arrested for making allegations of abuse of power against the country's chief executive.

There are no such restrictions on members of the press in the United States, and stories of police corruption are front-page and prime-time news. Newspapers and television networks gain more readers and viewers when they expose scandals involving police corruption and often relish printing or broadcasting breaking stories of police brutality, abuse of power, or illegal behavior. Many incidents of police aberrant behavior have been exposed by the news media, affecting public opinion of the police.

■ **What is the role of investigative journalism in oversight of the police? What might be potential problems with media oversight in the United States?**

campaigns for professionalism in law enforcement through training and provides extensive training for state and local police departments at its national academy in Quantico, Virginia. The FBI National Academy annually trains nearly 1,000 police officers from across the country in technical subjects such as criminal investigations, legal topics and case law, and management. In addition, FBI field agents provide free on-site training for hundreds of police departments.

The FBI does not have the power to intervene on its own authority in alleged corruption or abuse of power at the local or state level. However, the FBI will extend assistance to local and state departments on request. The FBI then provides personnel and technical assistance to investigate complaints against police officers. However, when a possible violation of civil rights is involved, the FBI can initiate an investigation or intervene against lower court rulings. In these cases, the FBI promotes professionalism through criminal investigations of alleged illegal activities by law enforcement and through sting operations to uncover corrupt law enforcement and court officers, including judges and lawyers.

The Rodney King incident, in which a police beating of a suspect was captured on video and later aired on national television, was an example of direct FBI intervention. When the officers involved in the Rodney King police brutality case were found not guilty in a California state court, the FBI assumed jurisdiction and brought a case against the officers in federal court for violating King's civil rights. The officers were found guilty and were brought to justice. Another example of direct jurisdiction was an undercover sting operation in the Chicago area in which the FBI obtained evidence that judges and lawyers were conspiring to accept bribes from defendants in exchange for not-guilty verdicts.

Police departments often desire to "police themselves," whereas the public often demands some role in investigating and disciplining officers accused of corrupt practices or misconduct. The major sources of oversight in this debate are (1) the internal affairs unit of the police department, (2) investigative commissions and citizen review boards, and (3) significant community groups such as the news media.

Internal Affairs

One of the most visible means of dealing with unprofessional police behavior is the internal affairs unit of the police department. In response to the call by the public to upgrade the professionalism of police departments, Congress passed legislation in 1967 providing technical and financial assistance to police departments through the newly created office of the Law Enforcement Assistance Administration (LEAA). One of the provisions to be eligible for the generous financial assistance provided in the form of grants by LEAA was that police departments had to have an internal affairs unit to investigate complaints of misconduct.

Internal affairs units are the police who police the police. The internal affairs unit is similar to an investigation unit or detective unit. The officers work in plain clothes, often conduct covert investigations, and are responsible for uncovering violations of the department's rules and criminal laws. As the name implies, the internal affairs unit is completely under the command and control of the police department. The internal affairs unit normally is a small unit of veteran officers, and in the chain of command, it reports directly to the chief of police.

The internal affairs unit investigates alleged violations of departmental rules, complaints of unprofessional and violent behavior, and criminal wrongdoing. This unit reacts to citizen complaints filed with the police department and to allegations of police brutality or misconduct made public by the media or other external agencies. The unit also undertakes investigations on its own initiative, often acting similar to sting operations conducted by detectives. The only difference is that the target of the sting is police officers. Also, the internal affairs unit may randomly target police officers for investigation. This investigation can include following the officer during the course of duty, gathering data about an officer's lifestyle, habits, and relationships.

The internal affairs unit is normally charged with the responsibility of conducting random drug tests. Also, internal affairs units normally investigate serious police incidents involving alleged brutality or corruption. When a police officer is involved in a shooting, for example, the internal affairs unit will conduct an investigation to determine if the police officer was justified in the use of deadly force. If justified, it will decide if the officer followed department rules and policies. The internal affairs report is forwarded to the chief of police, who has the authority to act on the information.

Internal affairs units are controversial in that critics claim they cannot be objective or effective or trustworthy, because of their secrecy and the fact that they pit police officers against their colleagues and, worse, that they are in a position to cover up police misbehavior.[62] It is difficult to establish an external and independent internal affairs unit. Officers for internal affairs are recruited from the department in which they work—and to which they will return after their tour of duty in internal affairs. Officers know that when they leave the unit, they may be ostracized by other officers because of their conduct while in internal affairs, and that new internal affairs investigators may be friends of officers they investigated. Police dislike for the internal affairs unit is reflected in the many degrading names used to refer to internal affairs officers. It is no wonder that police officers find service in internal affairs stressful.

internal affairs units
Detective units within police departments that investigate alleged violations of department rules, citizens' complaints of police conduct, and criminal wrongdoing by police officers.

Finally, who watches the watchers? No one in the department has the responsibility to check the honesty and integrity of the internal affairs officer, another reason that internal affairs officers are rotated through the department. For many, the internal affairs unit represents federal intrusion into local and state powers, because federal grants to police departments are contingent on having internal affairs units. Federal funding with "strings attached" thus has had a significant impact on defining desirable police conduct. Federal grants also have been instrumental in raising training standards, promoting higher educational requirements, achieving better record keeping and the gathering of statistics useful in making decisions, and regulating working conditions. However, federal control of local and state police through funding requirements is seen by some as a violation of Article X of the U.S. Constitution and traditional checks and balances on national government.

Dissatisfaction and distrust of the effectiveness of internal affairs units has led the public to seek other ways to check police misconduct. Citizens are often skeptical of internal affairs investigative units under the complete control of the police. The perception is that citizen participation is often minimized by the internal affairs unit in its investigation.[63] A report of the National Advisory Committee on Criminal Justice Standards and Goals observed that many citizens were reluctant to bring complaints against the police because of fear of reprisal or harassment, and because of complex and cumbersome filing procedures. In some departments, a citizen who filed an unsubstantiated complaint against a police officer could be arrested for making a false report. People called for an independent means of investigating complaints against police officers.

Two approaches used by the community are (1) investigative commissions and (2) citizen review boards. The **investigative commission** is a special municipal, state, or national body appointed to investigate specific complaints and is disbanded after its task is complete. The **citizen review board** is a more permanent oversight body comprised of civilians with the power to inquire into alleged incidents of police misconduct.

Investigative Commissions

One of the earliest government-sponsored investigations of the police was the National Crime Commission in 1925. President Coolidge, alarmed by widespread accusations of police incompetency and abuse of power, appointed a panel of prominent citizens and professionals to inquire into the state of affairs. The **National Crime Commission,** better known as the **Wickersham Commission** after its chairperson, former U.S. Attorney General George W. Wickersham, issued 14 reports. Two of the reports, the "Report on Lawlessness in Law Enforcement" and the "Report on Police," addressed public concerns about the professionalism and competency of the police. The public had come to believe that the police were lax in the enforcement of Prohibition laws and that some were coconspirators with the bootleggers. There were also serious concerns that political agendas and the patronage system had led to the corruption of police departments. The reports of the Wickersham Commission suggested that the public was right.

Investigative commissions are useful in helping to define the extent and nature of police corruption or incompetence and in bringing about change. For example, the 1972, **Knapp Commission** reported that an important source of New York City police corruption was control of illegal gambling, narcotics, loan-sharking, and prostitution. It also found that not all police officers were equally corrupt. The 1994 **Mollen Commission** in New York City pointed out that by keeping silent about crimes of other officers, the police were acting as criminal gangs. Crime commission findings help shape anticorruption strategies, which must address the diverse motivations of officers as well as opportunities for crime. However, although crime commissions can publish critical reports that attract public attention and may affect public policy, they have no power to directly punish or correct the police departments or law enforcement officers they investigate.

At the local level, most police departments in medium to large cities are governed by a **police commission**—a board of civilians appointed by the mayor or city council

investigative commission Municipal, state, or national body appointed as needed to investigate specific complaints about police behavior, such as the Wickersham, Knapp, and Mollen crime commissions.

citizen review board Permanent oversight body comprised of civilians with the power to inquire into alleged police misconduct.

police commission Board of civilians appointed by the mayor or city council to act in an oversight role.

Figure 5.4

Major Investigative Commissions

Year	Crime Commission	Context	Purpose	Results
1919	Chicago Crime Commission	Progressive era and concerns about urban crime	Improve operations of the criminal justice system to reduce crime.	Similar investigations in 24 states. Improvements in police organization, administration, technology, and training. Creation of the National Crime Commission in 1925.
1931	Wickersham Commission (National Commission on Law Observance and Law Enforcement)	Prohibition era and concerns about violations of the 18th Amendment	Determine why Prohibition enforcement was breaking down	Machinery for enforcing federal laws found inadequate. Federal agents were engaged in corruption. Self-policing units established.
1957	U.S. Commission on Civil Rights (established by Congress in 1957)	Civil Rights era and concerns about violations of the 14th Amendment	Report on investigations into complaints of police misconduct in violating citizens' civil and human rights, including racial discrimination	Recommendations for recruitment and training of new officers, greater oversight of police, and external review of complaints of abuse. 1981 report, *Who Is Guarding the Guardians?* Related studies in Boston, Chicago, and Los Angeles.

to act in an oversight role. Usually, the most important functions of the police commission are to conduct a search for the job of chief of police and to call for a chief's resignation. The idea behind the police commission is to demand accountability of the police department. However, in reality, a police commission with a political agenda can turn the police department, including the position of chief of police, into a political patronage system. In such cases, the police department, including the chief of police, becomes responsive to the political agenda and the city commissioners instead of promoting professionalism in policing.

Citizen Review Boards

The citizen police review board is intended to provide both oversight and justice, determining punishment when police misconduct is proved. The primary functions of all

Figure 5.4

Major Investigative Commissions (*Continued*)

Year	Crime Commission	Context	Purpose	Results
1967-1973	National Crime Commissions	Protest era and public concern about crime rate, civil unrest, and public safety	Find ways to meet demand for more and better police services	Law Enforcement Assistance Administration (LEAA) of 1968 spent more than $6 million on crime control programs and college education for police officers.
1972	Knapp Commission	Sen. Kefauver's earlier (1957) investigations into organized crime, public concerns about vice control, and dramatic case of Frank Serpico of the NYPD	Determine why local law enforcement was breaking down. Investigate charges of institutionalized corruption in the NYPD.	Officers were taking bribes for not arresting prostitutes and gamblers. State Special Prosecutor post created to prosecute officers for corruption. Similar investigations in other cities and states.
1992	Mollen Commission	Public concerns about police corruption related to the war on drugs	Investigate charges of police involvement in drug trafficking in New York through police brutality and a "code of silence"	Officers prosecuted for protecting and assisting drug traffickers, drug trafficking, unlawful searches and seizures, perjury, and falsifying records. Internal Affairs reorganized. Similar investigations in PA, NJ, Washington, DC, and other states.

police review boards is to receive complaints by citizens regarding misconduct of police officers, to evaluate the charges, and to recommend sanctions. Boards can review complaints involving alleged violations of departmental procedures, criminal law, civility, or use of excessive force against citizens. Each community is responsible for determining if there is a need for a police review board in their community and the type of board they will adopt. Thirty-two of the 50 largest U.S. cities have instituted civilian review procedures.[64] The Police Executive Research Forum and the powerful International Association of Chiefs of Police have expressed interest in promoting police review

The National Association of Civilian Oversight of Law Enforcement maintains a roster of state resources for civilian oversight of the police at http://www.nacole.org/Roster_Oversight.html. ■

boards. In 1985, the **International Association for Civilian Oversight of Law Enforcement** was established to develop civilian oversight.

Police review boards are of three types: (1) the citizen monitor model, (2) the citizen input model, and (3) the citizen review model.[65] The models represent a continuum from minimum to maximum oversight. The model providing the least oversight is the **citizen monitor model.** The members who review complaints against police officers are civilian employees of the police department. Boards operating under this model have no power to operate independently of the police department. Under the **citizen input model** non-sworn police department personnel have the power to receive and investigate complaints independent of the police department, but they do not have the power to recommend sanctions against police officers when complaints are substantiated. That is to say, a citizen can file a complaint directly with the review board and not the police department or internal affairs unit. However, the review board cannot punish officers found to have engaged in improper conduct.

The model in which civilian oversight has the greatest power is the **citizen review model,** in which members of the police review board are not employees of the police department but are appointed by a governmental agency. The members of the review board have their own budget and personnel, do not answer to the police department, and are not under the authority of the police department. The review board is empowered to investigate complaints independently of the police department or the internal affairs unit, to hold a hearing, to summon witnesses, and to review evidence.

citizen monitor model Minimum oversight of police by civilian employees of the police department who monitor complaints.

citizen input model Moderate oversight of police by non-sworn personnel who investigate complaints independently of the police department.

citizen review model Maximum oversight of police by civilians appointed by a governmental agency that does not answer to the police department.

If a complaint is substantiated, the review board has the power to forward to the police administration recommendations for sanctions. The review board can recommend disciplinary action but cannot enforce its recommendations. Thus, the police administrator who chooses to ignore the findings of the review board may do so. The only enforcement power of the review board lies in public and political pressure that may result if the recommendations of the board are ignored. The civilian review model has grown in popularity over the other two types of review boards in the last three decades.

Opponents of the civilian review model claim that these boards interfere with the crime-fighting effectiveness of the police and cause antagonism between the police and the public. Also, police officers may close ranks in support of accused officers because of perceived unfairness, bias, or naïvete of a civilian police review board. Proponents argue that citizen review board actions often are preferable to seeking redress through

Civilian review boards evaluate claims of misconduct by municipal and state police. However, civilian review of federal law enforcement officers does not exist at present. Complaints of misconduct by federal law enforcement officers are investigated by administrative staff or by Congress and are handled though criminal or civil court action. Why is the use of civilian review boards controversial? What are some alternative forms of public oversight of the police?

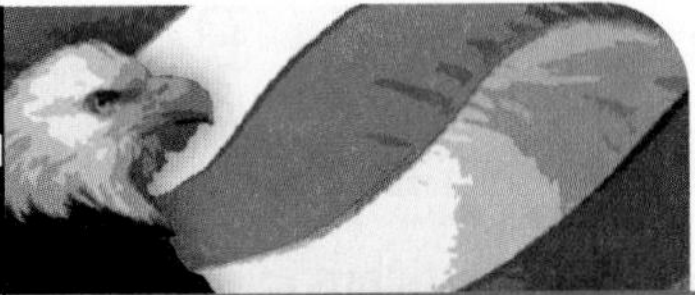

criminal justice in the world

Oversight of the Police in Britain and France

The use of police review boards is not uniquely American. Their use by other countries depends on the relationship between the police and the citizens of the country. In countries like Japan and Sweden, where the police enjoy strong public support and police corruption and brutality are rare, there is little or no public demand for the adoption of police review boards. In Sweden, for example, 80 percent of the respondents of a survey indicated that they did not think that the police used excessive force or abused their authority in the performance of their duties.

France has a national police force and has found that it is easier to regulate police misconduct through central administrative rule, the French Code of Criminal Procedures, and the French Penal Code. The office of inspector general of police is responsible for investigating all allegations of misconduct by members of the National Police and a similar office exists to investigate misconduct by members of the National Gendarmerie. Given the highly centralized nature of the French police, misbehavior is easier to regulate without civilian participation.

Britain has a national but comparatively decentralized police system. The Police Act of 1976 established the Police Complaints Board to handle complaints of police misconduct. The Board is composed of citizens and magistrates (lower court judges). Citizens can file complaints with the Police Complaints Board or directly with the police. The police investigate the complaint regardless of where it is filed. The Board can recommend sanctions, but only the chief constable (similar to the chief of police in the United States) has the power to impose recommended sanctions.

The British have similar complaints about their Police Complaints Board as Americans do about police review boards. These boards are seen as reactive only, limited in scope of inquiry to individual incidents of misconduct, and conservative in finding officers guilty as charged and imposing sanctions.

■ **What factors do you think might account for national differences in policing the police? What are some advantages and disadvantages of centralized oversight of police conduct?**

the courts and that civilian boards provide a realistic check and balance of police actions. While civilian oversight boards have increased, there is no evidence that they are having a great impact on police behaviors.[66] Few complaints result in actual disciplinary action, with most review boards finding in favor of the complainant only 4 to 6 percent of the time. In addition, police unionism can seriously impact the ability to administer the recommended disciplinary action of an oversight board. For example, in a 1995 case in Honolulu, Hawaii, a district court judge blocked the release of the names of disciplined police officers, although disclosure was permitted under state law. A clause in the police union's Memorandum of Agreement between the city and police prohibited the public release of the names of disciplined officers.

JUST THE FACTS 5.6

How do legislatures, the courts, and prosecutors have oversight over the police? How do government agencies such as the FBI influence police behavior? What are the roles of investigative commissions and internal affairs units? What are the different ways that civilians and the media have oversight over the police?

Prosecution of Police Officers

THE MAIN IDEA

Law enforcement officers in all jurisdictions can be prosecuted in criminal court, and police departments and officers can be named in civil suits.

As a nation that practices the rule of law, all citizens are subject to the laws of the land, including police officers. While police officers are the agents who enforce the laws of the land, they are also liable for punishment if they violate the laws that they are charged to enforce. Police officers who violate the law can be charged, prosecuted, and convicted in local, state, and federal courts.

Police Corruption

Corruption among police can take many forms, including drug dealing, bribery, extortion, or other felony crimes. Police officers also may be involved in conspiracies to falsify testimony, tamper with evidence, or brutalize suspects. Reports of corruption in big-city American police departments—with allegations of torture, beatings, secrecy, and death of suspects in custody—are shocking to most Americans. For example, an Amnesty International report in June 1996 focused on reports of police misconduct, corruption, brutality, deaths, and cover-ups in the New York Police Department (NYPD). This human rights watchdog organization found more than 90 cases of excessive use of force by NYPD officers, resulting in ill-treatment of suspects, deaths in custody, and unjustified shootings. Amnesty International alleged that police brutality and unjustifiable force were widespread problems that administrators and the Internal Affairs Division deliberately ignored. Police officers simply made false charges, such as "resisting arrest" against innocent victims of their brutality to cover up the abuse.

Police corruption also can take the form of the so-called Dirty Harry syndrome, named for a Clint Eastwood movie in which a city cop takes the law into his own hands to keep the bad guys from getting off the hook. Sometimes it may appear that the law protects the guilty and punishes the victim. Murderers may go free on technicalities, rapists may stay out of jail because of loopholes in the law, and child molesters may escape punishment because of court misgivings about police aggression in pursuit of suspected pedophiles. In the **Dirty Harry syndrome,** an officer feels that he or she knows best how to fight crime and that the public and the criminal justice system cannot be trusted to do the job. Tragically, the officer thus feels justified in breaking the law or violating constitutional rights in the belief that the end justifies the means.

Survey documented examples of police corruption in the United States in the 1990s at http://www.drugwarfacts.org/corrupt.htm. ■

Criminal Prosecution

At the local level, oversight of the police through prosecution for violation of local laws is fairly rare and ineffective. The primary reason is that local police officers are the primary agents who enforce local (city and county) laws, which are usually misdemeanor violations. It is uncommon to find cases of local police officers arresting fellow officers for violations of misdemeanor offenses. Thus, to a certain degree, local police officers often appear to be immune from prosecution for violation of municipal ordinances, such as laws against speeding. However, it is not uncommon for city officers to receive speeding tickets from highway patrol officers, officers in other states, or officers in other cities. For example, the enforcement of the prohibition against carrying concealed weapons is frequently enforced against off-duty police officers in out-of-state jurisdictions.

Dirty Harry syndrome
Form of police corruption in which police officers take the law into their own hands in the belief that they are achieving justice.

Oversight through arrest for criminal conduct is more common when it comes to state agents arresting local police or federal agents arresting local and state police. Federal and state police agencies have often used undercover operations for the express purpose of catching local police officers engaging in criminal or unconstitutional behavior. The FBI and the Drug Enforcement Agency utilize this oversight power more than any other agency. Often, these agencies conduct criminal surveillance and arrests at the invitation of local and state police departments.

Local police administrators have a genuine concern to rid their department of corrupt police officers. When they suspect police officers in their department are performing illegal behaviors such as drug dealing, bribery, or serious felony crime, and they have been unsuccessful in gathering sufficient evidence to prove these charges, police administrators may invite a federal (or state) police agency to help them with the investigation.

If a police officer is convicted of a criminal offense, he or she does not receive any special consideration by the court. Some argue that, if anything, the officer receives a more severe sentence than the "average" person because of the expectation that police officers should demonstrate greater moral behavior because of their position. If convicted of a crime and sentenced to serve time in prison, the officer will have to serve time in a state or federal prison. Thus, while it is rare to correct illegal or corrupt behavior of police officers through arrest and criminal prosecution, the threat of serving time in prison is a great deterrent to the average police officer.

In 1999, LAPD officer Rafael Perez reached a plea agreement with prosecutors in the Rampart police corruption scandal. Perez admitted to assaulting suspects, violating suspects' civil rights, filing false police reports, and planting evidence. He also implicated his partner, Nino Durden, and 69 other officers in misconduct. Since that time, more than 100 convictions were overturned, 12 officers were suspended, 7 resigned, 5 were terminated, and 6 had criminal charges filed against them. The first criminal case brought against Rampart cops came to trial in October 2000, in which three officers were found guilty. Durden reached a plea agreement in March 2001.

Civil Suits against the Police

Before the mid-1980s local, state, and federal law enforcement officers were protected from civil law suits for harm done to individuals in the line of duty. Under the doctrine of **sovereign immunity,** local, state, and federal governments claimed that they were "above the law" and thus could not be sued for tort actions in a civil court. The doctrine of sovereign immunity dates back to the early kings of England. In the United States, the doctrine was based on the philosophy that any monetary award against the government essentially punished all citizens, because the government would have to collect taxes and tariffs from innocent citizens to pay for any award made by the court. Thus, civil suits that sought monetary awards were prohibited. As modern legal philosophy led to the erosion of the concept of sovereign immunity, cities, states, and even the federal government relaxed their laws prohibiting civil suits. Today, citizens can sue law enforcement officers.[67]

Local and state law enforcement agents have more liability in a civil law suit than do federal law enforcement agents. State courts allow citizens to bring suit for negligent actions by officers that result in harm or injury to the citizen. The most common law suits are based on the allegations of **negligent practices:** negligent hiring, negligent training, negligent supervision, or negligent retention of personnel.

sovereign immunity The historic claim of local, state, and federal governments that they were "above the law" and thus could not be sued in civil court.

negligent practices Negligent hiring, training, supervision, or retention of personnel as grounds for civil suits against the police.

NEGLIGENT TRAINING, SUPERVISION, AND RETENTION The desire of local and state police departments to screen out unqualified candidates is motivated by the desire to hire the best-qualified people but also to reduce legal liability. Departments

table 5.1 Civil Suits against the Police: Federal District Court Awards against Police, 1978–1996

Civil Rights Violations	Average Awards ($)
False arrest	90,312
Excessive force	178,878
Assault/battery	117,013
Unlawful searches	98,954
Inadequate supervision	119,114
Strip search	24,329
Malicious prosecution	53,306
Inadequate training	105,450
Vehicular pursuit	1,250,000
Average awards against police departments	118,698

Some Facts

- In 1976, citizens filed 13,400 suits against police.
- By 1981, suits cost $780 billion nationally.
- Average suits filed annually today: 30,000.
- About 40% of police liability suits are for misconduct.
- Police lose only about 8% of civil suits filed.
- Between 1987 and 1991, New York paid $44 million in claims for police misconduct.
- In 1991 alone, the LAPD paid $13 million.
- Between 1994 and 1997, 508 law enforcement agents were convicted of corruption in cases investigated by the FBI, about half drug-related (and many more in noncorruption cases).

Source: Bureau of Justice Statistics; *Sourcebook of Criminal Justice Statistics*, 2000.

can be liable if they are found to have been negligent in their hiring process, the training an officer receives, or the retention of an officer who is unfit for duty.[68] If a person with characteristics that render him or her unfit for police duties is hired or retained, and if that person commits a tort or injury on another, the police department can be held liable for the officer's actions. In performing their duties, police officers are considered to be acting on behalf of their employer. By the principle of *respondeat superior,* or responding to one's superior (boss), if an officer injures someone, the department is considered liable for that injury. The injured party can sue both the individual officer and the police department. To minimize their liability to lawsuits alleging negligent hiring, negligent training, and/or negligent retention, police departments have adopted stringent hiring standards, training standards, and supervision practices.

SECTION 1983 LAWSUITS A problem that arose with civil lawsuits against local police officers and departments was the inability of the plaintiff to obtain a judgment against the police. Juries were reluctant to award large damage claims to plaintiffs, because a large cash award ultimately would have to be paid for by the citizens of the community through increased taxes. A solution was to bring the case to a federal court, because federal juries would be more impartial. Plaintiff's attorneys used a federal law passed in 1871 to protect freed slaves from being denied their constitutional rights. Title 42, Section 1983 of the United States Code of Federal Court declared it a tort to deny anyone a constitutionally protected right "acting under color of state law."[69] The law was aimed at prohibiting restrictions being placed by state and local governments on freed slaves that prevented them from voting. Over a hundred years later, innovative plaintiffs' attorneys successfully argued in court that Section 1983 applied to local and state law enforcement officers who denied citizens constitutionally protected rights acting under the color of state law. The federal courts accepted this argument, opening a new avenue for pursuing tort actions against police. Cases filed under this federal law are called **Section 1983 lawsuits.**

LAWSUITS AGAINST FEDERAL AGENTS During this period, local and state law enforcement agents could be sued in state court and federal court, but federal law enforcement agents were still protected from civil suits. Federal agents were protected against tort actions in a state court by the fact that the federal government claimed that federal agents acting "under color of law" were immune from civil liability in a state court. It was asserted and accepted by the courts that federal agents were only liable for tort actions in a federal court. The problem was the lack of a legal venue to bring a civil suit against a federal law enforcement agent.

A favorable ruling for the plaintiff in a 1971 federal case, ***Bivens v. Six Unknown Federal Agents,*** opened up the federal courts for suits against federal government officials for denial of constitutional rights.[70] However, **Bivens actions,** as they are called, restrict the lawsuit to the individual law enforcement agents, and not the U.S. government. The plaintiff cannot seek damages against the United States or its agencies.[71]

Most lawsuits against federal law enforcement agents are governed by the Federal Employees Liability Reform and Tort Compensation Act of 1988. This act, commonly known as the **Westfall Act,** provides for broad immunity against civil suits for federal government agencies and their employees. Under the act, if a federal employee is certified by the attorney general to have been acting within the scope of his or her office or employment at the time of the incident out of which the claim arose, the United States can be substituted for the employee as the defendant.

Some citizens who have won suits against law enforcement agents and agencies have received substantial awards. The philosophy behind large monetary awards is that they will act as a financial deterrent against police misconduct, brutality, and unprofessional behavior. When police departments have to pay out millions of dollars for civil judgments, the citizens of the community will demand and be willing to pay for corrective actions to prevent future liability. However, as a check on police misconduct, tort liability places a heavy burden of time and attention on the individual citizen seeking redress. The financial burden of finding an attorney to handle the civil suit is the responsibility of the citizen, and civil suits may take years to make their way through the courts.[72]

Section 1983 lawsuits Civil suits based on a federal law making it illegal for anyone "acting under color of state law" to deny a citizen's constitutional rights.

Bivens actions Civil suits against federal law enforcement agents for denial of constitutional rights.

JUST THE FACTS 5.7

What measures have been taken to deal with police brutality and police corruption? How effective is criminal prosecution in deterring police crimes? Can a police officer and his or her police department be sued by a citizen? What are the most common claims in civil suits against police?

conclusion:

Police Accountability

During the 1960s, police departments were frequently described as "closed societies." Phrases such as "the blue curtain" described the isolation of police from the public and the solidarity of the police against public scrutiny. Although the blue curtain has not disappeared, it has definitely parted. Both the public and police administrators have taken steps to make the operation of the police more open to view and more accountable. The Police Executive Research Forum and the powerful International Association of Chiefs of Police have promoted police review boards. In 1985, the International Association for Civilian Oversight of Law Enforcement was established to promote interaction among individuals involved in civilian oversight.

The police have modified their behaviors in response to changing social values. There is still the need for oversight, however, as there will always be police officers who abuse their power, and there will always be differences of opinion between the police and the public regarding what constitutes professional and acceptable law enforcement practice. And while police are concerned with efficiency in fighting crime and maintaining social order, the public is also concerned with preserving constitutionally protected rights. These concerns often clash. Practices that would promote effective law enforcement are the very practices that could threaten citizens' rights.

As a result, the oversight of the police is an incredibility complex business involving many different and diverse participants, such as law makers, police administrators, internal affairs units, the news media, the courts, investigative commissions, citizens' review boards, and so on. No one voice speaks authoritatively to the problem of police professionalism and abuse, and no one standard defines acceptable professional practice for all time. In the future, as in the past, the desire to be free of the fear of crime is counterbalanced by the desire to be free of abuses of police power.

Chapter Summary

- Rules of evidence influence police procedures in conducting searches and seizures, gathering evidence, making arrests, and conducting interrogations.
- The exclusionary rule, which defines legal versus tainted evidence, was extended to state as well as federal jurisdictions in the landmark case of *Mapp v. Ohio*.
- The Fourth Amendment protects Americans from unreasonable search and seizure.
- Exceptions to the exclusionary rule include search incident to lawful arrest, plain-view searches, consent to search, and the search of automobiles. The right to conduct a pat-down search of a person without probable cause was established through *Terry v. Ohio*.

- Other exceptions to the exclusionary rule concern public safety, fleeing felons, good faith mistakes, and some intelligence activities, such as wiretaps.
- The Fifth Amendment protects Americans from self-incrimination, such that confessions may not be obtained through torture, lies, deceptions, unfair lineups, or denial of civil rights.
- Rules of evidence also define lawful arrest, which may not involve entrapment. The landmark case of *Miranda v. Arizona* has had a significant impact on police practice during arrests and interrogations.
- Factors influencing police professionalism and accountability are checks and balances in the criminal justice system, criminal and civil prosecutions of police who break the law, and government agencies with preventative oversight functions, such as the FBI.
- The legislative branch of government has oversight powers through the ability to pass and amend laws, such as regulation of wiretaps.
- The courts, especially the U.S. Supreme Court, have indirect oversight power through rulings relating to the exclusionary rule and search and seizure, interrogation, and arrest.
- Prosecuting attorneys or district attorneys can refuse to prosecute cases if they suspect the police have acted improperly.
- The FBI provides professional training, investigates alleged illegal activities by law enforcement, and assists local and state agencies in investigations of police conduct.
- The internal affairs unit is the primary means that the police department uses to hold its police officers accountable.
- Local, state, and national investigative commissions are formed periodically to examine the behavior of the police.
- Citizen review boards have been developed to provide citizen oversight of police behavior. Three models of citizen review boards are the citizen monitor model, the citizen input model, and the citizen review model.
- Local, state, and federal police officers can be arrested, tried, and convicted for criminal behaviors and can be sued in civil court. The most common grounds for civil suits against police departments are negligent training, supervision, and retention.

Vocabulary Review

arrest, 156
Bivens actions, 169
Carroll Doctrine, 147
citizen input model, 164
citizen monitor model, 164
citizen review board, 161
citizen review model, 164
clear and present danger, 151
deadly force, 151
Dirty Harry syndrome, 166
entrapment, 157
exclusionary rule, 143
fleeing felon doctrine, 151
Fruit of the Poisoned Tree Doctrine, 144
good faith exception, 152
indigent defense, 156
internal affairs units, 160
investigative commission, 161
Miranda rights, 156
negligent practices, 167
pat-down search, 147
plain-view search, 146
police commission, 161
police lineups, 155
probable cause, 145
procedural law, 142
public safety exception, 150
rules of evidence, 143
search incident to lawful arrest, 146
Section 1983 lawsuits, 169
self-incrimination, 153
sovereign immunity, 167
warrant, 145
wiretapping, 152

Names and Events to Remember

Argersinger v. Hamlin, 156
Ashcraft v. Tennessee, 153
Bivens v. Six Unknown Federal Agents, 169
Brown v. Mississippi, 153

Carroll v. United States, 147
Communications Assistance for Law Enforcement Act of 1994, 152
Earl Warren, 158
Electronic Communications Privacy Act of 1986, 152
Escobedo v. Illinois, 156
Fifth Amendment, 153
Florida v. Jimeno, 146
Fourth Amendment, 145
Gideon v. Wainwright, 155
Harris v. United States, 146
In re Gault, 156
International Association for Civilian Oversight of Law Enforcement, 164
Jacobsen v. United States, 157
Katz v. United States, 152
Knapp Commission, 161
Leyra v. Denno, 154
Mapp v. Ohio, 144
Miranda v. Arizona, 156
Mollen Commission, 161
National Crime Commission, 161
Olmstead v. United States, 152
Silverthorne Lumber Co. v. United States, 144
Star Chamber, 153
Telecommunications Act of 1996, 152
Tennessee v. Garner, 151
Terry v. Ohio, 147
Weeks v. United States, 143
Westfall Act, 169
Wickersham Commission, 161
Wolf v. Colorado, 144

Think about This

1. Assume that Mr. Green is a drug dealer who has been convicted twice for sales of drugs to minors. A police officer who knows of Mr. Green's past criminal record sees Mr. Green driving down the street. Mr. Green is not violating any traffic laws and his vehicle is properly registered, insured, and licensed. The police officer pulls Mr. Green over on a "hunch" that he may get "lucky." When the officer pulls Mr. Green over, Mr. Green behaves in a "suspicious" manner. The police officer asks for permission to search Mr. Green's car and Mr. Green refuses. The police officer takes the keys to the car and opens the trunk. The police officer finds over $1 million in heroin. From this example, it is obvious that Mr. Green was engaged in illegal behavior. Should the police officer be punished? Should the drugs be allowed as evidence in a trial?
2. Where would you draw the line between public safety and personal privacy? Do you think existing case laws surrounding the Fourth and Fifth Amendments to the Constitution sufficiently protect citizens' rights to privacy and due process? What, if any, exceptions to these rights do you think are justifiable for protecting public safety? What criteria should law enforcement officers use when abridging citizens' civil liberties? Are law enforcement officers ever justified in abridging citizens' civil rights?

ContentSelect

Go to the ContentSelect web site and conduct a search using the keyword phrase "ethics training." Read the *FBI Law Enforcement Bulletin,* "Ethics Training: Using Officers' Dilemmas," written by criminal justice instructors Joycelyn Pollock and Ronald Becker. On the basis of this article, answer the following questions.

1. How is "ethical dilemma" defined? What are the characteristics of ethical dilemmas?
2. What five elements do police officers everywhere commonly identify as the central code of ethics for being a good police officer?
3. What are the five most common types of ethical dilemmas that police officers face?
4. What is police discretion, and how does it relate to ethical choice? What is a specific example of an ethical dilemma involving police discretion?

5. What are some examples of ethical dilemmas officers may face involving their duty, honesty, and loyalty? What factors can complicate decisions in these areas?

6. What is a gratuity? How can gratuities and gifts become serious issues for both police officers and police departments or agencies?

7. How can ethical dilemmas be resolved? What are four ethical frameworks officers can use to resolve ethical dilemmas? Which framework or combination of frameworks would you use?

1920s Police Patrol
How did modern American policing develop?

Homicide Investigation
What are the roles and functions of the police?

Highway Patrol
How does police work differ at the local and state levels?

Federal Law Enforcement
What are the goals of federal law enforcement agencies?

Campus Police
What needs do private and special police forces address?

Community Policing
How do police relate to the communities they serve?

The Police

The development of policing in the United States has followed European models and unique developments in American nationhood, government, and law. The story of policing is a story of professionalism and leadership in order maintenance and crime control, and it is a story of accountability to the communities police serve.

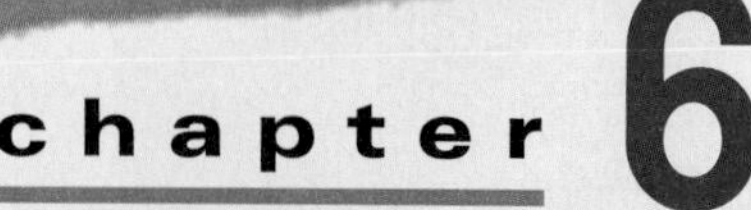

chapter 6 Historical Development of American Policing

outline

arning
ojectives

er reading this chapter
will understand:

- low American policing has been influenced and shaped by various historical events.
- The importance of Sir Robert Peel's London Metropolitan Police as the prototype for most modern police departments.
- Regional developments in policing in the American colonies and during the 1800s.
- How social values influenced the types of police agencies that evolved in the United States.
- The factors that revolutionized policing beginning in the early twentieth century.
- The origins of federal law enforcement agencies and why they differ from local and state police agencies.

Police Look for Shooting—Sniper Link

FALLS CHURCH, Va.—A dragnet covered suburban Washington on Tuesday as authorities searched for a cream-colored van spotted moments after a woman was killed in a mall parking lot by a single bullet to the head. The shooting led to fears that the sniper terrorizing the area had killed a ninth person.

Police swiftly closed highways . . . around Falls Church, about 10 miles west of the nation's capital.

Members of a Maryland task force investigating the sniper attacks were conferring with Fairfax County authorities to see if the shooting was the work of the sniper who has killed eight people and wounded two in the last two weeks. . . .

The victim was felled by a single shot about 9:15 p.m. as she stood in the parking lot of the blocks-long shopping center. . . . Shopper Raymond Massas said he "heard one shot. Not very loud, like a snap. After that I heard people start panicking." Two police helicopters circled the scene as bystanders looked on.

"It hasn't been this frightening since 9/11," said Bob Bakley as he stared across Route 50. . . .

Many schools in the region remained under lockdown Monday, meaning outdoor recess and physical education classes were canceled, and students were kept indoors all day. One of the sniper's targets was a 13-year-old boy who was wounded outside his school.

"Everyone is edgy," said Montgomery County Police Chief Charles Moose, who is heading the investigation. "People are hearing things that may normally be overlooked."

Earlier Monday, the longest lull yet in the Washington sniper's killing spree brought little relief as jittery residents flooded police with calls after hearing a car backfire, firecrackers or breaking glass.

"I'm looking around for every white van I see," said Richard Spears, who was mowing grass at James Monroe High School in Fredericksburg, Va. "It makes you a little leery."

President Bush said the "cold-blooded" attacks have made him sick to his stomach. "I weep for those who have lost their loved ones," he said. "The idea of moms taking their kids to school and sheltering them from a potential sniper attack is not the America that I know."

—From "Police Look for Shooting—Sniper Link," reprinted with permission of The Associated Press.

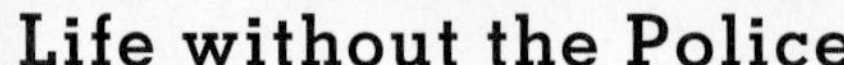

introduction:

Life without the Police

Crime and fear of violent crime are not unique to Falls Church, Virginia. In cities across the United States, crime is a major concern of citizens. The wave of spree shootings in and around Washington, D.C. in October, 2002, made citizens afraid to do everyday tasks such as fill up their cars with gas at service stations. When the spree shooter wounded a child dropped off at school, parents suddenly feared for their children's safety in a place that they had believed, just the day before, kept their children out of harm's way. In the face of such violence, citizens are comforted to some degree, however, by the fact that they can call 9-1-1 to summon the services of professionals trained to deal with crime. Perhaps it is difficult to imagine a time, a society, without the police. But one does not have to go back very far to find a time when the United Sates had no local police, no state police, not even the Federal Bureau of Investigation (FBI).

What would you do if you were to be awakened late one night by a noise that sounded like someone was breaking into your house, or if your automobile was stolen while you were shopping at the mall, or if you saw a suspicious person loitering around a public park where children were playing? One of the first responses of many people would be the desire to contact the police. People call the police because they believe that the police are trained and equipped to handle these kinds of problems and that the police have the authority to do something. Most people believe that it is the responsibility of the police to fight crime and maintain order. If there were no police, what would you do? Who would have the training and authority to do something?

Fifty years ago, people could summon the police to assist them, but without the benefit of the 9-1-1 telephone system. A hundred years ago, the police were there to render assistance and crime fighting, but telephones to summon them were not in use and police arrived on foot or horseback. In the early 1800s, there were no full-time, uniformed police to call for help.

The creation of the police was an inevitable product of the modern industrial state.[1] The employment of full-time, paid, uniformed personnel by cities to fight crime and perform public services is a relatively new social experiment in public order and justice. The first full-time, paid, uniformed police officers did not begin patrolling the streets of metropolitan London, England, until 1829. The first similar London-style police officer would not become common in American cities until the end of the nineteenth century.

Problems of social order and crime fighting were minimal in a predominately rural, agrarian society with limited mobility of citizens in the few major cities. The problems of social order and crime were significant concerns of the citizenry nevertheless. Before the advent of governmentally employed, full-time, uniformed police officers, the streets were not as safe, and life and property were less secure.[2] Tracking down criminals was primarily the responsibility of the person who had been victimized. The lack of police clearly affected personal liberties, commerce, and public order. One measure of the success and necessity of the police is that in just one century, society has come to depend on the police to maintain civility. The police have augmented, perhaps even to some degree replaced, other social institutions of order maintenance, such as family, religion, schools, and work.[3]

The contemporary role of the police is "to control those who cannot conform . . . , as well as to remind others of the cost of nonconformity to the accepted norms."[4] The police are perceived as authorized, trained, equipped, and omnipotently able to troubleshoot the problems of society. The role of the police has developed rapidly during the twentieth century and continues to evolve. This chapter examines the historical role of the police and points out how this role continues to change and expand as it is shaped by social expectations and public policy.

A Short History of the Evolution of Policing

THE MAIN IDEA

American methods of maintaining social order and dealing with crime have roots in ancient Europe.

American policing has influences and outcomes that are significantly different from those of other countries. All cultural groups and nations have had to find solutions for maintaining social order, but the main influences of American policing can be traced to England, Europe, and the Roman Empire.[5]

For documents, photos, and on-line activities on the history of policing, go to http://www.ablongman.com/criminaljustice. ■

September 29, 1829, is a landmark in the history of policing as it marked the beginning of Sir Robert Peel's London Metropolitan Police, the first documented, full-time, uniformed, paid police department in the world. The formation of the London Metropolitan Police and the subsequent adoption of this style of policing by most other nations in Western Europe and America was preceded by events stretching back to the Roman Empire and order maintenance during the Middle Ages. Many of the terms and concepts of contemporary policing, such as *sheriff, marshal,* and *constable,* can be traced to this heritage. The term *police* has its roots in the Greek word *poli,* or "city."[6]

Law and Order in the Ancient World

Civilization requires social order. Thus, even the oldest civilizations had the modern-day equivalent of civil and criminal laws to govern the behavior of its citizens. The **Code of Hammurabi** from the Babylonian period is the oldest surviving set of laws. More than 4,000 years ago (2050 B.C.), King Hammurabi of Babylon issued 282 laws regulating civil and criminal behavior.[7] These criminal and civil laws were carved in stone and erected in a public place for the citizens to read. These were the laws of the land in Babylonian civilization, and they prohibited acts similar to those prohibited in contemporary laws. For example, it was against the law to strike and kill someone. It was against the law to steal. It was against the law to try to obtain property by fraud, such as moving a survey marker defining the ownership of property. Punishments for violations of the law included fines, corporal punishment, and death. Other civilizations, including those of the Sumerians, Greeks, Hebrews, Egyptians, Persians, and Romans, also had laws to regulate citizen behavior. None of these civilizations, however, had a police department as we know it. Without a police department, order maintenance and crime fighting were the responsibility of individual citizens, extended families, religious leaders, and the military.

Code of Hammurabi
Earliest example of legal codes defining crimes and civil offenses.

Most people in the ancient world lived in rural agrarian communities and enjoyed little mobility. Few people traveled more than a day's walking distance from the place of

What special military units did Rome and other ancient states have to maintain order and enforce laws? Whose interests did these special military units serve? In ancient Rome, the office of magistrate reduced the role of the military in civilian law enforcement. The office of magistrate also made law enforcement a matter of local concern in a far-flung, diverse empire. Praetors, with the aid of their assistants, quaestores, investigated crimes, made arrests, interpreted laws, and acted as judges. As conquerors, the Romans influenced the development of policing in Europe, including England.

their birth. In such societies, disputes among neighbors or civil or criminal offenses were usually settled through some form of community mediation. Punishment by imprisonment was virtually unknown, as the goal of justice was to restore the peace of the community and minimize the loss to the victim or to punish the offender.[8]

In the ancient world, it was often difficult to separate religion, law, and crime; there was little or no separation between church and state in such societies. Thus, religious laws and religious leaders held prominent roles in everyday life, including the law, and religious leaders played a central role in maintaining public order and administering justice. When mediation failed or religious leaders could not exercise sufficient influence to resolve a dispute, the parties frequently simply turned to violence to resolve the dispute on the principle that "might makes right."

Ancient governments participated in maintaining public order only when a disturbance appeared to threaten the peace of state or kingdom and when actions appeared to disrupt commerce, the primary source of income for a country. Intervention by the government in these areas was similar to what today would be called "martial law." For example, in England during the Middle Ages, the crime of "disturbing the peace" referred only to disturbing the peace of the king, not that of your neighbor.[9] Disturbing the peace was any action that caused the monarch to feel insecure in his or her rule, such as raising a local army larger than deemed necessary or conspiring with others to undermine the rule of the king. Monarchs obtained their office by birth or by overthrow of the reigning king or queen through the use of force. The crime of disturbing the peace was punishable by death.

Commerce was essential to the economic stability of countries, and anything that threatened to disrupt commerce, such as piracy, theft, and fraud, provoked a governmental response. For example, both Egypt and London, whose commerce depended on the ability to move goods by river, developed a river patrol to ensure the safety of ships and goods. These military units would patrol the river to prevent piracy and the harbors to prevent theft. Military units used to enforce the law were not civilian-controlled but operated under the authority of the monarch. The loyalty of the military was exclusively to the monarch, and citizens did not enjoy guaranteed rights.

Roman Empire and the Middle Ages

Through a highly successful and aggressive military strategy, the Romans were able to dominate most of the Mediterranean region and far-flung lands in Europe, western Asia, and northern Africa. The uniting of diverse cultural groups under Roman law and the separation of the society into distinct social classes, including a class of slaves, created the need for new ways to maintain law and order. It was not feasible to depend on a system of community mediation and religious institutions because of cultural diversity and conflicting religious values and local versus Roman gods.[10]

Urban Cohort Roman Empire era military unit used to maintain law and order in the cities.

To maintain public order and enforce laws, the Roman government developed specialized military units. Augustus, Emperor of Rome (27 B.C.–14 A.D.), developed a specialized military unit, called the **Praetorian Guard,** to protect the emperor and his property, and another military unit, called the **Urban Cohort,** to maintain public order among the citizens.[11] The function of the Praetorian Guard was similar to the responsibilities of the U.S. Secret Service in protecting the president and the White House.

Soldiers in the Urban Cohort acted as keepers of the peace. It was their responsibility to protect the patricians, or upper class of Roman citizens, from disorder, riots, or attacks by the plebeians, a lower class of citizens, or slaves.[12] These peacekeepers had final authority over non-Roman citizens and slaves; that is, when the peacekeepers apprehended an accused person, they had the power to act as judge, jury, and executioner. Justice was swift and often brutal, and there were no courts of appeal for lower classes or noncitizens.

Unchecked police power concentrated in the hands of a few has the potential for abuse. Greek and Roman civilizations also prized justice, so the office of magistrate emerged as a check on the power of the military over civilians. Magistrates, called **praetors,** were trained in the law and had the power to act as judges to replace the summary justice administered by the Urban Cohort and Roman Legion.[13] **Quaestores** assisted the praetors in a role somewhat similar to that of police detective. The quaestore would assist the praetor with the arrest and investigation of those accused of breaking the law, thus reducing the role of the military in civilian law enforcement. These Roman offices were the seeds of a criminal justice system separate from military domination.

JUST THE FACTS 6.1

In what areas of society and social life did early governments focus their efforts to maintain public order?

Roots of American Policing

THE MAIN IDEA

Roots of the American policing system are in England, beginning in the Middle Ages.

The fall of the Roman Empire brought a new system of justice administration. With the demise of the centralized power of the Roman Empire and the elimination of special military units to maintain public order, a new system developed based on local control linked to land ownership. In the Middle Ages, there was no stable central authority to replace the role of the Roman Empire. Public order at the local level was primarily the responsibility of feudal lords who exercised nearly absolute control over the serfs and peasants who lived on their land.[14] In a feudal system, serfs were virtually economic slaves. They did not have the right to leave the manor without the permission of the lord of the manor.[15]

King Charlemagne had set up a code of laws that divided the land into units called "manors," and a lord appointed by the king was charged with the responsibility of maintaining public order. At the same time, public order and crime fighting were regarded as the responsibility of every citizen. Whoever saw a crime was supposed to raise a hue and cry, and it was the responsibility of every citizen to join in the pursuit of suspected felons.

Dependence on Kinship for Safety in Medieval England

The **frankpledge** or **tithing system** was the primary means of maintaining public order and fighting crime in England during the Middle Ages. The tithing system required that every male above the age of 12 join a group, or tithing.[16] It was the responsibility of the

praetors Roman Empire era officials who assisted in the investigation of charges against a person.

quaestore Roman Empire era judicial official whose responsibilities were similar to those of a magistrate judge.

frankpledge System of policing by use of kinship associations common in the Middle Ages in England.

tithing system System based on kinship and civilian responsibility and used to maintain social order and provide criminal justice for medieval England.

tithing to defend its members and territory and to assist neighboring tithings. A tithing consisted of 10 to 12 men and their extended families. Family ties made the tithing system effective. The tithing was based on patriarchy, and females could not belong to one independently of their husbands or fathers. Females did not have equal rights, and the inclusion of females in the criminal justice system and the securing of equal rights for them were not goals of ancient civilizations.

Twice a year, the **sheriff,** who was appointed by the king, conducted a review of the tithings to ensure that all eligible males were affiliated with a tithing and that each tithing has its proper number of members.[17] It was during these biannual inspections that the head of a tithing, called "the tithing man," was obligated to report to the sheriff any crime(s) the members had observed and to report on the action they had taken. At this time, the sheriff would also collect a fee from each tithing and update the inventory of weapons possessed by the tithings, as tithings were also used for military conscription in time of war.

In medieval England, the social order was organized around social class, an inherited status. One did not move from one class to another, and upward mobility was nearly impossible. One's role, identity, and behavior in society were based on birth.[18] Society was bound together by "personal relationships of reciprocal behavior entered into contractually and described by kinship terminology."[19] Although this inflexibility of social class restricted liberty, it promoted individual safety. Without the protection of guaranteed legal rights and governmental agents, people's safety was in the company they kept, and there was safety in numbers. The stronger the tithing, the more secure people were.

The English Office of the Sheriff

In addition to maintaining social order, the tithing also had responsibilities for defense and warfare. At a time when there were no permanent or standing armies, the citizens filled the ranks of the military in time of attack or warfare. The tithing was used as the primary mechanism for fulfilling military obligations. For the purpose of combining the local tithings into a larger military unit, the various tithings were organized into 10 groups of approximately 100 free males. (Women had no military role.) These 10 tithings were organized by geographical areas called *shires,* equivalent to counties, boroughs, or parishes in the United States. The person responsible for all of the tithings within the shire was known as the "reeve." He was the *reeve-of-the-shire,* or the **shire-reeve.** He had the power to summon the various tithings under his command to help defend against attack, to act as troops in warfare, or to pursue criminals.[20]

This office of the shire-reeve was to develop into the office of the sheriff, with the power to summon citizen assistance, known as ***posse comitatus.*** In nineteenth-century America, *posse comitatus* was an important power of the sheriff, who, for example, might mobilize a citizen posse to pursue outlaws. In the United States, the military was given the power of *posse comitatus* initially, but this power was revoked by Congress.[21] The separation of the military from civilian law enforcement is a distinct feature of the American criminal justice system.

In the eleventh century, political unification of England lessened the effectiveness and efficiency of the tithing system. On uniting England by military conquest in 1066, William, Duke of Normandy, better known as William the Conqueror, used the office of the sheriff to centralize his political, military, and economic control of the land.[22] William appointed sheriffs who were accountable only to the king. The sheriffs' allegiance was to the king, not to the community they served. Loyalty to the king was a more important job qualification than honesty, fairness, or competency.

The sheriff became a key instrument used by the king to raise revenue. The sheriff was the person responsible for assessing and collecting the various taxes. For example, just as lords could provide land to vassals, who in return provided a fixed annual rent for the privilege of farming the land (today this is known as "sharecropping"), the revenues from the borough farm or fee-farm was the basic lump sum of money from a

sheriff County-level law enforcement official whose origin is from medieval England.

shire-reeve Early English Middle Ages name for "sheriff."

posse comitatus The power of a law enforcement officer to utilize civilians or military troops to assist in law enforcement work.

ethics in the system

How the Tithing System Worked

The tithing system was based on the values of family honor, community harmony, and group (rather than individual) justice. If a member of a tithing committed an injury against another in the tithing, the tithing, acting as a group, worked to resolve the conflict. If a member of the tithing was accused of committing an injury against a member of another tithing, the two tithings were expected to resolve the dispute. If a member of a tithing was convicted of stealing property from someone in a different tithing, the most common punishment was restitution. The offender would be required to return what was stolen and an additional value as punishment.[23] For example, the theft of one pig might have required that the offender give the victim as many as seven pigs. Victims could, in a sense, profit from the theft, and there was no burden or expense to the society, such as would be incurred by incarceration of the offender. In reality, crime did not pay under this system.

If the individual who committed the theft did not or could not make restitution, it was the responsibility of the other members of the tithing to make the payment.[24] Because of limited mobility and close-knit families in a feudal society, offenders could not easily leave rather than pay the restitution. If the offender did leave, the other members of the tithing would be responsible for the restitution.[25] In the event of a serious crime, such as murder, for which the punishment could be death, the tithing would be responsible for delivering the offender for punishment. Again, if the offender could not be delivered, someone else from the tithing would be required to submit to the punishment. The logic of this arrangement was that the tithings would police themselves. If a member of the tithing chose to flee rather than provide restitution or forfeit his life, the other members of the tithing would be held accountable. Thus, the burden of paying a fine or finding an offender who fled fell on the tithing, not on either the state or the victim. The tithing system was an ingenious, practical, cost-effective method to handle crime at the local level, given the social context.

■ **On what moral and ethical principles was tithing based? Would the tithing system be regarded as fair in your community today? Why or why not?**

town that had to be paid to the king's treasury each year. It was the sheriff of the county who was responsible for delivering that payment.

■ *Legis Henrici:* The State as Victim

Fifty years later in 1116, King Henry I issued the ***Legis Henrici,*** or the Law of Henry.[26] These laws divided England into 30 judicial districts and identified certain offenses as violation of the "king's peace."[27] This marked the shift from a focus on the individual as victim to the idea that the state also could be the victim in certain crimes. Thus, the state, not the individual victim, assumed the responsibility of bringing the offender to justice.[28] This concept of the state as victim and party to the crime is a central theme of modern criminal justice systems. The state has the duty to apprehend, prosecute, and punish the offender. Even in cases in which the individual victim does not wish to pursue legal prosecution, the state, also a victim, has the ability and duty to do so.

Legis Henrici Laws of England issued by King Henry I that established judicial districts and gave the government new powers in regard to the criminal justice system.

■ The Magna Carta: The Origins of Due Process

Increased centralized control by the monarch without checks by a Constitution or Bill of Rights increased the potential for abuse of authority and the repression of individual liberties. The zenith of this abuse appeared to have occurred under King John I

(1199–1216). By the end of the twelfth century, the sheriff had become the primary enforcement agency of the Crown for collecting taxes, maintaining the king's peace, and bringing law violators to justice.

Faced with the need to raise the revenues necessary to support England's participation in the Crusades, the various military campaigns waged by King John, and the royal comfort of the king, the citizenry was taxed more and more. When taxation failed to raise the needed revenues, the government used fraudulent actions to raise them.[29] A common abuse was to falsely accuse a landowner of crimes against the king, because a person convicted of such a crime forfeited his property and wealth to the king. Under King John, liberal use of this corrupt strategy provoked outlaws such as Robin Hood, whose retaliation against King John has become an enduring legend of the period.

Concerned about the abuse of the law exercised by the sheriff, with the approval and apparent complicity of the king, the noblemen of England organized, armed themselves and met King John on June 15, 1215, on the plains of Runny Meade. There they put the request to him, backed by a significant show of force, that he sign a document that provided protection against the illegal seizure of lands. Understanding that he could sign or be put to death, King John signed the document, which he later tried unsuccessfully to renounce. The document signed by the king is the **Magna Carta,** or "Great Charter." It is England's equivalent to America's Bill of Rights. The purpose of the Magna Carta was to reform the corrupt practices of the office of sheriff, to provide a certain degree of autonomy regarding local matters, and to place limitations on the power of the king's authority over the criminal justice system.

The Growing Problem of Crime in the Cities

With the onset of the Industrial Revolution and the growth of the cities, crime in England's cities became a major problem. Previous systems depending on citizen volunteers and individual responsibility proved ineffective and inefficient as mechanisms for maintaining order in the growing urban population centers. In 1653, Oliver Cromwell tried a military solution to the problem of maintaining law and order in the cities. He divided England into 12 districts and placed a military general, who exercised discretionary police powers, in charge of each district. This strategy of policing by the military proved effective in lowering the crime rate, but it also reduced personal freedoms and was in sharp contrast to rising expectations of democratic values. The citizens of England found this solution worse than the problem. They expressed their dissatisfaction through public protests and rioting, resulting in the rescinding of Cromwell's scheme of military rule of the country.

Fire, the Industrial Revolution, and Gin

Fire, the Industrial Revolution, and the invention of gin are three important factors in the development of policing in England.[30] The large concentration of people and factories in the cities created a great fire hazard. In an era when all heating, cooking, and lighting was by use of fire and roofs were made of straw or wood, fires were common and devastating. One of the great fire threats was a night-time fire that would go undetected until it was too large to extinguish, given the limited fire-fighting technology of the time. Such a fire could spread and engulf the entire city.

Magna Carta Secured civil and criminal rights for English noblemen and similar to America's Bill of Rights in establishing due process for citizens of Great Britain.

THE NIGHT WATCH To guard against the hazards of fire at night, the cities of England developed what was called the "night watch." The night watch was a group of men charged with the responsibility of patrolling the streets at night to watch for fire. If they found a fire, they were to awaken the citizens so that they could help put out the fire. The night watch was staffed by volunteers; when not enough volunteers could be found, it was staffed by men who had been found guilty of various infractions of the city

For many American cities, the historical roots of the police as well as of the fire department can be found in the paid night watch, an English institution for neighborhood security. Why did cities in the American colonies adopt England's night watch? How did the functions of night watch expand in the U.S.? Who paid for the services of the night watch, and how did that affect the development of policing in both England and America?

laws. Soon the night watch was charged with both fire duty and crime fighting. However, those who participated in the night watch had neither training nor weapons to prepare them for crime fighting, and a common response of the night watch was simply to make sure that they did not see any crime.[31] While essential as a fire-fighting strategy, the night watch was not effective as a crime-fighting strategy. As the population and area of the cities increased, it became impractical to staff the night watch with offenders and volunteers. In 1737, King George II allowed city councils to levy taxes to pay for the night watch.

The night watch as a precaution against fire was adopted by many cities in the American colonies and continued after the Revolutionary War. For many American urban cities, the historical roots of the police can be found in the paid night watch.

INCREASING FEAR OF CRIME The Industrial Revolution, with the construction of factories in the cities and the resulting immigration of strangers, was what finally destroyed the ability of policing based on individual responsibility, kinship groups, and volunteers. As the population of London increased, fear of crime increased. The Industrial Revolution threw together people from different social classes into one setting. The nobility and the merchant class found themselves sharing streets and public places with people whom they viewed with suspicion and fear. This fear was fueled by the public rowdiness and drunkenness of the lower classes.

Before the invention of gin, the available alcoholic beverages consisted of beer, wines, and liquors. Most commoners found that beer was the only alcoholic beverage they could afford. Then in the early eighteenth century, gin, a highly alcoholic beverage (80–90 proof), became available at a very low cost. A popular saying of the time was that "one could get drunk for a penny, and dead drunk for twopence."[32] The availability of gin, the concentration of poorly paid or unemployed factory workers, and the lack of an organized police force contributed to an increase in street crime. Public drunkenness, theft, robbery, and public disorder became common problems in London and other large cities of the Industrial Revolution.

JUST THE FACTS 6.2

What factors made the tithing system successful during the Middle Ages, and what changes in society ended its success? How did the night watch influence the development of the police?

The English Response to Crime

THE MAIN IDEA

Increasing crime in English cities forced the development of a paid police force under the leadership of Sir Robert Peel.

The English government attempted to respond to the problem. In 1745, Parliament appointed a committee to study crime. The committee found that crime was a problem in the cities and predicted that it would get worse. The city of Westminster took more positive steps, enacting the **Westminster Watch Act of 1774** to deal directly with the problem of public law enforcement. Focusing on working-class leisure activities, the act was intended to control sex, swearing, drinking, and brawling.[33] Using a system of night watchmen, bailiffs, and gate guards, Westminster attempted to make its streets safer. Of course, such policing required financing, and in 1777 it was necessary for King George IV to modify the Tax Act of 1737, which allowed cities to levy taxes to pay the night watchmen, to allow for the payment of police wages and equipment. This is one of the earliest uses of government revenues to pay for policing.

Bow Street Runners and Thames River Police

Despite various reform efforts, street crime in London continued to grow worse. When city merchants demanded that street crime had to be reduced for the sake of commerce, the government responded by creating a special agency of "theft-catchers," the **Bow Street Runners.** In 1748, Brothers Henry and John Fielding were appointed as administrators or chief magistrate of a uniformed, full-time police force to provide policing on foot in the inner city, on horse patrol in the suburbs, and a special unit to catch thieves and criminals.[34] The headquarters for this agency was on Bow Street in London; hence, the name "Bow Street Runners" was applied to the agency's officers. In 1800, theft from the docks of the Thames River also threatened the health of commerce, and the Thames River Police Act established the Thames River Police. These officers were charged with reducing theft from the docks.[35]

Sir Robert Peel and the London Metropolitan Police

On June 2, 1780, Lord George Gordon led a mob protesting the Catholic Relief Act passed by Parliament in 1778, and rioting ensued. The City of London had no police to call on to restore order. By the time a sufficient military force was in position to control the violence, it was necessary to use deadly force against the rioters.[36] The rioting lasted for several days and hundreds of people were killed. The loss of control by the government clearly demonstrated the need for some means to maintain public safety and order in the city. Previous attempts using the military had proved very unpopular. Other attempts using fragmented agencies with specialized duties or part-time volunteers or poorly paid officers who lacked training had also failed to provide an effective means of maintaining law and order in the city. The citizens of London were ready for a new approach.

Sir Robert Peel, Secretary for Ireland from 1812 to 1818, had such an approach. As secretary, his job was somewhat like that of a governor in the United States.[37] One of the problems Peel had to deal with in Ireland was that of crime and public order. To combat the problem, Peel developed a system of paid magistrates and constables recruited from the ranks of honorably discharged, noncommissioned army officers.

Read about Sir Robert Peel and the history of the London Metropolitan Police at http://www.met.police.uk/history/. ■

In 1828, Peel was appointed to the office of Home Secretary of England. As home secretary, he needed to deal with the growing problem of street crime in London. Peel lobbied for an act of Parliament that would allow him to do something for the City of London similar to what he accomplished in Ireland. He wanted to create a system of full-time paid constables to be used to fight crime. In 1829, Parliament passed "An Act for Improving the Police in and Near the Metropolis," better known as the **London Metropolitan Police Act.** Under the leadership of Sir Robert Peel, a full-time, paid, uniformed police agency was established to promote public safety, enforce the criminal codes, and bring criminals to justice.[38]

Sir Robert Peel and the London Metropolitan Police Act of 1829 transformed law enforcement in England and America. What principles of law enforcement did Peel promote? How were these English "bobbies" chosen as police officers? How were they equipped to do their job? How were American police modeled after the "bobbies" but equipped differently? Why were Peel's bobbies referred to as "blue devils"? Negative initial public reaction reflected two ongoing challenges in policing: balancing individual liberties with the public good and applying laws equally regardless of social class.

PEEL'S BOBBIES Peel's belief was that the absence of police promoted crime, and he measured the success of his new police force by the impact they had on the crime rate. Peel emphasized both the importance of reactive crime fighting (identifying and arresting offenders) and preventing crime through a highly visible police presence.[39] Although he staffed his police agency with former military personnel and used a military-style command and control structure, Peel believed that his civilian police should be clearly differentiated from the military.[40] One way to distinguish the civilian law enforcement officers from military troops was to dress the police in distinctively different uniforms. The standard military uniform of the day was bright red with white trim, but Peel's police officers wore blue uniforms. Peel's police officers also were unarmed, were expected to be engaged with the community, and were recruited from the community they served. Peel recruited his new officers from the ranks of the working class, but officers were required to be literate, an unusual requirement at the time. Typical duties of the officers included not only crime fighting, but also checking on the well-being of citizens. For example, officers were expected to check in on elderly citizens to "see how they were doing" and render assistance to them when needed.[41]

Peel equipped his officers with a whistle for communication, a tall hat for visibility in the crowd, a distinctive uniform, and a short baton or stick that the officer concealed inside his coat. A full-time paid constable with a hat, whistle, baton, and blue uniform was the cutting-edge of policing technology in 1829.

Despite Peel's efforts, the initial reaction of the citizens to the police was negative to the point of violence. The police were seen as an intrusion into the individual freedoms of the citizen by government. They were called "blue devils." Members of the upper class opposed the idea that the constable's power of search and seizure extended not only over the lower class but to them as well. Members of the lower class saw the police as an instrument of the upper class to control them. However, the police's effect on public order was soon recognized, for the streets of London became safer for all classes of people. Within 10 years, Peel's police agents were accepted by the average citizen as an essential element in public order.[42] Peel's strong association with the formation of the London police is evident in that the street name for the new officers was "bobbies," named after Robert (or Bob) Peel.[43]

THE ORIGINS OF CIVILIAN POLICING Peel introduced a new philosophy in maintaining public order. He visualized police as a civilian-staffed and civilian-controlled means to promote public safety and justice. For his role in establishing the London Metropolitan Police or London-style policing, Peel is frequently referred to as the Father of Modern Policing.

Peel's concept also moved the responsibility of public safety to the government and out of the realm of individual responsibility or the military or part-time agencies. Also revolutionary was the concept of a police force with broad powers to enforce the laws of the land, including the powers of arrest and search and seizure. Initially, the London Metropolitan Police Act provided police services only within approximately a 10-mile radius of London; however, services were quickly extended to other parts of the city and throughout England. Only 6 years later, the Municipal Corporations Act of 1835 required standardized police forces in all cities.

Peels' police force brought social order to the cities of England and was to become the model for policing in most nations in western Europe and America. Striking a balance between the need for law and order and the competing need for liberty and personal freedoms, Peel's civilian-staffed police departments provided citizens a safe environment while preserving individual rights.

JUST THE FACTS 6.3

What factors led English cities to adopt London-style policing during the 1800s? What characteristics did London-style police share?

The Development of Policing in America

THE MAIN IDEA

American policing, shaped by unique regional politics and economics, gave precedence to local law enforcement and "home rule" by states.

The eastern coast of the United States was settled primarily by the British, and it is not surprising that policing prior to 1776 was modeled after British-style policing. In the Colonies, kings were replaced by local authorities such as governors. The monarchy of England provided land grants in the New World to various English patrons of the Crown, who in turn became the absolute authority in the Colonies. Because these colonial governors received their appointment from the Crown, it was difficult to lodge a complaint about how they ruled the colony. The prospect of an average colonist being granted an audience with the king to lodge a complaint against a colonial governor was virtually nonexistent. However, without the feudal system of England, which tied the serf to the manor, and with vast expanses of unexplored and unclaimed lands in the New World, social order took a unique turn. The tithing system, which depended on close kin relationships and a strong tie to the land, was useless.

Law and Order in the Colonies

Because most of the early settlements in the New World encountered a harsh and sometimes violent environment, social order was based on the "good of the community." For example, in the Jamestown colony in Virginia, founded in 1608, adherence to Dale's Law—the law of the colony—was strictly enforced for the survival of the community.[44] Those who would not conform to the laws of the community would be ostracized, which could have the same effect as a death sentence in the hostile environment. Likewise, the settlers of the Plymouth colony signed the Plymouth Compact, in which they pledged to conform their behavior to activities that promoted the good of the community.[45]

As the settlements in the New World gradually evolved into ports, farms, towns, and cities, the system of maintaining public order more and more resembled the British system of sheriffs, constables, and magistrates. Towns and cities adopted the British system of the night watch staffed by volunteers and convicted offenders.

Find out about the history and goals of the International Police Association at http://www.ipa-usa.org/.

Policing in America, 1776–1850

The American Revolutionary War in 1776, or the "Revolt of the Colonies," as it was called in England, occurred before the adoption of Sir Robert Peel's new London-style policing. Unlike policing in England, there is no definite date at which one can say that American cities adopted London-styled policing. However, by the 1890s, the London-style policing system had become the general practice in large American cities. Gradually, the various municipalities abandoned the use of part-time personnel and volunteers and adopted London-style policing in an effort to provide for public safety. For example, Philadelphia created night-watch and day-watch police forces in 1830, funded largely by a donation from Stephen Girard, a wealthy manufacturer who felt a London-style police department would be beneficial. New York City combined its day and night watch into a single police department in 1844.[46] Boston established a single police department in 1855.[47] By the 1880s, some 50 years after Peel had introduced the concept of a full-time, paid police force to London, London-style policing had become widespread in American cities.

With independence from Britain, the new United States of America pursued its own ideas of policing. Wary of strong central government, the United States adopted a system of shared and fragmented power that favored local control of policing. Local, state, and federal governments shared power in a complex system of checks and balances.

Article X of the U.S. Constitution states that any power not enumerated in the Constitution as a federal government power is a state government power. Policing was not mentioned in the Constitution as a federal power, so policing was considered a local matter. Thus, the new federal government had limited police powers. For example, when the federal government was first formed, the only federal law enforcement agencies were the U.S. Postal Inspectors and the U.S. Marshals. The U.S. Marshals Office performed few law enforcement duties, and the U.S. Postal Inspectors focused on promoting the safety and reliability of the delivery of the mail. For approximately 100 years, agencies such as the FBI, the Drug Enforcement Agency (DEA), and the Bureau of Alcohol, Tobacco, and Firearms (BATF) did not exist.

Initially, there also were no state or municipal police agencies. At the local level, the sheriff's office was the only police agency, and the sheriff departments occupied most of their time with jail operations, courtroom security, and the serving of court papers. Furthermore, the powers of the sheriff were limited in several ways. The office became an elected rather than an appointed position. In fact, today the sheriff is still the only law enforcement administrator to gain office by election. Furthermore, many counties limited the sheriff to a single 2-year term of office to prevent him or her from accumulating too much power. While these restrictions may have prevented abuse of power, they did little to create efficiency and effectiveness in law enforcement.

Policing in America, 1850–1900

In the United States, as in England, urbanization was the primary influence on the development of a new policing system. In the mid-1800s, rapid social change occurred through changes caused by the Civil War and dramatic population growth due to immigration. The population of New York City, for example, increased from 250,000 in 1845 to 620,000 in 1855. By the beginning of the Civil War in 1861, the city's population was near 800,000 and nearly half were foreign-born.[48] These immigrants often were seen as a "dangerous" class of people, the source of crime.[49] Several criminological theories of this era were based on the assumption that crime is class-specific, a characteristic of the

Article X Article X of the United States Constitution proscribes that all powers not explicitly granted to the federal government are reserved as state powers.

poor, who typically were minorities.[50] Often the mix of minorities and newly arrived immigrants created social and economic conflict, resulting in violence and even riots.

As in England, public safety or the lack of it, in urban centers was the impetus for the development of new concepts in policing. However, there were significant differences between the London-style metropolitan police and the American police. The major difference was the lack of centralized government control, professionalism, and focus on crime prevention. The source of these differences can be traced to the power of home rule.

Under the principle of home rule, the state can delegate to the municipalities the power to establish a municipal government, tax its citizens, establish its own laws, raise a police force, and establish courts and correctional facilities. Thus, each city, separate and autonomous from other cities, from the state, and from the federal government, can establish a criminal justice system and a police force of its own design. Furthermore, each municipal department is under the absolute power of the municipal government. Police departments during this period were often seen as merely the enforcement branch of the political machines that ran the city. Also, because of the perception and use of the police for politically partisan purposes, there was little emphasis on selecting and training qualified officers. Selection was based largely on political loyalties and favors.[51] Thus, American-style policing mimicked London-style policing more in form than in function.

The Civil War had a positive impact on American-style policing. After the war, trained, experienced ex-military men who could find no other work often entered policing.[52] The Civil War also spurred significant advances in firearms, especially multiple-shot, reliable sidearms adopted by the police as standard equipment. In an era without radios, without any means to summon help, and with no rapid way for help to arrive, the officer's revolver must have seemed critical to his self-protection. Unlike the British experience, the American police officer was armed. In fact, a common symbol of the authority of the American police officer is the weapon he or she carries.

Vigilantes and Posses in the Wild West

Use searches to read first-person accounts by Edward Riley and Elizabeth Roe about their experiences with western frontier justice in the 1870s at this Library of Congress site: http://memory.loc.gov/ammem/. ■

A unique chapter in the history of policing is the development of policing in the American West during the late 1800s. While New Yorkers lived under relatively civilized conditions in the second half of the nineteenth century, conditions were quite different for people living in the comparatively uninhabited "Wild West." A philosophy of national expansion, the discovery of gold, an uncommonly strong sense of self-importance, and a reckless disregard for the rights of people who differed from those of European background resulted in numerous injustices and frequent violence toward Native Americans and others. The tales of the gold, Indians, violence, lawlessness, and opportunity for unrestrained individual freedom lured the farmers, miners, ranchers, fortune seekers, immigrants, and an assorted lot of adventurers westward.

vigilantism The system by which citizens assume the role and responsibility of official law enforcement agencies and act independently, often without observation of due process and rights, to take justice into their own hands.

The West was a place where none of the historical models of policing applied. Often, a small number of white settlers, gold miners, or trappers migrated westward in hopes of better fortune and settled in remote cities such as Kansas City, Dodge City, and Denver, and territories such as Nebraska, Oregon, Texas, and California. Not until the end of the 1800s, when the train and the telegraph helped connect these places and reduce their remoteness, did cities in these areas begin to resemble their eastern counterparts. Public safety was maintained primarily by personal defense, **vigilantism,** town marshals, U.S. marshals, and the U.S. Army. In this environment, justice was often quick, brutal, or nonexistent. Without convenient access to the court system, farmers, ranchers, and gold miners frequently made their own justice, and the use of firearms and lynch mobs became the trademark of justice in the West. Outlaws were much more likely to be shot or lynched by posses than tried in a court of law and imprisoned.[53]

The development of policing in America varied regionally. Cities of the East followed English models early, with a trend toward full-time, paid, uniformed police forces. Uniquely American conditions delayed this development in other regions, however, such as in the "Wild West." When under threat, citizens of the West banded together temporarily to protect property and secure public order. They joined mounted posses to pursue outlaws and often made quick, harsh judgments about the guilt or innocence of alleged offenders and the punishment they should receive. With few official law enforcement officers, judges, law courts, and correctional facilities, vigilante justice was almost always violent or deadly. How was the development of American local law enforcement affected by the unique situation of slavery in the South?

In settlements near a military post or fort, the U.S. Army was the official provider of law and order. Because most of the West was territorial land and not states, settlements did not have the power of home rule and thus could not legally form their own local police agencies. The U.S. Marshal's Office assumed responsibility for civilian law enforcement but often lacked enough manpower to cover the vast geographical area. The history of the U.S. Marshal's Office during this period is frequently described as "colorful."

Beginnings of Private Policing

The lack of competent local police during the nineteenth century created business opportunities for some. Merchants, railroads, banks, and even the federal government were in need of professional security and investigative services. With no public agency to fulfill these needs, they turned to private agencies. During the mid-1800s, private security agencies such as Brinks, Pinkerton, and Wells Fargo provided investigative services and protection of private property. These private agencies filled the void created by the widespread corruption found in local police and the geographical jurisdiction limitations of local police in the absence of state or federal police.

Today, private policing is a multibillion-dollar business. There are five or six times more private police agents than there are public police agents.[54] Brinks, Pinkerton, and Wells Fargo continue to be world leaders in private security. Merchants and citizens still hire private police for about the same reasons they did in the mid-1800s: to protect private property, to secure the services of professional guards, and to investigate matters that, while important to the client, may be of lesser importance to the public police.

Slave Patrols, Black Codes, and *Plessy v. Ferguson*

The need for a night fire watch, the growth of the cities, and the resulting fear of street crime have been cited as the roots of the police force. In the southern states, policing also had its roots in "slave patrols."[55] **Slave patrols** were established as early as the 1740s in the colonial southern states. Southern states passed laws giving any white freeman the right to stop, search, and apprehend any black person—slave or free. In fact, the law of most southern states presumed all blacks to be slaves.[56] Free blacks were required to carry proof of their liberty with them at all times. The membership of the slave patrols was loosely defined. In Georgia, "all urban white males aged 16 to 60, with the exception of ministers of religion" were considered members of the slave patrol, and it was their duty "to search and examine all Negro-Houses for offensive weapons and ammunition."[57] In addition to the powers of search and seizure, the slave patrols had the power to "inflict corporal punishment on any slave found to have left his owner's property without permission."[58]

The uniqueness of policing in the West has evoked many legends and is the plot for countless movies and television series, such as *Gunsmoke,* which is about the exploits of Matt Dillon, marshall of Dodge City, Kansas. However, the history of policing in the South has been largely ignored. Most likely, the reason for this neglect is the racial bias and violence that characterized the Civil War period. The pre–Civil War slave patrols brutally oppressed blacks. Many southern whites feared that a violent insurrection by the slaves was an imminent possibility. To prevent insurrection, many southern cities with large slave populations organized "foot and mounted patrols to prevent slaves from congregating and to repress any attacks upon the racial and social status quo."[59]

BLACK CODES After the Civil War, the southern states circumvented the emancipation of the slaves by adopting **Black Codes.** Virtually all of the former Confederate states adopted laws aimed specifically at nullifying the rights granted to the recently freed slaves.[60] Black Codes in South Carolina, for example, restricted former slaves from any occupation other than farmer or servant unless they paid an annual tax, ranging from $10 to $100, which was considered an enormous amount of money at the time.[61] Blacks were prohibited from renting land in urban areas. They could be punished by fine or involuntary plantation labor for such criminalized behaviors as using "insulting" gestures or language, doing "malicious mischief," and preaching the Gospel without a license.[62] Interracial marriage was prohibited by state law.[63] The belief and practice of both society and the legal system was that blacks had fewer civil rights than whites, and the emphasis was on maintaining this inequality.[64]

Southern police departments defined their mission as protecting the white population from the threat of violence at the hands of the slaves and later, freed slaves.[65] So intense was this fear that laws often were enacted to protect the white citizens from even the most remote threat posed by blacks. For example, in the early 1800s, Charleston, South Carolina, passed the Negro Seaman's Act, requiring free black seamen to remain on board their vessels while in Carolina harbors or to be imprisoned at night.[66] If the seamen came ashore, they were subject to arrest and could be sold into slavery. Similar statutes were enforced by other coastal slave states. (The jail that was built in Charleston to house "free Negro seamen," including Jamaicans, still stands and is now a tourist site.)

slave patrols Civilian groups in the southern states whose primary role was to protect against rioting and revolts by slaves.

Black Codes Laws passed by southern states after the Civil War to disenfranchise freed slaves.

diversity in the system

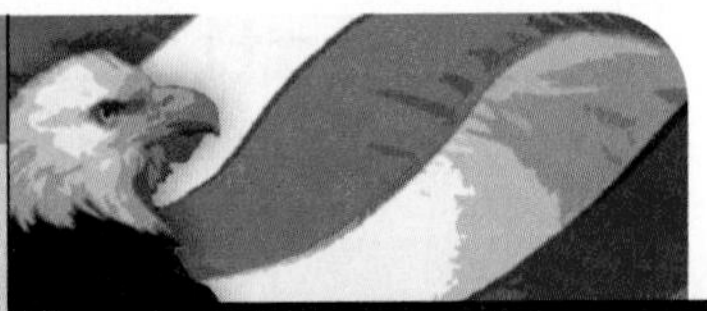

The First Black Police Officers

Hubert Williams and Patrick V. Murphy gathered data documenting the first appointments of black men as police officers.[67] According to their research, the first black police officers appeared after the Civil War as a result of Reconstruction in the southern states. The first appointments were in Selma, Alabama, in 1867; Houston, Texas, in 1870; and Jackson, Mississippi, in 1871. New Orleans, which had a police board composed of three black members out of five, appointed a police force that included 177 blacks by 1870. The first black police officer in the North was in the city of Chicago in 1872. By 1894, there were 23 black police officers in Chicago. Washington, DC, appointed its first black officer in 1874; Indianapolis in 1876; Cleveland in 1881; and Boston in 1885.

According to Williams and Murphy, these early appointments of black males to the police department were not well received by other officers and the white population of the cities. For example, when black males were appointed to the Philadelphia Police Department, several white officers quit the force in protest. When black males were appointed in July 1868 to the Raleigh, North Carolina, police department, the local newspaper, the *Daily Sentinel,* ran a headline that read "The Mongrel Regime!! Negro Police!!" The article concluded that the appointment of the four black police officers was "the beginning of the end."

The black officers did not receive equal treatment, pay, or responsibilities. Whereas most white officers were recruited from the ranks of the laboring class, black police officers frequently were overqualified in both education and previous experience. Despite the above-average qualifications of the black police, they were frequently restricted to working only in black communities. Because black police officers were generally poorly received by the white citizens of the community, they had limited authority and were not permitted to stop, search, or arrest whites. Race riots occurred in Jackson and Meridian, Mississippi, when black police officers attempted to exercise authority over whites. Chicago required that black police officers work in plain clothes to avoid drawing public attention to them.

■ **Where, when, and in what historical context were African Americans first hired as police officers? How did race affect their role and function as officers of the law?**

PLESSY v. FERGUSON The different treatment of blacks under law came to the attention of the Supreme Court in the landmark decision of ***Plessy v. Ferguson*** (1896).[68] The Supreme Court found state laws that required segregation of the races in public accommodations to be constitutional. This court case established the doctrine of "separate but equal" treatment of minorities, specifically African Americans. The result of this official recognition of the constitutionality of segregation was immediately seen in police departments. The employment of black police officers, both in the South and in northern cities, was suspended. Even the New Orleans Police Department, which employed 177 black officers in 1870, employed no black officers by 1910.[69] The lack of employment of black police officers remained the norm until strong civil rights legislation was passed in 1967.

Use searches to read more about the Black Codes, *Plessey v. Ferguson,* and Jim Crow laws at http://afroamhistory.about.com. ■

Plessy v. Ferguson (1896) U.S. Supreme Court landmark case that established the "separate but equal" doctrine that allowed racial segregation.

JUST THE FACTS 6.4

What developments in law enforcement were uniquely American? How did Article X of the U.S. Constitution and *Plessy v. Ferguson* affect the development of policing?

Foundations of Modern American Policing, 1900–1930

THE MAIN IDEA

Urban growth and professional practices introduced by August Vollmer changed the American policing system.

The emergence of the United States as a world-class industrial leader after World War I brought significant changes to all aspects of American society and government. Increased population density in New York, Boston, Philadelphia, Detroit, and Chicago increased ethnic diversity and strained social service agencies, including schools, public health, and housing. This strain was reflected in social disorder. After World War I, most people considered the primary threats to public order to be street violence, gangs, and vices such as gambling, drinking, and prostitution.[70] The widespread adoption of the electric light allowed citizens to continue their activities—including their criminal activities—all night long, both indoors and out. The automobile, the airplane, and the telephone changed opportunities for crime, and advances in weapons, including automatic weapons and semiautomatic pistols, increased the firepower of both criminals and police.

Labor Conflicts and Local Police

Many blamed the problems of social disorder on immigrants, the poor, and the lower class. New York Police administrator Raymond Fosdick in 1914, for example, declared that crime was caused by the unrestrained lower class. Also, labor strife between companies and the newly emerging unions was a significant source of public disorder.[71] Labor conflicts and strikes were frequent and often violent, even deadly. There were

August Vollmer's ideas for reforming police organization and professionalizing police work had a dramatic impact on law enforcement practices in the United States. In what ways were Vollmer's ideas like those of England's Sir Robert Peel a century earlier? What reforms in police organization and mission did Vollmer propose? In what ways did he seek to professionalize police work? What were some of his innovations in police recruitment, training, and technology? Why were his proposals unpopular in his day, and which of them are in effect in police departments today?

57,000 labor strikes between 1899 and 1915.[72] Citizens and governments turned to the local police officer as the front-line defense against public disorder.

The local police officer of the early 1900s was far different from his contemporary counterpart. For example, a veteran Boston police officer of 1913 was recruited from the working class and made $1,400 per year after 6 years of service. A cop on the day shift worked 75 hours a week, and one on the night shift worked 87 hours a week. He received 1 day off in 15. He received little or no training prior to being hired, or afterward. He was hired on the bases of his obedience to authority, physical strength, and size.[73] Many departments had a 6-foot minimum height requirement. Officers worked without the benefit of radio communications and patrolled their beats on foot or horseback.

During these early years of policing, an important debate occurred. The police, for the most part, were being used to maintain social order through enforcement of the laws and a forceful, sometimes brutal response to law breakers. Local police departments were seen primarily as extensions of the political parties that ran the cities. As Americans universally began to adopt local policing systems to combat crime and public disorder, debate arose regarding the role and function of the police. The presence of an armed police force empowered with the rights of search and seizure raised the question of how to balance individual rights and public safety. The use of police departments by corrupt politicians and powerful private business owners called into question the difference between criminal justice and social justice. One of the key persons who was influential in shaping American policing was August Vollmer.

August Vollmer and the Professionalizing of Policing

August Vollmer was the chief of police of Berkeley, California, from 1905 to 1932. Vollmer's vision of policing was quite different from most of his contemporaries. He believed the police should be a "dedicated body of educated persons comprising a distinctive corporate entity with a prescribed code of behavior."[74] He was critical of his contemporaries and they of him. San Francisco police administrator, Charley Dullea, who later became president of the International Association of Chiefs of Police, refused to drive through Berkeley in protest against Vollmer.[75] Fellow California police chiefs may have felt their opposition to Vollmer was justified, given his vocal and strong criticism of other California police departments. For example, Vollmer publicly referred to San Francisco cops as "morons," and in an interview with a newspaper reporter, he called Los Angeles cops "low grade mental defectives."[76]

Because of his emphasis on education, professionalism, and administrative reform, Vollmer often is seen as the counterpart of London's Sir Robert Peel and is sometimes called the "father of modern American policing." Vollmer was decades ahead of his contemporaries, but he was not able to achieve significant change in policing during his lifetime. It remained for Vollmer's students to implement change. For example, O. W. Wilson, who became chief of police of Chicago, promoted college education for police officers and wrote a book on police administration that reflected many of Vollmer's philosophies.[77] It was adopted widely by police executives and used as a college textbook well into the 1960s.

Vollmer is credited with a number of innovations. He was an early adopter of the automobile for patrol and the use of radios in police cars. He recruited college-educated police officers. He developed and implemented a 3-year training curriculum for police officers, including classes in physics, chemistry, biology, physiology, anatomy, psychology, psychiatry, anthropology, and criminology. He developed a system of signal boxes for hailing police officers. He adopted the use of typewriters to fill out police reports and records, and officers received training in typing. He surveyed other police departments to gather information about their practices.[78] Many of his initiatives have become common practice within contemporary police departments.

Vollmer lobbied for greater use of scientific crime detection practices, including the use of fingerprints, the polygraph, and scientific evidence. He also promoted the role of the police as social workers. For example, he delivered an address to the International Association of Chiefs of Police in 1919 on the subject "The Policeman as a Social Worker," which generated considerable opposition.[79] He advocated the selection of both police officers and administrators based on ability as measured by performance tests. This was a radical proposal at the time but now is common practice and a legal requirement for departments. Among the tests he considered important was the intelligence test. He believed that police officers needed to be above average in intelligence, an idea not shared by most of his contemporaries. His innovations brought him national recognition. Although Vollmer was not successful in changing the course of policing during his lifetime, he was important in signaling the direction it should and eventually did go.

JUST THE FACTS 6.5

How did immigration and urbanization influence policing in the United States? How did August Vollmer contribute to the development of professional American police forces?

Origins of Federal Law Enforcement

THE MAIN IDEA

Federal law enforcement agencies developed independently of local and state policing systems.

The history of policing prior to 1900 is largely one of the development of local (municipal and county) policing. Most federal law enforcement agencies were developed after 1900 in response to emerging needs that could not be filled by local or existing law enforcement agencies. During the 1800s, federal law enforcement agencies played a very limited role in law enforcement. However, contemporary federal law enforcement agencies have assumed more and more responsibilities and play a major role in law enforcement. The U.S. Marshals Service and the U.S. Postal Investigation Service are the oldest federal law enforcement agencies in the United States.

U.S. Marshals Service

The **U.S. Marshals Service,** whose roots were in the English system, was established by the Judiciary Act of 1789. The federal Marshals Service has had a colorful past, as it was the primary law in the western territories in the late nineteenth century. Legionary figures of the Wild West, such as Wild Bill Hickok, Buffalo Bill Cody, Bat Masterson, and the outlaw Bob Dalton all served as deputy U.S. marshals. Presently, the 94 U.S. marshals and their deputies are occupied chiefly by responsibilities such as the execution of federal arrest warrants, the movement and custody of federal prisoners, the capture of inmates that escape from federal penitentiaries, the security of federal court facilities and personnel, and the protection of witnesses who testify against organized crime.

See the U.S. Marshals Service at http://www.usdoj.gov/marshals/. ■

One of the first significant and far-reaching influences on contemporary law enforcement brought about by the actions of the Western federal marshals of the late nineteenth century was the ***Posse Comitatus*** **Act of 1878.** During the late 1800s, the federal marshals were responsible for maintaining law and order in the western territories, but they often lacked the necessary manpower and resources to carry out such responsibilities. To supplement their manpower, federal marshals were authorized to enlist the service of civilians and the military to help them perform their duties.[80] During the era of "Bleeding Kansas," when proslavery and antislavery factions had violent exchanges, the federal marshals were granted the power of *posse comitatus.* This authority granted them the power to deputize or command the assistance of private citizens and/or the military to assist the marshal in performing law enforcement duties. Because the federal government had to pay private citizens for their service, the federal marshal frequently used military troops. Thus, from 1854 to 1878, it was quite common for the federal marshal to command the assistance of military troops to help perform civilian law enforcement duties. The cost of maintaining order with the use of military troops quickly became too expensive for the federal government, and the power of *posse comitatus* was revoked in 1878.[81] This prohibition against using federal troops for civilian law enforcement has continued to be a guiding principle in American law enforcement.

The U.S. Marshals Service often works with other law enforcement agencies, assisting city, county, and state police with their fugitive cases, and is the primary American agency responsible for returning fugitives wanted in the United States from foreign countries. While the sheriff provides court security for state courts, it is the U.S. Marshals Service that provides court security for federal courts in the United States and its territories. Because of the large number of federal prisoners who are transported through partnership with the Immigration and Naturalization Service (INS), the Marshals Service operates the Justice Prisoner and Alien Transportation System. The fleet of jet and turboprop aircraft, frequently acquired through asset forfeiture, operates to move prisoners economically and safely through the United States.

One of the unique jurisdictions of the U.S. Marshals Service is the Missile Escort Program. Deputy marshals are specially trained to provide security and law enforcement assistance to the Department of Defense and the U.S. Air Force during the movement of nuclear warheads between military facilities. Also, the U.S. Marshals Service has jurisdiction to investigate cases in which individuals have reneged on debts owed to the government for criminal fines, financial fraud, or medical training. The deputies identify debtor assets, facilitate prejudgment and postjudgment remedy planning, and enforce other judgment requirements. The deputy marshals selected and trained for these duties are part of the Judgment Enforcement Team (JET) program.

U.S. Postal Investigation Service

The **U.S. Postal Investigation Service** is a highly specialized agency responsible for the security of the United States mail, mail carriers, and the investigation of mail fraud. Like the Marshals Service, the U.S. Postal Investigation Service dates from the founding of the nation. Its agents are called postal inspectors and are employed by the United States Postal Service. The Postal Investigation Service has always had a low-key profile despite the fact that it is one of the larger staffed federal law enforcement agencies and has an impressive record of effectiveness.

U.S. Secret Service

Another early federal law enforcement agency was the **U.S. Secret Service.** Today, most federal law enforcement agencies are under executive control (i.e., under presidential control). The U.S. Secret Service, founded in 1865, is under the control of the Department of the Treasury, and was first charged only with investigating the widespread counterfeiting and currency violations that followed the Civil War. Immediately following the Civil War, there were numerous "legal" currencies in circulation. Unlike today, it was

See the United States Postal Investigation Service at http://www.usps.gov/websites/depart/inspect/.

Figure 6.1

Historical Development of American Policing Prior to World War II

1000–1700

The tithing system, Office of Sheriff, and principles of due process and home rule develop in Europe during the Middle Ages.

- 1116 Henry I issues the *Legis Henrici* (Law of Henry)
- 1215 John I signs the Magna Carta
- 1608 Dales Law in England's American colony of Virginia
- 1653 Oliver Cromwell establishes military districts

1700–1800

The Industrial Revolution and gin influence the development of policing in England. The American Revolution sets the United States on a different course.

- 1737 George II levies taxes for a night watch
- 1748 Bow Street Runners in London
- 1774 Westminster Watch Act establishes public law enforcement in England
- 1787 U.S. Constitution ratified by the states
- 1787 U.S. Postal Investigation Service established
- 1789 U.S. Marshal Service established in the United States by Judiciary Act
- 1791 First ten amendments to the Constitution (Bill of Rights) ratified

1800–1850

Paid, uniformed, full-time police become the norm in European and American cities.

- 1800 Thames River Police established
- 1828 Sir Robert Peel appointed as Home Secretary for England
- 1829 London Metropolitan Police established by an act of Parliament
- 1830 Philadelphia establishes a night watch and a day watch
- 1835 Municipal Corporations Act standardizes metropolitan police forces in England
- 1844 New York City combines day and night watches into London-style police department

1850–1900

The Wild West, slavery, and the American Civil War uniquely affect the development of policing in America.

- 1865 U.S. Secret Service established
- 1867 First black police officers appointed in Alabama
- 1878 *Posse Comitatus* Act grants U.S. marshals the power to deputize
- 1896 *Plessy v. Ferguson* institutes racial segregation

1900–1930

World War I, urbanization, and labor conflicts influence the development of American policing.

- 1905–1932 Contributions of August Vollmer, chief of police of Berkeley, California, lead to the modernization and professionalization of American police departments.

legal for large companies, banks, and states to print and mint legal tender, or money. Also, the technology for printing money used by the federal government was relatively primitive, and the forgery of acceptable quality counterfeit money was not difficult. Some estimates place the percentage of counterfeit money in circulation immediately after the Civil War as high as 50 percent.[82] Initially, the U.S. Secret Service was responsible only for fighting counterfeiting and bringing counterfeiters to justice, but later its duties were expanded to include protecting the president.

Prior to 1900, no agency was charged with protecting the president from assassination or harm. The president, like any other citizen, went about his duties and life without the protection of federal bodyguards. Motivated by the assassination of President William McKinley at Buffalo, New York, in 1901, the duties of the Secret Service were expanded to include the protection of the president and eventually certain members of his family. One of the reasons that these duties fell to the Secret Service is that by the turn of the century, they had been so successful in combating counterfeiting and along with the vastly improved technology for printing money, the problem of counterfeiting had declined, so additional duties could be taken on. Today, the U.S. Secret Service is still responsible for fighting counterfeiting, but protection responsibilities occupy most of its time. In addition to the president, they protect the president's family, the vice president and designated members of his family, former presidents and their minor children, and widows of former presidents. With the assassination of Robert Kennedy, Congress again expanded the protection responsibilities of the Secret Service to include major presidential and vice-presidential candidates. The U.S. Secret Service also protects visiting heads of foreign governments. On occasion, the Secret Service has even been given the responsibility of protecting national treasures such as the Declaration of Independence, the Constitution of the United States, the United Nations Charter, and other valuable documents and works of art, including the Magna Carta when it was brought to the United States for exhibit.

JUST THE FACTS 6.6

What were the first three federal policing agencies to develop in the United States, and how have their responsibilities changed?

conclusion:

Life with the Police

The history of the development of American policing is the record of how society has attempted to cope with social and economic changes that disrupt social order. One of the common themes in the development of policing is the fear of street crime. Policing is a paradox; on one hand, the police promote social order, but on the other hand, they reduce individual liberties. Societies have found the balance between social order and freedom a moving target. As new ways of policing are developed to achieve just the right balance of order and liberty, social and economic changes are introduced that disrupt that balance. While policing as it is known today is a relatively new social experiment in maintaining law and order, it is difficult or impossible to imagine that society will ever return to a system of individual responsibility. Thus, the challenge is to develop a system of policing that ensures a safe society and controls social interactions, but at the same time does not achieve social order at the expense of those values that are esteemed by society, such as personal liberty, decentralized control, and local control of policing.

Chapter Summary

- A modern police force as we know it only began to emerge after 1829. The fear of crime was one of the major factors that caused the development of the police.
- The creation of the police was an inevitable product of the modern industrial state.
- There has always been the need to find a formal way to maintain social control in all societies. Thus, even the oldest civilizations developed ways to fight crime.
- The roots of American policing are in England. During the Middle ages, England used the tithing system to maintain order. This system emphasized individual responsibility and depended heavily on a rural, agrarian society with limited mobility.
- The industrial revolution brought numerous people into the cities of England, which resulted in a serious crime problem. London and other major cities experimented with several methods of policing. The forerunners of the modern police department include the night watch and the Bow Street Runners. Under the leadership of Sir Robert Peel in 1829, London adopted the first full-time, paid police force similar to the modern police department of today.
- In America, it took about 50 years for London-style policing to become widespread. The Constitution made police a power of the local, not federal government, and local policing prior to 1850 relied primarily on the office of the sheriff.
- The rapid increase of urban populations from 1850 to 1900 spurred the adoption of London-style police in America.
- American policing does not have a pattern of linear and progressive development. There were vast regional differences in the development of American policing. The Wild West and the slave patrols and Black Codes of the South were unique chapters in American policing.
- August Vollmer is the Father of American Policing. However, he was largely unsuccessful during his lifetime in getting other police departments to adopt his progressive philosophy.
- Federal law enforcement agencies developed over hundreds of years. As existing local and state police proved ineffective in combating new challenges of crime, federal law enforcement agencies were developed. The oldest federal agencies are the U.S. Marshals Service, the U.S. Postal Investigation Service, and the U.S. Secret Service.

Vocabulary Review

Article X, 189
Black Codes, 192
Code of Hammurabi, 179
frankpledge, 181
Legis Henrici, 183
Magna Carta, 184
Plessy v. Ferguson (1896), 193
posse comitatis, 182
praetors, 181
quaestores, 181
sheriff, 182
shire-reeve, 182
slave patrols, 192
tithing system, 181
Urban Cohort, 180
vigilantism, 190

Names and Events to Remember

August Vollmer, 195
Bow Street Runners, 186
London Metropolitan Police Act, 187
Posse Comitatus Act of 1878, 196
Praetorian Guard, 180
Sir Robert Peel, 186
U.S. Marshals Service, 196
U.S. Postal Investigation Service, 197
U.S. Secret Service, 197
Westminster Watch Act of 1774, 186

Think about This

1. American policing was developed using a model of decentralization and "home rule" because of the fear of strong central government control. Is this model still valid today or should policing be centralized?
2. The reason given for making the sheriff an elected office is that it increases accountability and makes abuse of power more difficult. What would be the advantages and disadvantages of having local police chiefs obtain their office by popular election?
3. Based on patterns and trends in the history of policing, what forces do you think will shape the development of the police in the twenty-first century?

ContentSelect

Go to the ContentSelect web site and type in the keyword *embezzlement*. There you will find an interesting in-depth analysis by Richard Soderlund of the development of industrial policing in eighteenth-century England. Consider the case of Martha Pimlott, who was punished for embezzlement when she stole bits of woolen yarn ("short-reeled" a spool) from the factory where she was employed as a spinner. Sample the article to answer the following questions.

1. What conflicts arose as a result of the industrial revolution that affected the definition and treatment of workplace crime?
2. How was embezzlement defined and punished? Why was embezzlement regarded as a serious crime in the worsted (wool) industry of the nineteenth century?
3. What means did manufacturers use to try to prevent workplace crimes in both cottage industry and factories? On what values of early capitalism was wage work based?
4. What strategies did manufacturers try to increase the supply of yarn and why were they unsuccessful?
5. What form of private policing emerged in factories as a result of the industrial revolution? Do manufacturers employ that form of policing today?
6. Where in this chapter might you use this article as an example of factors that influenced the history of policing?

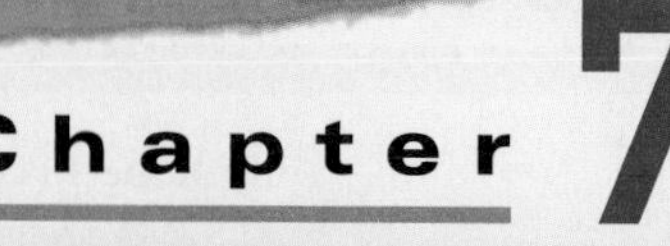

Chapter 7

Roles and Functions of the Police

outline

Learning Objectives

After reading this chapter, you will know

- What the local, state, and federal police agencies are and how they are both similar and different in organization and function.
- The characteristics and major responsibilities of the various local, state, and federal law enforcement agencies.
- The different jobs that police personnel perform in a police department and how officers develop their careers in law enforcement.
- How issues of decentralization and jurisdiction affect the continuing development of American policing.
- How law enforcement agencies have been changed in response to terrorist threats against the United States.

Bad Day at the Bank

SHAWNEE, KS—It wasn't a particularly well planned bank robbery, as the robber chose the busiest time on a Friday afternoon to rob a bank in Shawnee, Kansas. He had written out in advance his note to the teller, demanding the money, and had prepared his disguise, a paper bag with two holes cut out for his eyes. So as not to attract attention, he put the paper bag over his head after he entered the bank and removed the revolver from his pocket while holding the demand note in his other hand and proceeded toward the tellers. Apparently he had overlooked two small details. One, he had failed to cut the holes in the paper bag so that he could see out of them. Two, he had either not cased the layout of the bank lobby or forgot, in his excitement, that you had to walk down two steps once you entered. The bank robber missed the steps, fell, and broke his leg. As he lay in pain, the bank security guard walked over, removed the gun from his hand, read the demand note, and placed the bank robber under arrest. The bank robber was taken to the hospital for medical treatment. Bank robbery is both a federal offense and a state offense; therefore, he could be arrested by either the Federal Bureau of Investigation or the Shawnee Police Department, or both. Neither agency made any move to charge the suspect. He lay in the hospital for several days while the two agencies argued over who should arrest him. The problem was that neither agency wanted to arrest him. In the end, he was charged in state court. Why did neither agency want to arrest him? Neither agency wanted to arrest him because the arresting agency would have to pick up the suspect's hospital bill and assume liability for future medical treatment.

—"Bad Day at the Bank" by James Fagin.

introduction:

Who Are the Police?

The police are the most visible representative of the government in American society. For many people, most of their knowledge about the police comes from the media either in the form of entertainment shows or news coverage. While the media can give the viewer insight into the world of policing, the media can also be the source of some ill-conceived notions about the police. For example, televison's long-running police show *Hawaii Five-O* prompted many tourists to desire to visit the famed police agency while vacationing in Hawaii. Not only is there no such police agency, Hawaii is one of the few states without a state police agency. One needs to look beyond the media to examine the police and what they do. Many people do not know what the police actually do, how they are organized, or the source and limits of their authority. This chapter provides an overview of the responsibilities and organizational structure of the law enforcement agencies in the United States.

One of the most distinctive characteristics of policing in the American criminal justice system is that it is performed by over 17,000 fragmented, semi-autonomous law enforcement agencies.[1] Most of these agencies (over 12,000) are under the control of a city government. Over 3,000 law enforcement agencies are sheriff's departments. There are approximately 1,700 special police and 49 state police agencies.[2] There are less than 100 federal law enforcement agencies and of this number, only about 6 are well known to the public.[3] Each police agency is autonomous; has its own chief administrator, headquarters, rules and regulations, jurisdiction, training standards and facilities, retirement plan, salary scale, and uniform. While the uniform worn by the officers of the various police may appear identical to the casual observer, each department has its own unique uniform, badge and identification card.

For more information on the roles and functions of the police, go to http://www.ablongman.com/criminaljustice. ■

Furthermore, there is no single agency that has oversight responsibility for all of these different police agencies. There is no central authority, person, or agency to coordinate police activities, to enforce compliance with rules, to investigate charges of police abuse of power, or just to see to it that the police are doing a good job. Given the great number of police agencies and the lack of centralized control, it is not surprising that there are frequently overlapping jurisdictions and responsibilities and even duplication of services.

Understanding Jurisdiction

THE MAIN IDEA

Jurisdiction refers to both geographic region and official duties covered by an agency.

jurisdiction Geographical area of responsibility and legitimate duties of an agency, court, or law enforcement officer.

In trying to understand the American system of policing, a good starting point is to examine the **jurisdiction** of the various agencies. Each law enforcement agency's powers, responsibilities, and accountability is determined by its jurisdiction. Jurisdiction refers to the geographical limits such as the municipality, county, or state in which officers of the agency are empowered to perform their duties. Jurisdiction also refers to the legitimate duties that the department can perform. Some agencies have a relatively small geographical jurisdiction but a large number of legitimate duties. Other agencies have an expansive geographical jurisdiction but limited legitimate duties. For example, the geographical jurisdiction of the municipal police officer ends at the city limits, but Federal Bureau of Investigation (FBI) agencies have geographical jurisdiction in all of the 50 states, the District of Columbia, U.S. territories, and certain federal reservations. However, the legal jurisdiction of the FBI is limited to federal laws mandated by the Congress. Federal law enforcement agencies and courts do not have the common law jurisdiction of municipal police. FBI agents do not enforce traffic laws, do not make arrests for disorderly conduct, do not patrol the streets of the city and or respond to 9-1-1 calls. Furthermore, FBI agencies can only investigate a crime if it meets certain conditions, such as occurring on federal property or violating a federal law. Using jurisdiction as a criterion, the thousands of police agencies can be divided into five different types depending on their jurisdiction: county, municipal, state, special, and federal law enforcement.

JUST THE FACTS 7.1

What is jurisdiction? How do the jurisdictions of law enforcement agencies differ?

County Law Enforcement Agencies

THE MAIN IDEA

County law enforcement is performed primarily by the elected office of sheriff.

The sheriff's office is the oldest local policing authority in the United States. When the United States was founded, the Office of the Sheriff was the primary **local law enforcement** agency, as police agencies under the jurisdiction of the city did not become common until the late 1800s. The Office of the Sheriff came from England, but in the American system, rather than being appointed by the Crown, the **sheriff** was elected by popular vote of county residents. In contrast, police chiefs and directors of state and federal law enforcement agencies obtain their positions through political appointment.

While the normal term of office for the sheriff in the 1800s was 2 years, most modern sheriffs are elected to 4-year terms. In many county elections, sheriffs are expected to affiliate with a political party and to raise funds to campaign for the position. Qualifications to run for sheriff are minimal. The most common requirements are a minimum age and no felony convictions. Campaign, political affiliation, and public appeal are more important in obtaining the office of sheriff than job experience, education, or law enforcement abilities. It is not uncommon for some sheriffs to have no previous background in law enforcement prior to being elected.

local law enforcement Municipal or county law enforcement officer; also includes certain special police agencies with limited jurisdiction, such as campus police.

sheriff Chief administrative officer of the Office of Sheriff. The only elected position in law enforcement.

Jurisdiction of the Sheriff

The geographical jurisdiction of the sheriff is the county. Thus, the number of sheriff's departments in a state is largely determined by the number of counties. The state of Texas, with 255 counties, has more sheriff's departments than any other state. The District of Columbia and the state of Alaska do not have an office of the sheriff. In Hawaii, the sheriff's department is a state office, and the sheriff is appointed by the governor.[4]

The Office of the Sheriff provides law enforcement at the county level. Unlike other policing authorities in America, the sheriff is elected by popular vote. Campaigning, political affiliation, and public appeal are some of the characteristics important in an election. What is the origin of this practice? What are the minimum legal requirements to become a candidate? How long is the term that a sheriff serves? How is the Office of the Sheriff different from municipal, state, or federal organizations?

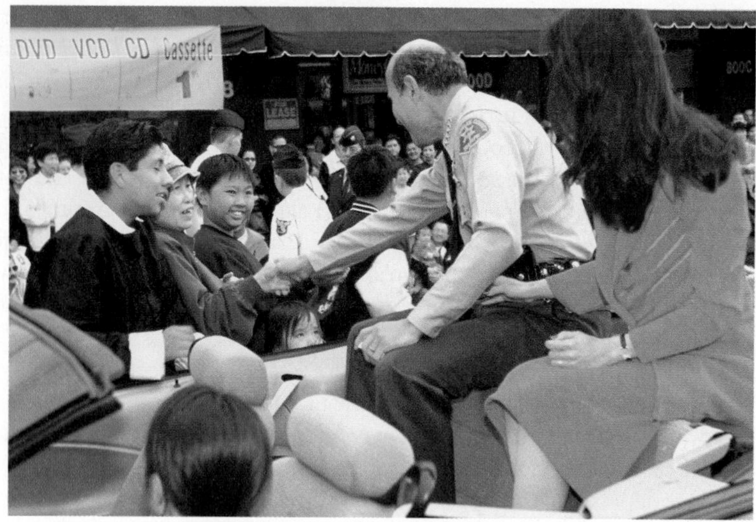

Because the sheriff has countywide jurisdiction, whereas local police departments have only municipal jurisdiction, the sheriff is generally designated as the **chief law enforcement officer** of the county. The chief law enforcement officer of the state is the attorney general, and the chief law enforcement officer of the United States is the U.S. attorney general.

Administrative Structure of the Sheriff's Department

The sheriff is empowered to appoint officers to help him or her carry out the duties of the office. These officers are called **deputy sheriff** officers. The second in command of the sheriff's office sometimes retains the old English title of undersheriff.[5] Deputy sheriffs wear different uniforms than local police within their county to distinguish the two departments. The star-shaped badge worn by the deputy sheriff is a carryover from the old English office of the sheriff, whereas officers in most police departments wear shields.

chief law enforcement officer Title applied to the sheriff of the county because his or her jurisdiction is greater than that of the local police agencies within the county.

deputy sheriffs Law enforcement officers working for the Office of the Sheriff. All law enforcement officers in the sheriff's office, regardless of rank, are deputy sheriffs.

officer of the court Law enforcement officer that is used by the court to serve papers, provide courtroom security, and transport defendants.

During most of the nineteenth and twentieth centuries, deputy sheriffs were selected for their jobs based on political patronage. The sheriff could personally select any one he or she wanted for the job without regard for qualifications for the position or competitive examination. The deputy sheriffs selected to help carry out the duties of the office were chosen because of their personal loyalty to the sheriff. Deputy sheriffs did not have job security or protection against casual dismissal. They retained their job "at the pleasure of the sheriff" and could be dismissed even without cause.

This system of selecting deputy sheriffs was based on the belief that an elected sheriff should be able to appoint employees on the basis of loyalty. Deputy sheriffs were expected to assist in the sheriff's reelection campaign, and this support was more important than job knowledge, ability, or skills. Until the mid-twentieth century, deputy sheriffs were even expected to contribute financially to the sheriff's campaign. If a sheriff failed to win reelection, the incoming sheriff had the authority to dismiss the deputy sheriffs and award the jobs as political patronage to those who helped him or her win office. Thus, new deputy sheriffs could assume their jobs immediately without the benefit of training.

Today there are state-mandated minimum training requirements for law enforcement officers. As a result of court rulings prohibiting the dismissal of deputy sheriffs for failing to campaign for the sheriff (or in some cases campaigning for the sheriff's

careers  in the system

Working in the Sheriff's Office

Most sheriff's departments have few employees, despite the large geographical responsibility and multipurpose nature of the sheriff's departments. Of the 3,000 sheriff's departments in the United States, only 12 have more than 1,000 sworn personnel and fewer than 100 have more than 250 sworn personnel. Most sheriff's departments (43%) employ fewer than 10 full-time officers. In some cases, the department can be very small, as about 50 departments employ just 1 or no full-time officers other than the sheriff.[6]

Overall, the salaries for entry-level deputy sheriffs tend to be slightly lower than those of entry-level municipal police officers. Also, the salary of the sheriff tends to be lower than that of the chief administrative officer of a municipal police department.[7]

The functions and organizational structure of the sheriff's department are major considerations in making career choices. The sheriff's department traditionally had three major areas of responsibility: law enforcement, court security and **officers of the court,** and jail operations. Court security and the serving of court orders is the duty most commonly performed by sheriff's departments today.

To meet the need for people in each of these areas of responsibility, some sheriff's departments have a dual-entry system and others have a single-entry system. In the dual-entry system, you apply specifically to be either a deputy sheriff in patrol or a correctional officer in county jail operations. Correctional officers receive different training, have different duties, and receive different pay. Individuals who enter as correctional officers usually are not "sworn" officers with the power of arrest and the right to carry a firearm. Jail personnel go through a shorter academy and often receive lower pay; in fact, some sheriff's departments have been known to transfer a deputy sheriff from road patrol to jail operations as punishment for errant behavior.

At the same time, in some county jails, personnel are supervised by sergeants, lieutenants, and captains who are in the deputy sheriff track. In those cases, deputy sheriffs eligible for promotion may find that they have to choose between transferring to a position in jail operations or declining the promotion and staying in road patrol at their present rank.

In a single-career track, all personnel in the sheriff's department enter as jail personnel. After serving a period of time, usually 1 year, as a correctional officer, a person can apply for promotion to deputy sheriff and undertake police training at the academy. This system is used by small- and medium-sized sheriff's departments that have difficulty getting qualified applicants to work in the jails. The deputy sheriff also may have to work in court security or prisoner transport.

■ **If you worked in a sheriff's department, what would you do? How would your career progress if you were in a dual-entry system? How would your job compare with that of a municipal law enforcement officer?**

table 7.1 Comparison of Entry Salaries of Sheriffs' Departments and Local Police

Median Salary	Sheriff	Local Police
Large population group	$30,200	$30,600
Medium population group	24,000	30,500
Small population group	20,100	23,500

Source: Bureau of Justice Statistics, *Sourcebook of Criminal Justice Statistics* 2000. <www.albany.edu/sourcebook/1995/pdf/t148.pdf; www.albany.edu/sourcebook/1995/pdf/t149.pdf>.

opponent), most sheriff's departments use a civil service selection process for the appointment of sworn officers. Deputy sheriffs are selected based on competitive examinations that test job knowledge, skills, and abilities and can be dismissed from their jobs only for legitimate reasons.

Law Enforcement Duties of the Sheriff

The Office of the Sheriff was the first and only local law enforcement agency in the late eighteenth and early nineteenth centuries. The sheriff and his deputies were empowered to enforce the laws of the county and state, to make arrests, to engage in preventative patrol, and to carry firearms. The law enforcement jurisdiction of the sheriff exceeded that of the municipal chief of police. As municipalities grew, both geographically and in population, many city limits extended to the limits of the counties in which they were located. With the rise of municipal policing in the latter half of the twentieth century, the role of the sheriff in providing law enforcement services has diminished. Today, in practice it is often the municipal police who assume major responsibility for law enforcement and the sheriff's department that provides police services for citizens who live in unincorporated or rural areas of the county. However, in some major metropolitan areas very little of the county is unincorporated, and the law enforcement services of the sheriff overlap those of municipal police. In some cases, the sheriff's department provides few or no law enforcement services. In other cases, duplication of functions and overlapping jurisdictions lead to cooperation or conflict between departments. A classic example of conflict was between the Los Angeles Sheriff's Department and the Los Angeles Police Department over the Tate-La Bianca murders committed by followers of notorious Charles Manson. Conflict between the two agencies hindered the investigation of the crime, as both agencies claimed jurisdiction.[8]

Serving the Court and Operating the County Jail

The sheriff's department is the law enforcement agency used by the state court system to serve warrants, summons, and papers of the court; to provide court security; and to transport prisoners to and from the courtroom. For this reason, deputy sheriff officers are known as "servants of the court." Initially, the serving of court papers was a major source of income for the sheriff. Most sheriffs received little pay for their position and were allowed to keep for their personal use some or all of the fees charged to serve the papers of the court. This practice has not completely disappeared, and in many counties the sheriff's department still gets to keep part of the fees paid to serve court papers. The historical reason for this practice is that the concept of financing government operations from personal income taxes was not instituted until the passage of the Seventeenth Amendment, which made the collecting of personal income taxes constitutional. Throughout the nineteenth century, all government agencies and services were financed by a system of fees, tariffs, or property taxes. Modern practices allow for the budgeting of law enforcement from public funds.

The third responsibility of the sheriff's department is the operation of the county jail, also originally a source of income for the sheriff. The sheriff would be given a budget by the county to take care of the prisoners in the county jail, but could keep unspent funds for his personal use. The sheriff could also charge other agencies such as cities, the state, or the federal government to temporarily house prisoners in the county jail. In the late 1800s and early 1900s, the sheriff's office and the jail were frequently housed in the county courthouse. In some of the rural counties, the sheriff's personal living quarters were also attached to the county jail, as the sheriff was the primary security for the jail at night. Today, many counties have transferred the responsibility of jail operations to special correctional agencies.

table 7.2 Comparison of Responsibilities of Sheriffs' Departments and Local Police

Responsibility	Sheriff	Local Police
Preventative patrol	Some departments do not perform this function.	Primary responsibility
Traffic enforcement	Some departments do not perform this function.	Primary responsibility
Order maintenance	Some departments do not perform this function.	Primary responsibility
Crime investigation (detectives)	Some departments do not perform this function.	Primary responsibility
Correctional officer	Personnel work in county jail	A few departments have holding cells.
Service of court papers	Primary responsibility	Do not perform this function
Provision of court security	Primary responsibility	Do not perform this function (except for municipal court)
Juvenile unit	Sheriff's departments will not have a juvenile unit if they do not perform law enforcement duties.	Common in even small police departments
Transportation of prisoners	Primary responsibility	Minor responsibility

JUST THE FACTS 7.2

By what titles are chief executive officers of law enforcement agencies known, and how do they obtain their positions? What are the three traditional duties of the sheriff's office?

The City Police: "The Cops"

THE MAIN IDEA

The municipal police force is the most local and visible representation of government in the community.

When most people refer to "the police" they mean the municipal police—not the sheriff, state police, or federal police. Many town and city residents appear not to appreciate or notice the difference among deputy sheriffs, state police, and municipal police officers. The municipal police department and police officer have become the most visible representation of government authority in the community. Commonly referred to simply as "the cops," municipal police officers far outnumber all other types of law enforcement officers combined. (The origin of the term *cops* is lost in history. Many believe it is the English slang "coppers," referring to badges made of copper metal that early night watchmen wore around their necks, or an acronym for "**c**onstable **o**n **p**atrol.")

Each incorporated town or city in the United States has the power to establish its own police department and laws. Thus, there are over 12,000 municipal police departments. Typically, the size of the municipal police department increases as the population of the city increases, and the largest police departments are found in the largest cities, as shown in Table 7.3.

While large cities may employ thousands of police officers, most municipal departments are much smaller. Over 90% of the municipal police departments employ fewer than 50 officers and serve populations of less than 25,000.[9] The police department is one of the major expenses of the city. The budget for a small police department will average about $1.7 million per year, and large departments may have budgets that exceed $300 million.[10]

Jurisdiction of Local Police

In the United States, the geographical jurisdiction of the municipal police officer is limited to the city limits. Once outside his or her municipal jurisdiction, a local police officer's powers to arrest, search, or even carry a firearm may not be recognized. For example, if a Los Angeles police officer were to take a vacation to Hawaii, he or she would have no police powers in Hawaii and would be prohibited from carrying a concealed firearm.

While the geographical jurisdiction of municipal police officers is limited compared to county, state, and federal agents, their legal jurisdiction is the most comprehensive of all of the police agencies. Municipal police officers have the authority to enforce both city and state laws, and often their authority is based on common law rather than statutory law. Common law authority gives the officers broad discretion in determining which behaviors are illegal.

As cities have merged into large metropolitan areas, police departments have

table 7.3 Ten Largest U.S. Police Departments

State	Agency	Number Sworn Personnel
New York	New York Police Department	39,099
Illinois	Chicago Police	13,307
California	Los Angeles Police	9,573
Pennsylvania	Philadelphia Police	7,013
Texas	Houston Police	5,433
Michigan	Detroit Police	4,016
District of Columbia	Washington Metropolitan Police	3,443
Maryland	Baltimore Police	3,005
Florida	Metro-Dade County Police	2,949
Texas	Dallas Police	2,858

Source: Bureau of Justice Statistics, *Sourcebook of Criminal Justice Statistics* 2000. <www.albany.edu/sourcebook/1995/pdf/t158.pdf>.

responded by expanding the geographical jurisdiction of the municipal police officer through intercity agreements. In large metropolitan areas such as Dade County (Florida), Los Angeles, and Las Vegas, intercity and county agreements have established the **metro police.** These agreements provide for greater geographical jurisdiction to avoid the problems that would develop if the police did not have any powers outside of their city limits.

Go to http://www.communitypolicing.org/ for more information on community policing. ■

Administrative Structure of the Municipal Police

The chief administrative officer of the police department is usually called the **chief of police.** The chief obtains his or her position by appointment. In smaller cities, the chief may be directly appointed by the mayor or city council. In larger cities, the chief may be appointed by a police commission appointed by the city council. Unlike the sheriff, who is elected for a specified number of years, the chief has no guarantee of the term of his or her appointment. For this reason, chiefs are said to "serve at the pleasure of the mayor or the city council." This political relationship between the chief and city administrators has influenced local policing.

The second-in-command of the police department is usually called the **deputy chief** or assistant chief. This person is selected by the chief from among the higher ranking police administrators. Promotions among other ranks and the hiring of new police officers for the department are usually accomplished through competitive civil service exams based on job-related skills, abilities, and knowledge. These officers are called "sworn" personnel because they must take an oath to uphold the laws of the city, state, and county and to execute faithfully the responsibilities of their office.

"Non-sworn" personnel of the police department, such as secretaries, office workers, and technicians, are referred to as "civilian" employees. Civilian employees do not have the powers granted to sworn police personnel of arrest, search and seizure, and the right to carry a firearm. Sworn personnel normally enjoy what is referred to as "civil service protection," which means that after completing their probation period of employment, they cannot be dismissed from their jobs without cause and due process.[11]

Police departments have a system of military-style ranks in a hierarchical pyramid, with a chain of command from officer to chief.[12] This is termed a *command-and-control structure,* as in the organizational chart in Figure 7.1 on page 212. Although also

metro police Local police agency that spans several geographical jurisdictions, such as cities or city and county.

chief of police Title of the chief administrative officer of a municipal police agency. The chief obtains his or her position by appointment of the mayor, city council, or other designated city agency, such as the police commission.

deputy chief Title of the second in command of a municipal police agency. This is an appointed position by the chief of police.

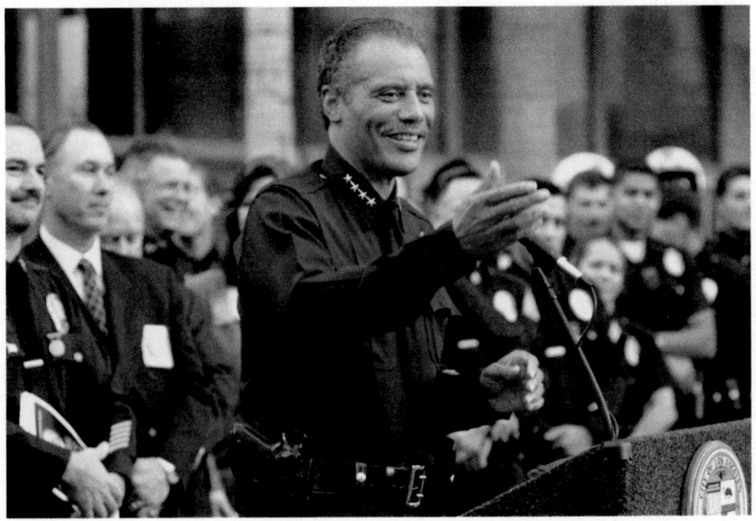

Local police departments have a paramilitary system of ranks, with a police chief as the chief law enforcement officer. What is the order of ranks in the hierarchy? How are ranks indicated? How are ranks filled? How do officers move through the system in the course of their careers? What might be some strengths and weaknesses of a hierarchical organizational structure with a pattern of linear advancement? What are some benefits and drawbacks of lateral career moves in law enforcement?

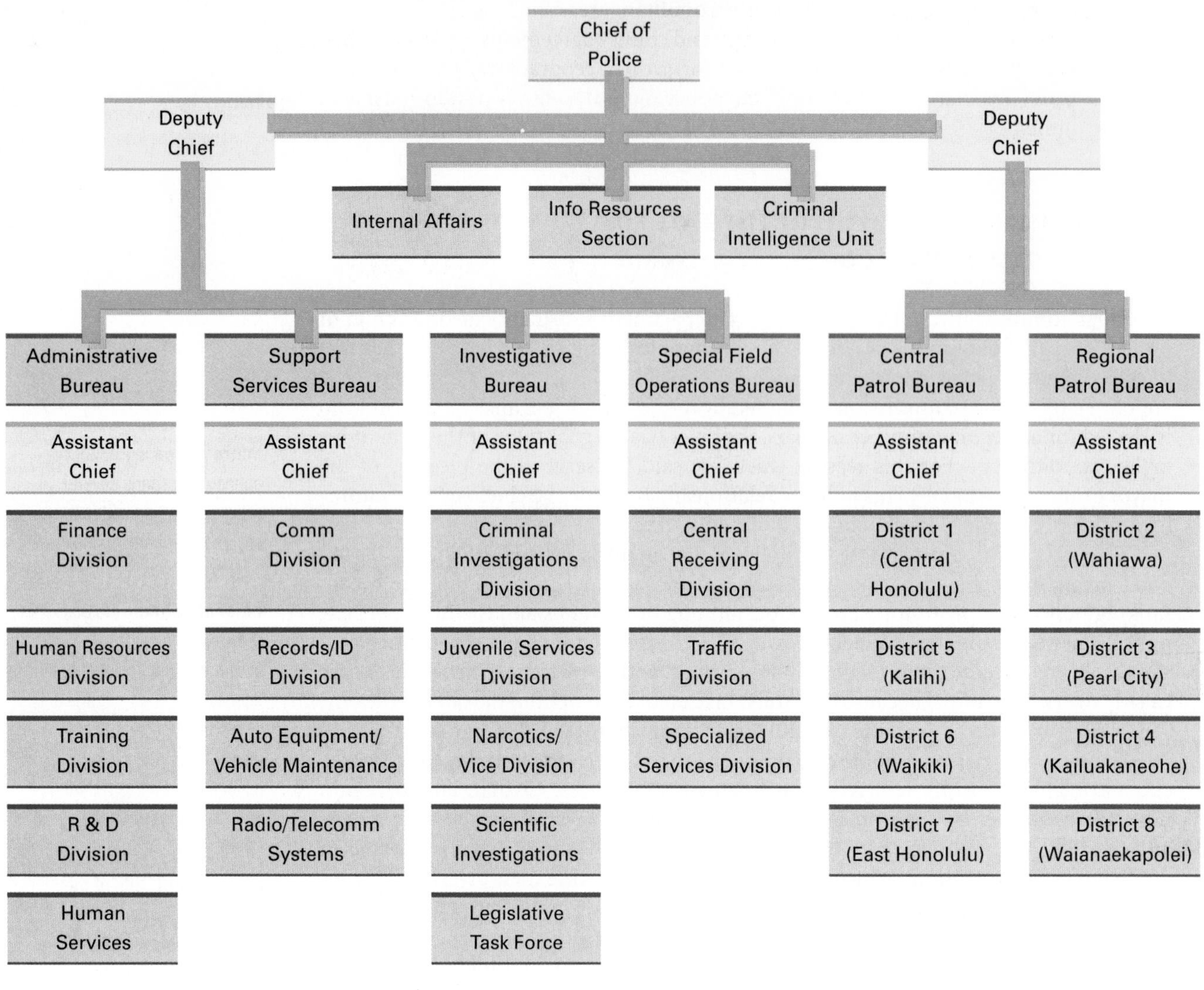

Figure 7.1

Command-and-Control Structures (Honolulu Police Administration)

Source: Reprinted by permission of the Police Department of the City and County of Honolulu, Hawaii.

organized in terms of a command-and-control structure, federal law enforcement agencies do not use military titles but titles such as field agent, supervisor, agent-in-charge, and director.

The police organizational chart differentiates among the various functions that the department performs. The most common divisions are patrol, detective services, and support services. The patrol division is the largest organizational unit. Detective services include the investigation of crimes such as fraud, burglary, arson, and homicide. Larger departments allow for specialization among detectives, including juvenile officers, vice squad (gambling and prostitution), and other divisions based on types of crime. Support services might include special units for community crime prevention, drug education in schools, juvenile delinquency, child abuse, missing children, drunk drivers, gangs, domestic violence, repeat offenders, hate crimes, victims' services, and more.[13] Specialty support units include the police training academy, the air patrol unit, the bomb squad, and the reserve or auxiliary police (volunteers who assist in police duties).

careers

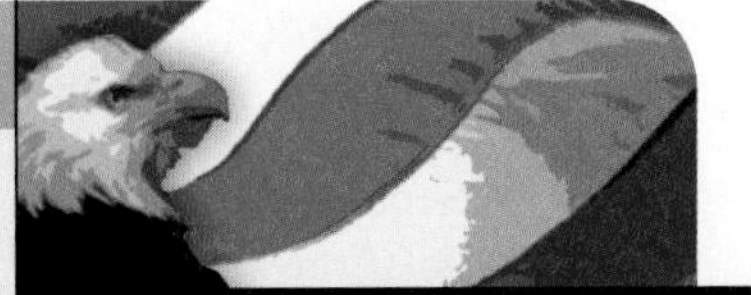

in the system

Police Ranks and Promotions

Ranks and specialties usually are identified by uniform insignia. For example, in many departments, advancement is indicated by stripes on the sleeve of the officer's uniform or the "collar brass" that the officer wears. In some departments, the badge an officer carries is another distinction. When promoted from patrol officer to sergeant, an officer might trade in his or her silver or "tin" badge for a gold badge, indicating the supervisory powers of a sergeant. Rank also may be distinguished by the color of the uniform or of the braid on the hats officers wear.

In the United States, until recently all police officers had to start at the bottom of the pyramid as a patrol officer. It was not possible to start as a sergeant, detective, or lieutenant without working your way up the pyramid. Even higher ranking officers with previous experience usually are started at an entry-level rank if they move to another department, although progressive departments permit officers to retain the same rank. A college degree, highly desired among recruits, mainly allows an officer to shorten the length of time before he or she can take the sergeant's exam.

Advances in rank bring additional power, prestige, and administrative responsibilities, as well as increases in salary. A sergeant is a "field supervisor" or "line supervisor," and a patrol sergeant may supervise as many as 30 patrol officers. Lieutenants usually have responsibility for a complete unit, such as "day watch" or "detectives." Larger departments have a greater number of higher ranking positions and thus greater opportunity for promotion.

While young officers might be attracted to a small city, advancement in a small police department is limited because advancement is possible only when a higher position is vacated.

Many departments have minimum qualifications for officers seeking to be detectives. Commonly, patrol officers are expected to serve 1 to 5 years before becoming eligible to be a detective, and some departments require a minimum rank of sergeant. After successfully passing the sergeant's examination, the officer's name is placed on a promotion list. Officers who make the highest scores are placed at the top of the list and are promoted to administrative patrol duty or detective until open positions are filled. Patrol sergeants and sergeant detectives hold the same rank and receive similar base pay.

Lateral, or horizontal, career moves are available in addition to steps for upward mobility. In a lateral transfer—as often as every 2 or 3 years—an officer remains at the same rank but assumes new duties. A patrol officer could request transfer to the police academy and work as an instructor. A detective could work his or her way up to burglary, sex crimes, or homicide investigator. An officer could ask to be transferred to personnel, research and development, or the crime lab, or to diverse special assignments, such as SWAT team member or school officer.

■ **As a municipal police officer, how would you most likely begin your career? What career choices would you have along the way, and how would those choices affect your mobility in the system?**

■ Police Patrol, Crime Prevention, and Other Services

Municipal police are responsible for a wide variety of services. The most commonly demanded services of the municipal police include traffic enforcement, accident investigation, patrol and first response to incidents, property crime investigation, violent crime investigation, and death investigation. Municipal police departments also end up assuming de facto responsibility for many things that are not their job, because they are one of the very few government agencies available 24 hours a day, 7 days a week, and they will dispatch an officer to the scene. Thus, it is common to find that municipal police agencies also have responsibilities for animal control, search and rescue, emergency medical services, civil defense, communication and technical support services, jail operations, **order maintenance,** and even fire fighting in some cities.

order maintenance
Non-crime-fighting services performed by the police, such as mediation, providing for the welfare of vulnerable persons, and crowd control.

table 7.4 How Police Officers Spend Their Time

Type of Activity	Percentage of Time
Preventative patrol	29.45
Crime-related activity	26.34
Administrative activity	12.3
Traffic-related activity	11.32
Order-maintenance activity	8.73
Unavailable for assignment	5.13
Medical-related activity	2.26

Source: "What Police Do" by Jack R. Greene and Carl B. Klockars in *Thinking about Police,* 2/e edited by Carl B. Klockars and Stephen D. Mastrofski, pp. 273–284, 279. Reprinted by permission of The McGraw-Hill Companies, Inc.

In an effort to save money, some smaller cities have combined the police department and the fire department. Commonly called the Department of Public Safety, the officers of these departments receive training in both law enforcement and fire fighting. A small number of full-time fire-fighting personnel are employed by the city to staff the fire station and drive the fire engine, but most of the fire fighters are police officers. These officers perform routine patrol but carry fire-fighting equipment and uniforms in the trunk of their patrol cars. If there is a fire, they respond to the scene of the fire and perform fire-fighting duties.

Contrary to the image promoted in the media of the police officer as primarily engaged in crime fighting, the reality of police work is that most police officers spend only a small portion of their time in crime-fighting activities.[14] Unlike the police officers in television series who receive misdemeanor and felony calls each episode, most real police officers are more likely to receive numerous calls for service and order maintenance. It is not uncommon for officers to complete a shift without making any arrests for criminal behavior.

Serving Shifts and Districts

The organizational structure of the police department is also based on geography. Departments divide the geographical area for which they are responsible into small units called districts, beats, or precincts. Each geographical unit is given a name or number relating to its location, its natural boundaries, or its place in the local economy, such as business district, warehouse district, waterfront, or downtown. The size of a unit, and the number of officers assigned to it, is based on population density and demand for police services in the area.[15]

Finally, the organizational structure of the police department is shaped by time. Unlike many businesses, the police must provide services all day, every day, 365 days a year. To provide this coverage, it is necessary to have "shifts" or "watches," each with its own administrators and support personnel. Days typically are divided into three 8-hour shifts, and rookies typically are assigned "new officer watch," the 11 P.M. to 7 A.M. shift. It is common practice to rotate personnel among shifts, but more popular and innovative schemes include shifts of 4 days a week at 10 hours a day with 3 days off every week.

JUST THE FACTS 7.3

What is the jurisdiction of the local police? How are police departments organized, and what are their job functions in the community?

The State Police

THE MAIN IDEA

State police agencies enforce traffic laws and investigate criminal activities.

state law enforcement Law enforcement agencies under the command of the executive branch of the state government, such as the highway patrol and state police.

The geographical jurisdiction of the state police is limited by the state boundaries, and their legal jurisdiction is determined by legislation. **State law enforcement** agencies can be divided into three major types: traffic enforcement, general criminal investigation, and special investigation. Some states, such as Kentucky, have a single state police agency that is responsible for both general criminal investigation and traffic enforcement. Other states have created distinct agencies for each function. The state of Kansas, for example, has two separate agencies: the Kansas Bureau of Investigation, which is responsible for general criminal investigations and the Kansas Highway Patrol, which is responsible for statewide traffic enforcement. Some states, such as Missouri, do not have a state police agency empowered with general criminal investigation authority. The state of Hawaii has neither a state highway patrol nor a statewide general criminal investigation agency. The state legislature of each state has the authority and discretion to establish the state police agencies that they think most appropriate for the needs of their state.

Use links at http://www.policeemployment.com/ to compare and contrast local, state, and federal law enforcement agencies and opportunities. ■

Highway Patrol

State police agencies that focus on traffic enforcement are commonly called "highway patrol." The legal jurisdictions for these agencies are limited to enforcing the traffic laws and promoting safety on the interstate highways and primary and secondary roads of the state. State traffic enforcement officers do not provide general preventative patrol services to neighborhoods, as do municipal police, or engage in the investigation of crimes. Using automobiles, motorcycles, airplanes, and helicopters, state highway patrol officers enforce the various traffic laws of the state, render assistance to motorists, and promote highway safety. Highway patrol officers have the powers of arrest and search and seizure, and are allowed to carry firearms.

The chief executive officer of the state's highway patrol agency is normally called a "director," and he or she receives his or her appointment from the governor of the state. Candidates for the highway patrol are selected through the use of competitive civil service procedures. Highway patrol officers are state employees and may be transferred throughout the state. Whereas municipal police officers are commonly called "cops," state highway patrol officers are commonly called "troopers." Because of the distinctive wide-brimmed hat worn by some state police highway patrol, which is similar to that worn by "Smokey the Bear" (from the advertising campaign to prevent forest fires), highway patrol officers are also often called "Smokey the Bear," "Smokies," or just "the Bear."

States with toll roads can use revenues collected from tolls to hire highway patrol officers who are employed by the turnpike authority. The geographical jurisdiction of officers employed by the turnpike authority is limited to the toll roads of the state. Their tour of duty may require that they patrol a hundred miles or more of turnpike in a single shift. Some states may restrict such officers from carrying concealed firearms off duty.

Criminal Investigation

State police agencies may have law enforcement powers similar to the municipal police in that they are authorized to conduct criminal investigations, perform routine patrol, and provide police services. So as not to duplicate the law enforcement services provided by municipal and county police, state police focus on the investigation of statewide crimes, such as those involving drugs and narcotics, or crimes that occur in more than one jurisdiction, such as a mobile crime ring, organized crime, or serial murder. In counties in which the sheriff's department cannot provide police services to unincorporated areas in the county, the state police may provide services to these areas. Sometimes, small towns or villages will contract with the state police to provide police services for a fee rather than attempt to have their own police department.

State police can also have jurisdiction for investigation of crimes where the municipal or county police may appear to be biased. In cases in which there are charges of political corruption of local officers, voter fraud, or bribery of state officials, it may make sense to give jurisdiction for these investigations to the state police.

JUST THE FACTS 7.4

What are the various types of state law enforcement agencies and their responsibilities?

What are the chief responsibilities and powers of state law enforcement officers? What is their jurisdiction? How does their job differ from that of officers in municipal police departments? In what ways might their jurisdiction and duties overlap or conflict with both local and federal law enforcement?

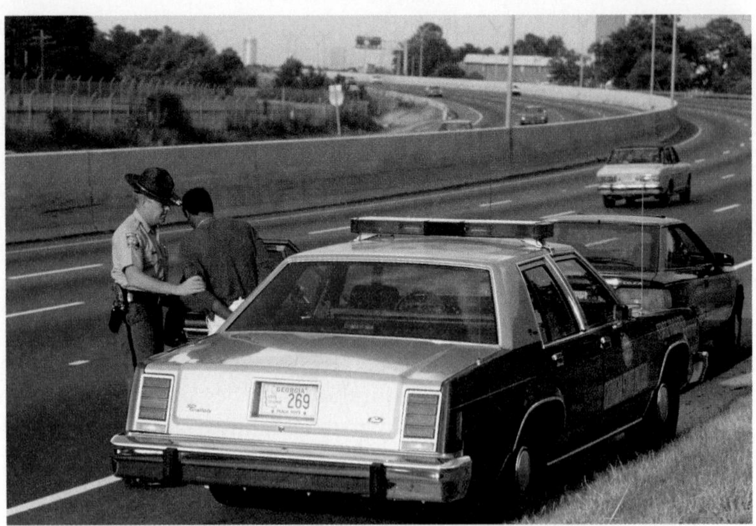

Special Police

THE MAIN IDEA

Special police agencies have limited jurisdictions, responsibilities, and powers.

Special police agencies include both state and local agencies that have limited geographical jurisdictions, such as airport police, park police, transit police, public school police, college and university police, public housing police, game wardens, alcoholic beverage control agencies, and special investigative units. The largest single employer of special police is the New York City Transit Police, with over 4,000 full-time officers, nearly one-third of all special police officers in the United States. Most special police departments are small; about two-thirds of the special police departments have fewer than 10 full-time employees.

Special police have limited jurisdiction both in geography and police powers. They are hired, trained, and equipped separately from municipal police officers, sheriff's deputies, and state officers. Special police officers seldom receive much attention from the public, and because of the nature of their work, they may often be mistaken for security guards. They are not security guards, because they are government employees with police powers. For example, state colleges and universities have to provide security for the campus. Many of the state colleges and universities have a police department rather than a security department.[16] The employees of these campus police have general police powers on the state campus, have the right to make arrests and conduct searches, and have the authority to carry and use firearms. They are a police department, but they provide services only for the campus. They do not provide routine patrol services other than on the college campus nor do they provide other police services to the general community. While the special police agencies perform essential services, are the source of a substantial number of jobs, and contribute significantly to the public safety of citizens, they have had little impact or influence on the development of the criminal justice system.[17]

special police Police with limited jurisdiction. Special police have very narrowly defined duties and sometimes extremely limited geographical jurisdiction.

JUST THE FACTS 7.5

Who are the special police? How are special police different from municipal and state police?

The jurisdiction of campus police extends only to the property boundaries of the public or private college or university that employs them. How might the powers and duties of these officers differ from those of other special police? What other kinds of special police work are there? Why are special police needed in addition to county and municipal police, state police, and federal police agencies?

Federal Law Enforcement

THE MAIN IDEA

Three types of federal law enforcement agencies are the military, civilian, and Indian Tribal police. Civilian law enforcement agencies, particularly the FBI, have been reorganized to respond to terrorist threats.

Federal law enforcement agencies are similar to local and state law enforcement agencies in that they are decentralized and specialized. Federal law enforcement agencies, each with a different jurisdiction and administrative leadership, have been developed to handle the enforcement of federal laws. Federal law enforcement agencies are under the administrative control of the executive branch of the federal government. The president, with the approval of the Senate, appoints the chief executive officers of the various federal law enforcement agencies. The title for the head of a federal law enforcement agency is "director." Directors are not appointed to a term with a specified time limit, but like chiefs of police they serve at the pleasure of the U.S. president. Although the president needs the approval of the Senate to appoint a director, he or she does not need the approval of the Senate to remove a director. This relationship creates an atmosphere in which directors of the various agencies have to work to maintain the appearance of neutrality and fairness, yet must not make decisions contrary to the goals and mission of the president. If the director were to fall into disfavor with the president, he or she could find that the job terminated.

Federal Jurisdiction and Police Powers

Unlike the limited geographical jurisdiction of local and state police, most federal agencies have jurisdiction in all 50 states, the District of Columbia, and U.S. territories. The legal jurisdiction of federal law enforcement agencies is fragmented and overlapping. The legal jurisdiction of each agency is determined by legislation and executive orders. Also, federal agencies are often charged with the same responsibilities as state and local law enforcement agencies. For example, both the FBI and state and local law enforcement agencies have jurisdiction over bank robberies, kidnappings, and drug crimes. There is no hierarchy of authority, as local, state, and federal law enforcement agencies are independent of each other. In contrast, many foreign governments have chosen to

federal law enforcement Law enforcement agency under the control of the executive branch of the federal government.

Follow links at http://www.indiancountry.com/?2757 to learn more about tribal police and issues concerning tribal jurisdiction. ■

centralize the law enforcement function within their country. Countries such as Canada, France, Great Britain, Japan, Mexico, and Sweden have much more centralized control of their law enforcement agencies.

Federal agencies with police powers can be divided into three types: military, Indian Tribal police, and civilian agencies. There is some overlap in this classification, as some federal civilian agencies also have jurisdiction on Indian and military reservations.[18] There is a difference between military and civilian police agencies, because federal legislation prohibits the military from performing civilian law enforcement duties. This prohibition against the use of military troops to perform civilian law enforcement was established by the Posse Comitatus Act passed in 1878. Recently, exceptions have been made to allow various military agencies to assist in law enforcement efforts against international drug trafficking. However, for the most part, military personnel are still prohibited from exercising civilian law enforcement duties.

Military Police and Tribal Police

Local and state police agencies do not have jurisdiction to enforce federal laws on military and Indian reservations. To maintain order, to provide criminal and noncriminal investigative services, and to provide police services to service personnel and on military bases and installations throughout the world, the various branches of the U.S. military service use military personnel who have the power to make arrests and carry firearms. For example, the **U.S. Army Criminal Investigation Command** provides services similar to those provided by detectives in civilian police departments. The U.S. Army Military Police duties are very similar to those provided by municipal police. The **military police** are responsible for preventative patrol, responding to reports of illegal or disruptive activities, arresting law violators, traffic control, crowd control, handling of emergencies, or other law enforcement responsibilities as would be handled by their civilian counterparts in a municipal police department. The U.S. Navy has taken a different approach to investigating serious crimes. Unlike the Army, the Navy employs civilians to provide investigative services. The **Naval Investigative Service** employees are not military personnel but civilians hired by the Navy to provide services on Navy bases and installations similar to duties performed by civilian police detectives.

Indian reservations are considered sovereign territories, where local and state police have no jurisdiction. Federal police and the military have limited jurisdiction on Indian reservations. Each Indian reservation has the legal authority to establish its own **tribal police** to provide police services. In addition to tribal police departments, police services on tribal lands are provided by the FBI and the Bureau of Indian Affairs. The jurisdiction of each agency is not easily defined and in the past has been the subject of conflict, particularly between the tribal police and the FBI.[19]

military police Military personnel with special training and jurisdiction to provide law enforcement services on military installations.

tribal police Police agency that provides police services on Indian reservations. Tribal police operate independently of local, state, and federal police due to a special relationship between the United States and Native Americans living on reservations.

Research suggests that public safety on Indian reservations has been neglected by the American criminal justice system, resulting in a public safety crisis on the reservations.[20] The rate for violent victimizations per 1,000 Native Americans age 12 or older for 1992–1996 (124 violent crimes per 1,000 Native Americans) was more than twice the rate for the nation (50 per 1,000 persons).[21]

The issues of policing Native American tribal lands is complicated by questions concerning the legal jurisdiction of tribal police. Although tribal police have jurisdiction over Native Americans living on tribal lands, their jurisdiction over nontribal residents is restricted.[22] Another issue is that the tribal police are not held to the same state or federal training requirements as other police officers.

The federal government has recognized this problem, and since 1999 federal grants totaling $89 million have been awarded to reservation police departments nationwide to increase the ranks of uniformed officers, enhance community policing efforts, and sustain trial courts.[23] Additional revenues are being requested. In 1995, the attorney general established the **Office of Tribal Justice** to coordinate tribal issues for the Department of Justice. Intended to increase the responsiveness of the Department of Justice to Native criminal justice 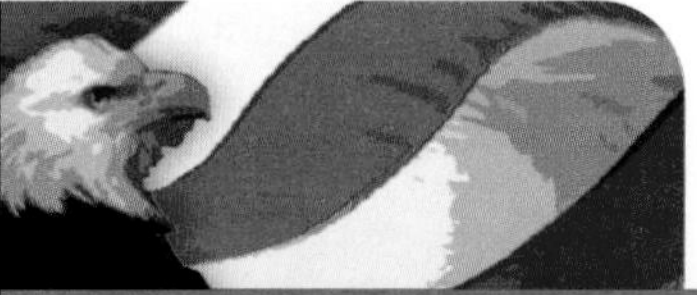 in the world

Jurisdiction in England and France

A centralized federal- or state-controlled law enforcement system might result in more effective and efficient law enforcement. Just a quick look at the difficulties of enforcing the various state and federal drug and firearms laws can illustrate this. With enforcement divided among local police, state police, the FBI, Drug Enforcement Agency (DEA), U.S. Treasury, and U.S. Customs, it is easy to understand the difficulties that can be encountered.

As mentioned, other countries have adopted more centralized control and organization of the police. England has local control of the 43 provincial police forces (provinces are similar in size to counties). The equivalent of the American chief of police for the 41 provincial forces of England is called the chief constable, and his or her second in command is the deputy chief. The chief constable obtains his or her position by appointment. The chief administrative officers for the Metropolitan Police of London and the City of London are called commissioners and are appointed, respectively, by the monarch and by the home secretary. However, the English constable is a servant of the Crown and not an employee of the provincial police authority that hired him or her. Thus, unlike the American police officer, who exercises a delegated authority, the English constable has original authority, and the English constable's jurisdiction is not limited by local political geographical authority.[24]

France has two national police agencies: the National Gendarmerie and the French National Police. The National Gendarmerie has jurisdiction in towns with populations of less than 10,000. The French National Police has jurisdiction in towns with populations of more than 10,000. Recruitment for the two agencies is national rather than local, and recruits are trained by the state. French citizenship is a requirement for employment in either police agency. There is no local control of the police in France similar to that exercised by American cities and counties over their police and sheriff departments.[25]

The fragmented nature of law enforcement in the United States is no accident. The political philosophy found in the U.S. Constitution and espoused by the founders—and a contemporary value—is the mistrust of large centralized governmental agencies. A centralized law enforcement agency, whether state or federally controlled, is viewed with suspicion and mistrust. The inefficiency of a fragmented system is considered one of the prices to pay for freedom in a democratic government. A centralized law enforcement system might be better but is seen by many Americans as a sign of a potential threat of dictatorship. This conflict is difficult for the various agencies who must try to fulfill the demands for law and order, yet work in a system in which the checks and balances build in inefficiency and roadblocks.

■ **How do the English and French law enforcement systems balance local control and unity of command? How does the United States compare?**

American tribes and citizens, the purpose of the Office of Tribal Justice is to ensure better communication by serving as a permanent point of contact between the Department and federally recognized tribes.[26] A 1997 report by the Department of Justice concluded, "in sharp contrast to national trends serious and violent crime is rising significantly in Indian country and law enforcement in Indian country, as it presently exists, often fails to meet basic public safety needs."[27] The report also concluded that tribal governments do not consider the FBI to be an appropriate provider of police services on tribal lands. Due to the isolation and sovereignty of Native American tribes, the problems of policing on tribal lands do not readily parallel those of local or state police agencies.

Civilian Federal Law Enforcement

The United States does not have a national police agency. Instead, the United States has adopted a system of semi-autonomous agencies under the command of various departments in the federal government. Rather than an agency with general police powers

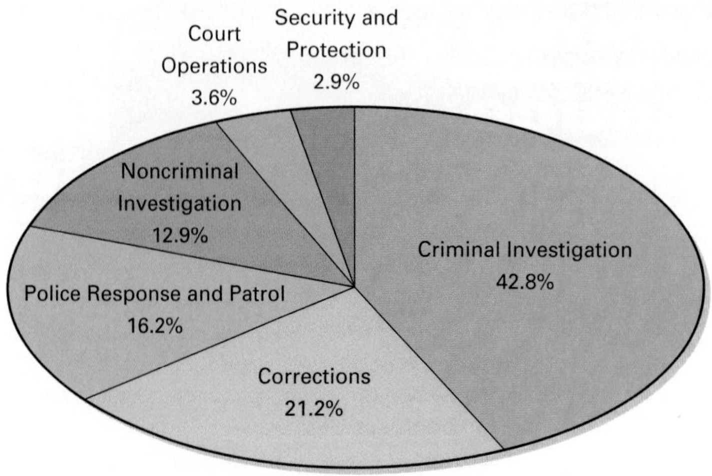

Figure 7.2

Responsibilities of Civilian Federal Law Enforcement Agencies

similar to the local police, each federal agency has a specialized function, and its jurisdiction is limited by legislative authority or statutory law. Federal police agencies do not enjoy the freedom and expansive jurisdiction provided by common law, as their legal jurisdiction is established by legislation. The legal jurisdiction of the various federal law enforcement and investigative agencies is limited to the enforcement of federal laws.

Well-known federal law enforcement agencies include the FBI, the U.S. Marshals Service, the Drug Enforcement Agency, and the Bureau of Alcohol, Tobacco and Firearms. In 2000, the largest employers of federal officers were the Immigration and Naturalization Service (17,654), the FBI (11,523), the U.S. Customs Service (10,522), and the Drug Enforcement Agency (4,161).[28] Federal agencies categorize their personnel with arrest and firearms authority into one of six categories according to their primary area of duty: criminal investigation, corrections, police response and patrol, noncriminal investigation, court operations, and security and protection. Some agencies can have multiple duties. For example, the U.S. Marshals Service, described in detail in Chapter 6, has responsibility for court operations and criminal investigations. Likewise, the U.S. Secret Service, also described in Chapter 6, is responsible for protecting the president and investigating counterfeiting. Descriptions of some federal civilian law enforcement agencies follow (see Figure 7.2).

Changes in the Federal Bureau of Investigation

The **Federal Bureau of Investigation (FBI)** was not created until the twentieth century; however, it is perhaps the most famous of the federal police agencies. The forerunner of the FBI, the Bureau of Investigation, whose agents were unarmed, was created by executive order in 1908 by President Theodore Roosevelt. The primary purpose of the bureau was to provide detective services to the executive branch of the government. The Bureau of Investigation at first focused on finding communist agents in the United States. Following the overthrow of the Russian czar at the beginning of the twentieth century, Americans feared that the newly formed Communist government would export its violence to the United States.[29] Following the bombing of several federal officials by radical communists, the United States used the services of the newly created Bureau of Investigation in an operation called the Palmer Raids to bring those responsible to justice and to round up and deport "dangerous" communists who were in the United States.

The FBI became a prominent federal police agency during the 1930s under the leadership of J. Edgar Hoover. During this time, agents of the FBI waged a war on crime that resulted in the FBI killing John Dillinger, Pretty Boy Floyd, Baby Face Nelson, Ma Barker, Alvin "Creepy" Karpis, and other gangsters. Unlike the negative publicity and critical review that results today when police agents use deadly force, the social context of the time was such that the killing of gangsters by the FBI was widely accepted as a great contribution to public safety.[30]

RESPONSIBILITIES OF THE FBI Since 1930 the responsibilities of the FBI have grown steadily. In 1930 the FBI was designated the national clearinghouse for the newly legislated *Uniform Crime Reports*. In 1935 the FBI established the National Police Academy. In 1939, in response to the needs caused by World War I, the FBI was charged by President Franklin D. Roosevelt with the responsibility for domestic intelligence matters relating to espionage, sabotage, and subversive activities.[31]

The investigative and enforcement authority of the FBI, like all federal police agencies, is strictly limited to federal laws and specifically delegated federal authority. Through legislation such as the Mann Act in 1910, the Lindbergh Law in 1932, the Fugitive Felon Act in 1934, and the National Firearms Act in 1934, the FBI has been able to assume additional criminal responsibilities. However, the FBI is not a national police force. They do not have control or jurisdiction over state and local police agencies.

Official duties of the FBI include investigations into organized crime, white-collar crime, public corruption, financial crime, fraud against the government, bribery, copyright infringement, civil rights violations, bank robbery, extortion, kidnapping, air piracy, terrorism, foreign counterintelligence, interstate criminal activity (including crime using the Internet), fugitive and drug-trafficking matters, and other violations of federal statutes. Recent federal legislation has expanded the jurisdiction of the FBI to include antigang authority and a greater role in terrorism, Internet, and computer crime.[32]

For information on the Federal Bureau of Investigation, go to http://www.fbi.gov/. ■

In addition to criminal investigation and domestic intelligence responsibilities, the FBI also maintains and operates a sophisticated crime lab and makes the technical expertise of the crime lab available on request to other police agencies free of charge. The FBI crime lab provides invaluable expertise to police departments (e.g., fingerprint identification). Unlike its British counterpart, Scotland Yard, which selectively collects fingerprints, the FBI has attempted to amass a universal personal identification system. As early as 1935, J. Edgar Hoover proposed to the public that every person in the United States, including children, should have his or her fingerprints on file with the FBI Civil Index Division. The idea of a universal fingerprint system has never been accepted, but the FBI has collected millions of them.

The FBI also maintains the National Crime Information Center (NCIC), the nation's largest databank of computerized criminal information on wanted felons, convicted (paroled) felons, and stolen items such as automobiles, boats, guns, and securities. Nearly every police agency participates in the NCIC, and it has been an invaluable tool in law enforcement in this highly mobile, contemporary society.

These officers are from different agencies in federal civilian law enforcement. They are collaborating in a raid on a transnational shipment because their jurisdictions and investigations in a drug-trafficking case have overlapped. What other civilian and governmental agencies compose federal law enforcement? How is federal police work different from police work in local and state police departments?

REORGANIZATION OF THE FBI FOLLOWING SEPTEMBER 11 Prior to the September 11 terrorist attacks on the United States, responding to terrorism was only one of the many missions of the FBI, and it was not the top priority. FBI agents were restricted from using the Internet as a tool for gathering information, and administrative guidelines prohibited "FBI field agents from taking the initiative to detect and prevent future terrorist attacks, or act unless the bureau learns of possible criminal activity from external sources."[33] Following the September 11 attacks, however, public and congressional scrutiny resulted in a significant reorganization of the FBI.

To combat future terrorism, FBI Director Robert Mueller asked for hundreds of new agents, better computer resources, and a redirected mission and priorities that will force the FBI to change its organizational culture and shed its traditional case-oriented focus on criminal activity.[34] Mueller hopes to build "a Federal Bureau of Prevention whose central mission is to collect, analyze and act on information that will help prevent attacks."[35] Mueller told Congress, "The FBI must become better at shaping its workforce, collaborating with its partners, applying technology to support investigations, operations and analyses, protecting our information and developing core competencies."[36] The new FBI priorities are:[37]

- Protect the United States from terrorist attack.
- Protect the United States against foreign intelligence operations and espionage.
- Protect the United States against cyber-based attacks and high-technology crimes.
- Combat public corruption at all levels.
- Protect civil rights.
- Combat transnational and national criminal organizations and enterprises.
- Combat major white-collar crime.
- Combat significant violent crime.
- Support federal, state, local, and international partners.
- Upgrade technology to successfully perform the FBI's mission.

The FBI also reorganized its Counterterrorism Division, established the Office of Intelligence, and placed more emphasis on coordinating with other agencies and using intelligence information more effectively. As a result of all the changes, the FBI is focusing its recruitment on candidates who possess skills beyond those associated with traditional criminal investigation. The critical skills that the FBI is now seeking in new agents include computer science, other information technology specialties, engineering, physical sciences (physics, chemistry, biology), foreign language proficiency (Arabic, Farsi, Pashtu, Urdu, Chinese, Japanese, Korean, Russian, Spanish, and Vietnamese), foreign counterintelligence, counterterrorism, military intelligence experience, and fixed-wing pilots.[38]

Other Civilian Federal Law Enforcement Agencies

U.S. CUSTOMS SERVICE AND THE IRS The Department of the Treasury has several law enforcement agencies under its authority, the largest of which is the **U.S. Customs Service.** The responsibility of this agency is to guard the nation's borders against the smuggling of contraband into the country. The Internal Revenue Service (IRS) Intelligence Division, a law enforcement agency with armed personnel, is under the authority of the Department of the Treasury. The primary function of the IRS Intelligence Division is the investigation of tax fraud and tax evasion. Its agents investigate what is best described as "white collar" crime and organized crime. The detective work of the IRS intelligence agent requires extensive expertise in accounting, computers, and other special investigative skills.

For information on the U.S. Customs Service, go to http://www.customs.ustreas.gov/. ■

BUREAU OF ALCOHOL, TOBACCO, AND FIREARMS Also under the Department of the Treasury is the **Bureau of Alcohol, Tobacco and Firearms (BATF),** another agency whose origins were related to the need to enforce tax laws. BATF, as its name suggests, investigates violations of federal laws regarding alcohol, tobacco, and firearms. Initially their activities were focused on tax evaders. Early in U.S. history, the taxing of alcoholic beverages became a significant source of income for the federal government. The BATF was popularized in the media for their campaign against the legendary and infamous rum runners and moonshiners during the Prohibition era. Recent social, legal, and economic changes have significantly curtailed the illegal production and sale of alcohol, and BATF is currently much more active in the investigation of firearms violations, illegal explosives, and avoidance of tobacco taxes. The illegal sale of tobacco products deprives the federal government of hundreds of millions of dollars in tax revenues.[39]

For information on the Bureau of Alcohol, Tobacco and Firearms, go to http://www.atf.treas.gov/. ■

DRUG ENFORCEMENT AGENCY Another high-profile federal law enforcement agency is the **Drug Enforcement Administration (DEA).** The DEA, founded in 1973, is a relatively new federal law enforcement agency. Its jurisdiction includes drug trafficking organizations in the United States and abroad. The DEA is the only federal law enforcement agency whose sole mission is to combat drug trafficking.[40]

Other Federal Agencies with Police Powers

Other federal agencies with law enforcement powers include the U.S. Postal Investigation Service and the U.S. Secret Service, described in detail in Chapter 6, and the Immigration and Naturalization Service (INS), the Internal Revenue Service (IRS), the National Park Service, the U.S. Capitol Police, the U.S. Fish and Wildlife Service, the GSA-Federal Protective Service, and the U.S. Forest Service. These agencies have more limited legal jurisdictions and are not as involved with conflict of interests with other agencies and local and state agencies.

Two agencies not included in the discussion of federal law enforcement agencies, but sometimes confused with such agencies because of their portrayal in the media, are the **Central Intelligence Agency** (**CIA**) and the **National Security Agency** (**NSA**). Both of these large government agencies have responsibilities related to national security, but their focus is threats posed by foreign governments and powers. Unlike other police agents, neither the CIA nor the NSA has the power of search and seizure, to make arrests, or to carry firearms. In fact, the CIA is prohibited by law from conducting any operations on American soil other than those that are administrative. Law enforcement operations related to domestic national security are handled by the FBI.

JUST THE FACTS 7.6

What are the types and responsibilities of federal law enforcement agencies?

conclusion:

Challenges of Decentralization

With so many different local, state, and federal law enforcement agencies, it is difficult to answer the question, "Who are the police and what do they do?" The men and women who work in law enforcement agencies represent a wide range of citizens. The duties of their jobs range from security to high-tech crime fighting. Their duties include so many functions that it would be easier to list what they do *not* do rather than what they do. This patchwork of law enforcement agencies is not without problems: duplication of services, fragmentation, and lack of control and oversight. In a sense, no one agency or person is really responsible for law enforcement in the United States. Every agency can blame another agency if there is a problem or failure in public safety. While one of the purposes of this system of law enforcement is to provide for specialization, each agency seems intent on expanding its legal jurisdiction, which defeats the benefits of specialization.

Despite the challenges of decentralization, it is impossible to imagine modern civilization without modern policing. Policing is a product of the complexity, technology, and impersonal nature of urban industrial society. The police perform a vital role in public order and justice, but that role has undergone major change, and there is no reason to assume that more change is not in store for the police in the future. Policing in the United States is a large, intricate system with many agencies. Change in any one agency requires changes in many others and in the way the agencies interact. Legislators, the press, the public, even the police are constantly suggesting new changes in policing. Today more attention is being given to the police function than at any prior time. Some of this attention is focused on the ignoble past of the police, but much of it is directed toward the future of policing. The organization of the police, the strategies used by the police, and the role of the police in society reflect the balance of power between the government and the individual. They reflect the values of society and the dreams of citizens. They reflect politics and morality. They are the very way in which society defines life, liberty, freedom, and the pursuit of happiness.

Chapter Summary

- The police are the most visible representative of the government in the community.
- America has a fragmented system of thousands of semi-independent local, county, state, and federal police. There is no hierarchy in this system, in that each law enforcement agency is independent. The FBI does not oversee "lower-level" police departments.
- The sheriff is the chief law enforcement officer of the county and has the traditional responsibilities of the sheriff, including law enforcement, court service and protection, and jail operations. The sheriff is the only elected chief executive officer of a law enforcement agency. Officers are called deputy sheriffs and usually wear a star-shaped badge.
- The municipal police are the most visible and numerous of the police agencies. While having limited geographical jurisdiction, municipal police have the broadest legal jurisdiction. Many cities have signed intercity agreements that allow metro police to expand the geographical jurisdiction of the city police. The chief of police is appointed by the mayor, city council, or police commission and does not have civil service job protection.
- Each state has a different structure for their state police. The common responsibility of the state police is traffic enforcement (highway patrol) or general criminal investigation, or both. The chief executive officer is the director and obtains his or her position by appointment, usually by the governor.
- There are many small, specialized law enforcement agencies with limited jurisdiction, such as the airport police, transit police, and public housing police. The New York City Transit Police is the largest of these types of agencies.

- There are several types of federal law enforcement agencies: military, Indian tribal police, and civilian law enforcement agencies. The largest federal agency is the Immigration and Naturalization service. The best known is the Federal Bureau of Investigation.

Vocabulary Review

chief law enforcement officer, 206
chief of police, 211
deputy chief, 211
deputy sheriffs, 206
federal law enforcement, 217
jurisdiction, 204
local law enforcement, 205
metro police, 211
military police, 218
officer of the court, 206
order maintenance, 213
sheriff, 205
special police, 216
state law enforcement, 214
tribal police, 218

Names and Events to Remember

Bureau of Alcohol, Tobacco and Firearms (BATF), 222
Central Intelligence Agency (CIA), 223
Drug Enforcement Agency (DEA), 223
Federal Bureau of Investigation (FBI), 220
National Security Agency (NSA), 223
Naval Investigative Service, 218
Office of Tribal Justice, 219
U. S. Army Criminal Investigation Command, 218
U.S. Customs Service, 222

Think about This

1. Have the increased mobility of American society and advancements in transportation and communication made local control of police obsolete? Should the American police be reorganized with greater centralization? Would centralization pose a threat to civil liberties and the checks and balance of government power?
2. Should the various federal law enforcement agencies, such as the AFT, DEA, FBI, Postal Inspectors and U.S. Marshals Service, which frequently have overlapping investigation and crime-fighting responsibilities, be merged into one federal police agency? What would be the advantages and disadvantages of such a consolidation? Would consolidation pose a threat to civil liberties and the checks and balance of government power?

ContentSelect

Go to the ContentSelect web site and type in the keyword phrase "Policing in America." Read the article by David Bayley to answer the following questions.

1. According to Bayley, what three characteristics distinguish policing in America from policing in other countries?
2. In what seven ways has American policing changed in the last 30 years?
3. How does the author assess police research and its application to police work?
4. What four factors are significantly shaping the future of policing in America?
5. How does this article relate to information given in this chapter by your textbook author?

Chapter 8

Police Professionalism and the Community

outline

Learning Objectives

After reading this chapter you will be able to

- **Trace the steps in the process of screening, hiring, and training police recruits.**
- **Describe the minimum standards and desired education for police officers.**
- **Use examples from history to explain the relationship between policing behavior and community expectations.**
- **Compare and contrast five policing styles.**
- **Define community policing and contrast it with traditional models of policing.**
- **Identify both positive outcomes and criticisms of community policing initiatives.**
- **Identify professionalizing influences on police departments that come from within the field of law enforcement.**

When There's No Cop in Sight

The police are the public and the public are the police; the police being only members of the public who are paid to give full-time attention to duties which are incumbent on every citizen. . . . This axiom . . . by the father of modern policing [Sir Robert Peel], could scarcely have been brought to life in a more brutal and dramatic fashion than it was on September 11 in the skies over western Pennsylvania. It was there, with police help literally miles away in any direction, and armed with only their own courage, that a group of 40 ordinary citizens—the passengers and crew aboard a hijacked Boeing 757—took matters into their own hands, vowing to go down fighting and thwarting a plot to crash the plane into a prominent U.S. landmark, quite possibly the White House or the Capitol.

It was in that light, then and after considerable soul-searching, that *Law Enforcement News* decided this year to honor the passengers and crew of United Airlines Flight 93 as our People of the Year for 2001—not simply for the stance they took in a desperate situation, extraordinarily courageous though it was, but as importantly, because they serve as standard bearers of a new and direct citizen engagement in fighting terrorism.

In some ways, it's a paradigm of informed citizen behavior . . . Because of cell phone technology, the passengers knew they were on a suicide mission and armed with that information, they took direct action to save lives.

One of the things the police profession has been slow to realize over the past couple of decades is just what citizens are capable of doing on behalf of the community when they do have sufficient information to act. . . . In some ways, what happened on the airplane was kind of a microcosm of citizen action on behalf of public safety.

—"When There's No Cop In Sight" by Jennifer Nislow from *Law Enforcement News*, Vol. XXVII, No. 567, 568, December 15/31, 2001.

introduction:

Impacts of Professionalism on Policing

To what extent were the actions of the passengers of Flight 93 exceptional? To what extent were they an expression of police and community values? Do you think law enforcement should expect that kind of dedication from citizens? What exactly is the relationship between police and community? What exactly is professionalism, and how do police personnel become "professionals" in the first place? This chapter addresses professionalizing influences on the police. For example, two powerful influences on police professionalism are (1) the selection and training of police officers and (2) the history of interaction of the police with the community.

Selection of Police Officers

THE MAIN IDEA

Major influences on police professionalism are the quality of applicants hired and the training they receive.

Check out the Office of the Police Corps and Law Enforcement Education at http://www.ojp.usdoj.gov/opclee/. ■

Today, employment as a local law enforcement officer is open to many more people than it was 50 years ago, and as a result there is a significant difference in today's police officer compared with the typical officer then. Fifty years ago, police officers were recruited to a large degree based on size, strength, and the ability to follow orders, and nearly all officers were white men. This picture has changed substantially for the better.

Historically, police departments hired minimally qualified applicants, and often the new police officer received no training. As late as the mid-1960s, it was not uncommon for police and sheriff departments to hire new officers and put them to work without any training. In a number of departments, the only training the new officer received was on the job. The officer would be partnered with a veteran officer who was expected to teach the new officer everything he needed to know as they performed their daily patrol

In the early twentieth century, police officers were white men hired on the basis of their size, strength, and loyalty to their superiors. Today, police departments want their officers to reflect the diversity within the community and be motivated to continue their education. Police officers are trained to high standards of ethical behavior, and their loyalty tends to be to one another and to the communities they serve. What are the requirements for becoming a law enforcement officer today?

diversity

in the system

The Civil Rights Act of 1972

An example of the impact of legislation on police professionalism is seen in the passage of legislation regulating the hiring of police officers. Minorities and women were effectively barred from police work until the **Civil Rights Act of 1964** was amended in 1972. The Civil Rights Act of 1964 exempted governmental agencies from the provisions of equal employment opportunity. The 1972 amendment subjected governmental agencies to the same standards of equal employment requirements as private businesses. Until this legislation was passed in 1972, law enforcement agencies could and did refuse to hire women and minorities with impunity. As a result, prior to 1972, police departments were predominately staffed by white men. If a woman or person of color submitted an application to be a "policeman" (the most commonly used title for the position prior to 1972), she or he could be told that the application was refused simply because of gender or race. It was *legal* for police departments to discriminate in hiring. The argument advanced by the police departments and accepted by many in society was that policing was "man's" work and that women would not be able to perform police duties effectively. Men of color were refused employment primarily because of beliefs related to racial prejudice.

The 1972 amendment of the Civil Rights Act of 1964, prohibited discrimination in hiring based on gender, race, and religious affiliation. As a result, hiring standards that resulted in a bias toward the selection of white men came under scrutiny. When it could be demonstrated in court that the hiring standards used by a department resulted in a bias in the choosing of officers based on gender, race, or religious affiliation, the court issued binding rules that prohibited the practice.

For example, one the greatest obstacles for female applicants was the physical fitness test required by police departments. The physical fitness test of many departments prior to 1972 emphasized upper body fitness as measured by the ability to do push-ups, pull-ups, rope climbs, and wall climbs. Women failed these tests at a much greater rate than did male applicants. When women challenged these entrance tests, police departments were unable to defend them; they were not relevant to job-related skills and abilities. It is recognized that a police officer should have a certain level of fitness, but police departments could not justify that applicants who could perform 50 push-ups would make better police officers than those who could perform only 35 or 20. Some departments required that applicants be able to climb a 10-foot wall with the use of a rope. When challenged in court, however, departments were not able to show how in the course of an officer's daily duty he or she would have to climb a 10-foot wall. Today, police departments must demonstrate that all job requirements for the position of police officer are related to job knowledge, skills, and abilities.

While it can be said that minorities and women are still underrepresented in local policing, their representation is increasing. Many departments have undertaken very aggressive recruiting campaigns to increase the number of female and minority officers on their departments. Demographic and employment trends strongly suggest that employment by police departments will increasingly reflect American racial and ethnic diversity and trends toward gender equity.[1]

■ **How did the Civil Rights Act of 1972 change the way police departments are staffed and the way officers are recruited?**

duties. Today, the selection and training of police officers is highly sophisticated and the standards for hiring and training are among the highest for an entry-level position.

There is no universal hiring process that must be used by local police agencies. Each city and county department sets its own entrance requirements, salary levels, testing procedures, and timetable. Fortunately, while there are no universally required criteria and procedures, over the years—due to state regulations, public expectations, Supreme Court decisions, and civil and criminal liability cases—local police agencies have adopted a set of hiring procedures. These procedures are fairly uniform from department to department, despite the autonomy each department enjoys.

careers  in the system

Qualifications for Police Work

While local, state, and federal police agencies have similar standards for employment and frequently recruit from the same pool of applicants, there are some major differences in the conditions of employment among the various agencies. While municipal police, county sheriff, and state agencies will hire people as young as 21 years old and may require only a high school diploma, many of the federal agencies have a higher age limit and require a bachelor's degree.

One of the biggest differences between federal employment and local or state employment is related to the jurisdiction of the agency. Municipal and county police officers can expect that their job will always be located within the geographical limits of the city or county. A municipal or county police officer will not be transferred from one city to another or from one county to another. In federal agencies, especially the ATF, DEA, FBI, and Secret Service, agents can expect to be transferred several times in their careers.

Most federal police agents must complete their initial training either at the FBI Training Center in Quantico, Virginia, or the Federal Training Center in Glenyco, Georgia. After completion of the training academy, the federal agent is assigned to an office according to the need of the agency. Because of the nature of the work, ATF, DEA, and FBI agents may be transferred every several years. Secret Service agents can expect frequent and sometimes extended travel, including foreign travel. If the president or other protected person travels overseas, Secret Service agents travel in advance to check the security arrangements and travel with the president or protected member during the entire trip. If staying in one place is an important consideration for the type of job one wants, the choice between a federal or local police agency is critical.

Persons interested in and qualified for law enforcement employment may also possess similar characteristics that make them desirable to the CIA or NSA. While recruitment by both agencies is by competitive examination of job-related abilities, skills, and knowledge, these agencies tend to be secretive about the actual job duties of their employees. Both agencies actively recruit from the ranks of military personnel. Other desirable characteristics for those seeking employment in the CIA or NSA are a high IQ, a good memory, foreign travel, and fluency in a foreign language.

■ **How might qualifications for employment in local, state, and federal law enforcement agencies differ?**

Equal Employment Opportunity

Supreme Court decisions have required that hiring standards must reflect job-related requirements, cannot be arbitrary, and cannot discriminate on bases of race, national origin, religion, or sex.[2] The major impact of these decisions has been to eliminate minimum height requirements, which were once as high as 6 feet for some departments; to eliminate non-job-related physical tests such as climbing 10-foot walls; and to eliminate discrimination based on race, color, and gender.

The hiring process for police officers is normally regulated by municipal, county, or state civil service rules. Civil service rules mandate that positions in law enforcement be filled by competitive evaluation of candidates based on job-related criteria. The usual process for hiring includes a written test, an oral interview, a physical examination, fitness testing, psychological testing, a background check, a drug-screening test, and, in some departments, a polygraph examination.[3]

The requirements for employment used by local police departments are much more rigorous than those used by private businesses for entry-level jobs. Local police departments use an extensive screening-out procedure, leading to a lengthy employment process. It is not uncommon for the application process to take months for a

table 8.1 Police Officers by Sex, Race/Ethnicity, 1997[a]

		Percentage of Full-Time Sworn Employees Who Are:											
		White			Black			Hispanic			Other[b]		
Population Served	Total	Total	Male	Female	Total	Male	Female	Total	Male	Female	Total	Male	Female
Local Police Departments													
All sizes	100	78.5	72.2	6.3	11.7	9.1	2.5	7.8	6.8	1.0	2.1	1.9	0.2
1,000,000 or more	100	64.7	57.1	7.6	17.8	12.5	5.4	15.6	12.9	2.7	1.9	1.6	0.2
500,000 to 999,999	100	63.1	56.2	7.0	23.4	17.7	5.7	7.0	6.1	0.8	6.6	6.1	0.5
250,000 to 499,999	100	69.6	60.6	9.0	19.1	15.2	3.9	9.3	8.3	1.0	1.9	1.7	0.2
100,000 to 249,999	100	78.9	71.7	7.2	11.6	9.7	1.9	7.2	6.6	0.6	2.3	2.2	0.1
50,000 to 99,999	100	85.4	79.3	6.1	7.5	6.5	1.0	5.4	4.9	0.5	1.6	1.5	0.1
25,000 to 49,999	100	88.5	83.1	5.4	6.0	5.2	0.8	4.6	4.3	0.3	0.8	0.8	[c]
10,000 to 24,999	100	91.9	87.3	4.6	4.3	3.9	0.4	2.7	2.6	0.1	1.1	1.0	0.2
2,500 to 9,999	100	89.1	84.8	4.3	4.8	4.3	0.4	4.1	3.9	0.2	2.0	1.8	0.2
Less than 2,500	100	89.3	86.8	2.5	5.3	5.0	0.2	3.2	3.1	0.1	2.3	2.0	0.2
Sheriff's Departments													
All sizes	100	81.0	70.2	10.8	11.8	8.0	3.7	5.9	5.0	0.9	1.3	1.1	0.2
1,000,000 or more	100	67.1	57.9	9.3	16.9	11.4	5.5	13.5	11.4	2.1	2.5	2.2	0.3
500,000 to 999,999	100	74.8	62.8	12.0	17.2	10.6	6.6	6.2	5.1	1.0	1.9	1.6	0.2
250,000 to 499,999	100	83.7	71.8	11.9	9.8	7.3	2.5	5.6	4.7	0.8	1.0	0.8	0.2
100,000 to 249,999	100	84.2	73.0	11.2	11.5	7.9	3.6	3.5	2.8	0.7	0.8	0.7	0.1
50,000 to 99,999	100	92.0	80.4	11.6	5.8	4.5	1.3	1.8	1.7	0.2	0.4	0.3	0.1
25,000 to 49,999	100	88.0	78.0	10.1	8.6	6.0	2.6	2.3	2.0	0.3	1.1	1.0	0.1
10,000 to 24,999	100	88.6	79.4	9.1	8.3	6.1	2.2	2.6	2.3	0.3	0.5	0.4	0.1
Less than 10,000	100	93.2	82.1	11.2	2.2	2.0	0.2	3.7	3.3	0.4	0.9	0.7	0.2

Sources: U.S. Department of Justice, Bureau of Justice Statistics, *Local Police Departments 1997,* NCJ 173429 (Washington, DC: U.S. Department of Justice, 2000), p. 3, table 5; and *Sheriffs' Departments 1997,* NCJ 173428 (Washington, DC: U.S. Department of Justice, 2000), p. 3, table 5.

[a]Percents may not add to total because of rounding.

[b]Includes Asians, Pacific Islanders, Native Americans, and Alaska Natives.

[c]Less than 0.05%.

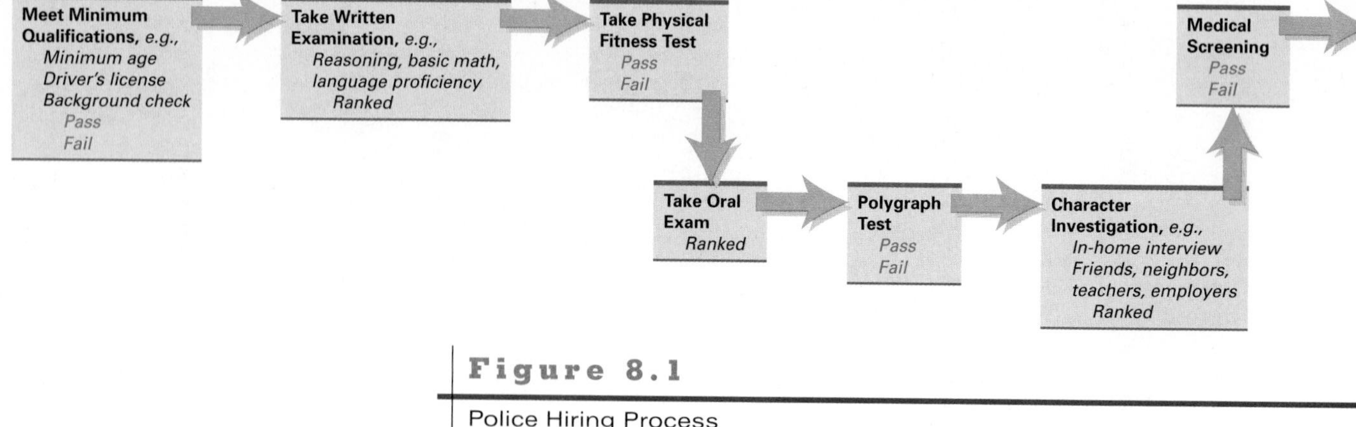

Figure 8.1

Police Hiring Process

candidate to complete. Some departments have recognized the hardship that a long application process may impose on a candidate and have taken steps to shorten it, but, as Figure 8.1 suggests, the hiring process is still lengthier than that used by private industry.

Minimum Job Qualifications

Police and sheriffs' departments employ approximately 1 million full-time sworn officers. Recruiting enough qualified men and women to fill the ranks of these agencies requires extensive screening, testing, and training of candidates. The selection procedure used to hire new police officers has some similarities to those used in the corporate environment, but police departments are permitted by law to utilize criteria that private companies cannot use to select new employees. For example, it is illegal for private companies to use pre-employment polygraphs to screen prospective employees, but this is a common practice in selecting candidates for the police department.[4]

The most common requirements among the various departments are that the applicant must be 21 years old, have a certain level of educational achievement, must have a valid driver's license, be in good physical health, and have good moral character.[5]

Age, Driver's License, and Residence

Because most state and federal laws that regulate the ownership of pistols require a person to be a minimum of 21 years of age, nearly all police departments require applicants to be 21 years old when they are sworn in as police officers. (Thus, some departments with academies that last 6 months will allow applicants to be as young as 20½ years old when they start the academy.)

The requirement of a valid driver's license is universally required by all departments. Because the operation of a motor vehicle is required by all police departments, a person who cannot obtain a driver's license or whose driver's license has been revoked can be denied consideration for employment.

Most departments have residence requirements. Residency rules can require either (1) that the candidate be a resident of the city, county, or state for a certain period of time prior to employment; or (2) that the person be a resident at the time of employment or shortly after being hired.[6] While the former was the norm in earlier times, the latter requirement is much more common today.

For information on the Office of Sheriff, see http://www.pasheriffs.org/pasheriffhistory.htm. ■

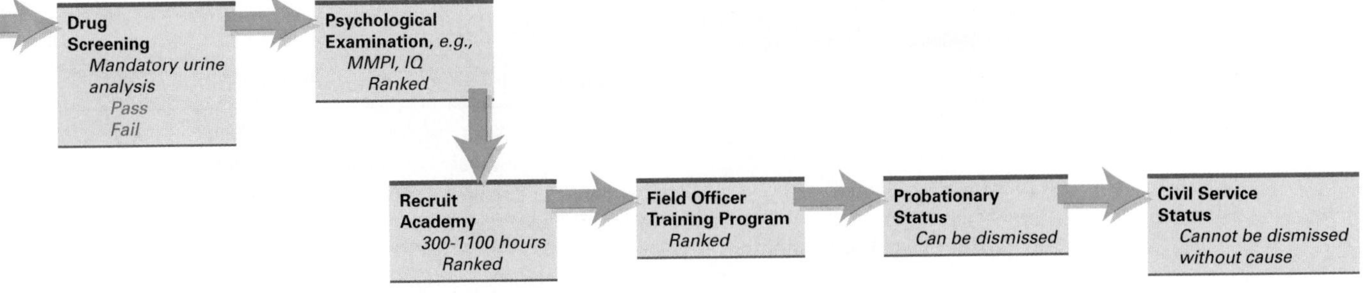

Education

A prominent change in minimum job qualifications has been an increased emphasis on recruiting from a more educated pool of applicants.[7] The requirement of a minimum of a high school education was not universal in the 1960s. College-educated officers were rare. Even college-educated police executives were rare, as it is estimated that less than 1 percent of local police chiefs had a bachelor's degree in the 1960s. Today, nearly all local police departments require a minimum of a high school diploma or general equivalency degree (GED) to apply for employment.[8,9]

See the Federal Law Enforcement Education Training Center at http://www.fletc.gov/. ■

A 1967 presidential commission recommended that a 4-year college degree should be the minimum requirement for employment as a local police officer.[10] Although this standard has not been adopted universally, a number of police departments require some college or a 4-year college degree to apply for the position of police officer.[11]

A major factor that promoted the emphasis on college-educated police officers was the federal **Law Enforcement Assistance Administration (LEAA)** program. From the late 1960s to the early 1980s, the federal government administered an educational loan and grant program under the LEAA, called the **Law Enforcement Educational Program (LEEP),** to encourage criminal justice personnel and applicants to attend college. Under LEEP, college students who indicated their desire to join a police department after graduation, as well as employed police officers, could obtain student loans to attend the colleges of their choice. In return for remaining in the criminal justice system after graduation from college, their educational loans were forgiven. Nearly 100,000 students took advantage of this government program.[12] The impact was so great that hundreds of community-college and 4-year college programs started offering criminal justice majors to meet the demand.

The LEEP program was discontinued in the early 1980s, but the number of college-educated police officers has continued to grow. Other factors, such as the adoption of new communication and computer technologies by the police, continue to increase the demand for college-educated police officers. For example, computer literacy is becoming a common job requirement for police officers, as all police departments serving more than 50,000 people use computers, and nearly 25 percent of larger departments (100,000–1,000,000) use laptop computers.[13]

Minimum educational standards must be met before someone is allowed to apply for the position of police officer, but the hiring process is competitive, and it is often the candidates with greater-than-minimum qualifications who are selected. For example, in one Midwest sheriff's department, while the minimum educational level was a high

table 8.2 Education of Police Officers, 1997[a]

Population Served	Total with Requirements	High School Diploma	Some College[b]	2-Year College Degree	4-Year College Degree
	Percentage of Agencies Requiring a Minimum of:				
Local Police Departments					
All sizes	97	83	5	8	1
1,000,000 or more	100	63	31	6	0
500,000 to 999,999	100	63	25	12	0
250,000 to 499,999	100	74	15	6	4
100,000 to 249,999	100	72	17	10	1
50,000 to 99,999	100	71	14	13	3
25,000 to 49,999	100	76	9	11	3
10,000 to 24,999	99	79	6	11	2
2,500 to 9,999	98	85	4	8	1
Less than 2,500	95	84	4	6	1
Sheriff's Departments					
All sizes	97	86	3	7	1
500,000 to 999,999	96	89	3	4	0
250,000 to 499,999	100	85	7	4	4
100,000 to 249,999	99	83	6	9	1
50,000 to 99,999	97	86	4	6	2
25,000 to 49,999	99	78	7	13	1
10,000 to 24,999	96	83	2	10	1
2,500 to 9,999	98	88	4	6	1
Less than 2,500	94	90	1	3	0

Sources: U.S. Department of Justice, Bureau of Justice Statistics, *Local Police Departments 1997*, NCJ 173429 (Washington, DC: U.S. Department of Justice, 2000), p. 5, table 7; and *Sheriffs' Departments 1997*, NCJ 173428 (Washington, DC: U.S. Department of Justice, 2000), p. 5, table 7.

[a]Percents may not add to total because of rounding.

[b]Nondegree requirements.

school diploma or GED, 14 percent of the deputy sheriffs had an associates degree, 9 percent had a bachelor's degree, and one deputy sheriff had a master's degree.

Because of better working conditions, increased pay, and the adoption of competitive written examinations, departments find that they can recruit candidates with above-minimum qualifications. In addition, as more police departments adopt competitive written examinations for recruiting and promotion, college-educated candidates frequently find that they have an advantage over those without a college education.

Some police departments attempt to recruit college-educated candidates by offering additional pay for employees who have college degrees. For example, 64 percent of local police departments with 100 or more sworn officers offer educational incentive pay and reward officers for educational achievement beyond the high school diploma.[14]

Despite arguments by some that college-educated officers are overqualified for the job because of the routine nature of the work,[15] the trend continues toward recruiting from a pool of college-educated applicants.[16]

Written Examination

The written examination is usually the first competitive hurdle in the quest for employment. Applicants are given a written examination and their scores are ranked. The examination tests the reading, writing, comprehension, and basic math abilities of the candidate. The examination does not test the candidate's knowledge of the law, police procedures, or other job-related knowledge. This information will be taught in the police academy. The purpose of the written examination is to test for basic skills that will not be part of the academy curriculum. If candidates do not score above a certain minimum score, usually 70 percent, they are notified that they cannot continue to the next requirement. Candidates who score above 70 percent are ranked according to their score and are allowed to proceed to the next screening step.

Oral Interview

The next competitive screening process usually is the oral interview. Most departments have adopted what they call a "stress interview" format. The purpose of the interview is not only to gather information about the candidate, but also to assess the character and suitability of the candidate for police work.

The interview is usually done by a panel that includes officers from the department and often also civilians from the community. In the oral interview, the candidate is asked ethical and decision-making questions that cannot be answered "correctly." No matter what answer candidates give, the members of the interview panel press them to explain why they answered as they did.

For example, candidates might be asked if they would give their mothers speeding tickets. If they answer "no," they will be challenged that they are not upholding the law and are exhibiting favoritism. They will be questioned to determine where that favoritism ends. If candidates answer "yes," they will be challenged as to their truthfulness. They may be told that no one would actually give their mother a speeding ticket, so they must be lying. If they are lying about this answer, what other answers would they lie about? The interviewers are examining the candidates' ability to remain calm and respond appropriately under stress as well as their truthfulness. Honesty is considered a very important characteristic for new recruits.

Certain questions cannot be asked by law. During the interview, candidates cannot be asked about their religion (unless it would interfere with job performance, such as the inability to work on certain days because of religious prohibition) or their ethnic origin. Candidates cannot legally be denied employment based on their accents. Female candidates cannot be asked about their plans for marriage, childbearing, or birth control.[17]

This applicant for police officer will be interviewed by a hiring panel. Because police officers frequently work with minimum supervision, they must make decisions very quickly—often with life-and-death consequences—without consulting anyone. The oral interview attempts to evaluate the candidates' ability to perform in this type of environment. The panel typically asks, "Why do you want to become a police officer?" If the candidate tells the panel that she wants to join the police department to "help people" or "fight crime," she might receive a low score. Why?

Medical and Physical Examination

Candidates have to pass a medical examination. Some departments allow candidates to be examined by qualified medical doctors of their choice, but other departments insist that candidates be examined by departmental medical doctors.

The physical and medical requirements used by police departments vary. All requirements have to be job related, but each department may have slightly different medical or physical standards. Almost universally, candidates will be eliminated if they are color-blind, but departments have different standards regarding eyesight and hearing. Some departments still require near-perfect eyesight (20/40 is the standard usually used by the Department of Motor Vehicles to drive without corrective lenses). Some departments are more relaxed in their vision requirements and require only that the applicant's vision can be corrected to near normal, assuming there is no significant medical problem or blindness.

Weight must be proportional to height, but the U.S. Supreme Court has virtually banned the use of minimum height requirements.[18] Departmental procedures for the physical fitness examination also vary. For some departments, candidates must take a physical fitness test that evaluates their abilities on certain job-related physical strength and aerobic-fitness criteria. Common physical strength tests include pull-ups, sit-ups, push-ups, and timed running. Many police departments use an aerobic test of fitness that requires the candidate to run a certain distance within a specified time and also places a maximum limit on the pulse rate. This pulse rate limit is adjusted for age and gender.[19]

The physical fitness test has endured as a controversial issue because, historically, the physical fitness test disproportionately discriminated against female applicants. Physical fitness tests have been challenged in court, and now all physical fitness tests must be reasonably related to a job requirement. Some departments have eliminated the physical fitness test as a pre-employment requirement and give the physical fitness

Figure 8.2

An Example of Physical Fitness Tasks for Prospective Law Enforcement Officers

Most physical fitness tests for prospective law enforcement officers include minimum standards for performance in the leg press, bench press, sit-up, sit-and-reach, and 1.5-mile timed run. In this example of a physical fitness test, applicants actually dress as police officers and perform physical activities relating to actual police work.

1. The uniformed and equipped candidate sits in a patrol car and

2. hears a description of a fleeing felony suspect.

3. On "Go," the candidate runs 130 yards,

4. climbs a 6-foot chain-link fence,

5. crawls under two tables,

6. and climbs through a small (30 × 30 inches) window opening.

7. The candidate then identifies the proper suspect from 4 possible targets,

8. and, grabbing a 150-pound dummy representing the suspect, moves the dummy 5 feet.

examination near the end of academy training. In such cases, academy training includes training to prepare the candidate for the physical fitness test. The purpose of moving the physical fitness test is to allow candidates time to develop the necessary strength and endurance to pass the test. If a candidate is successful in obtaining employment as a police officer, many departments continue to require regular physical and medical examinations as a condition of continued employment.

Good Moral Character

Candidates are required to be of good moral character. The first step in establishing good moral background is usually the lack of any felony arrests or arrest for serious misdemeanors. Serious misdemeanors include arrests for violence, carrying a weapon, domestic assault, or drugs. Other factors also are considered. A conviction for driving while intoxicated usually disqualifies a candidate. In some departments, speeding tickets issued in the last year can disqualify a candidate. A new federal law prohibiting anyone from possessing a firearm who has ever been convicted of domestic abuse has added a new requirement.[20] Because this law is a federal regulation, all police departments must abide by this restriction. The law does not provide for any exemption, and a single conviction, misdemeanor or felony, no matter how long ago, disqualifies a candidate. Furthermore, any serving police officer who has ever been convicted of domestic violence, no matter how long ago, is now effectively prohibited from carrying or owning a firearm.

The domestic violence legislation has had a far-reaching impact on the police.[21] The inability to carry or own a firearm clearly interferes with the ability to carry out one's duties as a police officer. Police departments across the county have had to come to grips with this problem and find ways to handle such cases. Some police officers affected by the law have appealed to the governor of their state for an ex post facto pardon of the offense to wipe it off their record. Other officers have challenged the constitutionality of the law, but so far no challenge has been successful. In many cases, officers have had

Figure 8.3

"Officers Seek Pardons to Save Jobs"

Officers Seek Pardons to Save Jobs

Associated Press

HILO, Hawaii — With a pardon already granted to one Big Island police officer, more officers are seeking pardons for domestic violence convictions that may cost them their jobs.

The police union, the State of Hawaii Organization of Police Officers, has helped 16 officers apply for pardons.

A 1996 federal law prohibits possession of a firearm by anyone convicted of using or attempting to use physical force on an intimate partner or family member.

The law is retroactive, applying to old and new convictions — and gives no exemption to the military or law enforcement officers, making it nearly impossible for an officer to do his job.

All 16 of those officers the union is helping with appeals were convicted before the law was enacted, said union attorney Michael Green.

"The union's position is that these officers did not know they were going to lose their jobs at the time their cases were resolved," Green said. "They changed the rules of the game after the game was over."

Besides helping these officers get pardons, the union also is considering challenging the constitutionality of the law, Green said.

Source: "Officers Seek Pardons to Save Jobs" reprinted with permission of The Associated Press.

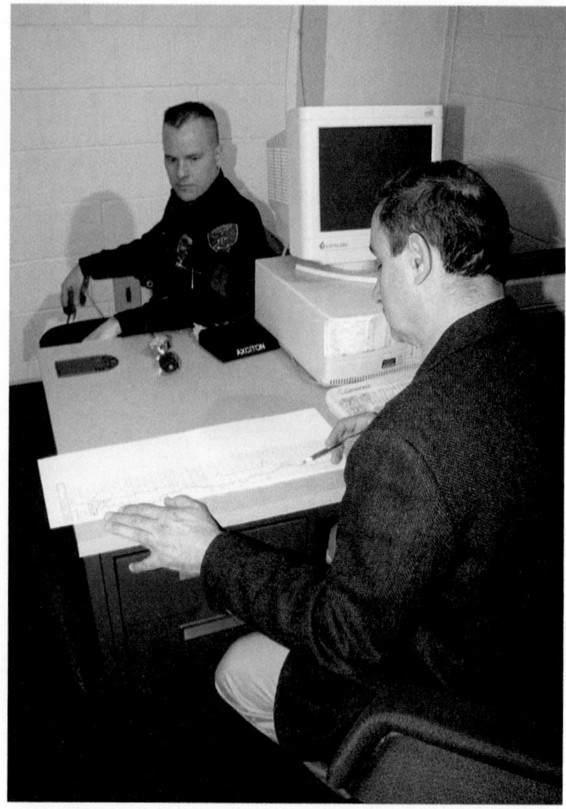

The polygraph measures responses to stress, such as blood pressure, breathing rate, and galvanic skin response. To the extent that a subject finds lying stressful, a polygraph examiner can determine whether he or she is being deceptive in answering the questions. Although the polygraph is not permitted as evidence in a criminal court, scientific research has indicated that it is 85 to 90 percent reliable in detecting deception. The most common behaviors about which subjects lie are drug use, immoral or illegal sex, homosexuality, concealed medical problems, concealed debts (e.g., gambling debts), and other vices that would disqualify the candidate. Why is deception an undesirable trait in law enforcement?

to be terminated or transferred to duties that do not require the use of a firearm, such as administrative duty, the booking desk, or corrections.

Most departments interview character references, employers, neighbors, and teachers to assess the candidate's character. Not only will they interview the people that the candidate puts down as character references, but the department's investigator will also attempt to find other people who know the candidate and interview them. In this investigation, the department is looking for indicators of drug use; alcoholism or binge drinking; prejudice against other people because of race, color, religion, or national origin; excessive debt; and loyalty to the United States. In conjunction with the background interview, a credit check is usually conducted to see if the candidate has excessive debt or a bad credit history, which can be a disqualification.

One of the goals of a background investigation is to determine whether the candidate has used illegal drugs or abused legal drugs. In most departments, a candidate who admits to selling drugs or using hallucinogenic drugs is disqualified. Two or three decades ago, any admitted drug use would have automatically disqualified a candidate. However, the social ethics of drug use have changed. Changing social acceptance and widespread use of marijuana have caused many police departments to reevaluate their standards related to marijuana use. Many local departments permit "casual experimentation" or "historical use" of marijuana. The Federal Bureau of Investigation asks candidates the following questions: Have you used marijuana during the last 3 years more than 15 times? Have you used any illegal drug(s) or combination of illegal drugs, other than marijuana, more than 5 times during the last 10 years?

Some departments are also interested in a candidate's sexual preference. In about half of the states, sexual acts between persons of the same sex are still considered crimes. In these states, a candidate can be disqualified for homosexual activity. A candidate also may be disqualified for extramarital affairs or fornication, which is also a crime in some states.

Psychological and Polygraph Examinations

Nearly 80 percent of police departments require a psychological evaluation as part of the selection process.[22] A little more than half of the departments (55%) reserve the right to require a polygraph examination.[23] The psychological evaluation is performed by a professional who administers various tests to assess a candidate's personality and sometimes his or her intellectual potential. The **polygraph,** when used, is normally performed by a person employed by the department who is trained and certified to administer polygraph examinations.

polygraph Lie-detector test given to help screen law enforcement applicants.

Both examinations are designed to help the department "select-out" candidates with undesirable traits. Neither examination can be relied on by itself to indicate that a candidate is not qualified. It is usually the "red flags" indicated by these examinations, combined with additional information gathered through interviews or background checks, that result in the dismissal of a candidate from further consideration. Because of the cost and time involved, these tests normally are given to candidates who have passed the preliminary stages of the job application, such as the written, oral, and physical examinations.

careers in the system

Psychological Examinations in Recruitment

There are three types of psychological tests that may be administered as part of the selection process for police officer: achievement tests, intelligence tests, and personality tests. Any test administered must test for job-related skills, knowledge, or abilities. While the various departments use different tests, two commonly used tests are the MMPI, or Minnesota Multiphasic Personality Inventory, and the Weschler Intelligence Test.[24] The following interview with Robert Santee, Ph.D., Ed.D., professor of psychology at Chaminade University of Honolulu, answers some frequently asked questions about these tests.

Q: What information can be obtained by using a personality test?

Dr. Santee: A personality test will measure the characteristics of a person. It can't tell you how you acquired these characteristics or when you acquired them. There are two kinds of personality tests: "pen-and-paper" self-report inventories and projective tests. Projective tests are more subjective. In a projective test, a person might be shown an ambiguous picture or drawing of two persons and asked, "What is happening in this picture?" It is assumed that their interpretation of this ambiguous image will reveal what they are thinking. For example, I once administered a projective test to a client and part way through the test, instead of describing the actions of the figure by saying, "He did this or that," he started saying ". . . and then I did . . . ." That's a pretty good sign that the test is assessing his personality. A personality test can act as an effective filter if you know what are the characteristics which are associated with a "good" police officer.

Q: The Minnesota Multiphasic Personality Inventory, or MMPI, is one of the more commonly used personality tests. What does it measure?

Dr. Santee: The MMPI is a self-report inventory of about 600 true-false questions about personal habits, attitudes, beliefs, and fantasies. The MMPI was not designed to assess if people would be good police officers. It was designed to measure pathology or problems with personality. Most likely, it has been adopted for use as an employment screening test because of its reliability. It has been tested across a wide variety of populations. It provides scores on 10 clinical scales: Hypochondriasis, Depression, Hysteria, Psychopathic Deviate, Masculinity-Femininity, Paranoia, Psychasthenia, Schizophrenia, Hypomania, and Social Introversion. Obviously, some of these would have a direct bearing on the suitability of a person to be a police officer. However, your scores on the MMPI alone would not be enough to act as an effective filter, but they do serve as a red flag—areas of one's personality that should be further examined.

Q: If you know what personality traits the department is looking for, instead of answering the questions truthfully, is it possible to answer the questions in a way that will result in the personality profile the department wants?

Dr. Santee: The test has a way to test to see if the person is "faking bad" or "faking good." It also has checks on carelessness, misunderstanding, malingering, response set, and test-taking attitude. Because the test was designed to be administered to people even with extreme personality problems, the possibility that the person would attempt to be deceptive on the test has been given careful consideration. It would be difficult for the person to do what you suggest and not be detected.

Q: If you are rejected for police work because of your MMPI personality profile, can you do anything to change your personality profile?

Dr. Santee: No. Personality is fairly stable.

Q: What is the difference between achievement tests and intelligence tests?

Dr. Santee: Achievement tests measure competencies and knowledge a person has. Achievement tests commonly measure reading, writing, and knowledge. Most achievement tests peak at the high school level, as there is little reason to measure beyond that unless it is for graduate school. An IQ test measures the potential reasoning and memory abilities of a person.

Q: What are the classification ratings for IQs?

Dr. Santee: The normal range for the Wechsler IQ test, which is similar to the Stanford-Binet and McCarthy Scales, is a score between 90 and 109. A score of 80 to 89 is low average, and a score of 110 to 119 is high average.

(continues)

Q: If you score low on the IQ test, could you improve your IQ by going to college?

Dr. Santee: No. IQ scores are very stable. They are more reliable than the MMPI. If you score low on the IQ test, you probably couldn't get into college. IQ is a measure of one's potential, so that isn't going to change. You can't study for an IQ test.

Q: Are these personality tests and IQ tests accurate?

Dr. Santee: Yes. They have good discriminate validity.

Q: Are these personality tests and IQ tests biased?

Dr. Santee: In my class, I asked my graduate students how many thought IQ tests were culturally biased, and nearly everyone raised their hand. But it's not true. There is a difference between culture loading and culture bias. All tests have cultural loading. They are designed to be used in a particular culture and test for certain cultural values. An IQ test might ask, "What you would do if you saw smoke coming from a house?" This question assumes the person has certain cultural knowledge about houses, fire departments, the use of telephones, and so forth. Modern IQ tests have been shown to have good reliability across subgroups in prediction.

Q: Can you get a copy of the test to study ahead of time?

Dr. Santee: Absolutely not! That would be a serious breach of professional ethics.

Q: Can anyone give these personality tests and IQ tests?

Dr. Santee: There is a difference between a person trained to administer the test and a person trained to interpret the test. The MMPI is a test booklet that almost anyone could administer. However, to interpret the scores, you have to be a qualified professional. The companies that make the tests will not sell them to someone unless they are qualified to interpret them. These qualifications are usually established by state regulations or the American Psychological Association. A police administrator could not just write off and get a copy of the MMPI or an IQ test and give it to applicants. In fact, one of the red flags that a test situation may be unethical is the use of a photocopied test. All legitimate tests are original copies.

■ **What is the purpose of tests such as the MMPI and the Wechsler in recruiting police personnel? Do you think your performance on those tests would indicate that you are well suited to police work?**

JUST THE FACTS 8.1

Who are the police? How are police officers selected? What are the requirements for becoming a law enforcement officer?

Training of Police Officers

THE MAIN IDEA

Systems are in place to ensure that newly recruited police officers receive the training they need to be effective and professional in their jobs.

State laws have had a great impact on the training that police departments must provide to new officers and on minimum standards for yearly training.[25] Starting in the late 1960s, the states have passed laws requiring higher and higher minimum training standards. Today, most new police officers must receive between 400 and 1,100 hours of training before they are allowed to exercise their powers as a police officer.[26] In addition, many states have required that every police officer must complete a minimum number of hours of training each year to retain their police powers. As a result of such laws, the job knowledge of new police officers today is far more extensive than in the past.

Selection for the Academy

After candidates are interviewed, tested, and screened, a number of selected candidates are given notices to report to a **police academy** and undertake up to 1,100 hours of training. Larger departments have a permanent staff, physical facilities, and resources for the academy, but smaller departments may have to send officers to regional academies, where officers from several different departments are trained.

Once in the academy, the recruit receives full pay and benefits from the department, but during the academy does not have police powers and cannot carry a weapon or make arrests. Academies frequently are more similar to military training than to college classes.[27] The academy emphasizes academic learning, physical fitness, and development of the recruits' aptitude for police work. In the academy, the recruit learns the specific laws of the state, county, and/or city of his or her jurisdiction.[28]

The typical training academy includes instruction in the following categories:

- Patrol and traffic
- Criminal law, evidence, and investigations
- Physical training
- Firearms training
- Department orientation, policy, and procedure

police academy Facility or programs for the education and training of police recruits.

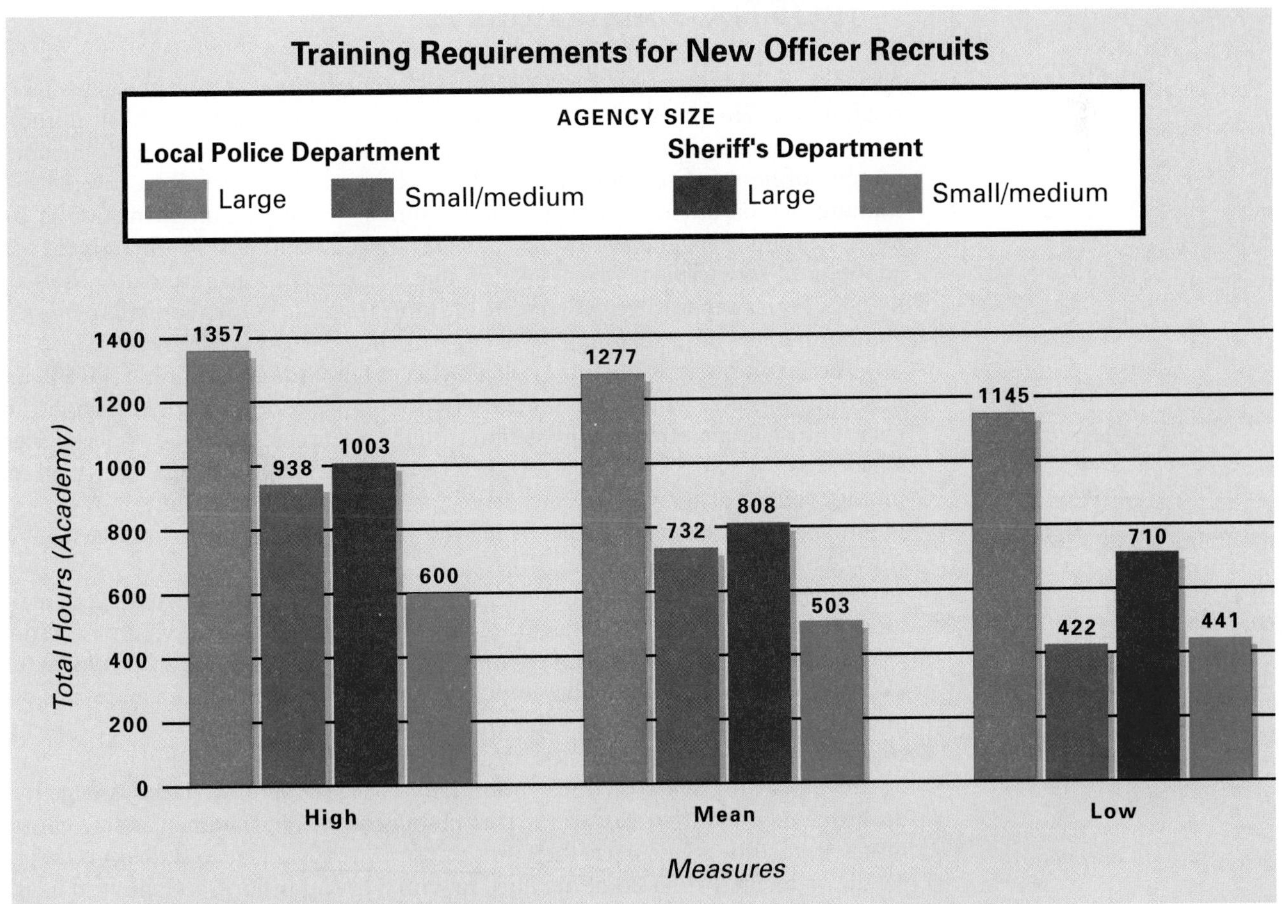

Figure 8.4

Average Number of Training Academy Hours Required*

*Classroom hours + field training hours.

Visit the Centre for Law Enforcement Education in Nigeria at http://www.cleen.kabissa.org/. ■

- Community relations and human behavior
- First aid
- Cooperation with other agencies
- Miscellaneous topics such as animal control, civil defense, typing, note taking, computer training, English grammar and spelling, hospital etiquette, SCUBA certification, and so on.

The average length of training for all department academies is about 600 hours. Larger departments tend to have longer academies, an average of 1,000 hours.[29]

There are two philosophies concerning the selection of candidates for the academy. One model assumes that because all candidates have been thoroughly screened, everyone will pass the academy. Only the number of officers needed to fill the new positions are selected for training. On completion of the academy, each officer is guaranteed a position with the police or sheriff's department. The other model assumes that some candidates will drop out of the academy or will be dismissed for various reasons. In this case, more officers are chosen for the academy than there are positions available in the department. On graduating from the academy, the recruits are ranked and jobs are filled, starting with the top-ranked candidate. If there are not enough jobs for all graduates, some will go on a waiting list and may be offered a job at a later date.

Police Officer Standards and Training (POST) Commissions

An innovation in training is the POST certified community-college criminal justice curriculum. Certain states have formed state-level commissions to establish minimum state-wide training standards for police and sheriff officers. These standards include the number of hours of training new officers receive and the topics to be covered in the training. Standards also include minimum annual training requirements for all commissioned officers and codes of ethical behavior and standards for the trainers.[30] The adoption of statewide standards ensures that all police officers, no matter the size or budget of their department, will receive the same training. POST standards help ensure a uniformity of competency across all departments.

These commissions are called **Police Officer Standards and Training (POST) commissions.** In states with POST standards, community colleges can establish criminal justice curriculums, often in conjunction with the requirements for the associate degree, which satisfy the POST standards. Students graduating from such POST-certified community-college programs are considered to have met the state's minimum training requirements for hiring and may be hired by a police department without having to complete academy training.

When an officer who has completed a POST-certified community-college curriculum is hired, the police department usually will provide a short period of additional training, about 1 or 2 weeks. This training covers department-specific knowledge, such as department orientation, policy and procedures, and local ordinances. (States without POST commissions do not allow students who have completed the POST-certified curriculum in another state to be exempted from the training academy in their state.)

In states with POST-certified community-college programs, the advantage to the departments is that they can accrue tremendous savings in training costs, as community-college students must pay their own tuition. The advantage to students is that they get the opportunity to become qualified for entry-level positions, and thus can increase their chances of employment. Another advantage of POST standards has been that when all departments within the state have the same minimum training standards, many local police departments have been receptive to interdepartmental transfers. A police officer can transfer from one department to another within the state without having to go back to the academy for basic training. Prior to POST standards, interdepartmental transfers without retraining were rare. As a result, police departments have a wider pool of talent from which to recruit when looking for new police officers or police supervisors.

While several studies have suggested that community-college-trained recruits perform better on certain aspects of police work involving interaction with the community than do police academy recruits, this system of training usually is used only by small- or medium-sized departments.[31] Larger police and sheriff departments usually prefer to operate their own academies and do not exempt newly hired officers from completing academy training, even if they have completed a POST-certified community-college program.

Police and sheriff's departments do not allow a candidate to substitute general college credits or a college degree for completion of the training academy. A candidate with an associate's degree, bachelor's degree, or even master's degree in criminal justice (or other major) is not exempted from completing any portion of the training academy.

Field Training and the Probationary Period

Most departments use some form of in-service training or **field-training program** to further evaluate the suitability of the candidate for police work after graduation from the training academy.[32] During this period of time, the academy graduate works directly under the supervision of an experienced officer. The experienced officer evaluates the "street-sense" and attitude of the new officer and assesses his or her ability to be a good cop.[33]

The field-training program may last only several weeks, but most departments keep the newly hired officer on a probationary status for up to a year. During this time, the department reserves the right to dismiss the officer without having to show cause. For example, during the probationary period, an officer could be dismissed for unprofessional behavior, which, if committed after the probation period, would result only in a reprimand or temporary suspension.

JUST THE FACTS 8.2

What training standards and benchmarks must police recruits meet?

Policing Strategies

THE MAIN IDEA

Styles of policing reflect community values and the history of police-community relations.

Recruits receive training in policing strategies and professional behavior. One of the more powerful influences on police professionalism and community satisfaction with police services is how the police go about their job of providing services and what services the police think are most important to provide.[34] Police scholar James Q. Wilson proposed that rather than viewing police behavior as random and independent of community values, the style of policing and hence the behavior of the police officer should be viewed as closely related to the type of city government and community expectations. Wilson assumed that even neighboring police departments could have different styles of policing reflecting the differences of each in city government and community expectations.[35]

field-training program
Probationary period during which police academy graduates train in the community under the direct supervision of experienced officers.

Read an an article on the impact of women in law enforcement on policing styles at http://www.csmonitor.com/atcsmonitor/specials/women/work/work011200.html. ■

Five Styles of Policing

To test this theory, Wilson observed several police departments in the Northeast. From his observations he concluded that there were three classifications of police departments or styles of policing: watchman style, service style, and legalistic style. Also, he said that the style of policing used by the department was not random, but was related to the type of city government and community values. In cities of homogenous populations with strong, traditional, mayor-controlled police departments, Wilson observed that the police tend to adopt the watchman style of policing. The **watchman style** of policing emphasizes order maintenance and a great deal of use of discretion by the officer to divert most people from the criminal justice system. The community expects the police to maintain order but not actually to intrude very significantly into the average person's life. In some ways, this style of policing has the police performing more as a private security force for the city rather than as a police department.[36]

The **service style** of policing emphasizes the importance of the service roles of the police rather than crime-fighting activities. In the service style of policing, the police department emphasizes social service roles. Rather than emphasize the law enforcement powers of the police, the community expects the police to demonstrate an attitude of service and helpfulness. For example, rather than arrest the parties to a domestic disturbance, the police are expected to counsel the parties.[37]

The **legalistic style** of policing emphasizes the role of the police officer as crime fighter and rule enforcer. It minimizes the discretion of the police officer, transferring that discretion to other criminal justice agencies, such as the courts and prosecuting attorney. The legalistic style of policing seems to emerge in heterogeneous communities with city council governments. By emphasizing strict enforcement of the rules on all people at all times, this strategy attempts to portray the image that the police are fair, unbiased, competent rule enforcers of the community.[38]

Other studies of the police strategies have come to similar conclusions regarding the link between the behavior of the police and the values of the community. For example, a study by James Hernandez of municipal police departments in California concluded that there were two distinct policing styles: white-collar and blue-collar.[39] Police departments with **white-collar policing** are characterized by a more educated group of officers. They reflect many of the characteristics of Wilson's legalistic style of policing. Hernandez proposed that this style of policing is more likely to be found in college towns and suburbs. Hernandez's second classification is the style of **blue-collar policing.** Departments that have adopted this style of policing tend to have a less educated police department. Education is not as important because the policing environment seems to require more physical interactions between police and citizens. Hernandez says that the population of these cities tends to be "more physically expressive."[40]

watchman style Style of policing emphasizing order maintenance, police discretion, and diversion.

service style Style of policing emphasizing community service and social service over crime-fighting activities.

legalistic style Style of policing emphasizing the role of the police officer as crime fighter and rule enforcer.

white-collar policing Style of policing emphasizing education and upper middle class values, often found in college towns and suburbs.

blue-collar policing Style of policing emphasizing physical expression and interaction between police and public and reflecting the values of lower middle class and urban communities.

Core Values

An important point to emerge from the studies of Wilson and Hernandez is the premise that there is a link between police behavior and community values. The police do not act randomly, nor do they develop values in a vacuum. Police strategies reflect a department's values, which reflect community values. This premise introduces another perspective regarding police strategies: the assertion that police strategies *respond* to community values.

This view suggests that community values influence everything the police do. Community values influence attitudes, behaviors, and policies. However, values cannot be assessed merely by examining the published codes of conduct or value statements of the community or the department. Conflict can exist between a police department's explicit values, that is, what it says it does—"protect and serve"—and their implicit values, that is, what they actually do—"maintain the status quo." Values can determine the policies adopted by a police department even when there are rules on the books that prohibit such actions.[41]

For example, mayors and city mangers often tell police chiefs to "clean up the gangs in the park." Because the police do not have the necessary resources or authority to clean up the gangs in the park, the only way that this goal can be accomplished is by breaking the rules. If the police chief believes that cleaning up the park has primary importance, the concern with "don't break the law" simply becomes "don't get caught breaking the law."[42]

The police distinguish between implicit and explicit values. They distinguish between what the community says it wants and what it really wants. When policy strategy is determined by community values, "there are ... written rules that are never enforced, and unwritten rules that are strictly adhered to."[43] How the police carry out their duties, how they see their role in society, how they relate to the community, what tactics and technology they use, and how they measure success and failure are influenced by the relationship between the police and the community.

Read "Ethics, Integrity and Police Culture" at http://www.interpol.int/Public/Publications/ICPR/ICPR483_1.asp. ■

Changing Police-Community Relations

Over the last 100 years, the relationship between the police and the community has changed. Ideas about competent, professional police behavior ultimately come from broader social forces. For example, in 1988, members of the Executive Session on Policing, sponsored by the John F. Kennedy School of Government at Harvard University, consisted of prominent criminal justice and government leaders. This panel of experts surveyed the history of police professionalism and came to the conclusion that this history can be divided into three eras: the political era, the progressive era, and the reform era. During each of these eras, the behavior of the police and character of the department were influenced by prevailing social values and beliefs to create a predominant style of policing in that era.[44]

POLITICAL ERA The so-called political era dates from the introduction of London-style municipal policing in the United States in the 1840s to the early 1900s. The Executive Session concluded that this era demonstrated a progression of police professionalism from *Keystone Cops* to *Dragnet*. During the political era, the police were far less independent of municipal government and politics. District or precinct officers often could not be hired without the approval of the political machine of that area. Chiefs were appointed by strong mayors who expected absolute loyalty to themselves and to the political party. During this era, there was little discussion of police professionalism. Under these conditions, policing was beset by corruption, abuse of power, incompetence, and political control for personal gain.[45]

PROGRESSIVE ERA The progressive era dates from the early 1900s to the 1930s. Dissatisfied with the state of affairs during the political era, reformers advocated professionalization and a break from corrupting political influences. Police reformers such as August Vollmer represented the ideal leader during this era. It was also during this period that **J. Edgar Hoover** began elevating the image of the Federal Bureau of Investigation to international status. Hoover served as director of the FBI from 1924 to 1972, and despite the controversies about his role and activities as director, it is difficult to deny the professionalism brought to the FBI during Hoover's tenure.[46]

REFORM ERA The reform era dates from the 1930s to the 1960s. The ideal image of reform-era policing is presented in the TV images of the Los Angeles Police Department of the 1960s depicted in the TV series *Dragnet* and *Adam 12*. Technological developments are credited with stimulating the evolution of police professionalism. In the

criminal justice  in the media

What Is the Truth about Police Work?

How accurately does the media portray the truth of police work? The public image of the police is strongly influenced by broadcast media, especially television, and this image has changed over time. For example, Chief **William H. Parker** (1950–1966) was credited with improving the image of professionalism and honesty of the Los Angeles Police Department through a collaboration with network television. Parker consulted with Jack Webb on the then-popular TV show, *Dragnet.* In *Dragnet,* the TV personae of Detective Sergeants Joe Friday ("Just the facts, ma'am") and Bill Gannon became the image of police professionalism, for which, as a result, the LAPD received a worldwide reputation. In the 1990s, that reputation was shattered by the Ramparts corruption scandal, and, again, the media—in the form of investigative journalism—played a prominent role in public perceptions of the police.

Police series on television and police movies, both action dramas and comedies, are among the most popular genres in the United States, and these media emphasize the violence, danger, and excitement of police work. Live-action television, referred to as "reality TV," features series such as *COPS* and depicts car chases, bank robberies, hostage events, and shoot-outs. Even real cops watch TV shows and movies about the police, and, for better or worse, the job expectations of candidates for positions of police officer are influenced by what these potential recruits see in the media.

■ **What image of the police and police professionalism is popularized today, compared with Chief Parker's day? Overall, are portrayals of the police in the media positive or negative? To what extent do you think the portrayals are "real"?**

reform era, the two most important technological influences were the automobile and the development of centralized dispatch using the telephone and police radio. According to Kelling and Moore, "The patrol car became the symbol of policing. . . . It represented mobility, power, conspicuous presence, control of officers, and professional distance from citizens."[47]

As a result of changes during the reform era, policing moved away from the politics of city government, away from decentralized geographical control, and away from foot patrol. The ideal police department of the reform era was an independent, professional, centralized crime control agency quickly responding to calls for crime fighting. During the reform era, the police assumed an identity as part of the criminal justice system.[48] The police department and the community emphasized the role of the police officer as having technical knowledge and skills and being guided in his or her actions by the law. Reformers fought to eliminate police corruption.

thin blue line A metaphor for the police as lonely heroes forming a barrier between criminals and law-abiding citizens.

Unfortunately, police strategies used in the reform era to achieve professionalism, minimize corruption, and increase efficiency resulted in a significant decrease in personal interactions between police and the community. The metaphor that developed described the police as the **thin blue line.** Kelling and Moore explain, "It connotes the existence of dangerous external threats to communities, portrays police as standing between that danger and good citizens, and implies both police heroism and loneliness."[49] Another characteristic of the reform era was the attempt by the police to develop an image of omnipresence "to deter criminals and reassure good citizens."[50] Through the use of centralized dispatch, communications technology, and the patrol car, the police attempted to provide instant response. Response time to the scene of a crime became one of the important measures of police effectiveness.

PROTEST ERA It can be proposed that the reform era became a protest era of policing during the 1950s. Police values and practices that were commonplace and even looked on by the community as characteristic of effective policing are considered abhorrent today. One of the major characteristics of the police-community relationship during the 1950s–1970s, for example, was the schism between the police and the community based on race.[51] This was a time in American society characterized by racial segregation. During this period, the police were identified with the status quo, and communications technology helped spread this image of the police. The evening television news showed the police using violence against civil rights activists and Vietnam War protesters, and these images were very upsetting to many citizens. Images such as the police unleashing police dogs to attack peaceful civil rights marchers or of Chicago police officers using unrestrained violence on political protesters shocked the public and provoked demands for new policing strategies.[52]

During the 1960s and 1970s, the crime rate began to climb. Cities burned. Drugs, gangs, and crime became pandemic. The image of police omnipresence proved to be a myth as cities were consumed with disorder and riots that the police could neither prevent nor control. Fear of crime, increasing violence, mistrust of the police, and serious doubts about the professionalism of the police resulted in widespread dissatisfaction with police services—especially with the municipal police.[53] It is not surprising that since the late 1980s new policing strategies have been adopted by many police departments as a reflection of the public's dissatisfaction with traditional policing. One of these new policing strategies came to be known as "community policing."[54]

JUST THE FACTS 8.3

What are five styles of policing, and how do they reflect changing public expectations of the police in different eras?

Community Policing

THE MAIN IDEA

Community policing is based on community involvement in maintaining public order, crime prevention, and alternatives to arrest.

Community policing developed during the 1960s and 1970s as citizen disenchantment with police services and criticisms of police professionalism led to experimentation with different policing strategies.[55] One of the early strategies used during this period was team policing.[56] **Team policing** attempted to establish small units of police personnel who would assume responsibility for public order and crime control within a geographical area. It was thought that this decentralization would encourage more police-community involvement. Unfortunately, because of the incompatibility of the decentralized decision-making strategy of team policing and the highly centralized command-and-control administrative model of policing, team policing was strategically incompatible. Team policing enjoyed only brief and limited popularity. Most citizens and police saw little organizational change in policing under team policing. It was more of an add-on rather than a radical new strategy.[57] Community policing is enjoying far more success than team policing.[58]

team policing Decentralizing development during the 1960s and 1970s in which small units of police personnel took responsibility for a particular geographical area.

Community policing involves citizens in quality-of-life issues in their neighborhoods that, if addressed, may reduce delinquency and crime. How does community policing differ from traditional policing models? According to this chapter, what are some drawbacks of community policing? What have been some unexpected negative and positive outcomes of community policing efforts?

See the Community-Oriented Policing Services site at http://www.usdoj.gov/cops/. ■

What Is Community Policing?

Despite its popularity and widespread use, there is no universally accepted definition of **community policing.** As a result, many police departments have declared that they have adopted community policing; however, each community policing program is different.[59] The common characteristics of community police are these:

- Focus on decentralized strategies that promote crime prevention rather than rapid response, crime investigation, and apprehension of the criminal[60]
- Focus on promoting the quality of life of the community and public order rather than law enforcement[61]
- Use of alternatives other than arrest and force to solve the cause of the problem rather than responding to the symptoms of the problem[62]

The common elements of community policing are proactive police services that emphasize decentralized crime prevention, preventing the recurrence of crime and promoting the quality of life in the community.

Broken Windows and Zero Tolerance

community policing
Decentralized policing programs that focus on crime prevention, quality of life in the community, public order, and alternatives to arrest.

broken window theory
Belief that ignoring public order violations and disruptive behavior leads to community neglect, which fosters further disorder and crime.

Although each police department has approached community policing differently, an underlying theme of community policing is a partnership between the police and the community. In this partnership, the police become problem identifiers, dispute resolvers, and managers of relations rather than crime fighters, law enforcers, and the "thin blue line."[63]

Underlying this strategy of public order is the philosophy of the "broken window."[64] In an interesting experiment, an automobile was parked in a neighborhood and left. It was discovered that the automobile was more quickly vandalized if a window on the parked automobile were broken than if the automobile were left undamaged. The message sent by the broken window was, "Nobody cares"—other acts of vandalism are okay.

When applied to a neighborhood, the **broken window theory** means that if vacant buildings are left untended; if graffiti is tolerated; and if public order violations such as public drinking, disruptive behavior by youths, and vandalism are permitted, these will

ethics in the system

Limits of Zero Tolerance

According to New York City Police Commissioner Howard Safir, "People involved in minor crime are often involved in major ones. When you enforce the small things, it sends a message that you won't tolerate any criminal behavior. It has a ripple effect."[65] New York included in its zero tolerance policy a strict enforcement against subway fare evaders, people who attempt to ride the subway without paying the fare. One of the things discovered was that people who would try to avoid the fare would also break other laws. Thus, when police began arresting fare jumpers, they found that the people arrested often were also wanted for other crimes or were carrying drugs or firearms.

New York residents were delighted when aggressive policing strategies inspired by the broken window philosophy resulted in lower crime rates, but they became confrontational when the police turned their attention to jaywalking. In a crackdown on crime, which was threatening both the quality of life for residents and potential income from tourism, the police adopted the community policing strategy of zero tolerance of law breaking, including even failing to cross at crosswalks. What was the reaction of the community when the police turned to the strict enforcement of jaywalking laws? Citizens protested. Despite the fact that, in general, the strict-enforcement strategy appears to have been instrumental in significantly reducing the crime rate in New York, many citizens felt that enforcement of the jaywalking laws went too far. As one New York City resident said, "I don't rob banks, I don't stick people up, and I don't steal from the collection plate, but I draw the line at crossing at street corners. Nobody is going to tell me where to walk."[66]

Why did citizens in favor of zero tolerance react differently to jaywalking than to fare jumping? Do you agree with the broken window theory? How would you define the limits zero tolerance?

be signals to people that nobody cares about the community, leading to more serious disorder and crime.[67]

One of the strategies associated with the broken window philosophy is strict enforcement for minor violations of the law, such as public drinking, after-hours use of parks, loitering, and even jaywalking. This strict enforcement is called the **zero-tolerance** strategy, and the assumption behind this strategy is that it will send the message to more serious lawbreakers that if even such minor offenses are noticed by the police, then more serious offenses also will bring prompt police action. According to the broken window theory, tolerance by the police and the community for people breaking "small laws" demonstrates the community's apathy and leads to more serious crime.

Police Partnership and Public Order

Studies conducted in the 1970s indicated that much police work actually involved order maintenance as opposed to crime fighting.[68] In fact, in only about 5 percent of all dispatched calls in most cities does the officer have a chance to intervene or make an arrest. Despite the emphasis of the police on rapid response time, these studies suggested that rapid response time was, in general, an ineffective crime-fighting strategy. The philosophy of community policing holds that order maintenance, not law enforcement, is the root of crime fighting. If a community has a high degree of public order, more serious crime is less likely to develop.[69]

zero tolerance Strict enforcement of the laws, even for minor violations.

Frequently, when police seek to enter into a partnership with the residents of a neighborhood to promote public order and to fight crime, both sides must learn to trust each other and to communicate. Both the police and the community are not accustomed to working with each other. The old division between "us and them" or "police and civilians" had worked effectively to separate the community and the police. In working in partnership with the community, sometimes community expectations were quite surprising to the police. In one attempt to establish community policing in a public housing project, police officers thought that initially the residents would want to see the police direct their resources toward fighting drug dealing, violence, or youth gangs. To their surprise, the major complaint of the residents was illegally parked cars and abandoned vehicles.

In meetings with the residents of the housing project, community police officers learned that despite a long history of trying to get some response to their numerous complaints about abandoned vehicles, they had had no success. The residents had repeatedly called 9-1-1 but had been advised that abandoned vehicles were handled by another city department. Calls to this department failed to produce any results. Taking up the challenge, community policing officers assigned to the housing project coordinated efforts between the police and the city department that handled abandoned vehicles and, in one weekend, removed dozens of abandoned vehicles from the parking lot and streets surrounding the housing project. Once the police proved their ability to get a "small" thing done, such as removing abandoned vehicles, the housing residents developed more trust in the police and began to supply them with information about drug dealing and criminal activities in the housing project. As one resident summarized the situation, "If the police can't do anything about an abandoned car, what can they do about drug dealing?"

Problem-Oriented Policing

Community policing emphasizes attacking the root problem that causes crime instead of responding to the symptoms of the problem by arresting offenders and taking victimization reports. This approach to crime fighting is sometimes called "problem-solving policing" or "problem-oriented policing." **Problem-oriented policing** emphasizes three main themes:[70]

- Increased effectiveness by attacking underlying problems that give rise to incidents that consume patrol and detective time
- Reliance on the expertise and creativity of line officers to study problems carefully and develop innovative solutions
- Closer involvement with the public to make sure that the police are addressing the needs of citizens

Rather than being reactive, problem-solving policing emphasizes the role of the police as proactive—acting before the crime is committed. Traditionally, police are reactive. They respond to a crime or call for service. Once they respond, they take steps to solve the crime or catch the criminal or resolve the conflict. Seldom, or never, are they expected to take steps to find out what was the cause of the crime or conflict and what would prevent it from recurring.[71]

problem-oriented policing
Proactive type of community policing that focuses on solving the underlying problems of delinquency and crime.

If calls for police services were randomly distributed throughout the city and each call were unique, there would be little reason for the officer to attempt to find the cause of the crime or conflict and initiate strategies to address the cause rather than the symptom. Efforts to find and address the cause of a problem take considerably more time and resources than traditional policing. However, studies indicate that the demand for most police services comes from a relatively small portion of the city's residences and that police frequently respond repeatedly to the same problem or crime. Whether it is a domestic disturbance call, a burglary call, or a call reporting public drinking and disorderly behavior in a park, the police frequently find themselves returning to the same location to deal with the same problem. Problem-oriented policing focuses on resolution of the problem.

Scanning, Analysis, Response, and Assessment (SARA)

One commonly used technique in problem-solving policing is SARA. **SARA** stands for scanning, analysis, response, and assessment.[72] *Scanning* is the process of gathering data about the incident that would allow the officer to place it in a broader frame of reference. It allows the officer to define the problem. *Analysis* is the search for information that would let the officer understand the underlying nature of the problem and its causes and consider a variety of options for its resolution. *Response* requires the officer to work with citizens, businesses, and public and private agencies to implement a solution that would impact the cause of the problem. Instead of making an arrest, the goal of the officer is to prevent the crime from happening again. The final stage, *assessment,* requires the officer to follow up on the initiative taken to see if it has had the desired effect. If it has not, the problem requires reexamination for new solutions. SARA is based on the premise that if the police solve the problem that caused the crime, the extra resources used to solve the problem will be recovered by the time saved in repeat calls.

When the Newport News (Virginia) Police Department used this problem-solving approach on real-world problems, the results were impressive. Working on the crime problems of household burglaries, personal robberies, and larcenies from automobiles, the Newport News Police Department was able to reduce household burglaries by 35 percent, personal robberies in the downtown area by 39 percent, and larcenies from automobiles in the downtown area by 53 percent.[73] However, to accomplish this result, the officers had to do more than rapidly respond to 9-1-1 calls. Officers had to think

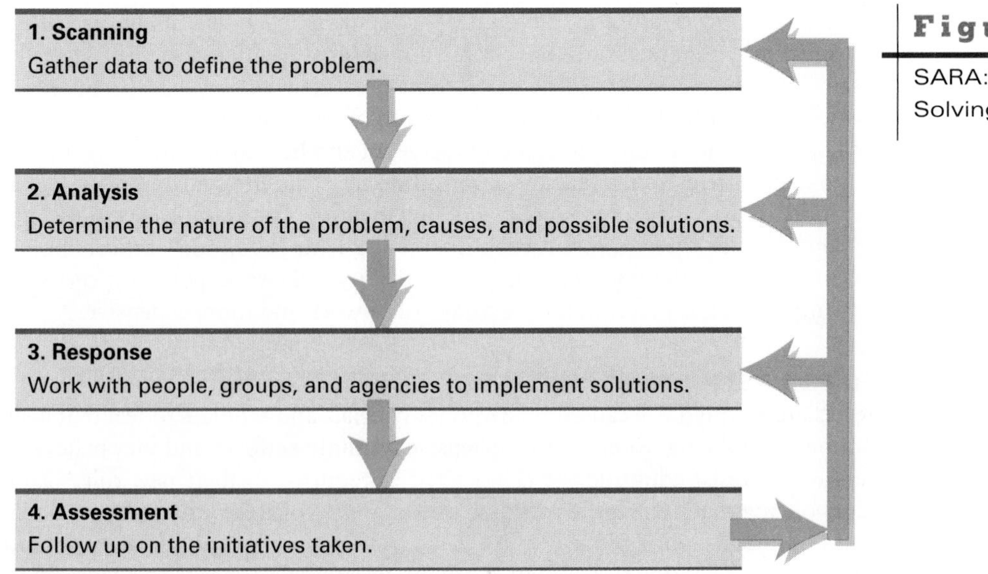

1. Scanning
Gather data to define the problem.
2. Analysis
Determine the nature of the problem, causes, and possible solutions.
3. Response
Work with people, groups, and agencies to implement solutions.
4. Assessment
Follow up on the initiatives taken.

Source: William Spelman and John E. Eck, *Problem-Oriented Policing* (Washington, DC: National Institute of Justice, January 1987), p. 4.

Figure 8.5

SARA: A Four-Step, Problem-Solving Process

through the cause of a problem, assess the community resources for solving the problem, and implement a solution. This strategy is significantly different from traditional policing, which emphasizes rapid response to calls, high-speed cars, high-tech weapons, and impressive arrest statistics.[74] For example, to reduce the burglary rate, the Newport News Police Department found that it was necessary to get involved in enforcing building codes, tracking down "slum landlords," and educating residents about crime prevention.[75] Other cities have found that these strategies also to apply to the problems of gangs and prostitution.

Challenges of Community Policing

If community policing is so great, why isn't everyone doing it? Community policing is not without its critics, who believe that community policing, like team policing before it, will soon be a historical footnote in policing strategies. Critics argue that community policing will not last because, like team policing, it requires that decision making be decentralized in the police administrative structure. Problems are solved through decisions made by the lowest ranking persons in the organization. Unless there is the need to involve greater organizational resources, such as a concern with a citywide problem, problems are addressed at the bottom of the organizational pyramid rather than the top.[76]

DECENTRALIZATION OF DECISION MAKING The decentralization of decision making runs counter to the traditional paramilitary command-and-control organizational culture of the police. Community policing strategies require the "shifting of people and authority out of headquarters and specialists units back to field commands."[77] Despite the criticisms of traditional police command-and-control structures, after over 100 years of use, many police officers, especially the command-and-control officers, have grown accustomed to it and even prefer it over the newer community policing strategies. Some opponents argue that "despite scholarly opinions, the street cops tend to prefer the quasi-military style."[78] This argument is based on the assumption that the traditional law enforcement strategy gives the police officer a better sense of control, structure, and direction in an otherwise chaotic environment.

The Lakewood (Colorado) Police Department's experiment in nontraditional police uniforms and ranks seems to support this observation that police officers prefer traditional structures. Under Chief Charles Johnson, Lakewood Police Department officers switched from traditional police uniforms to blazers and gray trousers. They also discarded the use of military ranks such as sergeant and lieutenant. After 3 years, however, the department found that the nontraditional structure and uniforms created more problems than they solved and abandoned their use. For example, personnel from other departments were confused when interacting with Lakewood's officers because they were unable to identify their rank and authority. Lakewood police officers found the new uniforms less practical for everyday police work and more expensive.[79]

NEED FOR RETRAINING The change in the police role when community policing strategies are adopted has caused many police officials and scholars to feel that a shift to community policing would require extensive retraining efforts, and they believe that officers would resist adopting the characteristics required in their new role.[80] Community policing requires a more educated officer and an officer with creative problem-solving abilities.[81] Police officers must view members of the public as a potential resource in crime fighting rather than as potential criminals. It has been suggested that this shift in viewpoint may be difficult for many police officers.[82] While all citizens are supposed to be treated fairly and in a professional manner, some police officers have developed critical attitudes that make it difficult for them to apply this standard. It is possible that many officers would not want to become more sensitive and open to their environment or more involved in the day-to-day lives of the people in the community.[83] The police officer's separation or isolation from the community makes it possible for him or her to engage in grisly interactions such as assaults, accident victims, and shootings, day after day as duty demands, without becoming impaired by emotional overload. According to Hernandez, "For the cop, a certain amount of insensitivity may be synonymous with survival."[84]

If some officers resist the change to a community policing style, it can cause an increased burden on other officers, resulting in burnout. One of the findings in surveys of departments that adopt community policing strategies is that not all officers "get with the program." As a result, other officers must make up for their work. For example, in the Minneapolis "Cop-of-the-Block" program, officers were supposed to make personal contacts with residents of the community. A survey found that one officer alone accounted for about half of all recorded personal contacts.

CRIME DISPLACEMENT VERSUS ELIMINATION Other concerns about community policing strategies refer to the displacement of crime to non-community-policing areas.[85] While community policing and problem-solving strategies may reduce robberies, burglaries, prostitution, or car thefts in one neighborhood, they may not eliminate the crimes but merely drive them to another part of the community or to another community, where they become someone else's problem. For example, when Wichita, Kansas, responded to the community demand to clean up prostitution, extensive police and community efforts were effective not in eliminating the street prostitute, but only in moving them to another part of the community that was less vocal about the problem. Several years later, the same pattern repeated when the police initiated a campaign to clean up drug activity. A crackdown on drug dealing in one part of town merely resulted in its moving to another part of the community. Many believe that the dislocation of crime is a major problem with community policing.

MINORITY COMMUNITIES Some people have expressed serious concern over the ability of community policing strategies to work in minority neighborhoods.[86] They cite the fact that "empirical studies have shown that community-oriented approaches that are effective in most neighborhoods work less well, or not at all, in areas inhabited by low-income blacks and other minority groups."[87] Supporters of community policing dispute this claim, and it is not clear what effect the minority race or ethnicity of an officer has on community policing efforts in minority neighborhoods.

TYRANNY OF NEIGHBORHOODS A final concern over community policing strategies is the "potential tyranny of neighborhoods" that would suppress "persons who for one reason or another are considered objectionable."[88] Most community residents would support the efforts of neighborhood watch groups and police to reduce public intoxication in parks, drug dealing in housing projects, and gang violence near schools, but what happens when the police and community turn their attention to other goals? For example, some community groups have been active in opposing the release of paroled offenders back into their communities. Such community opposition has attracted the attention of the American Civil Liberties Union, which has expressed concern over potential violations of constitutional and privacy rights.

In an effort to promote quality of life and fight crime, neighborhoods may mistake diversity and tolerance for crime and disorder. As neighborhoods can be places of congeniality, sociability, and safety, they can also be places of smallness, meanness, and tyranny. The minority youth walking in a white neighborhood may find that he becomes a target of the police and the community because he is different, not because he is criminal.

table 8.3 Community Policing, 1997–1999

	Community Policing Officers					
	1997			1999		
Population Served	Percentage of Agencies Using	Number of Officers	Average Number of Full-Time Sworn[a]	Percentage of Agencies Using	Number of Officers	Average Number of Full-Time Sworn[a]
All sizes	34	15,978	3	64	91,072	11
1,000,000 or more	75	1,111	93	100	27,724	1,728
500,000 to 999,999	75	726	40	88	4,536	216
250,000 to 499,999	76	1,729	49	91	5,018	119
150,000 to 249,999	82	1,183	22	93	4,221	68
50,000 to 149,999	75	3,171	9	93	11,613	27
25,000 to 49,999	64	2,170	5	88	7,976	13
10,000 to 24,999	54	2,354	2	77	10,902	8
2,500 to 9,999	33	2,000	1	64	11,200	4
Less than 2,500	21	1,535	1	54	7,880	2

Source: U.S. Department of Justice, Bureau of Justice Statistics, *Community Policing in Local Police Departments, 1997 and 1999,* Special Report NCJ 184794 (Washington, DC: U.S. Department of Justice, February 2001), p. 2.

The term *community policing* refers to a law enforcement approach that seeks to address the causes of crime and reduce the fear of crime and social disorder through problem-solving strategies and police-community partnerships (Source, p. 1). In 1997, agencies were asked for the number of full-time sworn personnel whose regular assigned duties included serving as a community policing officer. In 1999, this definition was revised to ask for the number of full-time sworn personnel serving as community policing officers, community resource officers, community relations officers, or others regularly engaged in community policing activities (Source, p. 11).

[a]Excludes agencies that did not employ any full-time community policing officers.

The Future of Community Policing

The jury is still out on the benefits of community policing strategies, although they are popular with the public. It is too early to tell if community policing strategies will be universally adopted. As more police departments document their efforts at community policing strategies, data will accumulate. It may be that community policing strategies might have little impact on crime rates, but a much greater impact on the community's fear of crime.

Traditional police strategies have emphasized crime fighting and investigation and have paid little if any attention to citizens' fear of crime. Police have assumed that fear is caused by criminal victimization. They reasoned that if criminal victimization is reduced, fear of crime would naturally diminish. However, research has shown that the causes of fear of crime do not stem so much from criminal victimization as other interactions and environmental cues.[89] The level of fear of crime does not necessarily go down as the crime rate drops. Community policing may be an effective strategy for reducing citizen's fear of crime, because one of the positive effects of the adoption of community policing strategies seems to be that it promotes the belief by citizens that the community has been empowered. Citizens feel less helpless in the face of rising crime rates. Even in communities where crime rates do not decrease with the adoption of community policing strategies, the self-confidence of the community seems to improve and the fear of crime decreases.

It still remains to be seen how flexible police administrations are willing to be in restructuring police departments, because the classical organizational structure of policing has endured since Robert Peel's first police department. One of the important tests will be whether the organizational structure and culture will reward the individual officer who participates in community policing. If officers who participate in community policing are seen by the police culture as not doing "real police work" and are passed over for choice assignments and promotions, officers will soon abandon their commitment to community policing despite encouraging crime statistics or community accolades.

JUST THE FACTS 8.4

What are some specific community policing strategies that have been tried, and on what factors does their success depend?

Professionalizing Influences on Police Departments

THE MAIN IDEA

Police departments are continually improved by individuals and groups within the profession.

As you have seen, perhaps the most powerful professionalizing influence on the police has been the public it serves.[90] Just as influential are professionalizing forces within the field of law enforcement. For example, police administrators and administrative rules are very important internal factors in regulating police behavior to achieve compliance with the standards set by law, ethics, and the community.[91]

See the International Association of Chiefs of Police at http://www.theiacp.org/. ■

Police Administration and Leadership

Police professionalism and accountability are influenced by the quality of leadership that the department and the community exercise over the police department. Thus, police officers are influenced by senior leadership in the department, which must be expected to model competent, professional behavior.[92] Administrators often conduct their own research and development and take initiative in implementing the latest strategies, remedies, and technologies in police work. Under police administration and leadership, police departments developed extensive rules and regulations—standard operating procedures—to govern police behaviors.

standard operating procedures (SOP) Standard departmental rules, regulations, and punishments for infringements, designed to promote police professionalism.

Standard Operating Procedures (SOP)

Standard operating procedures (**SOP**) were developed as a management tool to ensure that all officers were aware of the standards of conduct, to define appropriate and inappropriate behavior, to set punishments for violations of the rules, and to issue instructions to clarify existing rules and regulations. It was believed that an extensive SOP rule book would promote police professionalism by ensuring proper conduct and providing consistent and fair punishments for improper conduct. The use of such a book has become nearly universal in police departments.[93]

A major topic in the police academy is to acquaint the new officer with the rules, regulations, and policies that govern their behavior. The rules in the SOP govern all aspects of police officers' behavior, both on-duty and off-duty. Some of the rules are obvious in their intent to promote professionalism. For example, officers are prohibited from sleeping on duty. Other rules concern the private lives of police officers. Departmental rules may prohibit officers from incurring excessive debt, cohabitation without marriage, or adultery.

Despite their intent to promote professionalism, some department rules, it can be argued, may violate the rights of police officers. Examples include requirements that police officers live within the city limits of the municipality that employs them, prohibitions against making critical remarks to the public about any aspect of the police department or its leaders, prohibitions against homosexual activity, and regulations dictating hair length or forbidding facial hair. Also questionable are rules against "unprofessional behavior" that are so vague as to leave serious doubt as to when officers have violated the rule.[94]

Accreditation of Police Departments

The concept of accreditation of police departments is fairly new. **Accreditation** is a common practice in education: Colleges and universities must meet certain minimum standards to receive approval from state or national accrediting agencies. Even college or university professional programs, such as teacher certification programs, nursing programs, medical doctor and dentist programs, veterinary programs, and so forth, may require additional accreditation before graduates are eligible for professional employment. Graduates of professional programs typically also need to take national qualifying examinations to obtain a license to practice in a particular field.

At present, there are no mandatory accreditation requirements for law enforcement agencies. Other than complying with state and federal laws and POST standards, police departments do not have to meet accreditation standards. The **Commission on Accreditation for Law Enforcement Agencies (CALEA)**, established in 1979, has worked to promote voluntary adoption of accreditation standards by law enforcement agencies. Of the more than 12,000 agencies in the United States, only about 400 have chosen to comply with the voluntary accreditation standards of the Commission. CALEA has no power to compel adoption of accreditation standards. Furthermore, CALEA standards assume that departments use traditional reactive police strategies rather than community policing strategies. Critics argue that standards based on the assumption of traditional police strategies do not help identify the gains in professionalism being made by departments adopting community policing strategies.[95] Accreditation may become more or less of an influence in promoting police professionalism in the future.

accreditation Voluntary rating of police departments according to standards set by the Commission on Accreditation for Law Enforcement Agencies (CALEA), designed to promote police professionalism.

police unions Labor unions of diverse types that represent the interests of law enforcement personnel.

Police Unions and Professional Organizations

Other professionalizing influences on the police are professional associations, including police unions. **Police unions** have been very important in helping to establish standards of conduct and a system of punishment for violations. The Boston police strike of 1919 set the tone for police unionism. In 1919, in protest to the horrible working conditions, low pay, and political cronyism that influenced the management of the police

Figure 8.6

Police Professional Organizations

Selected International Associations
International Association of Women Police: www.iawp.org
International Association of Chiefs of Police: www.theiacp.org
International Narcotics Interdiction Association: www.inia.org

Selected National Associations
International Association of State Troopers: www.statetroopers.org
American Deputy Sheriffs Association: www.deputysheriff.org
American Police Officers Association: www.apoa.com
Federal Law Enforcement Officers Association: www.fleoa.org
National Black Police Association: www.blackpolice.org
National Internal Affairs Investigators Association: www.niaia.org

Selected State and Local Organizations
Boston Police Patrolmen's Association Inc.: www.bppa.org
Colorado Police Protective Association: www.cppa.net
Activist Law Enforcement Organizations: www.officer.com/activist.htm
Los Angeles School Police Association: www.lausd.k12.ca.us/orgs/poa/
Maryland Coalition of Police and Deputy Sheriffs: marylandcops.org
Florida Gang Investigators Association: www.fgia.com

Selected Police Unions
Southern States Police Benevolent Association: www.sspba.org
National Association of Police Organizations Inc.: www.napo.org
National Police Defense Foundation: www.npdf.org

during the political era, the police officers of Boston organized and went on strike. The public reaction to the strike was immediate and severe. All striking officers were fired and did not get their jobs back.[96] Governor Calvin Coolidge declared that police officers did not have the right to strike, regardless of the reason or working conditions. Public opinion was so polarized by the police strike that legislation was passed in Massachusetts and nearly every other state making it illegal for police officers to strike. In many states, it was a felony for a police officer to strike. Most states prohibited police officers from joining a union by making it a crime.

When the National Labor Relations Act of 1935 extended the right of collective bargaining to private-sector employees, police officers were excluded from the benefits of the law. Management in police departments was unilateral. Officers had no input as to working conditions, rules and regulations, or compensation. Officers could not find anyone to support their right to have input into their working conditions. For example, a 1944 statement by the International Association of Chiefs of Police (IACP) simply concluded that police unions could accomplish nothing.[97] This state of affairs was to continue until 1959, when Wisconsin granted relief to police officers by authorizing public-sector collective bargaining.

From 1959 to the 1980s, police officers fought to obtain the right to have a voice in their working conditions and pay. Sometimes the battle was unprofessional and violent. Eventually, through U.S. Supreme Court victories and state legislation, police officers won the right to organize, to engage in collective bargaining, and, in some states, even the right to strike.[98] Today, officers in most large police departments are represented by a union or a collective-bargaining unit.[99]

Professional organizations for police officers include labor unions, benevolent associations, and professional associations, not to mention local informal interest groups and support groups run by and for police officers. These organizations and associations contribute to the professionalization of police work, and extend the police presence into the community as members of the community themselves. In this photograph, members of a police association work with individuals in their community.

Some police officers are represented by local units known as **benevolent associations**, such as the New York City Patrolmen's Benevolent Association or the Boston Patrolmen's Benevolent Association. Other police officers belong to unions such as the American Federation of State, County, and Municipal Employees; the International Union of Police Associations; the Service Employees International; the Communications Workers of America; the American Federation of Government Employees; the International Brotherhood of Teamsters; or the National Union of Police Officers. Regardless of whether the police officers are represented by local associations or national unions, such representation has come to have a significant impact on professionalism.[100]

One of the strongest influences that unions have had on police behavior is the union contract, or **memorandum of agreement (MOA)**, that is negotiated between the bargaining unit and the police department. In the past, the standards for police behavior were set entirely by the chief of police. As mentioned earlier, police officers had no say in standards of behavior or punishment for violation of rules.

One of the centerpieces of nearly every contract, or MOA, is the section that defines misconduct, appropriate punishments, and the rights of the officer. These provisions are fully enforceable through the courts. Therefore, police administration has had to give careful consideration as to what will be the standards of professional conduct and what punishment will follow for violation of these standards. Also, by enumerating the standards of professional conduct and agreeing to the justness of the punishments, police officers can be held to a code of conduct. Negotiations between police management and police officers as to what this code of conduct is to cover, what punishments will be enforced, and how violations are to be treated cause each side to seriously consider appropriate standards of professionalism.

benevolent associations Local or municipal collective bargaining units.

memorandum of agreement (MOA) Union contract negotiated between the bargaining unit and the police department.

JUST THE FACTS 8.5

What are some influences on police professionalism that come from within the profession?

conclusion:

The Police and the Public

During the 1960s, police departments were frequently described as "closed societies." Phrases such as "the blue curtain" described the isolation of police from the public and the solidarity of the police against public scrutiny. Although the blue curtain did not disappear, it definitely parted. The public and police administrators have taken steps to make the operation of the police more open to the public. The police have responded to social values and modified their behaviors. There is still the need for oversight, as there will always be those police officers who abuse their power or honest differences of opinion between the police and the public regarding what constitutes professional and acceptable law enforcement practices.

One of the problems concerning police oversight and professionalism is the concern of the police with efficiency in fighting crime and maintaining social order and the concern of the public with preserving constitutionally protected rights. Often the two concerns are antagonistic. Practices that promote efficiency in law enforcement could undermine the rights of citizens.

Recruitment, screening, education, training, administration, and leadership all contribute to the development of police professionalism and accountability to the community. However, achieving acceptable standards of police professionalism must remain an ongoing goal. The standards that define acceptable professional behavior and practices today may be condemned tomorrow by the public, the courts, the media, or even progressive police administrators as unacceptable.

Chapter Summary

- Police professionalism is achieved through extensive testing of applicants who apply for the position of police officer, including written, oral, physical, medical, moral character, psychological, and polygraph examinations.
- Personnel selected for the position of police officer attend a police academy, followed by a period of field training and probation.
- How the police enforce the law and what laws they enforce are related to community values, which have influenced policing through the political, progressive, reform, and protest eras.
- Five styles of policing—watchman, service, legalistic, white-collar, and blue-collar—reflect different goals and priorities of law enforcement.
- Community policing attempts to develop a partnership between the police and the community and emphasizes crime prevention and quality-of-life issues rather than crime fighting.

- Criticisms of community police strategies include the decentralization of authority, lack of training, displacement of crime, ineffectiveness in minority communities, and the potential tyranny of neighborhoods over personal liberty and community diversity.
- Other professionalizing influences are police administration and leadership, standard operating procedures, accreditation of police departments, and police unions and professional organizations.

Vocabulary Review

accreditation, 256
benevolent associations, 258
blue-collar policing, 244
broken window theory, 248
community policing, 248
field-training program, 243
legalistic style, 244
memorandum of agreement (MOA), 258
police academy, 241
police unions, 256
polygraph, 238
problem-oriented policing, 250
service style, 244
standard operating procedures (SOP), 255
team policing, 247
thin blue line, 246
watchman style, 244
white-collar policing, 244
zero tolerance, 249

Names and Events to Remember

Civil Rights Act of 1964, 229
Commission on Accreditation for Law Enforcement Agencies (CALEA), 256
J. Edgar Hoover, 245
Law Enforcement Assistance Administration (LEAA), 233
Law Enforcement Educational Program (LEEP), 233
William H. Parker, 246
Police Officer Standards and Training (POST) commissions, 242
SARA, 251

Think about This

1. If you had the power to determine the minimum qualifications for police officers, what qualifications would you require, and why?
2. The U.S. military services have programs allowing people to enter the various branches of the service as commissioned officers without having to serve any time in the enlisted ranks. Should the police department allow college graduates to enter the police department directly as detectives or lieutenants? Do you think that college graduates should be required to attend the same training academy as non-college graduates, or should they be allowed to attend an accelerated course?
3. Civil rights legislation has required equal employment opportunities for women and minorities. However, women still make up only about 6 to 11 percent of the average police department. Even in police departments that are aggressive in recruiting female officers, the percentage of female officers is relatively low. Why?
4. Can community police strategies that require a trust relationship between the police and citizens work in minority neighborhoods where, historically, the police and the community have been at odds with each other? In neighborhoods with high gang activity? In neighborhoods with a history of rioting and anti-police demonstrations?
5. Based on what you have learned so far, how would you characterize the era of policing from the 1970s to the present?

ContentSelect

Visit the ContentSelect web site and type in the keyword phrase "community policing." This search will turn up several articles on the subject. Read the January 2001 *FBI Law Enforcement Bulletin,* "International Community Policing Partnership." This bulletin describes an unusual partnership between a local police department in Ohio and a constabulary in Northern Ireland. The partnership was started for the purpose of sharing strategies and programs for community policing. Read the article, and answer the following questions.

1. How did Chief Hanwell and Constable Young develop the community policing partnership? What forms did the chief's leadership and research take?
2. How is community policing in Ballymena, Northern Ireland, different than in Medina, Ohio?
3. What Medina community policing strategies did the Ballymena Neighborhood Police Unit adopt?
4. What successful and award-winning community policing programs has the Medina Police Department put into effect since 1995?

The Court System
What is the structure of the American court system, and how does it work?

Court Jurisdictions
How are the federal and state court systems similar and different?

Plea Bargains and Trials
By what process does a criminal case get to trial?

Order in the Court
What are the roles and responsibilities of all the players in a trial?

Crime and Punishment
What are the types and goals of criminal sanctions?

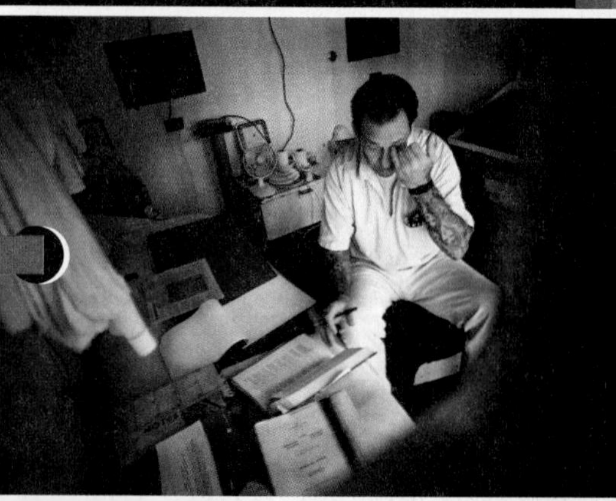

Sentencing and Death
How are sentences restricted, decided, administered, and debated?

The Courts

Local, state, and federal courts are the hub of the criminal justice system. The court system is based on jurisdictions, prosecutorial discretion, pleas, and appeals. Each stage of a trial is governed by procedural rules designed to bring about just judgment of liability for crimes. The trial process, which ends with a verdict, is designed to protect the rights of the accused. In a criminal trial, the prosecutor represents the government, which acts on behalf of the victims. Defense counsel represents the accused. A judge sentences convicted criminals as punishment for their crimes. Sentences cover a continuum of sanctions from probation to the death penalty and are meted out for different purposes from retribution to rehabilitation.

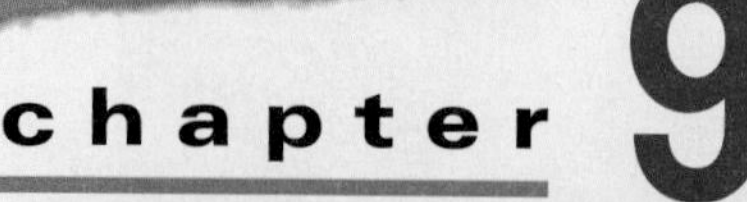

chapter 9

The Court System

outline

earning Objectives

er reading this chapter, you l know

- The history and dual structure of the court system.
- The difference between criminal and civil law.
- How the federal court system is organized and the responsibilities of each level of the federal courts.
- How the state court system is organized and the responsibilities of each level of the state courts.
- The education and testing required of lawyers.
- How judges are selected and issues concerning the judiciary.

What's a Judge to Do?

HARRISBURG, PA.—J. Michael Eakin and Kate Ford Elliott both want to be a Supreme Court justice for the Commonwealth of Pennsylvania. Both are appellate-level Superior Court justices and both appear to be well qualified for the position. Eakin is a Republican and Elliott is a Democrat and to obtain the position of Supreme Court judge they will have to run for office in a partisan election. Whoever gets the most popular votes will be the next state Supreme Court judge. Both candidates received top recommendations from a commission of the Pennsylvania Bar Association. How is the voter to decide for whom to vote? The problem is that ethical rules prohibit the two candidates from discussing their positions on issues. Despite the fact that Eakin and Elliott face each other as Republican and Democratic opponents and will spend up to $400,000 each to campaign for the $133,643-a-year judgeship, they cannot make campaign promises, engage in debates over the issues, or issue statements saying what they are for or against.

Because many important issues will come before the Supreme Court following the election, the outcome is expected to be important to the Supreme Court, where Democrats are in a slim majority by a 4 to 3 margin. The candidates have issued statements criticizing each other. Each opponent has claimed that the other has violated the spirit of the prohibition against campaigning. Elliott criticized Eakin supporters for being the only ones in the country to campaign negatively in the weeks after the September 11 terrorist attacks.

Elliott has campaigned for the high court twice before, in 1995 and 1997. Eakin, in addition to his other accomplishments and awards, is known as the "rhyming judge." The reputation comes from three opinions Eakin wrote in poetic verse, garnering widespread media attention. One opinion filed in a dispute between two businesses in the Philadelphia suburb of Limerick read:

"'Limerick Auto' and 'Limerick Collision'
Are so close one may clearly envision,
That the two are the same, So a limerick I frame,
And join in my colleagues' decision."[1]

—From "Race Tests Limits of Rules against Candidates Debating Issues" by George Strawley. Reprinted with permission of The Associated Press.

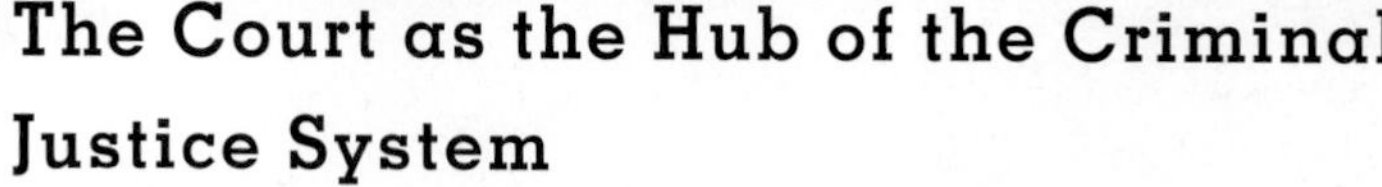

introduction:

The Court as the Hub of the Criminal Justice System

Judges are at the center of the court, yet the criminal justice system is still trying to find a way to select judges that is impartial and results in the selection of the most qualified candidates. Judge Eakin won the race for Pennsylvania Superior Court justice, but should candidates for state judges be required to run for election as if the office were just another political position to be won by clever and effective campaigning?

If there is a center to the American criminal justice system, it is the courts. All law enforcement and prosecutorial agencies work to move defendants into the court system, and from the courts defendants are removed from the system if found not guilty or are directed toward the various correctional agencies. The role of the judicial system is very important in the criminal justice system. The judicial system has many characteristics that make it different from police and corrections. However, as in law enforcement and corrections, the judicial system is a dual system: There are federal courts and state courts. This chapter reviews the roles and characteristics of the dual court system.

The judicial system is rooted in the U.S. Constitution and state constitutions. Unlike the various police and correctional agencies that evolved over a period of time, the federal court system was established by Article 3 of the Constitution. Article 3 established the Supreme Court, authorized Congress to ordain and establish inferior courts as necessary, set an indefinite term of service for federal judges, and provided that the compensation of a judge cannot be reduced during his or her continuance in office. Article 3 also required that the trial of all crimes, except in cases of impeachment, shall be by jury.

From the beginning the nation's founders saw the judiciary, especially the federal courts, as an integral part of the system of checks and balances of power. Thus, unlike police and correctional agencies that are subordinate to various political powers, the federal courts have a degree of independence, even power over the other two branches of government. The U.S. Supreme Court has equality with the executive and legislative branches of government in that it has the power to declare laws and executive orders unconstitutional. At the same time, the federal court system is lacking in political power in that it cannot directly make laws, and the federal court system is completely dependent on the legislative and executive branches for financial resources. The courts, both federal and state, have no "police" to enforce their rulings or to require agencies or personnel to cease and desist practices declared to be unconstitutional. Police and correctional agencies are not seen in the same light as essential to the checks and balances of political power.

From its humble beginning, the United States has crafted a complex judicial system with power to declare an act of Congress unconstitutional,[2] to settle disputes, and to sentence a person to death for violation of the law. The law as interpreted by the judicial system has become the primary arbitrator of right and wrong behavior. The

United States is a nation of law, and everyone is assumed to be subject to the law. As Kenneth Starr, independent counsel for the Clinton impeachment trial, declared, "No one—absolutely no one—is above the law."[3]

The Role of the Judicial System

THE MAIN IDEA

The United States has a dual system of courts, federal and state, which adjudicate criminal and civil cases.

Over the centuries, society's ways of dealing with harms against another have changed. At one time, people felt that if another person harmed their reputation, they could challenge the offending party to a duel to the death. In 1804, Aaron Burr, third vice president of the United States, killed Alexander Hamilton, secretary of the treasury, in such a duel. In the western frontier of the late nineteenth century, disputes sometimes were settled by gunfights. Today, however, people are prohibited from seeking private revenge and personal justice through the use of violence. The government requires that all wrongs—whether accidental, negligent, or criminal—be handled by the criminal justice or civil justice system.

The concept of a "court" vested with the power to arbitrate disputes can be traced back to the earliest times. One of the earliest references to *court* refers to the power of kings, rulers, and nobility to resolve disputes. Disputes were brought before the king or ruler, and the parties to the dispute argued their case. The opinion of the monarch frequently was unchallengeable and based primarily on his or her personal power, values, and interpretation of the dispute. As society became more sophisticated, it was necessary to develop a system of **jurisprudence**—a philosophy of law—to settle disputes, to replace the arbitrary authority of kings and rulers. In such a system, there is a body of written law to regulate interactions. As you read in Chapter 4, these laws or codes provide people with guidelines that regulate behavior.

The Babylonian Code of Hammurabi of the eighteenth century B.C.E. is one of the earliest legal codes that has been preserved. However, the jurisprudence system of the United States was influenced primarily by the Justinian Code, the Napoleonic Code, and the common law of Great Britain. The Justinian Code, developed under the Roman emperor Justinian I, was influential in shaping the civil law of Europe and of Spanish colonies in Mexico and Latin America. The Napoleonic Code, designed by Napoleon Bonaparte to unify the laws of his empire, became the basis of the legal system of the state of Louisiana, a French colony. English common law was the main foundation on which the American jurisprudence system was built. The earliest colonies in North America were English or became English territories, and jurisprudence in the colonies essentially was the same as in England. After the Revolutionary War, the newly created government of the United States continued to use the English common law model of jurisprudence.

jurisprudence The science or philosophy of law.

dual court system The political division of jurisdiction into two systems of courts, federal and state. Under this system, federal courts are separate from but have limited jurisdiction over state courts.

Dual Court System

In the **dual court system,** the court systems of the various states are sovereign governmental jurisdictions, each equal in importance. The federal courts are distinct from the state courts but do have limited jurisdiction over the state courts. This political division of jurisdictions between the federal and state governments is called a dual court system. The term *dual* means that there are two systems of courts. Thus, within both the federal and state systems, there are many further distinctions and divisions of the jurisdiction of the courts. The jurisdiction of the federal courts is defined in **Article 3, Section 2 of the U.S. Constitution** (Figure 9.1).

The **Eleventh Amendment,** ratified in 1795, restricted the jurisdiction of the federal courts by declaring that a private citizen from one state cannot sue the government of another state in federal court. The **Tenth Amendment** provided that powers not specifically delegated to the federal government were reserved to the states. Under this authority, each state has the responsibility and power to establish their own court system. Modern American jurisprudence, both federal and state, includes codes of civil, criminal, and public law as well as codes of civil and criminal procedures.

Civil versus Criminal Law

Individuals are responsible for seeking redress in a civil court when they are harmed by violation of a civil law. **Civil law** is referred to as private law because it addresses the definition, regulation, and enforcement of rights in cases in which both the person who has the right and the person who has the obligation are private individuals. Private law includes (1) redress for harm done to another that is not criminal and (2) contract law regulating the many and varied legal transactions such as inheritance, real and personal property, business organizations, and negotiable instruments.

Harm to another that is noncriminal in nature includes injuries due to the accidental actions of another, the carelessness of another, or the failure of another to act. An example of harm due to carelessness would be a doctor who performs an operation and carelessly leaves foreign objects in the patient. The patient may even die from this mistake, but it may not be a crime. Likewise, a person may be harmed or even killed in an automobile accident, but there may be no criminal intent by the party that caused the injury or death. Civil law also recognizes that a person may be harmed by libel, slander, or fraud.

civil law (private law) Civil law (private law) covers the law concerned with the definition, regulation, and enforcement of rights in cases in which both the person who has the right and the person who has the obligation are private individuals.

torts Private wrongs that cause physical harm to another.

Torts are private wrongs that cause physical harm to another. If you get angry and strike another, you have committed a tort. Striking another person is also a crime. Thus, some behaviors can be both a tort and a crime. Even serious offenses such as sexual assault can be both a tort and crime. Defendants charged with behaviors that are both a tort and a crime can be (1) prosecuted by the government in criminal court and (2) sued in civil court by the person who was harmed. Even if the governmental prosecution of the defendant for a crime is unsuccessful, the plaintiff can file suit in a civil court and may be successful. One of the major reasons for the different outcomes is the standard of proof required in civil court versus criminal court. The burden of proof in a civil court is a "preponderance of the evidence," while the burden of proof in a criminal court is "beyond a reasonable doubt." The O. J. Simpson case for the alleged murder of his ex-wife Nicole Brown Simpson and Ron Goldman is an example in which the government

Figure 9.1

Article 3, Section 2 of the U.S. Constitution

"The judicial power shall extend to all cases, in law and equity, arising under this Constitution, the laws of the United States, and treaties made or which shall be made, under their authority; to all cases affecting ambassadors, other public ministers and consuls; to all cases of admiralty and maritime jurisdiction; to controversies in which the United States shall be a part; to controversies between two or more states; between citizens of the same state claiming lands under grants of different states, and between a state or the citizens thereof, and foreign states, citizens, or subjects."

In the early republic of the United States, when the justice system was still a European import, Aaron Burr killed Alexander Hamilton in a duel to settle a grievance as a matter of honor. How would their grievance toward each other be handled in the American justice system today?

was unsuccessful in proving the criminal charges against the defendant, but the victims' families were able to obtain a monetary judgment for damages in civil court.

PRIVATE PARTIES MUST INITIATE CIVIL CASES Redress for civil wrongs, contract violations, and torts must be initiated by the individual and fall within the jurisdiction of the civil court. Civil cases far outnumber criminal cases, and the jurisprudence system is driven primarily by the courts' role as mediator in civil cases.

As you will recall from Chapter 2, the criminal justice system is responsible for detecting, prosecuting, and punishing people who violate criminal laws. After a criminal law is passed, it is the responsibility of the police to detect law violators. The responsibility of the court is to determine whether a person violated the law. Finally, the responsibility of corrections is to punish offenders for violation of the law. The criminal justice system exists for the purpose of enforcing obedience to laws that have been created by political bodies such as the city, county, state, or federal government.

The criminal justice system and civil justice system have certain features in common. They both have courtrooms, judges, and juries, and both use the law as the criterion for settling conflicts between parties. However, there are very significant differences between the criminal justice system and the civil justice system. The civil justice system is for the resolution of private wrongs and injuries. In the civil justice system, both parties to the dispute are private parties (corporations and the government may be treated as private parties in civil cases). Both sides are responsible for their own expenses in pursuing justice. In the civil justice system, one party is said to "sue" the other party. The party that "brings suit," or files the lawsuit, is the **plaintiff,** and the party alleged to have done the harm is the defendant. Civil cases are not heard in criminal court, and civil judges are different from criminal judges.

PUNISHMENT IN CIVIL VERSUS CRIMINAL CASES The rules of evidence for civil cases are different from the rules used to conduct criminal cases. In a criminal case, the jury is required to come to a unanimous opinion as to the guilt of the accused. In a civil case, a strong majority vote of the jury is permitted to hold the defendant responsible for the harm he or she is alleged to have caused.

The punishments in a civil case and a criminal case also are different. In a criminal case, the defendant can be fined, sentenced to imprisonment, or even executed. In a civil case, the defendant cannot be sentenced to prison or executed. Most civil cases are settled by fines or orders of the court requiring defendants to do what they promised to do in a contract or agreement or to pay the defendant for injuries or damages.

plaintiff The party that brings suit in court.

In a criminal case, the government prosecutes a defendant accused of violating a criminal law. The government bears all expenses related to the prosecution of the defendant. The government may choose to prosecute the defendant even if the person harmed by the defendant does not desire it. In a criminal case, the defendant is alleged to have harmed society.

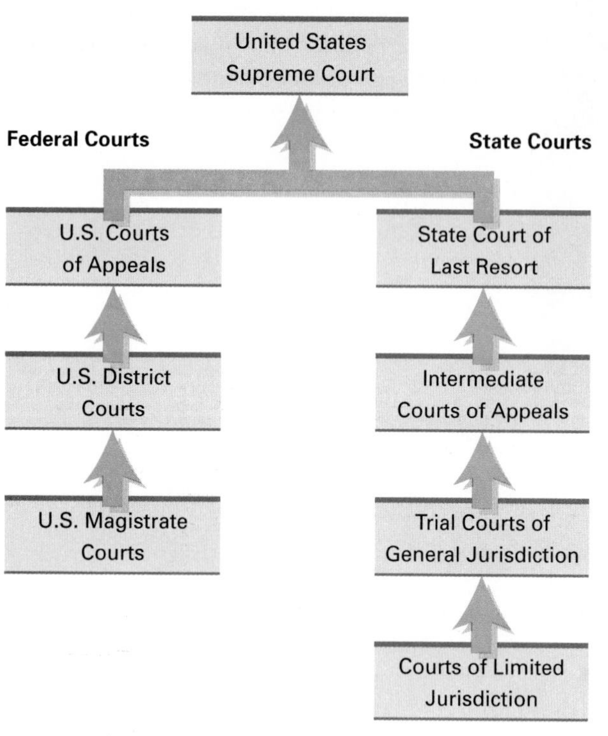

Figure 9.2

Hierarchy in the Judiciary

As this figure suggests, the number of cases appealed up the judicial hierarchy continually decreases. The great majority of cases in both the state and federal court systems are disposed in the lower courts.

NAMING OF CASES A civil case can be distinguished from a criminal case by the way the case is named. Civil cases involve conflict between private parties, so the name of the case will be the last names of the two parties, with the plaintiff listed first, as in *Smith v. Jones* or *Hazelwood v. Cranberry*. In a criminal case, the government is the prosecutor, and the defendant is the person who is alleged to have committed the crime. The case will first be identified by the government agency prosecuting the case, followed by the name of the defendant, as in *State v. Smith, Commonwealth v. Hazelwood,* or *United States v. Bostick*. When the first name of the case is that of an individual and the second name is that of a government agency or employee, as in *Hurtado v. California, Kent v. United States,* or *Ruiz v. Estelle,* this indicates that an individual has filed a lawsuit against the government or is appealing a lower court verdict.

A civil lawsuit can be related to a criminal case, as in cases in which defendants allege that their civil or constitutional rights were violated. For example, in *Klopfer v. North Carolina,* the U.S. Supreme Court ruled that the Sixth Amendment right to a speedy trial applies in state as well as federal proceedings, and in *Mapp v. Ohio,* the Supreme Court ruled that evidence obtained in violation of the Fourth Amendment must be excluded from use in state as well as federal trials. Also, civil trials in which the defendant files a lawsuit against someone in the criminal justice system, such as a warden or police chief, can impact the criminal justice system. In *Ruiz v. Estelle,* for example, the federal court decision declared that the Texas prison system had engaged in unconstitutional practices, and in *Rhodes v. Chapman,* the Supreme Court ruled that cell overcrowding is in itself neither cruel nor unusual punishment as prohibited by the Constitution.

Hierarchy in the Judiciary

Unlike the thousands of police departments that operate independently of each other, the courts are organized in a hierarchy of authority whereby the decisions of each lower court can be reviewed and reversed by a higher court (Figure 9.2). Also, unlike the police, wherein federal agencies have no authority over state and local agencies, federal courts do have some authority over state courts. Each state has a final court of appeals, but it is possible to appeal a state decision to the U.S. Supreme Court, which may or may not choose to hear the case. Decisions of lower federal courts also can be appealed to the next higher court and ultimately to the U.S. Supreme Court. When the U.S. Supreme Court makes a ruling regarding the constitutionality of a law, due process right, or rule of evidence, that decision is binding on all federal and state courts. When a U.S. Court of Appeals decision is rendered regarding constitutionality, all lower courts in that district are bound by the ruling. It is possible that U.S. courts of appeals in different districts may adhere to different constitutional interpretations. If there is ever a conflict

Go to www.courttv.com for information on current and famous trials, both criminal and civil. ■

between federal courts in the 13 federal judicial circuits, the final interpretation of the constitutionality of an issue will be made by the U.S. Supreme Court.

State courts follow a similar hierarchical arrangement as the federal courts. The decisions of a state's final court of appeals are based on the state constitution and are binding on all lower courts in that state. A decision from a state's intermediate court of appeals is binding on all of the lower courts under the authority of that court but not on other courts in other judicial circuits. The decisions of a court in one state, even the state's supreme court, regarding the constitutionality of a practice or issue is not binding on any court in another state. States are independent and equal political entities. If a conflict arises between states, the U.S. Supreme Court has the authority to arbitrate the conflict.

JUST THE FACTS 9.1

What is meant by a dual court system? How do civil law and criminal law cases differ? What is the hierarchy of the judiciary system?

The Federal Court System

THE MAIN IDEA

The federal court system has a hierarchical structure, including lower courts, courts of appeals, and the Supreme Court.

The authority for establishing a federal court system is in Article 3 of the U.S. Constitution. Congress created the lesser courts referred to in Article 3 on September 24, 1789. Congress passed the federal Judiciary Act that established 13 courts, one for each of the original states. Initially, the federal courts had few cases, as there were few federal laws. The Supreme Court originally consisted of six justices, but today there are nine justices—one chief justice and eight associate justices—on the Supreme Court.

MARBURY v. MADISON For the first 3 years of its existence, the Supreme Court had virtually nothing to do and did not review any judicial decisions. The landmark decision that established the power and role of the Supreme Court and, by inclusion, its lesser courts was ***Marbury v. Madison* (1803)**. In *Marbury v. Madison,* under the leadership of Chief Justice John Marshall, the Supreme Court claimed the power to review acts of Congress and pronounce whether congressional acts were constitutional. This claim gave the Supreme Court the power to nullify acts of Congress. It also asserted that the Court has the power to review congressional acts without having to wait for a case to be brought before the Supreme Court. This power to declare congressional acts unconstitutional—the power of judicial review—has been the most important power that the Supreme Court exercises. The Supreme Court sees its primary mission as the guardian of the Constitution and accomplishes that goal by exercising its power of judicial review.

The federal court system has undergone significant revisions during its history. Today, instead of 13 courts, the federal judiciary has a unified, four-tier structure of over 100 courts covering the United States and its territories. The federal judiciary is divided into 13 federal judicial circuits that cover various geographical jurisdictions. The geographical jurisdictions of the federal court are much larger than those of the state courts. For example, the Eighth Federal Judicial Circuit includes seven states, the Ninth Federal Judicial Circuit includes nine states, and the Tenth Federal Judicial Circuit includes six states (Figure 9.3 on page 272).

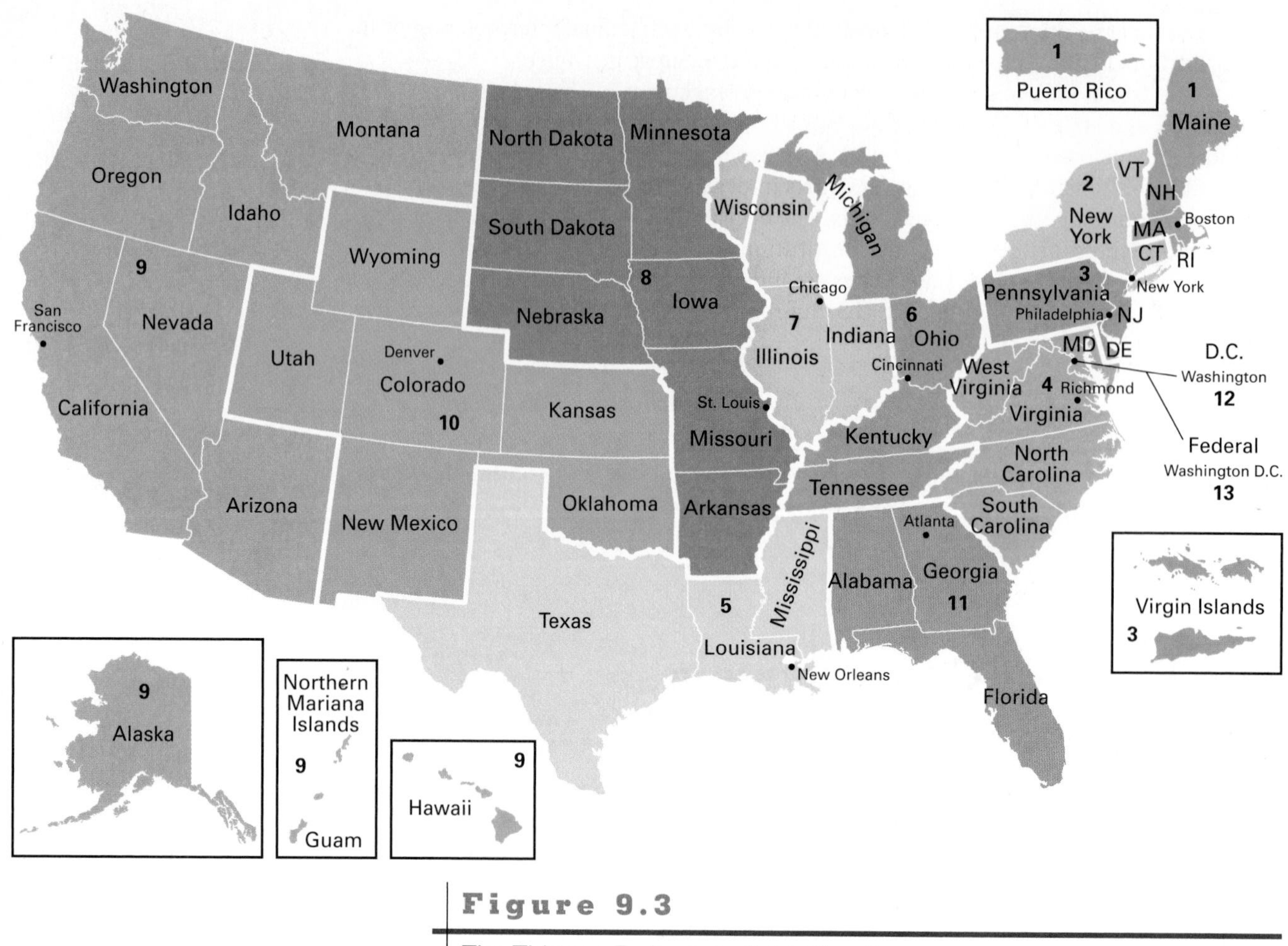

Figure 9.3

The Thirteen Federal Judicial Circuits

See http://www.uscourts.gov for a wealth of information on the various U.S. federal courts, as well as useful links and employment opportunities. ■

The federal court system is responsible for the enforcement of all federal codes in all 50 states, U.S. territories, and the District of Columbia. This includes responsibility for civil, criminal, and administrative trials. The federal court system is also responsible for the trials involving local codes and ordinances in the territories of Guam, the Virgin Islands, and the Northern Mariana Islands. If a person violates a federal law, they can be tried at any federal district court within the circuit. Thus, a person accused of mail fraud in Oklahoma could be tried in Oklahoma, Arizona, Colorado, Kansas, New Mexico, Utah, or Wyoming.

As mentioned, the federal court system is responsible for both civil and criminal cases. The focus of this book is on the criminal justice system, but there are twice as many federal district court civil trials as there are criminal trials. Criminal trials, especially trials for violent crimes, are only a small part of the work load of the federal court. For example, in 2000, there were only 313 homicide trials, and of this number, only 247 were for first-degree murder.[4] Of the criminal trials handled by the federal district court, the majority of defendants are tried for drug offenses. In 2000, there were 27,220 defendants tried for drug offenses.[5]

As shown in Figure 9.4, the federal court is divided into four tiers of responsibility: the U.S. magistrate courts, the trial courts, the appeals courts, and the U.S. Supreme Court.

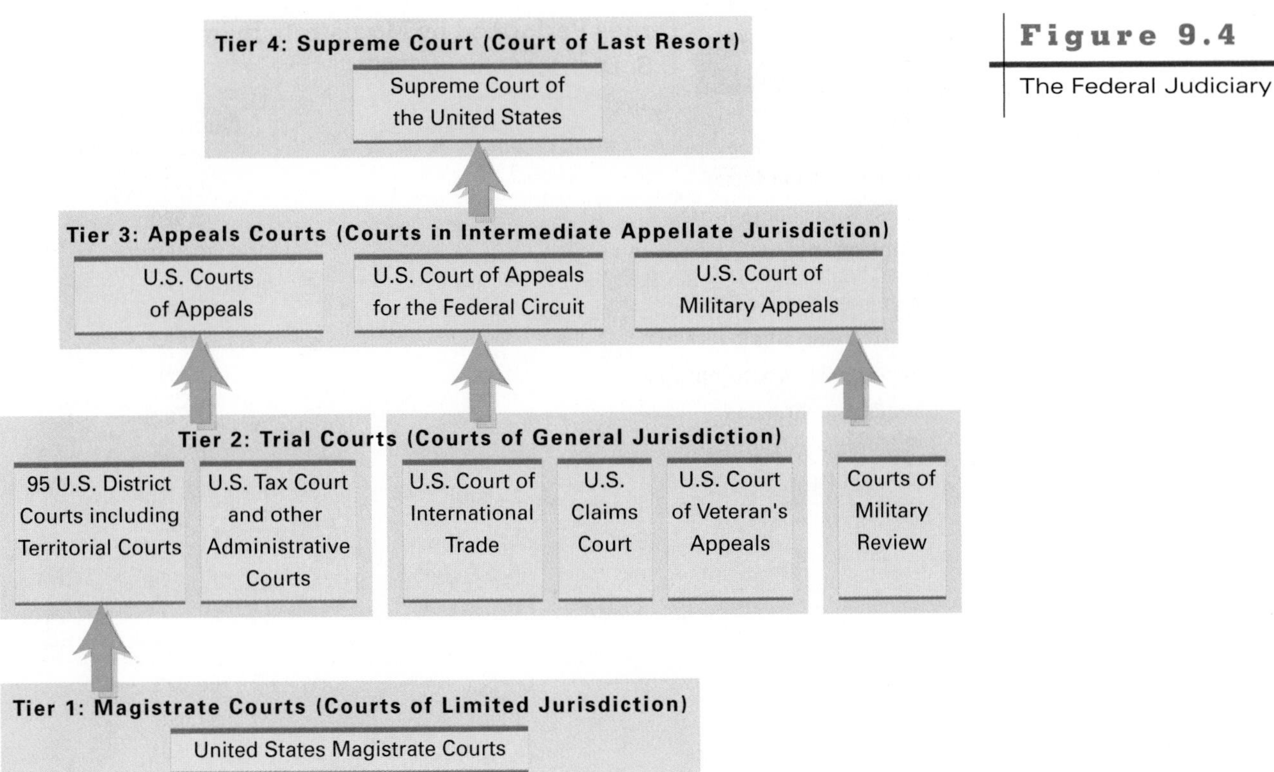

Figure 9.4

The Federal Judiciary

U.S. Magistrate Courts

U.S. magistrate courts are federal lower courts whose powers are limited to trying lesser misdemeanors, setting bail, and assisting district courts in various legal matters. Federal magistrate courts were created by the **Federal Magistrate's Act of 1968,** which phased out the former ineffective system of part-time U.S. commissioners. U.S. magistrate courts try class A misdemeanors and petty offenses as well as performing such duties as issuing search and arrest warrants, hearing initial appearances, and presiding over preliminary examinations, arraignments, detention hearings, and bail reviews. Magistrate courts are also responsible for hearing pretrial motions and evidentiary hearings. Federal magistrate courts also handle prisoner litigation, such as requests for habeas corpus, civil rights appeals, and evidentiary hearings. Duties of magistrates are summarized in Table 9.1 on page 274.

U.S. magistrate courts Federal lower courts with powers limited to trying lesser misdemeanors, setting bail, and assisting district courts in various legal matters.

United States District Courts

U.S. district courts are the trial courts of the federal system. They are the courts of original jurisdiction for all federal trials in the 50 states, the District of Columbia, Puerto Rico, and the U.S. territories of Guam, the Virgin Islands, and the Northern Mariana Islands. **Original jurisdiction** means that they are the first court to hear the charges against the defendant and to render a verdict regarding the charges against the defendant. It is the district court that decides if a defendant is guilty. Some federal district courts—such as the United States Tax Court, the United States Court of International Trade, the United States Claims Court, the United States Court of Veteran's Appeals, and the Courts of Military Review—have specific responsibilities.

U.S. district courts Trial courts of the federal system.

original jurisdiction The first court to hear and render a verdict regarding the charges against the defendant.

table 9.1 Duties Performed by Magistrate Judges in U.S. District Courts, 2000

Activity	Number
Trial Jurisdiction Cases	88,449
Class A misdemeanors	8,990
Petty offenses	79,459
Preliminary Proceedings	264,997
Search warrants	29,824
Arrest warrants/summonses	26,880
Initial appearances	77,752
Preliminary examinations	16,589
Arraignments	49,740
Detention hearings	37,490
Bail reviews	10,741
Other	15,981
Additional Duties	404,712
Criminal	108,823
Motions	67,099
Evidentiary hearings	1,990
Pretrial conferences	10,965
Probation/supervised release	3,109
Guilty pleas	10,614
Other	270,876
Civil	270,876
Settlement conferences	24,255
Other pretrial conferences	49,724
Motions	171,659
Evidentiary hearings	501
Social Security	5,516
Special masterships	734
Others	18,487
Prison Litigation	25,013
State habeas corpus	10,125
Federal habeas corpus	3,469
Civil rights	11,419
Evidentiary hearings	800
Civil Consent	11,481
Without trial	10,181
Jury trial	750
Non-jury trial	550
Miscellaneous matters	36,813
Total	806,452

Source: Sourcebook of Criminal Justice Statistics Online, http://www.albany.edu/sourcebook/1995/pdf.

District courts hear both civil and criminal cases but, as mentioned, the majority of cases are civil cases. Cases brought to district court include a wide variety of topics, including treason, homicide, copyright infringements, traffic offenses on federal reservations, violation of the Securities and Exchange Acts, and violations of federal regulations such as the Endangered Species Acts and the Meat and Poultry Inspection Acts.

There are 95 district courts distributed throughout the United States and the U.S. territories. Each district court has one or more courtrooms with one or more federal district judges. Each courtroom has numerous support personnel attached to it, such as federal prosecutor, U.S. Marshal Service personnel, and civilian court employees. Courtroom personnel are discussed in greater detail in Chapter 10.

United States Courts of Appeals

Appeals are guaranteed by congressional act. Rather than have the Supreme Court handle all appeals, the federal judiciary uses **U.S. courts of appeals** to hear appeals from U.S. district courts. The right of appeal applies to both civil and criminal cases, but the focus of this discussion is on criminal appeals. Criminal appeals to the U.S. Court of Appeals must be based on the claim that the defendant was denied a fair trial or that the law which the defendant was convicted of violating was unconstitutional. Defendants cannot appeal on the grounds that they are innocent. The question of guilt or innocence is a question of original jurisdiction and is addressed in the U.S. District Court: The judge or the jury heard the facts of the case and rendered a decision regarding the criminality of the defendant's behavior. Thus, the U.S. appeals court will not conduct another trial to determine the guilt of the defendant.

In 2001, defendant Robert Phillip Hanssen, a former FBI agent, was tried for espionage and treason. Since 1985, he had worked for Moscow, passing secrets to the Russians about American defenses and spy operations. In what court jurisdiction do you think he was tried, and why? What difference does court jurisdiction make in the American system of jurisprudence?

A fair trial does not mean that the defendant's trial was without error, but it does mean that there was no substantial judicial error that could have affected the outcome of the court's decision. During the defendant's trial in district court, it is the responsibility of the defendant's attorney to object to any procedure or court ruling that is thought to be unfair or unconstitutional. The district judge makes a ruling on the objection raised by the attorney, and the trial proceeds based on the judge's ruling. The objection of the defense counsel is entered into the transcript of the trial. After the trial, if the defense council believes that the ruling of the district judge was not correct, the judge's ruling can be appealed. If at the time of the trial the defense attorney fails to object to an unfair practice, the absence of such an objection can be considered a reason to deny the appeal.

The role of the U.S. Court of Appeals is to determine (1) whether the district judge made a judicial error, and (2) whether the error could have substantially affected the court's decision? If the appeals court determines that (1) the judge correctly interpreted the law or rule or (2) a judicial error was made but the error did not substantially affect the trial's outcome, the appeal can be dismissed. If the appeals court determines that a judicial error was made and the error could have substantially affected the trial's outcome, the appeals court will review the appeal and issue a ruling regarding the error. In criminal trials, judicial error includes, for example, the following:

U.S. courts of appeals The panel of federal judges that hears appeals from the U.S. district courts and determines if a judicial error was made that could have substantially affected the court's decision.

- Admitting evidence that has been improperly obtained
- Allowing prosecutorial evidence and witnesses not relevant to the trial
- Disallowing defense evidence and witnesses

- Improper trial conduct
- Misbehavior by the jury
- Instructions by the judge prohibiting the jury from considering a lesser offense
- Improper instructions by the judge to the jury

One must remember that there is a difference between judicial error and innocence. The defendant may indeed have committed a criminal act and is, without question, guilty in the eyes of the public. There may be videotape or eyewitnesses that document the defendant's commission of the crime, and the public may be outraged when a conviction is reversed on appeal. However, to convict the defendant in a court of law, rules must be followed and the rights of the defendant must be protected. The difficult balance between protecting the public from criminals and protecting the rights of defendants has been discussed in previous chapters. Often, it is the courts of appeal that decide what balance will be struck.

U.S. Courts of Appeal are required to hear the cases brought to them on appeal from the federal trial courts within their circuit. The U.S. Court of Appeals does not conduct a jury trial. Rather, a panel of federal appeals judges, usually three, review the case. A review does not mean that the defendant appears before the appeals court. The appeals court may decide to review only the written briefs submitted by the attorneys and to make a decision based on the information contained in the briefs. If the appeals court decides to hear oral arguments, the attorneys come before the court and present their reasoning. Often, there are legitimate differences of opinion among legal professionals regarding an interpretation of a law, constitutional right, or court decision. The attorneys attempt to persuade the panel of judges that their interpretation is the correct one. The appeal focuses on a rule of law and not the guilt of the defendant, so no witnesses or evidence is presented during the appeals hearing. If the U.S. Court of Appeals decides that a substantial judicial error has been made, the court reviews the case and determines the appropriate action to be taken to correct the error. The decision of the appeals court may mean that the defendant receives another trial in which the judicial error is corrected, or the sentence of the defendant may be modified.

There are 13 U.S. circuit courts of appeals and over 165 federal courts of appeals judges. Each of the 13 federal judicial circuits has one location that is the principal seat of federal courts of appeal, and there are two courts of appeals located in Washington, DC. (One of the Washington, DC, courts of appeals handles civil cases related to patents, copyrights, tax disputes, and claims against the federal government.) Appeals court circuits were first established in the original Thirteen Colonies and spread westward as the United States expanded. The geographical jurisdiction of the courts of appeals is called a **circuit court** because, originally, federal appeals judges literally traveled a circuit from one federal district court to another to hear appeals. This geographical origin of the various federal appeals circuits resulted in a disproportionate division of circuit courts east and west of the Mississippi River. There are only 4 U.S. circuit courts of appeals west of the Mississippi River.

As a result of the shift of the population centers from the east coast to the west coast, western U.S. circuit courts of appeals have more cases to review and also greater diversity in the values and cultures of the people within a circuit. The Ninth U.S. Circuit Court of Appeals, for instance, includes the western states Alaska and Hawaii and the U.S. territories of Guam and the Northern Mariana Islands. When there is widespread diversity, judges of the U.S. courts of appeals do not always have the same interpretation of the Constitution, the law, or criminal procedures. Nevertheless, the federal court system requires that decisions of the U.S. Circuit Court of Appeals are binding on all U.S. district courts within that circuit. For example, an opinion regarding the constitutionality of a search without a warrant in the Ninth U.S. Circuit Court of Appeals would be binding on all U.S. district courts in the Ninth Circuit, though not binding on the district courts in the other circuits. While not binding, decisions from other jurisdictions can be cited as guidelines.

circuit court Any court that holds sessions in various locations within its jurisdiction.

This circuit court judge rode from courthouse to courthouse over a vast western territory. Which court jurisdiction did he represent? What was his specific role and function in the criminal justice system? How did his rulings relate to the rulings of judges in lower courts in the states and territories he visited? Does the same system operate today?

The U.S. Supreme Court

The **U.S. Supreme Court** is the highest court in the American judicial system. This means that there is no higher authority to which to the defendant can appeal a decision of the Supreme Court. A decision by the Supreme Court is final and cannot be overruled by Congress. The only way to affect Supreme Court decisions is for Congress to pass a statute or constitutional amendment altering the wording of a law that the Supreme Court has declared constitutional. For example, in 1919 Congress passed the Eighteenth Amendment, which prohibited the manufacture, sale, or transportation of intoxicating liquors, and in 1933 repealed the prohibition with the Twenty-first Amendment. As another example, when the Supreme Court ruled that laws to collect federal personal income tax were unconstitutional (because they violated Article 1, Section 9 of the Constitution), Congress passed the Sixteenth Amendment, authorizing the federal government to lay and collect taxes on personal incomes.

In addition to its role in the criminal justice system, the Supreme Court exercises other important judicial powers. The Supreme Court is the legal mediator for lawsuits between states and between the United States and foreign countries. The Supreme Court also is the final authority for legal opinions binding on the federal government. For instance, when controversy arose over the legality of ballots cast in the state of Florida in the 2000 presidential election, the Supreme Court provided the final judgment regarding the vote count.

U.S. Supreme Court cases that determine how the Constitution is to be interpreted are called **landmark cases.** A landmark case is important, because once the U.S. Supreme Court makes a ruling, the lower courts have to fall in line with that ruling. Landmark cases end diversity in practices and rulings among the various circuit courts of appeals. U.S. Supreme Court rulings on constitutionality also are applicable to the state courts. Landmark cases are important in determining the constitutional rights of the defendant.

U.S. Supreme Court The highest court in the American judiciary system, whose rulings on the constitutionality of a law, due process rights, and rules of evidence are binding on all federal and state courts.

landmark cases U.S. Supreme Court cases that mark significant changes in interpretations of constitutionality.

REVIEWING CASES Unlike the U.S. circuit courts of appeals, the U.S. Supreme Court does not have to hear a criminal case on appeal. The Supreme Court chooses cases that the justices believe address important constitutional issues. Technically, the Court must review cases when (1) a federal court has held an act of Congress to be unconstitutional, (2) a U.S. Court of Appeals has found a state statute to be unconstitutional, (3) a state's highest court of appeals has ruled a federal law to be unconstitutional, and (4) an individual's challenge to a state statute on federal constitutional grounds is upheld by a state's highest court of appeals. In all other cases, the Court can decline to review a case. In reality, if a majority of justices does not want to review a case, the Court simply affirms the lower court's decision. If the Court decides not to review a case, there is no further appeal to the Court's decision.

In its role of judicial review of a case, the Supreme Court does not conduct jury trials and does not determine whether the defendant is guilty or innocent. The purpose of the Supreme Court's review is to determine whether a significant judicial error has been made and if so, determine the appropriate remedy. The Supreme Court has the power to review civil lawsuits, criminal cases, and juvenile hearings. The Court is very selective in deciding what cases to review and will not hear a case until all other appeals have been exhausted. For a state case, that means that the case must have been reviewed by the state's highest court before the Supreme Court will consider it for review. Furthermore, the case must involve a substantial federal or constitutional question. In the federal fiscal year 2000, over 8,000 cases were filed or pending for review, and only 99 cases were selected for review,[6] including 12 criminal cases.[7]

The process by which the Supreme Court chooses which cases to review begins with a clerk for a Supreme Court justice—an attorney who performs legal research for the justice. Clerks review the numerous cases that petition to the Supreme Court, select those that may merit consideration, and forward them to the Supreme Court judges. Each judge reviews the case and decides whether the case has the potential to raise a significant federal or constitutional question. If four or more members of the Supreme Court feel that the case meets this criterion, it is selected for review. For cases selected for review, the Court issues a writ of certiorari. This authority to select cases for review is known as **certiorari power.** A **writ of certiorari** is an order to the lower court, state or federal, to forward the record of the case to the Supreme Court. Table 9.2 shows the disposition of writs of certiorari for 2000.

certiorari power If four members of the Supreme Court believe a case meets its criteria for review, a writ of certiorari is issued, ordering the lower court to forward the record of the case to the Supreme Court.

writ of certiorari The power of the U.S. Supreme Court to choose what cases it will hear.

brief A concise statement of the main points of a law case.

When the Supreme Court selects a case for review, this does not mean that the defendant is innocent, is freed, or is immediately entitled to a new trial. The Court has several options in reviewing a case. The Court can

1. examine the trial record and facts of the case and determine that no further review is necessary;
2. ask the attorneys representing the appellant to submit a written statement, called a **brief,** stating the substantial federal or constitutional issue they think needs to be decided. (The attorney from the other side submits a rebuttal brief, and the Court decides on the basis of information in the briefs); and
3. decide that the case deserves a hearing.

table 9.2 **Petitions for Review on Writ of Certiorari to the U.S. Supreme Court Filed, Terminated, and Pending, 2000**

	Pending Oct. 1, 1999	Filed	Terminated			Pending Sept. 30, 2000
			Granted	Denied	Dismissed	
Criminal	778	1,786	12	1,779	0	773
U.S. civil	455	956	29	935	12	435
Private civil	1,175	2,763	51	2,416	32	1,439
Administrative appeals	90	128	7	106	1	104
Total	2,498	5,633	99	5,236	45	2,751

Source: Sourcebook of Criminal Justice Statistics Online, http://www.albany.edu/sourcebook/1995/pdf.

At a hearing, the two sides are invited to present oral arguments before the full Supreme Court, but these oral arguments do not resemble a trial. There are no witnesses and no jury, and no evidence as to the guilt or innocence of the defendant is presented. This hearing is not to determine guilt or innocence, but to determine whether the case involves a substantial federal or constitutional issue, and the attorneys must confine their arguments to this issue. The Supreme Court justices will ask questions of the attorneys, but few cases are decided by this method. In 1999, only 38 cases were argued before the Supreme Court.[8]

After reviewing a case, the Court declares its decision and can issue a written opinion explaining the reasons for their decision. A case that is disposed of by the Court without a full written opinion is said to be a **per curiam opinion.** The Court can affirm the case or reverse the lower court's decision. In affirming a case, the Supreme Court finds that there was no substantial judicial or constitutional error and the original opinion of the lower court stands. In a criminal case, this means that whatever sentence was imposed on the defendant may be carried out or continued. If the Court is hearing an appeal by the government, which lost the case in lower court, then an "affirm" might mean that the lower court's decision stands.

REMEDIES FOR JUDICIAL ERROR Reversing the case means the Court found that a judicial error or unconstitutional issue was central to the lower court's decision. Most cases are not reversed. In 1999, the Court reversed only 25 percent of all of the cases decided on merit.[9] In a criminal case, reversal does not mean that the defendant is freed, is innocent, or receives a reduced sentence. It means that the Supreme Court found the conviction of the defendant to be flawed and that conviction is "vacated." After the case is reversed, it is remanded. **Remanded** means that the case is returned to the court of original jurisdiction—the court that first convicted the defendant—with the instructions to correct the judicial error, called a "remedy."

If the judicial error involved the introduction of inadmissible evidence, such as an illegal confession or search and seizure or inappropriate testimony, then the remedy requires a new trial in which the inadmissible evidence cannot be used. If a conviction cannot be obtained without this evidence, the prosecution may decide not to ask for a new trial. In that case, the charges are dismissed and the defendant is set free. If the prosecution decides to retry the case, the defendant may or may not be convicted at the new trial.

Not all judicial errors require a new trial. Judicial errors also can involve an incorrect sentence being assessed against a defendant, and the court of original jurisdiction may be instructed to recalculate the sentence. A common criminal appeal for a reduction of sentence is the appeal for a reduction of a death sentence to the lesser sentence of life in prison.

When a long-incarcerated individual appeals on a writ of habeas corpus, an appeal to the Supreme Court can take decades. Long delays are unusual, however, although in some cases defendants have served the length of their sentence by the time that the Supreme Court hears their case. Delays often are due to the large case load of the Supreme Court and its limited ability to review and decide on appeals. Some critics of the judicial system have argued that such a delay in justice is the same as justice denied. There appears to be no immediate solution to this problem, as new issues raised by terrorism and bioterrorism have only enlarged the number of legal cases involving substantial questions of constitutional rights, due process, human rights, and civil liberties.

per curiam opinion A case that is disposed of by the U.S. Supreme Court that is not accompanied by a full opinion.

remanded The reversal of a decision by a higher court and the return of the case to the court of original jurisdiction with instructions to correct the judicial error.

JUST THE FACTS 9.2

How was the federal court system established? What cases do magistrate courts hear? What cases do district courts hear? What is needed to have an appeal heard? How does the U.S. Supreme Court operate?

Characteristics of the State Court System

THE MAIN IDEA

State courts have jurisdiction to settle legal disputes and criminal matters for violation of local, or state, criminal ordinances.

State courts are authorized and organized autonomously by each state. If there is a legal dispute between states, the federal courts have jurisdiction. The purpose of state courts is to try defendants charged with violations of state laws or the state constitution. A state also contains smaller political jurisdictions, such as cities and counties, and each of these has its own legal codes. Therefore, states must establish court systems that provide for a defendant to be tried for allegedly violating a city or county ordinance. Like the federal court system, the state court system has a number of specialized courts dealing with noncriminal cases. Also as in the federal courts, criminal trials compose only a small percentage of the state court's activities.

State court systems uniquely reflect the history of each state. For example, Pennsylvania's judiciary began as a disparate collection of courts, some inherited from the reign of the Duke of York and some established by William Penn. They were mostly local, mostly part-time, and mostly under control of the governor. All of the state courts were run by nonlawyers, and final appeals had to be taken to England. The Judiciary Act of 1722 was the colony's first judicial bill. It established the Pennsylvania Supreme Court and the Court of Common Pleas. The court system changed again with the Pennsylvania Constitution of 1776 and the Constitution of the United States. After that, the most sweeping changes in Pennsylvania's judiciary came in 1968. The Constitution of 1968 created the Unified Judicial System, consisting of the supreme court, superior courts, and commonwealth courts; common pleas courts; the Philadelphia municipal court; the Pittsburgh magistrate court; Philadelphia traffic court; and district justice courts. Pennsylvania's judicial system is shown in Figure 9.5.

Each state is a sovereign government and has the authority to establish its own system of state courts. Like Pennsylvania, most states designed their state court system when they were admitted into the Union. Thus, the states consisting of the original Thirteen Colonies have the oldest state courts, and the states of Alaska and Hawaii have the newest. Over time, the philosophy, mission, and values of the citizens of the states

This is a Pennsylvania superior court today. Where do superior courts stand in the hierarchy of Pennsylvania's state court system? How and when was the system established and changed? Each state has a unique system, but all state court systems have an equivalent hierarchy of jurisdictions. How does the state hierarchy of courts compare with federal court jurisdictions?

Figure 9.5

Pennsylvania's Judicial System

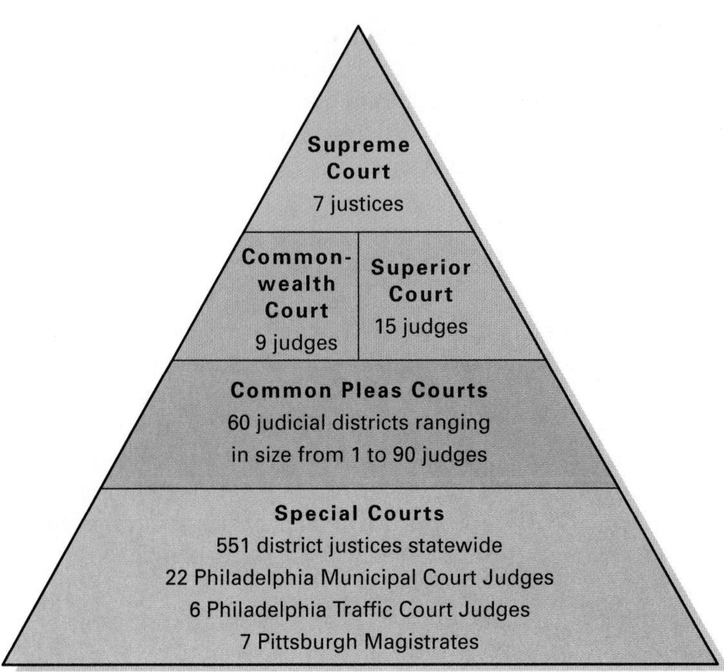

Source: http://www.courts.state.pa.us/index/ujs/courthistory.asp, "A History of Pennsylvania's Courts."

change, and many states have found it necessary to redesign their state court system. Most of those states have chosen models that resemble the four-tier federal court system. The four-tier system consists of (1) courts of limited jurisdiction, (2) courts of general jurisdiction, (3) courts of intermediate appellate jurisdiction, and (4) courts of last resort. Each state has unique names for the various courts within its system. Each state has granted different jurisdiction to the various courts within its system based on geography, subject matter, and hierarchy. Each state has a hierarchy of appeals from the lowest court to the court of last resort.

See http://www.ojp.usdoj.gov/bjs/pubalp2.htm#sco, an excellent reference that describes each of the state court systems, is a publication of the Bureau of Justice Statistics. See *State Court Organization 1998,* by David Rottman et al. ■

Courts of Limited Jurisdiction

State courts with original jurisdiction—the power to determine whether or not the defendant is guilty—are divided into courts of limited jurisdiction and general trial courts. Courts of limited jurisdiction are known as justice of the peace courts, municipal courts, and magistrate's courts. General trial courts are called circuit courts, superior courts, district courts, courts of common pleas, and court of first instance.

Courts of limited jurisdiction frequently are not **courts of record**—courts in which the trial proceedings are recorded. For example, traffic courts, municipal courts, and county courts frequently are not courts of records because no written record is made of the trial in these courts. Thus, a case that is appealed to a higher court from a limited jurisdiction court must have a trial de novo, or new trial. A new trial is required because there is no written record of the lower court's proceedings to determine whether a judicial error occurred.

courts of limited jurisdiction State courts of original jurisdiction that are not courts of record (e.g., traffic courts, municipal courts, or county courts).

courts of record Courts in which trial proceedings are transcribed.

Justice of the peace courts and municipal courts perform similar functions, hearing minor criminal cases involving municipal and traffic laws, issuing search and arrest warrants, setting bail, and arraigning defendants. Traditionally, justice of the peace courts are associated with rural geographical jurisdictions, while municipal courts are associated with urban geographical jurisdictions. Another court of limited jurisdiction is the county court, where counties can try defendants for violations of county laws. Most courts of limited jurisdiction also perform noncriminal functions, such as processing civil suits, accepting passport applications, and performing marriages. Some courts of limited jurisdiction try civil cases with limited dollar amounts. These courts are commonly referred to as "small claims courts."

Courts of General Jurisdiction

The **general trial courts** of the state judicial system are the workhorses of the criminal justice system. State general trial courts handle all kinds of criminal cases—from traffic violations to murder. In 1998, state courts convicted nearly 1 million adults of a felony. State felony convictions account for 95 percent of all felony convictions in the nation. The largest number of felony convictions in state courts in 1998 was for drug offenses (33.9%), followed by property offenses (30.5%) and violent offenses (17.8%). Despite the public's perception of the prevalence of violent crime, only 1 percent of the felony convictions in state courts were for murder, 3.2 percent for sexual assault, and 4.2 percent for robbery.[10]

General trial courts are courts of record. A full transcription (i.e., a word-for-word recording of the proceeding) is made for every trial in a general trial court. Nearly all appeals for criminal cases originate from state general trial courts.

Appellate Courts

Most states have an intermediate appellate court that acts in a similar capacity as the U.S. Court of Appeals. Some common names for these are Court of Criminal Appeals, Court of Appeals, Appellate Court, Court of Special Appeals, Appellate Division of Superior Court, Superior Court, and Commonwealth Court. These **appellate courts** do not have original jurisdiction and review cases for judicial error and other significant issues concerning due process, civil rights, and federal and state constitutional questions.

Courts of Last Resort

Each state has a court of final appeals. The names given to these various **courts of last resort** are Supreme Court, Supreme Judicial Court, Court of Appeals, and High Court. Oklahoma and Texas have two separate courts of last resort: The Supreme Court of Criminal Appeals handles criminal cases, and the state Supreme Court handles all other cases. Each state determines the number of judges that sit on the court of last resort, typically five to nine justices.

The state court of last resort has appellant jurisdiction and acts much like the U.S. Supreme Court. Its primary purpose in criminal cases is to review a selected number of cases that may have a significant state or federal question. After reviewing the case, the state's court of last resort can decide to affirm the case or to reverse and remand the case. After a criminal defendant has exhausted all appeals in the state court system, he or she can appeal the case to the U.S. Supreme Court.

general trial courts State courts of original jurisdiction; often called circuit courts, superior courts, district courts, courts of common pleas, and courts of first instance.

appellate courts Appellate courts have the authority to review the proceedings and verdicts of general trial courts for judicial errors.

court of last resort A state court that reviews lower court decisions and whose decisions can be appealed to the U.S. Supreme Court.

JUST THE FACTS 9.3

What is the four-tier system of state courts? In which court would you appear for a traffic violation? A misdemeanor charge? A violent felony? A civil rights violation?

Lawyers and Judges

THE MAIN IDEA

Lawyers must receive legal training and pass the bar examination to practice law, while judges are appointed or elected to positions.

Of all of the personnel in the criminal justice system, judges and lawyers receive the most prestige. According to data from The Gallup Organization, most people (85%) say that the honesty and ethical standards of judges are average or "able." Nearly half of the respondents (47%) rated judges as above average.[11] While judges share a common background with lawyers, lawyers do not rate as highly as judges in the public eye. Unfortunately, the public's perception of the honesty and ethical standards of lawyers had dropped over the past 25 years. Twenty-five years ago, 25 percent of respondents rated the honesty and ethical standards of lawyers as above average, whereas in 2000 only 17 percent rated lawyers as above average.[12] Only a little over half of respondents (59%) to the 2000 survey rated the honesty and ethical standards of lawyers as average or above average.[13]

Two factors that may contribute to the positive image of the judge and the lawyer is the mandatory higher education required for these positions and the above-average salaries (Tables 9.3 and 9.4 on page 284). The formal educational standard for lawyers

table 9.3 Highest and Lowest Salaries of State Judges, 2000

Highest Five Salaries		Lowest Five Salaries	
Highest State Court			
National Average	*116,184*		
Illinois	153,052	American Samoa	74,303
New York	151,200	Montana	83,550
Florida	150,000	Oregon	93,600
District of Columbia	149,900	Wyoming	93,000
California	149,686	New Mexico	90,407
Intermediate Appellate Court			
National Average	*114,280*		
Georgia	146,994	New Mexico	85,887
Illinois	144,049	Puerto Rico	90,000
New York	144,000	Oregon	91,500
New Jersey	141,176	Oklahoma	93,530
California	140,332	Mississippi	95,500
General Trial Court			
National Average	*104,349*		
District of Columbia	141,300	Puerto Rico	65,000
New York	136,700	New Mexico	81,593
New Jersey	133,330	Wyoming	83,700
Florida	130,000	Oregon	85,300
Northern Mariana Islands	120,000	Oklahoma	88,511

Source: Sourcebook of Criminal Justice Statistics Online, http://ww.albany.edu/sourcebook/1995/pdf.

table 9.4 Annual Salaries of Federal Judges, January 1, 2001

Judicial Office	Annual Salary
Chief Justice of the United States	$186,300
Associate Justices of the Supreme Court of the United States	178,300
United States Circuit Judges	153,900
United States District Judges	145,100
Judges, United States Court of International Trade	145,100
Judges, United States Court of Federal Claims	145,100
United States Bankruptcy Judges	133,492
United States Magistrate Judges (full-time)	133,492

Source: Sourcebook of Criminal Justice Statistics Online, http://wwwalbany.edu/sourcebook/1995/pdf.

has risen from nothing at the end of the eighteenth century to graduate school in the twenty-first century.

While the newly formed United States adopted a legal system similar to its former colonial ruler's, it did not adopt the corresponding British system for lawyers and judges. In fact, until after the War of 1812, fear and hatred of British ways were prevalent in the American court system.[14] Lawyers in nineteenth-century America were poorly educated, as the practice of law emphasized common sense and apprenticeships. Formal education was not a requirement for entry into the practice of law. A person could study under the apprenticeship of a practicing attorney and receive his or her license to practice law by passing a state examination. Abraham Lincoln is probably the most well known attorney in America who did not have a formal law education.

Until recently, the right to be a lawyer or a judge has been restricted to white men. Margaret Brent was the first nonofficial female lawyer in the country. She arrived in the colonies in 1638 and was involved in 124 court cases in Maryland. Because of her sex, however, she was denied recognition for her contributions. Belle Babb Mansfield passed the Chicago bar examination in 1869. That same year **Myra Bradwell** passed the Illinois bar exam with honors, but she was refused admission to the state bar because she was a woman. This decision was upheld by the U.S. Supreme Court in ***Bradwell v. Illinois.*** In 1872, Alta Hulett became the first practicing attorney in Illinois by an act of the legislature. Other states followed suit in the 1870s and 1880s as educated women began to seek careers in the justice system. In 1890, Myra Bradwell finally was admitted to the Illinois bar, and in 1892, just 2 years prior to her death, she became the first woman to receive a license to practice before the U.S. Supreme Court. The American Bar Association recognizes Myra Bradwell as the first female lawyer in the United States.

The law profession has been self-regulating in other ways. For example, the legal system investigates charges of ethical violations of standards of behavior involving lawyers and judges. Judges or lawyers who violate criminal laws find themselves in court as defendants. The **Center for Judicial Conduct Organizations** conducts annual surveys of judicial watchdog organizations. These organizations typically are state agencies created by statute or constitutional amendment with the mandate to receive, investigate, and dispose of complaints regarding judicial misconduct. Examples of judicial misconduct are prejudice or bias, slow processing of orders, procedural or administrative irregularity, courtroom demeanor, and conflict of interest. As an illustration, Table 9.5 shows the types and dispositions of complaints against judges for **judicial misconduct** in the United States during 1999.

judicial misconduct
Unprofessional or illegal behavior by a judge that is considered inappropriate for his or her position or prejudicial to the persons involved in a trial.

ethics in the system

Ethical Violations by Lawyers

What do you do if your lawyer is in jail? When defense attorney Gary Modafferi, 38, a former city deputy prosecutor for the City and County of Honolulu, was arrested for charges related to possessing crystal methamphetamine, the 150 state and federal clients that he was defending had to decide that very question. Few of his clients requested a new lawyer. Ironically, most of his clients were facing criminal charges involving drugs.[15]

After his arrest, Modafferi was freed on $100,000 bail and placed under house arrest. Modafferi asked the court to remove the house arrest restriction so that he could better defend his clients. However, on his first appearance in federal magistrate court, representing his client Raymond Dongon on charges related to heroin, cocaine, firearms, and money laundering, the prosecution argued that Modafferi should be removed from the case on the grounds that the defendant could later challenge his conviction by saying Modafferi was on drugs and could not effectively represent him. The judge agreed, and over the objections of his client, removed Modafferi from the case. Modafferi eventually was convicted of the charges against him and was prohibited from further representing clients while in prison.

If an attorney is accused of a violation of ethical standards of behavior that are not criminal in nature, the agency responsible for the discipline of the attorney is the state bar association in which the attorney is licensed to practice law. The state bar association has the power to conduct inquiries and hearings concerning the ethical standards of practice of the attorney and to issue punishments. Punishments can range from reprimands or orders that the attorney perform certain actions (usually to correct defects or work not done) to disbarment. Disbarment is the most serious punishment that the bar association can issue. When an attorney is disbarred, he or she is prohibited from practicing law in any capacity in that state. The attorney cannot charge clients for legal advice and cannot represent clients in court or other legal proceedings. Obviously, the financial impact of disbarment can be significant. Attorneys can be disbarred for a certain amount of time, such as 3 months or a year, or they can be disbarred indefinitely. In many states, if the attorney is disbarred for more than 1 year, he or she must retake and pass the state bar examination before practicing law again. Even presidents of the United States are subject to the censure of the bar association. The California Bar Association disbarred President Richard Nixon after his involvement in the Watergate scandal. President Bill Clinton was disbarred by the Arkansas Bar Association for charges related to perjury.

■ **Is it enough that a bar association is responsible for investigating its own members, or should an unbiased panel be appointed to investigate and punish unethical lawyers? Do you believe that President Clinton should have been disbarred for lying about having an extramarital affair?**

Education for Lawyers

Today, the formal educational standard for lawyers is 2 to 3 years of graduate study beyond the bachelor's degree. The most common career path for modern lawyers is to complete a bachelor's degree followed by law school. Law schools do not require a specific undergraduate curriculum for admission but recommend a good liberal arts background with emphasis on writing, comprehension, and analytical thinking. In addition to an undergraduate degree, nearly all law schools require the student to take the **Law School Aptitude Test (LSAT).** The LSAT is a standardized test that measures the student's analytical thinking and writing abilities. The LSAT does not measure the student's knowledge of the law. The typical law school requires 2 years of course work and may also require one year of internship to obtain the J.D., or juris doctorate degree (Doctor of Law). There are some law schools that shorten the time required for graduation by providing accelerated coursework or cooperative programs with undergraduate

table 9.5 Judicial Misconduct Complaints (by Type of Disposition and State, 1999[a])

	Complaints			Disposition of Complaints										
	Pending at Beginning of Reporting Period	Received during Reporting Period	Pending at End of Reporting Period	Dismissed without Formal or Informal Action	Approximate Percentage of Dispositions That Were Dismissals	Informal Action Taken	Judge Vacated Office during Investigation	Judge Privately Censured, Admonished, or Reprimanded	Judge Publicly Censured, Admonished, or Reprimanded	Judge Suspended as Final Sanction	Fine Imposed	Judge Removed from Office	Recommendation Pending	Other[b]
Alabama	37	215	44	203	94	11	2	(c)	0	0	(c)	1	1	0
Alaska	14	48	9	42	79	2	0	1	0	0	(c)	0	1	0
Arizona	48	260	50	225	79	30	0	30	2	1	(c)	0	1	1
Arkansas	160	243	162	232	96	1	0	(c)	6	0	0	1	1	3
California	108	1,125	120	1,021	94	53	2	3	9	(c)	(c)	0	1	1
Colorado	0	143	0	142	99	0	0	1	0	(c)	0	0	0	0
Connecticut	8	77	10	63	84	NA	NA	0	1	0	(c)	0	1	11
Delaware	0	10	3	7	100	0	0	0	0	0	(d)	0	0	0
District of Columbia	2	14	2	14	100	0	0	0	0	(c)	(c)	0	0	0
Florida	6	454	10	392	87	13	0	(c)	0	(c)	0	0	4	5
Hawaii	14	34	11	31	84	6	0	1	0	0	(c)	0	0	0
Idaho	5	195	10	185	95	3	0	2	0	0	0	0	0	0
Illinois	223	447	78	483	82	105	2	(c)	0	0	(c)	0	0	0
Indiana	0	231	15	183	85	20	0	0	4	1	0	0	0	0
Kansas	9	305	6	276	90	10	0	1	0	(c)	(e)	0	0	1
Kentucky	13	218	3	206	94	12	0	6	1	2	0	0	0	1
Louisiana	105	427	120	279	68	11	0	2[f]	2	0	(c)	0	1	2
Maine	9	41	10	40	100	3	0	0	0	0	0	0	0	0
Maryland	36	96	39	91	98	5	1	1	0	(c)	(c)	0	0	0
Michigan	177	650	152	639	87	10	5	10	0	1	(g)	0	5	0
Minnesota	17	144	20	132	94	8	1	(c)	1	0	1	0	0	0
Mississippi	34	336	36	294	84	24	0	9	2	0	1	0	5	11
Missouri	46	210	46	197	94	11	2	11	0	0	(c)	0	0	0
Montana	6	39	11	32	94	1	0	1	1	0	(c)	0	0	0
Nebraska	9	78	7	80	100	(c)	0	(c)	0	0	(c)	0	0	2
Nevada	41	143	40	138	96	3	0	(c)	0	(c)	0	0	1	4
New Hampshire	30	53	9	56	76	0	0	5	0	0	(g)	0	0	0

New Jersey	63	249	35	257	93	3	0	14	1	0	(c)	1	0	2
New Mexico	24	94[h]	20	67	68	18	8	11	1	0	0	1	0	82
New York	178	1,424	183	1,283	90	54	20	(c)	14	(c)	(c)	4	2	1
North Carolina	25	347	17	318	90	0	1	20	1	(c)	(c)	0	1	13
North Dakota	10	92	35	62	93	0	1	0	0	1	(c)	0	0	1
Ohio	20	697	61	545	83	(c)	0	(c)	0	2	0	1	1	1
Oregon	3	137	7	131	98	3	0	(c)	0	0	(c)	0	0	1
Pennyslvania	9	522	43	444	93	31	0	(c)	0	0	(c)	1	1	1
Rhode Island	6	21	6	20	83	2	0	1	0	0	(c)	0	0	0
South Carolina	60	198	60	140	71	50	0	1	5	(c)	(c)	0	0	4
South Dakota	1	16	5	11	92	1	0	0	0	0	0	0	0	0
Texas	360	776	281	729	85	28	2	16	11	1	(c)	1	1	11
Utah	66	125	46	122	82	17	0	9	5	0	(c)	0	1	42
Vermont	5	66	11	44	73	(c)	0	(c)	1	0	(c)	0	0	0
Virginia	NA	47	10	42	NA	0	0	(c)	0	(c)	(c)	0	0	0
Washington	167	318	146	313	92	(c)	1	(c)	8	2	(c)	1	3	0
West Virginia	28	252	26	252	99	0	0	(c)	3	0	0	0	0	4
Wisconsin	10	434	13	431	99	3	0	(c)	1	0	(c)	0	3	2
Wyoming	7	17[i]	3	21[i]	100	1	0	0	0	(c)	(c)	0	0	0

Source: American Judicature Society, Center for Judicial Conduct Organizations, *Judicial Conduct Reporter,* Vol. 22, No. 2 (Chicago: American Judicature Society, Summer 2000), pp. 2, 3. Table adapted by *Sourcebook of Criminal Justice Statistics* staff. Reprinted by permission.

Note: The Center for Judicial Conduct Organizations conducts annual surveys of judicial conduct organizations. These organizations are typically State agencies created by statute or constitutional amendment with the mandate to receive, investigate, and dispose of complaints regarding judicial misconduct. The judicial conduct organizations handle complaints such as judicial prejudice or bias, slow processing of orders, procedural or administrative irregularity, courtroom demeanor, and conflict of interest. (The Center for Judicial Conduct Organizations, *Judicial Conduct Reporter* 3 (Fall 1981), p. 2.) Information was not available for Georgia, Iowa, Massachusetts, Oklahoma, and Tennessee. Cross-jurisdiction comparisons should be done cautiously due to differences among the states in reporting periods, definitions or complaints, authorized sanctions, and recording practices. For the states of Alabama, California, Kentucky, Mississippi, North Carolina, and South Carolina, any discrepancies in totals are due to multiple or consolidated complaints and/or dispositions.

[a]Judicial conduct organizations use varying periods. Most of the above data are for either calendar year or fiscal year 1999. Other reporting periods are: 1998 for California, New Hampshire, Ohio, and Wisconsin; 8/99 to 6/00 for Indiana; fiscal year 2000 for Maryland; 1/98 to 12/99 for North Carolina.

[b]This category encompasses a number of statutes including misconduct cases that were pending before the supreme court, judges who were suspended as an interim sanction, orders for education, retirement, and disability.

[c]Sanction not available in the jurisdiction.

[d]The Delaware Constitution empowers the Court on the Judiciary to "censure, remove or retire" any judicial officer. The constitution does not specifically provide that the court may suspend, fine, or assess fees or costs; however, case law has made it clear that the power to suspend a judicial officer is inherent in the express powers granted to the court by the constitution. Whether the court has the inherent authority to impose other lesser sanctions, such as a fine or interim suspension, is not clearly settled.

[e]Fines not specifically authorized but supreme court's plenary power may encompass imposition of fine.

[f]The Judiciary Commission does not impose sanctions, but it does counsel.

[g]It is not clear whether a fine is an available sanction.

[h]Seventy-two unverified complaints and 912 inquiries also were received by telephone or in person.

[i]Indicates verified complaints received.

Go to http://www.abanet.org, the official web site of the American Bar Association, for a wealth of information on careers in law, current events, the ABA perspective on current events, and much more. ■

institutions in which students take courses during their junior and senior years that will count toward the law degree.

There are two kinds of law schools: **American Bar Association (ABA)** approved and non–American Bar Association approved. Lawyers are in a self-regulating profession. The American Bar Association and the various state bar associations govern professional standards of conduct, education, and ethics. After graduation from law school and before one can practice law, it is necessary to pass a standardized state examination covering the laws and procedures of that state. This standardized examination, similar to the professional examination required for doctors and nurses, is drafted by members of the state bar association, who also evaluate the examinations taken by law school graduates.

A student can go to law school in any state but must pass the **bar examination** for the specific state in which in which he or she wants to practice law. To practice law in more than one state, lawyers are required to pass the bar examination of each state in which they want to practice.[16]

The bar examination is named after the divider in a courtroom that separates the court personnel from the public audience. In the past, this low, usually wooden rail was the "bar" or barrier that divided the professional courtroom work group from the public. Only qualified personnel could cross this barrier, a tradition practiced today in contemporary courtrooms. Historically, in English tradition, before an apprentice could pass through this barrier and become part of the court work group, he had to pass an oral examination. This practice became known as "passing the bar." Of course, it is still necessary for lawyers to pass the bar before they can be licensed to practice law in a state.

The bar examination is rigorous and requires specific knowledge of the laws and procedures of the state. (After graduation from law school, the aspiring attorney often takes a course specifically to prepare for the state bar examination.) Students who graduate from ABA-approved law schools are allowed to take the state bar examination in any state of their choice. The ABA has examined the curriculum and institutional capacity of the approved school and has determined that it has met a minimum standard of excellence. Not all law schools are ABA-approved, but law schools approved by a state's department of education are also legitimate. Students who graduate from non-ABA-approved law schools can take the bar examination in the state in which the school is located but may be prohibited from taking the bar examination in any other state.

bar examination A rigorous test of the laws and procedures of a state that must be passed in order to practice law in that state.

Most law schools do not prepare the student for a specialty in the practice of law, but provide a general grounding in legal theory and the knowledge necessary for the lawyer to develop his or her special area of interest. Students may choose to practice civil

What are the principal differences between the British and American court systems? In the British system, the king or queen appoints judges who remain in their posts until mandatory retirement age. What are some advantages and disadvantages of selecting judges by that method? What are the advantages and disadvantages of the methods of choosing state and federal judges used in the United States?

criminal justice

in the world

The English Legal Profession

Although the United States adopted the English system of common law, courts, and trial by jury, it developed a substantially different method of legal education and practice. The criminal cases of Great Britain are handled in the Crown courts, which have exclusive jurisdiction for all major criminal cases and handle appeals from the magistrate courts. Magistrate courts handle traffic offenses and minor crimes and are similar to bench trials in that the magistrates determine the outcome of cases without a jury. As in American courts, trials in the Crown courts are heard by a judge and a jury.

According to Richard J. Terrill, there are several significant differences between the American and British legal professions.[17] Great Britain has a two-tier legal profession consisting of solicitors and barristers. Solicitors provide legal advice to the public and handle other civil matters, such as drawing up contracts, conducting land transactions, handling probate, and providing legal services in divorce issues. Solicitors are not required to have college degrees but must complete 3 years of undergraduate education, followed by a 2½-year internship with a practicing solicitor. Alternatively, the candidate can complete a year of education at a college of law, followed by a 4-year internship with a practicing solicitor.

Solicitors must pass a series of examinations at the end of their internships and then apply for admission to the Law Society. If accepted, there is a 3-year waiting period before the newly licensed solicitor can establish a legal practice. During these 3 years, he or she must work for a partnership or law firm.

Two important differences between the American system and the British system are that (1) the fees that a solicitor can charge a client are regulated by law and (2) solicitors have only limited rights to argue a case before the court. Solicitors may argue cases in magistrate courts and county courts, which have jurisdiction only in civil cases over matters such as contracts, small claims, and estates and trusts below a certain value.

Criminal cases in the Crown's courts and appeals courts are argued by barristers. The Crown's court is similar to the American courts of general jurisdiction (i.e., district courts). Barristers are legal specialists who carry on the English tradition of oral arguments so central to British legal procedure. Solicitors do not make the oral arguments before the court but seek the services of a barrister to present a case to a judge and jury.

To become a barrister, the candidate must first obtain a law degree from a university and then join one of the four Inns of Court: Gray's Inn, Lincoln's Inn, the Inner Temple, and the Middle Temple. The inn provides the student with additional knowledge regarding the more practical aspects of the law and the process of arguing cases before the court. The course of study at the inn also prepares the student for the bar examination. As in the American legal system, the prospective barristers must successfully pass a bar examination. Unlike the American system, however, after passing the bar examination, the student is not licensed to practice law on his or her own. Rather, the student finds a junior barrister who will allow him or her to complete an internship for a period of 1 year. The apprentice is called a "pupillage."

After apprenticeship, students seek admission as a junior barrister and sit behind the Queen's counsel in the courtroom. Two types of barristers are the junior barrister and the Queen's counsel. After approximately 15 to 20 years of practice, a junior barrister is qualified to apply to the lord chancellor, the head of the judiciary, for promotion to Queen's counsel. If appointed as Queen's counsel, a process known as "taking silk," the barrister can wear silk robes in court rather than the cotton robes worn by junior barristers.

Most judges are selected from the ranks of Queen's counsel. Judicial appointments are made by the monarch on the recommendation of the lord chancellor or the prime minister. The appointment is not subject to a confirmation hearing before Parliament and is not reviewed by the Bar of England and Wales. The judicial appointment lasts until the judge reaches the age of retirement. Because of the length of time it takes to achieve the rank of Queen's counsel, most judges are in their forties or fifties when appointed.

■ **What are the principal differences between the American and British judiciaries? Should the United States consider a two-tiered system of lawyers, using solicitors to do basic legal work for a lower price? What benefit might the British selection of judges have over the selection of federal judges in the United States?**

law or criminal law, but most graduates of law schools enter into the practice of civil law. Criminal lawyers are further divided into defense attorneys and government prosecutors. As you have read, defense attorneys defend accused persons for a fee or are appointed as public defenders. Public defenders are discussed in more detail in Chapter 10. Prosecutors work for the city, county, state, or federal government.

Selection of Federal Judges

Judges for state trial courts and the federal judiciary are selected from the ranks of practicing attorneys. Judges for state courts of limited jurisdiction come from diverse backgrounds and may not have any formal legal education. Federal district judges, courts of appeals judges, and Supreme Court justices are nominated by the president, and their nominations must be confirmed by a majority vote of the Senate. There is no constitutional requirement that the president's nominees have formal legal education and be practicing attorneys; however, as a rule, this is true of all nominees. The ABA reviews the nominations and issues a statement stating whether it considers the nominee qualified for the appointment. Neither the president nor the Senate is required to give consideration to the ABA's evaluation, but the ABA's endorsement is considered an important political factor.

Federal judges are appointed for life and can be removed from office only by the impeachment process. Furthermore, the salary of a federal judge cannot be reduced or withheld during his or her tenure in office. The purpose of these conditions is to provide the federal judge with a degree of independence from the executive and legislative branches of the government. Federal magistrate judges are appointed to full-time or part-time positions by federal district court judges.

On first appearance, the salary of federal judges appears very attractive (see Table 9.4). Full-time federal magistrate judges earn over $133,000 per year, and the chief justice of the U.S. Supreme Court earns over $186,000 per year.[18] While this is well above the national median salary, and a lot more than a police officer or correctional officer's salary, it is not considered competitive enough to attract the most qualified attorneys into the judicial system. Successful attorneys of the caliber required for appointment to a federal judgeship often have a greater potential for income in private business rather than in government service.

Selection of State Judges

There is no one system for selecting state judges, as each state has a different system for selecting them. The most common method of selecting state judges are (1) appointment by a nominating commission, (2) appointment by the governor of the state or legislative appointment, (3) partisan election, and (4) nonpartisan election (Table 9.6). Not only does the selection process vary from state to state, but the responsibilities and terms of service also vary. The terms of office for state judges range from 1 year to life tenure. Salaries also range widely, as do qualifications for office. In 1998, there were 208 statewide general and limited jurisdiction trial court systems in the United States, the District of Columbia, and Puerto Rico. About 9,065 full-time authorized judges served in the 71 statewide trial court systems of general jurisdiction.[19] In all but two states, Maine and Massachusetts, general jurisdiction trial court judges are required to have a law degree.[20]

The states have struggled to find fair and impartial ways to select judges. One of the more contemporary methods is to use a nominating committee, which usually is composed of members of the state bar association and other community members. In Hawaii, for example, the nominating committee runs advertisements in the newspaper and invites practicing attorneys who meet the minimum qualifications to apply for the position of judge (Figure 9.6 on page 292). The nominating committee screens and interviews candidates and forwards a list of qualified candidates to the governor. The governor

table 9.6 Method of Selecting State Judges and Length of Initial Term

Method of Selection	Initial Term
Partisan Election	
Alabama	6 years
Illinois	6 years
Indiana	6 years
Louisiana	6 years
Michigan (most counties)	6 years
Missouri (most counties)	6 years
New York	14 years
Ohio	6 years
Pennsylvania	10 years
Tennessee	8 years
Texas	4 years
West Virginia	8 years
Nonpartisan Election	
Arkansas	4 years
Florida	6 years
Georgia	4 years
Idaho	4 years
Kentucky	8 years
Minnesota	6 years
Mississippi	4 years
Montana	6 years
Nevada	6 years
North Carolina	8 years
North Dakota	6 years
Oklahoma	4 years
Oregon	6 years
South Dakota	8 years
Washington	4 years
Wisconsin	6 years
Elected by Legislature	
Virginia	8 years
Appointment by Governor	
Maine	7 years
New Hampshire	To age 70
New Jersey	7 years
Choice of Nonpartisan Elections or Appointment by Governor	
California	6 years
Nominating Commission	
Alaska	Until general election, not less than 3 years
Arizona (most counties)	Until general election, not less than 2 years
Colorado	Until general election, not less than 2 years
Connecticut	8 years
Delaware	12 years
District of Columbia	15 years
Hawaii	10 years
Iowa	Until general election, not less than 1 year
Kansas (most districts)	Until next general election

(*continues*)

table 9.6 Method of Selecting State Judges and Length of Initial Term (*Continued*)

Method of Selection	Initial Term
Nominating Commission (*cont.*)	
Maryland	Until general election, not less than 1 year
Massachusetts	To age 70
Nebraska	Until general election, not less than 3 years
New Mexico	Until next general election
Rhode Island	Life tenure
South Carolina	6 years
Utah	Until general election, not less than 3 years
Vermont	6 years
Wyoming	Until general election, not less than 1 year

Source: Based on data from American Judicature Society, *Judicial Selection in the United States: A Compendium of Provisions,* 2nd ed. (Chicago: American Judicature Society, 1993); and in *Sourcebook of Criminal Justice Statistics Online* http://www.albany.edu/sourceboo/1995pdf/t176pdf, Table 1.76, Method of Selection and Length of Initial and Retention Terms of General Jurisdiction Court Judges.

makes the final selection by appointing judges from the nominating committee's list to a 10-year term. After 10 years, the judge is reviewed by the nominating committee and is either renewed or dismissed. In 15 states, general jurisdiction trial court judges are selected by gubernatorial appointment and in 3 states by appointment by state legislatures. In these states, the governor or legislature has wide latitude in selecting judges.

In 28 states, general jurisdiction trial judges are selected by popular vote. Two methods of selecting judges by election are by partisan election and nonpartisan election. Ten states use partisan elections that require candidates for judge to declare their affiliation

Figure 9.6

Selecting Judges in Hawaii

Source: "Notice of Anticipated Vacancy in Judicial Office" from Judicial Selection Commission, State of Hawaii.

NOTICE OF ANTICIPATED VACANCY IN JUDICIAL OFFICE

The Judicial Selection Commission, State of Hawaii, announces that it is accepting the submission of names of applicants for the office of **Judge, District Court of the Fifth Circuit**, State of Hawaii. This vacancy will be created by the retirement of **The Honorable Gerald S. Matsunaga** on December 30, 1998. The names of qualified individuals may be submitted by any interested person, including an applicant for the judicial office referred to in this notice.

The Constitution of the State of Hawaii provides that the Chief Justice shall fill a vacancy in the District Court by appointing a person from a list of not less than six nominees presented by the Commission. The Constitution requires that persons selected by the Commission be residents and citizens of the State of Hawaii and of the United States and have been licensed to practice law by the Hawaii Supreme Court for a period of not less than five years preceding nomination. All names submitted to the Commission will be kept confidential by the Commission and should be delivered by mail to the following address not later than January 28, 1999.

B. Martin Luna, *Chair*
Judicial Selection Commission
State of Hawaii / P.O. Box 2560 / Honolulu, HI 96804

with a political party and campaign for office just as a candidate for any other political office would. In partisan elections, judges must raise sufficient funds to pay for their campaigns and win the popular vote to get elected. Judges elected through partisan elections usually serve a 6-year term and then must run again to retain the office. Nonpartisan elections, used in 18 states, prohibit the candidate for judge from declaring a political party and "campaigning."

The purpose behind each system is to obtain fair and honest judges who will be accountable to the public but are insulated from immediate public opinion. Each system claims to accomplish that end. States that use gubernatorial or legislative appointment claim that because these politicians are accountable to the public, they will make wise choices or risk being removed from office. Furthermore, it is argued that making judges run for office would subject the candidates to undue pressure from the voters or would create potential conflict of interest due to financial contributions to the candidate's campaign by special interest groups. States that use nominating committees claim that theirs is the most efficient method of selecting qualified judges, because the selection of candidates is made by legal professionals from a qualified pool of candidates. States that require judges to obtain office through election argue the public approval is the best method of ensuring that judges are fair and honest. Critics of the election process argue that the public is not the best judge of judicial merit and that the election process and the requirement to raise campaign funds may introduce bias or the appearance of bias into the judiciary.

Judges for courts of limited jurisdiction often are not required to have any formal legal training or college education. Frequently, these judges are appointed by a city or county political official, and their courtrooms may consist of a meeting room in city hall or the gymnasium of the local school. Only 31 states require initial or pre-bench education for these judges.[21] The salaries of the judges and the cost of running the court typically are paid out of fees collected by the court. Until the practice was declared unconstitutional, justices of the peace in Ohio were paid from costs assessed to convicted defendants.[22]

State courts of limited jurisdiction are used as background settings for television comedies such as *Night Court*. More serious criticisms include studies showing that these courts are overcrowded and provide rushed justice devoid of any quality.[23] Many problems and criticisms of the judiciary stem from state courts of limited jurisdiction.

JUST THE FACTS 9.4

What training and testing are required to become a practicing attorney? How are federal judges chosen? How are state judges chosen? What are some issues concerning the way the judiciary works?

conclusion:

The Judicial System as the Protector of Constitutional Rights

The dual court system of the United States forms a unified judicial system in which a case in the lowest state court ultimately could be reviewed by the U.S. Supreme Court. Likewise, a judicial decision by the U.S. Supreme Court is binding on all federal and state courts. The U.S. Constitution provided the initial authority for a judicial system at both the federal and state levels. Both federal and state courts have undergone extensive revisions since their founding, but the basic principle has remained that the judiciary is an independent, self-regulating, equal power with the legislative and executive branches of the government.

The judiciary not only acts as impartial arbitrator in many matters both civil and criminal, but also serves a very important role in providing checks and balances on the power of the legislative and executive branches. The federal courts, especially the Supreme Court, have assumed the role of defender of the Constitution, and state courts have adopted a similar identity and mission. As defender of the Constitution, the judicial system often is criticized as being more concerned with the rights of the criminals than the guilt or innocence of the defendant and the harm to the victim. In opinion polls over the last 30 years, 50 to 70 percent of college freshmen responding say that there is too much concern in the courts for the rights of criminals.[24] Despite these and other criticisms, such as the slowness of processing cases through the courts and the issues of choosing judges, the courts are still considered fundamental protectors of constitutional rights.

Chapter Summary

- The judiciary is the center of the criminal justice system and is the primary and ultimate arbiter of right and wrong.
- The federal judiciary is a branch of government with the power of checks and balances to prevent abuse by the executive and legislative branches of government.
- The U.S. dual court system consists of a four-tier federal court system and a state court system for each state. In the judicial system hierarchy, higher courts have power over lower courts, and the U.S. Supreme Court has power over the state courts.
- The courts are responsible for both civil and criminal judicial oversight. Most of the court's resources and time are taken up by civil cases.
- The federal court system is a four-tier, unified judicial system composed of magistrate courts, district courts, courts of appeals, and the Supreme Court. The federal courts are divided into 13 geographical circuits. Cases are initially tried in magistrate or district courts. Appeals courts review cases for judicial error. Cases cannot be appealed on the basis of a claim of innocence.
- The U.S. Supreme Court is the absolute court of last resort. Appeals to the U.S. Supreme Court do not resemble trials; for example, the Court does not utilize a jury to hear appeals.
- Each state has the power to organize its own judicial system. Most states have four-tier organizational structures like those of the federal judiciary.
- Lawyers and judges are respected personnel in the criminal justice system. A high salary and mandatory higher education contribute to this rating. The typical lawyer is required to complete 2 to 3 years of study beyond the bachelor's degree and must pass a bar exam.
- Federal judges are nominated by the president, approved by the Senate, and appointed for life tenures.
- State judges are selected by a number of different methods, including partisan election, nonpartisan election, a nominating commission, and appointment.

Vocabulary Review

appellate courts, 282
bar examination, 288
brief, 278
certiorari power, 278
circuit court, 276
civil law, 268
court of last resort, 282
courts of limited jurisdiction, 281
courts of record, 281
dual court system, 267
general trial courts, 282
judicial misconduct, 284
jurisprudence, 267
landmark cases, 277
original jurisdiction, 273
per curiam opinion, 279
plaintiff, 269
remanded, 279
torts, 268
U.S. courts of appeals, 275
U.S. district courts, 273
U.S. magistrate courts, 273
U.S. Supreme Court, 277
writ of certiorari, 278

Names and Events to Remember

American Bar Association (ABA), 288
Article 3, Section 2 of the U.S. Constitution, 268
Myra Bradwell, 284
Bradwell v. Illinois, 284
Center for Judicial Conduct Organizations, 284
Eleventh Amendment, 268
Federal Magistrate's Act of 1968, 273
Law School Aptitude Test (LSAT), 285
Marbury v. Madison (1803), 271
Tenth Amendment, 268

Think about This

1. Should all states have uniform laws and courts? Consider whether it is fair that an action that is legal in one state may be illegal in another state. Should individual states be able to set their own laws according to their culture and diverse populations?
2. Why are there different systems for choosing judges? What are the advantages and disadvantages of those systems? How do you think judges should be chosen, and why? Should standards and methods for choosing state and federal judges be uniform?
3. The U.S. Supreme Court hears few of the cases sent to it for review. Why? Should the Supreme Court be expanded, perhaps into divisions for civil and criminal cases, to handle more cases? Should there be a Supreme Court for each federal court district? What would be some pros and cons of expanding the U.S. Supreme Court?

ContentSelect

Go to the ContentSelect web site and type in the natural language search phrase "civil versus criminal"; also click on the box requesting search of "General Interest Publications." Read "Justice Delay: Stark Reality of Vacant Benches" by Warren Richey in the May 21, 2001, issue of the *Christian Science Monitor*. This article discusses how delays in choosing federal judges may be causing long delays for civil cases. Sample the article to answer the following questions.

1. Why are civil cases filed in federal courts being delayed?
2. According to the article, opposing political parties have kept judicial vacancies from being filled. What difference would the political party of the judge make in his or her role as a judge?
3. Consider the statement from the article that "justice delayed is justice denied." Do you agree? Explain your answer.
4. According to this text, federal judges are appointed to life terms. Given the delay in bringing on new judges, do lifetime appointments make sense? Would the political process involved in removing unfavorable judges create more vacancies?

Chapter 10

Courtroom Participants and the Trial

outline

Learning Objectives

After reading this chapter, you will know

- How to differentiate among the three types of criminal trials.
- How charges against the defendant are determined.
- The major proceedings before a criminal defendant goes to trial, including bail, competency testing, and plea bargaining.
- The laws regarding the right to a speedy trial and rules of evidence.
- The major pretrial motions.
- The roles of the people who participate in a criminal trial.
- The proceedings in the actual criminal trial.

Lawyers Force Removal of Crime Statue

ASSOCIATED PRESS, MINEOLA, NY. January 13, 1998—A sculpture of a drunken-driving crime scene has been removed from a courthouse lawn after lawyers said it could influence jurors.

The sculpture, titled "Stand Up and Speak Out," was created by artist Michael Alfano, 28, whose girlfriend was killed by a drunken driver as she crossed a New Jersey street in 1992.

Defense attorneys began grumbling about it almost immediately after it went up in September.

If the statue stirred sympathy among jurors, they said, it could prevent drunken-driving defendants from getting fair trials.

—From "Lawyers Force Removal of Crime Statue" reprinted with permission of The Associated Press.

introduction:

The Adjudication Process

Many factors can influence a trial other than protest art. A criminal trial is a complex event involving many participants who do their work behind the scenes. The public's perception of a criminal trial is strongly influenced by the media, as few people outside of the criminal justice system have the interest and patience to observe a criminal trial. Many people, however, have watched criminal trials on television and in movies. Some media presentations of trials are pretty much complete fiction. The guilty party rarely, if ever, bursts forth from the public seating and confesses to the crime in the middle of the trial. Most criminal trials last only a couple of days. Furthermore, often people fail to appreciate the difference between a civil trial and a criminal trial. Court TV and other public broadcasts of actual criminal trials, on the other hand, provide the public with an accurate view of a criminal trial. The challenge is to keep fact separated from fiction. This chapter provides a description of the criminal trial process, the people involved in this process, and the decisions that have to be made in bringing a defendant to trial.

Jurisdiction

THE MAIN IDEA

Criminal trials take place in three types of courts, chosen on the basis of the jurisdiction and severity of the crime.

There are three types of criminal trials: criminal trials in courts of limited jurisdiction, criminal trials in state courts, and criminal trials in federal courts. Criminal trials in state and federal courts tend to be complex and involve many more people than criminal trials in courts of limited jurisdiction. As you read in Chapter 9, courts of limited jurisdiction include justice of the peace courts, municipal courts, and county courts. The criminal jurisdiction or authority of these courts is limited to the misdemeanor laws of the municipality and county.

Trials in Courts of Limited Jurisdiction

These cases usually concern crimes such as simple assault, disorderly conduct, trespass, and larceny. In a typical case, the defendant is arrested by a local police officer and appears before the court for a trial within a few weeks. Usually, the defendant is not guaranteed the right to an attorney, because the punishment does not exceed the threshold at which the government must provide defendants with an attorney if they cannot afford legal counsel. It is not uncommon in a court of limited jurisdiction for the judge and the prosecutor to be part-time employees of the municipality. Most trials consist of the police officer telling the judge what law the defendant is alleged to have violated and the evidence supporting his or her assertion, followed by the defendant's rebuttal. For the most part, these trials are fairly simple affairs. Few witnesses are called to testify, and only a minimum of evidence is introduced.

As mentioned in Chapter 9, courts of limited jurisdiction are not courts of record, and no transcript is made of the proceedings. Scheduling of trials is simple in that many defendants are given the same trial date and time. The court starts the day with the first case and proceeds through the others as time permits. These are not jury trials, and the judge renders an immediate decision following the conclusion of the arguments. The defendant has the right to appeal the decision to a court of general trial jurisdiction.

Each local or municipal court has its own distinctive procedures, depending on factors such as the legal training of the judge, the judicial resources of the municipality or county, and the number of cases that the court hears. In rural areas, the justice of the peace court may be held only once a week, whereas in large urban cities, the municipal court may hear cases daily. Because of the diverse and variable nature of trials in courts of limited jurisdiction, the focus of this chapter is on trials in state courts of general jurisdiction and federal district courts.

Go to http://www.uscourts.gov/districtcourts.html, the official web site of the federal judiciary, for information about district courts, including many links. ■

Trials in Courts of General Jurisdiction and Federal District Courts

Most felony criminal trials occur in state courts of general jurisdiction or United States district courts. Because there are more felony crimes committed in violation of state laws than federal laws, the number of state felony criminal trials is much higher than the number of federal felony trials. Trial procedures for state and federal courts of general jurisdiction are similar. This chapter discusses the general procedures that apply to both state and federal courts and highlights when there is a difference between the two.

One of the first decisions that must be made when a person is arrested for a felony crime is which court has jurisdiction. The general guidelines for determining jurisdiction have to do with which laws were violated and the geographical location of the crime. If the crime was a violation of both federal and state law, the defendant may be tried in either or both courts. Violation of federal and state laws are considered different offenses and do not constitute trying the person twice for the same offense, which is prohibited by the Fifth Amendment of the Constitution. Thus, if the crime is in violation of both federal and state laws, it is not considered **double jeopardy** to try the defendant in both federal court and state court. As a practical matter, however, most defendants are not tried in both federal and state court. Usually, the federal or state prosecutor with the strongest case takes the lead in bringing the case to trial. Bank robbery, both a federal crime and a state felony, is one crime in which this question frequently arises. Federal and state prosecutors could both choose to try the defendant for bank robbery, but usually only one prosecutor files charges. Often, the arresting agency is a factor in determining who files charges. If the bank robber is arrested by the Federal Bureau of Investigation, federal charges are filed, and if the defendant is arrested by the state or local police, state charges are filed.

Federal courts claim jurisdiction for crimes committed in the United States; its territories; maritime jurisdictional limits; federal, Native American, and military reservations; and U.S. registered ships at sea. For a state court to have jurisdiction of a case, all or part of the crime must have been committed within the state. If part of the crime is committed in a state, the state may claim jurisdiction over other parts of the crime, even crimes committed in another state. It is not considered double jeopardy to try a defendant in two or more states for what would appear to a layperson to be the same crime. States are sovereign political entities; thus, violation of the laws of several states is not considered the "same crime," and each state retains jurisdiction.

double jeopardy The defendant can be charged only once and punished only once for a crime. If tried and found innocent, the defendant cannot be retried if new evidence of his or her guilt is discovered.

For example, if a person is abducted in one state and transported across the state line, where he or she is murdered, both states can claim jurisdiction over the crime. Both states could try the defendant for kidnapping and murder, even though the kidnapping happened in one state and the murder happened in another. If two (or more) states claim jurisdiction over a crime, the state officials must negotiate to determine who will first prosecute the defendant. The states also will have to negotiate whether the defendant will be tried in both states if he or she is convicted by the first state. If the defendant is convicted and is to be tried in the second state, the states must negotiate whether the trial will occur before or after the convicted defendant has served his or her sentence for the crime. If the crime is first-degree murder and one state has the death penalty but the other state does not, the decision concerning in which state to try the defendant becomes even more important.

JUST THE FACTS 10.1

What cases are brought before the courts of limited jurisdiction? What types of courts hear felony trials? What role does the arresting agency have in determining where a felony case will come to trial? How is jurisdiction determined?

Charges and Proceedings before Trial

THE MAIN IDEA

The police and prosecutor work together to determine the charges to be brought against the defendant. After the arrest but before the trial, decisions also must be made about setting bail, determining the defendant's competency to stand trial, and plea bargaining.

The Constitution requires that citizens must be informed of the charges against them before being tried in a court of law. The first step toward bringing a person to trial is the arrest and booking of the person, which formally charges them with having committed a crime. The process of bringing a person to trial involves the joint activity of the police and the prosecutor. One of the first questions to answer is whether the defendant will be arraigned before a state court or in the U.S. magistrate court. The defendant must be arraigned before the court, federal or state, that will exercise jurisdiction over the case. Usually, federal agents take the accused to a U.S. magistrate court for arraignment, whereas local and state law enforcement officers take the accused before the appropriate state court. Because both courts may have jurisdiction in the case, a defendant who is first arraigned before one court may later be arraigned before another.

Determining the Charges: The Police and the Prosecutor

When the accused is first arrested, the law enforcement officer files a report charging the person with a crime. After the person is booked, a magistrate reviews the charges filed against the accused and determines that the police have filed constitutional charges against the person and have provided the person with his or her constitutionally protected rights. The police and the prosecutor then work together to bring the case to trial and secure a conviction, without violating due process.

As you read in Chapter 4, historically the British Crown abused its authority both in England and in the colonies. One common abuse of authority was to charge a person with a crime where no evidence existed to support the charge. After separation from England and to prevent this abuse by the new government, the framers of the Constitution of the United States included the provision that due process must be used in bringing a person to trial for a criminal offense. You will recall that due process has been interpreted to mean that the government needs to present evidence to an impartial judicial body that a crime has been committed and that there is reasonable belief that the person accused committed the crime. The prosecutor, not the arresting officer, is responsible for presenting this evidence.

After reviewing the police reports and in some cases talking to the arresting officers, the prosecuting attorney must decide if he or she wants to proceed with the case or drop it. The fact that the police have arrested and booked a suspect is no guarantee that the prosecutor will see the same merit in the case that the police did. The prosecutor may decide that the police do not have sufficient evidence to prove the charges beyond a reasonable doubt and may refuse to move the case forward. Table 10.1 gives you an idea of the number of federal offenses declined for prosecution in the period between 1999 and 2000.

It is also very common for the prosecutor to modify the charges alleged by the police before moving the case forward. The prosecutor has the option of dropping charges,

table 10.1 **Disposition of Suspects in Matters Concluded by U.S. Attorneys, by Offense, October 1, 1999–September 30, 2000**

	Suspects in Criminal Matters Concluded						
	Total Number of Suspects	Prosecuted before U.S. District Court Judge[b]		Concluded by U.S. Magistrate[c]		Declined Prosecution[d]	
Most Serious Offense Investigated[a]		Number	Percent	Number	Percent	Number	Percent
All Offenses[e]	117,450	73,090	62.2%	13,916	11.8%	30,444	25.9%
Violent Offenses[f]	5,641	3,403	60.3	329	5.8	1,909	33.8
Property Offenses	27,713	14,675	53.0	1,978	7.1	11,060	39.9
Fraudulent[f]	24,186	12,988	53.7	1,368	5.7	9,830	40.6
Other[f]	3,527	1,687	47.8	610	17.3	1,230	34.9
Drug Offenses	37,009	28,917	78.1	1,966	5.3	6,126	16.6
Public Order Offenses	46,238	25,841	55.9	9,275	20.1	11,122	24.1
Regulatory	5,840	1,862	31.9	637	10.9	3,341	57.2
Other	40,398	23,979	59.4	8,638	21.4	7,781	19.3
Weapons	7,753	5,026	64.8	161	2.1	2,566	33.1
Immigration	16,110	13,414	83.3	2,199	13.6	497	3.1
Tax law violation[f]	941	627	66.6	12	1.3	302	32.1
Other	15,594	4,912	31.5	6,266	40.2	4,416	28.3
Unknown or Indeterminable Offenses	849	254	29.9	368	43.3	227	26.7

Source: Bureau of Justice Statistics, *Federal Criminal Cases Processing, 2000* (Washington, DC: Department of Justice, February 2001), p. 9.

[a]Based on the decision of the assistant U.S. attorney responsible for the matter.

[b]Includes suspects whose cases were filed in U.S. district court before a district court judge.

[c]Includes defendants in misdemeanor cases that were terminated in U.S. district court before a U.S. magistrate.

[d]Includes suspects whose matters were declined for prosecution by U.S. attorneys upon review.

[e]Includes suspects whose offense category could not be determined.

[f]In this table, "Violent offenses" may include nonnegligent manslaughter; "Fraudulent property" excludes tax fraud; "Other nonfraudulent property" excludes fraudulent property and includes destruction of property and trespassing; and "Tax law violation" includes tax fraud.

adding additional charges, or reducing the charges. The police may have arrested the person for first-degree murder, but the prosecutor may believe that the evidence only warrants charges of second-degree murder. This power of prosecuting attorneys is called **prosecutorial discretion.** The prosecutor also exercises power in the preliminary hearing, information, indictment, and arraignment, described in Chapter 2.

Law enforcement and the prosecution are each autonomous criminal justice agencies, but without cooperation between them it is difficult to achieve a successful prosecution. When the police arrest a suspect, the prosecutor has a very short time to decide if the charges are appropriate and if the evidence, even though incomplete at this stage, is sufficient to bring the case to trial. The relationship between the prosecutor and the arresting officer(s) is an important factor in this decision. Serious felony crime is most likely to be handled by veteran detectives who have an ongoing relationship with the prosecutor. The prosecutor depends on the professionalism and competence of these detectives in making the decision to take the case.

In some major cases, the police and the prosecutor work together prior to the arrest of the suspect. In important cases, taking months or years to investigate and compile the necessary evidence, the prosecutor may be an active partner with the police. Some prosecutors even have their own investigative staff that can gather additional evidence to help support the charges. In major felony cases in which the prosecutor and law enforcement officers work together, the prosecutor may want to use the grand jury to obtain an arrest warrant rather than have the police arrest the suspect on probable cause (see Chapter 2).

Checks and balances against police and prosecutorial power are provided by the initial screening of the first appearance and preliminary hearing. In addition, the prosecutor must present evidence to the court at the arraignment that the defendant should be tried for the offense. At the arraignment hearing, the prosecutor has the dilemma of how much evidence he or she should present to convince the court. The arraignment is the final stage before the trial, and the charges filed at this time are the charges on which the defendant will be tried. The prosecutor needs to present enough evidence to convince the court that the defendant should be held over for trial. However, the more evidence that the prosecutor presents, the more information the defense has to prepare for the trial. Thus, the prosecutor wants to present enough evidence to secure a trial date but not so much that the defense will be able to determine the entire prosecution strategy. Three other important decisions that are made before the trial are (1) setting bail, (2) determining the competency of the defendant to stand trial, and (3) plea bargaining.

prosecutorial discretion The power of prosecutors to decide whether or not to charge the defendant and what the charge will be and to gather the evidence necessary to prosecute the defendant in a court of law.

bail In the American criminal justice system, bail is a system of pretrial release of the accused in a criminal proceeding based on a guarantee by the accused—not a custodian—that the defendant will appear in court as required.

Bail

One of the hallmarks of the American criminal justice system is the assumption that the criminal justice system will treat defendants as if they are innocent until they are proven guilty. Essential to the fulfillment of that principle is the premise that the defendant will not be incarcerated prior to conviction unless absolutely necessary for public safety. As defined in Chapter 2, the mechanism to provide for the pretrial release of the defendant is **bail.**

Bail has its roots in English history and has been used since before the Norman Conquest in 1066. In an era before prisons were used to detain people prior to trial, the English magistrate would place prisoners with private parties who would guarantee that they would be delivered to the court when it was time for trial. To ensure that these custodians would perform their duties properly, they were required to sign a bond, known as a private surety, promising that if they failed to produce the prisoners on the trial date, they would forfeit a specified sum of money or property. The new American government adopted a variation of this pretrial procedure. Rather than entrust the accused to a custodian, the **Eighth Amendment of the Constitution** recognized the concept of bail and also specified that excessive bail should not be required of the accused. In the American criminal justice system, bail is a system of pretrial release of the accused in a criminal proceeding based on a guarantee by the accused—not a custodian—that the accused will appear in court as required. The most common method of guaranteeing the appearance of the defendant is to require a cash bond or some property of value.[1]

The Eighth Amendment does not specifically state that a defendant is guaranteed bail. It only states that excessive bail should not be required. The U.S. Supreme Court has interpreted the wording of the Eighth Amendment to mean that the defendant does indeed have a right to bail.[2] Initially, the Constitutional guarantee of bail was not a state requirement but applied only to the federal courts.[3] However, the question of whether or not a state defendant has a guarantee of bail has never been a significant constitutional issue, as state constitutions and judiciary practices have provided defendants with this right. Both the federal and state courts have recognized that the right to bail is not an unrestricted right. The controversy over bail has centered around (1) what is excessive bail, (2) when can bail be denied, and (3) does the bail system discriminate against the poor?

In posting bail this defendant is legally bound to return to the court for trial. How did the bail system originate, and what is the reason for it? What standards and criteria did the judge use to determine whether or not to allow release on bail in this case? How was the amount of bail determined? In what circumstances might the defendant have used a bail bondsperson? What are some alternatives to the cash bond system? What can happen if the defendant does not show up for the trial?

EXCESSIVE BAIL The Supreme Court has declared that excessive bail must be based on standards relevant to guaranteeing that the defendant will not take advantage of his or her freedom and flee prior to the trial.[4] Thus, there are no standard limits of excessive bail that apply to all cases. The court has the power to consider each case individually, based on the totality of the circumstances. The court can consider factors such as the seriousness of the crime, the defendant's prior criminal record, the strength of the state's case, and the defendant's financial status. In some cases, the court has set bail at millions of dollars and this has not been considered excessive. Table 10.2 gives you an idea of the variability in setting bail.

table 10.2 **Bail Amounts for Felony Defendants in the 75 Largest Counties, by Percentage**

Excessive bail is prohibited. Bail must be relative to the charges against the defendant. Bail for most defendants charged with public order offenses is less than $5,000, whereas bail for most defendants charged with murder is in excess of $25,000.

Most Serious Arrest Charge	Number of Defendants	<$5,000	$5,000–$9,999	$10,000–$24,999	>$25,000
Violent offenses	7,090	22%	17%	20%	40%
Property offenses	10,380	42	20	21	17
Drug offenses	13,784	34	22	24	20
Public order offenses	3,298	43	18	19	20
All offenses	30, 479	34	20	22	25

Source: Bureau of Justice Statistics, *Felony Defendants in Large Urban Counties, 1998* (Washington, DC: Department of Justice, November 2001), p. 18.

DENIAL OF BAIL Bail is not an absolute guarantee, and defendants, under some circumstances, can be denied bail (*U.S. v. Salerno*).[5] Initially, the Supreme Court narrowly defined the purpose of bail as ensuring that the defendant would appear for trial. Both the federal judiciary and state judiciaries recognized cases in which the defendant's pretrial release could pose a potential danger to society and bail should be denied. Starting in the 1970s, state judiciaries started enacting danger laws that allowed the court to deny bail for certain offenses in which public safety could be a concern. The most common use of this denial of bail was for allegations of murder and drug offenses. The 1984 federal Bail Reform Act provided the same authority to federal judges.[6] The **1984 Bail Reform Act** allowed the court to make the assumption that the defendant may pose a danger to others or to the community. Once the court makes this determination, it is the burden of the defendant to demonstrate that he or she is not a flight risk and is not a danger to persons or the community.[7] California law prohibits the court from releasing a defendant on bail who is charged with multiple murder on the presumption that the defendant would be a danger to the community. The O. J. Simpson trial for murder was an example of bail being denied based on the presumption that the defendant could be a danger to the community. Despite arguments of the defense that Simpson was not a flight risk and was able to post a high bail, the state of California denied bail. Figure 10.1 shows the percentages of felony defendants detained on bail and denied bail in a recent year.

For most misdemeanor offenses, bail is set based on a set fee schedule; that is, for most common offenses, a predetermined bail is set by the judge in advance, committed

Figure 10.1

Pretrial Detention of Felony Defendants (Percentage Denied Bail)

Bail is not an absolute right of a defendant. While most defendants charged with minor crimes are released on bail, nearly half of murder defendants are denied bail.

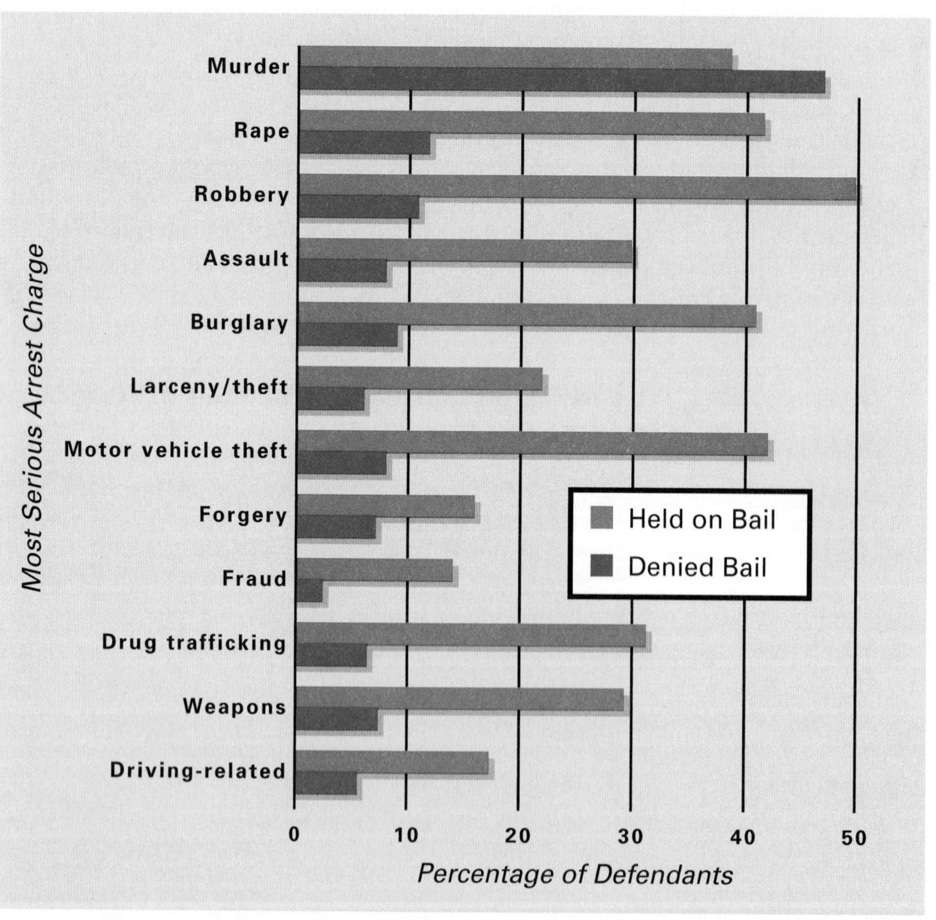

Source: Bureau of Justice Statistics, *Felony Defendants in Large Urban Counties, 1998* (Washington, DC: Department of Justice, November 2001), p. 16.

to written record, and used by booking to know what bail to set without a judge's instructions. Bail is an integral part of the initial appearance. For more serious felony cases, there is a bail hearing in which the prosecutor and the defense argue before the judge the merits of pretrial release. In the federal judiciary, bail hearings are held before magistrate judges. In most state courts, bail hearings are handled by courts of limited jurisdiction. Bail hearings are not heard and decided by a jury, and following short oral arguments, the judge has wide discretionary powers as to granting bail and setting the amount.

DISCRIMINATION AGAINST THE POOR If bail requires the posting of a cash bond, it seems obvious that low-income defendants are not going to have access to the right of bail because of their lack of available money. Without the ability to post a cash bond, the poor are condemned to remain incarcerated until their trials. Given the fact that even simple felony cases may take months before they come to trial, the possibility arises that the poor may spend more time in jail awaiting their trials than the length of sentences they may receive at the end of their trials. (When this does happen, defendants are credited with time already served and are released.) Accused persons who are not incarcerated have greater opportunities to assist in their defense. Thus, if bail discriminates against the poor, the poor may not receive the same quality of justice as the rich. Recognizing that a cash bail system may discriminate against the poor, the judiciary has established alternatives.

THE BAIL BONDSPERSON In actuality, many people cannot afford the bail that may be required for pretrial release. In felony criminal cases, it is not uncommon for bail to set at tens of thousands of dollars. The court does allow the bail to be secured by lien on property, and family and friends can help contribute to the bail. Most people, however, simply do not have access to the amount of money required for bail. As a result of this situation, the judiciary provides for a bail bond business. The **bail bondsperson** is an agent of a private commercial business that has contracted with the court to act as a guarantor of the defendant's return to court. The bail bondsperson is not a state or federal employee but is a private party operating a for-profit business.

The bail bondsperson acts as an intermediary and posts the bond for the accused. If the defendant shows up for all scheduled court appearances, the court returns the amount of bail posted by the defendant and the defendant pays the bail bond company a nonrefundable fee for its service. This fee is usually 10 percent of the bond but may be higher, as there is no set limit on the bail bond company's fee. At a 10-percent fee, a person whose bail is set at $1,000 would have to pay the bail bond company $100 for its services. A person whose bond is set at $50,000, a more realistic figure for a serious felony crime, would have to pay $5,000. Bail bond companies can refuse to underwrite the bail of a defendant if they do not believe the defendant is a good risk.

BOND JUMPERS AND BOUNTY HUNTERS A person who fails to show for a court appearance is said to have "jumped bond." When a person jumps bond, the court will allow the bail bondsperson (bondsagent) a certain amount of time to return the defendant to the custody of the court before revoking the posted bond. The bail bond businesses are not criminal justice agencies, but when they post bail for a defendant they are considered to be agents of the court. This power allows the bail bondsagent to require the defendant to sign a legally binding contract, waiving the right of extradition. This means the agent can track down and bring back the bond jumper.

As an agent of the court, the bail bondsagent, who is not a law enforcement officer, does not have to observe the restrictions placed on the police in seeking the return of the person who fails to show for his or her court appearance. Essentially, the bondsagent may use any means necessary to return the person to the jurisdiction of the court. The bondsagent is authorized to carry firearms, can use the threat of force to compel the defendant to return, and can kidnap the defendant and forcibly return him or her to

bail bondsperson An agent of a private commercial business that has contracted with the court to act as a guarantor of a defendant's return to court.

Go to http://www.bailacademy.org/index1.html, the site of the Pacific Northwest Bail Enforcement Academy, for a description of the training and duties of bail enforcers, also called "fugitive recovery." ■

the court against his or her will. The bondsagent does not have to have an arrest warrant to enter a private residence where the defendant has sought refuge, and can trespass anywhere the defendant is hiding. The bondsagent is allowed to pay a third party to search for and return a bond jumper. There are no minimum requirements or mandated training for people who track down and return defendants. Commonly called "bounty hunters," bondsagents have greater powers than police officers in the pursuit of bond jumpers.

ALTERNATIVES TO CASH BOND Despite the widespread use of the bail bonds system, there are criticisms of it and of the conduct of bail bondsagents in returning bond jumpers. One of the primary criticisms is that even with fees at 10 percent of the total bond, the bail bonds system still discriminates against the poor, and a disproportionate number of the poor who are accused of crimes and have bail set are persons of color. Charges of institutionalized racial discrimination have led both federal and state courts to implement a number of alternatives to the cash bond system.

release on recognizance (ROR) Provides for the pretrial release of the accused, based merely on the defendant's unsecured promise of return for trial.

unsecured bond Release based on the defendant's promise to pay the court an amount similar to a cash bail bond if the defendant fails to fulfill a promise to return for trial.

signature bond Release based on the defendant's signature on a promise to return for trial.

One of the early experiments in alternatives to the cash bond system was the **Manhattan Bail Project.**[8] In the 1960s, the Manhattan Bail Project tested the use of **release on recognizance (ROR).** ROR provides for the pretrial release of the accused based merely on the defendant's unsecured promise that he or she will return for trial. The success of the project has caused many states to adopt the use of ROR. ROR is most appropriate for nonviolent offenses when the defendant has ties to the community and is not a flight risk.

Unsecured bond and signature bond are pretrial release systems that allow the defendant to be released on his or her promise to return for trial. An **unsecured bond** releases the defendant, who signs a promissory note to pay to the court a predetermined amount similar to that set by a cash bail bond if he or she does not fulfill this promise. The percentages of pretrial releases of felony defendants on ROR on different types of bonds are shown in Figure 10.2.

A **signature bond** is commonly used for minor offenses, such as traffic law violations. It is similar to ROR but much simpler. There are no prequalifications for a signature bond, and no one makes an assessment of the defendants' flight risk or danger to the community. A signature bond allows the police officers, acting as agents of the court, to release the accused immediately after they are charged with the offense if they sign a promise to appear in court. When a police officer asks a motorist to sign a traffic citation, the motorist's signature is not a confession of guilt but a promise to appear in

Figure 10.2

Pretrial Release of Felony Defendants

The most common form of bail is for the defendant to post a cash bond or to use the services of a bail bondsperson to post a cash bond.

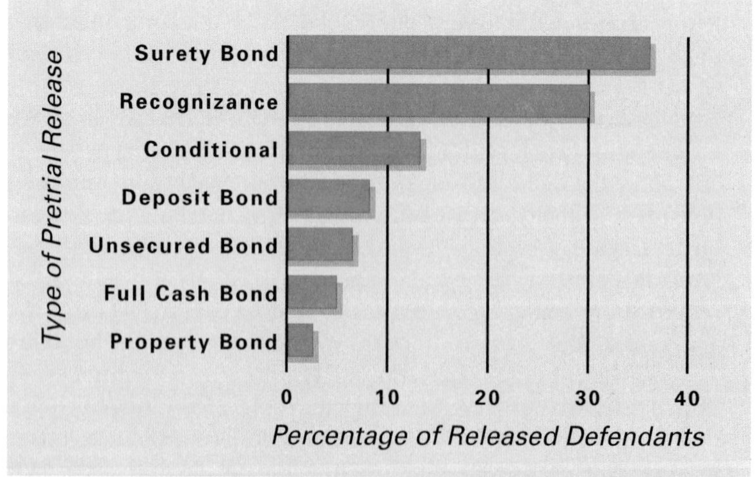

Source: Bureau of Justice Statistics, *Felony Defendants in Large Urban Counties, 1998* (Washington, DC: Department of Justice, November 2001), p. 17.

table 10.3 Time from Arrest to Release for Felony Defendants, 1998

Most defendants are quickly released after being arraigned. About half of all defendants are released within 1 day, and over 90% are released within 30 days.

	Released Felony Defendants in the 75 Largest Counties			
		Percentage Who Were Released Within:		
Most Serious Arrest Charge	Number of Defendants	1 Day	1 Week	1 Month
Violent offenses	6,949	49	75	91
Property offenses	10,183	58	81	94
Drug offenses	13,449	53	82	94
Public order offenses	3,298	56	82	95
All offenses	33,878	54	80	94

Source: Bureau of Justice Statistics, *Felony Defendants in Large Urban Counties, 1998* (Washington, DC: Department of Justice, November 2001), p. 19.

court. If the motorist does not sign the citation, he or she forfeits the right to a signature bond and the police officer has the authority to take the motorist into custody. After booking, the motorist will be required to post bond.

Conditional release and third-party custody are interesting alternatives to cash bail. Conditional release and a closely related type of bail, called supervision release, require the defendant to agree to a number of court-ordered terms and restrictions. Common terms of conditional release include participation in drug or alcohol treatment programs, attendance of anger-management classes, compliance with a restraining order, and regular employment. Supervision release adds the additional stipulation that the defendant, similar to someone on parole or probation, must report to an officer of the court at regular intervals. Table 10.3 gives data on the time from arrest to release on trial or bail alternative.

conditional release A bail alternative in which the defendant is released from custody if he or she agrees to a number of court-ordered terms and restrictions.

Third-party custody allows the court to release a pretrial defendant to the custody of an individual or agency that promises to be responsible for their behavior and to guarantee their participation in the legal process. The two most common conditions are placing a defendant with his or her family or with attorneys who assume responsibility for their clients. Youthful offenders are the most likely candidates to be placed with their families. An adult member of the family assumes responsibility for a defendant's day-to-day behavior and appearances for scheduled court appointments. Table 10.4 on page 308 gives data on percentages of felony defendants who fail to return to court.

PROS AND CONS OF BAIL The advantage of alternatives is that the defendant does not have to pay the necessary money to post the bond, and there is no bail bond fee to pay to a third party. Also, it is to the court's advantage to release as many pretrial defendants as possible. Pretrial defendants who are denied bail are a special category of incarcerated persons. By law, they are not guilty of any crime and cannot be confined as punishment nor placed in a state penitentiary. Most pretrial defendants are incarcerated in county jails, which is costly to the state. Jails are overcrowded, and pretrial defendants take up valuable space that could be better used to house convicted offenders and to relieve overcrowding.

table 10.4 Percentage of Released Felony Defendants in the 75 Largest Counties Who Failed to Appear in Court

One of the criticisms and concerns about the bail system is that some defendants take advantage of their release and flee. Between 11 and 22 percent of defendants fail to return for court appearances, and between 3 and 7 percent of defendants flee and never return, unless rearrested.

Most Serious Arrest Charge	Number of Defendants	Failed to Return to Court	Remained a Fugitive
Violent offenses	7,090	11	3
Property offenses	10,380	18	5
Drug offenses	13,784	22	7
Public order offenses	3,298	14	4
All offenses	34,695	18	5

Source: Bureau of Justice Statistics, *Felony Defendants in Large Urban Counties, 1998* (Washington, DC: Department of Justice, November 2001), p. 21.

Prosecutors and police often are critical of economic arguments encouraging bail and the pretrial release of defendants in general. Their view is that the defendant will continue to engage in criminal activity. Police argue that some defendants use pretrial release as an opportunity to commit further crimes to pay for their legal fees. Figure 10.3 gives an idea of the rate of misconduct by felony defendants out on bail. It is not uncommon for prosecutors to ask for high bails in an effort to keep pretrial defendants incarcerated.

Competency to Stand Trial and the Insanity Defense

Prior to the trial, it is the responsibility of the court to determine that the defendant is competent to stand trial. **Competent to stand trial** means that defendants comprehend the charges against them and are able to assist their attorneys in their defense. Competency to stand trial usually is determined by the ruling of a federal magistrate court judge or similar-level state judge. Health is one of the most common reasons a pretrial defendant may not be competent to stand trial. A defendant who has a serious disease and is undergoing treatment can experience serious side effects that affect his or her judgment. A defendant who is wounded by the police may not be competent to stand trial because of the need for medical treatment. A defendant with a medical condition affecting intellectual capacity may be considered incapable of understanding the charges against him or her. Declaring a pretrial defendant not competent to stand trial is a temporary ruling. When the defendant becomes competent to stand trial, the court will order that the trial proceedings resume or begin.

competent to stand trial
The concept that defendants comprehend the charges against them and are able to assist their attorney in their defense.

The claim that a defendant is not guilty by reason of insanity, as discussed in Chapter 4, is an affirmative defense that must be made prior to the trial. After the insanity defense is declared, the court orders a series of psychiatric examinations to assess the defendant's mental state. The results of examinations are admissible as evidence during the defendant's trial. A finding of not guilty by reason of insanity is not determined by the medical professionals who examine the defendant, however, but by the jury.

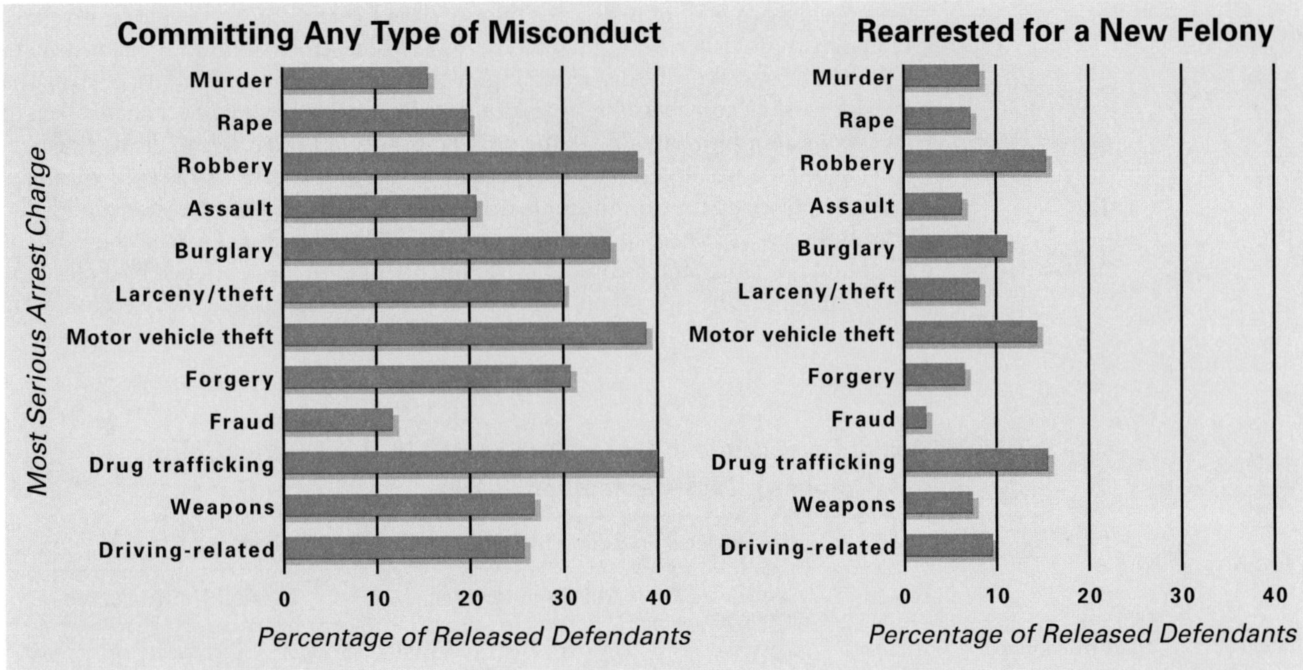

Source: Bureau of Justice Statistics, *Felony Defendants in Large Urban Counties, 1998* (Washington, DC: Department of Justice, November 2001), p. 22.

Figure 10.3

Misconduct Prior to Case Disposition by Released Felony Defendants

More serious than the failure to return for a court appearance is a defendant released on bail who commits another crime while on bail. As many as 40 percent of defendants released on bail commit new crimes while on bail.

Plea Bargaining

Another pretrial activity is plea bargaining, defined in Chapter 2, and a great majority of cases are disposed by this method without ever going to trial. Both the police and the victim often object to the practice of plea bargaining, but the prosecutor must make the best use of the resources of his or her office. The police and the victim object to plea bargaining on the grounds that the offender typically is not punished to the fullest extent of the law. After working to gather the necessary evidence and witnesses to help convict the defendant, law enforcement officers would like to see the defendant prosecuted on the most serious charges. Victims often want the same thing but for revenge or retribution or satisfaction that justice has been provided. Yet the prosecutors decide to offer defendants the opportunity to plead guilty to lesser charges. Why?

One reason is that preparation for trial is a time-consuming and costly endeavor. The prosecutor's office has the actual responsibility for trial preparation and bears the majority of the costs associated with gathering evidence, interviewing witnesses, and other preparations. Most prosecutors have only a limited staff and budget and cannot possibly take every case to trial. Furthermore, the court has only so much time to hear cases. Thus, the prosecutor's office must select which cases to take to trial and which to offer a plea bargain. With few exceptions, plea bargaining is an integral part of the path in a criminal trial because it keeps the costs of justice affordable.

In deciding to offer or to accept a plea to a lesser charge, the prosecutor must make an important professional judgment as to how to best serve community interests with the limited resources of the department. A plea bargain guarantees a guilty verdict. The prosecutor wins a conviction in approximately 80 percent of the cases that are taken to trial, but without plea bargaining, the prosecutor would not be able to devote the personnel and resources necessary to prepare for trial in these cases. In a sense, plea bargaining helps free up time for the more difficult cases. Also, without plea bargaining, the prosecutor risks a substantial investment in time and resources, only to have the defendant found not guilty and escape all punishment. A guilty plea obtained by a plea bargain assures that the defendant will have a criminal record and will receive some punishment or treatment.

table 10.5 Disposition of Defendants in Cases Terminated in U.S. District Courts, by Offense, October 1, 1999–September 30, 2000

	Defendants in Cases Terminating in U.S. District Courts							
			Number Convicted			Number Not Convicted		
Most Serious Offense Charged[a]	Number of Defendants	Percentage Convicted	Total	Plea[b]	Trial[c]	Total	Dismissed[d]	Acquitted[c]
All Offenses[e]	76,952	88.6%	68,156	64,939	3,217	8,796	7,669	1,127
Felonies	65,656	91.5	60,059	57,404	2,655	5,597	5,008	589
Violent offenses[f]	2,964	90.3	2,676	2,480	196	288	238	50
Property offenses	14,080	91.0	12,814	12,248	566	1,266	1,152	114
Fraudulent[f]	11,590	91.0	10,550	10,102	448	1,040	943	97
Other[f]	2,490	90.9	2,264	2,146	118	226	209	17
Drug offenses	27,274	91.2	24,886	23,744	1,142	2,388	2,152	236
Trafficking	25,579	91.3	23,348	22,301	1,047	2,231	2,024	207
Possession and other	1,695	90.7	1,538	1,443	95	157	128	29
Public order offenses	21,338	92.2	19,683	18,932	751	1,655	1,466	189
Regulatory	1,229	86.6	1,064	1,014	50	165	141	24
Other	20,109	92.6	18,619	17,918	701	1,490	1,325	165
Weapons	5,049	88.4	4,461	4,089	372	588	493	95
Immigration	11,599	95.9	11,127	11,024	103	472	449	23
Tax law violation[f]	626	95.8	600	550	50	26	25	1
Other	2,835	85.7	2,431	2,255	176	404	358	46
Misdemeanors[f]	11,214	71.6	8,025	7,470	555	3,189	2,651	538
Unknown or Indeterminable Offenses	82	87.8	72	65	7	10	10	0

Source: Federal Criminal Case Processing, 2000 with Trends 1982–2000 (Washington, DC: BJS Federal Justice Statistics 2001), p. 11.

[a]Based on the offense carrying the most severe statutory maximum penalty.

[b]Includes *nolo contendere.*

[c]Includes bench and jury trials.

[d]Includes defendants in cases dismissed for lack of evidence or lack of federal interest.

[e]Includes defendants for whom an offense category could not be determined.

[f]In this table, "Violent offenses" may include nonnegligent manslaughter; "Fraudulent property" excludes tax fraud; "Other nonfraudulent property" excludes fraudulent property and includes destruction of property and trespassing; "Tax law violation" includes tax fraud; and "Misdemeanors" include misdemeanors, petty offenses, and unknown offense levels.

The irony is that the career criminals seem to benefit more from this practice than minor criminals or the innocent. Obviously, the innocent can only be harmed by the practice of plea bargaining. A defendant accused of a serious crime such as capital murder but who is not guilty may be tempted to accept or offer a plea bargain for a lesser crime that does not carry the threat of the death penalty for fear of being wrongfully convicted and executed. Plea bargaining most benefits major criminals such as the burglar who has committed 300 burglaries, the serial rapist who has committed numerous sexual assaults, or the drug dealer who has constantly engaged in the trafficking of drugs.

The prosecutor may not have sufficient evidence to convict a career burglar for all of the burglaries that he or she has committed. The prosecutor may not even know of all of the crimes the defendant has committed. If the prosecutor agrees to charge the defendant with only a single burglary in turn for a confession to 300 burglaries, what does the prosecutor gain? First, the prosecutor and the police get to "clear" the 299 burglaries, even though the defendant is not prosecuted for them. By accepting this offer, the police and the prosecutor can report a higher clearance rate to the public. Second, the prosecutor knows that even if a defendant is convicted of multiple offenses, he or she may end up serving the prison sentences concurrently instead of consecutively. Thus, the extra time and effort required to obtain the multiple convictions may make little difference in the actual outcome.

Finally, the prosecutor may not be completely confident of the evidence or witnesses. The prosecutor may believe that at the last moment a victim may refuse to testify. Witnesses to crimes committed by gang members or organized crime figure may become concerned about their safety or the safety of their families, for instance, and may refuse to testify or may give weak and inconclusive evidence. A young witness, especially a child, may pose special difficulties for the prosecutor. Or the prosecutor may believe that the reputation of the arresting police officer or reliability of evidence gathered by the police may not stand up to cross-examination. Any of these reasons may make the prosecutor reluctant to take the case to trial.

On advice of defense counsel and at the urging of the prosecutor, this defendant, seated, changed her plea to guilty on a lesser charge of serious bodily injury to a child. Authorities found the defendant's abused 8-year-old daughter living in a closet in the family trailer. As a result of the plea bargain, the case will be disposed without going to trial. What are the advantages and disadvantages of plea bargaining for the defendant? For the prosecutor? For the court? For the criminal justice system?

Plea bargaining can be initiated by the prosecuting or the defending attorney. Plea bargaining can center around the charges or the sentence. As explained in Chapter 2, at arrest the police and prosecutor typically charge the defendant with as many crimes as possible, beginning with the most serious crime. In return for dropping the more serious charges, the defendant offers his or her guilty plea. Plea bargaining can involve the police, the prosecutor, the judge, and defense counsel but seldom involves the victim. In some cases, the victim is not even informed of the decision to accept a plea bargain. The defendant may provide the police with information regarding other criminals or crimes in return for their help in convincing the prosecutor to accept the defendant's plea bargain. The defendant may not have been the principal offender and may offer to testify against other defendants in exchange for a plea bargain. Plea bargains for testimony against fellow partners in crime is risky, however, as the information often remains unconvincing to a jury.

In sentence bargaining, the defendant seeks leniency. Sentences can range from probation to life imprisonment. The defendant may offer to plead guilty to the charges in return for the prosecutor's recommendation to the judge for a minimum sentence. Most defendants—especially the guilty—want to avoid jail time, and a sentence of probation, even a long period of probation, is preferable to hard time in prison. Some defendants want to negotiate where they will serve their time or the type of facility or its security level. Because they control the charges to be filed against the defendant, prosecutors can bargain for reduction of the charges directly. However, the judge has control over the sentence, so sentence bargaining frequently involves pretrial negotiation among the prosecutor, defense counsel, and judge. In some cases, a judge may encourage a plea bargain, especially where guilt appears obvious and a trial would only take up the scarce resources of the criminal court. Judges may encourage plea bargaining by making it known that if convicted in a trial, a defendant will receive a more severe sentence than if he or she had pled guilty. Judge participation raises a serious question as to the role of the judge in the adjudication process. The American Bar Association standards recommend that the "trial judge should not participate in plea discussions."[9] The Federal Rules of Criminal Procedure also state that the court should not participate in negotiating guilty pleas.[10] Some states have similar prohibitions. Despite these prohibitions, judge participation in plea bargaining is a characteristic of the criminal justice system.

JUST THE FACTS 10.2

Who determines the charges to be brought against the defendant? What are the prosecutor's powers? How do prosecutors and the police work together to bring charges? How is bail set? Who determines if the defendant is competent to stand trial? What does it mean to be not guilty by reason of insanity? Why do victims and the police often object to plea bargaining? Why do prosecutors and defendants accept plea bargains?

Preparation for the Criminal Trial

THE MAIN IDEA

A criminal case that goes to trial must assure the defendant the right to a speedy trial and legal counsel; must follow specific rules of evidence; and must proceed with the judge, prosecutor, and jury serving specific roles in the trial.

After adjudication—assuming that the defendant is competent to stand trial, no alternative diversion is offered, and no plea bargain is struck—the case proceeds forward in the criminal justice process. It becomes one of the few arrests that actually results in a criminal trial. For a case to come to trial, it must be placed on the **court docket,** or calendar. Attorneys, defendants, and courtroom personnel must know when the case is scheduled for trial and how long the trial is expected to last, because the demand for judges and courtrooms exceeds the limited resources of the criminal justice system. Defendants released on bail, especially when guilty, may want to postpone their day in court. However, defendants awaiting trial in jail—especially those who are not guilty—want to hasten the day of judgment.

Once a case is on the docket, the actual time that a defendant must wait for his or her day in court is not left to the defendant or to the government. The **Sixth Amendment of the Constitution** guarantees that defendants will receive a speedy trial, but the Constitution does not define what constitutes *speedy*. The right to a speedy trial is not the same as the statute of limitations. The **statute of limitations** is the length of time between the discovery of the crime and the arrest of the defendant. Various crimes have different acceptable lengths of time between the crime and the arrest. Usually, less serious crimes have a shorter period for arresting the defendant, and more serious crimes have longer periods. Customarily, there is no statute of limitations for the crime of murder. The right to a speedy trial refers to the time between arrest and trial.

court docket The calendar on which court cases are scheduled for trial.

statute of limitations Legal limits regarding the length of time between the discovery of the crime and the arrest of the defendant.

The Sixth Amendment Right to a Speedy Trial

Like other Amendments in the Bill of Rights, the Sixth Amendment right to a speedy trial originally extended only to federal crimes in federal courts. It was not until 1967 that the Supreme Court made the Sixth Amendment applicable to state and federal courts as well.[11] Prior to then, states did not have to provide a speedy trial unless guaranteed by the state constitution. The definition of *speedy trial* differed substantially among states. Some states required that the trial take place in less than 2 months' time, and others allowed a case to come to trial years after the defendant was arrested. Initially, the Supreme Court did not provide specific guidelines to help determine what constitutes a speedy trial. The Court took the view that a speedy trial is a relative matter and may vary in length of time from arrest to trial because of the circumstances of the case.[12]

The judicial interpretation of the right to a speedy trial changed dramatically in the late 1960s and early 1970s, beginning with the 1967 case of ***Klopfer v. North Carolina.***[13] Peter Klopfer, a professor at Duke University, was arrested for trespass while engaged in a sit-in at a segregated motel and restaurant. Klopfer initially was tried for trespass, which resulted in a hung jury. In such cases, the state has the right to retry the defendant. The prosecutor decided not to bring the case to trial, but at the same time refused to dismiss the charges against Klopfer. The laws of North Carolina allowed the prosecutor to postpone a trial indefinitely, even over the defendant's demand for a speedy trial. At the time, the state of North Carolina did not guarantee defendants the right to a speedy trial.

Thus, Klopfer was left in a state of legal limbo. At any time the prosecutor could decide to reactivate the criminal charges against the defendant, and the defendant had no recourse due to lack of a speedy trial. Klopfer's case was appealed to the U.S. Supreme Court on the grounds that North Carolina denied him his constitutional rights. On appeal, the Supreme Court agreed and declared the North Carolina law unconstitutional. The right to a speedy trial was extended to state courts, and spurred by the Klopfer case, many states adopted speedy trial legislation. The Sixth Amendment right applies even if a defendant, for whatever reason, does not object to a delay. In 1972, in ***Barker v. Wingo,*** the Supreme Court issued a ruling that a defendant's failure to demand a speedy trial does not amount to a waiver of the Sixth Amendment right.[14]

While guaranteeing the right to a speedy trial, the Sixth Amendment does not specify the remedy if this right is denied. If a defendant is denied a speedy trial, what should the court do? After the *Klopfer v. North Carolina* ruling that extended this right to state courts, the Supreme Court found it necessary to review cases in which some state defendants failed to receive a speedy trial. In 1973, the Supreme Court decided that the remedy to be applied when a defendant does not receive a speedy trial is that the charges against the defendant will be permanently dismissed, and the prosecutor subsequently will not be allowed to bring these charges against the defendant. However, the Court also ruled that delays caused by the defendant's actions, such as requests for postponement, claims related to competency to stand trial, and other requests for delays, cannot be considered a denial of the right to a speedy trial.

The Speedy Trial Act of 1974

These Supreme Court rulings caused both federal and state courts to change the way they did business. Previously, the prosecutor could select some cases for prosecution and leave others to a later time without any concern for the delay in bringing a case to trial. After the Supreme Court ruling, the prosecutor had to be mindful of bringing all cases to trial in a timely manner or risk losing the ability to prosecute. The Speedy Trial Act of 1974 turned this concern into a crisis. **The Speedy Trial Act of 1974** required a specific deadline between arrest and trial in federal courts. Fully implemented in 1980, the act required that, except in a few well-defined situations and barring delays created by the defendant, the defendant would be brought to trial within 180 days of his or her arrest or the charges could be dismissed and could not be reinstated. When a federal defendant is charged with a crime, the clock starts, and the prosecutor has 30 days to seek an indictment or information. If the defendant is indicted, the prosecutor has 70 days after the indictment or information to start the trial.[15] The clock is stopped for delays attributable to the defendant, such as postponements or escape to avoid prosecution. The clock does not stop when the delay is attributable to the prosecutor, however, even if the delays are beyond the prosecutor's control. Basically, the Speedy Trial Act requires that federal cases be brought to trial 100 days after the arrest of the defendant (30 days from arrest to indictment plus 70 days from indictment to trial) or the prosecutor runs the risk of having the charges against the defendant dismissed. When this act was passed, many prosecutors were not prepared to bring a defendant to trial so quickly, and many courts were unable to accommodate the demand for speed. Prosecutors were forced to become more efficient and effective in bringing cases to trial, and courts were forced to utilize courtrooms and judges in a more productive manner. Court administrators and the Clerk of the Court came under new pressures to exercise effective management of the court's docket.

Rules of Evidence

See http://www.law.cornell.edu/rules/fre/overview.html, the Legal Information Institute at Cornell University, for a complete listing of the federal rules of evidence.

Each court is governed by certain rules of evidence. As you learned in Chapter 5, rules of evidence are laws that shape law enforcement and court practices, defining how the trial will be conducted, how evidence will be introduced, how the parties to the trial will act, and the order of the proceedings. Deviation from rules of evidence constitutes a judicial error, which leads to appeals. If a rule of evidence is violated, the prosecution or the defense can appeal the case. If the appeals court finds that the violation is a serious breach of the rules, the defendant has not received a fair trial.

Each state court and the federal courts have different rules. To represent clients in a particular court, attorneys are required to demonstrate that they have competent knowledge of the rules of evidence for the court hearing the case. To represent a client in a court of appeals or the state or federal supreme court, attorneys may need to pass an examination on the rules of evidence.

Usually, attorneys qualify for practice in state trial courts of limited and general jurisdiction by virtue of their good standing in the state bar association. The federal trial courts have different rules of evidence, requiring that the lawyer demonstrate competency in the federal rules of evidence before he or she can present a case in federal court. Also, a lawyer must demonstrate competent knowledge of a state's rules of evidence before being allowed to represent a client in that state's trial courts.

The rules of evidence regulate nearly every aspect of the trial. Rules of evidence can be mundane, such as the rule that only the original of a document can be introduced as evidence. In addition, rules of evidence determine what evidence is relevant, what evidence is permissible, what evidence cannot be introduced, what evidence an expert witness may present to the jury, what questions can be asked of witnesses, and what is required before an item of physical evidence can be introduced into the trial.

If during the trial the prosecutor or defense counsel believes that a rule of evidence has been violated, it is his or her duty to raise objections to the judge. To do this, the attorney says, "I object on the grounds that . . . ." For example, if the prosecution asks a witness a question that the defense feels the witness is not competent to answer, the defense attorney objects on the grounds that the question calls for the witness to make a conclusion that he or she is not competent to make. Objections include questions that are not relevant to the present case or that call for the witness to comment about the mental state of the defendant (e.g., whether the defendant was angry). If the judge agrees, he or she declares that the objection is sustained, and the witness is instructed not to answer the question or the evidence will not be presented to the jury. If the judge does not agree, he

careers

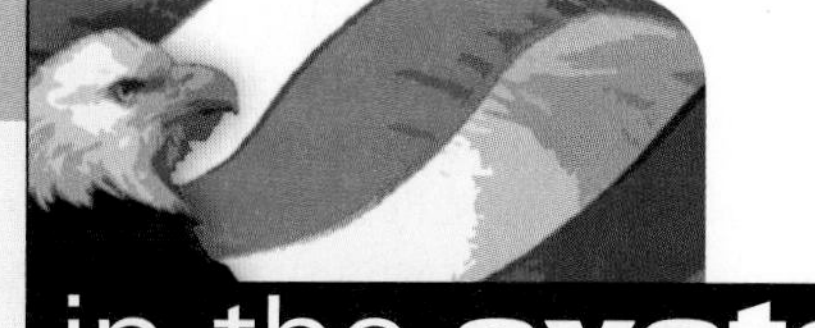

in the system

Court Administrators and Clerk of Court

The day-to-day management of the cases and paperwork of the court are the responsibility of the court administrator and the Clerk of Court. Court administrators can be judges or non-lawyer professionals hired for their management skills. In larger courts (five or more judges), often a professional position is created to handle the administrative matters of the court.[16] The court administrator works for the judges of the court. A professional court administrator does not perform judicial duties and is not a lawyer. Court administrators perform administrative and clerical duties, do strategic planning to increase court efficiency, manage the trial schedule of the court, and manage the budget. Court administrators also may have responsibility for supervising clerical staff who work for them, making effective use of jurors, and ensuring an adequate supply of jurors for the trials scheduled.

The **Clerk of Court** works directly with the trial judge and is responsible for the court records. Usually, each judge has his or her own Clerk of Court. Large courts may employ assistant clerks of court who help perform routine tasks and paperwork. The Clerk of Court and assistants are responsible for the paperwork generated both before and during the trial. The Clerk of Court issues summonses and subpoenas for witnesses, receives pleas and motions and forwards them to the judge for consideration, and prepares all case files that a judge will need for the day. During the trial, the Clerk of Court records and marks physical evidence introduced in the trial. It is the Clerk of Court who swears in the witnesses. In some jurisdictions, the Clerk of Court has certain signatory powers as an agent of the judge and can issue warrants or perform other judicial powers requiring court oversight.

As a result of the need to bring a case to trial in a timely manner, the job of the court administrator and Clerk of Court are important. Delays due to slow performance of routine tasks necessary to bring the trial to court is not an excuse to deny the defendant a speedy trial. The Clerk of Court and court administrator often are invisible to the public. Much of their work, however, is behind the scenes, but it is essential to the efficient operation of the court.

■ **What roles do court administrators and the Clerk of Court fulfill in the adjudication process? Why is their work important in criminal trials? If you wanted to be a court administrator or Clerk of Court, how could you find out more about these jobs?**

or she overrules the objection. As you read in Chapter 9, after the trial, the case can be appealed if the prosecution or defense believes the judge made a judicial error.

Pretrial Motions

Rules of evidence include procedures called motions, which are defined in Chapter 2. Motions are formal written requests, usually in a specified legal format, requesting that the judge make a ruling regarding some aspect of the trial prior to the start of the trial. The judge makes a decision regarding the motion and informs the parties of the decision. The most common motions are for continuance, discovery, change of venue, suppression, a bill of particulars, severance of charges or defendants, and dismissal.

MOTION FOR CONTINUANCE A **motion for continuance** is a request to delay the start of the trial. Either party to the trial can file this motion, but if filed by the prosecutor, the prosecutor will still be required to start the trial within the time limit specified by the Speedy Trial Act applicable to the court. Common reasons for delay include the health of the defendant, lawyer, or prosecutor; delays in obtaining laboratory results about evidence; difficulty in locating witnesses; and the defense's need for more time to prepare for the case.

Clerk of Court Government employee who works directly with the trial judge and is responsible for court paperwork and records before and during a trial.

motion for continuance A pretrial request to delay the start of the trial.

MOTION FOR DISCOVERY A **motion for discovery** is a motion filed by the defense counsel, requesting that the prosecutor turn over all relevant evidence and a list of witnesses that the prosecution may use at the trial. The prosecutor is required to turn over state's evidence and witnesses, but the defense is not required to provide the prosecutor with similar information. The right of discovery is based on the philosophy that the state is at an advantage. Furthermore, some of the evidence the government has collected may suggest that the defendant is not guilty. Failure to provide the defense with a complete list of witnesses and all physical evidence and evidentiary documents is considered a violation of due process.[17] Due process requires that all witnesses and all kinds of evidence, especially evidence not used by the prosecutor that may suggest the defendant is not guilty, must be delivered to the defense.[18] The defense has a right to see police files and interviews conducted by the police as well as witnesses and evidence developed by the prosecutor's office. This requirement allows the defendant's lawyer to mount a defense against the prosecutor's case.

The right of the defense to see a list of witnesses is related to the Sixth Amendment guarantee of the right to a public trial. A trial is public not only in the sense that the public has knowledge of the trial and may attend the proceedings, but also in that there can be no secret witnesses against the defendant. This right extends to undercover police agents and confidential informants used in the case. While children may be protected to some degree from public view while giving testimony at a trial, their identities must be revealed to the defense.

MOTION FOR CHANGE OF VENUE A **motion for change of venue** is a request, either by the prosecution or by the defense, to move the trial to another courtroom for a stated reason. The most common reason for a change of venue is the belief that it is not possible to obtain a fair trial due to local knowledge or perception of the crime. Local knowledge or perception of an offensive crime can make it impossible to obtain a jury pool that is not biased against the defendant.

Motions for a change of venue can ask only for a change to another court in the same jurisdiction. The jurisdiction of federal trial courts may include several states, however, such that in a federal criminal trial the defendant may ask for a change of venue to a court in another state within the same jurisdiction. Motions for a change of venue do not apply to an appeal, as the appellate court does not use a jury. The judge has the authority to grant or deny the motion and to determine the site of the new trial. A change of venue may involve considerable expense, and the court docket of the new court must be able to accommodate the trial and so the judge gives careful consideration to this request.

MOTION FOR SUPPRESSION A **motion for suppression** is made by the defense to prevent certain evidence being introduced in the trial. The motion is based on the claim that the evidence was gathered in a manner that violated due process or was unconstitutional.[19] Most motions for suppression are applied to physical evidence or confessions covered by the exclusionary rule, explained in Chapter 5. Suppression of evidence can influence the outcome of the trial. The case against the defendant may be seriously weakened if the prosecutor cannot use the defendant's confession or cannot use physical evidence gathered by the police at the scene of a crime. For example, if the defendant's confession is excluded, the jury will not know that the defendant confessed to the crime.

MOTION FOR A BILL OF PARTICULARS If a defendant is charged with possession of burglary tools, illegal weapons, drug paraphernalia, or illegal gambling paraphernalia, a **motion for a bill of particulars** allows the defense to receive more details as to exactly what items the prosecution considers illegal. For example, in a case involving a defendant charged with illegal possession of burglary tools, the prosecutor must provide the defense with a list of the tools that will be introduced as evidence of guilt. This list allows the defense attorney to prepare a defense against the charge. If the alleged

motion for discovery A pretrial motion filed by the defense counsel, requesting that the prosecutor turn over all relevant evidence, including the list of witnesses, that the prosecution may use at the trial.

motion for change of venue A pretrial request, either by the prosecutor or the defense, to move the trial to another courtroom.

motion for suppression A pretrial motion made by the defense to exclude certain evidence from being introduced in the trial.

motion for a bill of particulars Allows the defense to receive more details as to exactly what items the prosecution considers illegal if a defendant is charged with possession of burglary tools, illegal weapons, drug paraphernalia, or illegal gambling paraphernalia.

burglary tools are a screwdriver and a pry bar, the defense has the opportunity to persuade the jury that the defendant had legitimate use for these tools at the time and did not intend to use them to commit a crime.

MOTIONS FOR SEVERANCE OF CHARGES OR DEFENDANTS If Adam and Zelda commit a burglary and are captured by the police, the prosecutor may want to try both defendants at the same trial. If Jake has committed six burglaries, the prosecution may want to try Jake on all six counts of burglary at the same trial. Advantages to the prosecutor in trying multiple defendants or multiple offenses at a single trial are that these trials are cheaper, require less preparation, and provide some advantage in proving the guilt of the defendant.[20] Defendants may believe that being tried for a series of crimes at a single trial or being tried with alleged partners in crime may prejudice their right to a fair trial and therefore request a motion for severance of charges or defendants. A **motion for severance of charges or defendants** requests that the defendant be tried for each charge separately, or that defendants charged with the same crime be tried separately.

This jury is being sworn in to serve in a criminal trial. The lawyers representing the prosecution and the defense have filed pretrial motions with the judge, which are decided at the start of the trial. What might these pretrial motions have been? Who are all the other trial participants in the courtroom, and what are their roles in the trial process?

MOTION FOR DISMISSAL The defense attorney claims that the charges against the client should be dismissed on the grounds of lack of evidence, violation of due process, lack of jurisdiction, or any number of other reasons that the case should not proceed to trial. A judge can grant two types of dismissal: with prejudice and without prejudice. A **motion for dismissal** granted with prejudice means that the defendant cannot be recharged with the same crime. A motion for dismissal granted without prejudice means that the case will not proceed to trial, but the prosecutor may correct the defect and arraign the defendant again.

JUST THE FACTS 10.3

Why must the prosecutor ensure that the defendant is brought to trial in a timely manner? How does the Rules of Evidence affect what the jury gets to hear or see? What tests must evidence meet before it can be presented at the trial? What are seven common pretrial motions and what effect do they have on the trial?

Participants in the Criminal Trial

THE MAIN IDEA

Participants in the criminal trial include representatives of the government and representatives of the defendant, who are part of the courtroom work group, as well as witnesses.

A typical courtroom is shown in Figure 10.4 on page 318. Many people work behind the scenes to make a criminal trial possible, but only certain participants are present in the courtroom during the trial. Those present at trial can be divided into three groups:

motion for severance of charges or defendants
A pretrial request that the defendant be tried for each charge separately or that multiple defendants charged with the same crime be tried separately.

motion for dismissal
A pretrial defense motion that the charges against the defendant be dismissed.

Figure 10.4

A Typical Courtroom

The typical courtroom is designed for functionality. The three major areas in a courtroom are as follows: (*Bottom*) The public area for the public and the media provides limited seating on a first-come basis; often, for sensational trials, people wait in a line outside the courtroom, hoping to gain entry. The public cannot cross the "bar" that divides the public area from (*Middle*) the courtroom working area, where courtroom personnel conduct the business of the court. Behind the courtroom working area is (*Top*) the private work area, where the judge's office and the jury room are located.

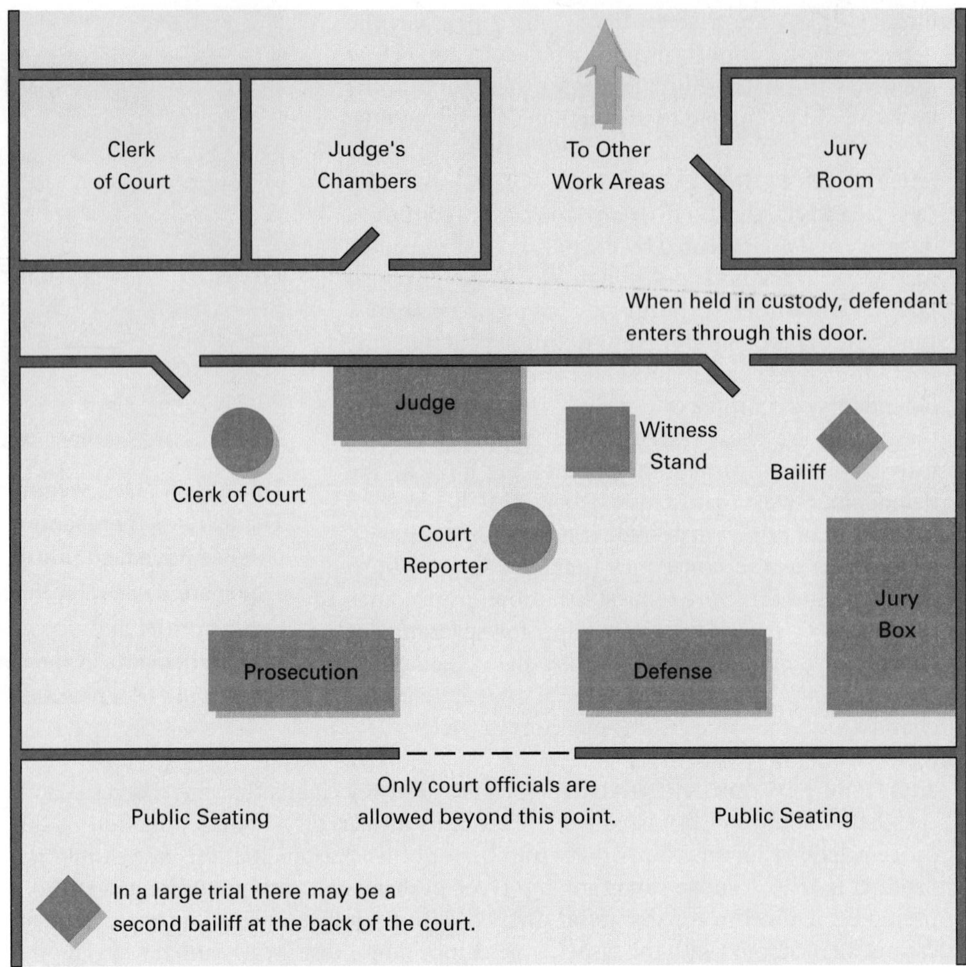

Source: Barbara Boland et al., The Prosecution of Felony Arrests, 1988 (Washington, DC: Bureau of Justice Statistics, 3, 1992).

(1) government employees, (2) the defendant and his or her legal counsel, and (3) witnesses and victims. The **courtroom work group** cuts across these distinctions.

On This Side, Representing the State

People at a trial, who are employed by the government, can be divided into four groups: (1) people who work to make the trial possible but do not take any side in the trial; (2) the prosecutor and his or her assistants, who have the responsibility of presenting evidence against the defendant; (3) the judge, who must exercise impartial management of the trial and make decisions regarding proper procedure and due process; and (4) the jury, a panel of citizens that has the authority to decide if the defendant is guilty or not guilty.

courtroom work group
Adversarial and neutral parties, usually the prosecutor, defense attorney, judge, and other court personnel, who get together and cooperate to settle cases with the least effort and conflict.

TAKING CARE OF THE BUSINESS OF THE COURT The Clerk of Court, court recorder, and bailiff perform important tasks to make the work of the court possible. The people are not part of the prosecution or the defense. Their job is to make it possible for the business of the court to be conducted efficiently and safely. As you have read, the judge's Clerk of Court has important pretrial duties.

The **court recorder,** also called the **court reporter,** transcribes every word spoken by the judge, attorneys, and witnesses during the trial. The court recorder is responsible for making a permanent written record of the court's proceedings. This written record is required, so if the court recorder is not present or cannot accurately transcribe the proceedings for any reason, the trial must be stopped. The court reporter also has the authority to stop a trial at any point if he or she cannot record what is being said. Skill in stenography is the basis on which court reporters are hired. They must be able to record up to 200 words a minute; to achieve this speed, they use a special system of phonetics and computer technology. Most courtroom reporters attend specialty programs that train and certify them for the position.

The **bailiff** is usually a county deputy sheriff or a U.S. deputy marshal. The county sheriff is responsible for providing bailiffs for court security for state courts, and the U.S. marshal is responsible for providing court security for federal courts. The bailiff is an armed law enforcement officer who has the power of arrest and the power to use deadly force if necessary. For most bailiffs, courtroom security consists of escorting the jury in and out of the courtroom and maintaining order in the court at the direction of the judge. However, responding to any breach of security, attempted escape of the defendant, violence, or attack on any person in the courtroom is the bailiff's responsibility. The bailiff may be called on in life-threatening emergencies, as defendants have been known to attack witnesses, judges, attorneys, and even members of the press.

THE PROSECUTOR The prosecutor is not an employee of the court but does represent the government. The role of the prosecutor is to bring charges against the defendant, gather the evidence necessary to prosecute the defendant, and present the evidence at trial. The prosecutor's primary goal is not to convict the defendant but to seek justice. The American Bar Association's Code of Professional Responsibility states that a prosecutor should not present evidence that he or she knows to be unreliable, nor should the prosecutor hide or withhold from the defense evidence that may suggest the innocence of the defendant. The prosecutor's job is to see that the person who committed the crime is brought to justice. The prosecutor's job is to demonstrate to the court that the evidence supports a conviction beyond a reasonable doubt.

THE JUDGE The judge is a central figure in the trial. The centrality of the judge's role is evident in that, during the trial, the attorneys will address the judge as "the court." The judge is a neutral party. His or her role is similar to that of an umpire or referee at a baseball or basketball game. This role can be complicated in a bench trial when the judge, rather than a jury, determines whether the defendant is guilty. In a bench trial, the judge must act as impartial mediator during the trial and, at the conclusion of the trial, must make a determination of guilt. As you read in Chapter 4, bench trials often are prohibited in cases involving serious felonies.

The judge determines what evidence can be presented at the trial, what witnesses can testify and what they can testify to, and when courtroom breaks are permissible. The judge has authority over the courtroom personnel, the attorneys, the jury, members of the media, and the public in the courtroom. The power of the judge lies in his or her absolute and immediate ability to fine or imprison people for **contempt of court.** If the judge believes that an attorney, either defense or prosecution, has violated a professional standard of conduct during the trial, he or she can impose a fine or term of imprisonment. Unprofessional conduct can include being late for court, continuing to argue with the judge when told to stop, or more serious violations regarding witness and evidence integrity. It is difficult to appeal a contempt of court decree. Contempt of court is not a crime and, thus, the person does not have the same rights as a defendant accused of a crime. Contempt of court can bring substantial penalty. For example, witnesses who will not testify may be held in prison for up to 2 years for contempt of court.[21]

The public, the jury, and the members of the media may be fined or imprisoned for contempt of court. If people in the courtroom are unruly, the judge can impose a fine or hold them in jail for contempt of court. The power of the judge even extends to

court recorder (court reporter) Stenographer who transcribes every word spoken by the judge, attorneys, and witnesses during a trial.

bailiff A county deputy sheriff or U.S. deputy marshal responsible for providing security and maintaining order in a courtroom.

contempt of court A charge against any violator of the judge's courtroom rules, authorizing the judge to impose a fine or term of imprisonment.

appropriate dress of persons in the courtroom. Jury members can be fined or imprisoned for violating the orders of the judge not to discuss the case. The media most often run afoul of the judge's authority by violating a **gag order**—an order that the evidence or proceedings of the court may not be published or discussed publicly. If disclosure of evidence or testimony may jeopardize the defendant's receiving a fair trial, the judge has the authority to order all parties to refrain from discussing or publishing this information. Members of the media who violate this order can be held in contempt of court.

THE JURY Jurors are citizens required by law to perform jury duty. The court wants jurors who are fair, competent, and able to serve, so citizens can escape jury duty for certain legitimate reasons. Selecting a fair and competent jury and deciding legitimate excuses for jury duty have been major challenges for the court.

The Constitution requires that people be tried by a jury of their peers. The Supreme Court has not interpreted this literally, however. A white, middle-class man does not get a trial by a jury of white, middle-class men. Rather, the jury pool is selected from a broad base of citizens who are representative of the community. Many jurisdictions have used voter registration lists as the pool from which to select jurors. Studies have clearly demonstrated, however, that this pool of candidates is biased, because voter registration lists underrepresent minorities and people with lower income.[22] The current practice in many courts is to select jurors from more representative sources, such as licensed drivers or people listed in the telephone book.

Citizens are paid for jury duty by the government, but the rate of pay is very low, ranging from only a few dollars to $40 per day. Most jurors serve for only short periods of time but may be asked to serve for extended periods; for some jurors, even a few days may impose a severe hardship. Also, some citizens may not be competent to serve as jurors. For these and other reasons, the court may excuse citizens from jury duty. Each jurisdiction determines the rules for excusing citizens from jury service, but the rules must not discriminate against a person because of race, gender, or other characteristics that are considered in violation of the law. For example, until 1975, many states automatically excluded women, especially women with children at home, from jury duty. In ***Taylor v. Louisiana*** (1975), the Supreme Court decided that the exclusion of women from jury duty created an imbalance in the jury pool and was not justified.[23] Legitimate reasons for excuse from jury duty include illness, conviction of a felony crime, or not being able to comprehend English. Members of certain professional groups, such as physicians, may be excluded from jury duty, based on the reasoning that jury service would be detrimental to community safety. Other members of professional groups, such as attorneys, police officers, and legislators, may be excluded from jury duty, based on the reasoning that they may not be able to be neutral and make decisions based only on the evidence presented in court. Most jurisdictions require jury service only once a year.

The Constitution does not require a jury of 12 persons. This number is a tradition but is not a legal requirement, and obtaining 12 people to serve on a jury can be a challenge. All states require 12 jurors for capital cases, and all but six states require 12 jurors for felony trials. Fourteen states allow misdemeanor trials with only six jurors. Other states allow criminal trials with a jury of seven or eight jurors.[24]

In a criminal trial, the jury is known as the "trier of the facts." The jury has the authority and responsibility to decide which evidence is to be accepted as credible and which is not. If the prosecution introduces witnesses and evidence indicating that the defendant committed the crime, but the defense introduces alibi witnesses who swear the defendant was with them at the time of the crime, the jury decides which evidence is the most credible. If the defendant pleads not guilty by reason of insanity, the jury decides if the defendant was insane. Each side can introduce expert witnesses who testify about the mental health of the defendant, but the jury is the ultimate judge of the defendant's mental state at the time of the crime. It is the jury that decides if the evidence and witnesses prove beyond a reasonable doubt the guilt of the defendant. This is an awesome responsibility, and it is given to 12 laypersons.

gag order A judge's order to participants and observers at a trial that the evidence or proceedings of the court may not be published, aired, or discussed publicly.

On This Side, Representing the Defense

The defendant and his or her attorney are the primary persons on the defense side, and these two sit together at a table at the trial. The defendant may choose to assist in his or her defense or may choose to remain passive and let the defense attorney handle the case.

In any criminal trial in which the maximum punishment exceeds 6 months in prison, the defendant is entitled to a jury trial and the right to be represented by an attorney.[25] There are two types of defense attorneys: public defenders and private defense attorneys. The defendant hires a private defense attorney and may choose any attorney registered to practice law before the court. The defendant may hire as many private defense attorneys as he or she can afford. In rare cases, the defendant may choose not to have a defense attorney but to represent him- or herself. The court discourages self-representation but cannot compel a defendant to hire or accept a defense attorney.

THE DEFENDANT If the defendant cannot afford to hire a private defense attorney, the court will appoint and pay for an attorney to represent the defendant. A defendant who cannot afford a private attorney is known as an indigent defendant. When a defendant is charged with a crime, a judge inquires as to the defendant's ability to afford an attorney. Defendants indicating they cannot afford an attorney are required to complete a financial statement and submit it to the court. The court examines the defendant's finances and decides on the matter. About half of all criminal defendants accused of a felony crime cannot afford an attorney, and for larger counties this number increases to 80 percent.[26] **Indigent defense** services represent a substantial expense in the criminal justice system. In 1999, an estimated $1.2 billion was spent by indigent criminal defense programs in the largest 100 counties. These programs handled approximately 4.2 million cases.[27]

CRIMINAL DEFENSE PROGRAMS Three types of indigent criminal defense programs are (1) assigned counsel, (2) public defenders, and (3) contract attorney programs. Assigned counsel programs and public defender programs account for approximately 40 percent of the indigent criminal defense programs, and about 20 percent of indigent criminal defense programs use contract attorney programs.[28]

The *assigned counsel system* is the oldest system of indigent defense. One of the professional codes of ethics of the American Bar Association is that lawyers are expected to provide **pro bono,** or free, counsel to defendants who cannot afford it. After ***Gideon v. Wainwright,*** many states adopted a version of this system. Under the assigned counsel system, the court appoints an attorney from the state bar association's list of attorneys in good standing. The court pays this attorney a fee for representing the defendant. Often, however, this fee is less than the market rate for a good defense attorney. In addition, the court will not pay for expenses associated with a good defense, such as independent investigators and laboratory tests. This is a drawback for both the defendant and the defense attorney.

Despite the widespread use of the assigned counsel system, there are numerous criticisms about (1) the competence of the attorney and (2) the attorney's effort in defending the client. As mentioned, the assigned counselor is chosen from a list of attorneys, but there is no guarantee that the counselor has experience in criminal trials. For instance, a tax attorney might be assigned to represent a defendant accused of murder, rape, or robbery. In theory, all attorneys are generalists and pass the same bar examination to practice law. They are supposed to be knowledgeable in criminal law and capable of defending clients in court. In reality, attorneys specialize and may not be competent to handle a criminal felony case. Inadequate representation by assigned defense counsel often plays a role in the conviction of the defendant. For example, Anthony Porter spent 16 years in prison for murder. His case was taken up by David Protess, a journalism professor from Northwestern University, and several of his students as a class project. Their

indigent defense Defense counsel for a defendant who cannot afford a private attorney.

pro bono Free counsel offered to indigent defendants.

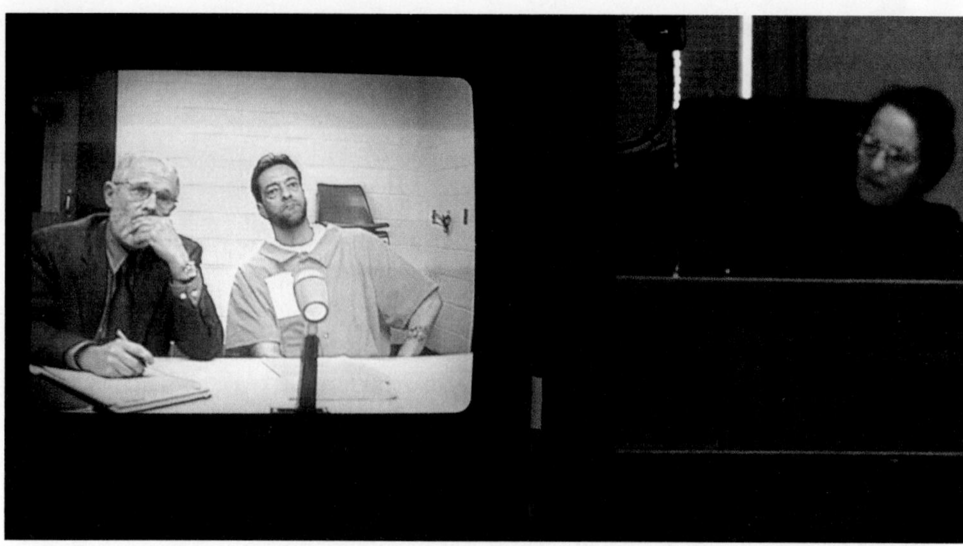

This defendant, Richard Dodd (center), appeared in court before Judge Sylvia Lewis (right) with his public defender via closed-circuit television. Dodd was already serving a life sentence for another kidnapping and rape. What difference did it make if Dodd had a public defender? How are public defenders different from private criminal lawyers, court-assigned attorneys, and contract attorneys?

investigation revealed that Porter was innocent and had received an inadequate defense. Porter was freed in 1999, largely due to Protess's efforts.

The second most used system of indigent defense is the public defender system. Public defenders, like the prosecutor, are employees of the state. **Public defenders** may be full-time or part-time attorneys hired to provide defense counsel to indigent defendants. Under this system, each court jurisdiction has a **Public Defenders Office** headed by a public defender and staffed with assistant public defenders, investigators, and support personnel. The pay for public defenders and assistant public defenders is low compared to the median salary of attorneys, and the workload is incredibly high. In an average state Public Defenders Office in a large county, a staff of less than 100 handles over 43,000 cases.[29]

Despite the more than $1.2 billion spent on public defenders, courts simply cannot afford to provide all the indigent defense services required. The demand for indigent services far exceeds the capacity of the Public Defenders Office. One result is that clients may not consult with their public defender until shortly before their trial. Thus, clients receive little representation in pretrial proceedings. Public defenders cannot devote the time and resources for an excellent defense in every case. Getting a good plea bargain for the client and disposing of the case quickly, rather than taking the case to trial, becomes a priority. A client who is not guilty must choose between accepting a good plea bargain or risking conviction and a long prison sentence, or death, due to incompetent representation. Nevertheless, unlike assigned counsel, public defenders typically are experts in criminal law and know how to try a criminal case in court. They are important members of the courtroom work group who contribute to obtaining justice through a speedy and fair trial.

The third indigent defense system is a system of *contract attorneys*—nonsalaried individual private attorneys, bar associations, law firms, consortiums or groups of attorneys, or nonprofit corporations that contract with a funding source to provide court-appointed representation in a jurisdiction.[30] Contract programs handle a larger percentage of juvenile cases than do public defender or assigned counsel programs.

public defenders Attorneys who are employees of the state, hired to provide defense counsel to indigent defendants as an alternative to the assigned-counsel and contract attorney systems.

JUST THE FACTS 10.4

What is the current legal requirement for a speedy trial? Explain rules of evidence, citing two examples. What are the seven most common pretrial motions? What problems arise from having court-appointed attorneys?

diversity

Defending the Guilty

in the **system**

The defense attorney's job is to represent the defendant's interests. A question often asked is how can a defense attorney defend a guilty client? However, everything must be done to mount an adequate defense, whether or not the client is guilty. The trial is an adversarial process in which the prosecution and the defense attempt to persuade the members of the jury through evidence and witnesses that their side is the most credible. The question of guilt or innocence is more complicated than whether the client committed the crime, for example, killed the deceased, took the property, or defrauded a victim. Thus, *guilt* and *innocence* are legal terms, not moral terms. A person could rob a bank and kill a police officer responding to the bank alarm, and the state could charge the defendant with first-degree murder and ask for the death penalty. The defense could argue that while there is little dispute that the defendant committed the acts alleged by the state, the defendant did not have the necessary intent (*mens rea*) for first-degree murder—that the defendant did not commit the crime with premeditation or intend to kill the police officer. Lacking the conditions required for first-degree murder, the defense could argue for second-degree murder, a lesser crime that does not carry the death penalty.

The morality of the robbery and death and the sinfulness of the defendant are not the central questions addressed in a trial. The purpose of a trial is to prove beyond a reasonable doubt that the defendant committed the act specified by the charges and with the necessary intent required by the law, and to do this while preserving the rights of the accused. The defense attorney may argue that the client is not guilty because he or she (1) did not commit the crime, (2) is insane, (3) lacked criminal intent (self-defense as opposed to murder), or (4) committed the act under mitigating circumstances (such as duress or necessity), or may use any number of other defenses.

Furthermore, defendants are tried for the crime with which they are charged, and past crimes cannot be considered in determining guilt. Knowledge of a past criminal record may prejudice the jury against the defendant, even if the defendant were not guilty of the particular crime being tried. Yet, it seems logical that a person arrested for possession of burglary tools and who has been arrested over two dozen times for burglary most likely intended to use the tools to burglarize another house. Unless a defendant is accused of multiple crimes simultaneously or of a crime that matches a profile of a serial crime, the jury will not be allowed to hear evidence of the defendant's prior criminal record.

Thus, the criminal justice system does not have the same definition of *guilt* as the religious practitioner, moral philosopher, or average citizen. Furthermore, the criminal justice system cannot always be trusted to properly identify the guilty party. Defense attorneys have seen many defendants falsely accused of crimes. In the final analysis, then, the defense attorney cannot refuse to represent a client because he or she believes the client is guilty. Every client is equal in the eyes of the law and must receive the best defense possible.

■ **What is the role of the defense attorney in a criminal trial? Should defense attorneys knowingly defend criminals who are guilty? Why, or why not?**

The Criminal Trial

THE MAIN IDEA

A criminal trial consists of jury selection, presentation of evidence and witnesses, and the closing arguments and verdict.

The criminal trial is a complex, unpredictable event in the criminal justice process. A defendant has anywhere from less than a 20 percent to nearly an 80 percent chance of being convicted and sentenced to incarceration.[31] The probability of conviction increases as the seriousness of the charge increases. Defendants have nearly an 80 percent chance of being convicted for murder but less than a 20 percent chance of being convicted for fraud. It is difficult to summarize all of the important decisions and strategies of the trial attorneys in a brief explanation. Therefore, this description of the trial process focuses on the sequence of events in an American criminal trial. The trial sequence can be divided into three stages: (1) trial initiation, (2) the presentation of evidence and witnesses, and (3) post-argument activities.

Trial Initiation

Once the courtroom work group has determined a case to settle by a trial, several major pretrial activities occur. First, attorneys from each side present pretrial motions (discussed previously) to the court. After the pretrial motions have been disposed of, the next step is to secure a time and judge on the court's docket. Based on past practice and experience, the attorneys attempt to secure a judge who may be favorably disposed to the arguments that they are planning to present in court. In addition, it is extremely important to obtain a jury that is favorably disposed toward one's side.

JURY SELECTION The jury is supposed to be neutral and unbiased. However, neither the prosecutor nor the defense attorney wants a completely unbiased jury, and both have some influence in shaping the composition of the jury through a process known as *voir dire*. Through the voir dire process, defined in Chapter 2, a jury is selected from eligible members of the jury pool. Eligible jury members are called from the jury pool to the courtroom to be interviewed by the attorneys and the judge. During the interview, each side and the judge ask the prospective juror questions. Questions usually concern whether the juror has ever been the victim of a crime (especially a crime similar to the one of which the defendant is accused), what the juror knows about the case from the media, whether the juror is related to anyone in the courtroom or the case, and whether the juror already has formed an opinion about the guilt of the defendant.

Some people assume incorrectly that if they provide obviously biased answers during voir dire they will be excused from jury duty. If they are excluded from serving on the jury for that trial, however, they must return to the jury pool and wait to be called for another trial. In many courts, a juror is required to serve in the jury pool for an entire week or in a trial lasting only 1 to 3 days.

See http://www.jri-inc.com/, the web site of the Jury Research Institute, a trial consulting firm, for descriptions of some strategies used by defense attorneys in jury selection. ■

In complex criminal trials, especially in which the defendant has retained the services of a private attorney, jurors may be asked to fill out questionnaires in addition to answering oral questions during voir dire. Some attorneys in high-profile cases retain the services of a jury consultant to help analyze the attitudes and characters of the jurors in order to shape a favorable jury through "scientific" jury selection.

VOIR DIRE AND PEREMPTORY CHALLENGE The attorneys shape a jury by exercising their right to challenge a juror's ability to serve on the jury, by asking the juror to be removed for *cause*. The goal of **voir dire** is to select 12 jurors and a number of alternative jurors, usually no less than 2. Alternative jurors are sworn in with the other members of the jury and sit with the jury during the entire trial. If a "regular" juror is unable to complete his or her service—for example, because of illness—an alternative juror replaces the excused juror. An objection to the seating of a juror for cause means that an attorney perceives some bias or characteristic that would prevent a fair trial. For instance, a juror who was recently the victim of a robbery may be excused for cause under the assumption that he or she may be biased against a defendant being tried for robbery. There is no limit to the number challenges for cause that each side may exercise. The judge makes the final decision as to whether or not a juror is excused.

voir dire The process through which a jury is selected from the members of the jury pool who have been determined eligible for service.

peremptory challenge The subjective evaluation of the attorney that is used to exclude jurors.

Each side also has a limited number of peremptory challenges it can use to exclude jurors. A **peremptory challenge** is based on a subjective evaluation by the attorney and need not be justified to the court. Until the late 1980s and early 1990s, it was permissible to use peremptory challenges to shape the jury by excluding jurors based on their race or gender.[32] In 1986, the U.S Supreme Court prohibited the exclusion of jurors based solely on race, and in 1994, prohibited the exclusion of a juror based on gender.[33]

criminal justice in the world

The French Trial

The French criminal system practices what is known as continental law, which is different from the American system of case law. The two systems also differ in how they handle a criminal trial. The purpose of the French trial is to discover the truth. The French trial is not based on the adversary system, as is the American trial. Also, the French criminal trial may include a suit for damages by the victim at the same trial rather than in a separate civil case.

The French system divides criminal offenses into felonies, misdemeanors, and violations. Misdemeanors are tried by three magistrates in the local court of major jurisdiction. The accused does not have right to trial by jury for a misdemeanor. The felony trial is handled by the Court of Assize and is prosecuted by the procurator of the republic. France has a centralized criminal justice system, and the procurator is more like a state attorney general than a district attorney.

In France, the investigation of a crime is supervised by the courts, not the police. An examining magistrate has the power to interrogate witnesses, the accused, and the victim. The accused has the right to know the charges, the right to remain silent, and the right to an attorney. Bail before a trial is considered an exception, as most defendants are detained in jail before the trial. If a defendant cannot afford an attorney, he or she is entitled to a court-appointed and -paid attorney.The following description of the trial is from Dr. Terrill's world criminal justice system.[34]

A criminal felony trial is presided over by three judges: a judge from the regional court of appeals and two additional judges for either the court of appeals or a court of major jurisdiction. The presiding judge is called the "president."

Jurors for a criminal trial are selected by a lottery method from the annual list of jurors. The lottery selects 27 potential jurors and 6 potential alternative jurors. The procurator is allowed up to four challenges of jurors, and the defense is allowed five challenges. Nine jurors are selected for a trial, and they are seated beside the three judges. The trial is usually open to the public.

Before the trial, each side is required to exchange a list of witnesses. At the start of the trial, the president asks the clerk to read the names of witnesses. After it is confirmed that all witnesses are present, the witnesses leave the courtroom, and then the clerk reads the charges against the accused, and the accused is given an opportunity to make a statement. After his or her statement, the accused answers questions from the judges, the jury, the procurator, the defense counsel, and the counsel for any civil charges being brought. The judges and procurator ask questions directly, but the other participants submit their questions through the president of the court.

Then the witnesses are called into the courtroom one by one to give testimony. They are witnesses for the court, not for the defense or the prosecution. Witnesses are allowed to tell their stories without interruption, and answer questions afterward. They then remain in the courtroom throughout the trial.

Counsel for the civil suit then presents arguments for awarding damages or reimbursement. The procurator presents his or her arguments, and then the accused or counsel offers a defense. The civil party and the procurator reply to the defense, the accused offers a final rebuttal, and the trial ends. There are no closing arguments.

The three judges and nine jurors retire to deliberate the case together. A verdict of guilty requires eight votes. Votes are by secret ballot, and both the judges and the jurors have an equal vote in conviction. If there is a civil claim, only the judges decide. If the defendant is convicted, the judges and jurors determine an appropriate sanction from a range of punishments prescribed by law. Convicted defendants may appeal for a review of the case to the court of cassation. Defendants found not guilty are released immediately.

■ How are French criminal courts and the adjudication process different from the American court system? How are cases argued? How are they decided? What might be some advantages and disadvantages of the French system compared to the American system?

■ Presentation of Evidence and Witnesses

When the jury is seated, the trial is considered to have officially started, and the trial proceeds to the opening arguments and the presentation of evidence and witnesses. Each side is given the opportunity to present evidence and witnesses to persuade the jury for or against the defendant. Usually, the length of the trial is determined in advance, and each side is allotted approximately half the trial time for their arguments.

OPENING STATEMENTS Before evidence is presented, however, each side has the opportunity to address the court, especially the jury, to explain what the case is about and to provide an overview of what to expect. The attorneys' arguments in the opening statements are not considered evidence. Also, the attorneys are not obligated to do everything they say they will do in their opening statements. The prosecution makes the first opening statement, explaining to the jury the crime of which the defendant is accused, the seriousness of the crime, and the strength of the state's evidence against the defendant. Many defense counselors choose not to present an opening statement or may present only a brief statement contradicting the prosecutor's allegations. The defense may want to hear the evidence of the prosecution and evaluate the strength of that evidence before making a commitment as to what the defense will prove.

THE STATE'S CASE AGAINST THE DEFENDANT The state has the burden of proof and must provide evidence and witnesses that convince the jury beyond a reasonable doubt of the defendant's guilt. The state can present four types of evidence: (1) real evidence, (2) testimonial evidence, (3) direct evidence, and (4) circumstantial evidence.

Real evidence is physical evidence such as a gun, a fingerprint, a photograph, or DNA matching. All real evidence is accompanied by an explanation of what the evidence is, how it was gathered, and how it connects the defendant to the crime. For example, the real evidence of an autopsy report on the cause of death is explained by the medical examiner who performed the autopsy. The police officer who found the real evidence of the firearm used to shoot the victim must identify the firearm and explain where it was found and how it was handled.

The explanations of real evidence are examples of **testimonial evidence**—the testimony of a witness. Testimonial evidence may be given by laypersons or experts. Laypersons can testify only to what they heard, saw, felt, smelled, or otherwise directly experienced. Laypersons usually cannot give second-hand or **hearsay evidence**—information about events they only heard from others. An example of hearsay testimony is that of a person who was told by another that the defendant bragged about robbing a convenience store. Expert witnesses, on the other hand, make inferences beyond the facts and give testimony based on their expert knowledge. For example, a medical doctor may testify that the victim was killed by a blow to the head with a blunt instrument and that a hammer found in the possession of the defendant could have been the instrument used to make that fatal wound. The doctor did not see the defendant strike the victim and does not know if the hammer was the murder weapon but is allowed to give expert testimony as to the probable cause of death.

Direct evidence is any real or testimonial evidence that connects the defendant to the crime. An eyewitness who can identify the defendant as the bank robber is an example of direct evidence. **Circumstantial evidence,** on the other hand, can be interpreted in more than one way and does not indisputably link the defendant with the crime. An example of circumstantial evidence is a witness who hears a shot, observes the defendant running from a room, and then enters the room and finds the victim shot. From this testimony, the jury may infer only that the defendant could have been the one who shot the victim. Circumstantial evidence does not prove guilt. In California and other states, the rules of evidence require that if there is more than one interpretation of circumstantial evidence and one of those interpretations is favorable to the defendant, the jury must accept the favorable interpretation as the best explanation.

Not all evidence meets the acceptable **legal standards of evidence** required by the rules of evidence. The evidence and testimony of witnesses must meet three criteria to be used in the trial: (1) The evidence must be competent—legally fit for admission to court. For example, the evidence must be reliable. Polygraph (lie detector) examinations are not accepted as reliable scientific evidence and, thus, are excluded as evidence in

real evidence Physical evidence such as a gun, a fingerprint, a photograph, or DNA matching.

testimonial evidence The testimony of a witness.

hearsay evidence Information about a crime obtained second-hand from another rather than directly observed.

direct evidence Evidence that connects the defendant with the crime.

circumstantial evidence Evidence that *implies* that the defendant is connected to the crime but does not *prove* the defendant is connected to the crime.

legal standards of evidence Evidence and the testimony of witnesses must be competent, material, and relevant.

criminal trials because they do not constitute *competent evidence*. (2) The evidence has to be material. *Material evidence* has a legitimate bearing on the decision of the case. For example, whether the defendant is a good father and husband is not material to the question of whether he committed arson fraud. (3) The evidence must be relevant. *Relevant evidence* is applicable to the issue in question. For example, evidence that the defendant has a history of domestic violence is not relevant to the question of whether he or she assaulted the victim in the case.

The prosecutor asks a witness to take the stand and give testimony. The prosecutor asks the witness questions to elicit the information about the crime that the witness has. This is called the "direct examination of the witness." The prosecutor cannot direct or coach the witness to get certain answers, however. For example, the prosecutor cannot ask the witness a "leading question," such as, "Did you see the defendant strike and kill the victim on the night of January 6th at about 8:00 P.M. in the Town Tavern?" Also, the prosecutor cannot ask the witness for information that he or she is not qualified to provide. For example, asking, "Was the defendant happy when he heard about the news of his wife's death?" is inappropriate because the witness cannot know how the defendant was feeling and can testify only to the defendant's actions.

When the prosecutor is finished, the defense attorney is allowed to question the witness. This is called the "cross-examination." The defense attempts to show that the witness's testimony is not credible or is contradictory. The defense may attempt to show, for instance, that, with insufficient light, the witness was too far away to recognize the defendant. After the cross-examination, the prosecutor may ask additional questions to repair any damage that the defense may have done to the witness's credibility. This is called the "redirect examination." Following the redirect, the defense has another opportunity to question the witness, called the "recross-examination." It is not necessary that the defense cross-examine or recross-examine a witness, however. If the defense chooses not to exercise these options, the prosecution has no further opportunity to question the witness. In the recross-examination and redirect examination, the defense and the prosecution, respectively, cannot introduce new evidence. Their examination is limited in scope to the credibility of evidence presented by the witness in the direct examination. When the prosecution has presented all its evidence and witnesses, the prosecution "rests." The court may offer a short break or may proceed to the first defense witness.

THE DEFENSE'S CASE Before presenting any evidence or witnesses, it is customary for the defense to ask for a motion for directed verdict on the face of the prosecutor's case. The prosecution has the burden of proof in the trial. If the prosecution has not established a *prima facie* case of guilty—that is, clear and convincing evidence of guilt—the judge can direct the jury to return a verdict of not guilty even before the defense presents its case. A request for a directed verdict is rarely granted.

The rules of evidence and the order of examination of the witnesses are the same for the defense as for the prosecution. The defense rests when it has presented all of its evidence and witnesses. The prosecutor may attempt to discredit the defense witnesses and evidence by calling its own witnesses to give testimony. This testimony is limited to refuting the evidence introduced by the defense and cannot introduce new evidence. This is called the "prosecutor's rebuttal" and may be followed by defense counsel's "surrebuttal." Both sides then have exhausted their opportunity to introduce evidence. Very few trials make use of all the opportunities to present and rebut evidence and cross-examine witnesses.

Post-Argument Activities

After all the evidence and witnesses are presented, each side is given the opportunity to summarize its case to the jury. This is called "closing arguments" or "summation." Neither side can introduce new evidence or arguments in the closing statements. The closing argument is a persuasive speech to the jury in which the prosecution argues that it has been proved beyond a reasonable doubt that the defendant is guilty, and the defense argues that the prosecution has failed to demonstrate this standard of proof. Closing arguments, especially in capital murder cases, can be emotionally charged speeches to the jury.

CHARGE TO THE JURY After the closing arguments, there is usually a short recess while the judge prepares the **charge to the jury**—a written document explaining to the jury how the law is applicable to the case. For example, in a murder case, the judge may instruct the jury about the different degrees of murder and homicide and the conditions necessary for each. The judge also summarizes the evidence and instructs the jury about any point of law concerning the evidence. For example, the judge may instruct the jury how to treat circumstantial evidence or the how to evaluate the truthfulness of contradictory evidence given by prosecution and defense witnesses. The judge also makes clear what evidence can and cannot be considered in arriving at a verdict. For example, the jury cannot perform any independent investigations, discuss the case with anyone other than fellow jurors during deliberation, or seek additional information about the case, especially from the media. The judge's instructions to the jury may be quite lengthy and technical, and sometimes are grounds for an appeal. If the judge has provided incorrect instructions about the law or the evidence, the defendant can appeal the case on judicial error. Likewise, a prejudicial statement to the jury by the judge can be grounds for appeal.

JURY DELIBERATIONS After receiving the judge's instructions, the jury retires to the jury room to deliberate. There is no requirement as to how long or short a time the jury should deliberate before coming to a verdict. In theory, the jury is supposed to withhold judgment until the conclusion of the trial. In practice, however, jurors may have already determined whether or not they believe the defendant is guilty. Jury deliberations can take minutes, hours, or days. The first order of business is for the jury to elect a foreperson who will lead the deliberations.

During deliberation, the jury cannot discuss the case with anyone outside of the deliberation room, nor can they read or listen to any media coverage of the case. Any juror who hears or sees media coverage of the case is required to report this to the judge, who can disqualify the juror and assign an alternate. If the jury cannot come to a verdict by the end of the day, the judge has the authority to sequester the jury to prevent the jury from obtaining outside information. This means that the jurors are required to remain under court supervision rather than return to their homes. Jurors are housed and fed at the expense of the state until they reach a verdict.

When the jury reaches a verdict, they notify the bailiff, who notifies the judge. The judge may ask for the jury's verdict in advance of announcing it to the public if he or she feels that the verdict may cause a strong public reaction that may create a public safety issue. If the jury cannot reach a verdict, the jury is said to be "deadlocked" or a "hung jury," in which case the judge declares a mistrial. Only about 6 percent of juries are unable to reach a verdict. As explained in Chapter 2, if the judge declares a mistrial, the prosecutor has the option of filing the same charges against the defendant and trying the case again, and there is no limit to the number of times a case can be retried due to a mistrial.

THE VERDICT The jury renders a verdict on each charge against the defendant. In some cases, as in murder, the jury has the option of finding the defendant guilty or not guilty of various lesser included crimes—such as homicide, involuntary manslaughter, or negligent homicide—instead of the charge filed by the prosecutor. When the defendant is charged with multiple charges, the jury can find the defendant guilty of some of the charges and not guilty of others.

If the jury finds the defendant guilty, but the judge believes that the verdict is contrary to the evidence presented or that the jury did not follow his or her charge in arriving at their verdict, the judge can enter a directed verdict of not guilty. This verdict overturns the jury's verdict. However, the judge cannot overturn a jury's verdict of not guilty, even if the jury violates the judge's instructions and ignores the law pertaining to the case. For example, if the jury refuses to convict the defendant even when the defense

charge to the jury Written instructions about the application of the law to a case that the judge gives to the jury to help them achieve a verdict.

does not satisfy the requirements of the law, a situation referred to as "jury nullification," the judge must accept the jury's verdict.

When the jury reaches a decision, they are brought back into the courtroom to announce the verdict publicly, and the judge asks the foreperson to read the verdict for each charge against the defendant. Each member of the jury is then polled to ensure they agree with the verdict, which must be unanimous. The jury is polled to make sure that no timid juror has been coerced to agree by peer pressure. Once the jury is polled, the verdict is final.

APPEALS Defendants found guilty may appeal their verdict to a court of appeals based on the claim of judicial error. The defendant also can ask for a new trial based on the claim that newly found evidence not available at the time of the trial has been discovered and would substantially affect the trial's outcome.

The defendant who is in state custody and is found not guilty is released as soon as possible. If the defendant is found not guilty, the prosecutor cannot ask for a new trial based on either judicial error or newly discovered evidence.

JUST THE FACTS 10.4

What is involved in selecting a jury? How does the prosecution's opening statement differ from the defense attorney's opening statement? What are the four types of evidence? What instructions are given to the jury before deliberation begins?

conclusion:

The Trial—Justice Is the Goal

Police charges against the defendant are merely suggestions to the prosecutor. The prosecutor's charges at arraignment are but a hope. The decision of guilt or innocence is decided at the trial. Despite a constitutional guarantee of a trial by jury, over 90 percent of those charged with felony crimes choose to forego this procedure and plead guilty. A great number of professionals come together to make a trial possible. In the American judicial system, the trial is a conflict situation between the prosecutor and the defense. At the trial, the playing field is not level, but is tipped in favor of the defendant. The American judicial system recognizes the awesome power of the state compared to the limited resources of the accused and takes a number of opportunities to balance the power between the state and the defendant. Thus, even if the defendant is convicted, he or she has the right to appeal, a right denied to prosecutors if they lose the case. The procedure and rules of the trial are well defined, but the strategy and risk that go into the decision making and presentation of evidence are left to the professional judgment of the participants in the trial. Despite the differences among the various courts, all work toward a common objective—justice.

Chapter Summary

- Three types of criminal trials are state trials in courts of limited jurisdiction, state trials in courts of general jurisdiction, and federal criminal trials.
- Trials in courts of limited jurisdiction are usually quick, involve misdemeanor crimes, and vary in the degree of professionalism and training of the judge and courtroom personnel.
- Most trials are conducted in state courts of general jurisdiction. State courts and federal courts have different procedures but are more similar than they are different.
- The police and the prosecutor must work together to bring charges against the defendant. This requirement also acts as checks and balances against abuse of power.
- Before the trial, the court decides if the defendant is to be granted bail. Three kinds of bail are cash bond, that provided by bondsagents, and unsecured bond.
- Despite reforms in the bail system, there are still many problems with bail discriminating against the poor.
- Before defendants can stand trial, the court must assess their competence to assist the attorney in their defense and to understand the charges against them. If a defendant is not competent to stand trial, the trial is postponed.
- Plea bargaining is a very important mechanism for disposing of cases, as over 90 percent of defendants plead guilty. Plea bargaining can center around the charges or the sentence.
- Because of the Speedy Trial Act of 1974, most defendants must be brought to trial within 100 days of arrest. This requirement places great stress on the resources of the prosecutor and the court.
- The court administrator and the Clerk of Court play an important role in managing the court docket.
- Prior to the trial, the parties to the case may make a number of pretrial motions, including motions for continuance, discovery, change of venue, suppression, bill of particulars, severance of charges or defendants, and dismissal.
- Many people participate in making a trial possible. The court recorder, also known as the *court reporter*, records every word of the trial. The bailiff is responsible for security. The prosecutor is responsible for presenting the evidence against the defendant.
- The judge is a neutral party to the trial. The judge must ensure that the defendant gets a fair trial. The jury decides whether the defendant is guilty or not guilty.
- Defendants are entitled to court-appointed counsel if they cannot afford a lawyer. The three types of court-appointed counsel are assigned counsel, public defender, and contract attorney.
- The criminal trial starts with the selection of the jury. The state presents its witnesses and evidence first, followed by the defense presentation. After the evidence is presented, the defense summarizes its case, followed by the state's summary.

Vocabulary Review

bail, 302
bail bondsperson, 305
bailiff, 319
charge to the jury, 328
circumstantial evidence, 326
Clerk of Court, 315
competent to stand trial, 308
conditional release, 307
contempt of court, 319
court docket, 312
court reporter, 319
courtroom work group, 318
direct evidence, 326
double jeopardy, 299
gag order, 320
hearsay evidence, 326
indigent defense, 321
legal standards of evidence, 326
motion for a bill of particulars, 316
motion for change of venue, 316
motion for continuance, 315
motion for discovery, 316
motion for dismissal, 317
motion for severance of charges or defendants, 317
motion for suppression, 316
peremptory challenge, 324
pro bono, 321

prosecutorial discretion, 302
public defenders, 322
real evidence, 326
release on recognizance (ROR), 306
signature bond, 306
statute of limitations, 312
testimonial evidence, 326
unsecured bond, 306
voir dire, 324

Names and Events to Remember

1984 Bail Reform Act, 304
Barker v. Wingo, 313
Gideon v. Wainwright, 321
Eighth Amendment of the Constitution, 302
Klopfer v. North Carolina, 313
Manhattan Bail Project, 306
Public Defender's Office, 322
Sixth Amendment of the Constitution, 312
Speedy Trial Act of 1974, 313
Taylor v. Louisiana, 320

Think about This

1. Although the accused is arrested by the police based on probable cause of a crime, the prosecutor ultimately is responsible for bringing charges against the person, plea bargaining, or dropping the case. Should the prosecutor have such broad powers? What kinds of checks and balances could be built into the legal system so that prosecutors do not abuse their power?
2. In 1994, in Manassas, Virginia, a defendant sought to explain his violent behavior as the product of temporary insanity. While receiving a speeding ticket, Lonnie Weeks shot and killed a state trooper. Weeks argued that he did not realize what he had done until afterward, when he had the gun in his hand. On the basis of information in this chapter, how did the police and the prosecutor determine the charge of first-degree murder? Why was bail denied? Why was the case tried rather than plea bargained? How did the defense prepare its case; did it make any difference that Weeks was guilty? What standard of proof was required for an insanity plea? What standard of proof was required for a conviction? Weeks was convicted of first-degree murder. After considering evidence of mitigating circumstances, the jury confirmed the sentence of death, and this sentence was upheld on appeal to the U.S. Supreme Court. After requests for clemency failed, Weeks was executed by the state of Virginia on March 14, 2000.

ContentSelect

Go to the ContentSelect web site and type in the natural language search phrase "rules of evidence." Read "Proving Guilty Knowledge" from the April 2000 issue of the *FBI Law Enforcement Bulletin.* The article discusses the rule of evidence requiring the government to prove that the possessor of an illegal drug knowingly possessed the contraband. A person possessing drugs without knowledge is not guilty. Sample the article to answer the following questions.

1. What are some ways that police can establish knowledge of possession in the case of hidden compartments in a vehicle?
2. Explain the concept of "willful blindness." What does the *Model Penal Code* say regarding willful blindness?
3. In the case of multiple passengers in a vehicle with hidden contraband, what standard must be established to convict a person on possession?
4. Is the receipt of an unopened package containing contraband sufficient to convict?
5. Your text points out that rules of evidence must be followed. The article shows how hard it can sometimes be to correctly present evidence at a trial. Explain how detailed knowledge of the rules of evidence would improve chances for convictions.

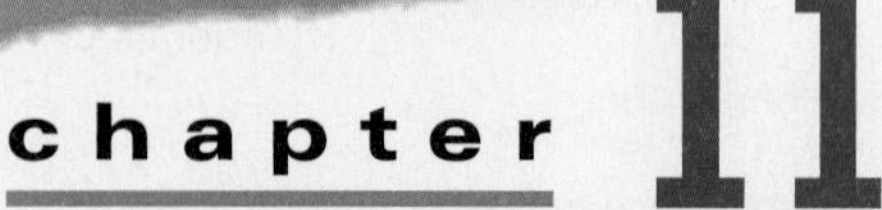

chapter 11

Sentencing and Sanctions

outline

Learning Objectives

After reading this chapter, you will know

- **The five contemporary philosophies regarding the purpose of punishment.**
- **The types of sentences used for persons convicted of misdemeanors and felonies.**
- **What takes place during presentencing investigations and sentencing hearings.**
- **How the "not guilty by reason of insanity" defense is used by defendants and what sanctions are imposed when an offender is pronounced insane.**
- **The differences between indeterminate and structured forms of sentencing.**
- **The reasons for controversies surrounding sentencing reform and the death penalty.**

Teen Sentenced to Four Hours of Polka Music

CAMBRIDGE, OH (AP)—A man was sentenced to listen to four hours of polka king Frankie Yankovic's greatest hits for driving through the city with his windows rolled down and his truck's stereo blaring.

Municipal Judge John Nicholson found Alan Law guilty of disorderly conduct and ordered him to pay a $100 fine or listen to polka tunes.

Law chose to face the music.

Nicholson picked Yankovic's music because he thought the 19-year-old Law would not be a fan of the Cleveland polka legend, who died in 1998.

"Most of the time I try to impart the Golden Rule to people: Do unto others as you would have others do unto you. You may enjoy listening to your music, but many people do not want to hear your music," Nicholson said.

Law listened to the full four hours of Yankovic's hits, which include "Blue Skirt Waltz," "Who Stole the Kishka" and "Too Fat Polka," in a police station interview room.

—"Teen Sentenced to Four Hours of Polka Music," reprinted with permission of The Associated Press.

introduction:

Convicted—Now What?

What was the purpose of Law's sentence? Did the punishment fit the crime? What would be the measure of its effectiveness?

Consider what happens once the defendant is convicted of a crime. Luis Alfredo Garavito, 42, confessed to killing 140 children in a 5-year spree in the South American country of Colombia. He was sentenced to 835 years in prison. The victims, mostly poor children of street vendors, were tied up, mutilated, and had their throats slit.[1] Rosemarie Radovan, 31, was sentenced to 3 months in jail and 5 years of probation for repeatedly leaving her 5-year-old and 7-year-old sons locked in the trunk of her car while she was at work. To drown out the boys' cries, she would turn up the radio.[2] A San Antonio High School basketball player threw an elbow, breaking the nose of an opposing player. The referees did not call a foul, but the young man was charged with aggravated assault and serious bodily injury and sentenced to 5 years in prison. The Bexar County prosecutor and the victim's parents argued that the punishment fit the crime. The defense attorney and mother of the defendant called the sentence "overkill in response to an unfortunate event." The defendant's mother vowed "to fight the prison sentence every step of the way, all the way."[3]

What is the appropriate punishment for these crimes? What is the purpose of punishment? Should perpetrators of crimes suffer pain similar to that which they inflicted on their victims? Are there crimes for which the death of the criminal is justified? Are some punishments too severe for the crime? This chapter examines sentencing and sanctions in the criminal justice system, including the death penalty.

Purpose of Criminal Sanctions

THE MAIN IDEA

Criminal sanctions are created to deter, incapacitate, seek retribution, or rehabilitate the offender and restore peace and justice in the community.

The history of punishment in the United States is rooted in economic sanctions, corporal punishment, and death. However, the concept of serving time in a prison or jail as punishment for a crime is a fairly new philosophy of the criminal justice system. Historically, punishments in England and the American colonies consisted primarily of fines, ordeals, and tortures. Criminals who could not afford to pay the fines imposed on them could be sold into economic servitude, a form of slavery, to pay the fines. **Corporal punishment** included whipping, branding, dunking, the stocks or pillory, and other pain-inflicting rituals.

corporal punishment The administration of bodily pain, based on the premise that a painful experience suffered as the result of criminal activity will deter future crime.

Five contemporary philosophies regarding the purpose of punishment are (1) deterrence, (2) incapacitation, (3) retribution, (4) rehabilitation, and (5) restorative justice. These are simple categories for classifying punishment, but often the law and circumstances are not so simple. Criminal sanctions may have more than one purpose and may have unstated or contradictory purposes.

Deterrence

Deterrence is based on the principle that punishment should prevent the criminal from reoffending. The problem is to identify what punishment or threat of punishment effectively prevents people from committing crimes or criminals from reoffending. Punishments based on deterrence include corporal punishment, threat of bodily harm based on the premise that people seek pleasure and avoid pain. Thus, a painful experience suffered as the result of criminal activity should, in theory, discourage the offender from committing future crimes.

CORPORAL PUNISHMENT Some people profess that corporal punishment is an effective deterrent to misconduct in raising properly behaved children and ensuring proper conduct in schools. As a result of this deeply rooted belief, attempts to pass laws prohibiting the use of corporal punishment against children and students by parents and teachers have been unpopular and unsuccessful.[4]

Although corporal punishment has been abandoned as an official punishment in the United States, many foreign countries continue to use some form of corporal punishment as an official sentence. In 2000, Nigeria introduced Islamic law, which sanctions the use of corporal punishment. Despite this, Nigeria received international criticism in January 2001 for flogging a 17-year-old Muslim girl 100 times for having premarital sexual relations, and later in August 2001, for sentencing a 20-year-old woman to 100 lashes with a cane for having an extramarital affair.[5] In August 2001, in just 4 days, Iran sentenced 20 people to be lashed. Their crime was drinking alcohol, an offense against Islamic law. Each offender received 80 lashes.[6] In November 2001, Saudi Arabia flogged 55 youths 15 lashes each for harassing women. They were arrested by a special police unit responsible for patrolling large shopping centers and educational institutions. Courts in Saudi Arabia routinely order lashings for minor crimes.[7] According to Human Rights Watch, in Iraq Saddam Hussein's government adopted the punishment of amputation of arms, legs, and ears for robbery, military desertion, and other crimes.

SPECIFIC AND GENERAL DETERRENCE Two types of deterrence are specific deterrence and general deterrence. **Specific deterrence** is when an individual who has committed a crime is deterred from committing that crime in the future by the nature of the punishment. Punishment with the power of specific deterrence would cause offenders not to drink alcohol again, for example, or not to harass women again, because of the unpleasant experience they suffered for their last offense.

General deterrence is the ability to prevent nonoffenders from committing crimes. General deterrence is based on the logic that people who witness the pain suffered by those who commit crimes will desire to avoid that pain and, hence, will refrain from criminal activity. Based on this belief, corporal punishment is often carried out in public so that others may witness the event. For example, in the Iranian flogging for drinking alcohol, over 1,000 people gathered in Vali-e-Asr Square in Teheran to watch the lashings. In England and the United States, hangings were once a public event, and parents brought their children to witness what happens when one breaks the law. Some advocates of general deterrence today propose that the death penalty would be a greater deterrent to crime if executions were broadcast live on television.

STERILIZATION AND DETERRENCE The dark side of deterrence is the historical belief, first made popular by Cèsar Lombroso, that crime is hereditary and criminals should be sterilized to prevent future crime. As you read in Chapter 3, sterilization of criminals was practiced in the United States during the early twentieth century. In the United States today, a chemical version of castration is legal, but the few cases in which it has been used have drawn criticism and protest. Supreme Court Justice Oliver Wendell Holmes argued for sterilization as an effective means to prevent crime. One criminologist has even argued that the drop in crime in the 1980s and 1990s was due to the

deterrence Philosophy and practices that emphasize making criminal behavior less appealing.

specific deterrence Deterrence based on the premise that an individual is best deterred from committing future crimes by the specific nature of the punishment.

general deterrence Deterrence based on the logic that people who witness the pain suffered by those who commit crimes will desire to avoid that pain and will refrain from criminal activity.

What philosophy of criminal sanctioning does corporal punishment reflect? How does making punishment public contribute to that goal? The administration of pain as a sanction against criminal offending has a long history and has been practiced at one time or another in most societies worldwide. What evidence is there that corporal punishment is effective in its goal? What are the other principal types of criminal sanctions?

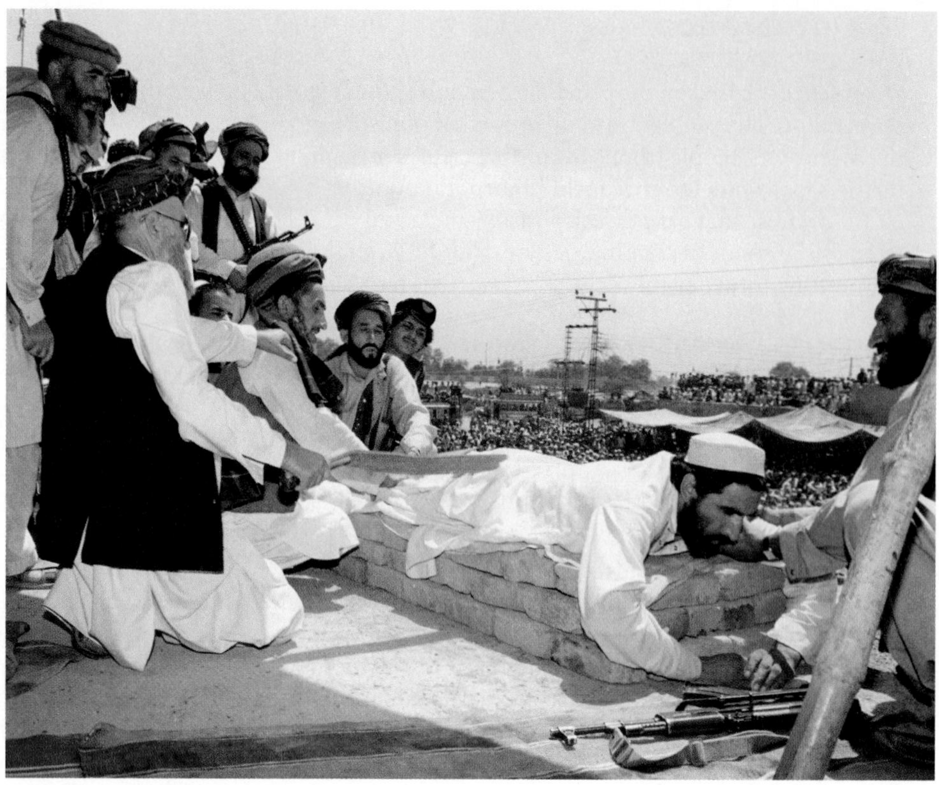

increase in abortion in the general population. Other countries have used sterilization to reduce the births of "socially undesirable" persons. Between 1935 and 1975, Sweden sterilized more than 63,000 citizens to improve Sweden's genetic stock. In addition, more than 200 mentally ill patients were starved to death between 1941 and 1943, and it is alleged that between 1944 and 1963, approximately 4,500 Swedish citizens were lobotomized, often against their will, as a form of treatment for homosexuality.[8] Until 1996, Japanese law allowed the forced sterilization of people with a broad range of mental or physical handicaps, hereditary diseases, and leprosy. Japanese Health Ministry statistics indicate that nearly 850,000 people were sterilized between 1949 and 1996.[9] The law was changed in 1996 due to a change in public sentiment.

Incapacitation

Another view of punishment is that if criminals cannot be deterred from committing further crimes, they should be prevented from having the opportunity to commit other crimes, a condition referred to as **incapacitation.** Katherine Mary Knight, 45, a slaughterhouse worker in Australia, was sentenced to life in prison without parole for the murder of John Price. Knight stabbed Price 37 times, decapitated him, skinned his body, and later included his flesh in meals for the son and daughter of the deceased. Australia does not have a death penalty. The sentencing judge, Justice Barry O'Keefe, said that Knight was a "very dangerous person" and ordered that she should never be released.[10]

incapacitation Deterrence based on the premise that the only way to prevent criminals from reoffending is to remove them from society.

banishment Removal of the offender from the community.

The concept of incapacitation as the purpose of criminal sanctions is based on the belief that there is no known way to prevent criminals from committing future crimes other than by removing them from society. Two of the oldest forms of incapacitation are banishment and transportation. Banishment as a criminal sanction may have begun in prehistoric times. **Banishment** removed offenders from society, often under the stipulation that if they returned, they would be put to death. This removal could be for a period of time or forever. In societies in which the protection and support of the group were essential to survival, banishment was considered a punishment nearly equal to death. Today, Georgia and Kentucky still use banishment. District Attorney Kelly Burke of Houston County, Georgia, favors legalized exile and has been successful in banning over 60 criminals from Houston county.[11] **Transportation** removed offenders from society by literally moving them to another place. England made extensive use of transportation as a criminal sanction. Until the American Revolutionary War, prisoners were transported to the American colonies. After the American Revolution, English convicts were transported to Australia until the mid-nineteenth century.[12] Transportation to penal colonies is not practiced today.

Modern means of incapacitation include confiscating the cars of accused drunk drivers and the property and valuables of drug dealers and members of organized crime. The argument of those in favor of the law is that without a car, it would be impossible to drive while intoxicated, and without wealth, it would be impossible to engage in illegal businesses like drug dealing. The most significant form of incapacitation, however, is imprisonment. Behind bars, a criminal is effectively prevented from having opportunities to commit more crimes.

Retribution

Retribution, or "just-desserts," argues that criminals should be punished because they deserve it. Retribution is associated with "get-tough" sentencing and the philosophy of an eye for an eye, which advocates that those who do wrong should pay for their crimes in equal measure. Traditionally, retribution was the victim's revenge. The victim was entitled to inflict punishment or to see that punishment was inflicted on the offender. Many who favor the death penalty argue that it is the most appropriate punishment for convicted murderers.

An example of this philosophy of retribution was the 2001 execution of a murderer by a 10-year-old boy under the Taliban's interpretation of Islamic law. Under this interpretation, relatives of a victim carry out the death sentence. Under the supervision of the Islamic court, the 10-year-old boy, the oldest male relative of the murdered man, shot the convicted man as thousands watched in southern Kandahar.[13]

Retribution relates to people's emotional response to a crime. For example, Kim Davis, 34, stole a car in Independence, Missouri. When he discovered that a 6-year-old child had been left in the vehicle, he tried to shove the boy outside. The boy became tangled in the seat belt, but Davis refused to stop. Horrified motorists who witnessed the awful scene pursued him for 5 miles before he was stopped. The boy did not survive the ordeal. Davis was charged with second-degree murder, robbery, child abuse, and kidnapping. A witness to the crime suggested that Davis should be "dragged himself, just like he dragged that kid."[14] In retribution, the criminal suffers—perhaps in a like manner—for the crime.

During the nineteenth and twentieth centuries, many prison officials and the public favored the idea that punishment was retribution. As a result, prison conditions often were deliberately harsh and cruel, and physical punishment was administered liberally to inmates. The public expected that prisoners would be punished while incarcerated.

Rehabilitation

Rehabilitation and restoration are more contemporary philosophies defining the purpose of criminal sanctions. **Rehabilitation** calls for criminal sanctions to "cure" the offender of criminality. The rehabilitation model often is referred to as the medical model in that it views criminality as a disease to be cured. Some believe rehabilitation

transportation Eighteenth-century practice by Great Britain of sending offenders to the American colonies and later Australia.

retribution Deterrence based on the premise that criminals should be punished because they deserve it.

rehabilitation Deterrence based on the premise that criminals can be "cured" of their problems and criminality and returned to society.

In Los Angeles, juvenile offenders work with severely disabled children at El Camino School as part of their jail time and rehabilitation program. Community service is a form of general restitution, which may be appropriate when it is not possible for an offender to remove the specific impacts of his or her crime on the victims. What are some other forms of restorative justice? How might restorative justice programs go hand in hand with rehabilitation programs? Goals of criminal sanctioning in the United States today tend not to focus on rehabilitating offenders and addressing the needs of victims. Why?

See http://www.curenational.org, the web site of CURE (Citizens United for Rehabilitation of Errants), a nonprofit national organization dedicated to reducing crime through rehabilitation programs and reforms of the criminal justice system. ■

of offenders is impossible. Advocates of rehabilitation favor approaches involving psychology, medical treatment, drug treatment, self-esteem counseling, education, and programs aimed at developing ethical values and work skills. Most rehabilitation efforts focus on juvenile delinquents and youthful offenders. The juvenile justice system is based on the principle that the primary purpose of the juvenile justice system is to rehabilitate. The criminal justice system and the public may accept that the purpose of criminal sanctions is to rehabilitate children and first-time offenders but often totally reject this premise for repeat and career offenders. Thus, the public may be willing to give the 14-year-old burglar the chance to turn his or her life around, but they would just as soon see the 45-year sexual offender spend the rest of his life in prison rather than give the system a chance to rehabilitate him.

Restorative Justice

restorative justice Model of deterrence that uses restitution programs, community work programs, victim-offender mediation, and other strategies to not only rehabilitate the offender but also address the damage done to the community and the victim.

Restorative justice focuses on rehabilitating the victims rather than the offenders. Rehabilitation often is criticized for forgetting the victim. The focus in rehabilitation is on the offender and what needs to be done to make him or her a productive, normal member of society. The restorative justice model does not argue against the rehabilitation of the offender, but it does advocate that the needs of the victim also must be central. Crime has a harmful effect on the victim and society, and justice requires that this harm be removed as much as possible. Restorative justice programs use restitution, community work programs, victim-offender mediation, and other strategies both to rehabilitate the offender and to address the damage done to the community and the victim. South Africa used this model to help heal the division between blacks and whites. South Africa's Truth and Reconciliation Commission allows those who committed hate crimes during apartheid, who confessed and repented of their crimes, to escape criminal sanctions. Table 11.1 shows the range of punishments given by state courts in a recent year.

JUST THE FACTS 11.1

What are the five main philosophies regarding the purpose of punishment? How do specific and general deterrence differ? What are the forms of incapacitation and retribution? How do rehabilitation and restorative justice differ?

table 11.1 Felons Sentenced to an Additional Penalty by State Courts

Judges may impose more than one sanction on a defendant. Felons who are sentenced to incarceration may also be fined, required to pay restitution, enter into treatment programs, or perform community service work.

Most Serious Conviction Offense	Percentage of Felons with an Additional Penalty of—				
	Fine	Restitution	Treatment	Community Service	Other
All Offenses	21%	13%	6%	6%	7%
Violent Offenses	18%	13%	5%	5%	6%
Murder[a]	9	10	1	3	2
Sexual assault[b]	16	11	8	4	7
Rape	12	10	9	3	8
Other sexual assault	18	12	8	4	5
Robbery	12	13	3	3	5
Aggravated assault	21	14	6	7	6
Other violent[c]	22	15	5	6	9
Property Offenses	21%	24%	5%	8%	7%
Burglary	19	23	5	6	7
Larceny[d]	21	21	4	7	9
Motor vehicle theft	12	21	5	5	17
Fraud[e]	24	29	5	11	5
Drug Offenses	22%	6%	6%	6%	7%
Possession	19	5	10	8	9
Trafficking	24	7	4	5	5
Weapon Offenses	18%	5%	4%	6%	6%
Other Offenses[f]	24%	9%	6%	6%	10%

Source: Bureau of Justice Statistics, *Felony Sentences in State Courts, 1998* (Washington, DC: U.S. Department of Justice, October 2001), p. 10.

Note: Where the data indicated affirmatively that a particular additional penalty was imposed, the case was coded accordingly. Where the data did not indicate affirmatively or negatively, the case was treated as not having an additional penalty. These procedures provide a conservative estimate of the prevalence of additional penalties. A felon receiving more than one kind of additional penalty appears under more than one table heading. This table is based on an estimated 927,717 cases.

[a]Includes nonnegligent manslaughter.

[b]Includes rape.

[c]Includes offenses such as negligent manslaughter and kidnapping.

[d]Includes motor vehicle theft.

[e]Includes forgery and embezzlement.

[f]Composed of nonviolent offenses such as receiving stolen property and vandalism.

criminal justice in the world

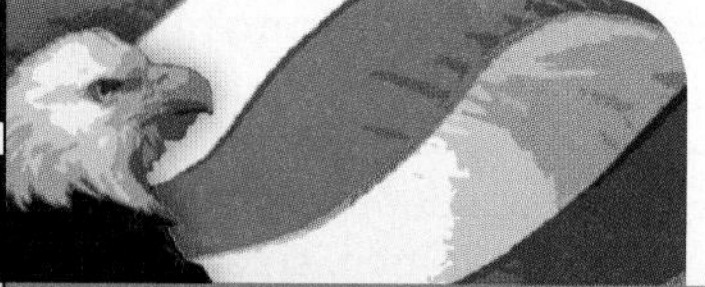

Terrorism: When the Punishment Does Not Fit the Crime

On October 18, 2001, just a few blocks from the smoking ruins of the World Trade Center, four disciples of Osama bin Laden were sentenced to life without parole. The four men were the first terrorists to be convicted in the United States by a civilian jury trial. The men were convicted of the 1998 bombings of the U.S. embassies in Kenya and Tanzania. In addition to the prison term, Judge Leonard B. Sand ordered each defendant to pay $33 million in restitution. In sentencing the terrorists, Judge Sand called terrorism "one of the most serious threats to our society... to the society of any civilized nation." Given the loss of life and destruction caused by the terrorists, some question whether the punishment fit the crime. Some critics argue that the criminal justice system cannot properly respond to crimes of terrorism. Israel, for example, has an aggressive military response to terrorism, involving the use of "targeted killings" rather than arrest and trial. Many object to Israel's policy of targeted killings of terrorists, but Israel's leader, General Sharon, protested that he finds little difference between his country's policy and the United States' policy of pursuing Osama bin Laden and Taliban terrorists in Afghanistan.[15]

Anticipating that the civilian criminal justice system may not prove adequate for the challenge, on November 13, 2001, President George Bush issued a controversial executive order that made terrorist defendants subject to trial by a military tribunal. The justification for this order was that members of al Qaeda had engaged in acts of international terrorism that could be considered violations of the laws of war, and that terrorism poses a national emergency. Under this executive order, the military has exclusive jurisdiction over any noncitizen accused of international terrorism who (1) is or was a member of al Qaeda, or (2) "has engaged in, aided or abetted, or conspired to commit acts of international terrorism, or acts in preparation therefor, that have caused, threaten to cause, or have as their aim to cause, injury to or adverse effects on the United States, its citizens, national security, foreign policy, or economy; or has knowingly harbored one or more [international terrorists]." The executive order also provides that its provisions may be expanded to include any other persons that the United States considers a threat.[16]

The executive order claims worldwide jurisdiction with

Sentencing

THE MAIN IDEA

Sentencing by a judge sets the punishment for an offense. State courts of limited jurisdiction oversee sentencing for misdemeanors, while state courts of general jurisdiction and U.S. magistrate courts oversee sentencing for felonies.

The jury (except in a bench trial) determines the guilt or innocence of the defendant, but the judge is responsible for determining the sentence the defendant receives. In **sentencing,** the judge evaluates the circumstances of the cases of everyone who pleads guilty or is convicted of an offense. The judge must also evaluate the possible sentences allowed by law and then select the sentence that best fits the case. All criminal laws passed by the state legislature or the U.S. Congress must specify the punishment or range of punishments that a judge can impose if a defendant is found guilty of violating that law. The only constitutional guideline for sentencing is the Eighth Amendment prohibition against cruel and unusual punishment. The U.S. Supreme Court has

sentencing The punishment for a crime as determined by a judge.

military tribunals at any time and place the Secretary of Defense decides. Persons subject to the order who are held by other agencies must be turned over for trial. The military tribunal may impose appropriate punishments, including life imprisonment and death.

Normally, aliens residing in the United States receive the same constitutional protections as United States citizens, but Bush's executive order negates these rights for persons accused of terrorism. The trial by military tribunal provides the accused with certain rights regarding admission of evidence and conduct of the prosecution but does not provide the same rights normally extended to non–United States citizens in civilian trials or to military personnel who are tried by military trial. For instance, the defense does not have the right to demand the disclosure of government intelligence methods before evidence is introduced, and conviction is by a two-thirds vote of the military tribunal. Persons conviction under the authority of the military tribunal cannot appeal.[17] Thus, the jurisdiction of the military tribunal is exclusive and final.

Defenders of civil rights attack the executive order for potential abuse through violations of constitutional rights and through racial and ethnic profiling. Other legal scholars argue that the order is necessary, given the extreme nature of the threat posed by international terrorism.[18] In the past, the U.S. Supreme Court has ruled that under certain circumstances, such as presidential assassinations and sabotage, persons may be denied due process.[19]

President Bush has defended trial by military tribunal. He argues that allowing international terrorists access to due process would be inappropriate. He said, "[We] must not let foreign enemies use the forums of liberty to destroy liberty itself."[20] Mr. Bush promised that military tribunal trials would be open to the public and the news media, and would have an appeals process.[21] Critics are most concerned about the lack of appeal to an independent authority, such as a judge or civilian court. They also fear the misuse of tribunals and the possible violation of international treaties, specifically the Geneva Convention. The Geneva Convention gives prisoners of war who are facing charges protections that include the right to choose their own lawyers, to be tried in courts that are independent of the prosecution, and to appeal convictions. Critics worry that if the United States suspends civil rights protections for international terrorists, other nations may retaliate and suspend the rights of United States citizens arrested in their jurisdictions.[22]

Some members of Congress see Bush's executive order an abuse of presidential power. The Bush administration maintains, however, that the president has the authority to enact such trial proceedings without specific congressional approval.[23]

■ **Do you think suspected terrorists should be given the same due process rights accorded to U.S. citizens? Why or why not? Do you think they should have the right to appeal their verdicts and sentences? How might the institution of military tribunals potentially change the American system of justice?**

allowed a broad interpretation of this amendment and, thus, few punishments have been found to be cruel and unusual.

The traditional criminal sanctions that a judge may impose are fines, imprisonment, probation, or some combination of these. Federal judges in U.S. District Court, military judges, and state judges in courts of general trial jurisdiction in states with the death penalty also may sentence a defendant to death. Federal and state judges have some flexibility in the sentences they can impose, so sentencing is not an automatic or routine function in which the outcome is always predictable. A comparison of state and federal felony convictions and sentences is shown in Table 11.2 on page 342, and characteristics of convicted felons are shown in Table 11.3 on page 344.

State judges in courts of limited jurisdiction (e.g., justice of the peace, municipal judge, etc.) and U.S. magistrate judges are more limited in the sentences that they can impose than are judges in state courts of general trial jurisdiction. As you read in Chapter 10, courts of limited jurisdiction, both federal and state, handle mostly misdemeanor crimes and violations. State judges in courts of limited jurisdiction cannot try felony cases.

A misdemeanor is a crime for which the maximum sentence cannot exceed 1 year in jail or prison. Also, the amounts of the fines for conviction of a misdemeanor are

table 11.2 Comparison of Felony Convictions in State and Federal Courts

Felony defendants generally are more likely to be convicted in federal court, with the exception of murder and some property crimes. Overall, defendants convicted in federal court receive longer prison terms, an average of 39 months for state felons versus 61 months for federal felons. Drug felons are sentenced to terms over twice as long in federal court than in state court.

Most Serious Conviction Offense	Felony Convictions			Federal Felony Convictions as Percentage of Total
	Total	State	Federal	
All Offenses	978,211	927,717	50,494	5.2%
Violent Offenses	167,294	164,584	2,710	1.6%
Murder	9,455	9,158	297	3.1
Sexual assault	29,910	29,693	217	0.7
Rape	11,703	11,622	81	0.7
Other sexual assault	18,207	18,071	136	0.7
Robbery	40,564	38,784	1,780	4.4
Aggravated assault	71,336	71,060	276	0.4
Other violent	16,029	15,889	140	0.9
Property Offenses	294,341	283,002	11,339	3.9%
Burglary	88,050	87,957	93	0.1
Larceny	109,115	107,621	1,494	1.4
Motor vehicle theft	14,518	14,368	150	1.0
Other theft	94,597	93,253	1,344	1.4
Fraud	97,176	87,424	9,752	10.0
Fraud	52,423	43,975	8,448	16.1
Forgery	44,753	43,449	1,304	2.9
Drug Offenses	335,493	314,626	20,867	6.2%
Possession	120,893	119,443	1,450	1.2
Trafficking	214,600	195,183	19,417	9.0
Weapon Offenses	35,064	31,904	3,160	9.0%
Other Offenses	146,019	133,601	12,418	8.5%

Source: Bureau of Justice Statistics, *Felony Sentences in State Courts, 1998* (Washington, DC: U.S. Department of Justice, October 2001), p. 3.

The vast majority of all felony convictions in the United States occurs in state courts. Overall, federal courts account for a relatively small number.

- In 1998, federal courts convicted 50,494 persons of a violent, property, drug, or other felony. State courts convicted 927,717, bringing the combined U.S. total to 978,211 felons convicted. Federal courts accounted for 5% of the national total.
- Violent offenses comprised 5% of felony convictions in federal courts but 18% of those in state courts.
- In 1998, 82% of felons convicted in federal courts were sentenced to incarceration. The remaining 18%

Most Serious Conviction Offense	Percentage of Felons Sentenced to Incarceration (Prison or Jail)		Mean Maximum Sentence Length (in Months) for Felons Sentenced to Incarceration (Prison or Jail)	
	State	Federal	State	Federal
All Offenses	68%	82%	39 mo	61 mo
Violent Offenses	78%	92%	77 mo	89 mo
Murder	96	91	258	113
Sexual assault	82	87	94	75
Rape	84	88	125	138
Other sexual assault	80	86	74	37
Robbery	88	96	94	91
Aggravated assault	72	74	44	39
Other	67	86	37	115
Property Offenses	65%	59%	31 mo	23 mo
Burglary	75	52	39	27
Larceny	64	54	25	32
Motor vehicle theft	76	76	22	28
Other theft	62	52	26	33
Fraud	55	60	27	22
Fraud	49	60	30	23
Forgery	61	60	25	20
Drug Offenses	68%	92%	31 mo	79 mo
Possession	65	87	21	84
Trafficking	71	93	37	79
Weapon Offenses	66%	92%	29 mo	101 mo
Other Offenses	63%	81%	25 mo	32 mo

received probation. State courts sentenced 68% of felons to incarceration (prison or jail) and 32% to straight probation.

- The average federal incarceration sentence was just over 5 years in 1998. By contrast, state incarceration sentences (prison or jail) had an average of 3 years and 3 months.
- Federal drug offenders received incarceration terms that were about twice the length of drug offenders in state courts (6 years and 7 months versus 2 years and 7 months).
- In 1998, federal offenders released from prison served an average of 91% of their prison term before release. Felons convicted in state courts served a significantly smaller proportion of their total incarceration sentence. For instance, state prisoners (not including felons sentenced to jail) served about 47% of their total prison sentence in 1998.

table 11.3 Demographic Characteristics of Persons Convicted of Felonies by State Courts

Males account for 80% to 90% of all felony convictions. Most convicted felons are between 20 and 39 years old. Blacks appear to be disproportionately represented, as they comprise about 14% of the total population but 31% to 69% of convicted felons.

Most Serious Conviction Offense	Percentage of Convicted Felons											
		Sex		Race			Age at Sentencing					
	Total	Male	Female	White	Black	Other	13–19	20–29	30–39	40–49	50–59	60+
All Offenses	100%	83%	17%	55%	44%	1%	9%	39%	32%	16%	3%	1%
Violent Offenses	100%	90%	10%	53%	44%	3%	12%	41%	28%	13%	4%	2%
Murder[a]	100	92	8	42	57	1	12	49	21	12	4	2
Sexual assault[b]	100	97	3	69	26	5	7	34	31	16	8	4
Rape	100	98	2	67	32	1	6	36	32	16	7	3
Other sexual assault	100	96	4	70	23	7	7	34	30	16	8	5
Robbery	100	92	8	35	64	1	22	47	22	8	1	–
Aggravated assault	100	86	14	56	41	3	9	40	30	15	4	2
Other violent[c]	100	89	11	67	32	1	9	39	28	17	5	2
Property Offenses	100%	75%	25%	60%	38%	2%	10%	40%	32%	14%	3%	1%
Burglary	100	92	8	64	35	1	17	43	27	11	2	–
Larceny[d]	100	76	24	57	41	2	10	39	31	16	3	1
Motor vehicle theft	100	91	9	69	27	4	18	48	26	7	1	–
Fraud[e]	100	58	42	62	37	1	4	39	36	16	4	1
Drug Offenses	100%	82%	18%	46%	53%	1%	7%	39%	33%	17%	3%	1%
Possession	100	79	21	55	44	1	5	34	36	20	4	1
Trafficking	100	84	16	42	57	1	8	43	30	15	3	1
Weapon Offenses	100%	94%	6%	49%	50%	1%	10%	47%	26%	12%	4%	1%
Other Offenses[f]	100%	88%	12%	67%	31%	2%	7%	35%	34%	18%	5%	1%

Source: Bureau of Justice Statistics, *Felony Sentences in State Courts, 1998* (Washington, DC: U.S. Department of Justice, October 2001), p. 6.

Note: Data on sex were available for 773,028 cases; on race, 647,483; and on age, 748,225.

—Less than 0.5%.

[a]Includes nonnegligent manslaughter.

[b]Includes rape.

[c]Includes offenses such as negligent manslaughter and kidnapping.

[d]Includes motor vehicle theft.

[e]Includes forgery and embezzlement.

[f]Composed of nonviolent offenses such as receiving stolen property and vandalism.

limited. As a result of these limitations, judges in courts of limited jurisdiction give much shorter sentences than do judges in courts of general jurisdiction. Usually, conviction for a misdemeanor does not result in imprisonment. Imprisonment was imposed in only 14.7 percent of federal misdemeanor convictions in 1999. Twice as many defendants (28.4%) only paid a fine. In federal misdemeanor sentences of imprisonment, the sentence was for 4 months or less. Nearly half (48%) of defendants convicted of a misdemeanor in federal court were sentenced to probation.[24]

State judges in courts of limited jurisdiction rarely have a staff of people to help them in determining the best sentence. Some misdemeanor crimes may only allow for a maximum sentence of a few days (i.e., 10 to 30 days) or a fine not to exceed $100 to $500 dollars. With such limitations imposed by law, sentencing by judges in courts of limited jurisdiction is significantly different than that in state and federal courts of general trial jurisdiction.

JUST THE FACTS 11.2

What is sentencing? Where and how are offenders convicted of misdemeanors sentenced? How does court jurisdiction affect sentencing?

Presentence Investigation Report

THE MAIN IDEA

After a defendant is found guilty, a sentence is determined through a process of presentence investigation and sentencing hearings.

A presentence investigation involves gathering information about the convicted offender to help determine the best sentence. Personnel from Federal Probation and Parole conduct federal presentence investigations. State presentence investigators may be from the state office of probation and parole or from a separate staff employed by the court to conduct presentence investigations.

In courts of general jurisdiction, how do judges decide the right sentence for a particular case? Following conviction, either by plea or trial, the defendant is returned to jail and the judge begins the process of determining the appropriate sentence. Federal and state judges of general trial jurisdiction are assisted in this process by a staff of people who conduct a presentence investigation.

Go to http://www.flmp.uscourts.gov/Presentence/presentence.htm. This United States Probation Office site explains presentence investigation and provides downloadable questionnaires and forms used during this process. ■

Unlike the impression of trials and sentencing in television and the movies, in which arrest, trial, and sentencing follow in rapid succession, the process from arrest to sentencing is rather lengthy. The average length of time from arrest to sentencing for felony cases disposed by trial by state courts in 1998 was 352 days, and 216 days for cases disposed by guilty plea. Generally, the more serious the crime, the longer the time from arrest to sentencing.[25]

The **presentence investigator**—a probation and parole officer who works for the court—has the responsibility of investigating the life led by the offender, any previous crimes and punishments received, the offender's attitude toward his or her crime, and the impact of the crime on the community and victims. After conviction, a defendant is expected to cooperate with presentence investigators and does not have the right to remain silent. All previous crimes committed by the offender may be considered in the sentencing process. The defendant's employment history, family relationships, and reputation in the community may all be considered. Prior convictions for any crime are a significant factor in determining the sentence. The average prison sentence for all state

presentence investigator
The person appointed by the court to investigate the offender's life, previous crimes and punishments, and present attitudes, as well as the impact of the crime on victims and the community.

felony convictions is 51 months for defendants who have only one prior conviction but rises to 75 months for those with two or more prior convictions.[26]

The offender may be required to complete interviews and life history forms as part of the presentence investigation. Defendants who refuse to provide information may be classified as uncooperative, which can be a factor in sentencing. Convicted defendants who do not accept responsibility for their guilt or do not express remorse for their crime may receive a more severe sentence.

The completed **presentence investigation report** is forwarded to the judge for his or her review. The report contains a recommendation for a specific criminal sanction. For example, if the presentence investigation report recommends a fine, the investigator will already have investigated the convict's finances to determine what he or she can pay. If unable to pay a court-assessed fine, an offender may not be imprisoned in lieu of the fine. The judge forwards a copy of the report to the prosecutor and the defense attorney. The investigator's role is important. In over 90 percent of the cases, the judge accepts the recommended sanction outlined in the presentence investigation report.

Sentencing Hearing and Victim Impact Statements

The judge sets a date for a **sentencing hearing,** at which the prosecution and the defense have the opportunity to critique the recommended criminal sanction. Presentence investigators may be called to testify as to how they compiled the data for their report and what influenced them in making a specific recommendation for a criminal sanction.

The judge also may allow **victim impact statements** at the presentence hearing, in which victims of the crime get a chance to influence sentencing. Victim impact statements are controversial. Technically, defendants are punished for what they did, regardless of who the victims were. Sentencing is not supposed to be based on whether the victim was a homeless person or a beloved member of the community. Because of the emotional nature of the victims' testimony, some civil rights advocates consider victim impact statements prejudicial and biased.[27] Defenders of victim impact statements argue that the harm and suffering caused to others is an appropriate factor in determining the offender's sentence. Both the defense and the prosecutor can appeal the sentence.

presentence investigation report Personal information about a convicted felon and the circumstances of the crime that is used to help determine the most appropriate sentence.

sentencing hearing A gathering before a judge that hears appeals, in which the prosecution and the defense argue the accuracy of the presentence report and the appropriateness of the sentence.

victim impact statements Statements that the victims of a crime make at the sentencing hearing for the convicted offender.

JUST THE FACTS 11.3

What information is obtained during the presentence investigation? How does the presentencing report influence sentencing? What other presentencing events and offender actions may affect the sentence?

Sanctions and the Mentally Ill Offender

THE MAIN IDEA

The insanity defense exists for defendants who claim that they lacked the ability to understand the criminality or harm in their actions.

As you read in Chapter 4, the insanity defense is based on the legal principle that defendants lack the necessary *mens rea* to be held criminally liable for their actions. Criminal law provides a similar defense for young children and for people with diminished intellectual capacity or mental retardation. Because the insanity defense is based on the claim of mental illness, people often mistake insanity as a mental health term. However, *insanity* is only a legal term, not a mental health term.[28] Only a jury, and not mental health professionals, can pronounce that a defendant is insane.

See http://www.law.umkc.edu/faculty/projects/ftrials/hinckley/BACKLASH.HTM. This web site describes changes in the insanity defense after the Hinckley trial. ■

Defining Insanity

Federal courts and state courts have different standards for defining insanity, but all federal courts use the same standard. When John Hinckley attempted to assassinate former President Ronald Reagan, he was acquitted in federal court based on a plea of insanity. The federal test of insanity in the early 1980s was if defendants lacked the capacity to appreciate the wrongfulness of their conduct or to conform their conduct to the requirements of the law. Because of the public outrage over the laxity of the federal insanity standard, however, this standard was made more conservative, making it more difficult to prove claims of insanity. The U.S. Congress passed the **Insanity Defense Reform Act of 1984,** under which the federal courts adopted a new standard of insanity.[29] The defendant had to prove insanity at the time of the crime by clear and convincing evidence. Mental disease or defect was no longer considered sufficient to avoid punishment. "Psychiatric evidence which negates mens rea . . . negates an element of the offense rather than constituting a justification or excuse."[30]

As you read in Chapter 10, when the defendant pleads not guilty by reason of insanity, the court arranges for the defendant to be examined by mental health professionals prior to the trial. The court, the defendant, and the prosecutor have input as to who is selected to examine the defendant. At the trial, these mental health professionals are called as expert witnesses to give their opinion as to the defendant's state of mind at the time of the crime. The defense must prove that the defendant was guilty but insane, while the prosecution must present evidence that the defendant is sane. It is not unusual at a trial to have mental health professionals give very different assessments of the defendant's mental health. The jury must digest the evidence and decide whether the defendant's mental health meets the legal standard of insanity. If it does, the defendant is **not guilty by reason of insanity.** If it does not, the defendant is guilty as charged.

The Insanity Defense Reform Act of 1984

The Insanity Defense Reform Act of 1984 requires that, in federal courts, the defendant found not guilty by reason of insanity must undergo a civil commitment examination within 40 days of the verdict. The **civil commitment process** determines whether the defendant should be released or confined to an institution for the mentally ill. The purpose is to determine whether defendants are a danger to themselves or to the public. If found to be a danger to the public or themselves, defendants may be involuntarily confined to a civil mental health institution until the medical staff determines that they are no longer a danger. In addition, defendants may be forced to undergo medical and drug treatment and may be denied their liberty for the rest of their lives. Because a successful insanity defense usually leads to a sentence that differs little from life imprisonment, the insanity defense is not used for misdemeanors or lesser felonies but is almost exclusively used in first-degree homicide cases.

not guilty by reason of insanity A verdict in which the defense has proven to the jury's satisfaction that the defendant was guilty but legally insane.

civil commitment process Process by which a person found not guilty by reason of insanity can be either released or confined in a mental institution.

State Courts and the Insanity Plea

State courts have adopted diverse standards for a successful insanity defense. Some still use the right-wrong test, others have adopted the *Model Penal Code* substantial capacity test (see Chapter 4), and a few have adopted standards combining elements of both

In 1982, John Hinckley was found not guilty by reason of insanity in the attempted murder of President Reagan. Many believed that Hinckley "got away with murder," and in response to public outrage over the outcome of the trial, many states enacted a new type of verdict, "guilty but mentally ill." With this verdict, a defendant is sentenced to prison but is supposed to be given psychological treatment in that setting, whereas with the "not guilty by reason of insanity" verdict, a defendant is acquitted and civil commitment proceedings are undertaken to have the person confined to a mental institution. John Hinckley remains indefinitely confined at St. Elizabeth's Hospital in Washington, DC.

of these tests of insanity. A number of states have adopted a new verdict—**guilty but mentally ill.** Michigan was the first state to adopt this verdict in 1975. The verdict provides the jury the option of finding that the defendant was indeed mentally ill, perhaps suffering from a serious mental illness, but that the defendant was "sufficiently in possession of his faculties to be morally blameworthy for his acts."[31]

In states that have adopted it, the guilty but mentally ill verdict is an alternative to the not guilty by reason of insanity verdict. Thus, the jury has the option of finding defendants mentally ill but morally responsible for their acts, or insane and lacking the *mens rea* to be held criminally liable. In the latter case, the defendant is involuntarily confined to a civil mental health facility, but if found guilty but mentally ill, the defendant is sentenced to incarceration in a state prison following psychiatric treatment. During confinement at a mental institution, if doctors determine that the defendant is no longer suffering from mental illness, he or she is not released but is transferred to the state prison to serve his or her sentence. The time that the offender spent in the mental institution counts toward the sentence to be served. Once returned to the regular prison population, offenders may still be considered mentally ill to some degree, but their medical and psychiatric problems will not excuse them from incarceration for the crime.

Public Fear of the Insanity Plea

The public fear that the successful use of the insanity defense poses a grave danger because it allows defendants to escape incarceration does not appear to be justified. A very small number of defendants choose to plead not guilty by reason of insanity.[32] Offenders found to be not guilty by reason of insanity rarely obtain their freedom following the verdict.[33] Media coverage has sensationalized unusual cases, such as that of Lorena Bobbitt, who successfully pleaded insanity to a charge of cutting off her husband's penis and was freed completely within 2 months of the verdict, and John Hinckley, who escaped possible lifetime incarceration by use of the insanity plea. However, these cases are not typical of defendants found guilty by reason of insanity.

guilty but mentally ill An alternative verdict in capital cases based on the standard that the defendant was mentally ill but also was sufficiently aware (had sufficient *mens rea*) to be held "morally blameworthy" for the crime.

What happens in sentencing when a defendant is not successful in his or her insanity plea? The judge may require that the convicted offender undergo a mental competency examination. If the offender is found mentally unfit for incarceration in the state or federal prison, he or she is placed in a maximum-security mental health facility that can provide appropriate psychiatric treatment. Some states have special correctional facilities for such patients. Medical authorities determine if or when the offender can be returned to the prison population. The time spent in the medical institution counts toward the sentence to be served.

JUST THE FACTS 11.4

What is the difference between not guilty by reason of insanity and guilty but mentally ill? How are cases based on the insanity defense processed and disposed? What are the provisions of the Insanity Defense Reform Act of 1984?

Sentencing Models

THE MAIN IDEA

Two models that govern the practice of sentencing in courts of general trial jurisdiction are indeterminate sentencing and structured sentencing.

At one time, state and federal judges had nearly complete discretion in sentencing an offender, because most states and the federal courts used the indeterminate model of sentencing. The **indeterminate sentencing** model gives the judge the most power and flexibility in setting the sentence of the offender. In the late nineteenth century, as incarceration became a common punishment for serious crimes, the predominant correctional philosophy was that offenders should demonstrate that they had changed their criminal attitudes and lifestyles as a condition of release. Thus, judges were given wide latitude in the sentences they could impose for crimes. Because no one could predict exactly when offenders would demonstrate that they were rehabilitated, offenders were given sentences of indeterminate length. For example, an offender might receive a sentence of a minimum of 1 year and a maximum of 20 years in prison. The exact number of years to be served would be determined by the prisoner's behavior and progress toward rehabilitation.

Indeterminate sentencing came under criticism in the late twentieth century. In addition to giving the judge wide latitude in sentencing, indeterminate sentencing also gave extensive power to prison authorities. In reality, it was prison authorities, not the judge, who determined the term of sentence to be served. Prison officials could arbitrarily exercise this power with little or no oversight. To cure the ills of indeterminate sentencing, state and federal legislation adopted **structured sentencing** models, including (1) determinate sentencing, (2) mandatory sentencing and habitual offender sentencing laws, (3) sentencing guidelines, and (4) presumptive sentencing.

indeterminate sentencing A model of sentencing in which judges have nearly complete discretion in sentencing an offender.

structured sentencing A sentencing model—including determinate sentencing, sentencing guidelines, and presumptive sentencing—that defines punishments rather than allowing indeterminate sentencing.

determinate sentencing A sentencing model in which the offender is sentenced to a fixed term of incarceration.

Determinate versus Indeterminate Sentencing

In **determinate sentencing,** the offender is sentenced to a fixed term of incarceration. This term may be reduced by parole or good behavior, but other than that, the inmate knows when he or she is scheduled for release from prison. Determinate sentencing is also known as "flat sentences" or "fixed sentences." Determinate sentencing was a sentencing reform that emerged in the 1970s to provide more equity and proportionality in sentencing. Proponents claimed that it would eliminate racial discrimination.[34]

Determinate sentencing reform did not become popular, however. Only Arizona adopted a determinate sentencing model. A few other states (California, Illinois, Indiana, and Maine) adopted sentencing models based on determinate sentencing but still provided for discretion in sentencing.[35]

Go to http://www.ncjrs.org/txtfiles1/nij/184253.txt. Read a research paper on issues of determinate sentencing—for example, Joan Petersilia, *When Prisoners Return to the Community: Political, Economic, and Social Consequences* (National Institute of Justice, November 2000). ■

Mandatory Sentencing and Habitual Offender Laws

A controversial sentencing model is **mandatory sentencing**—the strict application of full sentences, adopted because of public perception that offenders were "getting off too light." Concerned that judges were too lenient in sentencing, many states adopted legislation mandating that offenders convicted of crimes serve the sentence for that crime as specified by law. Thus, sentencing was not left to the discretion of the judge. Mandatory sentences have been applied mostly to crimes involving drugs or the use of firearms. For crimes with mandatory sentences, if the defendant is convicted, the sentence for the crime is specified by the law, and the judge has no authority to change the sentence based on mitigating circumstances. For example, if the law states that the prison term for committing a crime with a firearm is 2 years, then the judge must sentence the defendant to 2 years.

Mandatory sentencing also has been applied to repeat offenders and domestic violence offenders through **habitual offender laws.** California has received much press concerning its **three strikes law,** in which repeat offenders receive longer mandatory sentences. Proponents argue that "getting tough on crime" reduces crime by taking repeat offenders off the streets. Opponents argue that the three strikes law creates situations in which offenders are receiving disproportionately long prison terms for minor crimes, such as possession of marijuana. A case in 1998 illustrated this argument when a man who stole four chocolate chip cookies from a restaurant was sentenced to serve 26 years to life in prison under the state's three strikes law.[36] California Judge Jean Rheinheimer sentenced the offender, who had previously been convicted of burglary and assault with a firearm, to this long prison term. The theft carried a maximum 3-year sentence, but Judge Rheinheimer sentenced the offender under the three strikes law. To the defense's request for leniency, Judge Rheinheimer commented, "I just see no reason to say Mr. Weber is anything other than the three-strikes defendant the people and the Legislature had in mind when they enacted this law."[37]

Concerned that the criminal justice system was ignoring domestic violence or not taking domestic violence cases seriously, several states adopted mandatory sentencing for conviction of domestic violence. Sometimes, these sentences are for short periods of time, such as 48 hours, or involve only probation. Nevertheless, the convicted offender finds that he or she can no longer escape punishment for domestic violence.[38] Critics of mandatory sentencing argue that there may be unique circumstances in a case that make mandatory sentences inappropriate. Judges are critical of mandatory sentences, as they greatly reduce the authority of the judge in determining the sentence.

mandatory sentencing The strict application of full sentences in the determinate sentencing model.

habitual offender laws Tough sentencing laws, such as "three strikes" laws, to punish repeat offenders more harshly.

three strikes law The application of mandatory sentencing to give repeat offenders longer prison terms.

sentencing guidelines A sentencing model in which crimes are classified according to their seriousness, and a range of time to be served is mandated for crimes within each category.

Sentencing Guidelines

Sentencing guidelines have been adopted by most states. In **sentencing guidelines,** crimes are classified according to seriousness, and a range of time is mandated for crimes within each category. Each state has its own classification for the seriousness of a crime and the corresponding length of sentence that can be imposed for that crime. Federal crimes are defined by Section 3559, U.S. Code, Title 18 into felonies and misdemeanors and are representative of the scheme used by most states in setting sentencing guidelines. The federal court distinguishes five classifications for felony crimes and three classifications for misdemeanors:

- **Title 18 Felonies**

  Class A felony—maximum sentence of life imprisonment or, if authorized, death

  Class B felony—a minimum sentence of 25 years' imprisonment to life imprisonment. The death penalty is not permitted

Class C felony—a maximum sentence of 25 years but no less than 10 years' imprisonment

Class D felony—a maximum sentence of 10 years but no less than 5 years' imprisonment

Class E felony—a maximum sentence of 5 years but more than 1 year of imprisonment

- **Title 18 Misdemeanors**

Class A misdemeanor—a maximum sentence of 1 year of imprisonment but no less than 1 month of imprisonment

Class B misdemeanor—a maximum sentence of 6 months' imprisonment but no less than 30 days

Class C misdemeanor—a maximum sentence of 30 days' imprisonment but no less than 5 days

The sentencing schedule of many states reflects this same graduated sentencing pattern but may have different cut-off points for classifying the sentence. In the sentencing guideline model, the judge must select a sentence corresponding to the seriousness of the crime as defined by the sentencing guidelines.

Presumptive Sentencing

Presumptive sentencing is a structured sentencing model that attempts to balance indeterminate sentencing with determinate sentencing. Presumptive sentencing gives discretionary powers to the judge within certain limits. The best known presumptive sentencing model is used by the federal court according to the Sentencing Reform Act of 1984. The **Sentencing Reform Act of 1984** set minimum and maximum terms of imprisonment for the various federal offenses. It then provided an adjustment for the offender's criminal history and for aggravating or mitigating circumstances. After conviction, the judge must sentence the offender using the ***Federal Sentencing Guidelines Manual.***[39] Based on the offense and the offender's history, a base sentence is determined in months (e.g., 135–180 months). The offender's sentence can be increased by adding months for aggravating factors such as the use of a firearm, failing to cooperate with arresting authorities, lack of remorse, failure to recover stolen property, and so forth. The offender's sentence also can be shortened by months for mitigating factors, such as cooperating with arresting authorities, making restitution, providing information to authorities leading to the arrest of others involved in the crime, and so forth. The judge literally calculates a sentence using the base sentence in months listed in the *Federal Sentencing Guidelines Manual* and the addition and subtraction of months to this base sentence based on mitigating and aggravating factors. If the judge departs significantly from the *Federal Sentencing Guidelines,* he or she must provide written reasons for this deviation at the sentencing hearing. The prosecution or defense can appeal the sentence.

Federal judges protested the imposition of the federal sentencing guidelines, arguing that they violated the separation of powers clause. The argument was that the legislative branch of the government did not have the authority to dictate sentencing guidelines to the judicial branch of the government. Ironically, the U.S. Supreme Court was the final arbiter of the dispute and ruled that Congress is within its powers to legislate sentencing guidelines.[40]

presumptive sentencing
A structured sentencing model that attempts to balance sentencing guidelines with mandatory sentencing and at the same time provide discretion to the judge.

The Sentencing Reform Act of 1984 restricted, but did not abolish, plea bargaining. First, sentence-reduction plea bargaining cannot permit the offender to receive less than the minimum mandatory sentence for the offense.[41] Second, if plea bargaining results in reduced charges, the court record and plea bargaining agreement must fully disclose the details of the actual crime. Thus, if the crime of sexual assault is reduced to burglary, the court record will still contain the details of the crime of sexual assault. This record is public information. Thus, offenders cannot hide their crimes from the public and the media by plea bargaining to a lesser included crime.

One consideration in the use of presumptive sentencing is that it abolishes parole, or early release from prison. This is a stumbling block for states that want to adopt a presumptive sentencing model similar to the federal court model. Parole provides for the possibility that an offender sentenced to serve 9 years in prison may only serve one-third of that time. Many states depend on parole to move offenders through the correctional system, as there are not enough prison beds to accommodate the number of sentenced offenders. Thus, before these states could adopt a presumptive sentencing model, they would have to build more prisons. The federal correctional system has the ability to move inmates throughout the United States, which allows the federal government to manage prison overcrowding by moving prisoners to less-crowded facilities. State corrections do not have this option, however. Hawaii, for example, utilizes all the bed space it has for prisoners and is forced to ship prisoners to other states because of the cost of and public objections to building additional prisons on the islands. It would be a great hardship on the state economy to complicate the problem by eliminating parole.

Truth in Sentencing

Because they cannot eliminate parole, some states have taken another approach, called "truth in sentencing." **Truth in sentencing** legislation requires the court to disclose the actual prison time that the offender is likely to serve. Some states (Arizona, California, and Illinois) have gone one step further and adopted what is known as the 85 percent requirement rule, which states that the offender must serve at least 85 percent of the sentence before becoming eligible for release. Thus, an offender sentenced to 10 years in prison would have to serve 8.5 years before being eligible for early release. Because offenders in many states routinely serve only one-third to one-half of their sentences, the 85 percent requirement significantly increases the actual time in prison.

JUST THE FACTS 11.5

What criticisms were leveled against indeterminate sentencing? What are the three major types of structured sentencing? What are the benefits, drawbacks, and potential abuses of each? How did the Sentencing Reform Act of 1984 change methods of structured sentencing?

truth in sentencing In the application of presumptive sentencing in states that cannot eliminate parole, the legal requirement that courts disclose the actual prison time the offender is likely to serve.

capital punishment The sentence of death.

Sentencing and the Death Penalty

THE MAIN IDEA

Capital punishment is an ongoing issue in American justice. Imposition of the death penalty requires special procedures in the courts.

Capital punishment—the death penalty—can be traced back to the earliest records of human history. In English common law, the roots of the American system of justice, even minor thefts could be punished by death, and the prisoner could be tortured in the process. The punishment for treason under English common law in 1776 was to be hanged but taken down while still alive, so bowels could be removed and burned before the prisoners, their heads cut off and their bodies quartered.[42] The American colonists did not shun the use of the death penalty. The criminal codes of 1642 and 1650 of the New Haven colony mandated the use of the death penalty not only for crimes of murder and treason, but also for crimes such as denying the true God and His attributes, bestiality, theft, horse theft, and children above the age of 16 striking their natural father or mother.[43]

Go to www.derechos.org; Derechos Human Rights is the first Internet-based human rights organization. This web site offers a plethora of links to sites with information on the death penalty. ■

Many Western countries, including England, France, Germany, and Italy, have banned the death penalty, while China and Japan have retained it. Some nations have retained the death penalty in forms that are alien to American values. China, for example, executes prisoners by shooting them in the back of the head. Execution by Sharia law, law based on Islamic religious values, also is harsh. For example, in March 2000, Judge Allah Baksh Ranja of Pakistan sentenced to death a man convicted of strangling and dismembering 100 children. The judge ordered Javed Iqbal, 42, executed in a Lahore park in front of his victims' parents. He told the prisoner, "You will be strangled in front of the parents whose children you killed. Your body will then be cut into a hundred pieces and put in acid, the same way you killed the children."[44]

In the United States, lethal injection is the predominant method of execution (36 of the 38 states with a death penalty). Eleven states authorize electrocution; 4 states, lethal gas; 3 states, hanging; and 3 states, firing squad. Eighteen states authorize more than one method—lethal injection and an alternative method—usually decided by the condemned prisoner. The federal government uses lethal injection for offenses prosecuted under 28 CFR, Part 26. Federal cases prosecuted under the Violent Crime Control Act of 1994 (18 U.S.C. 3596) call for the method used in the state in which the conviction took place.[45]

Opposition to the Death Penalty

As the poll in Figure 11.1 on page 354 shows, the death penalty as a legal sanction enjoys popular support from the public. Other data indicates it is also supported by politicians and medical doctors.[46] However, a number of people strongly oppose the death penalty as a criminal sanction. One of the earliest debates about the death penalty was recorded by the Greek philosopher Plato regarding Socrates, who was convicted by the Athenians of corrupting the morals of the youth and was sentenced to death. A friend tried to convince Socrates that he should escape because he was wrongfully convicted, and said that other cities would welcome him as a citizen because they would recognize that the sentence was unjust. Socrates refused, however, arguing, "But whether in battle or in a court of law, or in any other place, he must do what his city and his country order him; or he must change their view of what is just.... He who has experience of the manner in which we order justice and administer the State, and still remains, has entered into an implied contract that he will do as we command him."[47] This argument—that there is an implicit contract between the individual and the state—is the crux of one of the most controversial debates in sentencing—the role of capital punishment.

Those opposed to the use of capital punishment are called abolitionists. **Abolitionists** claim that capital punishment is ineffective in preventing crime, is unfairly administered, and is sometimes administered in error, but the central premise of their arguments is that government does not have the right to take a person's life.[48] For example, the **Southern Center for Human Rights** argues against the death penalty, quoting freed slave Frederick Douglass, who became a champion of civil rights: "Life is the great primary and most precious and comprehensive of all human rights... whether it be coupled with virtue, honor, and happiness, or with sin, disgrace, and misery, the continued possession of it is rightfully not a matter of volition;... [It is not] to be

abolitionists People opposed to the use of capital punishment.

Figure 11.1

Are You in Favor of the Death Penalty for a Person Convicted of Murder?

The majority of Americans support the death penalty as an appropriate punishment for murder. In recent years, support for the death penalty has declined slightly. This may be due to doubts about the fallibility of the criminal justice system due to the number of persons who have proved they were wrongly convicted and sentenced to death.

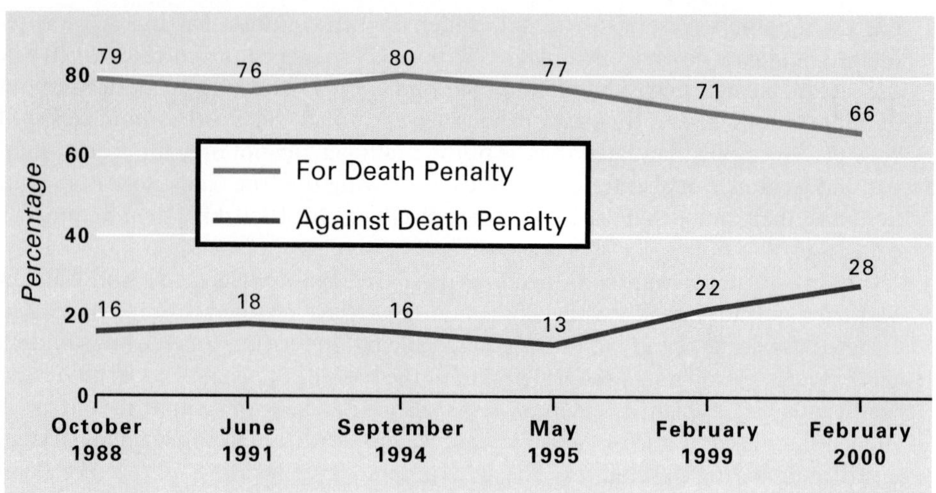

Source: From "A Life or Death Gamble" by F. Carter Smith and Corbis Sygma in *Newsweek,* May 29, 2000, p. 25.

deliberately or voluntarily destroyed, either by individuals separately, or combined in what is called Government."[49] Both abolitionists and proponents of the death penalty also argue for their views on the basis of religious values.

The first victory for abolitionists was the U.S. Supreme Court's ruling that potential persons could not be excluded from a capital murder jury simply because they opposed the death penalty. In ***Witherspoon v. Illinois***[50] (1968) the Court declared unconstitutional the common practice of prosecutors of excluding abolitionists from capital murder juries.

The Death Penalty and Civil Rights

In the United States, the death penalty sentence can be imposed by the state, the federal court, military courts, and military tribunals. The use of the death penalty by federal courts, military courts, and military tribunals is governed by federal laws, executive orders, and the U.S. Supreme Court. Each state has the option of adopting the death penalty as a legal punishment for crime, and 38 states have done so. States that use the death penalty as a sanction must preserve the civil rights of the condemned prisoner as defined by the state and federal constitutions. Appeal to the U.S. Supreme Court has been a common strategy of abolitionists. Appeals are based primarily on the Eighth Amendment, prohibiting cruel and unusual punishment, and the Fourteenth Amendment, providing for equality in justice. An early appeal to the U.S. Supreme Court based on the Eighth Amendment was ***Wilkerson v. Utah*** (1878).[51] Wilkerson appealed to the U.S. Supreme Court that his sentence of death by firing squad was cruel and unusual, but the Court upheld the constitutionality of the sentence. The first execution by electrocution took place at Auburn Prison (New York) on August 6, 1890. William Kemmler was sentenced to be executed for murder by use of the newly invented electric chair. Kemmler appealed to the Court that electrocution was cruel and unusual punishment. The Court disagreed, however, and execution by electrocution was added as another method of carrying out the death sentence.[52] In 1947, the Court was asked to take up another gruesome debate concerning electrocution: What if the person survives the first attempt at electrocution? Willie Francis, a 15-year-old black male, was convicted of killing Andrew Thomas by shooting him five times. The apparent motive was robbery;

Francis took the victim's watch and four dollars. When the state of Louisiana attempted to execute Francis, the electric chair failed to provide a fatal surge of electricity and Francis survived. He appealed a second attempt as cruel and unusual punishment, but the Court disagreed and he was electrocuted in the second attempt.[53]

The Death Penalty as Cruel and Unusual Punishment

On June 2, 1967, Luis José Monge was put to death in Colorado for the crime of murder. He was the last person to be executed for nearly 10 years, as in 1972 the U.S. Supreme Court effectively banned the use of the death penalty. In ***Furman v. Georgia***[54] (1972), the Court issued its most significant ruling regarding the death penalty. Rather than focus on the physical and emotional pain of the prisoner as the grounds for regarding capital punishment as cruel and unusual, Furman's defense argued that the death penalty, as applied, was arbitrary and capricious. This argument presented evidence that a person convicted of a capital offense may or may not be executed, because the law and the state courts did not systematically apply the death penalty. Who was executed and who was not appeared to be determined randomly. The only common element in executions was not the crime but the social-economic and racial characteristics of the offenders—poor and black. What patterns and trends do you observe in Table 11.4 on page 356 on characteristics of persons under sentence of death in 2000?

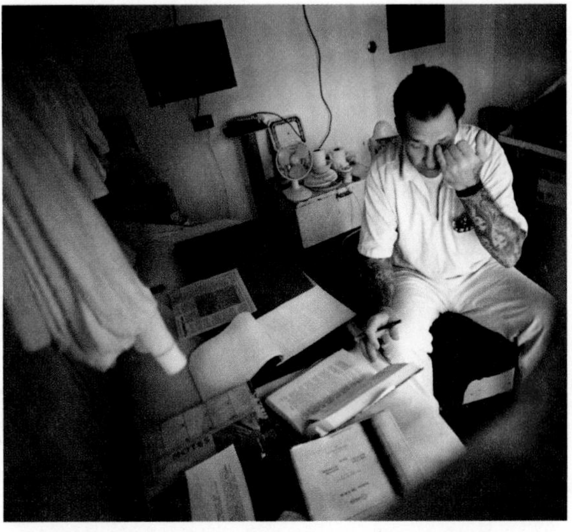

This death row inmate is awaiting execution by the state for a heinous crime. Why has capital punishment had such a long and troubled history in the United States? What legal issues relating to the U.S. Constitution have affected the use of the death penalty? What civil rights issues do abolitionists emphasize in their opposition to the death sentence? How have instances of official misconduct and error caused states to reexamine sentencing in capital cases?

There are two important points to note about the *Furman v. Georgia* decision. First, it did not declare that the death penalty was unconstitutional, only that the manner in which it was applied was unconstitutional. Second, all states were required to submit proof to the U.S. Supreme Court that their use of the death sentence was fair, equitable, and proportional to the crime. In effect, this ruling voided all existing death penalties and death penalty laws. Every prisoner in every state under the sentence of death was given a reprieve. However, rather than require new trials for all prisoners sentenced to death, the Court required only that the death sentence be reexamined. As a result of this ruling, each state that wanted to keep the death penalty as a sanction had to submit legislation to the Court for approval prior to resuming the use of the death penalty. Some states attempted to satisfy the criteria by adopting mandatory death penalties for first-degree murder. The Court refused to allow this strategy, however, and required states to be more specific in defining the criteria to be used in applying the death penalty.[55] The Court further defined its criteria for proportionate punishment when it struck down Georgia's statute authorizing the death penalty for rape.[56] The Court ruled that the death penalty was grossly disproportionate to the crime. As a result, nearly all death penalties are for the crime of first-degree murder with aggravating circumstances.

In 1976, the U.S. Supreme Court issued another landmark decision in ***Gregg v. Georgia***[57] (1976), which required a **bifurcated trial** structure in which trials for capital offenses had to be conducted in two separate parts. In the first part of the trial, the jury determines the guilt or innocence of the defendant. In the second part of the trial, after the defendant has been convicted, additional evidence can be introduced relevant to the punishment appropriate for the crime. There are three models for this two-part process.

bifurcated trial Two-part trial structure in which the jury first determines guilt or innocence and then considers new evidence relating to the appropriate punishment.

table 11.4 Demographic Characteristics of Prisoners under Sentence of Death, 2000, by Percentage

The profile of the prisoner under sentence of death is a single, white male with a high school education or less.

	Prisoners under Sentence of Death, 2000		
Characteristic	**Year-end**	**Admission**	**Removals**
Total Number under Sentence of Death	3,593	214	161
Gender			
Male	98.5%	96.3%	96.9%
Female	1.5	3.7	3.1
Race			
White	55.4%	57.0%	57.1%
Black	42.7	40.2	41.0
All other races*	1.9	2.8	1.9
Hispanic Origin			
Hispanic	10.6%	17.0%	8.6%
Non-Hispanic	89.4	83.0	91.4
Education			
8th grade or less	14.4%	17.6%	12.7%
9th–11th grade	37.3	34.1	39.6
High school graduate/GED	38.2	39.8	40.3
Any college	10.1	8.5	7.5
Median	11th	11th	11th
Marital Status			
Married	22.6%	23.5%	27.5%
Divorced/separated	21.0	18.7	25.4
Widowed	2.8	3.2	4.2
Never married	53.6	54.5	43.0
Missing Data by Category Were as Follows:			
Hispanic origin	382	67	22
Education	490	38	27
Marital status	329	27	19

Source: Bureau of Justice Statistics, *Capital Punishment 2000* (Washington, DC: U.S. Department of Justice, December 2001), p. 8.

*At year-end 1999, other races consisted of 28 Native Americans, 24 Asians, and 13 self-identified Hispanics. During 2000, 2 Native Americans and 4 Asians were admitted; 1 Native American, 1 Asian, and 1 self-identified Hispanic were removed.

Note: Calculations are based on those cases for which data were reported.

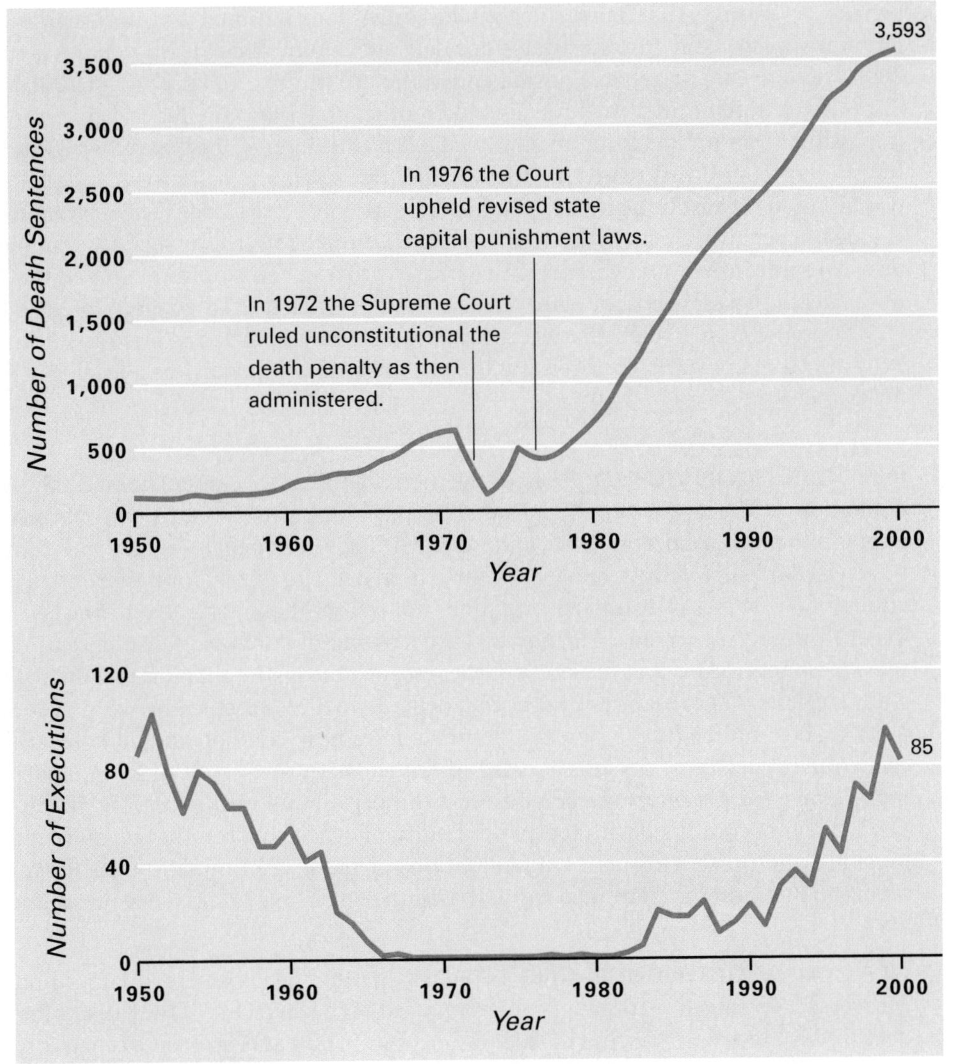

Source: Bureau of Justice Statistics, *Capital Punishment, 2000* (Washington, DC: U.S. Department of Justice, December 2001), p. 3.

Figure 11.2

Persons under Sentence of Death and Persons Executed, 1950–2000

There has been a tremendous explosion in the use of the death penalty since 1953, while the number of prisoners executed has declined. After a 10-year ban, the U.S. Supreme Court reinstated the death penalty in 1976. Since that time, 31 states have executed 683 prisoners. The number of executions has risen to about the level it was in 1950.

In the most common model, the jury can exclude the death penalty as an inappropriate sanction for the crime. In this model, if the jury does not authorize the death penalty, the judge may impose a lifelong prison term but cannot override the jury's decision. In the second model, the judge sets the punishment.[58] In the third model, the jury can recommend the death penalty, but the judge has final authority over the punishment.[59] Recent U. S. Supreme Court decisions have challanged the latter two models. Figure 11.2 shows the numbers of persons under sentence of death and executed in relation to the history of the death penalty in the United States.

Reconsideration of the Death Penalty

After 1976, more death sentences were overturned in Illinois than were carried out. Illinois Governor George Ryan announced in early 2000 that no more prisoners would be executed in Illinois until there was a thorough investigation into the use of the death penalty.[60] The American Bar Association has called for a national moratorium on capital punishment, and 16 other states decided to examine their death penalty laws in 2000.[61] After years of debate, Florida ended the use of the electric chair in 2001.[62] In response to much criticism, Texas joined 15 other states and the federal government in passing a ban on executing mentally retarded murderers.[63] In December 2001, the Kansas Supreme Court ruled that the way the state's death penalty was handed down was unfair and must be changed. The Kansas Supreme Court said, "The provisions of the death penalty violated the federal constitutional provisions against cruel and unusual punishment and the guarantee of due process." This opinion voided the use of the death penalty until the state can rewrite the sentencing language.[64] In 2002, the U.S. Supreme Court ruled that executing the mentally retarded is unconstitutional. Why are so many states reexamining the use of the death penalty as a legal sanction for crime?

INNOCENT CONVICTED Perhaps the most significant argument behind the reexamination of the death penalty is the alarming number of persons who have been wrongfully prosecuted, convicted, and executed. The death penalty is final and cannot be reversed or corrected. An apology by the criminal justice system for the wrongful execution of a prisoner is insufficient and does not restore the injustice done nor heal the harm to innocent persons. Furthermore, the wrongful conviction and execution of these prisoners means that the guilty parties escaped the justice that was due them. One study suggests that as many as 23 innocent defendants were executed between 1900 and 1988.[65] The criminal justice system is approaching a near-crisis of credibility regarding the wrongful deaths of persons accused of crime. Partly as a result of DNA evidence, many convicted prisoners are being freed from prison and death row. The impact of DNA evidence combined with recent revelations of official misconduct and corruption by police and prosecutors and with allegations of racial discrimination has led many people to question the continued use of the death penalty as a fair and just punishment.

OFFICIAL MISCONDUCT AND ERROR In 1998, Texas executed James Ronald Meanes, 42, seventeen years after he was convicted of murder. One of the reasons for the delay in his execution was that his file was lost for 7 years and prosecutors had forgotten about the case and sent the files to an archives office in Fort Worth.[66] Unfortunately, lost files are not the most serious examples of **official misconduct and error** associated with the death penalty. Malcolm Rent Johnson was convicted of rape and murder in 1982. Johnson claimed he was innocent, but forensic evidence disputed his protests of innocence. Johnson was executed on January 6, 2000. An investigation a year later into the accuracy of the forensic chemist's testimony, which was instrumental in convicting Johnson, strongly suggests that she gave false testimony about the evidence. Also, the evidence suggests that there may be at least two other cases in which the results stated in the lab report and confirmed by the state's forensic chemist contradict independent expert reexamination of the actual physical evidence.[67]

Some prisoners appear to have been wrongfully convicted because they were framed by police and/or prosecutors. Ronald Jones, who said police had beaten a confession out of him, was exonerated of the charges of rape and murder.[68] After Rolando Cruz was convicted of murder and sentenced to death, a reexamination of his case resulted in his release. In addition, charges of conspiracy to obstruct justice and to commit official misconduct were filed against the police and district attorney lawyers who prosecuted Cruz.[69] The investigation into the Los Angeles Police Department Ramparts scandal uncovered evidence that police framed numerous innocent citizens and obtained convictions on the basis of false evidence given by police officers.[70] Walter McMillian was released in 1993 after 6 years on death row, but the sheriff he claims framed him for the murder that put him there has not been prosecuted.[71] McMillian is

official misconduct and error A label for abuses of power and mistakes by people in the criminal justice system that can lead to wrongful convictions and wrongful incarceration.

one of 30 persons freed from death row who gathered in Chicago in 1998 for the first National Conference on Wrongful Convictions and the Death Penalty.

Some prisoners ended up on death row due to inadequate legal representation at trial. Gary Wayne Drinkard was convicted and spent 5 years on Alabama's death row. Drinkard was released after it was determined that his defense failed to introduce critical evidence and witnesses that would have proven his innocence. As an example of the need for death penalty reform, Southern Center for Human Rights director Stephen B. Bright presented Gary Drinkard as a witness at hearings on the Innocent Protection Act of 2001. Bright told the committee, "We have been very fortunate that the innocence of some of those condemned to die in our courts has been discovered by sheer happenstance and good luck.... The major reason that innocent people are being sentenced to death is because the representation provided to the poor in capital cases is often a scandal." The committee heard testimony that defendants were given lawyers fresh from law school or who had never before tried a death penalty case.[72]

In December 2001, a judge overturned the murder conviction of a man imprisoned for 27 years for murder. The judge ruled that the trial "was plagued by multiple problems which, cumulatively, present the inescapable conclusion that he was denied a fair trial." Even the widow of the murdered victim concurred, saying, "There's so much evidence that it wasn't him, and it doesn't look like there was any that says it was him."[73] Other prisoners who were wrongfully convicted have been released after 13 years,[74] 17 years,[75] and 24 years[76] of wrongful incarceration. Figure 11.3 traces the number of death-row inmates who have been exonerated since the 1970s.

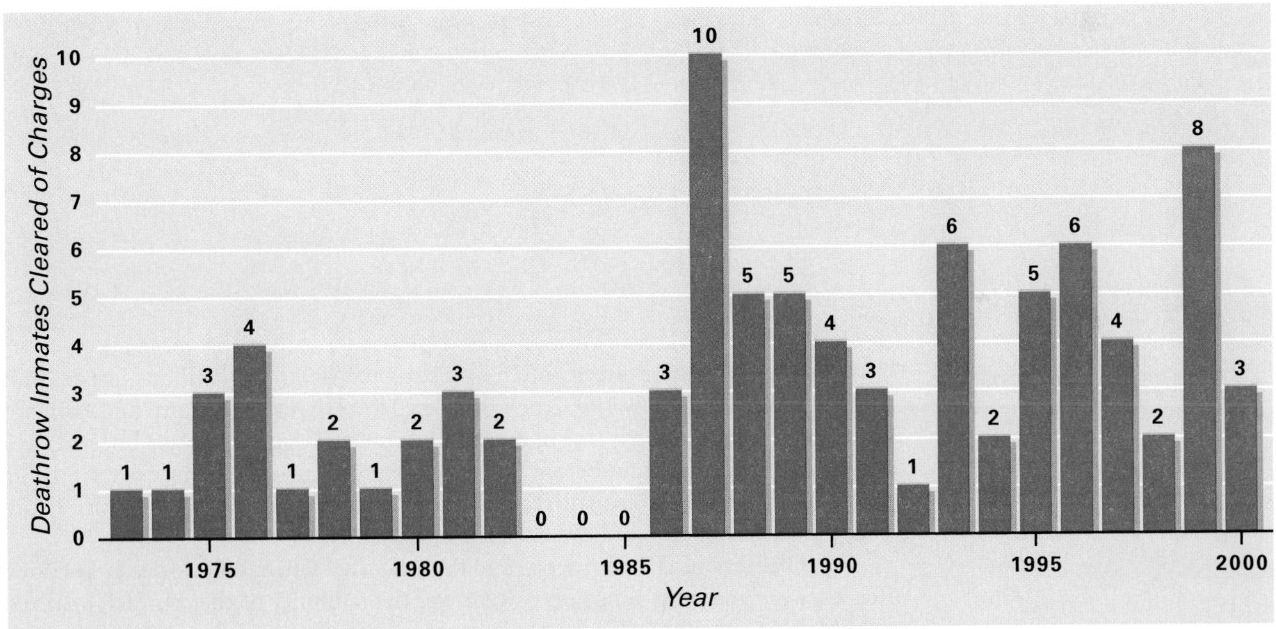

Source: From "A Life or Death Gamble" by F. Carter Smith and Corbis Sygma in *Newsweek*, May 29, 2000, p. 25.

Figure 11.3

Exonerated!

The increasing number of death-row inmates who are cleared of all charges has caused a crisis of confidence in the use of the death penalty. In 2000, Illinois exonerated more prisoners than it executed.

ethics in the system

And Justice for All

A report by the Leadership Conference on Civil Rights, a coalition of 180 civil rights groups, released in May 2000, concluded that blacks and Hispanics are treated more harshly than whites at every level of the criminal justice system, from investigation to sentencing.[77] A racially biased criminal justice system is deep-rooted in American history. In Virginia during the 1830s, there were only 5 capital crimes for whites but at least 70 for blacks.[78] Furthermore, there was a difference in severity of sentencing in which blacks could receive the death penalty for any offense for which a white would receive 3 or more years' imprisonment.[79]

In 1967, the President's Commission on Law Enforcement and Administration of Justice concluded, "The death penalty is most frequently imposed and carried out on the poor, the Negro, and the members of unpopular groups."[80] A 1973 study of offenders convicted of rape and sentenced to death shows that 13 percent of blacks convicted of rape were sentenced to death, but only 2 percent of whites convicted of rape were sentenced to death.[81] Blacks convicted of raping white women were more likely to be sentenced to death than blacks convicted of raping black women or white men convicted of raping either white women or black women.

Furman v. Georgia (1972) explicitly recognized the application of the death penalty as potentially arbitrary and capricious and sought to put an end to sentencing abuses once and for all. The effectiveness of ending racial discrimination in the use of the death penalty is debatable, however. A 1996 Kentucky study of death sentences between 1976 and 1991 found that blacks still had a higher probability of being sentenced to death than did homicide offenders of other races.[82]

Table 11.5 on page 362 shows executions by race between 1977 and 2000. Among prisoners executed between 1977 and 2000, whites had spent an average of 9 years and 8 months on death row, and black prisoners, 10 years and 8 months.[83] Blacks were more likely to have had prior felony convictions than were either whites or Hispanics. Among the 2,995 individuals who were removed from death row between 1997 and 2000, 52 percent were whites and 40 percent were blacks.[84] In 2000,

DNA EVIDENCE The advent of DNA testing has had a tremendous impact on the criminal justice system. By 1997, the FBI crime lab's DNA analysis unit had exonerated about 3,000 suspects. Nearly one in four of the suspects were exonerated but had already been charged with a crime before lab results were returned.[93] There are continuous reports of inmates freed from wrongful incarceration due to DNA evidence demonstrating that they could not have been the offender.[94]

The reliability of DNA evidence and the release of wrongfully convicted prisoners, often after serving years on death row, proves the fallibility of the criminal justice system. Often, the inmates who were released had to fight to get the court to reconsider their cases. Courts have adopted rules limiting the amount of time that may pass before new evidence will be considered[95] or have refused to allow DNA testing of prisoners who have already been executed.[96] In many cases, the criminal justice system has turned away from information that could be provided by DNA testing.[97]

DNA evidence has led to the release of more than 72 inmates from prison and 8 from death row. Yet, only two states, Illinois and New York, give inmates the right to use the latest DNA testing. Appeals procedures make it difficult to introduce DNA evidence

whites comprised 55 percent of all prisoners under sentence of death, blacks comprised 43 percent, and other races (1.9%) included 29 Native Americans, 27 Asians, and 12 persons of unknown race.[85] Recent statistics show a changing trend. Among the 683 individuals who were executed nationwide between 1997 and 2001, approximately 36 percent were black.[86]

Nevertheless, the racial bias of the death penalty continues to be controversial. In December 2001, a federal judge overturned the death sentence of Mamia Abu-Jamal. Abu-Jamal had been convicted for the first-degree murder of Philadelphia police officer Daniel Faulkner in 1981. Abu-Jamal claimed he was a political prisoner and victim of racial discrimination.[87] In another case, a federal judge asked prosecutors to explain why they were seeking the death penalty against three alleged Latino drug gang members but not against mob boss Joseph Merlino and three other co-defendants. Lawyers for the defense argued, "No distinction other than the race of the defendants . . . satisfactorily (or rationally) explains the filing of a death notice in the case at hand . . . and the decision not to return it in the Merlino matter."[88]

Despite the decades of statistical data indicating that the death penalty is not color-blind, the U.S. Supreme Court has refused to admit statistical evidence of racial discrimination as a justification for reversing death sanctions against blacks. In ***McCleskey v. Kemp*** (1987), the Court said that statistical data alone do not provide the level of proof necessary to claim that a specific death penalty violates the Eighth or Fourteenth Amendment.[89] A convicted person can obtain relief from the death penalty under the claim of racial discrimination only if (1) the decision makers in the case acted with discriminatory intent, or (2) the legislature enacted or maintained the death penalty statute because of an anticipated racially discriminatory effect.[90]

The report of the Leadership Conference on Civil Rights does not blame overt racial bias for the disparities in the criminal justice system. The report, written by lawyers, says that "a self-fulfilling set of assumptions about the criminality of blacks and Hispanics influences the decisions of police, prosecutors and judges in a way that accounts for the gap."[91] The report argues that these assumptions about the criminality of blacks and Hispanics are far-reaching and are a prime cause for such police abuses as false arrest reports, lying under oath, and planting evidence against minority persons.[92]

■ What is the evidence for racial discrimination in American criminal justice? Should this be accepted as a self-fulfilling prophecy? Would statistics about racial discrimination in sentencing influence a jury to give a lighter sentence? Would a defense attorney use this argument to appeal a death sentence or try to win a stay of execution?

after conviction. In some cases involving prisoners who have demonstrated through post-trial DNA testing that the trial evidence does not support their guilt, prosecutors still have refused to accept that the convicted defendant may be innocent.[98] The law does not protect the right of convicted inmates to appeal based on DNA evidence, and some states routinely destroy rape kits and other evidence that could be used to establish the prisoners' innocence.[99]

JUST THE FACTS 11.6

What methods of execution are used in the United States? Who are the abolitionists, and what is their cause? Why are trials for capital offenses conducted in two parts? On what grounds has the death penalty been declared unconstitutional, and what are the present rulings? Why are states reconsidering the death penalty today?

table 11.5 Executions of Inmates Sentenced to Death, by Race and Hispanic Origin, 1977–2000

Only about 10 percent of prisoners under the sentence of death have been executed. The backlog of death-row prisoners is creating a great strain on the resources of the courts and correctional system. More prisoners receive some other disposition than execution.

Race/Hispanic Origin[b]	Total under Sentence of Death 1977–2000[c]	Prisoners Executed		Prisoners who Received Other Dispositions[a]	
		Number	Percentage of Total	Number	Percentage of Total
Total	6,588	683	10.4%	2,312	35.1%
White	3,243	377	11.6%	1,187	36.6%
Black	2,722	246	9.0	956	35.1
Hispanic	524	49	9.4	136	26.0
All other races	99	11	11.1	33	33.3

Source: Bureau of Justice Statistics, *Capital Punishment, 2000* (Washington, DC: U.S. Department of Justice, December 2001), p. 11.

[a]Includes persons removed from a sentence of death because of statutes struck down on appeal, sentences or convictions vacated, commutations, or death by other than execution.

[b]White, black, and other categories exclude Hispanics.

[c]Includes persons sentenced to death prior to 1977 who were still under sentence of death on 12/31/00 (8), persons sentenced to death prior to 1977 whose death sentence was removed between 1977 and 12/31/00 (372), and persons sentenced to death between 1977 and 12/31/00 (6,208).

conclusion:

A Long Way to Go

What is the purpose of sentencing? Is it to punish the offender, to rehabilitate the offender, or to protect the community? The National Institute of Justice sponsored research that examined the crime-control effects of sentences over a 20-year period, based on 962 felony offenders sentenced in 1976 or 1977 in Essex County, New Jersey.[100] The purpose of this longitudinal study was to examine the effects of the different sanctions on the offenders' subsequent criminal careers. The study concluded that the main sentencing choices available to the judges had little effect on crime-control aims. Specifically, the study concluded that:[101]

- Except for the effect of incapacitation, whether the offender was sentenced to confinement made no difference in the rate of reoffending.
- Where the offender was confined made little difference—except for the unfavorable effect of placement in a youth facility.

- The length of the maximum sentence made no difference.
- The length of time actually confined made a slight difference.
- When jail was imposed along with probation, it made no difference.
- Fines or restitution made no difference.

The overall conclusion of the study was that empirical data suggested that there was little difference in sentences from a crime-control perspective.[102] Such data do not provide a happy ending to the discussion on sentencing. New and innovative sentencing strategies are constantly being tried. Laws defining the punishment for crimes and sentencing guidelines are being revised. People are examining the effect of sentencing and the fallibility of the criminal justice system, and are making new recommendations to improve the criminal justice system.

Sentencing is an important crossroad in the criminal justice system. It is harmful to convict the innocent and to impose sentences that do not deter criminality. It is harmful that there are so many possibilities for error in the use of the death penalty. Sentencing and sentencing reform will continue to be subjects of study and debate.

Chapter Summary

- Five purposes of criminal sanctions are deterrence, incapacitation, retribution, rehabilitation, and restorative justice.
- The jury determines guilt, and the judge determines the sentence the convicted defendant receives.
- Traditional sentences include fines, imprisonment, probation, or some combination. Certain states and the federal courts may impose the death penalty.
- Courts of limited jurisdiction impose short terms of incarceration and relatively small fines for minor offenses.
- Judges depend on information gathered in the presentence investigation report to set the appropriate sentence.
- The sanctions imposed on the mentally ill offender may be different. There is a legal difference between mental illness and insanity.
- Two major sentencing models are indeterminate sentencing and structured sentencing.
- Indeterminate sentencing is based on early release through the parole system.
- Structured sentencing includes determinate guidelines, sentencing guidelines, and presumptive sentencing.
- Mandatory sentencing, three strikes laws, and truth-in-sentencing laws are examples of structured sentencing.
- Research shows that the application of criminal sanctions often has discriminated against black and Hispanic males.
- Thirty-eight states, the federal courts, military courts, and military tribunals can sentence a defendant to death.
- While the public generally supports the use of the death penalty, there is strong opposition and much controversy.

- Many states are reconsidering the use of the death penalty due to the number of wrongful convictions that have been documented in recent years. DNA evidence has played a major role in freeing the wrongfully convicted.
- Data on the effectiveness of sentencing in reducing crime rates indicate that more study and experimentation are needed.

Vocabulary Review

abolitionists, 353
banishment, 336
bifurcated trial, 355
capital punishment, 352
civil commitment process, 347
corporal punishment, 334
determinate sentencing, 349
deterrence, 335
general deterrence, 335
guilty but mentally ill, 348
habitual offender laws, 350
incapacitation, 336
indeterminate sentencing, 349
mandatory sentencing, 350
not guilty by reason of insanity, 347
official misconduct and error, 358
presentence investigation report, 346
presentence investigator, 345
presumptive sentencing, 351
rehabilitation, 337
restorative justice, 338
retribution, 337
sentencing, 340
sentencing guidelines, 350
sentencing hearing, 346
specific deterrence, 335
structured sentencing, 349
three strikes law, 350
transportation, 337
truth in sentencing, 352
victim impact statements, 346

Names and Events to Remember

Federal Sentencing Guidelines Manual, 351
Furman v. Georgia, 355
Gregg v. Georgia, 355
Insanity Defense Reform Act of 1984, 347
McClesky v. Kemp, 361
Sentencing Reform Act of 1984, 351
Southern Center for Human Rights, 353
Wilkerson v. Utah, 354
Witherspoon v. Illinois, 354

Think about This

1. In late 2001 and early 2002, several states responded to a widening economic recession by closing jails, reducing sentences for nonviolent crimes, making it easier to win early release, and cutting prison education programs. How will such decisions affect offenders and their communities? To what extent do you think sentencing and parole decisions should be affected by economic considerations?
2. Which of the five purposes of criminal sanctions do you think might work best for a juvenile offender? A drug addict? An armed robber? A domestic abuser? Explain how your punishment fits the crime, yet would not be considered cruel and unusual. Which sentencing model do you prefer overall, and why?
3. Based on what you have learned in this chapter, if you were convicted of a crime, but you believed you were innocent, would you accept the guilty verdict and apologize or show remorse during the presentence investigation in the hope that this attitude would result in a recommendation for a shorter sentence? Why, or why not?

ContentSelect

Go to the ContentSelect web site and type in the natural language search phrase "mandatory minimum sentencing." Read "Mandatory Minimum Sentences: A Utilitarian Perspective," by Thomas Gabor from the July 2001 issue of the *Canadian Journal of Criminology*. The article discusses the problems of mandatory minimum sentencing in Canada and the United States. Sample the article to answer the following questions.

1. What reasons are given by the National Association of Women and Law (NAWL) against mandatory minimum prison sentences?
2. Under California's three strikes law, what crimes have been responsible for the majority of those convicted? Has the three strikes law reduced violent crime?
3. According to the article, how might mandatory sentencing affect an inmate who is unable to earn early release for good behavior? A substance-abusing repeat offender?
4. Do you agree with Judge Rheinheimer's application of the three strikes law in the cookie thief case? Why, or why not?

History of Jails and Prisons
What forces shaped the development of penal institutions in America?

Prison Populations
Who is in prison, and how do special prison populations challenge the system?

Correctional Officers
How are jails and prisons organized and administered today?

Parole Hearing
Are probation and parole effective as alternatives to incarceration?

Intensive Supervision
What is the role of intermediate sanctions in American corrections?

Day Reporting Center
Do community-based reentry programs for offenders work?

part five

Corrections

In the United States, the correctional system developed in response to the history of ideas about appropriate punishments for crimes and what the goals of punishment should be. After a defendant is found guilty and is sentenced to punishment, how and where and for how long should the sentence be carried out? Punishments may range from life imprisonment in near solitary confinement to probation under supervision in the community. Local, state, and federal correctional systems mirror the basic structure of law enforcement, the courts, and government in America. Penal reform goes hand in hand with judicial reform and centers on debates about the early release of offenders, the rights of victims and prisoners, the needs of special categories of prisoners, effective alternatives to incarceration, and corrections in the community.

chapter 12

Jails and Prisons

outline

Learning Objectives

After reading this chapter, you will know

- The history of punishments before jails and prisons.
- The reasons for the development of jails and prisons.
- How jails and prisons developed in the United States.
- The uses of federal, county, and municipal jails.
- How the state prison system is organized and administered.
- How prisoners are classified and assigned to levels of prison security.
- Career opportunities in state prison systems.
- The organization and development of the federal prison system.
- The reasons for and pros and cons of private prisons.

Abodes of Guilt and Wretchedness

The 1824 report of Daniel Rose, first warden of the Maine State Prison, after a 1-year investigation into the punishment of convicts and the establishment of a state penitentiary:

> State prisons should be so constructed that even their aspect might be terrible, and appear like what they should be, dark and comfortless abodes of guilt and wretchedness. No mode or degree of punishment which ever has been made or which ever can be adopted is in its nature so well adapted to purposes of preventing crime and reforming a crime, as close confinement in a silent or solitary cell, in which, cut off from all hope of relief during the term for which he shall have been sentenced, the convict shall be furnished with a hammock on which he may sleep, a block of wood on which he may sit, and which coarse, though wholesome food as may be best suited to a person in a situation designed for grief and penitence; and shall be favored with so much light from the firmament, as may enable him to read from the New Testament which shall be given him as his sole companion and guide to a better life. There his vices and crimes shall be personified, and appear to his frightened imagination as the co-tenants of his dark and dismal cell. They will surround him as so many hideous specters, and overwhelm him with horror and remorse.

—From: Law Enforcement Assistance Administration, *Two Hundred Years of American Criminal Justice: An LEAA Bicentennial Study* (Washington, DC: U.S. Department of Justice, 1976), p. 49

introduction:

Imprisonment—A Modern Invention

Maine State Prison today, shown in the chapter-opening photo, does not reflect Warden Rose's ideas on how prisons should look. In America in the 1800s, prisons were a new invention. Just as there was a time when uniformed, paid policing was unknown, there was a time when the concept of long-term **incarceration**—bodily (*carcas*) confinement in a prison—was unknown. Prisons were invented and the concept of prison was developed and refined. Warden Rose's vision of the perfect prison is a far cry from that advocated by correctional authorities today. It is difficult even to envision an institution such as the warden describes, so purposely designed to physically and psychologically abuse inmates, even assuming that such abuse would result in their rehabilitation.

The incarceration of accused defendants and convicted offenders has a sordid history. It is a history of violence against the inmate, brutal conditions of imprisonment, and theories of rehabilitation based on popular misconceptions and strongly held religious beliefs, all driven by economics. This chapter discusses the history of imprisonment, the development of the jail and state and federal prisons, and how jails and prisons have been, to a large degree, transformed into new institutions that are significantly different from their historical roots.

Before Jails and Prisons

THE MAIN IDEA

Until jails and prisons were built, punishments included branding, mutilation, public ridicule and pain, and whipping.

Life in the American colonies was difficult, as colonists struggled to provide basic necessities such as shelter, food, clothing, and a safe community. Most settlements in the New World were relatively isolated from other communities, a long way from their native lands and surrounded by a hostile and unexplored land. Imprisonment of offenders, especially as it is known today, was a luxury that colonial communities simply could not afford. Furthermore, as you will recall from Chapter 3, the social values and beliefs related to criminality were very different from contemporary values and beliefs. In the 1600s and 1700s, most people believed that crime was caused by weak character, sin, or free-will choice. Corporal punishments and capital punishment were the primary penalties for violation of the law. Punishments were painful, easily administered, required no long-term investment by the community, and were not costly. For example, in the mid- to late-1600s in colonial New Jersey, the whipping post, pillory (stocks), and gallows appeared to be the primary forms of punishment for lawbreakers.[1] The various mechanical devices and methods for inflicting pain on the offender were not used to extract confessions to crimes but to punish offenders.[2]

incarceration The bodily confinement of a person in a jail or prison.

As previously discussed, in colonial America, criminal codes were adopted by local communities and varied from community to community. Even after the Revolutionary War the United States retained this distinctive feature of local autonomy over the criminal code and punishment of offenders.[3] As a result, not only did laws and punishments vary from community to community, but each community had to rely on its own resources to finance its criminal justice system. Colonies could not rely on resources from England, and the early American states could not rely on the resources of the federal government to help finance their criminal justice systems. Communities had no excesses of resources that would have permitted punishments, such as long-term incarceration, involving the financial burden of housing, feeding, and caring for inmates. Other than capital punishment, the common punishments for offenders in colonial America and for the early years of the newly formed United States of America were branding, mutilation, public ridicule, and the infliction of pain through flogging, whipping, and other forms of striking of the offender. It was not uncommon for offenders to receive multiple punishments.

Branding

Branding is an old punishment dating back to the Code of Hammurabi. In England, **branding** dates back to the Fourth Century A.D., when offenders were branded on some part of their body with a mark or letter corresponding to the type of offense they had committed.[4] Each community specified the type of brand and location of the brand that the offender received. Some New Jersey communities, for example, variously required that persons convicted of burglary or robbery be branded with a letter T on the hand, the cheek, or the forehead. The location of the brand served to identify not only the offense, but also the number of offenses and their locations. For example, one New Jersey community required that for a first offense of burglary or robbery, a person would be burned with a letter T on the hand, and for a second offense be branded with a letter R on the forehead.[5] This community's version of the "three strikes" law required death as the penalty for the third offense.[6] In Gloucester County, New Jersey, a horse thief was branded on the right cheek with H.T."[7]

Branding served four functions: (1) It identified the offender to the community. Once identified by branding, the offender frequently was ostracized by other community members, and it was not uncommon for offenders to leave the community. (2) It acted as a general deterrent. The permanent brand served as a threat to both the offender and other potential offenders, as it was a visible reminder of what happened to those who violated community standards. (3) Branding was a method of identifying repeat offenders. In an era that lacked computerized criminal histories, fingerprints, DNA identification, and extensive court records, branding served as a simple but effective method of identifying repeat offenders to the court, even if the offender's identity and past offenses were unknown to the community. Thus, the court could take into account past offenses in determining the punishment to inflict. (4) Branding often was combined with other punishments, such as banishment. The branding of the offender made it possible to identify persons who had been banished. Although popular in the 1600s and 1700s, branding fell out of favor as a punishment in the 1800s. England officially abolished branding as a punishment in 1779.[8]

Mutilation

The cutting off of various body parts as punishment for criminal offenses was in common use in England beginning in the ninth century. In fact, **mutilation** was viewed as a humane substitute for capital punishment. Furthermore, mutilation, like branding, had the advantage of warning others throughout the offender's lifetime of the pain that would be inflicted on those who broke the law.[9]

branding Burning a mark or letter on an offender's body.

mutilation Cutting off of body parts as punishment for criminal offenses.

In colonial America, the most common forms of mutilation were the cutting off of ears and tongues. Mutilation often was combined with some other punishment, such as whipping, branding, or banishment. For instance, in Gloucester County, New Jersey, in 1771, the punishment for a horse thief included both branding and the cutting off of the right ear.[10] Cutting off the tip of the tongue or the pulling out of the tongue was usually the punishment for some verbal offense, such as blasphemy. The American colonies were founded by groups with strong religious values, and offenses such as swearing, taking the name of the Lord in vain, or profanity were considered serious offenses against community values.

Like branding, mutilation fell out of favor as a punishment by the 1800s. However, as discussed in Chapter 11, mutilation is still used by some countries as punishment for criminal behaviors. In some Middle Eastern countries, for example, the cutting off of hands or arms is still considered an appropriate punishment for certain property crimes, such as theft.

Public Ridicule and Pain

One of the most familiar methods of punishment for minor offenses in colonial America was the use of devices that inflicted public ridicule as well as pain. In small communities where everyone knew every other member of the community, punishments based on public ridicule were thought to be effective means of discouraging minor offenses. These punishments sought to label offenders and make their offenses known to the community. A common punishment based on this philosophy required offenders to wear some distinctive identification. The power of this punishment lay in the ridicule that it brought on the offender. In New York and Massachusetts, a common practice required offenders to hang a written notice describing the offense around their neck or to pin it to their chest.[11] Other communities required offenders to sew a symbol on their clothing, like the letter A for *adultery*.

pillory (stocks) In colonial America, a torturous restraining device in which offenders were forced to endure pain and public ridicule.

ducking stool In colonial America, forced immersion in water as punishment, through pain and public humiliation.

The use of stocks or the **pillory** combined public ridicule with pain and suffering. Tourists at reconstructions of colonial sites often view these devices with amusement, but persons confined in them suffered greatly, both psychologically and physically. The offender was humiliated by being pilloried in full view his or her neighbors.

Not as common as the stock and pillory was the **ducking stool**. This device lowered the offender into a body of water, frequently a river or lake. In some communities, offenders had their mouths held open with a bitlike device, forcing them to take in water while being submerged. Ducking was a public event and often a source of entertainment for the community. This punishment was most frequently used for women who continually nagged or used abusive language, but it was also used for other minor offenses

Offenders were positioned in the stocks or pillory in ways that caused intense pain over a period of days. During this time, offenders also were exposed to the elements, could eat or drink only when—or if—someone fed them, and were at the mercy of anyone, adult or juvenile, who wanted to taunt them or cause further injury. What goal of punishment did practices such as the stocks, pillory, and ducking stool reflect?

by both men and women.[12] Not only was the punishment painful and humiliating, if performed incorrectly it could result in the drowning of the offender. The last known ducking in England occurred in 1820 for the offense of wife beating.[13]

For a discussion of the history and current uses of corporal punishment as a deterrent to crime, go to the World Corporal Punishment Research site at http://www.corpun.com/index.htm.

Flogging and Whipping

Inflicting pain on offenders by striking them with some object is one of the oldest and most commonly used forms of punishment. This form of punishment includes whipping (or scourging), flogging, and caning. Offenders usually were struck with an implement especially designed for the purpose. Most commonly, offenders were struck across the back and, less commonly, on the soles of the feet. Whipping was a brutal form of punishment and could result in the death of the offender.

Whipping was an official punishment in sixteenth-century England. The **Whipping Act of 1530** set forth whipping as the punishment for vagrants. This punishment was applied to men, women, and children. The law provided that the offender was to be tied to the back of a cart, stripped naked, and beaten as they were pulled through the town or village until their bodies were bloody.[14] Sometimes, the severity of the punishment resulted in the death of the offender.

Whipping as a punishment was prevalent in colonial America and was used even into the middle of the twentieth century. In 1694 in West Jersey, the punishment for a first offense of burglary was 39 lashes on the back. In 1771, the New Jersey Assembly eliminated the punishment of death for stealing a horse and reduced the sentence to 30 lashes.[15] Pennsylvania abolished whipping in 1786, and the U.S. Congress abolished it in 1790. Most other states abolished whipping as a punishment by the end of the 1800s. However, Maryland retained whipping as a punishment until 1949, and Delaware continued to use whipping as a punishment until 1952 (the law was not repealed until 1972).[16]

Whipping as a punishment is firmly rooted in the classical criminological belief that criminality is controlled by the pain-and-pleasure principle. The infliction of a painful punishment is still thought by some to have more effect in preventing crime and recidivism than incarceration, which some perceive as lacking the appropriate degree of pain. In the United States, some proponents of corporal punishment continue to advocate the administration of pain as an appropriate punishment.

JUST THE FACTS 12.1

Why didn't the early American colonies build jails? On what basis were punishments chosen? What were the rationales for the four main types of punishment inflicted on criminals?

Origins of Incarceration as Punishment

THE MAIN IDEA

Societal changes, including industrialization and the growing population of cities, led to the need for prisons as an alternative to enslavement, banishment, and transportation.

Criminal codes in colonial America rarely included imprisonment as a punishment.[17] Today, the United States has one of the highest incarceration rates in the world. What

The New York Correction Historical Society site at http://www.correctionhistory.org/ includes detailed timelines, museum exhibits, and information on penal sanctions in New York from colonial times to the present. ■

caused this change? Why did the criminal justice system embrace incarceration of the offender as the primary punishment for law breaking? By around 1800, corporal punishment was gradually being replaced by imprisonment.[18] A major force underlying the use of incarceration as punishment was the impact of industrialization and the social changes it caused.

Punishments relying on shame and humiliation are most effective when administered in an environment in which the offender is connected to the community. Punishments relying on pain to deter crime are most effective when offenders rationally weigh the pain of punishment against the pleasure of the crime. Prior to industrialization, England and America were primarily rural, agrarian-based economies with stable populations. In such environments, the use of pain, shame, and humiliation as punishments were effective deterrents to crime. These punishments were based on Beccaria's and Bentham's classical theories of criminology (review Chapter 3). The basic premise of classical criminology theory was that crime is a rational act; offenders choose to commit crime and can be deterred from committing crime if the pain of the punishment exceeds the pleasure of the offense. This theory was the foundation for crime prevention, and as a result, punishments relied heavily on inflicting pain.

Jails and the Rise of the City

Cities began to flourish in Europe after the fall of feudalism, which had bound most commoners to a particular geographical community. Large numbers of persons were attracted to the city but could not find a means of earning a living there. As a result, cities became overpopulated by large numbers of unemployed persons who often turned to crime as the primary means of subsistence.[19] One of the first attempts to restore social order through incarceration was the use of the local jail. The jail, or "gaol" as it was called in England, was not so much a place for hardened convicts to serve long prison sentences as it was a place to remove from society a great and diverse number of persons who were considered the cause of social conflict and crime. Jails were intended to remove from society not only criminals but also vagrants, prostitutes, paupers, mentally ill persons, and even orphaned children and widowed women without means of support. The need for jails was considered so important in England that in 1166, Henry II ordered jails to be constructed in every shire (county).[20]

By the middle of the 1500s, jails had proven largely ineffective in controlling the social problems caused by poverty, economic hardship, and displaced agrarian workers. In an attempt to find a better way to handle the large number of people in poverty and the mentally ill, the city of London adopted the concept of the Bridewell, or workhouse. The **Bridewell** was a kind of poorhouse or almshouse. People who were unable to be productive members of society could be sentenced to the Bridewell, where they were supposed to receive the basic necessities and learn skills that would make them productive citizens. Bridewells were for men, women, and children. The concept of a workhouse or poorhouse proved to be so popular that in 1576, Parliament passed an act calling for each county to erect its own Bridewell.[21] This new treatment was thought to be more humanitarian than public whipping to control pauperism. As the populations of the cities continued to grow, however, the Bridewells were not effective in stemming the tide of impoverished migrants. People began to call for new means to deal with the poor and the crime that was blamed on them.

Bridewell A workhouse in London in the 1500s, in which basic necessities and skills to be productive were taught to the incarcerated poor and mentally ill.

By the beginning of the 1800s, the poor in the cities on both sides of the Atlantic were seen as a major cause of crime. New York civic and urban leaders chided paupers as "idle, ignorant, immoral, impious, and vicious." It was said of them that "they begged, stole, disturbed the peace, drank to excess, and committed shameful enormities. They sought charity but avoided work. They refused to conform."[22] The poor were seen as "a destructive evil which threatened social values and norms and thus became intolerable."[23] Unfortunately, the poor seemed to be everywhere. In 1815, more than one-fifth of New York City's inhabitants depended on public relief for subsistence.[24] Imprisonment was one of the options used to deal with this population of people who were perceived as threats to social order.

Enslavement and Transportation

During the 1600s and 1700s, enslavement or involuntary servitude was a commonly used punishment for criminal offenses, mainly because property crimes commonly required the offender to make restitution, often at several times the value of the property stolen. It was also common to require forced labor on public works as a punishment.[25] If the offender was unable to pay the required restitution, he or she would be sentenced to be sold into slavery to pay for the restitution.[26] The offender could be enslaved indefinitely or for a specified period of time. England combined the punishment of enslavement with transportation, defined in Chapter 11. From 1718 to 1769, 15 percent of the almost 17,000 felons convicted at the Old Bailey in London were executed for their crimes, while 69 percent were sentenced to transportation to the colonies.[27] It is estimated that nearly half of the colonists in the New World from the early 1600s to the 1700s did not enjoy new-found freedoms but arrived as indentured servants.[28]

THE HULKS ACT OF 1776 The American Revolutionary War caused a great strain on the English criminal justice system, as it abolished the practice of transportation. To replace transportation, England turned to the practice of long-term incarceration. Rather than house offenders in conventional jails, England used broken-down or abandoned war vessels and transport ships anchored in the Thames River to incarcerate prisoners. These vessels were called "hulks". The **Hulks Act of 1776** (the year of the Revolutionary War) called for offenders to be housed in these hulks. The prisoners were used to dredge the Thames River. The incarceration of prisoners in hulks continued until the discovery of Australia and the return of the use of transportation (to Australia) as punishment for crime.

THE FRENCH *BAGNES* Industrialization and technology also had a great impact on the criminal justice systems of Spain, France, and other Mediterranean nations. From the middle ages to the 1700s, oar-driven galley ships were commonly used to rid society of criminals and undesirables. Criminals and paupers were sentenced to serve time enslaved as oarsmen. When these ships put into port, prisoners were housed in secure stockades or prisons built in seaport cities for this purpose. When galley ships became obsolete, France turned to incarceration as a method to deal with these prisoners. France turned the seaport stockades into permanent prisons, called ***bagnes***.

In the *bagnes,* the prisoners provided products and services that were sold to help pay for the cost of housing them. Interestingly, these *bagnes* were operated by private businesses rather than government, and were a precursor of the industrial prison. The private businesses that operated these prisons expected to profit from the inmates' labors. In the late 1700s, France housed over 5,000 former oarsmen in just three *bagnes.*

JUST THE FACTS 12.2

What major social and economic changes led to the use of prisons over other forms of punishment? How did the philosophy of classical criminology support the idea of incarceration?

bagnes Private French seaport prisons of the 1700s housing former galley slaves.

Development of American Jails and Prisons

THE MAIN IDEA

The American prison system has developed from a system that abused and exploited prisoners into one that protects prisoner's rights.

The first institutions for incarceration of prisoners in colonial America and the United States were local jails, which served primarily for detention prior to trial or execution rather than for punishment or rehabilitation of the criminal.[29] In 1681, for example, the community of West Jersey required that condemned persons be kept in safe confinement until the next General Assembly after the governor had reviewed their cases.[30] Prisoners were confined until their punishments could be determined. Prisoners incarcerated in local jails were expected to work for their daily keep or to pay for it. Prisoners were not housed at the expense of the community.[31] In colonial America, jails for the most part were operated by private parties, and after the Revolutionary War, they were operated by the sheriff. Early jails were more like secure houses than the fortified structures of today. Apparently, early jails were not all that secure, however, as prisoners often escaped from them. The colony of New Jersey reported 1,830 escapes from jails between 1751 and 1777, an average rate of 67 per year.[32]

Early Jail Conditions

Conditions in early jails were deplorable, and all descriptions of them are difficult to imagine. As jails increasingly were used to incarcerate the mentally ill and the poor, overcrowding became a serious problem. One 1767 description of an early jail in Charles Town (Boston) reported that 16 debtors were housed in a single 12-by-12-foot room. The cell was so crowded that one of the prisoners died of suffocation but could not be removed until all of the other prisoners were first made to lie down to make room to retrieve the dead prisoner.[33]

In early jails, it was the prisoners' responsibility to provide for their basic necessities of life with their own funds or with the help of outside benefactors. Prisoners with the financial resources to provide for themselves could do so, but the state had no obligation to provide food or medical treatment for indigents. The more wealthy prisoners could buy additional cell space, food, and privileges, and even liquor was commonly made available to those who could afford it.[34] Prisoners who could not afford to pay for their accommodations were required to toil on public works projects in exchange for their keep. Those who could not work were allowed to beg passersby for food or money. Records indicate that some prisoners who were unable to provide for their daily needs were allowed to die of starvation.[35]

The portrait of American local jails at the birth of the nation is unpleasant. The jails were filled with all sorts of people—criminals as well as victims of misfortune. Men, women, and children were confined in the same cell, and no attempt was made to protect women and children from aggressive male prisoners. Sick prisoners were not separated from the healthy, so contagious diseases quickly and easily spread in the crowded and unsanitary conditions. Jails were not heated, did not have plumbing, and did not provide adequate per-person sleeping and living space. A primary factor in keeping the local jail population down was the death of many prisoners.[36] In 1777, English reformer **John Howard** traveled extensively in Europe, visiting jails and prisons. As a result, he wrote *State of Prisons,* a critical review of the brutality and inhumane conditions of Europe's penal systems. Howard's book was very influential and contributed to efforts at prison reform on both sides of the Atlantic.

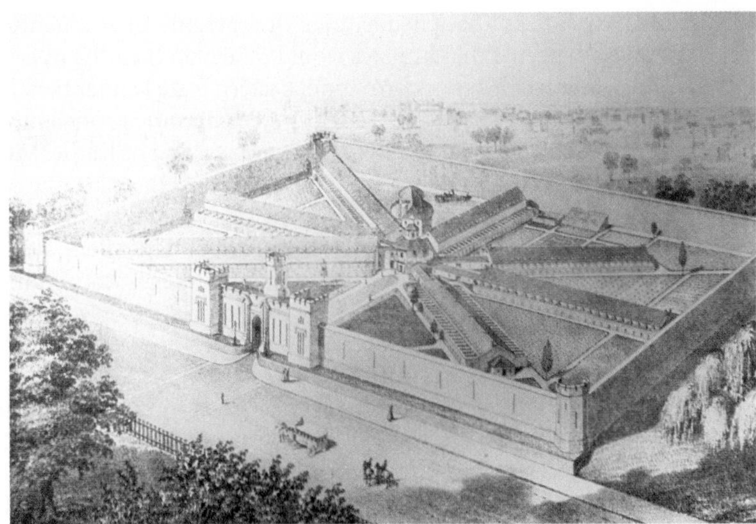

Based on principles demonstrated in the Walnut Street Jail, Pennsylvania's Eastern State Penitentiary became the blueprint for American state prisons of the early nineteenth century. The wheel shape of the penitentiary, with separated, large, single cells, reflected solitary, silent penitence and rehabilitation as the goals of incarceration. How did New York's Auburn system differ from Pennsylvania's penitentiary model?

Reform at Last: The Walnut Street Jail

In America, the prison reform movement had its origins with a group of Quakers called the **Philadelphia Society to Alleviate the Miseries of Public Prisons.**[37] In 1787, Benjamin Rush argued for prison reform at a meeting of the Society for Promoting Political Inquiries at the home of Benjamin Franklin. The Philadelphia Society to Alleviate the Miseries of Public Prisons was formed as a result, and this group lobbied the Pennsylvania legislature for humane treatment of prisoners. The group was successful, and in 1790, the Pennsylvania legislature passed a law calling for the renovation of the **Walnut Street Jail** in Philadelphia.[38] In addition to a humane physical facility and adequate food and water supplied at public expense,[39] the reform effort was successful in abolishing the practice of placing men, women, and children in the same cell and allowing prisoners to buy better treatment; prohibiting the consumption of alcohol by the prisoners; and separating the debtors and mentally ill from the criminal population. Children, many confined only because they were orphans, were removed from the jail and housed in a separate building.[40]

Prisoners in the Walnut Street Jail were required to work but were paid for their labor and could earn early release for good behavior. The new jail was a great improvement over previous conditions of imprisonment, and leaders came from other states to investigate the possibility of adopting the Walnut Street Jail model for their states.[41] However, the Walnut Street Jail ultimately failed because of overcrowding, which destroyed its ability to accomplish its mission. As a result of receiving state funding for renovation, the Walnut Street Jail became a temporary state prison, allowing prisoners from other cities in Pennsylvania to be housed there. The jail quickly filled beyond capacity.[42] Conditions deteriorated, and the cost of operating the jail became prohibitive. The goal of making prisons places for rehabilitation was crushed.

Bigger Is Better: Eastern State Penitentiary

By 1820, the hopes that Walnut Street Jail would be the model for prison reform were dashed, and overcrowding of the state's only prison required that a new institution be built. Pennsylvania's **Eastern State Penitentiary**, built in 1829, was an enormous investment of state resources and was based on a new philosophy of rehabilitation. Eastern State Penitentiary was built at the cost of $500,000 to house 250 prisoners. It was the most expensive public building in the New World and the first in the country to have flush toilets and hot-air heating.[43]

Eastern State Penitentiary was not designed as a jail or a prison but as a **penitentiary**. In a penitentiary, it was expected that inmates would reflect on their life of crime and change their ways. To encourage this transformation, Eastern State Penitentiary had an individual cell for each prisoner. Prisoners were required to become proficient at a skill that would support them after their release, such as woodworking or leatherworking. When not working or exercising, prisoners were expected to read the bible, the only literature allowed in their cells. Prisoners were kept in isolation from one another to avoid corrupting influences, and a "silent system" was enforced. The **silent system** required that prisoners communicate only with guards or prison officials; communication with other prisoners was forbidden. The goal of incarceration was to evoke penitence in the prisoner, with the idea that guilt and remorse or repentence would lead to rehabilitation, and prisoners could be released to lead normal, productive lives. This philosophy was compatible with the classical criminology theories and religious values of the period, emphasizing that crime was a rational choice made by the offender.

Eastern State Penitentiary was a maximum-security, walled, self-contained institution. It had seven wings like the spokes of a wheel that extended from a hublike center. Inmate cells were located on either side of the wings with outside windows. In the middle of the wing was a central passageway for use by guards and prison officials. Following the model of solitary confinement, the cells were designed so that inmates could not see any part of the prison other than what was directly in front of the cell. Cells were 12 feet long by 7.5 feet wide and had a window. Some inmates had a small outside exercise yard but seldom had a chance to leave their cells. The institution's design called for all activities—working, exercise, eating, and sleeping—to be performed within the individual prisoner's cell.

As with the Walnut Street Jail, many people came to view Eastern State Penitentiary to see if it could be a solution to their penal problems. The single-cell model reduced problems with inmate discipline. Inmates rarely had the chance to violate any rules, as they seldom left their cells or interacted with other inmates. As a result, corporal punishment was practically eliminated. Inmates were motivated to be productive and abide by the rules in exchange for the chance of early release and financial reward for their work.

The Auburn System

The single-cell plan was expensive, and as prison populations rose, the cost of construction became prohibitive. When the state of New York built a prison based on Pennsylvania's Eastern State Penitentiary, some significant changes were made. Built in 1816, **Auburn Prison** was a walled, maximum-security prison with inmate cells located in the center of a secure building. The cells in Auburn were smaller (7 feet long, 4 feet wide, and 7 feet high), with back-to-back cells stacked five tiers high. This arrangement made it possible to house many more prisoners cheaper and with much less space. Unlike the design of Eastern State Penitentiary, Auburn's design housed inmates in the center of the building without an outside window or exercise area. The cells were poorly lit and lacked access to fresh air. The cells stacked one on top of another created a unique prison architecture, called the **inside cell block**. This architectural model for housing prison inmates became a distinctive feature of the American penal system.

Auburn's cells were too small to be the inmate's "home," as in Eastern State Penitentiary. Auburn's cells were only for sleeping; during the day, inmates were moved to other areas to work and eat. This pattern is known as the **congregate work system**. Because inmates were moved from place to place within the prison, Auburn required a different type of administration. To minimize the opportunity for plotting escapes or uprisings, inmates were not permitted to talk to one another. However, unlike in the Eastern State Penitentiary, the silent system was more difficult to enforce, as inmates worked and ate together and met as they moved from place to place in the prison. To

penitentiary Correctional institution based on the concept that inmates could change their criminality through reflection and penitence.

silent system Correctional practice of prohibiting inmates from talking to other inmates.

inside cell block Prison construction in which individual cells are stacked back to back in tiers in the center of a secure building.

congregate work system The practice of moving inmates from sleeping cells to other areas of the prison for work and meals.

enforce silence, Auburn adopted a system of corporal punishment for violations of the rule. Flogging was administered as punishment, not for the crime but for violating prison rules. The floggings were designed to be painful but not to maim the inmate or require medical attention.[44]

Prisoners being moved from one location to another were required to march in a lockstep formation—marching in unison with one hand on the shoulder of the man ahead and all heads turned in the direction of the guard. When the inmates arrived at their destination, they continued to mark time until commanded to stop. Also, all prisoners had a similar short haircut and were required to wear distinctive clothing with stripes to clearly identify their status as prison inmates. Thus, the prisoners' schedule, movements, and appearance were strictly regulated.[45]

In 1821, the New York legislature passed a law requiring the "worst inmates" held at Auburn to be placed in **solitary confinement**.[46] These inmates were cut off from all contact with other people, including visitors, and were confined to their cells with only a bible to read. Unlike inmates at Eastern State Penitentiary, however, Auburn inmates in solitary confinement had no work to do, no exercise yard, and a very small cell. Lacking knowledge of the harmful effects of long-term solitary confinement (the sciences of sociology and psychology did not emerge until the 1900s), the legislature had created a prison environment antithetical to rehabilitation. Inmates in solitary confinement had mental breakdowns and committed suicide. The alarming debility and death rates forced the state to abandon this practice.[47]

Because inmates worked together in the Auburn system, the prison could combine their labor in larger and more profitable industries and construction projects. The sale of prison-made goods was so successful, the prison was virtually economically self-sufficient and required few resources from the state budget.[48] While the Eastern State Penitentiary model required more and more state resources to operate as the prison population rose, only 13 years after Auburn opened, the warden announced he no longer needed state funds to run the prison.[49] The Auburn system became the prototype of the American prison. The economic advantages appealed to other states, and between 1825 and 1969, 29 state prisons were built using the Auburn model. Many of these institutions, such as New York's Sing Sing, are still in use today.[50]

Southern Penal Systems

Many northern states used the Auburn system as a prison model. Southern states, however, developed their own unique prison system, based on different historical circumstances. The South retained an agrarian economy rather than building an industry-based factory system. Southern prisons practiced the **convict lease system** to supply the farm labor once provided by slaves. Rather than build large maximum-security prisons to produce prison-labor-made goods, southern states leased prisoners to private contractors. Inmate labor was used for agricultural work, some factory work, and construction work. The private contractor assumed all responsibility for the care and support of inmates and paid the state a fee for the inmates' labor. This prisoner lease system permitted southern states to deal with great increases in the prison population following the Civil War, without requiring the states to finance the construction of prisons. For some states, a significant amount of the state's income was derived from the sale of convict labor.[51]

Following the Civil War, approximately 90 percent of those incarcerated in the South were free blacks. Work and living conditions for inmates were wretched, and convicts worked 12 to 15 hours a day. States did not set minimum standards for living conditions and did not inspect the sites where inmates were housed. Inmates who performed agricultural work often were housed in temporary, portable cages near the work site. Thus, prisoners were no better off than during slavery, and discipline was brutal.[52] To prevent escapes when the prisoners worked in open areas, they were shackled

solitary confinement Practice of confining an inmate such that there is no contact with other people.

convict lease system In southern penal systems, leasing prisoners to work for private contractors.

The chain gang developed in the southern penal system, which reflected the legacy of dependency on cheap or slave labor for the South's agricultural economy. The reemergence of chain gangs in the 1990s led to a storm of protest and questions regarding the constitutionality of this treatment of prisoners. What parts of the U.S. Constitution might relate to the use of chain gangs?

Visit the web site of the Southern Center for Human Rights at http://www.schr.org. ■

together in what came to be known as the **chain gang.** The prisoner death rate in this system was over twice as high in southern prisons as in northern prisons.[53]

The prisoner lease system was used until the 1930s, when it was replaced by the **prison farm system**, or plantation system. Rather than lease prison labor to private contractors, the state used inmate labor to maintain large prison farm complexes. These prison farms were expected to be self-sufficient and profit-making. Some states expanded the concept and used prison labor to operate other profit-making industries. To reduce the costs of operating prison farms and prison industries, states often used inmates as guards and supervisors of other inmates.

Changing social consciousness in the southern states eventually ended for-profit prisons and use of inmate "trusties" to maintain security. Arkansas, however, continued to use the prison farm system, with its many abuses, until the 1960s.[54] A series of U.S. Supreme Court cases then ruled the penal practices in Arkansas unconstitutional.[55] The Court also decided that whipping for disciplinary purposes and the use of electric shock were cruel and unusual punishments. In its decision, the Court declared, "For the ordinary convict a sentence to the Arkansas Penitentiary today amounts to a banishment from civilized society to a dark and evil world completely alien to the free world culture."[56] The state of Texas also practiced the plantation farm system and came under public criticism and the scrutiny of the Court. As in the case of Arkansas, a series of U.S. Supreme Court rulings forced Texas to reform its prison system.

Modernization of Jails and Prisons

Contemporary jails and prisons may appear to the casual observer to be similar to the jails and prisons of the nineteenth century, but on examination, they are very different. Institutional corrections in the twenty-first century is being shaped by many forces which are transforming it, creating innovative strategies and causing an examination of the reasons for incarceration as a punishment for crime. The use of incarcerations as punishment for crime has resulted in a record incarceration rate for the United States. In 1997, a study of the world's incarceration rate by the Sentencing Project revealed that the United States and Russia had the highest incarceration rates in the world. From a rate of 426 prisoners per 100,000 population in 1991, despite a drop in the crime rate during the 1990s, the incarceration rate in the United States continued to grow every year.[57] The rate of growth slowed in 2000, but the prison population still was at an all-time high, with approximately 2 million people in federal, state, and local correctional facilities.[58] With only 5 percent of the world's population, the United States has 25 per-

chain gang In the southern penal system, convicts chained together during outside labor.

prison farm system In southern penal systems, using inmate labor to maintain large profit-making prison farms or plantations.

cent of the world's prisoners.[59] Incarceration must be viewed as a major industry and source of employment in the United States.

Prisons have come a long way from the model of self-sufficient, no-cost-to-the-state prisons of the nineteenth century. Today, prisons are a significant cost to local, state, and federal government, and employment in corrections accounts for 34 percent of the total employees in the criminal justice system.[60] The cost of prisons has increased over 300 percent since 1984. In 1996, states spent over $22 billion on prisons, and the federal government spent $2.5 billion.[61] The average annual cost of housing an inmate in a state prison is $20,100, and the average cost per year of housing a single federal inmate is $23,500. What happened between the nineteenth century and the twenty-first century to cause these changes?

In the late nineteenth century, the classical explanations of criminal behavior were overtaken by biological explanations, such as the criminological theories of Cesare Lombroso. As you will recall from Chapter 3, Lombroso argued that criminals are naturally inferior persons who cannot control their inborn criminality. If criminality is an inherited trait, it follows that attempting to rehabilitate them is futile, and thus is not a reasonable goal of the criminal justice system. Lombroso's theory influenced corrections in the late 1880s and early 1900s. Penal institutions abandoned a belief in criminals as weak-willed sinners and saw them instead as threats to civilization. The American criminologist Earnest Hooton argued that prisoners should be placed on self-contained, self-governing reservations completely isolated form society. Hooton favored the permanent incarceration of what he called "hopeless constitutional inferiors who on no account should be allowed to breed."[62] This philosophy was pervasive throughout the early 1900s. Prisons were operated under the premise that it was best to leave the fate of criminals to correctional authorities. Thus, for the most part, society abandoned the oversight of prisons. Even the courts adopted a hands-off policy. Once a person was incarcerated, he or she was denied access to the courts on any matter concerning his or her treatment or incarceration.[63] It was not until the 1960s that the courts interpreted the constitutional protections as extending to prisoners.

During the Great Depression of the 1930s, many states passed laws prohibiting the sale of convict-made products, which competed with local businesses on the open market. The operating capital that prisons had been able to generate through industries dried up, and prison industries turned to supplying products to the government.[64] During this era, for example, prisons became the exclusive manufacturers of license plates for state governments.

Continuing Prison Reform

Starting in the 1950s, post–World War II social changes, combined with deteriorating prison conditions, led to further prison modernization. The most influential force of change was the understanding by scholars and the public that social influences play an important role in crime causation. The criminal came to be seen as an ordinary person whose criminal behavior was in large degree influenced by his or her environment, social interactions, and economic opportunities. As you will recall from Chapter 3, the theory of biologically determined criminality gave way to sociological theories emphasizing peer interactions, learning theory, and lack of opportunities for legitimate success. In addition, prison conditions had deteriorated significantly after years of neglect and were brought to public attention through disasters such as fatal prison fires and inmate riots. Between 1950 and 1966, there were over 100 prison riots. Rioting continued in the 1970s and 1980s and often was deadly. In September 1971, forty-three prisoners died in the Attica State Prison riot. In February 1980, thirty-six died in the New Mexico State Penitentiary riots.[65]

The development that opened the floodgates of prison reform was the U.S. Supreme Court's rejection of the hands-off policy toward prisons. The Court decided

diversity in the system

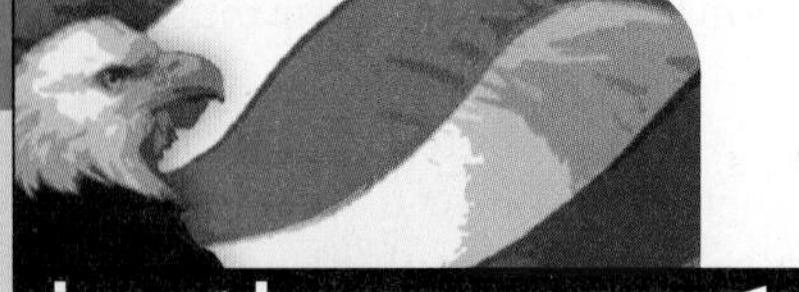

Institutional Racism and Incarceration

If the criminal justice system discriminates against minorities, an indicator of this discrimination is the ratio of minorities to whites in prison. While many other indicators may not show clearly that minorities are treated differently by the system, incarceration rates clearly demonstrate that there is a disproportionate confinement rate for minorities. If recent incarceration rates remain unchanged, an estimated 1 of every 20 persons (5.1%) will serve time in a prison during their lifetime.[67] However, the likelihood of going to state or federal prison is disproportionate when one examines the likelihood of going to prison by race. When the numbers are adjusted for percentage of the general population, the differences by race are enormous. A white male has a 1 in 23 chance of serving time in prison, while a Hispanic male has a 1 in 6 chance, and a black male has a greater than 1 in 4 chance.[68]

In the past 10 years, there has been little change in this incarceration rate, as the percentage of prisoners under state or federal jurisdiction by race has changed little.[69] In 1990, 35.6 percent of state or federal prisoners were white, 44.5 percent were black, and 17.4 percent were Hispanic. In 2000, 35.7 percent were white, 46.2 percent were black, and 16.4 percent were Hispanic. Furthermore, when one looks at the statistics for juvenile offenders held as adults, there is an even greater gap between whites and minorities in prison. Twenty-five percent of state prisoners under 18 are white non-Hispanic, whereas 58 percent are black non-Hispanic, and 15 percent are Hispanic.[70]

Some argue that the criminal justice system does not incarcerate innocent people; thus, all the black males in prison have committed a crime and deserve to be incarcerated. Others argue that the criminal justice system discriminates against minorities from the beginning, especially black males, as they are more likely to be stopped, arrested, charged, convicted, and sentenced to prison than are white males.

One of the effects of the 28.5 percent likelihood of incarceration for black males is their disenfranchisement from the political system. The District of Columbia and 46 states deprive felons of the right to vote while they are in prison. In addition, 32 states bar offenders from voting while they are on probation, and 29 bar voting while on parole. In 14 of these states, felons are barred from voting for life.[71] It is estimated that 13 percent of the nation's black male population cannot vote because they have been convicted of a felony.[72] In some states, such as Alabama and Florida, which have a higher percentage of black male inmates, it is estimated that one in three black men are denied voting rights because of felony convictions.[73]

According to the Sentencing Project, a Washington-based advocacy group for sentencing reform, and Human Rights Watch in New York, as a result of this policy and the disproportionate number of black males in prison and under the supervision of probation or parole, in a dozen states as much as 30 to 40 percent of the next generation of black men will permanently lose the right to vote.[74] The Sentencing Project report suggests that this trend will result in the loss of many of the gains made in the American civil rights movement. People denied the right to vote lack political and economic representation and may no longer see themselves as participants in the democratic process.

■ **How do you explain the disproportionate number of black and Hispanic males in prison? What might be some consequences of the widespread disenfranchisement of large numbers of black and Hispanic males? Should laws depriving convicted felons of the right to vote be repealed?**

that inmates have the right to sue in state and federal courts over living conditions, inmate rights, medical treatment, and prison policies. In some cases in which prison conditions were considered "beyond the ability or desire of the State to remedy," the Court appointed special masters to supervise and monitor the implementation of court-ordered decrees to improve prison conditions and guarantee the exercise of prisoner rights.[66]

Today, jails and prisons cannot hide from public scrutiny. Prisoners have access to the courts to file lawsuits regarding substandard living conditions and violations of constitutional rights; state and national watchdog organizations investigate and report on the correctional system; and work in corrections has become professionalized. The American Jail Association, for example, certifies jail managers as a voluntary process. Sworn or civilian personnel can be credentialed in full-time adult jail management as a professional specialty. Criticisms of corrections as well as other parts of the criminal justice system, such as concerns about institutional racism, contribute to ongoing prison reform.

jails Short-term, multipurpose holding facilities that serve as the gateway for the criminal justice system.

JUST THE FACTS 12.3

What were early jails and prisons like? What were the characteristics of the American penal systems developed in the Walnut Street Jail, Eastern State Penitentiary, and Auburn Prison? How and why was the southern penal system different? What post–World War II developments opened the floodgates of prison reform?

Jails

THE MAIN IDEA

Jails are multipurpose holding facilities and serve as a gateway for the criminal justice system.

The major institutions of modern civilian institutional corrections are the jail, the state prison, and the federal penitentiary. **Jails** are unique, short-term facilities that are used for more purposes than any other type of correctional institution. Jails hold defendants awaiting trial, defendants convicted of misdemeanor crimes, state and federal prisoners, mentally ill persons pending their movement to appropriate health facilities, adults of both genders, and juveniles. Jails hold local, state, federal, and military prisoners; convicted prisoners; absconders; and witnesses. However, the majority of inmates in local jails have not been convicted of a crime. They are waiting to be charged, tried, or transported to another institution. Jails hold everyone from accused murderers to persons detained for littering. Characteristics of jail inmates are summarized in Figure 12.1.

In addition to the fact that they are multipurpose, jails are unique as a gateway into the criminal justice system, and corrections in particular. When a person is detained or arrested for any crime, misdemeanor or felony, they first are confined in a jail. Only convicted offenders can be confined in state and federal prisons. Thus, all prisoners and most defendants enter the criminal justice system through jails.

Jails are primarily local institutions. There are only 11 federal jails under the supervision of the **Federal Bureau of Prisons (BOP)**, and these house a very small percentage of the jail population. In 1999, federal jails had about 11,000 prisoners, whereas the total local jail population was over 600,000 prisoners.[75] Federal jails do not house the diverse population of prisoners that is characteristic of local jails. The primary purpose of federal jails is to hold federal jail inmates awaiting adjudication or transfer. Federal jails have traditionally used local jails for this purpose, but the

Figure 12.1

Profiles of Jail Inmates

Most jail inmates are male. The South holds more jail inmates than do other regions. There are nearly equal numbers of whites and blacks in local jails.

Gender

Male	Female
528,998 (88%)	67,487 (11.2%)

Juveniles

Held as Adults	Held as Juveniles
8,598	860

Non-U.S. Citizens in Local Jails 5%

Inmates by Region

Northeast	90,716
Midwest	97,652
South	284,742
West	132,833

Race and Hispanic Origin of Jail Inmates

White, non-Hispanic	41.3%
Black, non-Hispanic	41.5%
Hispanic	15.5%
Other	1.7%

Source: Bureau of Justice Statistics, *Census of Jails, 1999* (Washington, DC: U.S. Department of Justice, August 2001), p. 3.

serious overcrowding in local jails has often resulted in local jails being unable to accept federal prisoners. Prisoners also are held in military prisons[76] and Native American jails,[77] and some terrorists are held in special military detention centers. These latter correctional institutions are significantly different from civilian correctional institutions and are not discussed in this textbook. The special topic of juvenile corrections is discussed in Chapter 15.

County Jails

There are over 3,300 local or county jails, and they vary significantly in size. About 47 percent of these jails have a capacity of fewer than 50 inmates. Less than 3 percent of the jails have a capacity of more than 1,000 inmates.[78] A few jails have very large populations. Two of the largest jails are the Los Angeles County Jail and the Maricopa County, Arizona, Jail. These jails house more than 7,000 inmates each. Counties must support their jails, so the size and condition of the facilities vary with the economic prosperity of the counties.

All states except Connecticut, Delaware, Hawaii, Rhode Island, and Vermont operate local jails, but these five states do have a combined jail–prison system operated by the state. Initially, local jails were operated by the county sheriff, and there was only one jail per county. In many states, this is still true, as about 78 percent of sheriff's offices operate a jail.[79] Jail operation is still a major responsibility of sheriff's offices. Fully one-third of all sheriff office sworn personnel work in jail-related positions, and 56 percent of civilian personnel work in jail-related positions.[80] As Table 12.1 shows, in sheriff's offices that operate jails, a significant percentage of the jail's personnel perform duties related to jail operations rather than to law enforcement or court security duties. Jails not operated by the sheriff's office are managed by a county department of corrections

table 12.1 **Large Sheriffs' Offices and Officers Performing Jail Operations**

In sheriffs' offices that operate jails, a significant percentage of personnel perform jail duties as opposed to law enforcement or court security.

Department	Total Number Full Time Sworn Officers	Percentage Performing Jail Operations
Los Angeles Co. (CA)	8,107	26
Cook Co. (IL)	5,768	58
Harris Co. (TX)	2,648	55
Broward Co. (FL)	2,419	50
San Diego Co. (CA)	1,999	53
Clark Co. (NV)	1,998	20
Wayne Co. (MI)	1,127	69
Nassau Co. (NY)	1,114	93
Salt Lake Co. (UT)	903	46
Suffolk Co. (MA)	817	98

Source: Bureau of Justice Statistics, *Law Enforcement Management and Administrative Statistics, Sheriffs' Offices, 1999* (Washington, DC: U.S. Department of Justice, May 2001), p. 2.

- Receive individuals pending arraignment and hold them awaiting trial, conviction, or sentencing.
- Readmit probation, parole, and bail-bond violators and absconders.
- Temporarily detain juveniles pending transfer to juvenile authorities.
- Hold mentally ill persons pending their movement to appropriate health facilities.
- Hold individuals for the military, for protective custody, for contempt, and for the courts as witnesses.
- Release convicted inmates to the community on completion of sentence.
- Transfer inmates to federal, state, and other authorities.
- House inmates for federal, state, or other authorities because of crowding of their facilities.
- Relinquish custody of temporary detainees to juvenile and medical authorities.
- Operate community-based programs with day reporting, home detention, electronic monitoring, or other types of supervision.
- Hold inmates sentenced to short terms (generally under 1 year).

Source: Bureau of Justice Statistics, *Census of Jails, 1999* (Washington, DC: U.S. Department of Justice, August, 2001), p. 2.

Figure 12.2

Functions of Locally Operated Jails

The following numerous functions performed by local jails make it difficult to operate the jail and manage the inmates. Inmates range from persons waiting to post bail to murderers. Many inmates are in jail for only a brief time. Some inmates are held only until they can be transferred to another institution.

employing only civilian personnel. Sheriff's departments and county departments of corrections otherwise perform the same jail functions (Figure 12.2).

As Figure 12.3 shows, the jail population has more than doubled since 1983. In 1999, in an effort to keep pace with the rising jail population, counties were constructing new jail facilities at the rate of about 500 new beds each week.[81] Some jails expanded so rapidly that it was not possible to construct enough new bed space, and prisoners were housed in corridors, outdoor tents, or trailers. Overcrowding in jails remains a serious problem for many states. State jails typically have occupancy in excess of 100 percent capacity. For example, in 1999, the District of Columbia jail population was occupied at 120 percent of capacity, Virginia at 118 percent, New Jersey at 110 percent, and Massachusetts at 105 percent.[82]

Visit the San Francisco County Jail at http://www.ci.sf.ca.us/sheriff/home.htm.

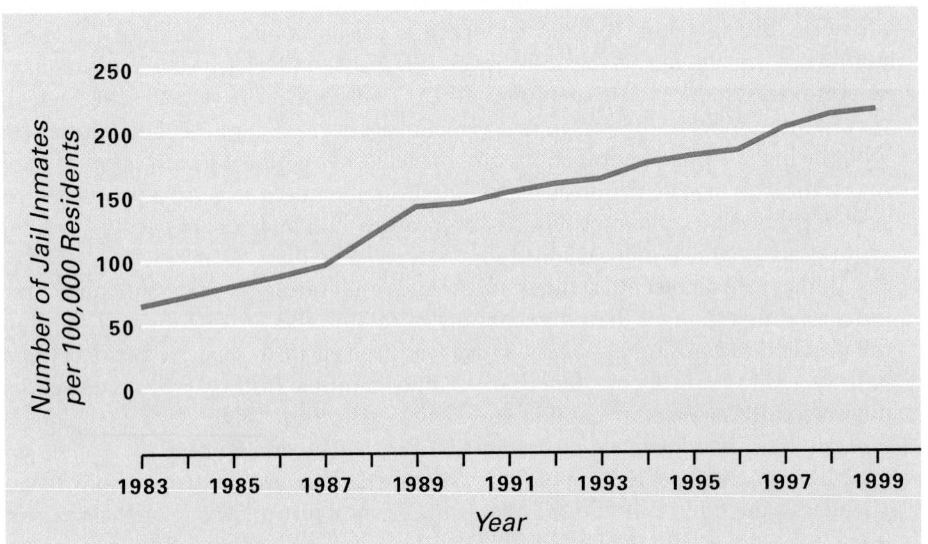

Source: Bureau of Justice Statistics, *Census of Jails, 1999* (Washington, DC: U.S. Department of Justice, August 2001), p. iii.

Figure 12.3

Trends in the Incarceration Rate

The jail incarceration rate has expanded so quickly that many local jails have not been able to construct the necessary bed space to accommodate new inmates. Overcrowding is a serious problem in local jails. In some jails, inmates are housed in outside tents due to lack of bed space.

Municipal Jails

Historically, local jails also included local prison facilities maintained by municipal police departments. In some counties, the sheriff maintained the county jail, and the police department maintained a separate municipal jail. These counties had both a municipal court and a county court, with each court housing its prisoners in the appropriate facility. Most municipalities have abandoned the use of the municipal or police jail. Recent state and federal regulations and standards regarding the housing of inmates have made it difficult for cities and towns to support local jails.

Municipal jails should not be confused with police holding cells, booking cells, or lock-up facilities. Nearly all police departments have secure detention facilities that may look like jail cells. The primary purpose of these holding cells is the temporary housing of arrestees until they can be booked and moved to another facility or pay their bail, or until detectives can determine if they are to be charged with a crime. These are not correctional institutions, and prisoners are not sent to these facilities to serve time as their punishment for a crime. Prisoners typically are confined in holding cells only for a period of 48 hours or less.

JUST THE FACTS 12.4

What are the types and functions of jails? Why are jails considered "gateways" into the criminal justice system?

State Prisons

THE MAIN IDEA

State prisons are correctional facilities with different security levels, prisoner classifications, and administration models for the incarceration of persons convicted of crimes.

Unlike jails, **state prisons** are correctional institutions containing only convicted offenders, usually felony inmates sentenced to prison as punishment for a crime. The number of inmates in state custody has doubled since 1990. Each state operates its own correctional system, and these systems differ significantly from state to state. States also vary in the number of inmates in the correctional system. Table 12.2 shows the ten states with the highest prison populations and the ten states with the lowest number of prisoners. Inmates in state prisons usually have been sentenced to serve a prison term of a year or more. Thus, different services, procedures, and policies are needed for prisoners than are provided in local jails.

state prisons Correctional facilities for prisoners convicted of state crimes.

In the early nineteenth century, most states built one large prison to house all state inmates. It was thought that this economy of scale would provide the best solution to the problem of housing prisoners. There was little effort to separate prisoners on the basis of age, type of offense, length of term, or criminal history. From the beginning, however, early state prisons, unlike early jails, separated prisoners by sex, maintaining separate facilities for female prisoners. Until the late twentieth century, women comprised a very small percentage of felony offenders. Thus, while early prisons for male offenders were built to house thousands of inmates, institutions for female prisoners usually were one-tenth the size. Furthermore, prison architecture reflected the assumption that male prisoners were more aggressive and dangerous, and that female prisoners were more docile and less violent.[83] Based on this assumption, correctional institutions for women often lacked the fortress-like architecture and brutal discipline of prisons for

table 12.2 States with the Highest and the Lowest Incarceration Rates, 2000

In comparing states, the number of inmates per 100,000 residents of the state is a more accurate measure, because of the great differences in the population size of states. For example, Louisiana has the highest incarceration rate of any state but has fewer actual inmates than the ten states with the highest prison populations.

	Number of Inmates		Incarceration Rate per 100,000 State Residents[a]
10 Highest			
California	163,001	Louisiana	801
Texas	157,997	Texas	730
Federal	145,416	Mississippi	688
Florida	71,319	Oklahoma	685
New York	70,198	Georgia	550
Michigan	47,718	Alabama	549
Ohio	45,833	South Carolina	532
Illinois	45,281	Nevada	518
Georgia	44,232	Arizona	515
Pennsylvania	36,847	Delaware	513
10 Lowest			
North Dakota	1,076	Minnesota	128
Maine	1,679	Maine	129
Wyoming	1,680	North Dakota	158
Vermont	1,697	New Hampshire	185
New Hampshire	2,257	Rhode Island	197
South Dakota	2,616	West Virginia	211
Montana	3,105	Vermont	218
Rhode Island	3,286	Nebraska	228
West Virginia	3,856	Washington	251
Nebraska	3,895	Utah	254

Source: Bureau of Justice Statistics, *Prisoners in 2000* (Washington, DC: U.S. Department of Justice, August, 2001), p. 5.

[a]The number of prisoners with a sentence of more than 1 year per 100,000 residents in the state population. The Federal Bureau of Prisons and the District of Columbia are excluded.

men. Today, states have numerous prisons within their jurisdiction and distribute inmates among them according to a system of prisoner classification.

Prisoner Classification

States have diverse prisons, and inmates can be placed in any prison throughout the state. Each prison is distinguished by its security level and the programs available to inmates at the institution. Before incarceration in a state prison, the inmate undergoes

diversity in the system

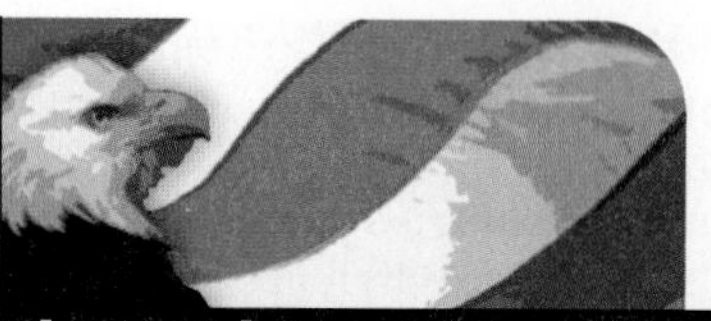

Women behind Bars

Until the nineteenth century, it was believed that female offenders were "fallen" women and could not be rehabilitated.[84] In the nineteenth century, there were few female offenders, and those few were housed in a wing or section of the men's prison and supervised by male correctional officers. Elizabeth Gurney Fry is credited with establishing the early theoretical and practical bases for women's corrections at Newgate Prison in London in the early nineteenth century. In America, between 1844 and 1848, Eliza W. B. Farnham instituted many of Fry's principles at the women's section of Sing Sing prison in New York. However, public outrage over "soft" treatment of the female offenders resulted in Farnham's dismissal. The first institution expressly for women was the Indiana Reformatory Institution for Women and Girls, built in 1873. The women's prison at Auburn, New York, did not open until 1893.

Female offenders have become more common and are routinely housed in separate facilities. Today, men are still nearly 15 times more likely than women to be in a state or federal prison. In 2000, the rate for inmates serving a sentence of more than 1 year was 66 sentenced female inmates per 100,000 women in the United Sates, compared to 961 sentenced male inmates per 100,000 men.[85] However, these figures do not reflect the growing crisis related to incarcerated female offenders. In 1983, there were 15,652 female offenders in local jails, but by 2000 there were 70,414.[86] In 1980, there were 13,400 female offenders serving a sentence of more than 1 year in a state or federal correctional institution. By 2000, that number had increased to 85,108.[87]

The shift to tougher sentences for drug offenses is a major reason for this dramatic rise in the incarceration rate for female offenders. In many states, the rate of incarceration of female offenders for drug offenses has nearly doubled since 1990.[88] Female offenders accounted for over 15 percent of defendants charged with a drug offense in U.S. district courts in 1999.[89] The number of boys charged with drug offenses in juvenile court from 1989 to 1998 dropped by 2 percent, but the number of girls charged with drug crimes rose by 2 percent.[90] Female offenders comprise 16 percent of the drug cases in juvenile court. In state prisons, 65 to 73 percent of female offenders admitted to regular drug use before incarceration.[91] Furthermore, it is estimated that many female offenders serving time for property and sex crimes were motivated to commit these crimes by the need to obtain money for drugs.

The skyrocketing increase of female offenders has created major problems for the correctional system. Female institutions are becoming overcrowded, and female offenders have less access to vocational, educational, medical, and rehabilitation programs. For example, the percentage of female offenders receiving drug treatment while in prison is declining significantly, despite the high rate of drug use among female offenders. Today, only 15 percent of state prison inmates and 10 percent of federal prison inmates obtain drug treatment while in prison, whereas in 1991, 29 percent of state and 19 percent of federal female offenders reported participation in drug treatment programs.[92]

While female offenders suffer many of the same physical and mental health problems in prison as do male prisoners, statistics indicate that the female offenders are

an extensive examination and assessment to determine an assignment to a particular facility. Because inmates remain in state custody for a relatively long period of time, the system attempts to determine the needs of the inmate and any characteristics that might influence placement. The correctional system also evaluates the security risks, staffing impacts, and institutional needs when deciding where inmates go.

prisoner classification
The reception and diagnosis of an inmate to decide the appropriate security level in which to place the prisoner and services of placement.

This process of **prisoner classification**, performed in a specially designated facility, is commonly known as reception and diagnosis. At the state's reception and diagnosis facility, the classification process includes identification of the inmate, examination of the inmate's criminal record, evaluation of the inmate's mental capacity and psychological stability, and the assessment of other factors that may influence his or her assignment, such as gang membership, age, and educational achievement.

more likely to suffer from HIV infection and mental illness than are male inmates. At year end in 1999, about 3.5 percent of female inmates in state prisons were infected with HIV, compared with about 2.2 percent of male inmates. About 24 percent of female inmates in state and federal prisons reported suffering from mental illnesses, compared with 16 percent of male inmates.[93]

Some see female offenders as victims of men.[94] You may recall from Chapter 3 that this is the view of feminist criminological theories, such as those of Freda Adler, Rita Simon, Kathleen Daly, and Meda Chesney-Lind. These criminologists argue that female offenders are victimized by a social and criminal justice system that is biased toward male dominance. Evidence of female offenders as victims of men is seen in the high rate of sexual and physical abuse reported by female offenders. About 57 percent of state female inmates and 40 percent of federal female inmates report that they were sexually or physically abused before admission, whereas only 16 percent of state male inmates and 7 percent of federal male inmates report that they were abused, and the proportions are similar for jail inmates.[95] Abuse of female offenders continues after incarceration, as there are frequent scandals involving correctional officers demanding sex from female inmates. Many former female inmates allege that during their incarceration, sex with male correctional officers in exchange for favors was commonplace. "Sexual favors are part of a hidden prison economy, in exchange for avoiding retribution, getting drugs, or obtaining extra privileges, such as staying up after hours."[96]

More than 1.5 million children in the United States have parents in prison.[97] The burden of incarceration falls heavier on female offenders than on male offenders. Families are more likely to be broken by a woman's confinement in the criminal justice system than by a man's.[98] On average, about 80 percent of female inmates have dependent children.[99] In 1998, 1,400 babies were delivered in prisons, only to be removed from their mothers shortly after birth.

Most mothers plan to return to their families after their release but frequently are poorly prepared for this task. Female offenders have fewer visits with family during their incarceration than do male offenders. One reason for this is that due to a lack of female prisons, female offenders often are incarcerated farther from home than are male offenders. Another reason is that when male offenders are incarcerated, custody of children typically remains with the mother, whereas when females are imprisoned, grandparents frequently become the caretakers of the children. Most data suggest that incarcerated women do not see their children at all.[100] Some innovative programs try to help keep female offenders united with their families. A promising program that is effective, inexpensive, and easy to administer is "Girl Scouts Beyond Bars."[101] The program provides for regular contact between mothers and daughters through Girl Scout programs conducted in prisons.

On their return to the community, female offenders are likely to face significant problems, including parental poverty, unemployment, substance abuse, low self-esteem, and ill health. Often, the problems of the parent are visited on the children, as child abuse and neglect are common outcomes. Children of incarcerated parents are five times more likely to offend than are children whose parents have not been incarcerated. This starts a vicious cycle of crime that is difficult to break.

While it is rare for female offenders to be executed, in 2000 there were 54 women under the sentence of death in 18 states.[102] Beginning with the earliest American colonial period, only about 561 women have been executed. Of this number, 137 executions have occurred since 1973.[103] Typically, 5 to 10 female offenders are executed per year. More than likely, the female murderer's victim was a family member, child, spouse, or boyfriend.

■ **What are some differences between male and female inmates? Why has female offending and incarceration soared in recent years? What special problems do women in prison face? What are the human costs of female incarceration?**

At the classification facility, the inmate is inducted into the state's prison system. Prisoners exchange their clothing for prison clothing, undergo extensive and intrusive searches for weapons or contraband, are photographed and fingerprinted, and are assigned an identification number or prisoner I.D. This process is similar to the booking process that occurs when a person is first arrested for a crime, but it must be repeated, because it is possible that the inmate reporting for prison is not the person who was convicted of the crime. Such a case was discovered in October 2000, when a federal prisoner walked away from a minimum-custody federal correctional facility. When police found and returned the escapee, prison officials found that he was an imposter.[104] The convicted offender had arranged for another person to report to prison

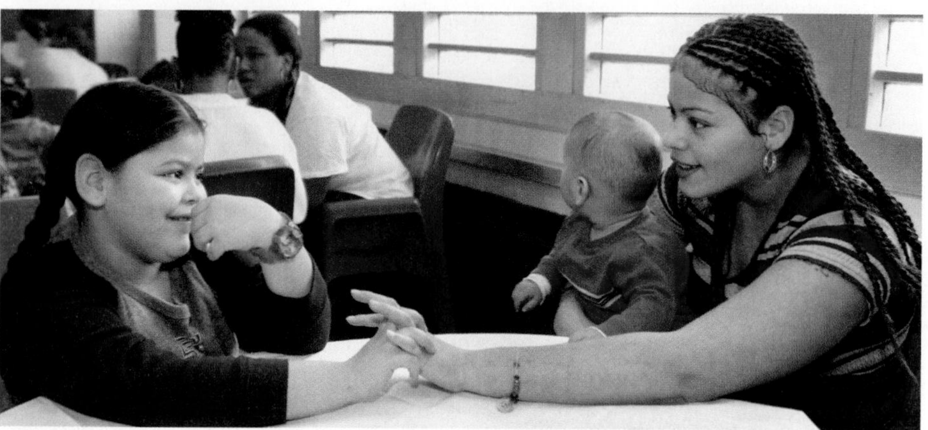

The experience of women in custody can be more troubling than what their male counterparts face. One major difference concerns children. Over half of female inmates have children under age 18, and the majority of the mothers were the primary caregivers at the time of their arrest. At the 1,800-bed detention facility for women at Rikers Island, New York—the nation's largest jail and detention complex—mothers reported that forced separation from their children was the most painful punishment they had to endure.

and serve time in his place. Officials had failed to detect this switch before the impostor had actually served 18 months of the other man's sentence.[105]

Security Levels

A primary purpose of classification is to determine what level of security is appropriate for the inmate. The security level of prisons is based on a scale from relatively few or mild security measures in place to prevent escape to many strong or harsh security systems to prevent escape. The levels are minimum security, medium security, and maximum security. Each state has a unique name or number system to identify security levels, but the basic principle is the same from state to state. Some state prisons have the capacity to house inmates with different security level classifications, such as having both medium- and high-security inmates being held in the same institution.

minimum-security prisons Prisons with few physical barriers to escape and many programs for inmates.

medium-security prisons Fortress-like, walled, self-contained institutions that offer inmates educational, vocational, and rehabilitation programs.

MINIMUM-SECURITY PRISONS **Minimum-security prisons** have few physical barriers to escape and may resemble a college campus or a farm. There are no walls, tower guards, or fortress-like structures at minimum-security prisons, and inmates have extensive freedom of movement. At a minimum-security prison farm, for example, an inmate may report to work in the morning and may work unsupervised in a remote area until the end of the day. Because of the lack of security, if an inmate flees from such an institution it is called a "walk-away" rather than an escape, although the offense and punishment are the same. Obviously, only prisoners that are not an escape risk are placed in a minimum-security prison.

MEDIUM-SECURITY PRISONS **Medium-security prisons** are fortress-like, walled, self-contained institutions. Armed correctional officers guard the perimeters of medium-security prisons, and the movement and activities of inmates are closely supervised. Medium-security prisons offer several living arrangements. The inmate can be assigned to a single cell, a shared cell, or a dormitory-like arrangement in which several

This Administrative Maximum Unit Prison (ADX) in Florence, Colorado, which opened in 1994, is the epitome of the super-maximum-security prison. It was modeled after the United States Penitentiary at Marion, Illinois, which was opened in 1963 to replace Alcatraz. Marion is in permanent lockdown, maintaining absolute physical and psychological control over inmates. As at Marion, prisoners at Florence remain in their cells almost all the time in a state of isolation and sensory deprivation. Out-of-cell time is a total of 9 hours a week, when an inmate is allowed to interact with one other person.

dozen inmates may share a common space. During classification, corrections officials determine which living arrangement is most appropriate for an inmate.

Medium-security state prisons offer educational, vocational, and rehabilitation programs for inmates. For example, inmates who have not completed high school routinely are required to complete the equivalency degree for a high school diploma. These inmates spend most of their day attending educational classes. Other inmates may enroll in vocational training programs such as automobile repair, refrigerator repair, printing, welding, or computer programming, or may work in a prison industry. The inmates' participation in these programs creates an inherent security risk, as inmates may have access to tools that could be used as weapons or to facilitate escape. Another security risk is created by inmates moving from work to their cells or to a dining facility. Unlike in the past, prisoners do not march in lockstep or observe the rule of silence. Thus, opportunities exist for inmates to plot escapes and equip themselves for this possibility.

MAXIMUM-SECURITY AND SUPERMAX PRISONS **Maximum-security prisons** are for prisoners who have been determined to be at high risk for escape or who are too violent to be placed in an environment in which they could attack another inmate or a guard. Maximum-security prisons are the most expensive of the prison facilities, and states have fewer maximum-security beds than any other type. Thus, prison officials must consider carefully who will be placed in a maximum-security prison, as these bed spaces are usually booked to capacity. Maximum-security prisons have few or no educational, vocational, or prison industry programs, because of the inherent security risks, and they provide prisoners with little freedom of movement. In extreme cases, a prisoner may be confined in the cell for 23 hours per day. Maximum-security prisons have extensive armed security, and the primary purpose is to ensure that inmates do not escape.

Some states have found it necessary to have one additional classification for especially violent or high-risk inmates—the super-maximum-security, or supermax, prison usually is a lockdown facility in which inmates remain in their cells and are moved only in chains and under guard. **Supermax prisons** offer no programs and restrict visitation rights and public access. These facilities are reserved for the most violent inmates within the state's prison system. Because supermax facilities are very expensive to operate, some states have chosen not to build them but to house their most violent inmates in a prison—a separate facility within the perimeter of a maximum-security prison. Some states also have built separate facilities for prisoners under sentence of death, who have little to lose by violating prison rules.

maximum-security prisons Prisons for inmates at high risk of escape or who are dangerously violent to other inmates or staff.

supermax prisons Controversial, extreme forms of maximum-security prisons.

Special Prison Populations

Some prisoners may not be suited to transfer to the general prison population. Because of age, mental illness, depression, other health status, or other characteristic, it may be necessary to keep the inmate out of the general population. During the classification process, the inmate is administered psychological tests to determine his or her mental stability. Incarceration can trigger intense depression, and as a result, some prisoners are high suicide risks. Prison officials attempt to identify such prisoners, provide assistance, and place them under constant observation in what is known as "suicide watch." As Table 12.3 suggests, inmate deaths from suicide and other causes also occur in local jails. Some inmates require psychiatric treatment and would be a danger to others or themselves if placed in the general population. During classification, these inmates are identified and often transferred to appropriate mental health care facilities.

During the classification process, prison officials also try to determine if the inmate's lifestyle or special needs should influence placement. Specific assignments may be based on the inmate's age, sexual orientation, gang affiliation, or physical health. Inmates with significant health problems, such as AIDS or tuberculosis, require extensive health care in prison. (The special case of inmates with HIV/AIDS is discussed in detail in Chapter 15.) Prison officials are responsible for providing appropriate health care and protecting other inmates and staff from infectious diseases.

Young prisoners, usually under 25 or 26 years old, may need to be separated from older, more hardened offenders. Elderly prisoners, an increasing challenge to correctional institutions, also may need to be protected from the general prison population. The "graying of inmates" is becoming more of a problem for prisons because of longer prison sentences and demographic factors such as aging baby boomers in the prison population.

Gang affiliation also is an important consideration in determining where to house a prisoner, and can be a real dilemma. Gang members placed together may post a security risk, as they will conspire together. However, an inmate placed in a housing unit with rival gang members may be assaulted. In some cases, groups of gang rivals forced to live together may engage in gang warfare.

A prisoner's classification may be changed based on behavior, a change in status, or other consideration. For instance, a prisoner assigned to maximum security may be reassigned to medium security based on good behavior and time served. A prisoner

table 12.3 Inmate Deaths in Jails

Very few inmates die while being held in local jails—less than two-tenths of 1 percent. The most common cause of death is illness, followed by suicide. Inmates suspected of considering suicide are placed on "suicide watch."

	Number	Percent
Illness/natural cause (excluding AIDS)	385	41.8
AIDS	78	8.5
Suicide	324	35.3
Homicide	28	3.0
Other	104	11.3
Total	919	

Source: Bureau of Justice Statistics, *Census of Jails, 1999* (Washington, DC: U.S. Department of Justice, August 2001), p. 8.

careers  in the system

Employment in State Prisons

In most state prison systems, the administrative staff is divided into two major categories: professional staff and correctional or custodial staff. Staffing also may be divided into three categories: administrative, treatment, and supervisory and security. A large prison, especially a medium- or maximum-security prison, is a self-contained city, and prison officials must provide numerous services to keep the prison functioning. These services relate to prison security and basic operations of providing services to the inmates and staff. Employees who work to maintain supervision and prison security are the correctional or custodial staff employees.[106] In most prisons, these are uniformed employees trained to oversee the safe movement and conduct of the inmate population. **Correctional officers** often have military-type ranks and titles similar to those used in police departments, such as sergeant, lieutenant, and captain. These officers may carry weapons in the performance of their duty and may be authorized to use deadly force to prevent prisoners from escaping. However, they do not have the power of arrest or search and seizure of citizens outside the prison, or the right to carry concealed weapons off-duty.

Entry-level correctional officers usually are required to have a high school diploma and other minimum qualifications, such as good moral character and a level of physical fitness, but the requirements are less stringent than those required for entry-level police officers. Entry-level custodial and security employees receive academy training similar to that provided to police officers, but the training academy for correctional officers normally lasts only about 2 to 6 weeks, followed by on-the-job training. Some states require that entry-level security officers undergo psychological and polygraph examinations, but many do not.

Employees in a prison who provide nonsecurity services, such as treatment staff and administrators, may be medical doctors, dentists, nurses, psychologists, counselors, teachers, recreational specialists, business administrators, secretaries, cooks, librarians, and so forth. If the prison has a prison industry, civilian employees supervise inmates' training and work. If the prison has an educational program, full-time teachers are employed to instruct inmates. The prison may have a hospital or clinic where medical personnel practice. All prisons have counselors who provide drug counseling or mental health services. Unlike the correctional officers, professional staff are civilians and do not wear uniforms. They do not have military-like titles and ranks, do not carry or use firearms, and do not have any police powers or receive academy training, and they are not required to meet physical fitness standards.

Correctional officers and treatment staff generally are civil service employees and obtain their positions by competitive examination and job-related qualifications. They do not serve at the pleasure of the warden or other administrator. In some prisons, the employees are unionized.

■ **How are correctional officers and law enforcement officers alike? How are they different? What other careers can be pursued in the correctional system? What are the key services that prisons, as "self-contained cities," must provide?**

assigned to minimum security who tries to escape, on the other hand, may be reassigned to a higher security prison.

■ State Prison Administration

State prison systems are the financial and administrative responsibility of each state and are therefore independent and unique. No federal agency has oversight responsibility for state prisons, although the federal government can influence state prisons indirectly through federal legislation, the U.S. Supreme Court, and conditions imposed on their remaining eligible for federal grants. The greatest impact of the federal government on state prisons has been U.S. Supreme Court rulings requiring minimum living standards and guaranteeing prisoner rights.

correctional officer Uniformed jail or prison employee whose primary job is the security and movement of inmates.

The web site of the American Correctional Association, at http://www.corrections.com/aca/, includes a career development section with job listings. ■

Formal oversight of state prisons is under the direction of the executive branch of the state government. The governor usually has the power to appoint the persons who run the prisons. The state legislative body controls the budget for the prison system, and the state courts rule on the legality of prison conditions and punishments. The chief administrative officer of a state prison is the **warden**, usually an appointee of the governor. The warden, in turn, appoints associate or assistant wardens, who run various units of the prison, such as security, education and recreational programs, and vocational programs. Associate and assistant wardens usually are civil service employees.

Informal oversight over state prisons occurs through organizations such as the **American Correctional Association** (ACA), which offers voluntary accreditation of 20 different types of correctional facilities and programs. Accreditation is based on compliance with national standards for the effective and professional operation and management of correctional systems. These standards cover administration and fiscal controls, staff training and development, physical plant, safety and emergency procedures, sanitation, food service, and rules and discipline. The ACA looks for practical, up-to-date policies and procedures that safeguard the life, health, and safety of staff and inmates.

JUST THE FACTS 12.5

What is the purpose of state prisons? By what process are inmates classified and placed? How are prison security levels defined? What considerations are given to special prison populations? What jobs are required to run a state prison? What do correctional officers do?

Federal Prisons

THE MAIN IDEA

Federal prisons are correctional facilities for inmates convicted of federal crimes.

The Department of Justice site at http://www.usdoj.gov/prisoninfo.htm has a list of all the federal prison facilities and explains how to get federal inmate information. ■

For over 100 years after the founding of the United States, there were no federal prisons. Federal prisoners were housed in state prisons for a fee. It was not until 1895 that the first federal prison for men was constructed at Leavenworth, Kansas. Using the labor of military prisoners at the nearby United States Disciplinary Barracks at Fort Leavenworth, the first federal prison was built in the architectural style of the times. Leavenworth prison was a walled, maximum-security prison based on the Auburn concept of inside cell blocks and congregate work. As in state prisons and local jails, the number of federal female offenders was only about one-tenth that of male offenders. The first federal prison for women was constructed in 1927. Like state prisons, oversight of federal prisons is balanced among the legislative, executive, and judicial branches of the federal government. The U.S. Congress funds federal prisons, which are under the executive control of the Office of the President. The U.S. Supreme Court has the power of judicial review and can declare that prison conditions are unconstitutional or that inmate rights have been violated.

■ The Federal Bureau of Prisons

warden The chief administrator of a prison.

Prohibition created many new federal offenses for trafficking in illegal alcoholic beverages, spurring the growth of federal prisons. In 1930, the federal government unified its prisons under the administrative control of the newly formed Federal Bureau of Pris-

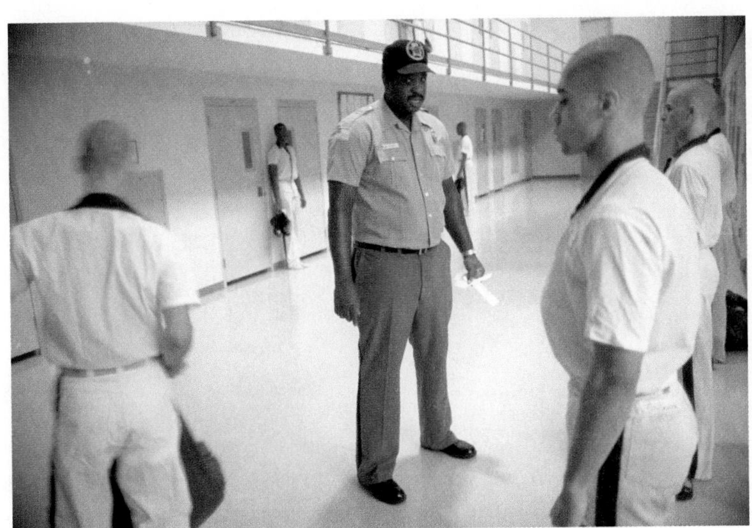

Correctional officers in federal penitentiaries typically must meet higher entry standards than those in state prisons, and they receive more training and higher pay. However, the custodial and security functions of correctional officers in state and federal institutions are basically the same. The goals are protecting the safety and security of inmates and staff and maintaining control over the smooth operation of all aspects of the facility.

ons. After repeal of prohibition, the number of federal prisoners continued to increase due to federal drug prosecutions, firearms violations, and, recently, mandatory sentencing. As the federal prison population exploded, overcrowding became a serious problem, and it was necessary to construct new federal prisons. Because of the nationwide jurisdiction of the federal prison system, new prisons could be built anywhere in the United States. Federal inmates could be housed in any federal prison in the country and could be transferred among the prisons at will. This authority to transfer federal inmates anywhere in the United States has been a great advantage of the federal prison system.[107]

In 1934, using this power, the newly formed Federal Bureau of Prisons built one of the most infamous prisons in U.S. history—the United States Penitentiary at Alcatraz, California, in San Francisco Bay. The most violent and highest security-risk inmates were then transferred from the various federal prisons to Alcatraz. **Alcatraz** was a maximum-security prison without any rehabilitation, educational, or treatment programs. Its primary goal was the incarceration of high-risk inmates and it gave little, if any, attention to rehabilitation goals, vocational programs, or educational programs. Alcatraz, which at one time housed Al Capone, prided itself on being escape-proof. In 1946, Alcatraz erupted in violence as two correctional officers and three inmates were killed during an escape attempt. Public perception of federal prisons was shaped by this event and by movies about notorious Alcatraz inmates. The prison was closed permanently in 1963 and today remains a popular tourist destination.

Federal Correctional Facilities

Today, the Federal Bureau of Prisons operates over 80 different types of federal correctional facilities throughout the United States, with a total inmate population of over 130,000.[108] The Federal Bureau of Prisons central office in Washington, DC, has six regional offices to oversee the operation of federal prison facilities. Federal prisons range from the supermax prison in **Florence**, Colorado, to minimum-security federal prison farms. The federal government even operates "coed" minimum-security correctional facilities, the largest of which is in Lexington, Kentucky. Some federal prison facilities serve primarily as medical centers for federal prisoners, and others as detention centers and prison camps. Table 12.4 on page 396 compares state and federal prisons in terms of prison populations.

Federal prisons use a security and classification system similar to that used by state prisons. New inmates are interviewed and screened to see which facility is most

table 12.4 **Number of Persons Held in State or Federal Prisons, 1990–2000**

The number of inmates in custody has nearly doubled since 1990. This increase occurred despite a decrease in the crime rate during the late 1990s.

Year	Total Inmates in Custody	Prisoners in Custody on December 31	
		Federal	State
1990	1,148,702	58,838	684,544
1995	1,585,586	89,538	989,004
1996	1,646,020	95,088	1,032,440
1997	1,743,643	101,755	1,074,809
1998	1,816,931	110,793	1,113,676
1999*	1,893,115	125,682	1,161,490
2000	1,933,503	133,921	1,178,433
Percentage change, 1999–2000	2.1%	6.6%	1.5%
Average annual increase, 1990–2000	5.3%	8.6%	5.6%

Source: Bureau of Justice Statistics, *Prisoners in 2000* (Washington, DC: U.S. Department of Justice, August 2001), p. 2.

Note: Counts include all inmates held in public and private adult correctional facilities.

*In 1999, 15 states expanded their reporting criteria to include inmates held in privately operated correctional facilities. For comparisons with previous years, the state count of 1,137,544 and the total count of 1,869,169 should be used.

Visit the Federal Bureau of Prisons at http://www.bop.gov/. ■

appropriate for them. Based on similar state criteria, the Federal Bureau of Prisons assigns prisoners according to a five-tier classification of its facilities: minimum, low, medium, high, and administrative. In the maximum-security prison, inmates are locked down, have little freedom of movement, and receive no recreational, educational, or vocational programs. At the minimum-security facilities, inmates have great freedom of movement and interaction with other inmates and have access to recreational opportunities and educational and vocational programs.

As in state prisons, the chief executive officer at a federal prison facility is the warden, who has various associates and assistants to help run the administrative units. Employees of the Federal Bureau of Prisons are federal employees, who generally receive better pay and benefits than state prison or local jail employees. Generally, however, the hiring standards are higher. Federal correctional officers must have a bachelor's degree, for example, whereas most states do not require a college degree. Federal Bureau of Prisons employees may transfer from one federal facility to another, so opportunities for advancement are greater than in state prisons or local jails. As in state prisons, staffing in federal prisons is divided between employees who primarily perform security duties and those who provide treatment services.

JUST THE FACTS 12.6

What events spurred the growth of federal prisons? How do federal prisons differ from state prisons in terms of goals, organization, and administration? What career advantages does employment in the federal prison system offer?

Private Jails and Prisons

THE MAIN IDEA

Because of overcrowding of correctional facilities and budget constraints in the face of the high costs of prison construction and staffing, state and federal prisoners are being housed in for-profit private jails and prisons.

A trend in corrections has been the **privatization** of jails and prisons. In 1999, there were 47 private jails housing 16,646 inmates and serving the same purpose as local jails. A number of counties unable to afford the cost of building and operating a jail have contracted with private security companies to house county inmates. Often, private jails are built in rural areas and house inmates from several counties. Unlike government-operated jails, private jails are for-profit ventures, which leads to concerns about oversight as well as about the quality of care and supervision inmates receive. The fewer services the private jail provides, the more profitable it is to house an inmate. Charges for housing an inmate in a private jail vary, ranging from about $25 per day per inmate to nearly $100 per day. The private jail must pay for all expenses from its revenues and still be able to show a profit.

Critics of the privatization of corrections argue that private companies provide less training and pay to jail personnel, and have higher inmate-to-correctional officer ratios than do county jails.[109] Proponents of privatization point to the cost and crowding of local jails. While the total number of inmates housed in private jails is small, the number of private jails has almost tripled since 1993. More counties have chosen to use private jails rather than build or expand their own jail facilities.

Private prisons are more numerous than private jails. In 2000, there were 264 privately operated state and federal prison facilities housing more than 87,000 prisoners. Private facilities held 5.8 percent of all state prisoners and 10.7 percent of all federal prisoners.[110] Some states had from 21 to 40 percent of their state prison population housed in a private prison, mainly because of overcrowding and associated high costs.[111] Figure 12.4 shows how state correctional expenditures rose between 1985 and 1996. In fiscal

privatization Trend toward the use of for-profit jails and prisons run by private companies.

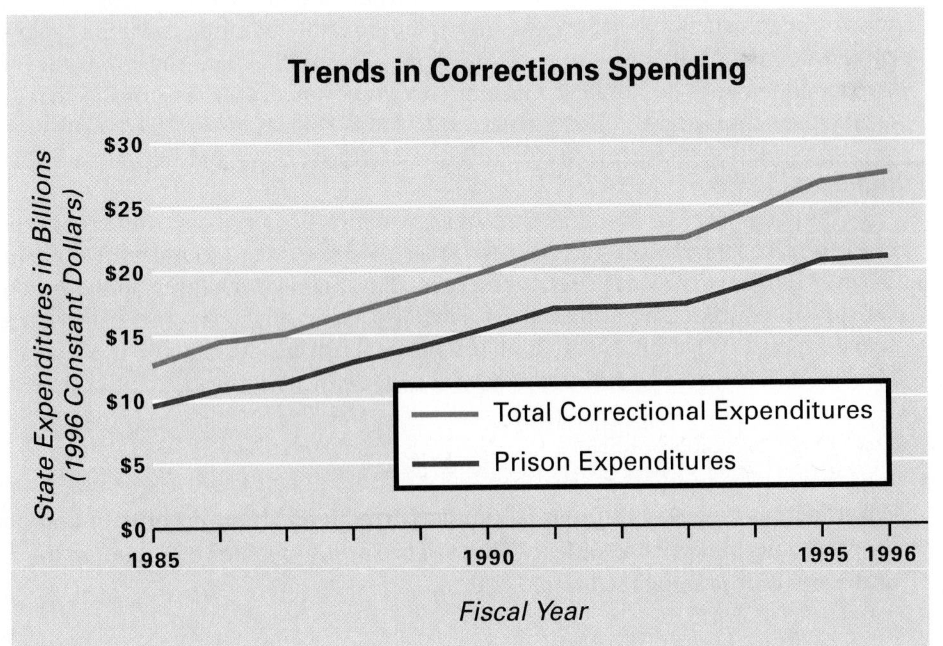

Source: Bureau of Justice Statistics, *State Prison Expenditures, 1996* (Washington, DC: U.S. Department of Justice, August 1999), p. 1.

Figure 12.4

Trends in Corrections Spending

The cost of operating correctional institutions, prisons in particular, have continued to rise. Each year between 1985 and 1996, states increased their spending for all corrections an average of 7.2%, and for prisons alone, an average of 7.3%.

Figure 12.5

State Spending on Prisons, 1996

Gone are the days when prisons did not cost the state any money to operate. Prisons are a major expenditure for states, and this has stimulated the growth of private correctional facilities.

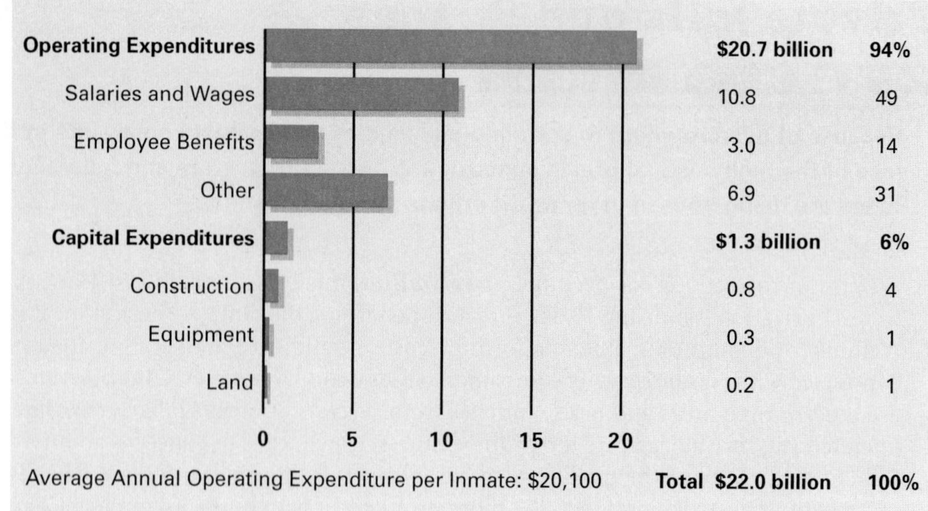

Source: Bureau of Justice Statistics, *State Prison Expenditures, 1996* (Washington, DC: U.S. Department of Justice, August 1999), p. v.

year 1996, states spent about $22 billion on prisons, and in 1997, this figure rose to more than $27 billion (Figure 12.5).

Many private prisons receive government assistance such as tax breaks, government financing, training grants, and construction help.[112] While private prisons help relieve the burden on overcrowded state and federal prisons, they often are criticized as detrimental to low-income communities, where most private prisons are located. Private companies market their services to the state on promises of providing jobs in low-income communities and providing inmate labor for community projects.[113] With some outstanding exceptions, pay and benefits, however, as well as prison conditions, often are below state standards.[114]

Another concern of critics is the issue of state liability for violation of inmates' constitutional rights and the abuse of inmates while housed in a private prison. Because it placed the inmate in the prison, the state retains liability but little control. Employees of private prisons are not government employees, and they and the companies that operate the prisons do not have immunity from certain lawsuits by inmates that government prisons enjoy.[115] Nevertheless, thousands of lawsuits are filed against state prisons as well as private prisons for violation of inmate rights and substandard prison conditions.[116]

A unique problem for private prisons is the jurisdiction of law enforcement over escaped prisoners. Not all states have enacted legislation that recognizes the potential status of inmates in private prisons as escapees. Thus, a prisoner who escapes from a private prison may not have broken a state law! Also, an assault by an inmate on a correctional officer at a private facility is an assault on a private citizen (a tort), whereas an assault on a state or federal correctional officer is defined as a more serious crime.

JUST THE FACTS 12.7

What factors have led to privatization in corrections? How do private and government jails and prisons differ? What are the arguments for and against the use of private correctional facilities?

conclusion:

Prisons—The Human Cage

Jails and prisons are designed to hold humans in a secure environment to prevent their escape. Frequently, the concern of the public is not the conditions of the jails or prisons but the perceived risk of escape and fear of harm caused by escaping prisoners. Most citizens strongly object to a jail or prison being built in their neighborhood.[117] Some citizens appear to have little sympathy for incarcerated inmates. For example, in response to a report on four suicides in a municipal jail, one editorial dismissed concerns about the deaths, arguing, "These suspects had been arrested for murder, kidnapping, burglary, drug dealing, assault and drunken driving. I do not consider these deaths as tragic losses. Rather, these four saved the overburdened taxpayers a great deal of money by taking their fates into their own hands."[118]

Jails and prisons represent a substantial financial burden and directly compete with other needed services. Often, people see every dollar that goes into jails and prisons as one less dollar to go to other services, such as schools, hospitals, medical care, public safety, and transportation. For example, when a Pennsylvania jail warden turned in a request for $500,000 for new computers for an educational program for Pittsburgh jail inmates, the county refused to process the invoice.[119] The computers were to be purchased from profits from the jail's commissary, where inmates buy candy, snacks, and toiletries, but the county government argued that the money should be returned to the taxpayers. As one official expressed, "We have taxpayers who can't even afford (computers). Before we give that type of convenience to prisoners, we should balance the budget. It's not our responsibility to educate and entertain the inmates."[120]

Recidivism rates show that jails and prisons have not proved as effective as desired. They have not protected the pubic from criminal activity in the long run. They have not deterred people from committing crimes through the threat or pain of incarceration, nor have they rehabilitated inmates, whether through penitence, educational training, or harsh discipline. Some have argued that prisons are nothing but warehouses in which inmates are placed because society cannot think of more effective solutions to an age-old problem. The public has become frustrated with the cost and lack of effectiveness of locking criminals in cages and waiting. The trend toward privatization has been one consequence. As the next chapters show, an emphasis on diversion, probation, early release, and community-based corrections is another response.

Chapter Summary

- Before jails and prisons, punishment was based on administering physical pain and public humiliation through branding, mutilation, and whipping, and on torture through devices such as pillories.
- Incarceration arose in societies that could afford it as an alternative to corporal punishment, banishment, enslavement, transportation, and execution. Widespread poverty as a result of immigration, urbanization, and industrialization led to the rise of jails and prisons.
- Bridewells, hulks, and *bagnes* were early European prisons. In the United States, Pennsylvania's Walnut Street Jail and Eastern State Penitentiary and New York's Auburn State Prison established uniquely American correctional models.
- Early American jails and prisons had rehabilitation as a goal. Prison labor was exploited, especially in colonies with indentured servitude and in southern penal systems, which operated on a convict lease system. Later, American jails and prisons had retribution as the chief goal.
- Prison reforms following World War II stemmed from the U.S. Supreme Court ruling that inmates have the right to sue the government over prison conditions and civil rights violations.
- Jails are short-term, multipurpose facilities that serve as a gateway to the criminal justice system. Federal jails are operated through the Federal Bureau of Prisons, county jails through sheriffs' departments, and municipal jails through police departments.
- State prisons contain only convicted offenders. States have their own systems, which vary significantly among states. Oversight comes through prison administration, headed by the warden, and through state and federal legislation and state and federal courts.
- States run reception and diagnosis centers to classify incoming inmates and place them in appropriate facilities—minimum-, medium-, or maximum-security prisons. Supermax prisons hold the most violent inmates in permanent lockdown.
- Prison populations include men, youths, the elderly, women, gang members, inmates living with AIDS, and persons with other health problems or mental illnesses, and these populations challenge the correctional system.
- State prison employees include correctional officers—civil service employees who perform security services—treatment staff, and other professional personnel. Most state prisons are like small, self-contained cities.
- Federal prisons such as Leavenworth and Alcatraz were built during the prohibition era and are run by the Federal Bureau of Prisons. The federal prison system parallels state prison systems in classification and administration, but federal prisons have higher standards for employment.
- Private jails and prisons developed as a result of overcrowding and the high cost of building and staffing correctional institutions. People disagree about the benefits and costs of privatization to both inmates and communities.

Vocabulary Review

Names and Events to Remember

Alcatraz, 395
American Correctional Association (ACA), 394
Auburn Prison, 378
Eastern State Penitentiary, 377
Federal Bureau of Prisons (BOP), 383
Florence, 395
John Howard (*State of Prisons*), 376
Hulks Act of 1776, 375
Philadelphia Society to Alleviate the Miseries of Public Prisons, 377
Walnut Street Jail, 377
Whipping Act of 1530, 373

Think about This

1. Two-thirds of inmates become repeat offenders. Is a system that is one-third effective acceptable? What do you think is a reasonable rate of success for prisons, and how would success be measured? After introducing restorative justice programs, countries such as New Zealand and Australia reported significant drops in repeat offending. Why might that be the case? Why haven't restorative justice programs received greater acceptance in the United States?
2. In early 2002, an inmate sentenced to life in prison received a heart transplant, at a cost to taxpayers of nearly one million dollars. Many other prisoners have received liver and kidney transplants. A case was presented before the courts to allow a transsexual inmate (serving a life term for murdering his wife) to receive a sex-change operation. Do you think inmates should have the right to such expensive health care? Why, or why not?
3. After reading about the history of punishment and prisons, which goals and method(s) do you think were most effective? How might earlier forms of punishment be updated to fit present-day realities?

ContentSelect

Go to the ContentSelect web site and key in the search word "prisoners." Read "Experience of Abuse among Women Visiting Incarcerated Partners" from the January 2001 issue of the journal *Violence against Women*. This compelling article discusses how partners cope with the incarceration of their spouses, how women view the private family visit, and how the women were more fearful of their encounters with prison authorities than with their potentially violent partners. Sample the article to answer the following questions.

1. According to the section "Living with a Partner in Prison," what life changes do partners of prisoners experience?
2. According to the section "Abuse and Fear Involving the Partner," how do prisoners try to maintain control over their partners from inside the prison?
3. How are female partners treated by the prison authorities? What does the article claim is the "paradox concerning the safety of women in PFVs"?
4. How do prisoners feel about conjugal visits? How do their partners feel?
5. According to the text, in what ways does the sentencing and incarceration of the accused take into account the needs of the accused's family? How could society better serve the family of a prisoner?

chapter 13

Probation and Parole

outline

Learning Objectives

After reading this chapter, you will know

- The differences between diversion, probation, and parole.
- The definitions and outcomes of mandatory and good-time release.
- The meaning of pardons and commutation of sentence.
- The origins and reasons for probation and parole.
- How a judge decides on granting probation.
- How a parole board decides on granting parole.
- The conditions of probation and parole and when probation and parole can be revoked.
- The advantages and disadvantages of probation and parole for offenders, communities, and the criminal justice system.
- The roles and functions performed by career probation and parole officers.

Rapist Hunted: Let Loose after Parole Violation

Cops are searching for a paroled rapist who was set free on $500 bail—even though he allegedly menaced a man September 11, claiming to be one of the terrorists responsible for the Trade Center attacks.

Michael Galgano, 38, walked up to a man on a blood-donor line at St. Vincent's Hospital shortly after the towers collapsed and declared, "I'm the reason for what happened," an NYPD spokesman said.

"He threatened to assault the victim, while reaching into his knapsack" as if he had a weapon, the spokesman said.

He was arrested and appeared before Manhattan criminal court Judge Gregory Carro two days later on charges of menacing and aggravated harassment. He was sprung on the low bail even though the prosecutor had asked for $2,000, according to a spokeswoman for the Manhattan DA's office.

She said Carro had been told Galgano was a paroled rapist.

Galgano is a registered sex offender who served 10 years in California for raping and choking two women and emptying a pistol at several others who spurned his advances, authorities said.

He had been given permission by California officials to move to New York in 1999, but he was required to register with local parole authorities.

Galgano lived for a while with his parents in Port Jefferson Station, L.I., but moved to a different address without telling officials, according to the Suffolk County DA.

His arrest in Manhattan constituted a parole violation. It was not clear why he was let go.

Officials could not immediately say why a more thorough probe was not launched in light of his claim to be a terrorist.

—Kieran Cowley, "Rapist Hunted: Let Loose after Parole Violation," *New York Post*, December 14, 2001, p. 26.

introduction:

Why Early Release?

Michael Galgano could be the poster child for those campaigning for a "get tough on criminals" policy of locking them up and throwing away the key. Galgano is every citizen's nightmare—a crazed sex-offender who is loose in the community not because he escaped from prison but because the criminal justice system released him. If the public is concerned that the criminal justice system releases inmates before they serve their complete sentence, they have good reason for concern. Approximately 4.6 million adult men and women were on probation or parole at the end of 2000. Of these 4.6 million offenders, how many are like Michael Galgano, a danger to the community? Why does the criminal justice system release prisoners before they have served their time or give them suspended sentences rather than prison time? Who is responsible for supervising the millions of inmates released on probation and parole, and how do they accomplish their job?

An important reason that persons convicted of crimes may not serve the entire length of their sentences is the growing cost of prison. As you read in Chapter 12, tough sentencing laws have increased the number of inmates despite a drop in the crime rate. Prisons are expensive, and many states are forced to evaluate whether they can afford to continue locking up criminals for long periods of time. Since the 1970s, the number of state prisoners has increased 500 percent, making prisons the fastest-growing item in state budgets.[1] Many states are finding that prison spending competes with other needs. Taxpayers are reluctant to keep spending money on corrections if that means there is less money to spend on schools.[2] As a result, many states are seeking ways to reduce prison costs, including drastic measures such as closing prisons. California closed five small, privately operated minimum-security prisons in 2002. Ohio, Michigan, and Illinois also have closed prisons. Michigan moved prisoners from jails back to prison to save the $500,000 needed to keep them in local jails. States also are reexamining their ability to pay for long prison terms. Prison terms for nonviolent offenders and habitual offender laws that result in 30+-year prison terms are expensive correctional policies.[3] Also, data on rehabilitation, comparative studies of other countries, and criminal justice scholars maintain that there may be alternatives to prison that provide community safety and better rehabilitation. As a result of these pressures, many states are using new correctional strategies to replace imprisonment.

Defining Diversion, Probation, and Parole

THE MAIN IDEA

Alternatives to incarceration include diversion for defendants, probation or suspended sentence for convicted offenders, and parole or early release for prisoners.

Before discussing alternative strategies, it is important to define and distinguish diversion, probation, and parole. Some offenders do not serve any of their prison time, while others are sentenced to prison but released prior to the end of their term of punishment. Offenders may not serve time because they are diverted from the criminal justice system or because their sentences are suspended.

In **diversion**, the defendant is offered an alternative to a criminal trial, possible conviction, and prison sentence, such as drug court, boot camp, or a treatment program. When a defendant is convicted in a criminal court and sentenced to prison, but the prison term is suspended, the defendant does not have to serve time in prison and is said to be on **suspended sentence**, or probation. Probation, a sentencing option of the trial judge, diverts the offender after conviction but prior to serving prison time.

In parole, the offender has been sentenced to prison, serves a portion of his or her time, and is released before the maximum term of the sentence. The decision to parole a prisoner is made by a parole board. Prisoners released under probation or parole are subject to continued supervision in the community and can be returned to prison if they violate the terms of their release. Other means by which a prisoner can be released from prison other than probation and parole include mandatory release, good-time release, pardon, and commutation of sentence.

For comparative information, log on to http://www.homeoffice.gov.uk/nps to view the web site of the National Probation Service for England and Wales.

Mandatory and Good-Time Release

When prisoners serve the entire length of their maximum sentence, it is required by law that they be released. This is called **mandatory release**. An inmate cannot be held in prison beyond the length of his or her sentence. Even if the prisoner obviously is not rehabilitated or prepared for reentry into society, he or she must be released after serving the time. These prisoners are released without any supervision, without any restrictions on their behavior, and frequently without any support or rehabilitation plan. Mandatory release requires that prison officials release a prisoner who has served the maximum sentence regardless of the danger that the prisoner may pose to the community. An argument for early release is that, unlike mandatory release, early release lets probationers and parolees back into the community with supervision and behavioral restrictions

Another form of mandatory release is when prisoners have served less than their full sentences but have earned good-time credit that entitles them to an early release. **Good-time credit** toward early release is a strategy to encourage the prisoner to obey institutional rules, refrain from violence and drug use, and participate in rehabilitation and vocational programs. In place of punishment for disobedience, good-time release gives inmates an incentive to comply with prison authority and rules. When the inmate is processed into the system, a percentage of the inmate's sentence is converted into good-time behavior. For many states, this is 15 percent or more of the time to be served. For example, an inmate with a 10-year sentence could receive a credit of 15 percent of the sentence or 1.5 years as good-time behavior. Good-time computation in the federal system is much less generous than in state prison systems. The **Comprehensive Crime Control Act of 1984**, which includes the Sentencing Reform Act of 1984, reformed the federal good-time provisions such that federal prisoners earn a maximum of 54 days annually after completion of the first year of a sentence.

Assuming a prisoner had a perfect record and received 15 percent credit for good time on a 10-year sentence, the prisoner's mandatory release date would be in 8.5 years. At that time, the prisoner would be released from prison without serving the entire sentence. However, if the prisoner is caught violating an institutional rule, time is deducted from his or her good time. For example, a prisoner sentenced to serve 2 years with 15 percent credit for good time would be required to serve 730 days (365 × 2) minus 109.5 days (15 percent good-time credit), or a total sentence of 620.5 days. However, if that prisoner gets into a fight, the punishment might be to have 30 days deducted from his

diversion A defendant is offered an alternative to criminal trial and a prison sentence, such as drug courts, boot camps, and treatment programs.

suspended sentence Another term for *probation*, based on the fact that convicted offenders must serve their full sentence if they violate the terms of release.

mandatory release After prisoners serve the entire length of their maximum sentence, it is required by law that they be released.

good-time credit A strategy of crediting inmates with extra days served toward early release, in an effort to encourage the prisoner to obey rules and participate in programs.

or her good-time credit. Now the prison term is 620.5 days plus the 30 days deducted from good time, a sentence of 650.5 days. If the prisoner continues to violate the rules, each violation costs additional good-time days. It is possible that the prisoner could exhaust the supply of good-time credit and find it necessary to serve the entire 2-year prison term. However, prison authorities cannot add to prison time beyond that sentenced originally by the court.

Prison authorities use the deduction of good-time days to regulate nearly every aspect of the inmate's behavior. Loss of good time can be used as a punishment for both minor and major offenses. An inmate can lose days for not lining up when told to do so, for reporting late to work, for being in a restricted area, for insubordination, for engaging in arguments, for attacks on other inmates or correctional officers, or for possession of contraband. With more serious violations, such as attempted escape or felony crime, the inmate is returned to court for trial and, if convicted, is sentenced to additional time. Table 13.1 presents data on average time served before release as a percentage of the full sentence. Figure 13.1 shows percentages of releases by types of parole from state prisons.

Pardon and Commutation of Sentence

Prisoners may not serve the entire length of their sentences because they are pardoned or have their sentences commuted. Pardon and commutation are forms of executive forgiveness, and are not a form of probation or parole. Pardons are sometimes referred to as clemency. Pardon and commutation of sentence can be performed only by the governor of the state for state prisoners or by the president of the United States for federal and military prisoners. Pardons and commutations of sentence are acts of mercy and do not indicate that an inmate is not guilty or innocent or was wrongfully sentenced.

There are no limitations on the number of pardons that governors and presidents may grant, and there are no guidelines or laws regulating who they may pardon and under what conditions. No one has the authority to revoke a pardon or to overrule the

table 13.1 Time Served in Prison before Release

In 2000, the average maximum prison sentence for states with truth-in-sentencing laws was 1 month less than for those states without such laws. Prisoners in truth-in-sentencing states served an average of 58 percent of their sentences, whereas prisoners in other states served an average of 54 percent of their sentences before being conditionally released. What percentage of their term should offenders serve before being eligible for parole?

	Average Maximum Sentence (in months)			Average Time Actually Served			Percentage of Maximum Sentence Served		
	1993	1996	2000	1993	1996	2000	1993	1996	2000
Truth-in-sentencing states	89	88	103	46	50	53	46%	52%	58%
Other states	129	113	104	53	54	55	42%	48%	54%
All states	108	99	103	46	50	53	46%	52%	56%

Source: Timothy Hughes, Doris James Wilson, and Allen Beck, *Trends in State Parole, 1990–2000* (Washington, DC: U.S. Department of Justice, October 2001), p. 6

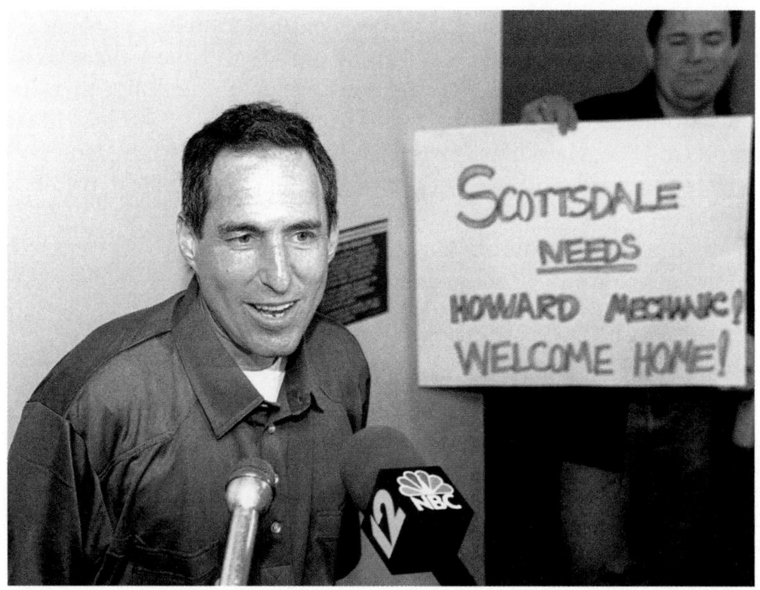

Most pardons are for mundane crimes. In 1997, for example, President Clinton pardoned a 74-year-old man convicted in 1947 of stealing 4 pounds of butter from his Navy base. There are no guidelines for state or federal pardons, but some undoubtedly have a political basis. In 1992, for example, George Bush pardoned six participants in an international scandal and in 1993 pardoned a wealthy Texas oilman, convicted of bank fraud, who had contributed substantially to his campaigns. Aside from executive pardon, what are the other forms of early release? Log on to www.bartcop.com/pardon.htm and www.time.com/time/nation/article/0,8599,101652,00.html to review some controversial presidential pardons.

governor or president. They may seek advice in issuing a pardon, but the absolute authority to issue pardons rests entirely within the executive authority. Also, there is no time limit for issuing a pardon. A governor or president can issue a pardon for a crime committed decades ago for which the person has already served the entire length of sentence, or can issue a pardon while an inmate is still serving time. Requests for pardons come directly from the inmate or the inmate's supporters.

One famous pardon was issued before the accused was even tried for a crime. On assuming the presidency after the resignation of Richard Nixon for his alleged involvement in the Watergate Scandal, Gerald Ford issued a presidential pardon to ex-President Nixon for any crimes that he may have committed in connection with Watergate. Many argued that President Ford exceeded presidential authority to issue a pardon in advance of conviction, but the pardon was never challenged in court.

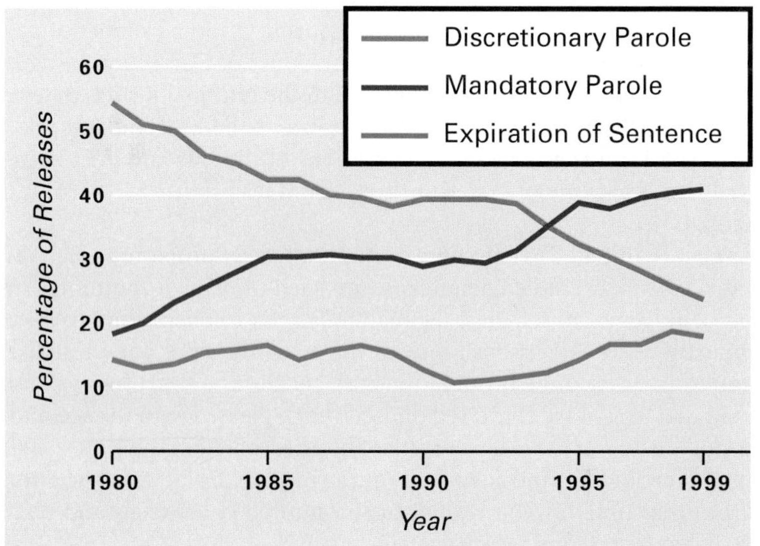

Source: Timothy Hughes, Doris James Wilson, and Allen Beck, *Trends in State Parole, 1990–2000* (Washington, DC: U.S. Department of Justice, October 2001), p. 4.

Figure 13.1

Percentage of Releases from State Prison

Since 1980, releases from prison for expiration of sentence have remained about the same. However, the use of discretionary parole has declined, and the use of mandatory parole has increased. Data indicate that inmates released on discretionary parole are more successful than inmates released on mandatory parole. Why do you think parole boards are granting fewer discretionary paroles?

Closely related to **executive pardon** is executive commutation of a prisoner's sentence. In **commutation of sentence**, the governor or president reduces the severity of an inmate's sentence. The most common use of executive commutation is to reduce a prisoner's sentence from death to life in prison and from life without parole to life with parole. For example, in 1997, Hawaii's governor John Waihee reduced the sentences of two inmates convicted of murder from life in prison without parole to life in prison with the possibility of parole.[4]

The powers of pardon and commutation give the executive branch checks and balances on the powers of the courts and legislature. By releasing prisoners, chief executives can intervene to correct or erase perceived abuses or errors in sentencing or corrections. However, there are no checks and balances on the executives' power to issue pardons, creating a potential for abuse. Some state governors have been accused of issuing pardons as a result of accepting bribes. Concerning the limits of executive power to issue pardons, the question arises whether executives can pardon themselves.[5]

JUST THE FACTS 13.1

What are diversion, probation, and parole? At what stage in the criminal justice process does each occur? How is mandatory release different from probation and parole? What are other forms of early release?

Origins of Probation

THE MAIN IDEA

Probation, which has rehabilitation as the goal, allows a convicted defendant to serve time under supervision while living in the community as long as he or she observes the court-ordered conditions of release.

Probation is a relatively new experiment in American corrections. The roots of probation can be traced to the efforts of **John Augustus** (1785–1859), a wealthy Boston shoemaker who devoted himself to bringing reform to the eighteenth-century criminal justice system. He intervened in Boston's municipal court to divert a number of defendants who were sentenced to serve time in the Boston House of Corrections. Augustus was not an officer of the court nor was he connected to the criminal justice system. As a private citizen, he used his personal finances to guarantee bail for defendants selected for diversion from jail. He was critical of the conditions of the jails and prisons of his time and believed that, for many offenders, prison would lead to further harm rather than rehabilitation.

In 1841, Augustus initiated what came to be known as probation. He was in Boston's municipal court when a defendant was convicted of being a common drunk. Augustus asked the judge not to sentence the man to jail but to release him to his custody instead. Augustus assumed responsibility for the man's behavior and provided for his rehabilitation. After 3 weeks, he brought the man back to the court for evaluation. Augustus reported that "the judge expressed himself much pleased with the account we gave of the man, and instead of the usual penalty of imprisonment in the House of Corrections—he fined him one cent and costs, amounting in all to $3.76, which was immediately paid." From that time on, John Augustus monitored court trials and rescued more than 2,000 defendants from incarceration.[6]

Other volunteers continued his work after his death until Massachusetts passed the first probation statute in 1878. By 1900, four other states had passed similar legisla-

executive pardon An act by a governor or the president that forgives the prisoner and rescinds the sentence.

commutation of sentence Reduction in the severity or length of an inmate's sentence, issued by a state governor or the president of the United States.

probation Conditional release of a convicted offender prior to his or her serving any prison time.

tion. By 1920, every state permitted juvenile probation, and 33 states had adopted a system of adult probation. Today in all states, more people are on probation and parole than are sentenced to prison. At the beginning of 2001, an estimated 3,839,500 adults under federal, state, or local jurisdiction were on probation, and about 725,500 were on parole.[7]

Office of Pretrial Services and Probation

State probation offices are organized in different ways and under different authorities. Five common organizational structures for state probation are (1) within the state executive branch, (2) within local (county or municipal) executive departments, (3) under the state judiciary, (4) under local courts, and (5) under various combinations of the first four.[8] Note, however, that probation is not under the authority of law enforcement or corrections. In many states, probation and parole services are provided by the same agency, employing probation and parole officers. Federal probation services are provided by the **Division of Probation and Pretrial Services**. Federal pretrial sentencing reports have five parts: (1) the offense, (2) the defendant's criminal history, (3) offender characteristics, (4) sentencing options, and (5) factors that may warrant probation. Using this information, the judge must decide if probation is an appropriate sentence for the offender, given the crime and the circumstances.

When determining whether to grant probation, local and county court judges typically have little information on which to base that decision. Because most criminals in these courts of limited jurisdiction are convicted of misdemeanors or violations, there is less risk to the community in the event that the judge grants probation when the criminal should have received a prison sentence. Local courts often use probation and fines liberally because of limited local correctional resources. Judges in state courts of general trial jurisdiction have much more extensive pretrial services available to them, and every sentence is based on the information contained in the presentence investigation report. Nationwide, approximately 9 percent of persons sentenced to probation abscond,[9] and about 43 percent of probationers are rearrested for a felony within 3 years of receiving a suspended sentence.[10]

Decisions to Grant Probation

Probation is a sentencing option of the judges in state courts of limited and general jurisdiction and in federal courts. Probation or suspended sentence for both juveniles and adults can be used as a sentence for both minor and serious crimes. An important factor in determining whether the defendant receives a suspended sentence is information about potential risks to the community if the offender is released. Judges must decide if the criminal's release poses a serious threat to the community. In many states with indeterminate sentencing, judges have great discretion in the use of probation and can suspend the sentences of those convicted of murder, burglary, theft, or traffic violations. The federal courts and some state courts have limited the judges' discretion through legislation requiring minimum sentences, mandatory sentencing, or structured sentencing. In these jurisdictions, judges may be prohibited from using probation for certain crimes.

Most defendants who receive probation are first-time, nonviolent offenders. A recent report states that slightly more than half (52 percent) have been convicted for committing a felony, 46 percent for a misdemeanor, and 2 percent for other infractions.[11] Women make up about 22 percent of the nation's probationers. Approximately 64 percent of the adults on probation are white and 34 percent are black.[12]

Probation is almost always combined with the requirement for supervision and treatment. Supervision demands that defendants report regularly to their probation

Probationers are among those attending this community-based drug treatment program. Conditions for release in both probation and parole can include regular attendance at an educational, vocational, or treatment program such as this one or Alcoholics Anonymous (AA). Probationers may even be required to participate in an organized religion of their choice. What are the other conditions of release? Why are probation and parole an advantage over mandatory early release?

officers on a daily, weekly, or monthly basis, depending on a number of factors. In addition, probationers may be required to seek professional treatment or counseling, and one justification for probation is that it allows the court to mandate treatment programs. Often, probationers must pay for treatment programs on their own. About 40 percent of federal probationers are drug offenders, and the conditions of their release require they complete drug treatment programs and submit to regular and frequent drug testing. Probationers must submit to drug tests whenever probation officers so order. Frequent mandatory drug testing has proved to be an effective strategy in drug rehabilitation.

Offenders with suspended sentences do not serve time in prison. Thus, the judge must conclude that (1) a sentence of prison time is an inappropriate punishment for the crime; (2) people would not be at serious risk from the offender having extensive freedom of movement in the community; (3) the offender would not benefit from any prison-based rehabilitation program or vocational program; (4) the offender can support him- or herself in the community, has a place to live, and is not suffering from serious mental illness; and (5) the offender will not commit another crime. The judge relies to a great extent on the presentence investigation report completed by the pretrial service officer (explained in Chapter 11) to make a judgment about the appropriateness of probation. The decision to grant probation as a sentence depends on the quality of information that the judge has about the defendant and his or her past record, social status, psychological profile, and employment status.

Advantages of Probation

The concerns associated with probation are fear of further criminal activity by the defendant and the lack of punishment for the crime committed. However, at a cost of about $1,000 per person per year, probation is much cheaper than prison.[13] If the probationer commits new crimes, however, the cost of the property loss or damage and the intangible costs of pain and suffering of the victims present a different picture. On the other hand, probation promotes rehabilitation through employment, opportunities for normal social relations, and access to community services and resources. Probationers are usually required to be employed or to attend school or vocational training. Employment enables offenders to support themselves and, if married, their families, and to pay taxes. The probationer is therefore not a burden to the taxpayer.

Probationers live in a "normal" environment. By remaining in the community, the probationer avoids the detrimental effects of the prison environment and retains relationships with family and other support groups and services. As you will recall from Chapter 3, a number of criminological theories of crime causation suggest that positive attachments to the community are a powerful factor in preventing criminal behavior.

Conditions of probation provide for supervision of the probationer's behavior and lifestyle. Standard conditions require that the probationer maintain employment, have a place to live, refrain from drug and alcohol use, and avoid socializing with known criminals. The probationer is monitored to ensure he or she abides by these conditions. Additional conditions may include successful completion of a drug or alcohol rehabilitation program. Probation sentences can be for as long as 10 years or more, during which time the probationer remains under supervision and must comply with all the terms and conditions of probation. Proponents of probation argue that long-term oversight of offenders at low cost to the community is superior to unsupervised release of prisoners.

Decisions to Revoke Probation

The decision to grant offenders probation is revocable, because probation is granted under the stipulation that offenders meet all the conditions of their release. Probation status can be revoked at any time if offenders test positive for drugs, are found in possession of a weapon, commit another crime, lose employment, fail to complete a treatment program, or commit any other offense. Offenders whose probation status is revoked are returned to prison to serve their entire sentences. For example, consider an offender sentenced to 5 years in prison with a suspended sentence who is on probation for 4 years but then commits a violation sufficient to have his or her probation revoked. The offender then goes to prison to serve out the 5-year sentence with no credit for any time spent under supervision as a probationer.

Prior to the Warren Court, probation was considered an "act of grace," and the Court did not recognize that the probationer has any due process rights following revocation of probation. In 1967, however, the Court reversed that opinion and ruled that probationers are entitled to due process hearings to establish that they violated their conditions of probation.[14] Today, the Court has ruled that probationers also are entitled to certain due process rights before their probation is revoked.[15]

The decision to revoke probation is initiated by the probation officer. The first step in the revocation process is the probation officer's allegation that the client has violated a condition of probation or has committed a new crime. In most jurisdictions, probation officers have the power of arrest and the authority to remove the probationer from the community immediately. Probation officers can apprehend the probationer and deliver him or her to a jail for detention. In some jurisdictions, the probation and parole officer must notify law enforcement authorities to apprehend the violator.

The probation officer writes a report detailing the alleged violation of probation and submits it to the court; a hearing is held to determine whether there is probable cause to revoke probation. If there is probable cause, the probationer's freedom is revoked and he or she is confined in a correctional institution until a second hearing is held. At the second hearing, the sentencing judge or other impartial judicial authority decides whether the alleged violation warrants revocation of probation and whether the evidence presented is sufficient and trustworthy to justify revocation.

Different rules of evidence apply in the sentencing hearing. For example, probation officers have the right of search and seizure of the probationer and his or her residence

Figure 13.2

Probation and Parole Violators Admitted to State Prison

Nearly half of new admissions to prison are probation and parole violators. What problems do you think are caused by the return of such large numbers of violators to prison in such areas as inmate management and inmate relations? Should technical violators be returned to prison or receive some other punishment? Should violators be denied a second chance at parole?

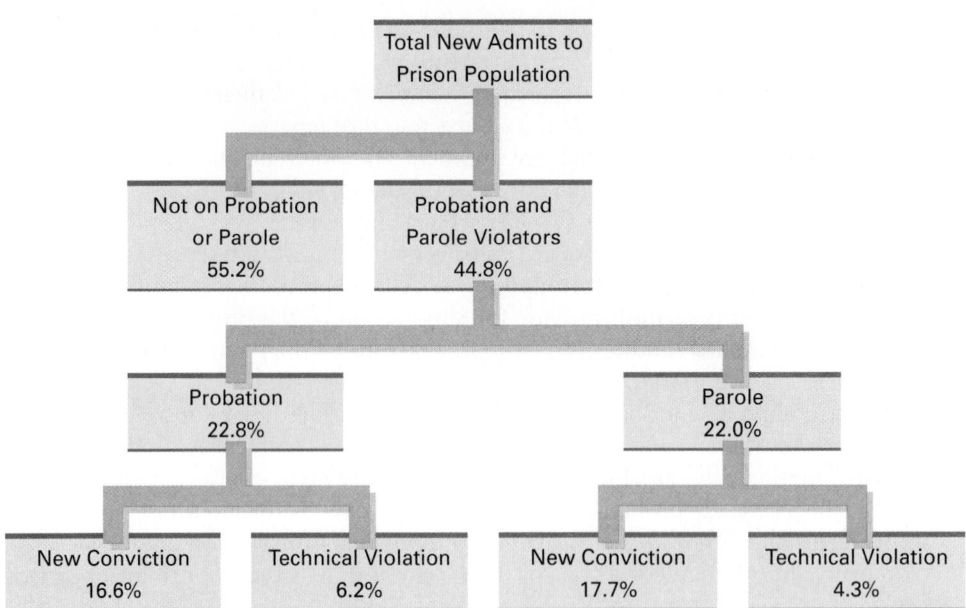

Source: Bureau of Justice Statistics, *Probation and Parole Violators in State Prison, 1991* (Washington, DC: U.S. Department of Justice, August 1995), p. 2.

without a search warrant, consent, or probable cause.[16] Probation officers do not have to advise probationers of their rights against self-incrimination, and probationers have only limited protection against self-incrimination.[17] Probation officers also can enter and search the probationer's vehicle at any time without permission. Probationers do have the right to counsel at their revocation hearing, and if they cannot afford counsel, they are entitled to a defense counsel paid for by the government.[18]

Imprisonment for violating a condition of probation is called a **technical violation**. Drug use is the most frequent reason that probationers are returned to prison for technical violations. Imprisonment for committing a new crime is not punishment for the new crime but for the crime they committed previously, for which they received probation. Offenders are re-arrested and tried for the new crime. If they are found guilty, their sentence for the new crime is added to the sentence they must serve for their previous crime. Even if the probationer is not convicted in court of committing the new crime, or if charges are reduced through plea bargaining or dismissed, the court still may revoke probation (see Figure 13.2).

Probationers cannot be returned to prison for technical violation for failure to pay a fine or restitution, if it can be proved that the probationer was not responsible for this failure. For example, probationers might lose their jobs through no fault of their own, incur medical bills that prevent them from making payment, or experience some other financial crisis not under their control. These probationers cannot be returned to prison because they lack the money to fulfill their conditions of probation. However, personal bankruptcy ultimately does not excuse the probationer from paying court-ordered fines or restitution.[19]

technical violation
Grounds for imprisonment of a probationer or parolee based on his or her violation of a condition of release.

JUST THE FACTS 13.2

How did probation originate? What are the important factors in deciding whether to grant a suspended sentence? What are the advantages and risks of probation? Under what circumstances can probation be revoked?

Origins of Parole

THE MAIN IDEA

Parole provides for the early conditional release of prisoners, is decided by parole boards, and is supervised in the community by probation and parole officers.

People often minimize the distinction between probation and parole, but the two are very different practices and have distinct characteristics. While the origins of probation can be directly traced to the early practices of John Augustus, the origins of parole are more diverse. The concept of parole encompasses the practice of conditionally releasing prisoners to the community and the supervision of the released prisoner, or the parolee, in the community. The parolee's early release from prison is conditional, based on compliance with the conditions of release and absence of criminal activity.

The historical roots of parole can be traced to practices of the French, English, and Irish. The term *parole* comes from the French phrase ***parole d'honneur***—the practice of releasing a prisoner for good behavior based on his word of honor that he would obey the law upon release.[20] **Alexander Maconochie** often is credited with developing the **mark system**, a forerunner of the parole system. Maconochie developed this early type of parole system between 1840 and 1844 while he was administrator of Norfolk Island, a prison colony off the coast of Australia. Maconochie pioneered the innovative penal strategy of releasing prisoners early on the basis of points, or marks, for good behavior and work performed in prison. The system operated according to a prison token economy in which the prisoner earned marks for good behavior. On imprisonment, each prisoner was assessed a debt in marks to be paid. Additional marks could be assessed against the prisoner for misbehavior or violation of prison rules. At the same time, the prisoner could earn good-credit marks for working, participating in educational programs, and good behavior. Prisoners who earned enough marks to offset the debt of their crime—and any additional debts they incurred while in prison—could buy their freedom. If prisoners had more than enough marks to buy their freedom, the extra marks could be redeemed for cash upon their release.

Maconochie's mark system was based on the premise that prisoners must demonstrate rehabilitation to earn their release from prison. This same basic assumption underlies the use of parole. Parole is based on the idea that prisoners should be released not because they have served a fixed amount of time, but because they have changed their ways. However, unlike modern-day parole, the **ticket of leave** that Maconochie's prisoners purchased with their marks granted them an unconditional release from prison. Released prisoners were not supervised in the community nor subject to any terms of conditional release. Today, on the contrary, parole is always conditional. Parolees can be returned to jail or prison for rule violations or other offenses.

Sir Walter Crofton pioneered the practice of conditional release for inmates prior to completing their sentences based on good behavior. In 1854, Crofton was chairman of the board of directors of Irish prisons. He adopted Maconochie's mark system and ticket of leave to solve the problem of prison overcrowding. However, Crofton's **Irish system** provided a continuum of conditions of supervision based on the prisoner's behavior. Initially prisoners were placed in solitary confinement but could work their way to greater freedom. In the final stages of the Irish system, prisoners were assigned to work programs outside the prison and could earn a ticket of leave entitling them to early release under supervision. If they disobeyed the terms of their release or committed a new crime, they could be summarily tried and, if convicted, have their ticket of leave revoked. Crofton's Irish system is the model on which the American parole system is based.

parole d'honneur Origin of parole based on the concept of releasing prisoners "on their honor" after serving a portion of their sentence but before the maximum term.

mark system Early form of parole invented by Alexander Maconochie in which prisoners demonstrated their rehabilitation by earning points for good behavior.

ticket of leave In the mark system, unconditional release from prison, purchased with marks earned for good behavior.

Irish system Early form of parole invented by Sir Walter Crofton on the basis of the mark system, in which prisoners were released conditionally on good behavior and were supervised in the community.

Pros and Cons of Parole

Good-time laws were passed as early as 1817 in New York, and they allowed the early release of prisoners with sentences of 5 years or less.[21] However, parole did not emerge as practice until the end of the 1800s. Even the term *parole* was not used in the United States until 1846.[22] The development of parole came with the use of indeterminate sentencing and efforts to address the correctional needs of youthful offenders. In 1869, Michigan adopted the first indeterminate sentencing law.[23] As explained in Chapter 11, an **indeterminate sentence** bases release on behavior that demonstrates signs of rehabilitation rather than on a fixed prison term. In indeterminate sentencing, the defendant is given a prison term with a minimum and a maximum number of years to serve. Indeterminate prison terms can have a wide range between the minimum and maximum number of years to serve, ranging from 1 year to life in prison.

The indeterminate sentence was extensively used at the **Elmira Reformatory** for youthful offenders in New York. Prior to the twentieth century and the adoption of the juvenile court system, youthful offenders were not entitled to special treatment in the criminal justice system. Warden **Zebulon Brockway** instituted the practice of early release at Elmira Reformatory in 1876 as a means to promote rehabilitation of youthful offenders, as opposed to punishment. Brockway's use of early conditional release combined with mandatory community supervision was the first significant use of parole in America.[24] As in the origins of probation, the first parole officers were volunteers.[25]

Although it promoted the rehabilitation of offenders in the community, parole did not become an overnight success. By 1900, twenty states had adopted parole statutes, but it was not until after World War II that every state had a parole system. The first federal parole statute was adopted in 1867, providing for the reduction of sentences of federal prisoners for good conduct. However, the federal parole system was not created until 1910. Even during Maconochie's time, the public was opposed to the concept of early release: Maconochie was removed as prison administrator because of opposition to his mark system.

In the United States, public opposition to parole is still widespread, and there are more than five times the number of people on probation as on parole.[26] This disdain for parole is reflected in the abandonment of the practice by the federal court system and many states. By the end of 2001, fifteen states had abolished parole board authority for releasing all offenders, and another 5 states had abolished parole board authority for releasing certain violent offenders. As a result of this movement, the number of inmates released on parole has dropped significantly. In 1990, 39 percent of the inmates who were released from prison were released as a result of a parole board decision. In 1999, this figure dropped to 24 percent.[27]

Parole is advocated as a correctional strategy for many of the same reasons as probation. However, it appears that the public is wary of the ability of the correctional system to accurately predict which prisoners have been successfully rehabilitated. Before going to prison, nearly two-thirds of inmates have been on probation.[28] Thus, to the public, those inmates did not take advantage of the "act of grace" that was offered them, and there is no reason to expect that they would do any better if offered a second chance through parole. This view is supported by the fact that in 1999, only 42 percent of state parolees successfully completed their terms of supervision.[29] Figure 13.3 shows the steady increase in parole violators being returned to state prisons. Table 13.2 identifies the crimes committed by probation and parole violators.

indeterminate sentence The defendant is sentenced to a prison term with a minimum and a maximum number of years to serve.

State and Federal Parole Boards

Parole requires the following elements in order to function: (1) the parole board, (2) an agency to supervise parolees on conditional release in the community, and (3) procedures to revoke parole for those parolees who violate their conditions of parole.

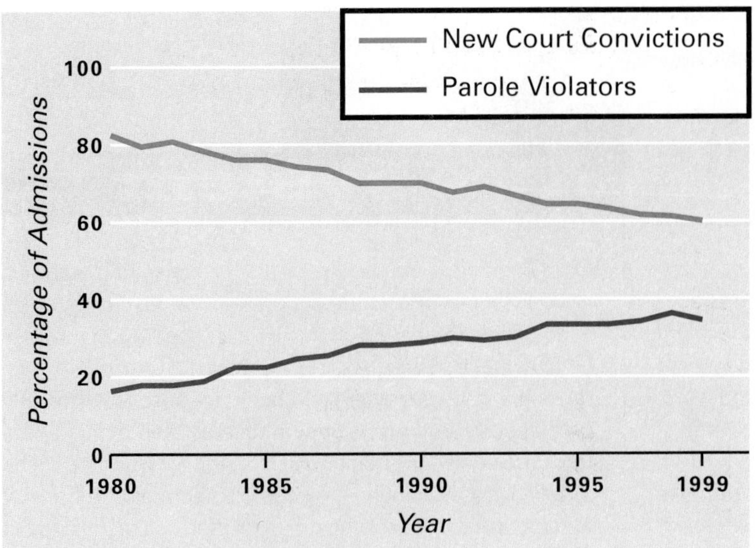

Source: Timothy Hughes, Doris James Wilson, and Allen Beck, *Trends in State Parole, 1990–2000* (Washington, DC: U.S. Department of Justice, October 2001), p. 1.

Figure 13.3

Admission to State Prison, by Type of Admission, 1980–1999

Since 1980, the crime rate and the number of new court convictions have dropped. However, the number of prison admissions for parole violation has almost doubled. If this trend continues, it is possible that parole violators could outnumber new court convictions. The rate of admission for parole violation has steadily increased for the past 20 years. In your opinion, what explains this increase? What could be done to promote the success of parolees released into the community?

The sentencing judge has the authority to grant probation, but parole is not under the authority of the sentencing judge. The **parole board**, not the judge, is responsible for deciding whether an inmate is to receive early release.

Each state establishes its own parole board, and no agency has oversight of all the state parole boards. State parole boards are established by state legislation and administered under the authority of the state's executive branch (i.e., the governor). The

table 13.2 Crimes Committed While on Probation and Parole

On the average, probationers were in the community for 17 months before being returned to prison for the commission of a new crime, and parole violators averaged 13 months on parole. During their time in the community, probation and parole violators committed the following crimes.

Probation Violators	Parole Violators
6,400 murders	6,800 murders
7,400 rapes or sexual assaults (33% of the victims were under the age of 12; 63% under 18)	5,550 rapes or sexual assaults (21% of the victims were under the age of 12; 47% under 18)
17,000 robberies	22,500 robberies
10,400 assaults	8,800 assaults
16,600 burglaries	23,000 burglaries
3,100 motor vehicle thefts	4,800 motor vehicle thefts

Source: Bureau of Justice Statistics, *Probation and Parole Violators in State Prison, 1991* (Washington, DC: U.S. Department of Justice, August 1995), p. 10.

If these offenders had remained in prison, it could be argued that these crimes would not have occurred. Often, the cost of the crimes committed by the probation and parole violator is not taken into account when calculating the cost effectiveness of probation and parole. Does the harm to the community committed by probation and parole violators negate the money saved by use of conditional release imprisonment? Is it fair to expose the community to this victimization by probation and parole violators?

parole board Individuals appointed to a body that meets in prisons to make decisions about granting parole release to inmates.

ethics in the system

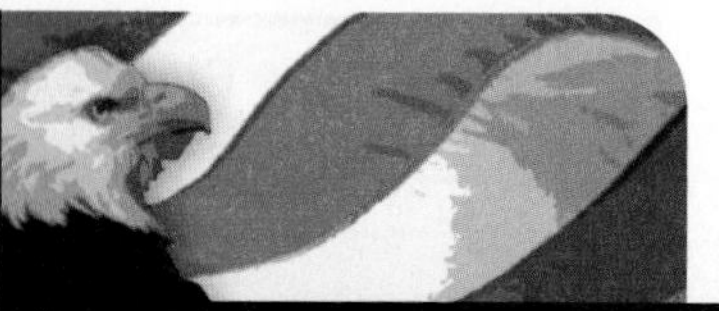

Who Should Know about Offenders Returning to the Community?

If they could have their own way, offenders released into the community on probation or parole probably would prefer that as few people as possible know of their status. However, the community and the criminal justice system do not see it that way. States have taken steps to make known to the public the presence of offenders on conditional release in the community.

In 1994, seven-year-old **Megan Kanga** was raped and murdered by a convicted sex offender on parole living near the child's New Jersey home. Neighbors were unaware her attacker was a convicted sex offender. Since that time, all 50 states and the federal government have passed some type of law requiring that sexual offenders released from prison must register with local law enforcement authorities. Sexual offenders must register for life, even after they have been completely discharged from the criminal justice system. They must register both in their home state and in states they visit for school or work. States that fail to establish mandatory **sex offender registries** can lose federal assistance money.[30]

In addition, a number of states have placed the names not only of sex offenders, but of all prisoners and parolees in an online database that can be accessed by any citizen. Online lookup sites enable neighbors, employers, victims—virtually anyone—to check to see whether any parolees live in their neighborhoods or have applied for a job. Parolees supported by the Florida Civil Liberties Union in Tallahassee, Florida, have complained that putting their names and criminal status on the Web makes it difficult for them to obtain employment or housing. However, victims' rights groups see the database as essential to public safety. In 2001, the states with online databases were New York, Pennsylvania, New Jersey, North Carolina, South Carolina, Georgia, Florida, Ohio, Kentucky, Michigan, Illinois, Indiana, Minnesota, Oklahoma, Arkansas, Texas, Colorado, Utah, and Arizona.

■ **Should inmates conditionally released back into the community have any rights of privacy? Should their status be public information, available on the Web? Should certain offenders, such as sexual offenders, be required to register with local law enforcement authorities for the rest of their lives?**

sex offender registries Open-access online databases identifying known sex offenders on parole, maintained to protect communities and potential victims.

independent model Decision making about parole is under the authority of an autonomous parole board.

consolidated model Organization of decision making about parole as a function of a state department of corrections.

legislature retains oversight through their powers of law making and budget approval. The governor appoints the director of the parole board and often the members as well. The state supreme courts and the U.S. Supreme Court have oversight powers in that they can declare certain parole practices unconstitutional.

Two models for administering state parole boards under the authority of the executive branch of government are the independent model and the consolidated model.[31] In the **independent model**, the parole board is an autonomous administrative unit with the power to make parole release decisions and to supervise all conditionally released inmates. In the **consolidated model**, the parole board is under the authority of the state Department of Corrections as a specialty unit within the department that makes decisions about conditional early releases.

State parole boards usually have fewer than a dozen members who may be full-time or part-time appointees. Final decision-making authority for selecting prisoners to release on parole lies with the parole board, but few states have qualifications for who can serve on the board. State parole board members are not required to have a minimum education, do not obtain their appointment by competitive civil service examination, and need not have any background in criminal justice or a related field such as psychology or sociology. A survey by the American Correctional Association revealed that, in the absence of minimum requirements, some state parole board members lack the educational and vocational experience to equip them to make such decisions.[32]

People who serve on state parole boards receive little pay, and there is little opportunity for advancement because of the small size and specialized nature of the job. Service on state parole boards can be a thankless task. Few appreciate the responsibility and hard work of the board, but everyone is quick to criticize the board if a released parolee commits a crime. Because the governor appoints members, the parole board often reflects the political agenda of the governor. State parole board members are neither correctional officers nor law enforcement officers. They do not have the power to carry concealed firearms, or the powers of arrest, search, and seizure. Their duties are mostly administrative, with a primary responsibility for making decisions about the early release of prisoners. All states have a parole board, even those that have abolished the practice, and states cannot retroactively revoke an inmate's right to parole. Thus, states that have abolished parole must nevertheless maintain the right to early conditional release for inmates sentenced prior to the abolishment of parole.

Go to http://www.cor.state.ky.us to view the Commonwealth of Kentucky's Offender Online Lookup. ■

The U.S. Congress created the United States Board of Parole in 1930, creating the first federal parole board. In 1976, the **Parole Commission and Reorganization Act** retitled the agency as the **United States Parole Commission**. The commission consists of a chairperson and commissioners appointed by the president, and regional offices are staffed by hearing examiners, case analysts, and clerical staff. Despite the increasing numbers of federal inmates, the U.S. Parole Commission is in the process of closing down its operations. The Comprehensive Crime Control Act of 1984 abolished eligibility for parole for federal offenders who committed crimes on or after November 1, 1987. Thus, only federal prisoners who committed crimes prior to that date are eligible for parole. Unless the law is changed, eventually there will be no need for the Parole Commission, and this agency will be abolished.[33]

Go to http://www.usdoj.gov/uspc to view the United States Parole Commission's web site. ■

The Parole Hearing

Parole boards make decisions through **parole hearings**. State parole boards have tremendous discretion in deciding which inmates to grant early conditional release, and inmates have little power to appeal these decisions. Parole hearings are not at all like trials, and each state and the federal Parole Commission have different procedures for conducting parole hearings.[34] Generally, hearings are brief, private rather than public, and held in the prison where the prisoner is housed. Parole hearings are convened by the parole board or by a hearing examiner who acts as the authorized representative of the parole board. The examiner presides over the hearing and makes a recommendation, which is forwarded to the parole board for formal action.

The board has great control over an inmate's eligibility for parole. When an inmate is processed into prison, his or her file is forwarded to the parole board for review to determine a first hearing date. The parole board reviews the circumstances of the crime and information about the offender and sets a date. For most offenders, the first parole hearing is set after serving one-third of their prison time. The parole board may recommend what they expect inmates to do during this time to increase their chances of obtaining parole. Usually, recommendations relate to participation in educational or treatment programs, vocational training sufficient to allow inmates to support themselves if released, and obedience to prison rules.

parole hearings Meetings with inmates, attorneys, and others in which the parole board decides whether to grant, deny, or revoke parole.

The power of the parole board to grant early release and the public expectation that the prisoner will serve out the sentence have created considerable public debate. In states using indeterminate sentencing, the sentence handed down by the judge may be quite different from the time actually served. The judge may sentence a defendant who has committed multiple crimes to two sentences of 10 years for each crime, to be served consecutively. In this case, the inmate is effectively sentenced to 20 years in prison.

The parole hearing is conducted in a meeting room with the parole board or its representatives. Few inmates expect or receive parole at the first hearing. Rather, the parole board sets the date of the next parole hearing. Some states require that all prisoners receive periodic opportunities for parole regardless of the circumstances of their conviction. Thus, a convicted serial killer would receive regular hearings despite the near impossibility that parole would ever be granted.

However, the parole board has the power to decide that the sentence will be served concurrently—the prisoner serves the time for both sentences simultaneously. The difference between these two interpretations has a great impact on calculating when an inmate is eligible for a first parole hearing. If an inmate is eligible after serving one-third of the sentence, an inmate serving two consecutive 10-year sentences is not eligible for parole until he or she serves one-third of 20 years, or about 6.6 years. If the sentences are served concurrently instead, then the inmate is eligible after serving one-third of the 10 years, or about 3.3 years. Often, the public is critical of parole boards that disregard the judge's instructions and permit concurrent sentences. This lack of truth in sentencing has led many states to adopt new sentencing guidelines that reduce or eliminate parole.

The parole hearing is conducted in a meeting room, not a courtroom. The board reviews the history of the case and all available information about the prisoner, and then the inmate is brought into the room to state his or her case for parole. All inmates are required to submit a parole plan, which contains detailed plans for employment, education, and living arrangements if released. These parole plans also contain statements explaining why inmates think they are ready for parole, what they have done to prepare for release, what they have done to rehabilitate themselves while in prison, and why they are sorry for the crimes they committed. In some states, inmates may request witnesses to appear at the parole hearing to testify in their behalf, but the parole board may deny this request. Inmates are not entitled to an attorney at their parole hearing. In many states, victims of a crime and law enforcement officers must be notified that an inmate is scheduled to receive a parole hearing, and these parties may appear before the board to testify for or against the release of the inmate. Law enforcement officers typically recommend that parole be denied. The prisoner is not entitled to cross-examine any witnesses that testify for or against his or her parole. The entire hearing lasts only a few minutes. Afterward, the parole board notifies the prisoner of the outcome. If parole is denied, the board is required to give written reasons for its decision.[35]

STANDARDS FOR GRANTING PAROLE The parole board's task is difficult, because predicting which prisoners are ready and able to reintegrate into the community is almost an impossible task. Board members often rely on feelings, common sense, and a sense of what the community would think. Some states and the U.S. Parole Commission have developed decision-making aids to help them make parole decisions. The probability or risk that a parolee will reoffend or be a danger to the community can be ranked on a scale from 1 to 10. However, in those states that use such an instrument, the parole boards are not bound by these devices and have the authority to deny parole even if the prisoner's score indicates a low risk. The American Law Institute has suggested a model protocol for parole boards based on identifying who should *not* be paroled rather than who should.[36]

PRISON OVERCROWDING AND PAROLE One of the most difficult decisions that parole boards have to make is who to release when the prison system is ordered to reduce its population due to overcrowding. If the conditions of imprisonment caused by overcrowding violate the **Eighth Amendment** against cruel and unusual punishment, the state or federal court may order a mandatory reduction in the number of inmates. Overcrowding in itself is not a violation of the Eighth Amendment, but when the overcrowding causes a significant deterioration in the standard of care, prisoners' constitutional rights are violated.

In 2001, for example, inmates of Morgan County Jail in Alabama filed suit on those grounds. The jail was built to hold 96 inmates, but the average prison population was 250. Most of the prisoners were waiting to be transferred to the state prison system, which had no room for them. The state prisoners thus remained crowded into the local jail, awaiting transfer. After a tour of the jail, the judge declared that the "sardine-can appearance of its cells more nearly resemble the holding units of slave ships during the Middle Passage of the 19th century than anything in the 21st century" and that conditions in the jail were "uncivilized, medieval, and barbaric."[37] The judge ordered the immediate reduction of the prison population, which, in the circumstances, constituted an order to release inmates. Many states have found themselves in a similar situation. In these cases, the parole board must meet and decide which inmates can be released immediately, even ahead of their scheduled release dates, to make room for new inmates.

At these "midnight parole hearings," the parole board must meet quickly and release inmates even before they have a parole plan in place. In the late 1990s, the state of Hawaii was under a court order to limit the state prison population to a capped number. To comply with the court order, if the evening prisoner count exceeded the cap, the parole board had to meet during the night to release prisoners before the official morning count. Such parole practices are not sound correctional policy but are political and legal necessities.

Prison overcrowding also has encouraged states to give inmates liberal good-time credit to speed releases. At the height of overcrowding in the Florida state prison system, some inmates were serving only a small percentage of their original sentences.[38] In 1990, states such as Arkansas, California, Indiana, and Louisiana were granting inmates more than 30 days' good-time credit per month![39] The parole board's task of deciding who to release early is complicated by mandatory sentencing laws. These laws prohibit early release for drug offenders, for example. Thus, parole boards are forced to give early release to violent offenders who are not serving mandatory sentences instead of to nonviolent drug offenders. Table 13.3 on page 420 compares percentages of successful parole discharges in discretionary versus mandatory releases over a 10-year period.

Conditions of Parole

Parolees are subject to conditions of release very similar to those for probationers. The conditions of release relate to security (will the parolee abide by the conditions of release?) and to plans for treatment and rehabilitation. Each state has different standard conditions of release, but most are similar to those of the U.S. Parole Commission. Federal parolees are required to abide by the following 14 **standard conditions of release.**[40]

standard conditions of release Federal and state guidelines with rules with which parolees must comply to meet their conditions of release.

table 13.3 **Percentage Successful State Parole Discharges, 1990–1999**

Between 1990 and 2000, the percentage of offenders who successfully completed parole declined slightly from 44.6 percent to 41.9 percent. Offenders released for the first time are much more successful than offenders rereleased, and offenders released on discretionary parole are much more successful than those released on mandatory parole. Why do you think inmates rereleased on parole and released on mandatory parole are less successful?

		Type of Release		Method of Release	
Year	All Discharges	First Release	Rerelease	Discretionary Parole	Mandatory Parole
1999	41.9	63.5	21.1	54.1	33.1
1998	43.8	62.9	20.5	55.3	32.2
1997	43.4	63.4	18.7	55.8	30.8
1996	45.2	67.4	19.4	55.9	30.2
1995	44.3	63.4	18.0	54.3	28.0
1994	44.3	56.7	19.1	52.2	30.4
1993	46.9	65.4	23.0	54.8	33.5
1992	48.6	57.4	22.5	50.7	29.8
1991	46.8	60.7	17.1	52.6	24.9
1990	44.6	56.4	14.6	51.6	23.8

Source: Timothy Hughes, Doris James Wilson, and Allen Beck, *Trends in State Parole, 1990–2000* (Washington, DC: U.S. Department of Justice, October 2001), p. 11.

1. A parolee must report to the assigned parole officer within 3 days of release. Most inmates are released to the jurisdictions in which they were sentenced and must have a place to live and a job. Parolees often must rely on family and friends to help them find a place to live and a job.
2. A parolee who cannot report to the assigned parole officer within 3 days of release must report immediately to the nearest U.S. probation officer.
3. Parolees cannot leave the geographical areas described in their certificates of release without written permission from their probation officers. Freedom to travel may be limited to a neighborhood, a city, or a state, and travel outside this geographical area for any reason without permission is a technical violation of the conditions of parole. Even if the purpose of the travel is to fulfill a legitimate purpose, such as attending a funeral, a parolee must have the parole officer's written permission.
4. Parolees who change their residence must notify their probation officers within 2 days.
5. Parolees must make regular, truthful reports to their probation officers and have little protection from self-incrimination. A parolee who does not truthfully answer all questions concerning his or her obedience to the conditions of release and any new crimes is committing a technical violation.
6. The parolee cannot violate any law and cannot associate with persons engaged in criminal activity. If arrested or questioned by a law enforcement officer, the parolee is required to report this fact within 2 days.

7. Parolees are prohibited from acting as informants for any law-enforcement agency.
8. Parolees are required to work and support their legal dependants and must report any change in their employment status within 2 days.
9. Parolees are prohibited from drinking alcoholic beverages to excess. If they are arrested for any public order crime due to drinking or for driving while intoxicated, this is a technical violation of the conditions of release.
10. Parolees cannot associate with persons who have a criminal record without the permission of their probation officers. It is not uncommon for family members of the parolees, including their spouses, to have criminal records, so this provision provides for exceptions approved by their probation officers. Illegal drug use is prohibited, as well as frequenting places where illegal drug use occurs.
11. Parolees are prohibited from owning, possessing, or using firearms, ammunition, and dangerous weapons.
12. Parolees must consent to allow their probation officers unlimited search and seizure of their residences, places of business, vehicles, or persons.
13. Parolees must make a good faith effort to satisfy any fine, restitution order, court costs or assessment, and/or court-ordered child support or alimony payment that has been imposed by the court.
14. Parolees must submit to a drug test whenever ordered, and parole officers can order drug testing as frequently as they think necessary. The officers are trained to administer drug screening tests, which can be done during regular appointments or home visits or at any time for any reason.

Revocation of Parole

Similar to probation, parole is revocable. Parole can be revoked for violation of a condition of release, a technical violation, or for commission of a new crime. Revocation of parole is common, as less than 50 percent of parolees are successful in maintaining their freedom after release.[41] Compared to probationers, parolees are more likely to be returned to prison for the commission of a new crime than are people on probation.[42] In 1997, seventy percent of parole violators in state prisons said that their parole had been revoked because of an arrest or conviction for a new offense, and 22 percent said they had absconded or otherwise failed to report to a parole officer.[43] An estimated 24 percent of prisoners were on parole at the time of the offense for which they were currently serving time in prison.[44] In 1999, parole violators accounted for more than 50 percent of state prison admissions in California (67%), Utah (55%), Montana (53%), and Louisiana (53%).[45] Prisoners released on parole (and probation) are prohibited from possessing firearms, yet 21 percent reported possessing a firearm while under supervision. Of those arrested for committing a new offense, almost 3 of every 4 reported being armed when they committed their offense (Table 13.4 on page 422).[46]

The U.S. Supreme Court has decided that parolees are entitled to certain due process rights, although these rights are substantially less than those of defendants in a trial. Most rights of parolees were established in the 1972 case of ***Morrissey v. Brewer***,[47] which gave parolees some protection against arbitrary and capricious revocation of parole. *Morrissey v. Brewer* secured the right to notice and a revocation hearing.

The supervising parole officer initiates proceedings for parole revocation by filing notice of a technical violation or a charge that the parolee has committed a new crime. As noted earlier, the parole officer can file notice of revocation of parole even if charges against the parolee are dropped. A standard of proof that is not sufficient for conviction in court may nevertheless be sufficient to revoke parole.

Revocation hearings most often are held in a prison facility and are conducted by the parole board or hearing officers representing the parole board. The parolee has the right to present evidence on his or her behalf and to cross-examine witnesses but may

table 13.4 Reason for Revocation among Parole Violators in State Prison, 1997

Offenders fail to complete parole for many reasons. What are some explanations why an offender on parole might commit a new crime or technical violation and risk return to prison? What do you think could be done to reduce the failure rate among offenders on parole?

Reason for Revocation	Percent*
Arrest/conviction for New Offense	69.9
Absconders	22.3
Failure to report	18.6
Left jurisdiction without permission	5.6
Drug-Related Violations	16.1
Positive test for drug use	7.9
Possession of drugs	6.6
Failure to report for drug testing	2.3
Failure to report for drug treatment	1.7
Other Reasons	17.8
Failure to report for counseling	2.4
Failure to maintain employment	1.2
Failure to meet financial obligations	2.3
Maintained contact with known offenders	1.2
Possession of firearm	3.5

Source: Timothy Hughes, Doris James Wilson, and Allen Beck, *Trends in State Parole, 1990–2000* (Washington, DC: U.S. Department of Justice, October 2001), p. 14.

*Note: Detail adds to more than 100% because some inmates may have had more than one violation of parole.

not have the right to representation by an attorney. The U.S. Supreme Court has ruled that states do not have to provide parolees with appointed legal counsel if they cannot afford one. Normally, it is the inmates' responsibility, not the states', to arrange for legal representation at revocation hearings.

Parole violators returned to prison are still entitled to additional parole hearings and may be released on parole again at a later date.[48] Only 16 to 36 percent of rereleased parolees successfully complete parole on their second attempts.[49] For most state and federal parolees, at least a portion of their "street time" will be credited toward their original sentences.[50] Usually, the parole time preceding the violation, noncompliance, or commission of a new crime is counted toward completion of the original sentence. For example, an offender with 5 years left on the original sentence who successfully completes 3 years of parole would have to serve only 2 years on return to prison to complete the sentence.

JUST THE FACTS 13.3

How did parole originate? How does the type of sentencing influence parole? What percentage of parolees successfully completes parole? What are the duties of the parole board? How is a parole hearing conducted? How is parole granted and revoked? What are the federal standard conditions of release?

careers  in the system

Probation and Parole Officers

Probation and parole officers enjoy a significant degree of independence in their work. They work directly with offenders, meeting clients in office visits and making scheduled and unscheduled visits to the clients' home and work. Probation officers specialize in supervision of juvenile offenders or adult offenders through separate agencies.

The position is moderately physically demanding, exposes the probation and parole officer to potentially life threatening situations, and is considered stressful. Federal officers receive hazardous duty pay, for example. Applicants for the position of federal probation and parole officer must be physically capable but may use a hearing aid or glasses. In most instances, the amputation of an arm, hand, leg, or foot will not disqualify an applicant from appointment. Unlike law enforcement officers, probation and parole officers do not attend a training academy, though they may receive brief orientation training. Applicants are expected to already have the necessary counseling and supervision skills required for the position.

Most agencies prefer mature applicants with previous related job experience. Federal probation and parole officers have a mandatory retirement age of 57 after 20 years of service; thus, they must be 37 years of age or younger when first appointed. Maturity is an important characteristic for the job, because probation and parole work requires one-on-one contact with felony offenders in a supervisory capacity. Nearly all successful job applicants have previous experience in counseling, social work, or criminal justice. Case loads of the probation and parole officer vary significantly. Officers with normal case loads supervise 80 to 150 offenders.

Unlike law enforcement agencies, probation and parole offices do not use a paramilitary structure or ranks. These officers wear civilian clothing, not uniforms. Frequent travel may be required. In rural areas, officers often must travel many miles to make home visits. Because the job is specialized and has limited duties, opportunities for advancement and horizontal job transfer are limited. Probation and parole officers work for the court, and each court has relatively few officers attached to it. Thus, throughout their careers, probation and parole officers continue to perform similar duties, unless they opt for a position in the administration and supervision of other probation and parole officers.

■ **If you wanted to be a police officer, would you find the position of probation and parole officer just as appealing? What problems do you think a beginning probation and parole officer might face in counseling and supervising older felony offenders? What level of education, skills, and experiences would help a person succeed as a probation and parole officer?**

Supervision of Probation and Parole

THE MAIN IDEA

Probation and parole officers are case workers with law enforcement powers who supervise convicted offenders in the community.

probation and parole officers State and federal professional employees who report to the courts and supervise defendants released on probation and offenders released from prison on parole.

The actual supervision of defendants released on probation and inmates released on parole is the work of state and federal **probation and parole officers**. As noted earlier, in many states and in the federal system, the same officers supervise both probation and parole and also perform pretrial investigation reports for the court. Probation and parole officers usually are considered law enforcement officers, with the power to carry concealed weapons and the power of arrest. At the same time, probation and parole officers are expected to perform rehabilitation work. This work strongly emphasizes social

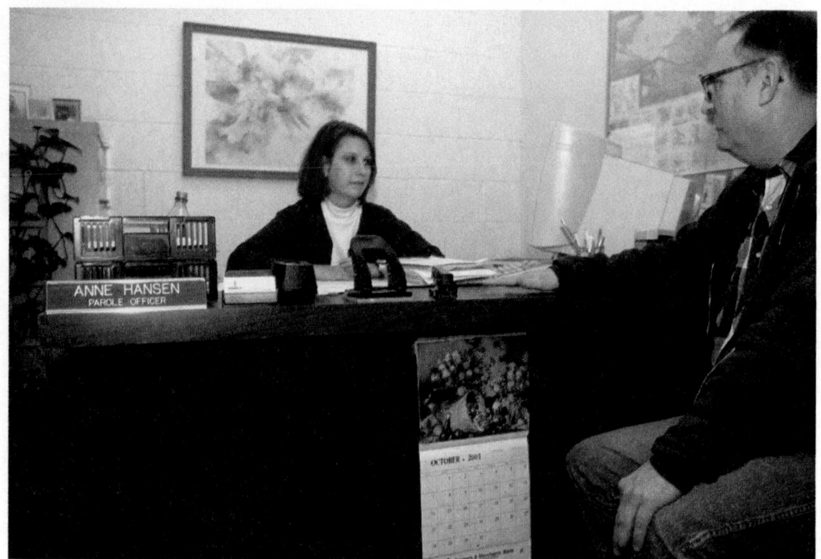

Most states and the federal government require that probation and parole officers have a minimum of a bachelor's degree, and many have a master's degree. Because of the strong social work component of the job, many probation and parole officers have degrees in social work, sociology, psychology, education, and public administration. Probation and parole began as volunteer initiatives and still make extensive use of citizen volunteers. The goal is to assist offenders and to help them succeed rather than arresting and punishing them.

Go to http://www.appa-net.org to view the web site of the American Probation and Parole Association. ■

work and rehabilitation skills as opposed to investigative and police skills. One indicator of the preference for this skill mix is the fact that a federal probation and pretrial services officer must have a bachelor's degree and postgraduate experience in fields such as probation, pretrial services, parole, corrections, criminal investigations, and substance abuse or addiction counseling and treatment. Basic experience as a police officer, a correctional officer, or a security officer does not meet this requirement.[51] Many probation and parole officer applicants have master's degrees.

In the supervision of clients, the probation and parole officer acts as (1) a case worker to help clients succeed in their reintegration into the community and fulfill the conditions of their release; (2) a resource broker to help clients to obtain services, treatment, social benefits, educational opportunities, and employment; and (3) a law enforcement officer and officer of the court empowered to enforce compliance with the court's orders and obedience to the law. The success of a probation and parole officer is judged not by the number of clients he or she returns to prison for violating the conditions of their release but by the number of clients who successfully complete probation and parole. To help the offenders succeed, in addition to providing counseling and guidance, the officer helps them obtain entry into drug treatment programs, vocational training, jobs, housing, medical care, rehabilitation services, and other referrals. The probation and parole officer protects the community from any harm that may be done by conditionally released offenders and deters and detects criminal activity on the part of the released offenders. The probation and parole officer also verifies compliance with the terms of release, authenticates the clients' residency and employment, and confirms court-ordered payments of fines or restitution and court-ordered attendance at rehabilitation or treatment sessions. Because of their power to initiate revocation proceedings to return clients to prison, probation and parole officers are more influential than social workers in motivating clients toward rehabilitation and treatment.

JUST THE FACTS 13.4

What are the job requirements for a probation and parole officer? What services are performed by the probation and parole officer? How do probation and parole officers help their clients?

conclusion:

You Can Lead a Horse to Water, But . . .

It is said that you can lead a horse to water, but you can't make it drink. The criminal justice system invests substantially in keeping offenders out of jails and prisons. Many people may think that the primary purpose of the criminal justice system is to detect law violators, convict them, and punish them. However, through probation and parole, the criminal justice system also tries to rehabilitate offenders and return them to the community.

In the beginning, concerned citizens, alarmed by the awful conditions of jails and prisons and the complete lack of emphasis on rehabilitation, looked for ways to move offenders out of jails and prisons and into treatment programs. Those volunteer initiatives became an integral part of the criminal justice system. Unfortunately, many offenders do not take advantage of the "act of grace" offered them. Unlike the successful early reforms of Augustus, Maconochie, and Crofton, many of today's conditional release programs appear to be failing both in rehabilitating the offender and in protecting the community. John Augustus's work was not formally evaluated, but he concluded that "most of his probationers eventually led law abiding lives."[52] Less than 3 percent of the 1,450 inmates discharged from Maconochie's penal colony under the mark system were convicted of new crimes.[53] Between 1856 and 1861, 1,227 tickets of leave were issued by Crofton's Irish system and only 5.6 percent were revoked.[54] Results like these are enviable in light of today's programs, wherein success rates are as low as 14 percent.[55]

Although many are critical of probation and parole, and the federal and state criminal justice systems have been abandoning the use of parole, there simply are too many offenders under correctional supervision to house them all in prison. Furthermore, despite the discouraging statistics, other data suggest that prison is not the most appropriate punishment for many offenders. As you will see in the next chapter, in corrections, the criminal justice system is undergoing major changes to attempt to provide rehabilitation services to offenders, to provide corrections in the community, and to prevent crime.

Chapter Summary

- The growing number of offenders and the high cost of prison have resulted in the early release of millions of inmates. Types of early release include mandatory release, good-time release, pardon, commutation of sentence, probation, and parole.

- The practice of probation originated with John Augustus of Boston in the mid-nineteenth century. Probation is a suspended sentence, granted by the trial judge on the basis of information in the presentence investigation report.
- Probation and parole have many advantages, including lower cost, reduction of overcrowding in jails and prisons, and the ability to use community resources to help rehabilitate offenders. Disadvantages include potential dangers to the community and repeat offending.
- Probation can be revoked for a technical violation, noncompliance with court orders, or the commission of a new crime. Probationers and parolees have some due process rights in the revocation of release.
- Parole is conditional early release from prison and is granted by a parole board, which is responsible for deciding which prisoners are released early. Parole hearings do not have to provide the same constitutional rights to inmates that they receive at criminal trials.
- The origins of parole are in Maconochie's mark system, Crofton's Irish system, and early release of youthful offenders at Brockway's Elmira Reformatory in the nineteenth century.
- Inmates who receive parole must abide by certain conditions and comply with laws and terms of release. Parole can be revoked, but the parolee is entitled to notice and a hearing.
- Probation and parole officers perform presentence investigation reports and supervise offenders on conditional release in the community. Probation and parole officers act as case workers, resource brokers, and law enforcement officers.

Vocabulary Review

commutation of sentence, 408
consolidated model, 416
diversion, 405
executive pardon, 408
good-time credit, 405
independent model, 416
indeterminate sentence, 414
Irish system, 413
mandatory release, 405
mark system, 413
parole board, 415
parole d'honneur, 413
parole hearings, 417
probation, 408
probation and parole officers, 423
sex offender registries, 416
standard conditions of release, 419
suspended sentence, 405
technical violation, 412
ticket of leave, 413

Names and Events to Remember

John Augustus, 408
Zebulon Brockway, 414
Comprehensive Crime Control Act of 1984, 405
Sir Walter Crofton, 413
Division of Probation and Pretrial Services, 409
Eighth Amendment, 419
Elmira Reformatory, 414
Megan Kanga, 416
Alexander Maconochie, 413
Morrissey v. Brewer, 421
Parole Commission and Reorganization Act, 417
United States Parole Commission, 417

Think about This

1. Mandatory release after serving a full prison term places a former convict into society with no supervision, no safety net, and no rehabilitation. Consider also that serving a full prison term means that the convict was not able to accumulate good-time credits and was not deemed eligible for parole. This is why some Americans say to "lock them up and throw away the key." Is that not an option? What is the solution?

2. In 2002, a Boston-area judge controversially decided to grant probation to several sex offenders. A media storm ensued that raised public fears and protest and jeopardized the safety of the released offenders. Do the mass media act responsibly in covering stories about criminals and the criminal justice system? How can a balance be achieved between the public's "need to know" and the many factors involved in making appropriate probation decisions?

3. Would you hire a convicted criminal to work in your company? Why, or why not? Would you pay higher taxes to support government employment of probationers and parolees as community service workers or aid workers abroad? How do problems of finding and keeping employment put released convicts at risk for reoffending, and what is the solution to this vicious circle?

ContentSelect

Go to the ContentSelect web site and key in the search word "parole." Read "Parole as Institutional Control: A Test of Specific Deterrence and Offender Misconduct" from the March 2000 issue of *Prison Journal.* This article discusses how the hope of parole—or the threat of being denied parole—can be used in prisons as a method of controlling behavior of inmates. Sample the article to answer the following questions.

1. How do prison officials use parole as both a remunerative reward and coercive punishment?
2. According to the section headed "Sample," how does the Nebraska prison system use the offender board review and parole hearing. What percentage of prisoners granted a parole hearing receives parole?
3. According to the section headed "Discussion," what explains the *increase* in misconduct by offenders granted parole hearings?
4. Why did the parole board deny parole hearings to prisoners with only a few months left to serve on their sentences?

chapter 14

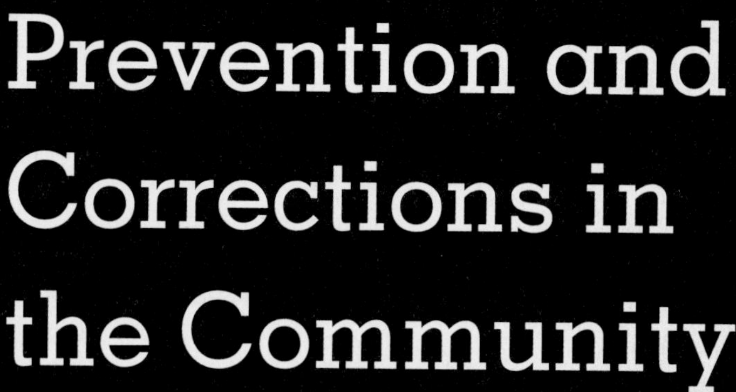

Prevention and Corrections in the Community

outline

arning
ojectives

er reading this chapter,
 will know

- The extent of the problems and rates of failure faced by prisoners returning to the community.
- The reasons that communities oppose the release of prisoners or local placement of correctional facilities.
- Why community corrections programs were developed.
- The types of intermediate sanctions, including intensive probation supervision, shock probation, shock incarceration, home confinement, and electronic monitoring.
- The role of programs that prepare the inmate for reentry into society, including work release, education release, halfway houses, and day reporting centers.
- New strategies designed to break the addiction-crime cycle, including a separate court system for drug offenders.

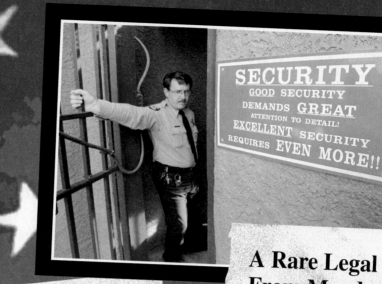

Prison Lifer Charged with 1997 Murder of Fellow Inmate[1]

HARRISBURG (AP)—A federal inmate already serving a 350-year prison sentence for kidnapping and bank robbery has been indicted in the 1997 murder of a fellow prisoner. Michael J. O'Driscoll, 48, was charged with the stabbing death of Robert M. Frankhouser, an inmate . . .

A federal judge in Colorado sentenced O'Driscoll to 300 years in 1984 for the kidnapping of a man who was later found dead in Kansas. In justifying the lengthy sentence, the judge said O'Driscoll "left nothing but carnage and devastation" in his wake. O'Driscoll also received two consecutive 25-year sentences for bank robberies in Colorado and Massachusetts. He is officially scheduled for release in the year 2222 and does not qualify for parole until 2082, when he would be 129 years old.

A Rare Legal Quest: From Murderer to Lawyer[2]

TEMPE, ARIZONA—If there is such a thing as final redemption for James J. Hamm, it is fast approaching: he may soon be practicing law in the same state where once the laws did not much matter to him.

As a drug-addicted drifter from Kansas, Mr. Hamm and a friend led two men into the Arizona desert near Tucson 27 years ago on the pretense of selling them drugs. Instead, they stole the money and shot the buyers to death.

Now . . . Mr. Hamm is trying to become a rarity in the legal profession: a lawyer with a murder conviction. Most states allow felons with proper credentials to practice law, but few have admitted anyone to the bar who has committed a homicide.

But for Mr. Hamm, the status of murderer-turned-lawyer specializing in prisoners' rights would not so much answer the age-old question of what rights should accrue to a man who has paid his debt to society as fulfill a commitment he made upon sentencing: that he would accept full responsibility for what he did and make the best of his situation. . . . The state prison, then, became his church, classroom, and lecture hall. He said he absorbed everything he could by reading, attending therapy sessions, and joining whatever educational courses were available to inmates, including a bachelor's degree program sponsored by Northern Arizona University, which he finished with a 3.964 grade point average and a degree in applied sociology.

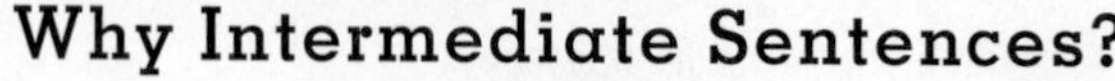

introduction:

Why Intermediate Sentences?

O'Driscoll will not be eligible for parole until he is 129 years old. He is not rehabilitated and does not appear to be headed in that direction. On the other hand, Hamm has turned his life around. What explains such a difference between two murderers? This question is important but is sometimes neglected by the criminal justice system. Many important changes are occurring in corrections, and chief among these changes is the challenge of finding ways to successfully transition the offender from prison to the community.

Criticisms of prison conditions and traditional probation and parole programs have resulted in new experiments in offender rehabilitation and community safety. Many of these new experiments are known as *intermediate sanctions*—sanctions somewhere between prison and traditional probation and parole—and are played out in the community rather than in prison. This presents a challenge: to rehabilitate the offender while ensuring community safety. This chapter examines why prisoner reentry is a crisis in the criminal justice system and discusses some of the many new prevention and community corrections programs that are being used to promote successful prisoner reentry.

The Failure of Incarceration to Prepare Offenders for Reentry

THE MAIN IDEA

Incarceration may get criminals off the street, but its failure to prepare inmates for returning to society has resulted in high rates of recidivism.

Hamm was released on parole for exemplary behavior. O'Driscoll will probably die in prison. Which case is more representative of felony offenders in the United States? O'Driscoll represents a very small percentage of inmates: inmates who will not return to the community. Nearly everyone who goes to prison returns to the community. In 2000, it was estimated that of the 1.2 million prisoners, a small number (about 3,300 per year) die in prison as a result of illness or other natural causes, suicide, execution, or for other reasons.[3] Despite the get-tough policy on sentencing, the abolishment of parole, and the use of mandatory sentences and structured sentencing guidelines, few prisoners receive a prison sentence so long that they do not return to the community.

The attempt to make communities safe by the use of incarceration is having the opposite effect. Most offenders sentenced to prison return to the community within 2 years. In California in any given year, about 40 percent of its prisoners are released back into the community. Tougher and longer sentencing strategies only result in more and more offenders being released back into the community.[4] Nationwide, nearly 600,000 inmates arrive yearly on the doorsteps of the community,[5] compared to fewer than 170,000 released offenders in 1980.[6] Figure 14.1 indicates that just about as many prisoners are admitted to state and federal prisons as are released from them.

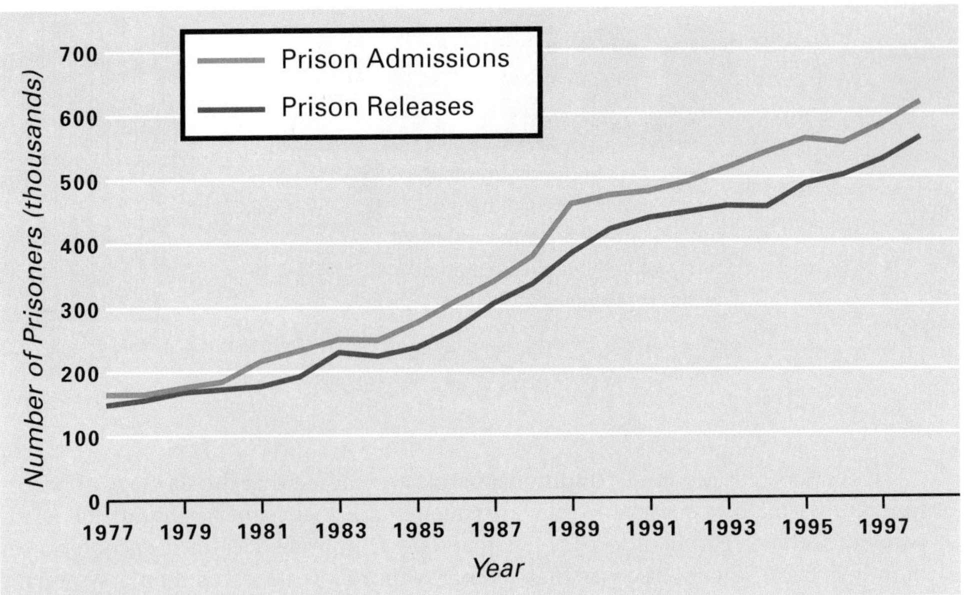

Figure 14.1

Sentenced Prisoners Admitted and Released from State and Federal Prisons

Source: Jeremy Travis, Amy Solomon and Michelle Waul, *From Prison to Home: The Dimensions and Consequences of Prisoner Reentry* (Washington, DC: The Urban Institute Justice Policy Center, June 2001), p. 4. Based on Bureau of Justice Statistics National Prisoner Statistics.

Unfortunately more than half of these released offenders do not make a successful reentry back into the community. Nearly 70 percent of California's paroled felons reoffend within 19 months. The failure rate of paroled inmates is so high that 71 percent of all admissions to California state prisons are parole violators.[7] In 1978, parole violators accounted for only 8 percent of the total felons admitted to prison.[8]

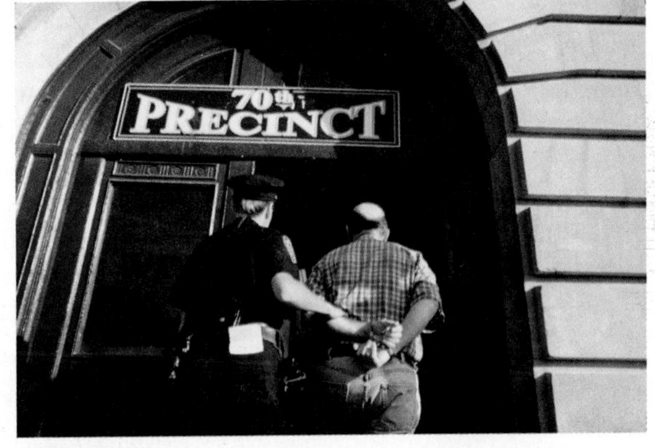

This ex-offender is being arrested for reoffending. Like many parolees returned to prison for violating the terms of release, he illustrates the correctional system's revolving door. The difference is that the ex-offender did not have access to probation and parole services. One of the problems created by the use of determinate sentencing is that when offenders serve the full term of their sentences, they are released back into the community without any supervision, support services, or parole plan. Prison does not prepare them for successful reentry, and without any supporting services, failure is predictable.

About 80 percent of offenders returning to the community are released on supervised release, and the remaining 20 percent will "max out," or serve their full sentences.[9] Prisoners reentering the community under traditional supervision and those returning under mandatory release are failing to make a successful reentry into the community. Most states require offenders to be returned to the counties where they lived before entering prison. According to Joan Petersilia, a leading researcher in corrections, "Since the vast majority of offenders come from economically disadvantaged, culturally isolated, inner-city neighborhoods, they return there upon release."[10] Once returned to their old neighborhoods, most offenders quickly fall into the lifestyles that led to their arrests. Most will last only 6 months on the street before they are rearrested. Two-thirds of all parolees are rearrested within 3 years.[11]

Often the term *revolving door* is used to describe the movement of offenders back and forth between the prison and the community. Offenders who routinely enter, leave, and reenter prison are said to be "serving a life sentence on the installment plan." This pattern of repeated incarceration and release is costly in terms of both dollars to the taxpayers and harm to the community. Figure 14.2 on page 432 shows how inmates enter and exit prison as in a revolving door without ever successfully integrating into the community.

Figure 14.2

The Revolving Door

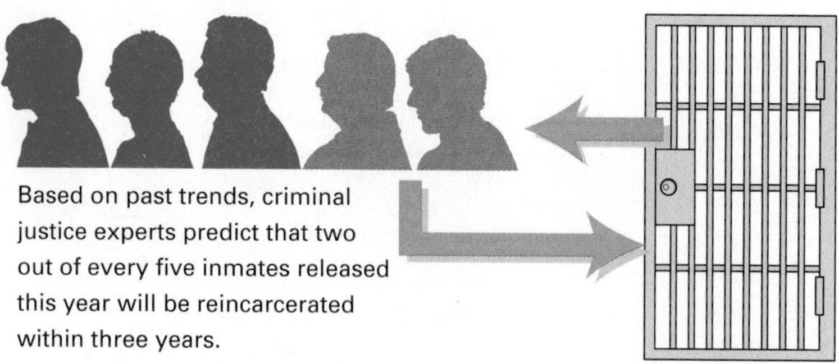

Based on past trends, criminal justice experts predict that two out of every five inmates released this year will be reincarcerated within three years.

Source: From *Why Planning for Release Matters* by Marta Nelson and Jennifer Trone, p. 2. Copyright © 2000, Vera Institute of Justice. Reprinted by permission.

Go to http://www.nicic.org/about/divisions/comm_corr.htm to view the community corrections web site of the National Institute of Corrections (Department of Justice). ■

Offenders released under traditional parole are finding that the shortage of probation and parole officers means they infrequently see their supervising officer. Many parolees see their parole officer for less than two 15-minute, face-to-face contacts per month.[12] They quickly discover that "parole is more a legal status than a systematic process of reintegrating returning prisoners."[13] There is little oversight of their activities and little assistance to help them successfully reenter the community. It must be remembered, "the majority of inmates leave prison with no savings, no immediate entitlement to unemployment benefits, and few job prospects. One year after release as many as 60 percent of former inmates are not employed in the legitimate labor market."[14]

The failure of offenders to be reintegrated into the community poses a serious problem for the criminal justice system. As these unprecedented numbers of offenders go home, their failure results in other social problems, such as increases in child abuse, family violence, the spread of infectious diseases, homelessness, and community disorganization.[15] The criminal justice system and society in general do not appear to have prepared for this problem. As Petersilia states, "Virtually no systematic, comprehensive attention has been paid by policymakers to dealing with people after release."[16] The rate of failure suggests that the criminal justice system lacks the organizational capacity to manage the integration of released offenders.[17]

Thus, as measured by recidivism, traditional probation and parole programs have not been successful. In light of serious threats to community safety, new community-based correctional programs and innovative sanctions are being developed and implemented to promote effective crime prevention, treatment, and offender reentry into the community.

JUST THE FACTS 14.1

What is the rate of recidivism, and what are some reasons that former inmates are rearrested? What social problems are caused by releasing unprepared inmates from incarceration? What is the role of intermediate sentencing in addressing these problems?

Concern for Community Safety

THE MAIN IDEA

Communities want offenders to be incarcerated but do not want to provide community-based corrections programs for released prisoners in their own neighborhoods.

Community-based corrections are sanctions that are alternatives to incarceration in jail or prison, such as boot camps or electronic monitoring, or supervision in the community after a sentence of incarceration has been served, such as furloughs, work releases, or halfway houses. Citizen opposition to locating community-based programs in their neighborhoods is one of the primary obstacles to community-based corrections. For example, when the Department of Probation wanted to acquire a building in a neighborhood in Phoenix, Arizona, a politician representing the neighborhood advised the backers of the program, "I won't stand in your way of moving into that building as long as every citizen in the neighborhood wants you there. But if there's one that doesn't, you're not moving there."[18] Few politicians are willing to risk the wrath of their constituents who are opposed to locating community-based treatment and prevention programs in their neighborhoods. Community opposition to locating prisons and correctional facilities in their neighborhood is so strong and common that there is even a name for it—NIMBY, or "not in my back yard."

Sometimes a single incident of harm to the community can close down an entire program. For example, Massachusetts adopted a weekend furlough program for offenders. In an effort to promote successful reentry into the community, offenders on **furlough** are allowed to live in the community unsupervised for short periods of time. Furlough programs offer inmates unsupervised release from prison for particular purposes for a certain period of time, usually only a few hours. While on furlough, inmates may attend a funeral, visit loved ones, go to a job interview, or otherwise attend to personal or family matters. In 1988, when an inmate on furlough committed a brutal rape, nationwide outrage was expressed at the danger to which this furlough program exposed the community. People called for the program's immediate suspension. Through the actions of a single errant offender, Willie Horton, an entire program was discredited.[19] Massachusetts adopted stricter guidelines to participate in the furlough program, but despite stricter guidelines, in 1994 another furloughed inmate shot a police officer.[20] These failures of the furlough program have had a great impact on public perception of the usefulness and dangerousness of community-based programs.

The dilemma is that while public demand for imprisonment is strong, those who are imprisoned are returned in a condition not much improved from the one that led to their imprisonment.[21] Consider the following data. In 1997, there were 5,400 persons under age 18 held in state prisons as adults, and the average maximum sentence for these offenders was less than 7 years. Even for violent offenders, the average maximum sentence was less than 8 and a half years.[22] Nearly all of these offenders will be released back to the community before they are 25 or 26 years old. How will their 7- or 8-year prison sentence prepare them for successful reentry into the community?

Many criminal justice professionals believe that the use of imprisonment creates a vicious cycle of offending. The more use made of imprisonment, the more demand there is by the public for effective postrelease supervision. Yet, in the absence of effective community-based treatment and prevention programs and intermediate sanctions, offenders revert to their criminal lifestyles. As mentioned previously, **intermediate sanctions** are punishments that restrict offenders' freedom without imprisoning them. These sanctions are stricter than probation but not as strict as prison. The failure of offenders to reenter the community without reoffending then causes the public to demand more use of imprisonment, and so on.[23] Imprisonment offers only a brief break in offenders' violation of the community, but this is not a permanent solution, because, as you have seen, nearly all offenders are returned to the community. In its extreme, this failure generates a total breakdown of the public's confidence in community-based treatment and prevention programs.

On the other hand, how should a community react to plans to place a community-based correctional facility in its neighborhood? Past experience has clearly demonstrated that community concerns for safety are not baseless. Thus, one of the greatest challenges for community-based treatment and prevention programs and intermediate

Go to http://www.uvm.edu/~vlrs/doc/furloughs.htm to read a critical review of media coverage of the Vermont furlough program. This site contains statistics about the crimes committed by furloughed prisoners in Vermont. ■

Go to http://www.ncjrs.org/pdffiles/165043.pdf to read the National Institute of Justice's report, "Intermediate Sanctions in Sentencing Guidelines." ■

community-based corrections Prevention and treatment programs to promote the successful transition of the offender from prison to the community.

furlough A reentry program for offenders, allowing them a chance to live in the community for a short period of time, in an effort to promote successful reentry into the community.

intermediate sanctions A term for punishments that restrict offenders' freedom without imprisoning them; community-based prevention and treatment programs to promote the successful transition of the offender from prison to the community.

Weed and Seed Nationwide federally supported crime prevention program that helps states reduce their crime rates by weeding out offenders and restoring neighborhoods.

sanctions programs is community opposition to the placement of these facilities in their neighborhoods.

JUST THE FACTS 14.2

How does the concept of NIMBY apply to community-based programs? Why do citizens oppose reentry programs such as furloughs? What are intermediate sanctions and community-based corrections?

ethics in the system

Conflict between Police and Community Corrections

Community policing programs such as Weed and Seed have emphasized the importance of improving quality of life as well as law enforcement response to crime. The U.S. Department of Justice oversees community **Weed and Seed** programs, a national strategy focused on crime prevention, initiated in 1991. The programs seek to restore high-crime areas through collaborations among law enforcement officers, residents, private businesses, churches, and civic organizations. These partnerships are to *weed* out crime—drugs, violence, and gangs—and to plant the *seeds* of community revitalization. To this end, local police departments in many states have community policing units. In the Edison neighborhood in Kalamazoo, Michigan, for example, the Weed and Seed program has the following goals:

1. Reduce Part I crime by 5%.
2. Eliminate rubbish, junk autos, and trash.
3. Reduce youth crime by 10%.
4. Reduce curfew violations by a visible amount.
5. Improve attendance at public schools by 10%.
6. Create a family-oriented retail shopping district.
7. Improve the appearance and safety of homes in the neighborhood.

However, some community policing programs have turned their attention toward preventing ex-felons from returning to the community. This strategy is in direct opposition to many community correction and treatment program goals. One of the most vocal critics of returning offenders to the community on probation is Chief Rubin Greenberg of Charleston, South Carolina. Chief Rubin instituted a "be on the look out for" (BOLF) list of ex-felons who had been paroled or returned to the Charleston community. Charleston police officers were instructed to stop these ex-felons on sight and let them know that the police were aware of their presence in the community and that if any crimes were committed in the neighborhood, they would be the first suspects. Also, when prisoners come up for parole, police officers from South Carolina police departments routinely attend the parole hearings to express their opposition to the granting of parole.

Other neighborhood community policing citizen groups have aggressively opposed the return of ex-offenders, especially sex offenders. Citizen groups have opposed the placement of community correctional facilities and programs in their neighborhoods, claiming that such facilities would promote crime, reduce property values, and expose persons in the neighborhood to danger. Citing the "broken window theory," some police departments have adopted zero-tolerance programs strictly enforcing even minor laws such as jaywalking (see Chapter 8). If offenders placed in the community under supervision are stopped and questioned by the police or are arrested, even for a minor violation, they are required to report this action to their probation officers. Offenders who are "hassled" by the police in the name of community crime prevention find that their chances of successful reentry into the community are jeopardized. Arrest, even for minor violations, could cost offenders their freedom.

■ **Is it appropriate for police to target probationers and ex-felons who have done their time? Is it in a community's long-term interest to reject correctional facilities and drug rehabilitation programs? How do you balance the community's concern for safety with the challenge of preparing offenders for successful reentry?**

Intermediate Sanctions and Community Corrections

THE MAIN IDEA

Intermediate sanctions were developed as a means of transitioning inmates back into society.

Community-based treatment and prevention programs were virtually unknown before the late 1960s. One of the pioneers of community-based programs was the **Vera Institute of Justice** in New York,[24] which in the 1980s spearheaded the use of community-based programs to promote the successful transition of offenders from prison to society. These programs were described as intermediate punishments and later as intermediate sanctions.[25] Many early programs addressed pressing concerns of prison overcrowding and skyrocketing costs and were not built on research and experimentation relating to criminological or correctional theory. Instead, early programs grew out of the search for practical and expedient solutions to pressing problems.[26] Thus, there is little surprise that many of programs have not lived up to expectations. Some have even resulted in substantial harm to the community. According to subsequent research, rehabilitation programs and new forms of supervision in the community have been faulted for not reducing recidivism or providing adequate safeguards for community protection.[27]

Visit the Vera Institute of Justice at http://www.vera.org. ■

Returning prisoners who cannot rejoin the community as law-abiding citizens can have a detrimental impact on the community's quality of life. The failures of the returning prisoners influence what are known as the "tipping points," beyond which communities can no longer favorably influence residents' behavior.[28] Sociologist Elijah Anderson argues that as more and more street-smart young offenders are released back into the community, they exert a strong influence on community disorganization, general demoralization, and higher unemployment. They can weaken the influence of family values and legitimate role models.[29] As the number of offenders in the community increases, their negative influence can reach the point where the community is powerless to exert stable positive influences over them. The structure of the community changes, disorder and incivilities increase, out-migration follows as desirable residents leave, and crime and violence increase.[30] This flood of returning offenders also increases the influence of gang activities in the community.[31]

Community-based intermediate sanctions are strategies aimed at stopping the revolving door of incarceration. This chapter discusses some of the most commonly used programs:

- Intensive probation supervision programs
- Shock probation and shock incarceration (boot camps)
- Home confinement and electronic monitoring
- Work and education release programs
- Halfway houses and day reporting centers

Intensive Probation Supervision

The three roles of the probation and parole officer, discussed in Chapter 13, include law enforcement officer, caseworker, and community resource broker. However, a factor contributing to the offender's failure is a lack of clarity or agreement about the purpose of probation and parole.[32] There also is a certain amount of conflict among these three roles. The probation and parole officer is faced with conflicting goals and objectives as he or she tries to both enforce obedience to the conditions of supervised release and at the same time act as counselor and encourager. Often, the role mix favors caseworker and community resource broker, and as a result, critics have charged that probation and parole officers have not been very good at ensuring that their clients fulfill the conditions of their treatment.[33] Sometimes, probationers or parolees simply abscond, and probation and parole officers are unable to locate them. In 1999, parole agents in California, for example, lost track of about one-fifth of the parolees they were assigned.[34]

In an effort to improve the effectiveness of probation and parole, to ensure community safety, and to promote greater success in reentry, probation and parole offices have adopted a new form of supervision of offenders, called **intensive probation supervision (IPS)**. In IPS, the probation and parole officer has a smaller caseload and more emphasis is placed on offender compliance with the conditions of supervision.[35] The offender may be supervised by a team of probation and parole officers. Instead of meeting briefly twice a month, the offender may be required to report daily as well as submit to on-site visits by the probation and parole officer. IPS can be used with either probationers or parolees. Its use dates back to the early 1950s when California Probation and Parole began to experiment with different-size probation caseloads.[36] Today, IPS programs have been implemented in every state, as well as in the federal system.

On reflection, even some probation and parole administrators admit that traditional programs may have been too lenient in enforcing the conditions of release.[37] Probation and parole officers often assumed incorrectly that released offenders would assume responsibility for compliance with the conditions of release. Leniency also stemmed from impossible caseloads and insufficient funding. Despite increases in spending for corrections, few dollars have gone to rehabilitation or probation and parole. Most of the new dollars have gone primarily to building new prisons, maintaining facilities, and paying for the correctional staff to operate institutions.[38] However, only about 5 percent of inmates complete a reentry program prior to release.[39]

Accustomed to being told exactly what to do and how to do it, parolees often expect their supervision officers to relate to them in the same way.[40] They assume that the probation and parole officer will find a job for them, provide them with the guidance they need to find a treatment program, and in general direct their actions to ensure compliance with the conditions of their release.[41] In traditional probation and parole, these expectations are unrealistic, and released offenders often need much more direct supervision than can be given to them.

IPS was designed to provide that direct supervision. As a result, IPS is more punitive and controlling than regular probation and is much more intrusive into the offenders' lives. Probation and parole officers may awaken them during the night with phone calls to verify that they are at home. Supervisors may visit offenders at work sites and at home and routinely conduct searches for possible evidence that they are not in compliance with the conditions of release. Officers search for drugs, child pornography, excessive alcohol, firearms, or expensive possessions that would not be consistent with the offenders' legitimate incomes.

In 1982, Georgia implemented one of the earliest IPS programs. In the Georgia IPS program, probation and parole officers acted more like law enforcement officers than caseworkers.[42] Offenders were held to strict accountability for compliance with the conditions of probation and parole. For example, officers would stake out an offender's home at night to ensure that he or she was not violating curfew. Offenders were required to bring their paycheck stubs to the probation and parole officer to verify their continued employment and hours worked.

intensive probation supervision (IPS) Probation supervised by probation and parole officers with smaller caseloads, placing a greater emphasis on compliance with the conditions of supervision.

New Jersey has one of the most successful and prominent IPS programs, which is designed to handle about 500 offenders at a time. The program provides strict supervision and requires such strict compliance with the terms of release that few offenders have been able to avoid being returned to prison. More than 25 percent of participants have been expelled from the program for violations.[43] However, of offenders who successfully completed the program and have been in the community for 5 years, fewer than 10 percent have committed new, indictable offenses.[44]

Successful IPS programs can save states such as New Jersey millions of dollars over the cost of imprisonment. It is estimated that Georgia's IPS program has saved that state over $20 million.[45] Ohio has had success with its IPS program and has realized substantial savings.[46] Many other communities have adopted similar programs that have achieved goals of accountability, public safety, and cost savings.[47] Still, some probation and parole officers complain that IPS programs substantially change the relationship they have with their clients. Probation and parole officers who view their primary role as counselor and facilitator find that the role of law enforcement officer often runs counter to many of the characteristics that promote effective counseling. In addition, the effective implementation of IPS requires new working conditions and hours, including nights and weekends. As a result, not all probation and parole officers are comfortable with the call for more IPS programs.

Split Sentencing and Shock Probation

When first-time, nonviolent offenders, especially youthful offenders, are convicted of a crime, they assume that they will receive a suspended sentence. Most of the time, they are correct in this assumption. As a result, these offenders often view their first convictions as a minor inconveniences, and their encounters with the criminal justice system do little to deter them from further criminal activities. What can a judge do when faced with a first-time offender who is wise to the ways of the system and is anticipating a suspended sentence? To deal with such an offender, judges have adopted the use of split sentencing and shock probation. Both sentences are similar in their goal of impressing on offenders the possible consequences of their behavior by exposing them to a brief period of imprisonment before probation.

In **split sentencing**, after a brief period of imprisonment, usually in a jail for as little as 30 days rather than in a long-term confinement facility, the offender is brought back to court. At that time, the judge then offers the option of probation. In split sentencing, to obtain his or her release from prison the offender does not have to apply for parole, have a parole hearing, or present a parole plan. Split sentencing is effective in two ways. First, the offender was not expecting any prison sentence. Thus, even a brief period of imprisonment comes as a shock. Second, the sentence exposes the offender to the realities of institutional confinement, but the offender is removed before he or she has time to adjust to institutionalization. The belief is that this "shock" will have a deterrent effect on future criminal behavior.

The sentence of shock probation is similar to split sentencing, but in **shock probation**, the offender is transferred to the custody of the state's department of corrections rather than the local jail and must apply for parole. Again, the offender serves only a brief period of incarceration before becoming eligible for parole. The major difference between split sentencing and shock probation is that in the former, the judge has control over the release of the offender, whereas in the latter, the offender's fate is in the hands of the Department of Corrections or the parole board. In shock probation, the offender must convince the paroling authorities that he or she should be released from prison. While technically this is a form of parole because of the very brief period of incarceration, it is commonly called shock probation rather than shock parole.

New Jersey's shock probation program is typical.[48] Offenders must serve a minimum of 30 days in prison before they can apply for release. They must submit a personal plan describing what they will do when released. This plan has many of the same requirements as a parole plan (described in Chapter 13). It must detail the problems the inmate has that may jeopardize successful completion of parole, such as alcohol or drug abuse, lack of anger management, or lack of legitimate employment. The plan must detail the community resources the offender can use to help with these problems. The offender also must have a community sponsor and is required to reside with the sponsor on release. If the paroling authority is satisfied with the offender's personal plan, he

split sentencing After a brief period of imprisonment, the judge brings the offender back to court and offers the option of probation.

shock probation Sentence for a first-time, nonviolent offender who was not expecting a sentence, intended to impress on the offender the possible consequences of his or her behavior by exposure to a brief period of imprisonment before probation.

In the typical boot camp, inmates rise early in the morning and participate in various physical training exercises and running. Following that, they practice military-style drill and ceremony marching, followed by work. Inmates are expected to obey commands promptly. As punishment for rule infractions, inmates perform push-ups or sit-ups or some other physical exercise. The inmates' day is strictly regulated. During the first weeks of boot camp, there may be no free personal time and no visitors.

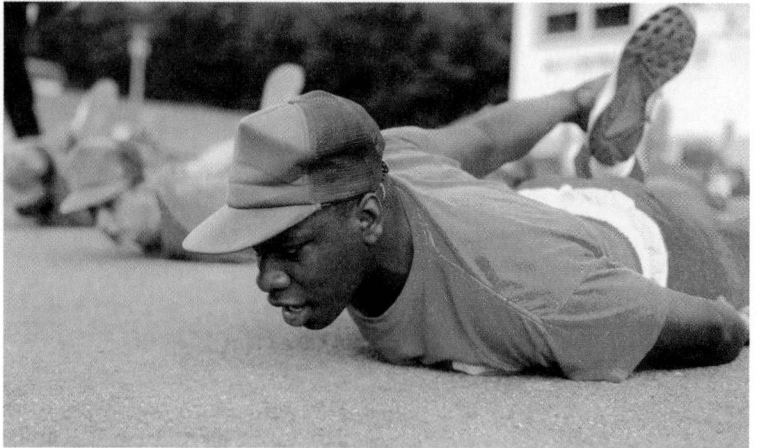

or she will be granted a 90-day trial release period. If the offender is successful in complying with the conditions of the release plan during this 90-day period, he or she is granted conditional early release, or shock probation.[49]

Shock Incarceration: Boot Camps

Shock incarceration programs are commonly called "boot camps" because they are modeled after military-style, entry-level training programs. Boot camps are designed to provide alternative sentencing for young, nonviolent offenders. Offenders who participate in boot camps are offered a reduced sentence followed by parole if they successfully complete the program.[50] If they do not complete the program, they are returned to the regular prison population. Although Ohio passed the first shock incarceration law in 1965, the practice did not become common until after 1980.[51] The first shock incarceration programs of nationwide significance began operating in 1983 in Oklahoma and Georgia.[52]

Shock incarceration programs adapt military-style physical fitness and discipline training to the correctional environment, as in basic training in military boot camps. Inmates participate in drill and ceremony, physical training, work (usually hard manual labor), and education. Inmates are organized into platoons of 50 to 60 inmates and may be required to wear military-style clothing. Correctional leaders are called drill sergeants, and inmates are expected to demonstrate unquestioning obedience to their orders. Inmates in boot camps frequently must perform community service work. Inmates of the New York shock incarceration programs, for example, help cut firebreaks, maintain public-use areas, help in the aftermath of emergencies such as forest fires and tornadoes, and assist local municipalities and community groups.[53] Shock incarceration programs are rigorous, and a substantial number of inmates do not complete them and are returned to the regular prison population.[54]

shock incarceration
Programs (boot camps) that adapt military-style physical fitness and discipline training to the correctional environment.

EFFECTIVENESS OF BOOT CAMPS Participation in boot camps is voluntary. The inducement to participate in shock incarceration programs is the opportunity for early parole. Inmates who participate in boot camps serve substantially shorter prison time. A typical boot camp may only be 6 months in length. One of the main purposes of brief, intensive, shock incarceration programs is to reduce the need for prison bedspace by permitting shorter terms of imprisonment. Although boot camps may be more expensive to operate on a per-day, per-inmate basis, they save money in the long run, because inmates serve less time in a boot camp than they would in a regular prison.[55]

The return-to-prison rate for offenders successfully completing adult boot camps is comparable to that of parolees who did not participate in or complete the program.[56] Supporters of the program argue that if the return-to-prison rate for offenders is comparable, boot camps pose no increased risk to the community, cost less than prison, and reduce the need to build more prisons, then they are indeed effective alternatives to prison.[57]

In shock incarceration, the inmate is released to the community well before the normal parole date. The underlying premise is that boot camps promote public safety by building character, instilling responsibility, and promoting a positive self-image so that nonviolent offenders can return to society as law-abiding citizens.[58] There is little direct evidence to support this claim, but boot camps remain popular with the public because they are perceived as being tough on crime.[59] Many state departments of corrections recognize the lack of research underlying the use of boot camps and describe their programs as "experiments."[60]

JUVENILE BOOT CAMPS Boot camps are popular treatment programs for juvenile delinquents.[61] The goal of treatment is to alter the character and values of the offender, and juveniles are seen as more likely to change than are repeat offenders or older offenders.[62] Some authorities are critical of this modality of treatment for juvenile offenders, however. They argue that the military-style strict discipline and group-oriented environment "is in direct opposition to the type of positive interpersonal relationships and supportive atmosphere that are needed for youths' positive development."[63] Figure 14.3 on page 440 compares characteristics of shock incarceration in juvenile boot camps and traditional facilities.

Another major criticism of juvenile boot camps is the lack of follow-up after release. Adults released from boot camp usually are released to the supervision of probation and parole. In fact, many adult shock incarceration programs release offenders into IPS programs rather than regular probation and parole supervision. Critics of juvenile boot camps express the concern that if juveniles are released back into the community after these brief periods in boot camps, without community-based supervision and follow-up support, they will "revert to their old ways of surviving in and relating to the community in which they live."[64] Research indicates that youths who participate in boot camps have more positive perceptions of their institutional environment than do juveniles in traditional facilities, but the lack of follow-up data makes it difficult to judge the impact of boot camps on recidivism rates.[65]

An interesting development in shock incarceration programs is the proliferation of private boot camps for troubled youths. These private camps mimic state-operated camps but charge parents for treatment programs that promise to help them with their delinquent or out-of-control children. While these private programs may appear similar to state-operated programs, many are unregulated businesses. One Arizona state senator, critical of the lack of regulation, said of private boot camps in the state of Arizona, "You have to provide more documents to get a fishing license than to run a camp for young boys. We require nothing to demonstrate you have the qualifications to engage in this type of activity."[66]

Nationwide, there are approximately 400 private boot camps for juveniles.[67] Many are not regulated by the state in which they operate, and there have been numerous complaints of child abuse and questionable therapeutic programs and practices. In Arizona, 10 children have died since 1989 while in the custody of these unregulated boot camps.[68] Nationwide, 30 children have died while attending private boot camps.[69] Often, parents who place their children in these facilities have high hopes but little knowledge of the practices and competency of the staff.[70] As a result of the numerous reports of abuse and questionable practices, there is a movement toward bringing proper oversight to private boot camps and strengthening state laws to regulate them to protect the children and youths they are intended to serve.[71]

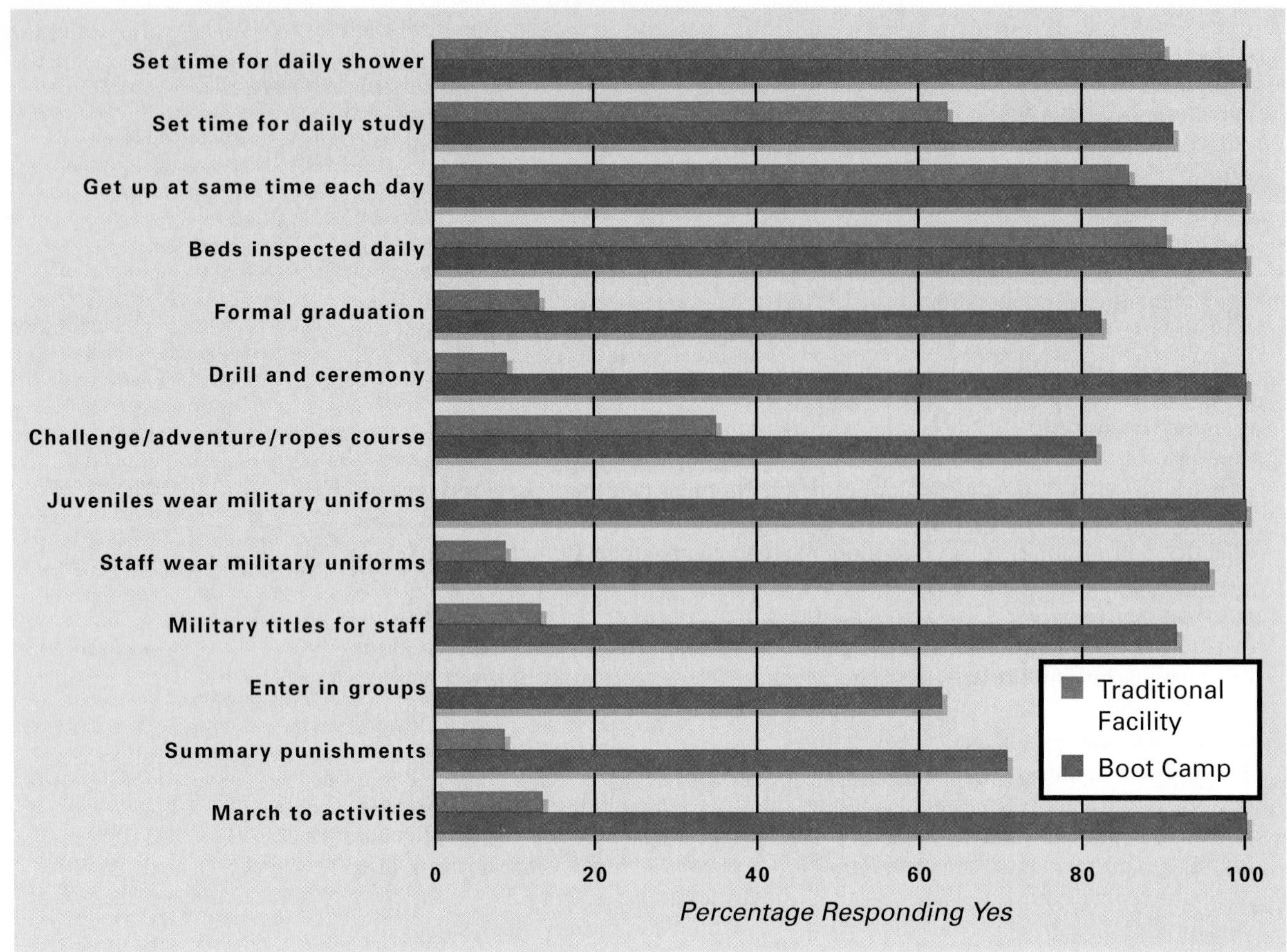

Source: Doris Layton MacKenzie, Angela R. Gover, Gaylene Styve Armstrong, and Ojmarrh Mitchell, *A National Study Comparing the Environments of Boot Camps with Traditional Facilities* (Washington, DC: U.S. Department of Justice, August 2000), p. 8.

Figure 14.3

Structure and Military Components in Juvenile Boot Camps and Traditional Facilities

Home Confinement and Electronic Monitoring

home confinement
A court-imposed sentence requiring offenders to remain confined in their own residences.

Home confinement is a sentence imposed by the court in which offenders are legally ordered to remain confined in their own residences.[72] Similar to parents telling their teenager that he or she is "grounded" as punishment for some misdeed, home confinement severely restricts the offender's mobility. Schedules are worked out that allow the offender to leave his or her home for work, medical appointments and services, court-ordered treatment or community service, grocery shopping, and other necessary responsibilities. Offenders cannot leave home for entertainment, to visit friends or family, to take vacations, or for any other purpose not explicitly authorized by the court. Rehabilitation was not one of the goals of early home confinement programs. Early home confinement programs were an intermediate sanction or punishment adopted primarily to reduce prison populations, reduce costs, and to increase control of offenders in the community.[73]

The sentence of home confinement is a kind of probation or suspended sentence that carries greater restrictions on the freedom of the offender in the community. Offenders must live in their own home or that of a sponsor (usually a relative) and must pay all of their housing costs. Thus, a prerequisite for home confinement is to have a place to live and a job or other financial resources for self-support. A difficulty of early home confinement programs was ensuring that the offender abided by the restrictions of his or her release and did not leave the home. Probation officers used a combination of phone calls and random home visits or stakeouts to verify that the offender was at home. These practices were labor intensive, however, and ineffective due to the shortage of probation officers to conduct a sufficient number of random home visits to ensure compliance.

The breakthrough in home confinement programs came with the use of electronic monitoring to ensure the offender's compliance. **Electronic monitoring** uses signaling technology to achieve a greater degree of certainty in compliance and at a fraction of the cost of using probation officers for this purpose. The first formal electronic monitoring program was implemented in 1983 in Albuquerque, New Mexico, when district court judge Jack Love, reputedly inspired by a "Spiderman" comic strip, placed a probation violator on electronic monitoring.[74]

Since 1983, the use of electronic monitoring has expanded rapidly. It has been adopted in all 50 states by local, state, and federal correctional agencies.[75] In 1987, only 826 offenders were monitored electronically. This number expanded to 6,500 in 1989, and by 1995, 21,275 offenders were monitored electronically.[76] In 1997, on any given day, about 5,000 adults were on probation under electronic monitoring.[77] Florida's Community Control Program has one of the most ambitious home confinement and electronic monitoring programs in the United States.[78] Spurred in part by an explosive rise in the need for prison bedspace, Florida's Correctional Reform Act of 1983 authorized the use of electronically monitored house arrest as a means to reduce the prison population.

TECHNOLOGICAL ADVANCES IN ELECTRONIC MONITORING In the past two decades, there have been significant changes in the technology for monitoring offenders sentenced to home confinement.[79] Early systems were passive-programmed contact systems, which used a computer programmed to make random calls to the offender at times when he or she was supposed to be home. A verification unit was attached to the offender, usually at the ankle or wrist, and when the computer called the home, the offender would have to insert the verification unit in a device attached to the telephone. The verification unit would then send a signal to the computer confirming that the inmate, or at least the inmate's verification unit, was at home. The inmate couldn't simply remove the verification unit and leave it with someone else to answer the computer's phone calls. When the inmate reported for face-to-face contacts with his or her probation officer, the unit was examined to ensure it had not been tampered with or removed. A variation on this technology is to use voice identification instead of a verification unit. When the computer calls the offender's home, the offender repeats a phrase for identification. The computer is programmed with the offender's voice print and can match the voice on the phone with the voice print.

The next generation of electronic monitoring systems used continuous signaling systems. The advantage of continuous signaling systems is that they monitor the offender's movements 100 percent of the time. The older passive-programmed contact systems have loopholes in that offenders willing to risk it could slip out of the house as long as they did not miss one of the programmed contacts. With continuous signaling technology, in contrast, the offender wore a receiver-transmitter device. Rather than the computer randomly calling the offender's home, a receiver-dialer device attached to the offender's phone constantly sent out a signal when the offender was supposed to

electronic monitoring An approach in home confinement programs that assures compliance through electronic means.

This parolee is wearing an electronic monitoring device that uses continuous signaling technology. Continuously signaling devices have several options not available with the passive-programmed technology. The signaling device can allow the probation and parole officer to verify that the offender is at a prescheduled location, such as the workplace, by emitting a signal that can be picked up by a portable monitoring device in the officer's car. Alcohol detection devices also can be added to the unit.

be at home. The transmitter-receiver device worn by the offender received this signal and sent a reply verifying his or her presence. The device was programmable and could be adjusted by the probation officer when the offender's schedule changed. Also, the device could be programmed by shaping the signal coverage area to allow the offender to have access to the yard. If there was an interruption in the signal between the receiver-dialer and the inmate's device, the unit was programmed to call the computer and alert the system to a potential violation.

With both the passive-technology-programmed reporting devices and the continuous signaling technology devices, the probation officer needs to confirm that an actual violation has occurred. When the offender fails to answer the telephone or when there is a break in the continuous signal during times when the offender is supposed to be home, a probation officer must contact the offender to confirm the violation.

The third generation of electronic monitoring devices began to emerge in 1997. They incorporated the advantages of Global Positioning System (GPS) technology, involving the use of satellites, not only to monitor the offender at home, but to have the ability to track every movement of the offender in real-time.[80] This technology allows the system to confirm that the offender not only is at home when he or she is supposed to be, but also is not violating restraining orders, visiting places where drugs are known to be sold or used, and frequenting off-limits places such as schools or playgrounds. Another advancement in electronic monitoring is the ability to monitor all communications by the offender on the Internet.[81] This ability is especially useful for monitoring sex offenders to ensure that they do not use the Internet for the purposes of contacting and enticing potential victims.

EVALUATION AND CRITIQUE OF ELECTRONIC MONITORING

Counting the number of people on electronic monitoring as potential prison inmates, there is no doubt that home confinement and electronic monitoring have saved the states money, compared with the costs of incarceration. There are significant start-up costs for the equipment purchases required to use home confinement and electronic monitoring, but even after factoring in these costs, most jurisdictions report that the program saves money over prison confinement.[82] Critics claim that this is a false savings, because offenders selected for release subject to home confinement and electronic monitoring are those who probably would have been given a suspended sentence.[83] Another criticism is that the system discriminates against the homeless and the unemployed. These offenders usually are excluded from home confinement programs because of their lack of a place to live, a telephone, and means of support.

A potentially serious criticism of electronic monitoring is that it may interfere with First Amendment and Fourth Amendment rights of offenders and of others with whom offenders come into contact.[84] New GPS tracking technologies combined with other emerging technologies possibly could identify people the offender contacts or could listen in on conversations. At what point will technological advances overintrude on people's privacy and other constitutional rights?

JUST THE FACTS 14.3

What are the five most common forms of community-based intermediate sanctions, and how effective is each? What is intensive probation supervision? What are the differences between shock probation and shock incarceration? What issues surround the use of boot camps? How can technology fulfill some of the roles of probation and parole officers?

Reentry Programs: Preparing Offenders to Take Responsibility

THE MAIN IDEA

Prison programs in which inmates participate prior to release can help to ease their transition to life in society as law-abiding citizens.

In addition to the intermediate sanctions of IPS, shock probation, shock incarceration, home confinement, and electronic monitoring, there is a need for treatment programs that focus on preparing inmates for reentry rather than punishing them.[85] Many states and the federal correctional system have implemented programs for preparing returning inmates through treatment and therapeutic programs such as work release, education release, halfway houses, day reporting centers, and drug treatment programs. For example, Ohio has taken initiative to move corrections "toward a new vision of the offender reentry dialogue,"[86] and Michigan has created the Office of Community Corrections with the specific purpose of improving rehabilitative services and strengthening offender accountability.[87]

Go to http://www.ojp.usdoj.gov/reentry/communities.htm for lists and descriptions of the many community-based reentry programs being implemented throughout the United States. ■

The federal system has recognized the importance of reentry programs. U.S. Code Title 18, Section 3624 requires that authorities should "to the extent practicable, assure that a prisoner serving a term of imprisonment spends a reasonable part" of the last 6 months or 10 percent of his or her sentence "under conditions that will afford the prisoner a reasonable opportunity to adjust to and prepare for the prisoner's reentry into the community."[88] The **Reentry Partnership Initiative** is a federal effort to help jurisdictions meet the challenges of offenders returning to the community. The goal is "to improve the risk management of released offenders by enhancing surveillance and monitoring, strengthening individual and community support systems, and repairing the harm done to victims."[89] Other federal legislation recognizes the need for effective community-based reentry programs for adults and juveniles that focus on treatment as well as punishment. Programs organized with the assistance of the **Serious and Violent Offender Reentry Initiative** divide reentry programs into three phases: (1) Protect and Prepare, (2) Control and Restore, and (3) Sustain and Support.[90] The programs discussed previously in this chapter tend to fulfill the goals of phase 1 and phase 2, while the following programs address the goals of phase 3 to help the offender be successful in reentry.

Work Release

How can state and federal programs help to sustain and support inmates in the community? Consider Samson Aguiar, who found his first job in prison working for Oahu's Community Correctional Center for 50 cents an hour plus lunch by grooming and repairing hiking trails along the Manoa Cliff Trail.[91] Unfortunately, despite his desire to work, it may be difficult for Aguiar to find employment once he leaves prison. Former inmates have more difficulty than other people in finding and keeping a job.[92]

Work release programs were first initiated under Wisconsin's Huber Law in 1913 but did not become commonplace until the latter half of the twentieth century.[93] Wisconsin's **Huber Law** permitted county correctional facilities to release misdemeanants for paid work in the community. In 1965, the **Prisoner Rehabilitation Act of 1965** authorized work release for inmates in federal institutions. By 1975, all 50 states and the federal system had some form of work release operating.[94]

work release Program allowing facilities to release inmates for paid work in the community.

OBSTACLES TO EMPLOYMENT The most serious obstacles facing offenders looking for jobs are (1) public prejudice against hiring ex-offenders, (2) lack of knowledge of how to find jobs, and (3) lack of the kinds of documentation required by employers. Public prejudice against hiring ex-offenders is strong. In a survey, 65 percent of all employers said they would not knowingly hire an ex-offender, regardless of the offense, and 30 to 40 percent said they check for criminal records when they hire employees.[95] Furthermore, ex-offenders are barred from many occupations that require occupational licenses, including law, real estate, medicine, nursing, physical therapy, dentistry, engineering, pharmacy, and education.[96] Often, employers refuse to hire offenders for fear of potential lawsuits through liability for negligent hiring should the offender commit a crime or harm the employers' customers.[97] These fears by employers are not groundless. For example, a family film company that hired inmates as telemarketers was sued by a woman who claimed a prisoner misused company information by sending her 14-year-old daughter a personal letter.[98]

Ex-offenders often lack the basic knowledge to conduct a successful job search. Many do not know how to fill out employment applications, how to conduct themselves during interviews, how to dress for job interviews, or how to present the attitude of self-confidence that employers want in their employees. Frequently, offenders have had little experience or success in employment prior to prison. Thus, they do not have basic life skills related to job hunting that are often taken for granted by the general population. Furthermore, offenders need to unlearn passive behavior patters that work well in prison but are a liability in searching for and retaining a job.[99] In prison, offenders become accustomed to being told what to do, when to do it, and how to do it. Obedience to the rules is one of the most important values in prison. When asked to show initiative, demonstrate decision-making skills, and be innovative, inmates often do not have these abilities.[100]

A unique problem that offenders have in getting employment is lack of proper identification (ID). Most people leave prison without a driver's license, passport, social security card, birth certificate, or other photo ID. Many are clueless as to how to obtain the identification they need.[101] Offenders find that even if they are successful in obtaining employment, they may lose their jobs because they cannot supply their employers with proof of identify and citizenship, as required by law.[102]

WORK RELEASE STRATEGIES Removing the obstacles to employment requires both community-based and in-prison programs. For example, Texas' Project RIO (Re-Integration of Offenders) provides in-prison vocational training programs to prepare inmates for the workforce and helps them obtain the IDs and documentation needed in the outside world, such as their birth certificate, social security identification, and state photo ID. Authorities hold the documentation for the prisoner and then forward it to the employer or agency as needed after the inmate is released.[103] New York provides inmates with a work release furlough for 6 weeks up to 3 months to allow them to find employment.

Recognizing the difficulty that ex-offenders face in finding employment, several states have laws that limit when and to what extent an employer may consider an applicant's criminal record. These laws make it illegal for an employer to discriminate against an ex-offender unless his or her conviction record is related to the duties of the job. Some states allow ex-offenders to seal or expunge their criminal records. Some states offer certificates of rehabilitation to ex-offenders who either have minimal criminal histories or have remained out of the criminal justice system for specified periods of time.[104] Title VII of the Federal Civil Rights Act of 1964 offers some protection against job discrimination against ex-offenders. The Equal Employment Opportunity Commission has determined that policies that exclude individuals from employment on the basis of their arrest and conviction records may violate Title VII, because such policies disproportionately exclude minorities.[105]

Many employers complain, however, that laws banning employers from considering a job applicant's criminal record is not "business-friendly." They claim that such laws "ignore the liability employers face regarding the actions of their workers. Employers get squeezed in the middle. If you don't hire, you get sued, but if you do hire and something happens to customers or other workers, you get sued."[106] To induce employers to hire ex-offenders, the federal government has made tax credits available to employers who do so and has established insurance programs to reduce the employer's exposure to liability for possible misdeeds by inmates.[107]

Some state correctional agencies are becoming more proactive in helping inmates find jobs after release by sponsoring job fairs. Some job fairs are held within the correctional institutions. Prison officials help the inmates prepare resumes and train them in job interview skills. Ohio's Department of Rehabilitation and Correction has sponsored more than 140 job fairs and even holds teleconferences for companies that cannot send representatives.[108] Other correctional agencies have entered into joint ventures with private businesses to offer inmates the chance to work for private companies while in prison and then to transition to civilian employment with the company when they are released from prison.[109] Such partnerships are made possible by changes in federal and state laws that formerly prevented inmates from working in private-sector prison jobs. In 1979, Congress enacted Public Law 96-157 (18 U.S.C. 176(c) and 41 U.S.C. 35), which created the **Private Sector/Prison Industry Enhancement Certification Program.** This program authorizes correctional agencies to engage in the interstate shipment of prison-made goods for private businesses, providing certain conditions are met.[110] The law allows private companies to operate businesses from within the prison and to use inmate labor. The law requires that inmates must be paid at a rate not less than the rate paid for work of a similar nature in the locality in which the work takes place. Prison officials allow the inmates to send some of the money to support their families and to keep a small portion for themselves, and the rest is retained for them until their release. These partnerships help reduce the burden on the state of supporting the inmates' families, provide a source of labor for the businesses, and help the inmates make successful transitions from prison to work after release.

Education Release

Education is recognized as a factor that can make an important difference in the successful transition of offenders from correctional systems back to their communities.[111] Education can make a tremendous difference for offenders, because many are high school dropouts and the work force has few positions for high school dropouts that pay a living wage. It costs an estimated minimum of $22,000 to $60,000 per year to incarcerate an offender, but the average cost of educating one student for 1 year is about $7,000.[112] Correctional officials have recognized the importance of education, and while in prison it is usually mandatory that inmates without a high school education be given the opportunity to earn a high school equivalency or general education development (GED) degree.

Some correctional institutions bring educational programs into the institution so inmates can further their education while in prison. Others provide education release opportunities for inmates both while in prison and as part of their parole plan. The typical education release program gives inmates the opportunity to attend college or university classes but requires them to return to the institution each day. When educational release is a part of an inmate's parole plan, the inmate is required to attend a vocational training program, community college, or university rather than go to full-time employment. However, inmates must have the means to support themselves and pay for their schooling.

Research has shown that offenders who participate in education programs are less likely to commit new crimes than are inmates who do not participate in such programs.[113] One study tracked 2,305 inmates over 3 years at the Bedford Hills Correctional

Facility, a maximum-security prison for women in New York that has an educational program sponsored by a consortium of private colleges. The study found that only 7.7 percent of the inmates who had taken college courses while incarcerated committed new crimes and were returned to prison after their release, while 29.9 percent of the inmates who did not take courses were jailed again.[114]

Halfway Houses

Halfway houses are transition programs that allow inmates to move from prison to the community in steps rather than all at once by simply opening the prison doors and having them enter the community directly. The first halfway houses in the United States were opened in the mid-1800s, but their use did not become commonplace until the 1950s.[115] The use of halfway houses was encouraged because such a program provided what was considered an essential transition, whereby an inmate could gradually adjust to freedom by a short stay, usually about 6 months, in a halfway house at the end of his or her sentence.[116]

Today, most halfway houses are nonprofit foundations.[117] The state departments of corrections contract with these nonprofit organizations to provide a gradual transition for the offender from an environment that maintains total control to one that permits partial control before the offender is released into the community. The typical halfway house provides services for 6 to 30 inmates in a minimum-security facility, often a residential home that has been converted into a halfway house. Inmates who do not follow the rules or who "walk away" from the halfway house are returned to prison or charged with the felony offense of escape. The combination of nearing the end of their sentence and risking return to prison with possible added time is an effective deterrent for most participants.

Halfway houses have full-time staff members who provide for the custody and treatment of the offenders. Offenders observe strict curfews, participate in treatment programs conducted by the house staff or community-based agencies, and seek employment or enroll in vocational training or college classes. The program allows a transition period from prison to freedom in that the offender is closely supervised but is given limited freedom within the community and is required to take responsibility for preparing for his or her successful reentry into the community. During the offender's stay in the halfway house, he or she does not have to report to a probation officer, as the house staff perform this function. Usually, the offender is released from the halfway house into the community under the supervision of a parole officer. As you read in Chapter 13, parole plans require that inmates have a place to live and resources for finding employment and appropriate treatment. Halfway houses are excellent opportunities for inmates seeking parole who do not have family or sponsors in the community to help them when they leave prison. Without halfway houses, many of these inmates would not be able to prepare an acceptable parole plan.

halfway houses Transition programs that allow inmates to move from prison to the community in steps.

day reporting centers An intermediate sanction to provide a gradual adjustment to reentry under closely supervised conditions.

correctional case managers Social work caseworkers who specialize in helping offenders adjust to life in prison, release from prison, and successful reentry into the community.

Day Reporting Centers

Day reporting centers are relatively new reentry programs dating to the early 1970s.[118] **Day reporting centers** provide for release from prison that is closely supervised by the state's department of corrections. Inmates live at home rather than being imprisoned or housed in a privately managed halfway house. As the name suggests, inmates report to supervisory centers on a daily basis. Inmates may be sentenced to day reporting centers rather than prison or may be released from prison to day reporting centers during the last months of their sentence. Inmates report to and leave from the center during the day to work, to participate in treatment programs, to attend classes or training programs, or to hunt for employment. Day reporting centers maintain daily schedules that

careers

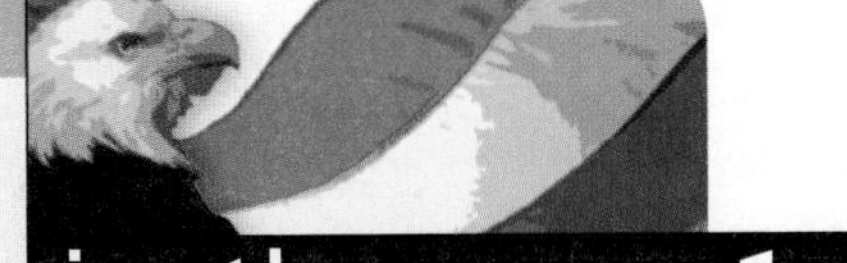

in the system

Correctional Case Manager

The author interviewed Jodie Maesaka-Hirata to get her opinion on what it is like to work with inmates in prison. Jodie Maesaka-Hirata is a Social Worker V for the Department of Corrections in the state of Hawaii and has worked with inmates and offenders since 1989. She started her career as a Social Worker II, working as a case manager inside Halawa Prison. She says that a big difference between the position of correctional officer and that of case manager is that inmates do not perceive case managers as authority figures. As a case manager, Maesaka-Hirata provides long-term and crisis counseling to inmates, writes evaluations for parole reports, makes housing classifications, and works with the inmates to help them adjust to prison life. During her career, she has worked at many different facilities in many different capacities.

Maesaka-Hirata has worked with both male and female inmates and notes that she has found male inmates to be less verbal, requiring her to be diligent in watching for signs of mood changes, and that they are more likely to exploit kindnesses. She finds that female offenders tend to play on emotions and have more complex social and emotional needs. Women offenders usually are single mothers; financially unstable; victims of physical, sexual, and psychological abuse; ethnic minorities; nonviolent; substance dependent; and homeless. The female offender usually is the primary caretaker for the family, and in Hawaii families usually are multigenerational.

From 1998 to 2000, Maesaka-Hirata worked with female offenders in the SISTERS program. This grant-funded program was a cooperative effort with the Department of Criminology and Criminal Justice at Chaminade University of Honolulu to help prepare female offenders for successful reentry into the community. Maesaka-Hirata teamed with professors from Chaminade to develop and implement a curriculum for female offenders, using volunteers from the university and community. SISTERS focused on teaching basic life skills and daily living skills, such as budgeting, banking, writing checks, planning menus, and buying groceries. Many inmates also were not knowledgeable about basic hygiene, physical health, and family planning. In addition, the program included topics such as self-confidence, interviewing for jobs, resume writing, how to live with AIDS and HIV, and decision-making skills.

According to Maesaka-Hirata, there is a great need for transition programs, and the most pressing need is for programs that emphasize daily-life skills and cognitive changes. The key to successful transition programs is working with the public and preparing the community, because transition programs need community support to be successful. They need the support of neighborhood boards, state politicians, human services agencies, and drug treatment programs.

Correctional case managers typically learn their jobs by shadowing another case manager for a few weeks in on-the-job training. Case managers also receive training on policy and procedures and day-to-day operational skills. New caseworkers may be required to take a medical and psychological examination, have a drug-screening test, and undergo a criminal background check. There is no physical agility testing, but case managers usually must have a minimum of a bachelor's degree, but a master's degree is preferred. Some states require some additional postgraduate coursework to qualify for the position.

Maesaka-Hirata says that working with inmates is not for everyone. There is a certain degree of danger in working with inmates, especially inside the prison and when conducting home visits. Yet, she says that corrections has been a rewarding career: interesting, diverse, and intense. There are good opportunities for upward mobility, and the field gives you the chance to make a positive difference in people's lives.

■ **What risks and rewards are involved in correctional case management? How is the work of a correctional case manager similar to and different from that of a correctional officer or a probation and parole officer?**

must accurately account for inmates' time while in the community. Participants must submit to certain conditions similar to those in a parole plan, such as random drug tests.

The purpose of the day reporting center is to act as an intermediate sanction for some inmates and to permit a gradual adjustment to reentry for others. Day reporting centers allow departments of corrections to reduce the need for prison bedspace by placing low-security-risk inmates in day reporting centers.[119] For inmates transitioning

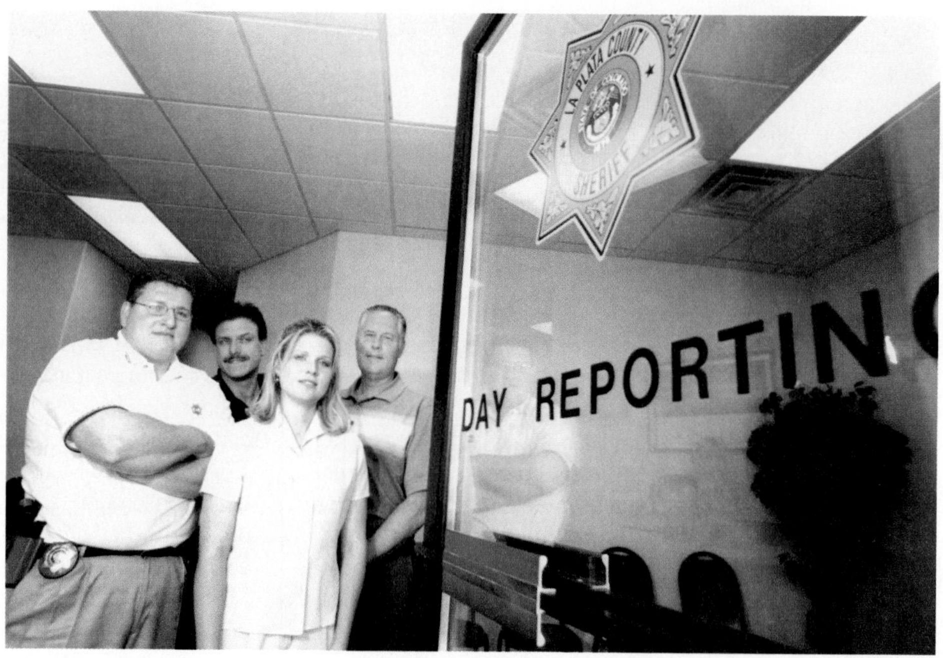

Day reporting centers provide close monitoring of offenders in the community. Inmates must report back to the day reporting center at predetermined times, depending on their schedules, which are tracked by computer. Participants who go to their own homes are required to report to the day reporting center each morning prior to starting their day. Some programs provide residential facilities, in which inmates participate in treatment and counseling programs during the evenings. Inmates usually can earn weekend furloughs, allowing them to leave the facility on a Friday night and return by Sunday evening.

from prison, day reporting centers allow them the opportunity to reenter the community under closely monitored conditions. Because day reporting centers are not widely used, extensive data are not available to judge their effectiveness. However, data from the Metropolitan Day Reporting Center in Boston, Massachusetts, indicate that inmates who enter the community from the day reporting center rather than directly from jail are less likely to commit new crimes and are more likely to be employed. Furthermore, only about 1 percent of inmates committed a crime while they were in the program.[120]

JUST THE FACTS 14.4

What programs in prisons and in communities are designed to help inmates transition to life in society? What obstacles to employment do ex-offenders face? What benefit do halfway houses offer to offenders?

Reentry Programs for Drug Offenders

THE MAIN IDEA

The rampant abuse of drugs among offenders has led to a separate system of drug courts and rehabilitation programs.

Drug Use Forecasting (DUF) Data collected on defendants in 23 cities indicates that 51 to 83 percent of arrested adult men and 41 percent to 84 percent of arrested adult women were under the influence of at least one illicit drug at the time of arrest.[121] In addition, drug use is a significant factor in property offenses, as 16 percent of adult prisoners indicated that they committed their offenses to get money for drugs.[122] While drug offenders may be nonviolent, during 1999, twelve percent of convicted federal drug defendants received a sentence enhancement for the use or possession of a firearm or other weapon.[123]

Drug crimes have occupied more and more resources of the criminal justice system. Between 1984 and 1999, the number of defendants charged with a drug offense in the federal courts increased from 11,854 to 29,306.[124] The Bureau of Justice Statistics estimates that two-thirds of federal and state prisoners and probationers could be characterized as drug involved.[125] In response to the increased frequency of drug crimes, the criminal justice system has enhanced drug law enforcement efforts and has adopted a get-tough sentencing policy for drug offenders. This tough federal stance has resulted in 62 percent of convicted federal drug defendants receiving statutory minimum sentences of at least 5 years or more.

However, enhanced enforcement and tough sentencing policies have failed to stem the number of drug offenders. Over 73 percent of state inmates reentering prison have admitted to drug or alcohol involvement while released.[126] Even when sentenced to prison, inmates continue to find ways to obtain drugs. Thus, incarceration in itself does little to break the cycle of illegal drug use and crime. Furthermore, the traditional case disposition process appears to lack the capacity to bring about any significant reduction in drug usage by persons convicted of drug offenses.[127] For a little over a decade, a new strategy to break the cycle of drug use and crime that has led to the revolving door syndrome for drug offenders has been the drug court. The **drug court** approach was started in 1989 as an experiment by the Dade County (Florida) Circuit Court. Today, nearly every state uses some form of drug court program to handle drug offenders. Drug courts have proved effective with adult and juvenile offenders and for use in tribal courts. Figure 14.4 lists the ten key components of drug court programs.

drug court An approach for dealing with drug offenders that is aimed at breaking the cycle of drug use and crime.

Figure 14.4

The Ten Key Components of Drug Courts

The operation and components of drug courts vary from jurisdiction to jurisdiction, but the following 10 key components identify state adult drug court programs as proscribed by the Drug Courts Program Office:

- Drug courts integrate alcohol and other drug treatment services with justice system case processing.
- Using a nonadversarial approach, prosecution and defense counsel promote public safety while protecting participants' due process rights.
- Eligible participants are identified early and promptly placed in the drug court program.
- Drug courts provide access to a continuum of alcohol, drug, and other related treatment and rehabilitation services.
- Abstinence is monitored by frequent alcohol and other drug testing.
- A coordinated strategy governs drug court responses to participants' compliance.
- Ongoing judicial interaction with each drug court participant is essential.
- Monitoring and evaluation measure the achievement of program goals and gauge effectiveness.
- Continuing interdisciplinary education promotes effective drug court planning, implementation, and operations.
- Forging partnerships among drug courts, public agencies, and community-based organizations generates local support and enhances drug court effectiveness.

Source: Defining Drug Courts: The Key Components (Washington, DC: Office of Justice Programs, Drug Courts Program Office, January 1997), pp. 1–3.

Adult Drug Courts

In states that have adult drug courts, adult offenders arrested for drug offenses are diverted from traditional case disposition processing as soon as possible. These offenders are offered the opportunity to participate in the drug court program rather than traditional case disposition, which results in incarceration. Drug court programs use intermediate sanctions, community-based treatment, and intensive probation supervision to achieve a two-fold purpose: (1) to get offenders clean and sober and (2) to compel offenders to participate in a comprehensive treatment program while being monitored under strict conditions for drug use. Almost all drug courts require participants to obtain a GED if they have not finished high school, to maintain or obtain employment, to be current in all financial obligations (including drug court fees and any court-ordered support payments), and to have a sponsor in the community. Some drug programs require offenders to perform community service hours.[128] Figure 14.5

Figure 14.5

Case Identification for Superior Court Drug Intervention Program

Drug court programs use a drug test after arrest to identify and divert drug users and drug offenders from traditional case processing as soon as possible. This figure illustrates how drug offenders are identified in the Washington, DC, Superior Court Drug Intervention Program.

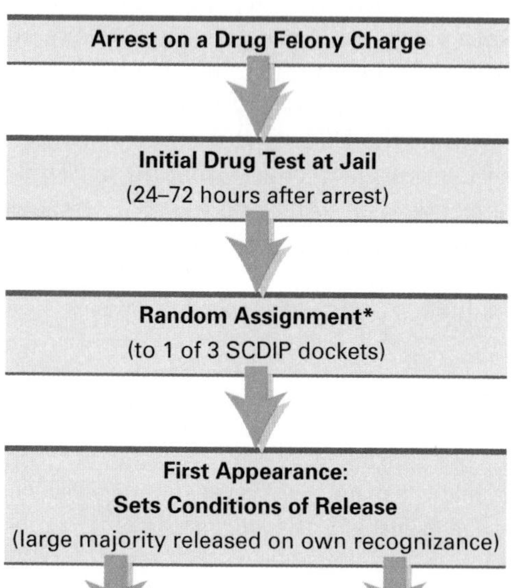

If initial post-pretrial release drug test **positive**, 2x per week drug test required

If released and initial drug test **negative**, no subsequent testing required

Regular hearings** on assigned SCDIP docket

Eligible for SCDIP as soon as 2 post-release drug tests are skipped or positive (about 40% on each docket)

Regular hearings** on assigned SCDIP docket

Eligible for SCDIP if judge finds evidence of drug use during hearings

* Defendants were not allowed to transfer to another SCDIP docket.

** Plea offers were made at regular docket hearings and could occur before, after, or at the same time as defendant became eligible for SCDIP, and the program offer was not contingent on acceptance of the plea. However, if the plea were rejected, defendants transferred out of the SCDIP dockets to a trial docket.

Source: Adele Harrell, Shannon Cavanaugh, and John Roman, *Evaluation of the D.C. Superior Court Drug Intervention Programs* (Washington, DC: U.S. Department of Justice, April 2000), p. 3.

illustrates how offenders are selected for inclusion in the Superior Court Drug Intervention Program.

If offenders accept the offer to enter into the drug court program and are accepted, "they are referred immediately to a multi-phased out-patient treatment program entailing multiple weekly (often daily) contacts with the treatment provider for counseling, therapy and education; frequent urinalysis (usually at least weekly); frequent status hearings before the drug court judge (bi-weekly or more often at first); and a rehabilitation program entailing vocational, education, family, medical, and other support services."[129] Figure 14.6 on page 452 shows the broad variety of treatment programs and support services that are available to participants in drug court programs.

Go to http://www.uvm.edu/~vlrs/doc/furloughs.htm for links to articles and statistics about drug courts throughout the United States. ■

In contrast to the traditional adjudication process in the criminal court, drug court programs are experiencing a significant reduction in recidivism among participants. Whereas about 45 percent of defendants convicted of drug possession will reoffend with a similar offense within 2 to 3 years, only 5 to 28 percent of drug court participants reoffend, and 90 percent have negative urinalysis drug reports.[130] Drug court programs also have been shown to save money. By avoiding the high cost of incarceration, some cities have been able to save up to $2.5 million per year in criminal justice costs.[131] By eliminating the revolving door syndrome, drug court programs not only save on the cost of incarcerating repeat offenders, but also save police, prosecutors, and courts the additional costs of processing the offenders through the system. Drug court programs also help save welfare benefits, as offenders who are employed when arrested often are able to maintain their employment and continue to support themselves and their families. By not having drug offenders repeatedly enter and exit the criminal justice system, criminal justice agencies are able to more efficiently allocate their resources to address more pressing needs and crimes.[132] Table 14.1 on page 453 shows how jurisdictions have been able to achieve substantial savings by the use of drug court programs. A testament to the effectiveness of drug court programs is that in a poll of 318 police chiefs, almost 60 percent advocated court-supervised treatment programs over other justice system options for drug users.

Juvenile Drug Courts

Drug use among teenagers is a significant problem in the criminal justice system, and juvenile drug courts are being used instead of traditional adjudication processes to work toward long-term success and rehabilitation of these offenders. According to the Office of Juvenile Justice and Delinquency Prevention, "juvenile drug courts provide (1) intensive and continuous judicial supervision over delinquency and status offense cases that involve substance-abusing juveniles and (2) coordinated and supervised delivery of an array of support services necessary to address the problems that contribute to juvenile involvement in the justice system."[133] Juvenile drug courts, like adult drug courts, have emerged only in the last decade but are quickly being adopted nationwide.

Juvenile drug courts are designed to respond as quickly as possible to delinquent activity so that offenders are held accountable and intrusive intervention can occur to provide treatment and sanction options.[134] Programs provide for court-supervised substance abuse treatment and core services addressing the needs of the juveniles and their families, including educational needs, behavioral problems, and family therapy. The hallmark of juvenile drug courts is the intensive, continuous judicial monitoring and supervision of participants.[135]

Juvenile drug court programs recognize the challenge of addressing family issues. The operating premise is that if family issues are not addressed, it is likely that the child will continue to be involved with drugs and delinquent activity. As a result, a number of programs require parent or guardian supervision and utilize the Multi-systemic Therapy (MST) approach to provide family-based treatment and to teach parenting skills.[136]

Types of Dedicated and External Treatment Programs

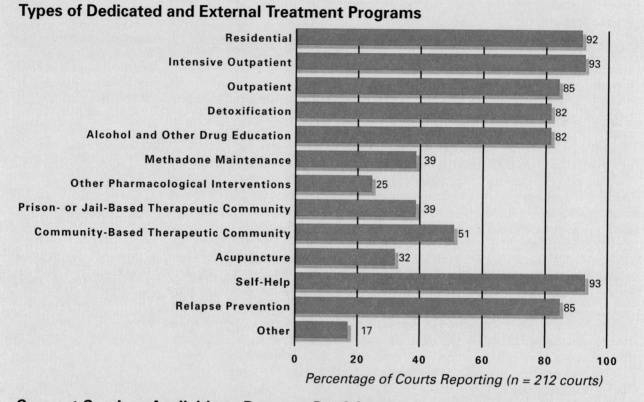

Program	Percentage
Residential	92
Intensive Outpatient	93
Outpatient	85
Detoxification	82
Alcohol and Other Drug Education	82
Methadone Maintenance	39
Other Pharmacological Interventions	25
Prison- or Jail-Based Therapeutic Community	39
Community-Based Therapeutic Community	51
Acupuncture	32
Self-Help	93
Relapse Prevention	85
Other	17

0 20 40 60 80 100

Percentage of Courts Reporting (n = 212 courts)

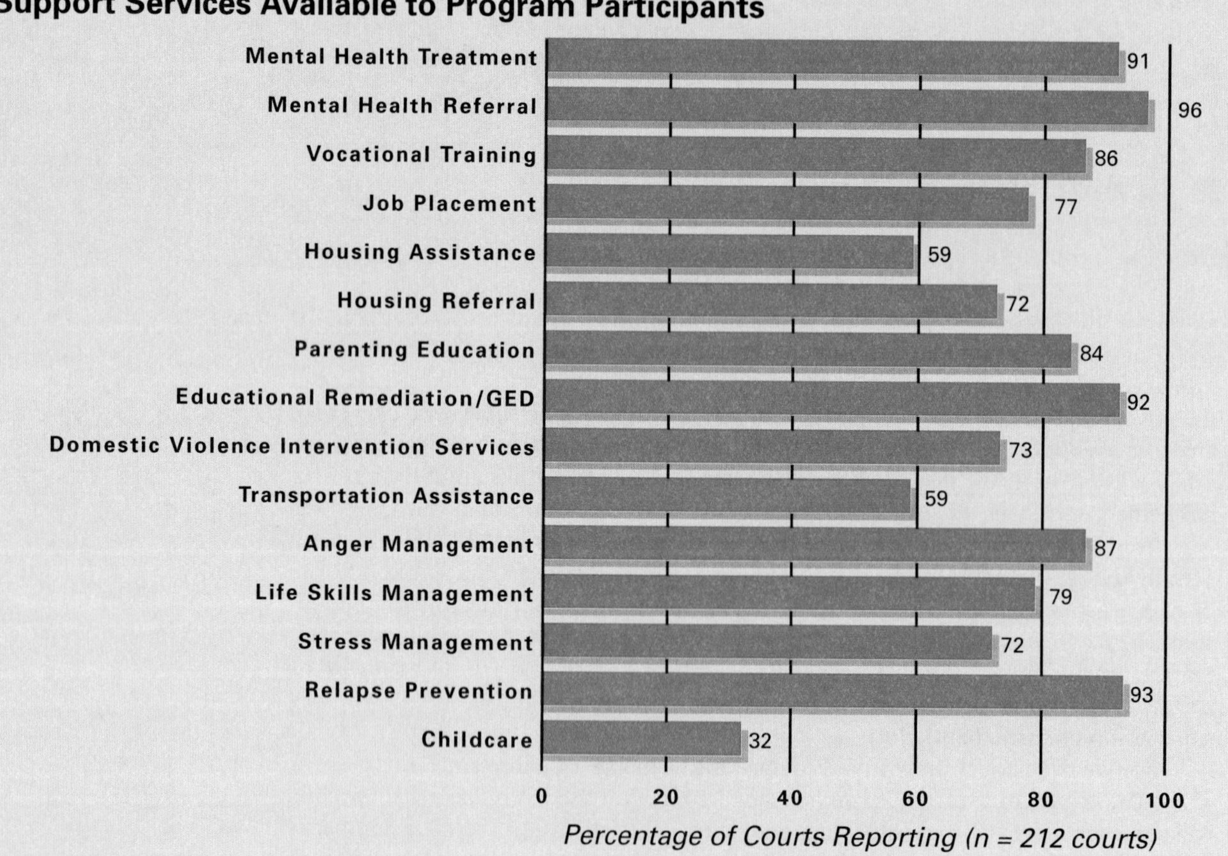

Source: Elizabeth Peyton, *Executive Summary Treatment Services in Adult Drug Courts: Report on the 1999 National Drug Court Treatment Survey* (Washington, DC: U.S. Department of Justice, May 2001), pp. 7–8.

table 14.1 Drug Court Program Savings

Jurisdiction	Savings Realized by Use of Drug Court Programs
Maricopa County (Phoenix), AZ	$112,077
Denver, CO	$1.8–$2.5 million
Washington, DC	$4,065–$8,845 per client in jail costs (amount fluctuates, depending on use of jail as a sanction while the defendant is enrolled in the drug court); and $102,000 in prosecution costs
Bartow, FL	$531,900
Gainesville, FL	$200,000
Kalamazoo, MI	$299,754
Klamath Falls, OR	$86,400
Beaumont, TX	$443,520

Source: Drug Court Clearinghouse and Technical Assistance Project, Office of Justice Programs, U.S. Department of Justice, http://www.ojp.usdoj.gov/dcpo/decade98.htm.

Extensive data are not available to evaluate the effectiveness of juvenile drug courts, but "judges anecdotally report that these programs are able to achieve greater accountability and provide a broader array of treatment and other services to youth and their families than traditional juvenile courts."[137] One-half to three-fourths of youths who enter juvenile drug court programs complete the program.[138] Initial analysis of indicators such as recidivism, drug use, and educational achievement seems to indicate that juvenile drug courts are providing better rehabilitation of youth than are traditional juvenile courts.[139]

Tribal Drug Courts

Unique problems of crime on Indian reservations include a disproportionately high rate of crime compared to general crime statistics. Alcohol and other substance abuse contributes substantially to the crime problem on Native American lands, as more than 90 percent of the criminal cases in most tribal courts involve alcohol or substance abuse.[140] In addition to alcohol abuse, many Native American communities have substantial problems with toxic inhalants. Drug courts were first adopted by Native American and Alaska Native tribal courts in 1997. Interest is growing, however, because drug court programs are more closely aligned with tribal justice concepts and methods than are traditional criminal justice processes.[141] Nevertheless, there are unique problems associated with adapting the drug court concept to meet the specific needs of Native Americans:[142]

Figure 14.6

Treatment and Services Provided by Drug Court Programs

A survey of 212 drug court programs illustrates the broad range of treatment programs and services provided by drug court programs.

- Tribal courts must address the specific cultural needs of their individual communities, including the challenge of incorporating tribal custom and tradition into the tribal drug court.
- The nature and high volume of alcohol abuse cases in most tribal courts present unique adaptation issues.
- Tribal courts face jurisdictional barriers that complicate their ability to implement an effective drug court process.
- Tribes seeking to establish drug court systems often face a broad range of other issues and challenges, including isolated rural locations, small-community issues, lack of resources and services, and lack of funding.

Tribal drug courts generally are called **Tribal Healing to Wellness Courts**. Some programs have developed individual names, using words from their native languages.[143] Healing to Wellness Courts may use traditional treatment processes involving tribal elders, traditional healing ceremonies, talking circles, peacemaking, sweats and sweat lodge, visits with a medicine man or woman, the sun dance, and a vision quest.[144]

Jurisdictional barriers to tribal drug courts include the lack of criminal jurisdiction over non–Native Americans, concurrent state jurisdiction, legal limits in sentencing (to 1 year or a fine of $5,000, or both), and a historically strained relationship with state courts and state agencies.[145] Also, more than 50 percent of the reservation population is under the age of 18,[146] requiring greater demand for juvenile drug court programs than is the case in the traditional criminal justice system. Data for traditional drug court programs are promising, however, and it is hoped that the drug court concept will prove flexible enough to work with traditional Native justice concepts and methods.[147]

TASC and RSAT

Federal assistance programs such as **Treatment Accountability for Safer Communities (TASC)** and the **Residential Substance Abuse Treatment (RSAT)** for State Prisoners Formula Grant Program have helped states adopt new comprehensive programs for drug offenders. Federal legislation designed to help states break the addiction-crime cycle of nonviolent, drug-involved offenders include the 1972 Drug Abuse and Treatment Act and the Violent Crime Control and Law Enforcement Act of 1994. Both laws provide federal funds to states to allow them to link the legal sanctions of the criminal justice system with the federally funded therapeutic interventions of drug treatment programs.[148] The major premise of programs funded by the grants is that criminal sanctions can be combined with the reintegration of offenders into the community, and that this can be done through a broad base of support from both the criminal justice system and the treatment community.[149] Combining intermediate sanctions and drug offender treatment programs is both effective and cost efficient. To prevent a return to drug use, these programs provide treatment both in prison and after release through postincarceration supervision. The combination of treatment strategies can reduce recidivism by about 50 percent. In addition to reducing recidivism, drug treatment costs are about $6,500 per year per inmate, whereas imprisonment costs are 4 to 10 times higher.[150]

TASC Treatment Accountability for Safer Communities, a federal assistance program to help states break the addiction-crime cycle.

RSAT Residential Substance Abuse Treatment, a federal assistance program to help states provide for treatment instead of prison for substance abusers.

JUST THE FACTS 14.5

What is the role of alcohol and drugs in criminal offending and crime rates? How do community-based programs address problems of substance abuse through state adult and juvenile drug courts? What special issues and challenges do tribal drug courts face? What are the benefits of federal programs that combine intensive supervision and therapeutic treatment for drug offenders?

conclusion:

Try, Try Again

The criminal justice system involves a dynamic process that is undergoing constant change, including the corrections component. Many correctional programs, philosophies, and challenges are new and evolving. Jails and prisons used for more than 100 years are being replaced by new structures that are radically different. Probation and parole, which emerged in the early twentieth century, are already being transformed by the new philosophies of intensive probation supervision (IPS) probation and parole and electronic monitoring. In the past 20 to 30 years, new intermediate sanctions have appeared that focus on control and treatment in the community. In the past decade, new programs for addressing the crisis of drug-addicted inmates are winning greater acceptance by the entire criminal justice system and the public.

Ways of looking at corrections are changing as new experiments in control and treatment are being tried. New research indicates that prisoners actually may prefer prison to many of the new intermediate and community-based sanctions. When polled as to their opinion of the harshness of punishments, many offenders say they prefer prison to the intrusiveness and control of IPS and other various community-based programs.[151] Fifteen percent of the participants who apply for early release under the New Jersey IPS program withdraw their application once they understand the restrictions and conditions of the program. When nonviolent offenders in Marion County, Oregon, were offered a choice between a prison term or release under IPS, one-third of the offenders chose prison.[152]

The perfect method to rehabilitate offenders and the perfect method to provide for community safety when offenders are released back into the community have not been found. However, like law enforcement and the judicial system, the correctional system continues to look for new and better ways to protect the community while providing for the successful reentry of offenders into the community.

Chapter Summary

- More offenders are returning from prison to the community than ever before. Often, they are unsuccessful in their attempt to reenter the community as law-abiding citizens. Because of disappointment with traditional probation and parole programs, new programs are being tried, with the aim of better protection for the community and more successful reentry of offenders into the community.
- New programs include intermediate sanctions and community-based corrections. Intensive probation supervision (IPS) emphasizes strict accountability to the conditions of probation and parole.

- Split sentencing and shock probation require the offender to spend a brief period of time in prison before being granted supervised release in the community. Shock incarceration is accomplished through boot camps for adult and juvenile offenders.
- Home confinement is an intermediate sanction that requires offenders to remain within the home unless specifically authorized to leave. Electronic monitoring effectively and efficiently ensures that offenders remain at home.
- Community-based treatment programs such as work release and education release help offenders obtain work or education so that they will be successful when they reenter their communities.
- Halfway houses are programs designed to help inmates make the transition from prison to community. Halfway houses provide offenders with limited freedom within the community during the last part of their sentences.
- Day reporting centers can be used as intermediate sanctions to keep offenders out of prison.
- Reentry programs for drug offenders emphasize the need to combine the power of the criminal justice system with the effectiveness of treatment programs under strictly supervised conditions. Adult, juvenile, and tribal drug courts are proving to be effective community-based treatment programs.

Vocabulary Review

community-based corrections, 433
correctional case managers, 446
day reporting centers, 446
drug court, 449
electronic monitoring, 441
furlough, 433
halfway houses, 446
home confinement, 440
intensive probation supervision (IPS) , 436
intermediate sanctions, 433
RSAT, 454
shock incarceration, 438
shock probation, 437
split sentencing, 437
TASC, 454
Weed and Seed, 434
work release, 443

Names and Events to Remember

Huber Law, 443
Prisoner Rehabilitation Act of 1965, 443
Private Sector/Prison Industry Enhancement Certification Program, 445
Reentry Partnership Initiative, 443
Serious and Violent Offender Reentry Initiative, 443
Tribal Healing to Wellness Courts, 454
Vera Institute of Justice, 435

Think about This

1. According to this chapter, a study has shown that female inmates who take college courses have a recidivism rate of 7.7 percent, compared with a rate of 29.9 percent for those who do not take courses. Why do you think college coursework reduces recidivism rates so dramatically? Would the same reasons and results apply to male inmates?
2. If incarceration does not reform prisoners, and most prisoners reenter society without the skills or opportunities to cope, why use prisons at all? Should only offenders who are sentenced to life or death be in prison? Would the money spent on prisons be better spent on rehabilitating offenders? What obstacles might such an option face?

3. If recidivism rates are so high, and communities are so unwilling to provide rehabilitation services, and employers are so reluctant to hire ex-offenders, should experiments with community-based corrections be ended and offenders simply kept in prison? Why, or why not? What is needed to make community-based corrections work?
4. Imagine that members of your family call and tell you that authorities have proposed starting a halfway house on their block. Your relatives are worried about the possibility of increased crime in the neighborhood, as well as a decline in the value of their home. What advice would you give them? Explain why you would be for or against the halfway house in the neighborhood.

ContentSelect

Go to the ContentSelect web site and key in the search term "drug courts." Read "Reintegrative Shaming and Recidivism Risks in Drug Court" from the October 2000 issue of *Crime and Delinquency*. This article discusses the effectiveness of drug courts in reducing recidivism. Sample the article to answer the following questions.

1. Read the section on Braithwaite's theory of reintegrative shaming. Describe the two types of shame associated with offenders reentering the community and how that shaming affects the offender.
2. Why does the article suggest that the drug court is more stigmatizing than conventional courts?
3. Consider the role that the judges play in the Miami and Las Vegas drug courts. How does the drug court judge role differ from that of a typical criminal court judge? Explain whether you believe the judge has too much power over the drug offender's life.
4. How do the conclusions in the article about the effectiveness of drug courts compare and contrast with views expressed in this chapter of your textbook?

Fear of Violent Victimization
Why do people fear becoming victims of violent crimes?

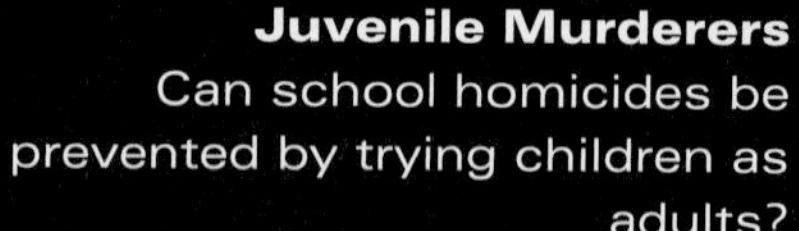

Juvenile Murderers
Can school homicides be prevented by trying children as adults?

Violence and Mass Media
To what extent are mass media a cause of crime?

Drug Addiction and Drug Crime
Should a medical model prevail over the war on drugs?

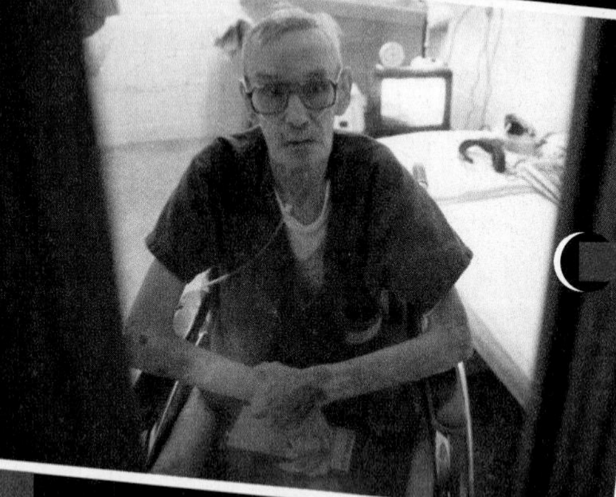

Prisoners and Public Health
Why must health and safety problems of prison populations be addressed?

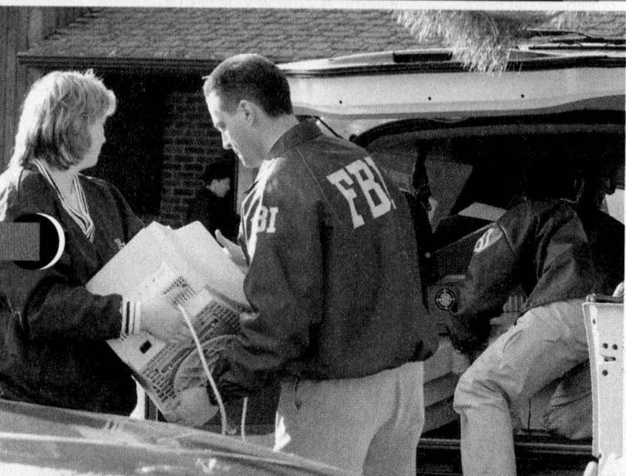

Technoterror and Cybercrime
What is the future of computer security and Internet freedom in the United States?

part six

Issues and Trends in the Criminal Justice System

For a final chapter, four unique challenges to the criminal justice system have been selected for special analysis. They have been selected because they represent comparatively recent, multifaceted problems with significant ongoing impacts on the criminal justice system. The problems include (1) the violent criminality of youthful offenders, including school violence, (2) the impacts of illegal drug use and trafficking on the criminal justice system, (3) burdensome physical and mental health problems in the offender population, and (4) the many new problems and opportunities that spring from developing technology. What new strategies, new laws, new skills, and new thinking will be needed to solve these and other problems today? How will interagency cooperation reshape responses to issues and trends in criminal justice?

chapter 15

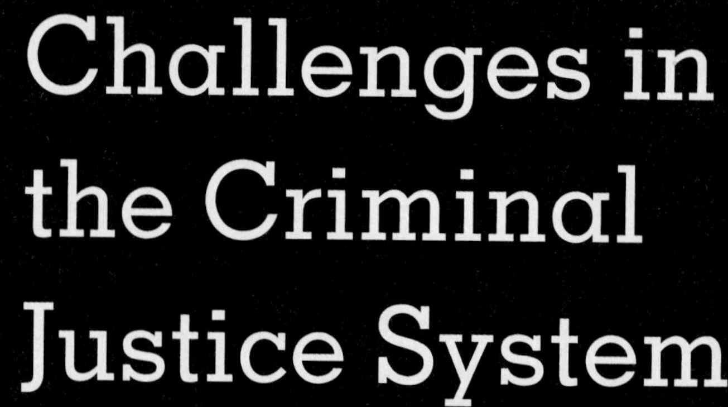

Challenges in the Criminal Justice System

outline

[Le]arning [O]bjectives

[Aft]er reading this chapter, [you] will know

- [F]our major challenges fac[i]ng the criminal justice [s]ystem in the twenty-first [c]entury.
- [T]he multifaceted problems [i]n responding to youth vio[l]ence and school [h]omicides.
- [D]rug law enforcement in [t]erms of the war on [d]rugs and the real-ties of addiction.
- [T]he strategies used [t]o reduce illegal drug [u]se in the United [S]tates and how to [c]ompare and contrast [t]hem.
- [T]he challenges of deal[i]ng with the physical and [m]ental health and safety [o]f prisoners and their [c]ommunities.
- [T]he impacts of new tech[n]ologies on crime, includ[i]ng cybercrime, corporate [c]rime, and terrorism.
- [T]he impacts of new tech[n]ologies on law enforce[m]ent and the criminal [j]ustice system.
- [T]he new roles and respon[s]ibilities required of crimi[n]al justice agencies and [p]ersonnel to meet new [c]hallenges.

Extreme Violence: Accused Slayer Is Also a Vampire

Santa Cruz, California.—A murder trial in Santa Cruz turned into a modern-day Dracula drama as prosecutors accused a 20-year-old woman of being a "vampire" that killed a neighbor and drank his blood. The "Lost Boys" trial accused Deborah Jean Finch, a former roller-coaster operator, with first-degree murder. Court watchers labeled the case "The Lost Boys" trial after a 1987 movie about teenage vampires that was filmed in Santa Cruz and neighboring towns. The defendant is alleged to have worshipped a Chinese vampire named Zwar, who she described as being 11-foot-8, with glowing gold eyes and the ability to control minds.[1]

—*Honolulu Advertiser*, June 4, 1992

Teenagers Kill Girl over Threat to Tell Plans

Clearfield, Pennsylvania.—A 15-year-old girl was strung up in a tree, and a friend clubbed her to death with a rock for threatening to reveal plans by a group of teens to run away to Florida. A group of 10 juveniles and young adults first put a rope around her neck and dragged her around a wooded clearing before hanging her from a tree until she passed out. When they noticed that she was still alive, one of the group bashed her head in with a rock. After killing her, most of the group left for a brief visit to Lakeland, Florida.[2]

—*Honolulu Advertiser*, May 22, 1998

introduction:

Beyond Crime and Justice

The teenage vampire killer and the brutal murder of a teen by her peers are examples of extreme youth violence—a growing challenge that the criminal justice system faces in the twenty-first century. Persistent, new, and growing challenges are many, making it difficult to choose which ones to discuss. In this last chapter, four challenges have been singled out for special discussion, and your instructor no doubt will have other special issues or trends in criminal justice that he or she wishes to discuss. This chapter focuses on (1) the violent criminality of youthful offenders, including school violence, (2) the impacts of illegal drug use and trafficking on the criminal justice system, (3) physical and mental health problems in the offender population, and (4) the many new problems and opportunities that spring from developing technology.

These four challenges have been selected because they are multifaceted and are having a significant ongoing impact on the criminal justice system. These and other challenges will require new strategies, new laws, new skills, and new thinking to solve them. They are beyond the ability of any one criminal justice agency to solve. For example, the police cannot fight the problem of youthful offender violence and school violence by themselves. Illegal drug use and trafficking will not be defeated by more enforcement and longer prison sentences. And it is not possible to improve the health of the offender population working only within the environment of jails and prisons. Thus, to find effective solutions, criminal justice agencies will need to cooperate much more extensively than they have in the past and to forge better partnerships with communities. As has been emphasized throughout this textbook, the criminal justice system is a dynamic system interlinked with the community, state, and nation.

The impact of new technology on the criminal justice system is almost beyond imagination. Technology is a two-edged sword. On one hand, it brings new tools to fight crime. On the other hand, it makes new crimes possible or makes it possible to commit old crimes in new ways. These challenges go beyond the discussion of crime and justice. Often, they require a discussion of the foundational values on which the criminal justice system is built. For example, new government policies regarding computer-based technologies give the criminal justice system new tools with which to fight crime. A result is debate about the balance of individual freedoms guaranteed in the Constitution and the need to fight computer-assisted crime.

Fear of Violent Crimes: No Safe Place

THE MAIN IDEA

Violence—youth violence in particular—presents a major challenge to the criminal justice system. The multifaceted causes and sources of violence make the problem hard to solve.

People fear becoming victims of senseless violent crimes. Despite the fact that most victims are harmed by someone they know and not a stranger, people fear being attacked by deranged murderers such as the young woman who thought she was a vampire or by a serial killer. Despite statistics indicating that **workplace violence** is decreasing, the public fears workplace violence, especially by postal employees, because of certain sensational cases. The public's perception of this danger is reflected in the term *going postal*, meaning becoming explosively violent in the workplace. Yet, an objective analysis of crime statistics does not justify this fear of violent crime. It seems clear that public perceptions influence people's fears more than do facts and figures. For example, the public's perception that post offices are more violent workplaces than other workplaces is not supported by comparative data. In fact, the data indicate a significant decline in violent crime over the past 30 years. For instance, while workplace violence appears almost daily in newspaper headlines, between 1993 and 1999 violence in the workplace declined by 39 percent.[3]

Nevertheless, people continue to be fearful of victimization, and this fear seems to be unrelated to facts and figures. For example, older people report greater fear of victimization, but less fearful younger people, especially non-white males, are much more likely to be victimized. The media play an important role in the public's fear of violent crime. A single incidence of violence can have a life of its own through media coverage. Wherever a violent crime occurs, it is quickly reported nationwide. A shooting in Hawaii,[4] California,[5] Miami,[6] Atlanta,[7] Pennsylvania,[8] or New York[9] is quickly and repeatedly reported in the news. The power of the media makes people fear that all crime is happening in their own backyards.

And, it appears that no place is safe. Big cities that were encouraged by dropping crime rates during the past decade are now seeing a rise in homicide rates.[10] Small towns, once considered safe havens from the violence of the big cities, are the scenes of spree killings.[11] Spree killings and random violence have occurred at homes, restaurants, motels, parks, and zoos. Churches and synagogues have been the sites of random acts of senseless violence and death.[12] Even the homeless have been targeted for random death at the hands of serial killers.[13] One of the places that until recently was considered safe was the school. Also, juveniles under the age of 18 were considered less capable of having *mens rea* (evil intent). However, the public has become very concerned over the safety of children in schools and the assumptions underlying the treatment of violent juvenile offenders.

Public Concern about Youth Violence

Of public concern is the alarming role of juveniles and youthful offenders in the violence in society. Media reporting of stories such as those at the beginning of this chapter cause people to fear the brutality of juvenile crime and to want to know why it happens. In 2000, law enforcement agencies made an estimated 2.4 million arrests of persons under the age of 18 (see Figure 15.1 on page 464). That year, juveniles were involved in 16 percent of all Violent Crime Index arrests and 32 percent of all Property Crime Index arrests.[14] Furthermore, juveniles, not adults, have been responsible for serious violence in the schools. Society does not seem to know how to respond to this threat.

Juveniles have committed serious violent crimes, such as murder, rape, robbery, assault, burglary, auto theft, and arson. In addition there is significant use of illegal drugs and underage drinking among juveniles. In about 12 percent of homicides, the perpetrator of the crime is a juvenile. Most (93%) juvenile murderers are male, and most (88%) are age 15 or older. Most victims of juvenile homicides are killed with a handgun. Of all victims killed by juveniles, 14 percent were family members, 55 percent were acquaintances, and 31 percent were strangers. In 1997, juveniles committed about 30 percent of the robberies and 27 percent of the aggravated assaults known to the

workplace violence
The use of violence in the workplace.

Figure 15.1

Juveniles Were Involved in 16 Percent of All Violent Crime Index Arrests and 32 Percent of All Property Crime Index Arrests in 2000

Note: The Violent Crime Index includes the offenses of murder and nonnegligent manslaughter, forcible rape, robbery, and aggravated assault. The Property Crime Index includes the offenses of burglary, larceny-theft, motor vehicle theft, and arson. Running away from home and curfew and loitering violations are not presented in this figure because, by definition, only juveniles can be arrested for these offenses.

One-quarter (25%) of all persons arrested for robbery in 2000 were under age 18, substantially above the juvenile proportion of arrests in other violent offenses: forcible rape (16%), aggravated assault (14%), and murder (9%).

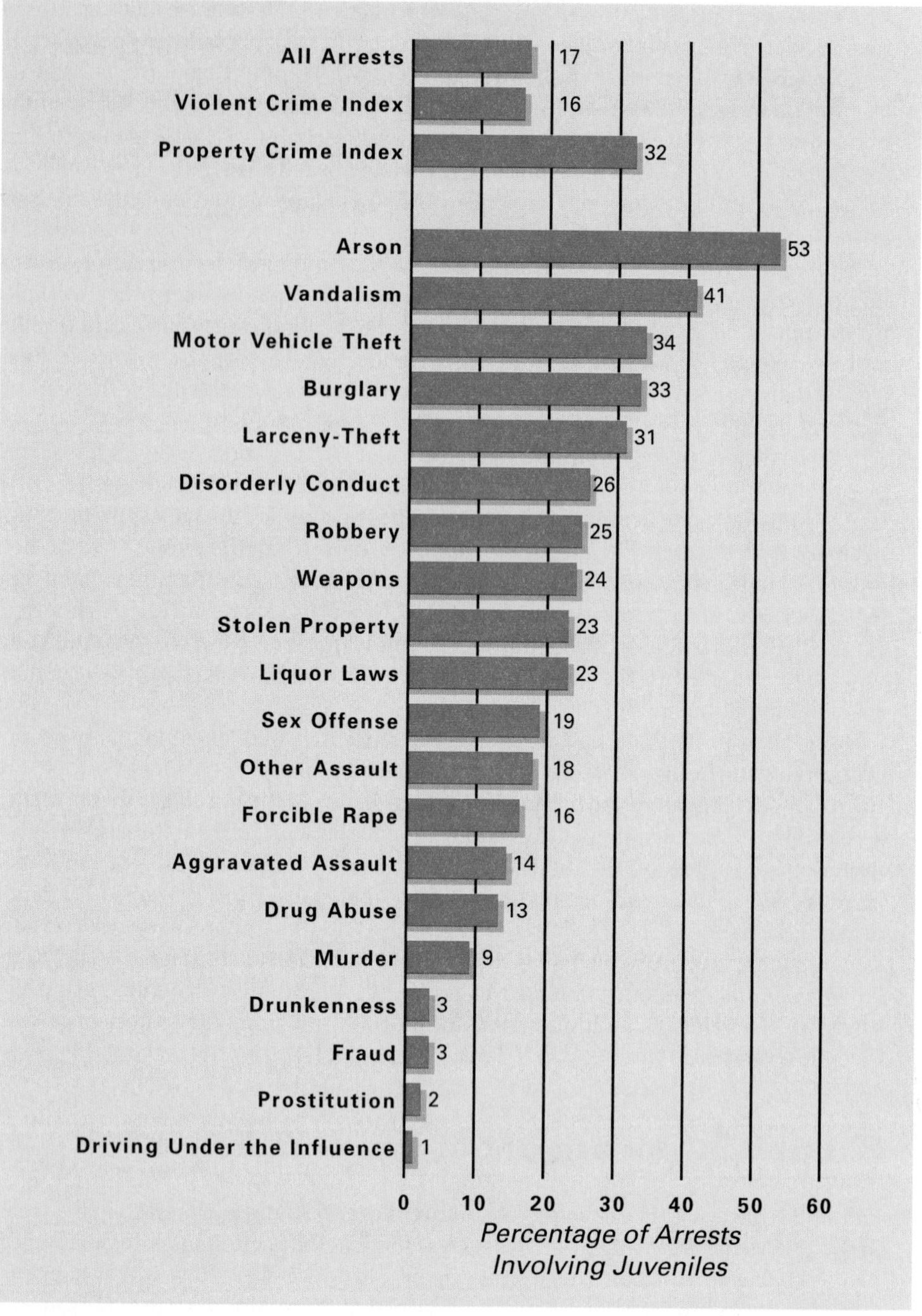

Source: Adapted from Snyder H., *Juvenile Arrests 2000* (Washington, DC: Office of Juvenile Justice and Delinquency Prevention, 2002).

police.[15] On average, juveniles were involved in one-fourth of serious violent victimizations annually over the past three decades.[16]

Statistics indicate that the actual rate of violent juvenile crime rose dramatically after 1980, peaked in about 1993–1994, and has declined since then.[17] Public perceptions of juvenile offending have been influenced primarily by media attention focused on high-profile incidents, such as homicides by young offenders and school spree shootings. These types of crimes are front-page newspaper stories and cover stories for magazines and receive the most air time on television. The public seems shocked and concerned by two characteristic of juvenile homicides: (1) how very young some of the offenders are and (2) how vicious and brutal the crimes of juvenile offenders can be.

Go to http://www.surgeongeneral.gov/library/youthviolence/ to read "Youth Violence: A Report of the Surgeon General" (released January 2001). ■

HOMICIDES COMMITTED BY VERY YOUNG OFFENDERS How young are juveniles who commit murder? In March 2002, a 4-year-old boy shot and killed an 18-month-old girl with her father's handgun as the two were watching a movie in a bedroom.[18] The police classified the shooting as an accident, and the boy's age makes prosecution on criminal charges impossible. However, there are examples of other homicides by very young offenders that are clearly deliberate criminal acts, often involving premeditation. In Decatur, Georgia, for example, a 7-year-old boy was arrested in the stabbing of a 4-year-old and a 6-year-old.[19] In New York, an 8-year-old boy was charged with criminally negligent homicide for allegedly stabbing to death a 4-year-old neighbor whom he had bullied for more than a year. The boy's 9-year-old brother was also arrested for assault for his role in the attack.[20] In Columbus, Ohio, police charged an 8-year-old girl with attempted murder for allegedly pouring poison into her great-grandmother's drink because the two did not get along.[21]

One problem is the public belief that the juvenile justice system cannot adequately punish young offenders for serious violent crimes like murder. The juvenile justice system assumes that very young offenders lack *mens rea*, a necessary element for a crime; therefore, often, very young offenders are simply released to a guardian or family member on juvenile probation. Very young offenders seem to get away with murder with impunity. Unfortunately, there appears to be no middle ground in the criminal justice system. An offender is either a juvenile and under the authority of the juvenile court system, which emphasizes rehabilitation rather than punishment, or the offender is an adult and faces the full force and punishment of the adult criminal justice system.

Lacking other alternatives, the criminal justice system must either leave offenders in the juvenile system or petition for their transfer to the adult court system. If that transfer is approved, the offender is tried as an adult. One of the nation's youngest offenders to be tried and convicted in adult court is Nathaniel Abraham, charged with second-degree murder in the shooting of a stranger when he was only 11 years old. When Abraham was in the sixth grade, he shot and killed an 18-year-old in what was described as a sniper-slaying outside a convenience store.[22] At his first court appearance, he was so small that his feet did not touch the floor when he sat in a chair, but the young boy was charged with first-degree murder and faced a possible life sentence if convicted.[23] In sentencing Abraham for second-degree murder, the judge said that the 1997 Michigan law that allowed the boy to be prosecuted as an adult is fundamentally flawed.[24] The judge took the option allowed by law to sentence Abraham to a juvenile detention until age 21 rather than the maximum sentence, which was life in prison with

This minor child is being tried as an adult for a homicide. The public is shocked at crimes of passion that children perpetrate against their parents. People also are shocked that youthful offenders seem willing to kill for petty reasons and to commit mass murder. Is incarceration and punishment in the adult criminal justice system the solution to the problem of youth violence?

criminal justice in the media

Violence—Entertainment or Cause of Crime?

The American Academy of Pediatrics says that "television viewing can affect the mental, social and physical health of young people."[25] The Academy recommends that children under 2 years of age should not watch television, older children should not have television sets in their bedrooms, and pediatricians should have parents fill out a media history along with a medical history.[26] In one of the first studies of TV violence, in 1977, researchers studied girls ages 6 to 10, then reinterviewed more than 200 of them 15 years later. The study concluded that girls who viewed violent TV shows and identified with aggressive TV heroines were more likely to be physically aggressive as young adults and more prone to criminal behavior.[27]

Following the Columbine High School (Littleton, Colorado) tragedy, U.S. representative Henry Hyde said before Congressional hearings, "Anybody that thinks rotten movies, rotten television, rotten video games are not poisoning, toxically poisoning, our kids' minds and making some kids think that conduct is acceptable just is not paying attention."[28] Gallup polls reported that 81 percent of American adults say they believe that violent entertainment is a cause of increased violence in society, and 73 percent say the government should restrict the access of minors to such materials.[29] Some critics assert that media violence directly causes real violence. For example, when 14-year-old Michael Carneal murdered three students and wounded five others during a shooting rampage at a Kentucky high school, he told homicide investigators that the shooting spree had been influenced by a murder scene he saw in the movie "The Basketball Diaries."[30]

Despite dire warnings and condemnations, **media violence** continues to be big business. The big hits continue to be television shows with violent content, such as *The Sopranos*, *Law and Order: Special Victims Unit*, and *OZ*, and events staged by the World Wrestling Federation (WWF). Game shows that titillate the audience with danger, such as *Fear Factor*, *Kidnapped*, and *Survivor*, are among the more popular shows, with viewers aged 18 to 34.[31] The Children's Defense Fund reports that by the age of 18, the typical child has watched approximately 200,000

the possibility of parole. While the judge in Abraham's case was lenient, other very young offenders have not been so fortunate in their sentencing. In Odessa, Texas, a 12-year-old boy convicted of beating a 45-year-old man to death with a tire iron for his social security check was sentenced as an adult and faces a prison term of 30 years.[32] After turning 21, he will be evaluated and if found to be not rehabilitated, he will be transferred to an adult prison to serve out the remaining years of his sentence.

The challenge of the criminal justice system is to find a way to handle very young offenders that balances justice with rehabilitation. Amnesty International used the **Abraham case** in a 1998 report condemning America's justice system as too harsh on juveniles.[33] However, laws that permit the trying of very young offenders as adults are the result of public frustration with a juvenile justice system that seems to be too lax. Concerned with the failure of the juvenile justice system to protect the public from juvenile violent offenders, the public has opted to hold some juveniles accountable for their crimes in adult court.

media violence The portrayal of violence in the media.

BRUTAL JUVENILE CRIME The second characteristic of violent juvenile crime that captures the attention of the pubic is the apparent complete disregard for life in some offenses. The public is alarmed not so much by the number of violent juvenile crimes but by the brutal or casual nature of the crime. In Camden County, New Jersey, a 16-year-old was charged with killing six people and wounding a seventh. Five of the

acts of violence in the media, including 25,000 murders. Voluntary rating systems, televisions with V-chips, and warnings on music covers seem to have done little to curtail the exposure of young children and adults to media violence. Video games, gangsta rap, and other music with explicitly violent lyrics have increased that exposure.

Congress has threatened to regulate media violence if the industry fails to adopt voluntary limits.[34] One proposed law would make it a crime punishable by up to 5 years in prison to sell, distribute, or lend violent movies, television programs, videos, books, and Internet material to children.[35] The City Council of Chicago summoned Jerry Springer before a hearing to question the violence on his popular TV show. One Alderman implied that the brawls on the show were no different from domestic fights that lead to thousands of arrests in Chicago. Springer countered that his show might curb violence because it shows domestic violence in an unattractive light.[36] Feminist-led protests and boycotts convinced MTV and retailers such as Wal-Mart and K-Mart to pull "Smack My Bitch Up," a hit song by the British techno group Prodigy. Groups complained that the video and the song have offensive lyrics that glorify violence against women.[37] However, small victories do not win the war on media violence.

Even if fictional violence could be reduced or eliminated from the media, there is the question of television coverage of real violence. In 1998, news stations broadcast live coverage of a man who set himself on fire and then killed himself with a shotgun.[38] In 1999, TV news coverage broadcast live a freeway chase that ended with the man being shot by police officers.[39] Nightly newscasts continue to show fires, high-speed chases, and homicide scenes. Popular reality-TV shows such as *COPS* and other programs that show the viewer actual video of high-speed chases, car wrecks, and assaults are based on real, not fictional, violence.

Mass media also exploit real-world violence. After the terrorist attacks on September 11, 2001, against the World Trade Center and the Pentagon, films such as *Collateral Damage*, in which Arnold Schwarzenegger seeks justice for a terrorist attack on Los Angeles, and *Black Hawk Down*, about the deaths of American soldiers in Somalia, were major hits. One defense of media violence is that viewers are not indifferent to the death and destruction portrayed, but that the vicarious assurance that they can survive it provides them with comfort that they can survive—even triumph over—the forces of violence in the world.[40]

■ Do you believe that media violence causes people, especially young children, to commit violent acts? What do you think should be the balance between the right of free speech and the regulation of media violence? If fictional violence can inspire people to violence, do reality-TV and newscast violence have the same power? If so, do you think broadcast violence should be regulated? If young offenders claim that they were influenced by media violence, is this a valid defense at their trials?

people apparently were killed to cover the assailant's tracks. Authorities described the killings as "chilling" and said "that a 16-year-old could kill six people and try to kill a seventh, and at least two of whom we believe had no connection with him, is just unimaginable."[41] Eighteen-year-old Seth Privacky confessed to killing his parents, grandfather, brother, and his brother's girlfriend. He shot the five in their heads at close range, execution-style. He said he killed them because his father had threatened to kick him out of the house.[42] In Boligee, Alabama, at least six boys watched as a screaming female classmate was stripped, held down by another group of boys, and raped in a high school locker room during school hours.[43] In Pensacola, Florida, a 13-year-old boy admitted killing his father with about 10 cracks to the head with a baseball bat, and his 12-year-old brother said the murder was his idea.[44] In Washington, DC, a 16-year-old opened fire at the National Zoo, wounding seven children.[45] These crimes sound more like those of hardened, depraved, repeat offenders than children as young as 12.

Violence in Schools

In August 1966, a student, Charles Whitman, dragged a foot locker filled with hunting rifles onto the observation deck of the clock tower at the University of Texas (Austin) and opened fire, killing 14 and wounding 31 others. The Whitman attack marked a new

What are the causes of youth violence? Why would high school students want to kill so many people? Is it family life, violence in the media, peer pressure, mental conditions? How can these crimes be prevented? To what extent does excessive and sensationalistic media coverage of school shootings encourage imitation as well as public overreaction? Are youths more prone to commit copycat crimes?

Go to http://198.246.96.2/nccdphp/dash/violence/index.htm to view the Centers for Disease Control and Prevention web site on "Federal Activities Addressing Violence in Schools." ■

and different terror—that anyone anywhere could be killed at random.[46] Prior to the Whitman attack, schools were considered one of the last safe places in the United States. About 30 years after the Whitman attack, school grounds again became killing fields in a series of spree killings on school campuses between 1996 and 1998. Young, white, mostly middle class boys with some signs of depression but no history of serious mental illness terrorized the nation with random acts of mass murder. Schools in Moses Lake, Washington; Pearl, Mississippi; West Paducah, Kentucky; Jonesboro, Arkansas; Springfield, Oregon; Littleton, Colorado; Conyers, Georgia; Edinboro, Pennsylvania; and Santee, California, are remembered for the violence and death that occurred on school grounds. The attack on Columbine High School students by Eric Harris and Dylan Klebold on April 20, 1999, was the most serious attack since the Whitman massacre. At Columbine High School, 1 teacher and 12 students were killed, and 23 others were wounded.

The Justice Policy Institute, the research arm of the Center on Juvenile and Criminal Justice, has declared that the chances of a child being killed at school are nearly 1 in 1 million.[47] Some experts have pointed out that despite the public fear of **school violence**, schools are still the safest place for children to be—safer than the streets, even safer than home.[48] Crime statistics indicate that these claims are true and that school violence, especially murders, appears to be declining. Despite these facts, calls continue for increased safety measures in schools. The nation's mayors called for 100,000 counselors to be placed in schools to spot and help troubled and violent kids. Mayors also recommended that students be required to wear uniforms and that conflict resolution programs be added to the curriculum.[49] Schools are screening students with metal detectors, expelling students for the slightest threat of violence, requiring students to report threats of violence or be expelled, placing full-time armed police officers in the schools, and drilling staff and students on procedures in case of a shooting.

school violence Violence that takes place at schools.

A report by the Office of Juvenile Justice and Delinquency Prevention acknowledged that many students are afraid to attend school, and many parents are concerned for their children's safety at school. However, the report criticized the media as a significant contributing factor to this fear. The report found that while violence in schools is a problem, statistics indicate that shooting sprees are rare, despite widespread headlines and special media reports. Less than 1 percent of the schools across the country have experienced a violent death on campus in the past 7 years.[50]

The Search for Accountability

One reason for public fear of school violence is that its cause appears to be mystery. Why does a child with an unremarkable history become a mass murderer who randomly kills teachers and classmates? The reasons that motivate juveniles to kill are diverse and, in a sense, do not seem adequate to explain the crime. Victor Cordova Jr., age 13, said he shot a 13-year-old classmate in the head because "other kids were bothering me."[51] A seventh-grader shot and killed his teacher because he had been sent home for throwing water balloons in class.[52] A 12-year-old student pulled a gun in class and threatened to shoot the teacher and classmates because he wanted to join his mother, who was in jail.[53] Two teens accused of killing two Dartmouth College professors did so because they were committed to "an evil-game of dare."[54] Two teens involved in the school shooting at Pearl, Mississippi, are believed to have been motivated by satanic beliefs.[55]

Numerous studies of violent offenders have attempted to understand what caused them to kill. Some studies focus on biological factors in juvenile violence, such as hormonal changes. These studies conclude that boys are "wired for aggression," which explains why juvenile violence is committed mostly by boys.[56] Studies by the Office of Juvenile Justice and Delinquency Prevention dispute this conclusion, however. A 1997 report warned, "This country can ill afford to continue to downplay their [juvenile females] significance in the full gamut of violence research, evaluation, prevention, intervention, and control."[57] Sociological theories point to diverse causes, such as environmental influence, peer pressure, lack of opportunity for legitimate advancement, and learned behavior. A study by Secret Service experts of 40 cases of school violence or shootings over 20 years concluded that there is no single profile of a school shooter.[58]

A California study concluded that the prevalence of serious juvenile delinquency could be reduced significantly by identifying and treating the small percentage of juveniles who are at risk of becoming chronic offenders when they first come into contact with the juvenile justice system.[59] The study reported that about 8 percent of juveniles account for nearly all significant violent juvenile crime. Furthermore, this small group of potentially serious, chronic offenders can be identified reliably at first contact with the juvenile justice system.[60] Identifying and treating these offenders could significantly reduce violent juvenile crime.

Many authorities claim that the availability of handguns is a major contributing factor in serious juvenile crime.[61] Proponents of gun control argue that school spree shootings are possible only because weapons are so easily available to children. They argue that gun control legislation mandating safer guns and penalties against adults who allow children to obtain guns would help promote a safer school environment. However, the criminal justice system does not know what causes violent juvenile behavior. More juveniles are being tried as adults in the belief that strict accountability will provide a solution. Others want to adopt programs to engage children in after-school activities and social and recreational programs. Others claim that the solution lies in understanding the chemistry of hormones and brain activity. With no solution in sight, many fear that not enough is being done to solve what many perceive as a serious and costly social problem (see Table 15.1 on page 470).

JUST THE FACTS 15.1

Why is there a public perception that violent crimes are increasing? What are some sources of violence in American society and culture? What problems does the criminal justice system face in dealing with young offenders? What are some factors that could cause youth violence?

table 15.1 Allowing One Youth to Leave High School for a Life of Crime and Drug Abuse Costs Society $1.7–$2.3 Million

Invoice

To:	**American public**
For:	**One lost youth**

Description	Cost
Crime:	
Juvenile career (4 years @ 1–4 crimes/year)	
Victim costs	$62,000–$250,000
Criminal justice costs	$21,000–$84,000
Adult career (6 years @ 10.6 crimes/year)	
Victim costs	$1,000,000
Criminal justice costs	$335,000
Offender productivity loss	$64,000
Total crime cost	**$1.5–$1.8 million**
Present value*	**$1.3–$1.5 million**
Drug abuse:	
Resources devoted to drug market	$84,000–$168,000
Reduced productivity loss	$27,600
Drug treatment costs	$10,200
Medical treatment of drug-related illnesses	$11,000
Premature death	$31,800–$223,000
Criminal justice costs associated with drug crimes	$40,500
Total drug abuse cost	**$200,000–$480,000**
Present value*	**$150,000–$360,000**
Costs imposed by high school dropout:	
Lost wage productivity	$300,000
Fringe benefits	$75,000
Nonmarket losses	$95,000–$375,000
Total dropout cost	**$470,000–$750,000**
Present value*	**$243,000–$388,000**
Total loss	**$2.2–$3 million**
Present value*	**$1.7–$2.3 million**

Source: Howard Snyder and Melissa Sickmund, *Juvenile Offenders and Victims: 1999 National Report* (Washington, DC: National Center for Juvenile Justice, September 1999).

*Present value is the amount of money that would need to be invested today to cover the future costs of the youth's behavior.

Drugs: War on Drugs or Addiction?

THE MAIN IDEA

Drug-related criminal activity has an impact on society on many levels, from crimes committed to obtain drugs to terrorist activities financed by money obtained from illegal drug sales. Different competing strategies exist for dealing with drug use.

The report of the National Drug Control Strategy proclaimed, "Over time, drugs will change people from productive citizens into addicts" and "tolerance of drug use is particularly corrosive for any self-governing people. Democracies can flourish only when their citizens embrace personal responsibility. Drug use erodes the individual's capacity to purse both ideals. It diminishes the individual's capacity to operate effectively. . . ."[62] President George W. Bush declared, "We must reduce drug use for one great moral reason: Over time, drugs rob men, women, and children of their dignity and of their character. Illegal drugs are the enemies of ambition and home. When we fight against drugs, we fight for the souls of our fellow Americans."[63]

Despite these dire warnings, illegal drug use continues to flourish in the United States. Approximately 2.8 million Americans are "dependent" on illegal drugs, and an additional 15 million fall in the less severe "abuser" category.[64] Illegal drug use is a problem in all communities. There seems to be no protection against the lure of illegal drug use, as evidenced by the arrest of two Amish men for selling cocaine to fellow members.[65] The men were from the conservative Old Order Amish of Lancaster County, Pennsylvania, known for its isolation from the outside world and prohibitions against the use of modern conveniences. Members ride horse-drawn buggies and dress in plain black clothes. Despite these shared, strong, conservative religious values, illegal drug use is a problem among some Amish youths.

The response of society and the criminal justice system to the challenge of illegal drug use generates great debate. Some accuse the criminal justice system of creating a "prison-industrial complex" that crowds jails and prisons with nonviolent drug offenders at the expense of cheaper and more effective treatment. Some point to the mockery of legalized alcohol and tobacco when marijuana is classified as a Schedule I narcotic on a par with heroin. Five times more deaths are attributed to alcohol and over 20 times more deaths are attributed to tobacco products than are caused by drug abuse.[66] The "War on Drugs" also is criticized for institutional racism. Human Rights Watch reports that 482 of every 100,000 black men are in prison for a drug crime, compared with just 36 of every 100,000 white men. Blacks make up 62 percent of the United States' imprisoned drug offenders, despite accounting for just 13 percent of the population.[67] Antidiscrimination activists have even accused the Central Intelligence Agency of introducing crack cocaine to Los Angeles.[68]

The American **War on Drugs** developed during the Nixon and Reagan eras. The ambitious goal of the Anti-Drug Abuse Act of 1988 was to create a drug-free America by 1995. In pursuit of that goal, the criminal justice system adopted extensive and harsh criminal penalties against drug users and drug trafficking. In fact, some of the highest criminal fines are for drug trafficking. The fine for trafficking in heroin can be as high as $10 million. Critics have pointed to the failure of the War on Drugs to reduce drug use, while at the same time inflicting much "collateral damage" on society. One critic compared the War on Drugs to Niagara Falls, saying, "'You take 10 buckets out one year, 100 buckets out the next. That's a 500 percent improvement, but the falls are still in place."[69] Government spends about two-thirds of its $19.2 billion drug budget on law enforcement and interdiction. The National Institute on Drug Abuse argues that drug abuse is a disease rather than a moral weakness, and users should receive medical treatment instead of imprisonment. Polls show that two-thirds of Americans favor treatment over jails.[70]

The extensive laws in the United States against the use, possession, and trafficking in illegal drugs are relatively recent criminal justice strategies. The first major federal law regulating drug use was the **Harrison Narcotics Act** of 1914. Until that legislation, opium, morphine, heroin, and cocaine were sold legally in the United States without prescription or prohibition. Many over-the-counter medicines contained these drugs. At one time, even beverages such as Coca-Cola contained cocaine. The Harrison Narcotics Act required that these drugs be dispensed only by prescription, and heroin continued to be legally available by prescription until 1920.[71] Marijuana was virtually unregulated until the **Marijuana Tax Act** of 1937, which levied a $100 per ounce tax on cannabis. It was not until the **Boggs Act** in 1951 that the use, possession, and sale of marijuana was made illegal and heroin was removed from the list of medically useful substances. The major piece of legislation that defines the criminal justice strategy in the War on Drugs is the **Comprehensive Drug Abuse Prevention and Control Act** of 1970. Title II of this act is known as the Controlled Substance Act. It created five schedules of psychoactive drugs, classified by their abuse potential and degree of psychoactivity, and established penalties. This schedule of drugs, shown in Table 15.2 on page 474, continues to be the basis for modern drug laws and strategies.

Additional legislation has strengthened the ability of the law enforcement agencies to take punitive measures against drug users and trafficking. The **Anti-Drug Abuse Act** of 1988 created the first cabinet-level post of drug czar and the **Office of National Drug Control Policy (ONDCP)**. It created new civil punishments for convicted drug offenders, such as denial of federal benefits. It also focused more attention on curbing recreational drug use. The Crime Control Act of 1990 created enhanced penalties for drug use or trafficking in "drug-free school zones," allowed federal agents to seize property associated with drug crime, and established federal funds for drug education programs at schools. The Violent Crime Control and Law Enforcement Act of 1994 budgeted federal money for treatment and drug courts, but endorsed the death penalty for drug trafficking and drug-related murders and established the "three strikes" law allowing a life sentence for violent felony or drug offenders. However, despite this increasingly tougher stance against illegal drugs, the criminal justice system has not found an effective strategy to win the War on Drugs.

Drugs and Crime

Some critics argue that the criminal justice system is losing the War on Drugs and should abandon its present course of action. They call for decriminalizing some drug offenses. Politicians and even former chiefs of police argue that the "holy war against drugs is having an insidious effect on law enforcement."[72] Governor of New Mexico, Gary Johnson, called for the legalization of drugs, from marijuana to heroin, with the idea that the best strategy is "Control it. Regulate it. Tax it. Educate people truthfully about its dangers. If we legalize it, we just might have a better society."[73]

Opponents to legalization point to statistics on the social harms as well as crimes associated with drug abuse. Annually, about 20,000 deaths are attributable to drug abuse, more than double the number from 1990.[74] About 110,000 individuals are estimated to have contracted HIV through intravenous drug use.[75] Total health care costs as a result of drug abuse are estimated at almost $15 billion per year, and productivity losses from drug abuse exceed $110 billion per year. The economic cost of drug abuse is projected to continue to rise almost 6 percent annually. The total economic cost to society in 2000 was estimated at $160 billion, a 57 percent increase from 1992.[76] Americans spent approximately $64 billion for illegal drugs in 2000—more than eight times the total federal outlay for research on HIV/AIDS, cancer, and heart disease.[77]

Drugs and drug-using behavior are linked to crime in several ways. Effects of drug use include criminal behavior—such as robberies, prostitution, or thefts to get money to buy drugs—and violence as a result of drug wars among rival traffickers. About 35 percent of all state and federal prison inmates and 15 percent of local jail inmates are incarcerated for drug-related crimes.[78] One alarming fact regarding the relationship between drugs and crime is that in 2000, between 52 and 80 percent of the adult males booked tested positive for drug use.[79] The crime-related costs of drug abuse exceed $100 billion annually. Over $500 million dollars is spent in private legal defense fees alone. Property damage for victims of drug-related crime exceeds $180 million annually. Nearly $5.5 billion is spent in legal adjudication.[80]

According to the National Institute of Drug Abuse (NIDA), failure to understand addiction as an illness may explain in part why historic strategies focusing solely on the social or criminal justice aspects of drug use and addiction have been unsuccessful. This viewpoint argues that zero-tolerance policies and incarceration of nonviolent drug users through tough sentencing are contrary to the growing body of scientific literature. What is the solution to drug use and drug-related crime?

Drug-related criminal behavior has far-reaching impacts on society. Marijuana growers ravage U.S. forests by growing marijuana on public lands, often in national parks. Their illegal operations endanger innocent persons who unsuspectingly trespass on their booby-trapped illegal farms. 1999, 452,330 marijuana plants with an estimated street value of about $700 million were removed from national forest land.[81] In December 2001, federal officials charged 35 people with running an international cocaine- and heroin-smuggling ring that used women traveling with infants to transport drugs in cans of baby formula.[82] Some of the infants were "rented" from poor families. In Chicago, parents were paid $200 to $2,000 to send their babies on the trips, and those who did so have had their parental rights terminated. Often, couriers ignored the needs of the infants in their charge. Children also may become victims of their parents in other ways. Studies have indicated that substance abuse by parents is a major underlying factor in nearly 90 percent of child endangerment cases.[83]

As cities are mounting antidrug strategies with some impact, small towns are facing an upsurge in drug dealing and drug crime. Many drug dealers are fleeing the cities and moving to the affluent suburbs. Relocation brings new law enforcement problems as small-town police officers clash with big-time drug dealers and cope with unfamiliar experiences with homicides, drive-by shootings, methamphetamine laboratories, increasing rates of drug abuse, and gangs. Small-town police often are ill-equipped and poorly trained to combat the rising drug problems they are now facing.[84] Local law enforcement agents have difficulty conducting undercover operations with limited resources.

Drug Abuse: Medical Model versus Criminal Justice Model

One of the most acrimonious debates regarding drug abuse is whether drug users are criminals who deserve to be punished by the criminal justice system or victims suffering from a treatable medical condition. The present model strongly suggests that drug users are criminals and incarceration in jails and prison is the appropriate punishment for their behavior. However, new research strongly suggests otherwise. The **National Institute on Drug Abuse** (NIDA) has concluded,

> Dramatic advances over the past two decades in both the neurosciences and the behavioral sciences have revolutionized our understanding of drug abuse and addiction. Scientists have identified neural circuits that are involved in the actions of every known drug of abuse, and they have specified common pathways that are affected by almost all such drugs. Research also has begun to reveal major differences between the brains of addicted and nonaddicted individuals and to indicate some common elements of addiction, regardless of the substance."[85]

table 15.2 Controlled Substances—Uses and Effects

Drugs	CSA Schedules	Trade or Other Names	Medical Uses	Dependence		Tolerance	Duration (Hours)	Usual Methods of Administration	Possible Effects	Effects of Overdose	Withdrawal Syndrome
				Physical	Psychological						
Narcotics											
Heroin	I	Diacetylmorphine, horse, smack	None in U.S, analgesic, antitussive	High	High	Yes	3–6	Injected, sniffed, smoked	Euphoria, drowsiness, respiratory depression, constricted pupils, nausea	Slow and shallow breathing, clammy skin, convulsions, coma, possible death	Watery eyes, runny nose, yawning, loss of appetite, irritability, tremors, panic, cramps, nausea, chills and sweating
Morphine	II	Duramorph, MS-Contin, Roxanol, Oramorph SR	Analgesic	High	High	Yes	3–6	Oral, smoked, injected			
Codeine	II, III, V	Tylenol w/Codeine, Empirin w/Codeine, Robitussin A–C, Fiorinal w/Codeine, APAP w/Codeine	Analgesic, antitussive	Moderate	Moderate	Yes	3–6	Oral, injected			
Hydrocodone	II, III	Tussionex, Vicodin, Hycodan, Lorcet	Analgesic, antitussive	High	High	Yes	3–6	Oral			
Hydromorphone	II	Dilaudid	Analgesic	High	High	Yes	3–6	Oral, injected			
Oxycodone	II	Percodan, Percocet, Tylox, Roxicet, Roxicodone	Analgesic	High	High	Yes	4–5	Oral			
Methadone and LAAM	I, II	Dolophine, Methadose, Levo-alpha-acetymethadol, Levomethadyl acetate	Analgesic, treatment of dependence	High	High	Yes	12–72	Oral, injected			
Fentanyl and analogs	I, II	Innovar, Sublimaze, Alfenta, Sufenta, Duragesic	Analgesic, adjunct to anesthesias, anesthetic	High	High	Yes	10–72	Injected, trans-dermal patch			
Other narcotics	II, III, IV, V	Percodan, Percocet, Tylox, Opium, Darvon, Buprenorphine, Meperdine, (Pethidine), Demerol, Talwin (Talwin, is not designated a narcotic under the CSA)	Analgesic, antidiarrheal	High-Low	High-Low	Yes	Variable	Oral, injected			
Depressants											
Chloral hydrate	IV	Noctec, Somnos, Felsules	Hypnotic	Moderate	Moderate	Yes	5–8	Oral	Slurred speech, disorientation, drunken behavior without odor of alcohol	Shallow respiration, clammy skin, dilated pupils, weak and rapid pulse, coma, possible death	Anxiety, insomnia, tremors, delirium, convulsions, possible death
Barbiturates	II, III, IV	Amytal, Fiorinal, Nembutal, Seconal, Tuinal, Phenobarbital, Pentobarbital	Anesthetic, anticonvulsant, sedative, hypnotic, veterinary anesthesia agent	High-Mod	High-Mod	Yes	5–8	Oral, injected			
Benzodiazepines	IV	Ativan, Dalmane, Diazepam, Librium, Xanax, Serex, Valium, Tranxene, Verstran, Versed, Halcion, Paxpam, Restoril	Antianxiety, sedative, anticonvulsant, hypnotic	Low	Low	Yes	4–8	Oral, injected			
Glutethimide	II	Doriden	Sedative, hypnotic	High	Moderate	Yes	4–8	Oral			
Other depressants	I, II, III, IV	Equanil, Noludar, Piacidyl, Valmid, Methaqualone	Antianxiety, sedative, hypnotic	Moderate	Moderate	Yes	4–8	Oral			

Stimulants											
Cocaine*	II	Coke, Flake, Snow, Crack	Local anesthetic	Possible	High	Yes	1–2	Sniffed, smoked, injected	Increased alertness, excitation, euphoria, increased pulse rate & blood pressure, insomnia, loss of appetite	Agitation, increased body temperature, hallucinations, convulsions, possible death	Apathy, long periods of sleep, irritability, depression, disorientation
Amphetamine/ methamphetamine	II	Biphetamine, Desoxyn, Dexedrine, Obetrol, Ice	Attention deficit disorder, narcolepsy, weight control	Possible	High	Yes	2–4	Oral, injected, smoked			
Methylphenidate	II	Ritalin	Attention deficit disorder, narcolepsy	Possible	High	Yes	2–4	Oral, injected			
Other stimulants	I, II, III, IV	Adipex, Didrex, Ionamin, Melfiat, Plegine, Captagon, Sanorex, Tenuate, Tepanil, Prelu-2, Preludin	Weight control	Possible	High	Yes	2–4	Oral, injected			
Cannabis											
Marijuana	I	Pot, Acapulco Gold, Grass, Reefer, Sxxx, Thai Sticks	None	Unknown	Moderate	Yes	2–4	Smoked, oral	Euphoria, relaxed inhibitions, increased appetite, disorientation	Fatigue, paranoia, possible psychosis	Insomnia, hyperactivity, and decreased appetite occasionally reported
Tetrahydrocanabinol	I, II	THC, Marinol	Antinauseant	Unknown	Moderate	Yes	2–4	Smoked, oral			
Hashish and hashish oil	I	Hash, Hash Oil	None	Unknown	Moderate	Yes	2–4	Smoked, oral			
Hallucinogens											
LSD	I	Acid, Microdot	None	None	Unknown	Yes	8–12	Oral	Illusions and hallucinations, altered perception of time and distance	Longer, more intense "trip" episodes, psychosis, possible death	Unknown
Mescaline and peyote	I	Mescal, Buttons, Cactus	None	None	Unknown	Yes	8–12	Oral			
Amphetamine variants	I	2,5-DMA, STP, MDA, MDMA, Ecstacy, DOM, BOB	None	Unknown	Unknown	Yes	Variable	Oral, injected			
Phencyclidine and analogs	I, II	PCE, PCPy, TCP, PCP, Hog, Loveboat, Angel Dust	None	Unknown	High	Yes	Days	Oral, smoked			
Other hallucinogens	I	Bufotenine, Ibopaine, DMT, DET, Psilocybin, Psilocyn	None	None	Unknown	Possible	Variable	Smoked, oral, injected, sniffed			
Anabolic Steroids											
Testosterone (Cypionate, Enanthate)	III	Depo-Testosterone, Delatestryl	Hypogonadism	Unknown	Unknown	Unknown	14–28 days	Injected	Virilization, acne, testicular atrophy, gynecomastia, aggressive behavior, edema	Unknown	Possible depression
Nandrolone (Decanoate, Phenpropionate)	III	Nortestosterone, Durabolin, Deca-Durabolin, Deca	Anemia, breast cancer	Unknown	Unknown	Unknown	14–21 days	Injected			
Oxymetholone	III	Anadrol-50	Anemia	Unknown	Unknown	Unknown	24	Oral			

Source: *Drugs of Abuse*, Drug Enforcement Administration, U.S. Department of Justice.

*Cocaine is designated a narcotic under the CSA.

Go to http://www.nida.nih.gov to view the NIDA web site. Typing "prison" in the site's search section provides access to information about drug use in prisons. ■

NIDA recognizes a gap between scientific knowledge concerning addiction and the response of the criminal justice system and the public. NIDA claims that the lack of appreciation of drug abuse as a public health problem is one of the major reasons why there has been "a significant delay in gaining control over the drug abuse problem."[86] Thus, NIDA criticizes conventional thinking about drug abuse as outdated from both clinical and policy perspectives. NIDA identifies the following barriers to solving the problem of drug abuse:[87]

- The tremendous stigma attached to being a drug user or addict. The criminal justice mind-set is that drug addicts are weak or bad people, unwilling to lead moral lives and control their behavior and gratifications.
- Ingrained ideologies. People are unwilling to revise their thinking about drug abuse based on new scientific knowledge. Even drug users and drug abuse treatment programs refuse to change their opinion of effective treatment strategies in the face of contradictory scientific evidence.
- Drug addiction is a chronic, relapsing illness, characterized by compulsive drug seeking and use. The dangerousness of a drug is not the physical symptoms associated with the cessation of use but the modification of brain functioning. Some changes in brain functioning are permanent or long lasting.
- Addiction is rarely an acute illness. For most people, it is a chronic, relapsing disorder. The standard for treatment success is not curing the illness but managing it, as is the case for other chronic illnesses.

Drugs, Organized Crime, and Narcoterrorism

In a report to Congress, President George W. Bush said, "Illegal drug use threatens everything that is good about our country. . . . It finances the work of terrorists who use drug profits to fund their murderous work. Our fight against illegal drug use is a fight for our children's future, for struggling democracies, and against terrorism."[88] The challenge of combating drug abuse is that many drugs are imported illegally into the United States and may even be bought and sold by nations to finance political movements and wars.

The drug trade is a vast international market. Moving drugs from nation to nation and then to the street level involves colossal management challenges. Problems include the cultivation of hundreds of thousands of acres of drug crops, **trafficking** hundreds of tons of illegal drugs across continents and through intermediaries and a maze of specialized border smuggling organizations, establishing a network of mid-level distributors, and selling the drugs to the users.[89] In addition, there is the problem of money. The drug trade relies on the international banking system to launder billions of dollars each year. As a result of **money laundering**, the drug trade often must resort to reverse smuggling, as it is necessary to smuggle out of the country enormous quantities of cash, which often weigh two to three times more than the drugs that were smuggled in.[90] To accomplish this task, the drug trade has had to organize into complex and vast international networks and alliances. Drug organizations are able to buy politicians, police, and judges to the point that they virtually operate without fear of apprehension by law enforcement. Sometimes, these so-called drug lords exercise such political and economic influence in countries that they constitute a shadow government, exercising great control over the legitimate government of the country. **Narcoterrorism**, ruling by fear and corruption, describes the practices of these drug lords.

trafficking Movement of illegal drugs across borders.

money laundering Concealment of the source of money.

narcoterrorism The redefinement of drug trafficking as terrorism, used to emphasize its significance.

The federal government has recognized the important role that international drug markets play in drug abuse in the United States and has undertaken new strategies for intercepting drugs at the borders and dismantling the drug networks that transport and distribute both the drugs and the illicit proceeds from their sale. This strategy addresses in part the criticism that the justice system has focused on sending users and low-level dealers to prison with excessively harsh sentences rather than focusing on the criminal elements that supply the drugs.[91] To correct this focus, the U.S. attorney general has directed the **Organized Crime Drug Enforcement Task Force (OCDETF)** to ensure that law enforcement efforts target the most significant drug-trafficking organizations.[92]

The primary law enforcement agencies involved in drug law enforcement have been the federal **Drug Enforcement Agency (DEA)** and state and local police. The OCDETF program, created in 1982, hopes to make a significant impact on reducing the supply of drugs in the United States. In fiscal year 2002, the OCDETF received $338.6 million for drug law enforcement. As part of the National Drug Control Strategy program, the OCDETF has the following goals:[94]

- Within 2 years, a 10 percent reduction in current use of illegal drugs by the 12–17 age group
- Within 2 years, a 10 percent reduction in current use of illegal drugs by adults age 18 and older
- Within 5 years, a 25 percent reduction in current use of illegal drugs by the 12–17 age group
- Within 5 years, a 25 percent reduction in current use of illegal drugs by adults age 18 and older

The OCDEFT program works collaboratively with other federal drug programs, such as the High Intensity Drug Trafficking Areas program and the Treasury Department's Financial Crimes Enforcement Network, to have an impact on the most sophisticated trafficking organizations. One of the lessons learned in drug law enforcement is that cooperation among the decentralized law enforcement agencies is effective in disrupting drug trafficking. This lesson has been applied to many other programs as local police and federal agencies have joined together to pool their resources to fight drugs. Table 15.3 on page 478 shows the federal trafficking penalties for marijuana and other drugs.

The law enforcement battle with drug traffickers was profoundly affected by the September 11, 2001, terrorist attacks on the World Trade Center and the Pentagon. As a result of these attacks, border and airport security was increased significantly. Initially, security efforts linked to counterterrorism reduced drug trafficking between borders, but subsequently, seizures of illegal drugs have been on the rise. Nationally, seizure of illegal drugs at airports, seaports, and border checkpoints increased by 17.1 percent in the last 3 months of 2001, compared with the same period the year before.[94] The Customs Service reported that while agents have found no terrorists, hardly a day goes by that they do not find drugs. Stricter inspections have revealed that drug trafficking has been more rampant than previously realized and that demand has increased. Afghan farmers have returned to cultivating opium poppies.[95]

New Strategies for the War on Drugs

Two major strategies for reducing illegal drug use in the United States are (1) supply reduction or elimination—a law enforcement approach—and (2) demand reduction—an education approach. **Supply reduction programs** attempt to stop illegal drugs from entering the United States, disrupt distribution networks in the United States, put drug dealers out of business, destroy illegal drug crops, control chemicals needed to make illegal drugs, and arrest sellers and buyers. **Demand reduction programs**, on the other hand, aim at reducing the demand for drugs by users through educational programs and persuasion. Demand programs target both the general public and specific groups such as school-aged children and teenagers. Today these two strategies, previously seen as competing and contradictory, are being combined in the effort to reduce drug abuse in the United States. The National Drug Control Strategy is committed to balancing supply reduction programs and demand reduction programs (see Table 15.4 on page 480).

supply reduction programs Programs attempting to stop illegal drugs from entering the United States, disrupt distribution networks in the United States, put drug dealers out of business, destroy illegal drug crops, control chemicals needed to make illegal drugs, and arrest sellers and buyers.

demand reduction programs Programs aimed at reducing the demand for drugs by users through educational programs and persuasion.

Debate over the effectiveness, and even the constitutionality, of drug reduction programs has divided public opinion. For example, in February 2002, New York governor

table 15.3a Federal Trafficking Penalties—Marijuana*

Description	Quantity	First Offense	Second Offense
Marijuana	1,000-kg or more mixture; or 1,000 or more plants	• Not less than 10 years, not more than life • If death or serious injury, not less than 20 years, not more than life • Fine not more than $4 million individual, $10 million other than individual.	• Not less than 20 years, not more than life • If death or serious injury, not more than life • Fine not more than $8 million individual, $20 million other than individual
Marijuana	100-kg to 999-kg mixture; or 100 to 999 plants	• Not less than 5 years, not more than 40 years • If death or serious injury, not less than 20 years, not more than life • Fine not more than $2 million individual, $5 million other than individual	• Not less than 10 years, not more than life • If death or serious injury, not more than life • Fine not more than $4 million individual, $10 million other than individual
Marijuana	50- to 99-kg mixture 50 to 99 plants	• Not more than 20 years • If death or serious injury, not less than 20 years, not more than life • Fine $1 million individual, $5 million other than individual	• Not more than 30 years • If death or serious injury, not more than life • Fine $2 million individual, $10 million other than individual
Marijuana **Hashish** **Hashish Oil**	Less than 50-kg mixture 10 kg or more 1 kg or more	• Not more than 5 years • Fine not more than $250,000, $1 million other than individual	• Not more than 10 years • Fine $500,000 individual, $2 million other than individual

Source: Drugs of Abuse, Drug Enforcement Administration, Washington, DC, U.S. Department of Justice, 2001.

*Includes hashish and hashish oil.

Marijuana is a Schedule I controlled substance.

table 15.3b Federal Trafficking Penalties

CSA	Penalty		Quantity	DRUG	Quantity	Penalty	
	2nd Offense	1st Offense				1st Offense	2nd Offense
I and II	Not less than 10 years. Not more than life. If death or serious injury, not less than life. Fine of not more than $4 million individual, $10 million other than individual.	Not less than 5 years. Not more than 40 years. If death or serious injury, not less than 20 years or more than life. Fine of not more than $2 million individual, $5 million other than individual.	10–99 gm pure or 100–999 gm mixture	METHAMPHETAMINE	100 gm or more pure or 1 kg or more mixture	Not less than 10 years, not more than life If death or serious injury, not less than 20 years or more than life Fine of not more than $4 million individual, $10 million other than individual	Not less than 20 years, not more than life If death or serious injury, not less than life Fine of not more than $8 million individual, $20 million other than individual
			100–999 gm mixture	HEROIN	1 kg or more mixture		
			500–4,999 gm mixture	COCAINE	5 kg or more mixture		
			5–49 mixture	COCAINE BASE	50 gm or more mixture		
			10–99 gm or 100–999 gm mixture	PCP	100 gm or more pure or 1 kg or more mixture		
			1–9 gm mixture	LSD	10 gm or more mixture		
			40–300 gm mixture	FENTANYL	400 gm or more mixture		
			10–99 gm mixture	FENTANYL ANALOGUE	100 gm or more mixture		

CSA	Drug	Quantity	1st Offense	2nd Offense
I and II	Others[1]	Any	Not more than 20 years. If death or serious injury, not less than 20 years, not more than life. Fine $1 million individual, $5 million not individual.	Not more than 30 years. If death or serious injury, life. Fine $2 million individual, $10 million not individual.
III	All[2]	Any	Not more than 5 years. Fine not more than $250,000 individual, $1 million not individual.	Not more than 10 years. Fine not more than $500,000 individual, $2 million not individual.
IV	All	Any	Not more than 3 years. Fine not more than $250,000 individual, $1 million not individual.	Not more than 6 years. Fine not more than $500,000 individual, $2 million not individual.
V	All	Any	Not more than 1 year. Fine not more than $100,000 individual, $250,000 not individual.	Not more than 2 years. Fine not more than $200,000 individual, $500,000 not individual.

[1]Law does not include marijuana, hashish, or hash oil (see separate chart).

[2]Includes anabolic steroids as of 02-27-91.

table 15.4 Supply Reduction and Demand Reduction Drug Programs

Program	FY 2002 Budget	Purpose of Program
Supply Reduction Drug Programs		
Safe and Drug-Free Schools Programs	$644 million	This program funds activities that address drugs and violence prevention for young people. To improve evaluation and better direct program activities, ONDCP will work with the Department of Education to develop a useful evaluation plan that will impose program accountability while alerting schools to problem areas.
Drug-Free Communities Program	$60 million	This program provides assistance to community groups on forming and sustaining effective community and antidrug coalitions that fight the use of illegal drugs, alcohol, and tobacco by youth. It includes funding for the National Community Anti-Drug Coalition to provide education, training and technical assistance for coalition leaders and community teams.
National Youth Anti-Drug Media Campaign	$180 million	The Media Campaign uses paid media messages to guide youth and parent attitudes about drug use and its consequences. Targeted, high-impact, paid media advertisements—at both the national and local levels—seek to reduce drug use through changes in adolescents' perceptions of the danger and social disapproval of drugs.
Parents Drug Corps Program	$5 million	This initiative funded through the Corporation for National and Community Service will encourage parents to help children stay drug-free by training them in drug-preventions skills and methods.
Demand Reduction Drug Programs		
Border Control and Enforcement	$76.3 million	This enhancement of the U.S. Border Patrol includes hiring an additional 570 agents to enforce national borders and to combat international drug trafficking.
Southwest Border Drug Prosecutions	$50 million	This program provides critical support to counties along the Southwest border for the costs of detaining and prosecuting drug cases referred to them by U.S. attorneys.
Andean Counterdrug Initiative (ACI)	$731 million	ACI includes enforcement, border control, crop reduction, alternative development, institution building, and administration of justice and human rights programs. For Colombia, funding will be used for several broad categories, including operations and maintenance of air assets; Colombian National Police and Army Counternarcotics Brigade operational support; resources for justice-sector reform projects; and herbicide application programs.

Source: National Drug Control Strategy (Washington, DC: The White House, February 2002).

George Pataki proposed that the state's harsh drug laws be revised: Mandatory prison sentences should be reduced, treatment options should be made available for nonviolent repeat offenders, and judges should have more discretion in drug sentencing. His proposal drew criticism from the state's district attorneys association, which considers the sentencing laws an effective tool in combating drug trafficking.[96]

Some antidrug strategies are challenged as to their fairness and constitutionality. When Illinois Bell disconnected public pay phones from 6 P.M. to 6 A.M. in high-drug-trafficking areas in an attempt to discourage drug dealers from using public phones to take orders, the American Civil Liberties Union (ACLU) protested that the plan discriminates against poor people and violates the rights of callers.[97] When federal agents used a thermal imaging device to determine whether an Oregon man was growing marijuana in his house, the Supreme Court overturned the conviction, arguing that the heat-imaging device violated reasonable expectations of privacy.[98] When officials of the White House Office of National Drug Control Policy offered to give television networks financial credits in exchange for weaving antidrug themes into their shows, the American Broadcasting Corporation (ABC) refused to submit television scripts to the government in advance of production.[99]

Antidrug strategies can affect nearly everyone in society, not just offenders. For example, as a result of a 1998 law banning the granting of student loans to drug offenders, 43,000 students with drug convictions may be denied aid.[100] The law requires applicants for federal grants, work-study funds, or subsidized loans to disclose if they have every been convicted of possessing or selling illegal drugs, and those who answer "yes" must provide details of their conviction. First-time offenders can be denied benefits for a year, and for a second offense, 2 years. Repeat offenders can be denied benefits indefinitely. Applicants who do not answer the questions are assumed to have been convicted of a drug offense and are not eligible for federal assistance. The American Council on Education, which represents colleges and universities, calls the restriction double punishment and says it discriminates against poorer students, who are in more need of financial aid. The Council also points out that conviction for more serious or violent crimes, such as murder, rape, and robbery, do *not* result in automatic denial of student aid.[101]

A 1988 law allows the Department of Housing and Urban Development to evict public housing tenants for drug use or possession, even when the use or possession is by guests or other residents. The law does not provide for any warning, and residents can be evicted for the first offense. Protests have erupted over cases in which elderly residents have been evicted because children, grandchildren, or caretakers have illegal drugs on or near the housing development.[102] Supporters of the law argue that it is the only way to keep tenants from ignoring the conduct of household members or guests.

People often strongly oppose programs for dealing with drug abuse that they see as improper, even when the programs are designed to protect public health. For example, the public may oppose needle exchange programs in the belief that making drug use safe promotes drug addiction. National Institutes of Health studies do not support this opinion and conclude that needle exchange programs reduce the spread of the human immunodeficiency virus that causes AIDS.[103] One public health program offered 57 women addicts $200 in exchange for being sterilized or using long-term birth control. The 57 women had been pregnant a total of 423 times. They had had 161 abortions and had given birth 262 times. Forty of those babies died, and 175 were placed in foster care. Nevertheless, critics claim the program is improperly based on bribery, interferes with reproductive rights, and supports addicts' drug habits.[104]

Even traditional programs can come under public scrutiny. The **Drug Abuse Resistance Education (DARE)** program is one of the most widely used antidrug programs in the nation. In 1999, federal education officials said they would no longer allow schools to spend money from the Office of Safe and Drug-Free Schools on the DARE program because it had not been scientifically proved effective. The program's curriculum emphasizing zero-tolerance policies was shown to be ineffective in preventing drug use among middle and high school students. In response to the criticism, DARE is developing a new curriculum that utilizes role-playing and discussion groups, with police acting as coaches instead of lecturers.[105]

In summary, progress toward reducing illegal drug use has been frustrated by (1) legalization efforts, (2) the diversity of strategies that emphasize supply reduction versus demand reduction, (3) the debate over whether illegal drug use is best addressed as a criminal justice problem or a medical addiction problem, and (4) the vast, organized, international network of drug traffickers who remain beyond the reach of the laws of the United States. In essence, drug control policy has just two elements: (1) modifying individual behavior to discourage and reduce drug use and addiction and (2) disrupting the market for illegal drugs.[106] Public policy and criminal justice strategies that integrate these two goals are more likely to succeed.

JUST THE FACTS 15.2

What are the economic costs associated with drug abuse? In what ways are drugs and drug-using behavior linked to crime? In approaches to the problem, what is the difference between the medical model and the criminal justice model? How do the supply-side and demand-side strategies work for reducing illegal drug use?

Offender Physical and Mental Health Challenges

THE MAIN IDEA

Another challenge to the criminal justice system is the health and safety of inmates and the communities to which they return. Special concerns include care of the elderly, inmates injured in prison gang violence, prisoners with HIV/AIDS or TB, and offenders with mental illness.

Daniel Tote, 47, missed his release date from prison. In fact, he remained in prison 10 months beyond the expiration of his sentence. Tote was not released because he was in a persistent vegetative state due to head trauma that he suffered in an attack while in prison. When his sentence expired, there was no place to send him. Nursing homes would not take him, because, as a prisoner, he was not eligible for Medicaid. He had no insurance and no family to care for him. Thus, he remained in the prison infirmary despite the fact that he was a free man. Eventually, the state found a nursing home in which to place him, at a cost to the state of about $40,000 a year.[107] Daniel Tote is an extreme example of a serious problem in the criminal justice system: The physical and mental health of offenders, both incarcerated and released, has become a costly and sometimes deadly public health problem with no end in sight.

Prisoners have significant physical and mental health problems. The health of the average 50-year-old prisoner approximates that of the average 60-year-old person in the free community.[108] In a survey by the Office of Justice Programs, about 40 percent of state inmates and 48 percent of federal inmates age 45 or older said they had had a medical problem since admission to prison.[109] While they are in prison, their health care is the responsibility of the state. When they are released from prison, as most are, these problems do not go away when they reenter the community. Often, the released inmate enters the community with significant physical and mental health problems that can have a serious—even deadly—impact on the public.

The trend toward incarceration of offenders has created an unintended consequence: the creation of long-term health-care obligations. As more prisoners are incarcerated and with longer sentences, the cost of prisoners' health care increases dramatically.[110] The impact of this problem can be seen in the fact that the most common Section 1983 lawsuit against jails and prisons involved claims of substandard medical treatment.[111] Many prison facilities now contain geriatric wings due to the high number of elderly inmates. These facilities provide long-term-care units staffed by nurses instead of correctional officers. Older, ill inmates receive a round-the-clock care that costs the state about $65,000 per year.[112]

Studies indicate that, statistically, the risk of recidivism drops significantly with age. However, prisons, especially federal prisons and prisons in states that have abolished parole, often cannot release these inmates. In other cases, elderly offenders cannot be released because they are serving mandatory terms or because there are no community-care facilities to release them to, as in the case of Daniel Tote. As a result, the care of geriatric inmates has become an expensive burden on the criminal justice system. In a system that is constantly competing for public funding of other needs—for example, drug treatment programs, juvenile rehabilitation programs, community policing, and even public schools and highways—it is difficult to justify spending $65,000 a year on care for each elderly prisoner. But can prisoners be released just because they are old and it is expensive to take care of them? About 45 percent of inmates age 50 and older were only recently arrested. Older felons tend to be locked up for more serious crimes, such as rape, murder, and child molestation.[113] These offenders need to be incarcerated for the protection of the public.

Three health-care problems with high potential impact on the public health of the general population are (1) violence in prison, including prison gangs; (2) HIV/AIDS and communicable diseases; and (3) mental health problems. These problems often have detrimental effects on public health and community well-being.

Violence in Prisons: Injuries

Prisons and jails are violent environments, and it is not uncommon that inmates are injured by violence while incarcerated. Prisoners can suffer injury caused by correctional staff, other inmates, or accidents. Information on injuries is lacking. In a special investigation of the medical problems of inmates, the Bureau of Justice Statistics found that the medical records of inmates were incomplete, missing, or stored in paper form, not electronically. The Bureau also found that 10 states did not collect data on the current medical condition of their inmates, and 18 states had data in forms unsuitable for statistical analysis. To gather information on the medical problems of inmates, the Bureau of Justice Statistics conducted personal interviews with a sample of inmates.[114] The survey revealed that injuries in prison were commonplace. Nearly half of state inmates who had served 6 or more years said they had been injured after admission.[115]

While most inmates report being injured accidentally while working or playing, a significant number of injuries are inflicted by correctional staff or other inmates. About 10 percent of state inmates reported that they had been injured in a fight.[116] The risk of being injured in a fight increased with time served. Men were 5 to 10 times more likely to be injured than were female inmates. Inmates age 34 or younger in both state and federal prisons were about twice as likely as those age 45 or older to report being injured in a fight. Nearly 16 percent of state inmates with a mental condition were injured in a fight, compared with 10 percent without a mental condition.[117]

Some inmates are injured by correctional officers. Despite the training and oversight of prison staff, there are numerous allegations of excessive use of force. Some cases are shocking, as in maximum-security Corcoran State Prison in California. The situation at Corcoran was described by a blue-ribbon panel as a "shooting gallery." Prison officers and superiors were accused of setting up fights between rival gang members and then using the fights as pretexts to shoot inmates in the recreation yards.[118] Correctional officers at Corcoran were also accused of staging gladiator-style fights between inmates.

There are many reasons why correctional officers may intentionally injure inmates. Working in prison affects correctional officers physically, psychologically, and emotionally. Correctional officers suffer abnormally high rates of heart attacks, ulcers, hypertension, depression, alcoholism, and divorce. The average age of death for correctional personnel is 16 years shorter than the average life span of the population at large.[119] The

Go to http://www.gangsorus.com/ to view the web site "Gangs or Us," which provides information on street and prison gangs.

stress of working in a violence-prone environment may cause some correctional officers to use violence as a method of discipline. For example, a lawsuit accusing Federal Bureau of Prisons guards of using excessive force to punish prisoners for minor violations of prison rules—for example, kicking on the door or pushing a food tray out of the door slot—was settled for $99,000.[126] The lawsuit alleged that a correctional supervisor, angry at an inmate who was kicking on the door of his cell, injured and brutalized the inmate with force to punish the behavior.

Prison status hierarchies and codes of honor also may explain inmate violence and violence against inmates by staff.[121] In jails and prisons, not all inmates are accorded equal status. At the bottom of the correctional status hierarchy are pedophiles, incest offenders, rapists, and those convicted of both rape and murder. In the middle of the hierarchy are thieves, burglars, and assaultive offenders. At the top of the hierarchy are murderers, drug offenders, and robbers. Sex offenders in prison are the "outcasts of the outcasts" and often are targeted for violence. Correctional staff or other prisoners may take it on themselves to punish lower social status offenders, especially pedophiles.[122]

Prison Gangs

Chapter 12 discussed the problem of gangs in jails and prisons. This discussion focuses specifically on the threat of violence that gangs pose in prison and in the community. Gang activity, a major factor in many prisons, has implications for in-prison and post-prison behavior.[123] The first prison gangs appeared in 1950. Prior to that time, strict control of prisoner movement, limited contact with the outside, absence of work release programs, and a harsh disciplinary code prevented the formation of gangs. Today, prison gangs, known as special threat or **security risk groups**, are a serious problem. For example, Rikers Island in New York has identified 44 security risk groups that operate within the prison.[124] Among the more common gangs operating in prison are the Aryan Brotherhood, the Black Guerilla Family, the Bloods, the Crips, La Nuestra Familia, Latin Kings, Mexican Mafia, Mexikanemi, Neta, and the Texas Syndicate. Most prison gangs are organized along lines of racial and ethnic identity.

Prison gangs pose special security risks and create a higher risk of violence because (1) gang codes of conduct discourage obedience to prison rules, and (2) gangs frequently are involved in trafficking of prison contraband and protection. Gang codes require absolute loyalty to the gang. Often, to show one's commitment to the gang, new members must pass initiation tests, rituals that require the new member to make a "hit" on a rival gang member or correctional staff member. The hit usually requires only that the gang member attack the person and draw blood.[125]

Gang membership extends outside the prison. Prison gangs use this characteristic to have fellow gang members smuggle contraband inside the prison during visitations, through staff members that have been bribed, or when the prisoner is outside the prison wall on work details or other forms of release. Prison gangs then use trafficking in **contraband**—such as drugs, cigarettes, money, pornography, and so on—to buy favors, recruit members, pay prison debts, and make a profit. Prisoners who compete with the prison gang business, who inform prison officials about gang activities, or who are unable to pay for gang contraband may become targets of gang violence.

security risk groups Groups that raise special threats, such as prison gangs.

contraband Smuggled goods, such as drugs, cigarettes, money, or pornography.

Many inmates join a gang for protection, so an unintended consequence of longer prison terms has been an increase in gang affiliation. Because prisoners have to stay in prison longer, they feel a greater need to be affiliated with a prison gang to provide them with protection from other gangs, from individual inmates, and from correctional staff members. Gang affiliation guarantees retaliation for any harm caused to a member by others. In extreme cases, such retaliation can lead to a vicious cycle of gang wars, as each gang continues to retaliate for the last attack. Because fear of gang retaliation may be much stronger than fear of official prison sanctions, whenever prison rules and gang codes conflict, gang members will obey their gang code.

Effective strategies for combating prison gangs have required the cooperation of many agencies in the criminal justice system. The New York City Department of Correction has adopted one of the more aggressive strategies to eliminate gang violence and the influence of prison gangs. In 1994, there were 100 stabbings and slashings per month on Rikers Island, and inmates and staff members were regularly assaulted and intimidated. Violence related to gang activities was estimated to cost $100 million per year in overtime costs. In fiscal year 2000–2001, however, the number of violent incidents was reduced to 54 for the entire year. How was this done?

To combat prison violence, the New York City Department of Correction felt it necessary to learn about the inner workings of gangs, both in and out of jail, and to work with other agencies.[126] A **Gang Intelligence Unit (GIU)** was formed to gather information about gangs, and this corrections unit works closely with the NYPD Gang Intelligence Unit and the federal High Intensity Drug Trafficking Area task force. Because gang crime is a national problem, the New York City Department of Correction has developed a database, called "Superbase," to track the activities of inmates identified as members of the 44 security risk groups on Rikers Island. A unique feature of Superbase is that the GIU can scan through tattoos as well as photographs and other identifications. The data allow the Department of Correction to adopt a zero-tolerance policy toward prison violence. The GIU investigates incidents of violence and seeks to make arrests, averaging two inmate arrests per day. Inmate violence that formerly was punished by administrative sanctions is now referred to the courts, where inmates are charged for the violent acts they commit in jail. This policy has dramatically reduced the rate of violence on Rikers Island.

In addition to punishing inmates for gang violence, the New York City Department of Correction wants to prevent gangs from gaining new members. An intense interagency training program helps members of the law enforcement community, parents, teachers, and citizens to understand the lure and dynamics of youth involvement in street and prison gangs.[127] Extensive interagency cooperation has been necessary to combat gang violence in New York municipal jails.[128] Interagency initiatives include:

- *Operation Guest House*—A joint program with the NYPD Warrant Squad, in which search warrant checks are conducted on individuals visiting prisoners
- *Operation Out House*—A joint program with NYPD, along with out-of-city jurisdictions, to check for outstanding arrest warrants upon discharge. Also, inmate visitors who are caught attempting to pass contraband to an inmate during a visit are arrested and checked for outstanding arrest warrants.
- *Operation GRIP (Gang Recidivist Interview Program)*—Former gang members are identified via database on rearrest and are interviewed by the GIU for information about organized gang activity in the communities where the individuals were arrested. Information gained from these interviews is passed on to the NYPD or other appropriate law enforcement agency.
- *Operation Hot Precinct*—The GIU works with the NYPD to identify and interrogate inmates who may have been involved in street crimes prior to arrest.
- *Operation World Trade Center*—Following the September 11 terrorist attacks, GIU investigators interviewed the correctional system's Muslim population in an effort to cultivate leads. The GIU takes the role of an intelligence clearinghouse, soliciting, tracking, and prioritizing World Trade Center leads and forwarding them to the FBI. Arrests have been made as a result, and a safehouse was discovered that contained fraudulent documents intended for terrorists.[129]

The strategies of the New York City Department of Correction illustrate how extensive interagency cooperation is necessary to combat gang violence in jails and prisons. Gangs have influence both in and beyond the jails and prisons, and only by working to prevent gang violence, bring violators to justice, and protect innocent inmates can prison gang violence be curbed.

HIV/AIDS and Communicable Diseases

Sexually transmitted diseases (STDs), including HIV/AIDS, and other communicable diseases pose serious challenges to administrators of both adult and juvenile justice systems.[130] The overall rate of confirmed AIDS cases among the nation's prison population is five times the rate in the U.S. general population. Official statistics indicate that a little over 2 percent of state prison inmates and less than 1 percent of federal prison inmates are known to be infected with HIV.[131] However, the rate of HIV/AIDS infection is not uniform throughout the criminal justice system. New York, for example, has an HIV-positive prison population of nearly 10 percent, and Florida has a rate of nearly 4 percent.[132] The percentage of HIV-positive inmates has remained fairly constant since 1995, but the total number of infected inmates has risen as the actual prison population has risen dramatically over the past decade.[133] The problem affects both male and female inmates, but a greater percentage of women (3.4%) than men (2.1%) is HIV-positive.[134]

AIDS-related deaths in prison have dropped dramatically, from over 1,000 in 1995 to fewer than 250 in 1999 (see Table 15.5).[135] However, in 1999, AIDS-related deaths still accounted for about 11 percent of all deaths in state prisons and 6 percent in federal prisons. The percentage of deaths because of AIDS is about twice as high in the state prison population than in the U.S. general population.[136] Because the number of inmates who are HIV-positive has continued to rise, the drop in the death rate is attributed primarily to advances in medical treatments available for HIV-positive patients and better identification and management of HIV-infected inmates by prison administrators.

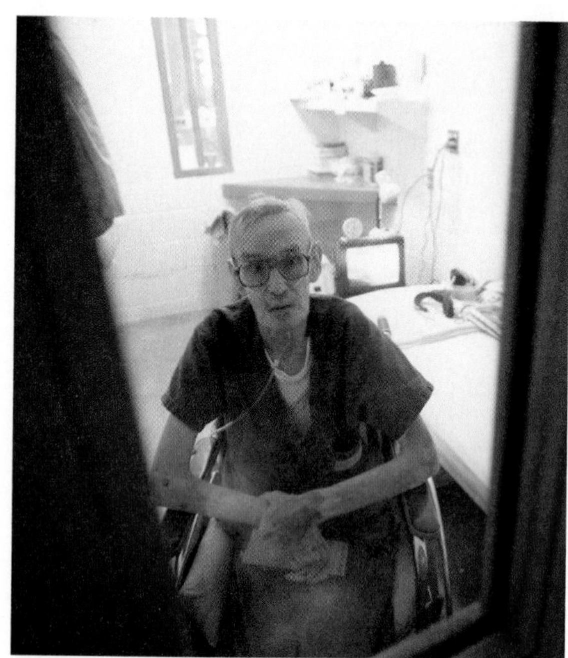

Why might you argue for keeping this prisoner in prison? Why might you argue for his release? In making such a decision, what would be your responsibilities toward the prisoner, the state in which he was imprisoned, and the community to which he would be returned? What if this prisoner had been convicted of a sex crime as a child predator? What if he were a member of a gang? What if he were a victim of prison violence? What if he were mentally ill? What if he were HIV-positive or had AIDS or TB?

Prisons are a critical setting for detecting and treating STDs. The testing of inmates for HIV/AIDS varies from state to state. About 19 states test all inmates at admission, whereas other states test inmates only on request or if the inmate belongs to a specific high-risk group. Most HIV-positive inmates were positive when admitted and thus did not become HIV-positive after admission to prison. Inmates contract HIV/AIDS from high-risk behavior, such as intravenous drug use or unprotected sex with partners who are infected. Many female inmates contract HIV/AIDS from prostitution. Because most inmates will be released back into the community, the identification of those with HIV/AIDS is important, as they constitute a significant percentage of the total number of Americans with HIV/AIDS.[137] Unfortunately, only 10 percent of state and federal prisons and 5 percent of city and county jails offer comprehensive HIV-prevention programs for inmates.[138]

Inmates who are HIV-positive pose special problems for correctional administrators. Those inmates cannot be completely isolated from the general prison population. In fact, federal laws regarding inmates' rights of privacy often prohibit prison administrators from making it generally known which inmates are HIV-positive. Thus, prison staff and other inmates may not be aware of which inmates are affected. This lack of knowledge creates concern among the prison staff, as they do not know if they are at risk of HIV infection when they handle inmates. Lacking this knowledge, the prison staff must treat all inmates as if they are potential infection risks. HIV-infected inmates may deliberately attempt to infect prison officials by biting them or by other means.

table 15.5 HIV in Prisons and Jails

The overall rate of confirmed AIDS among the nation's prison population (0.60%) was five times the rate in the U.S. general population (0.12%).

	HIV-Positive State and Federal Prison Inmates	Percentage of Custody Population	AIDS-Related Deaths	Death Rate per 100,000 Inmates
1995	24,256	2.3	1,010	100
1996	23,881	2.2	907	90
1997	23,886	2.1	538	48
1998	25,680	2.2	350	30
1999	25,757	2.1	242	20

Source: Laura M. Maruschak, *HIV in Prisons and Jails, 1999* (Washington, DC: U.S. Department of Justice, July 2001), p. 1.

When inmates who are HIV-positive are released back into the community, they may create a public health hazard without proper care or education. While in prison, inmates receive free medication and treatment, but after release, they may be responsible for their own medical expenses and treatment. Released inmates may pose a serious health hazard if they engage in unprotected sex or share needles from intravenous drug use. Female offenders pose a community health risk, as many return to prostitution to obtain the cash they need.

Prisons and jails also present optimal conditions of the spread of tuberculosis (TB).[139] TB can be more difficult to control than HIV because it is more easily spread by contact with active cases. TB-infected inmates released back into the community have the potential to spread the disease further, as TB can remain infectious for a long time. One study reported that in 31 state prison systems, 14 percent of inmates had positive tuberculin skin test results at intake.[140]

Inmates who receive only partial treatment for TB increase the threat of epidemic in the general population, because incomplete treatment raises the risk that the disease will become resistant to medications used to treat it and will not respond to subsequent treatment. Drug-resistant forms of TB could be transmitted to others, and the result could be a widespread public health disaster. Treatment of TB is complicated. A primary TB control measure is the complete isolation of infectious cases to prevent spreading the disease to other inmates. This type of isolation requires negative-pressure isolation rooms with ventilation that does not flow into the general ventilation system. Another complication of TB is that often inmates may be coinfected with both TB and HIV. Because TB can be spread through the ventilation system, prison administrators have to take precautions to keep general prison populations from being exposed. Failure to do so may result in a lawsuit.

Mental Health and Institutionalization of Offenders in Prison

Nearly one in five inmates in U.S. prisons reports having a mental illness.[141] A comprehensive Justice Department study of the rapidly growing number of incarcerated, emotionally disturbed people concluded that jails and prisons have become the nation's new mental health care facilities.[142] According to the report, "Jails have become the poor person's mental hospitals."[143]

In the 1960s, legislation was passed that made it difficult to commit mentally ill people who had not committed a crime to civil mental health facilities against their will. As a result, public mental hospitals were forced to release persons committed against their will unless the state could prove that the person was a danger to himself or herself or to the public. The intention of the legislation was that mentally ill people would receive community-based care instead of long-term hospitalization that differed little from incarceration. It was thought that with proper medication, community-based care would be a more humane alternative to long-term hospitalization.[144] Despite the good intentions of legislators, **deinstitutionalization** did not work as planned. There were too few community-based facilities, the mentally ill did not take their medications, and jails and prisons became the dumping ground for the mentally ill.[145] The mentally ill end up in jails and prisons for bizarre public behavior; petty crimes like loitering, public intoxication, and pan handling; as well as serious violent crimes such as murder, sexual assault, and property crime. About half of mentally ill inmates are in prison for a violent offense.[146]

THE MENTALLY ILL IN PRISON Because mentally ill inmates can be a danger to themselves or others, correctional facilities routinely screen inmates for mental illness on admission.[147] Inmates with mental illness can receive psychotropic medications and therapy or counseling by trained mental health professionals. In 2000, as a result of mental health screening, about 13 percent of state prisoners were receiving some mental health therapy or counseling services, and nearly 10 percent were receiving psychotropic medications. In six states (Vermont, Maine, Montana, Nebraska, Hawaii, and Oregon), approximately 20 percent of state inmates were receiving psychotropic medications. Another 2 percent were considered sufficiently mentally ill that they were housed in a 24-hour mental health unit.[148]

Mentally ill inmates frequently are unable to abide by prison rules and discipline. This is due in part to their mental illness and in part to the overcrowded conditions and stresses of the correctional institution. Also, because they are unable to have "normal" interpersonal relations—a difficult challenge even for the mentally stable in prison—they are more likely to engage in fights and other violent behaviors. Unable to conform to the rules or to restrain their violent behavior, the mentally ill spend many hours in solitary confinement or segregated housing. Unfortunately, this punishment greatly increases the likelihood of depression and heightened anxiety in the mentally ill inmate.[149] The experience of being incarcerated typically exacerbates the inmate's mental illness.[150] As a result, incarcerated, emotionally disturbed inmates in state prisons spend an average of 15 months longer behind bars than other prisoners. In many cases, the difference is attributed to their delusions, hallucinations, or paranoia, which makes them more likely to get into fights or receive disciplinary reports.[151]

The rates of mental illness while incarcerated vary by race and gender. The highest rate of mental illness is reported among white female state prisoners. About 25 percent of these women were identified as mentally ill, compared with about 16 percent of male offenders.[152] The rate of mental illness among black and Hispanic inmates is about half the rate of that of white inmates.[153] This finding has sparked debate as to meaning of this statistic. Are black and Hispanic inmates in better mental health, or does this statistic reflect an institutional bias. Some argue that the difference in rates between whites and non-whites is a result of the inexperience of white psychiatrists with minority patients.[154]

Prison environments contribute to mental health problems. Prisons are **total institutions**, a term sociologist Erving Goffman coined in his study of prisons and mental hospitals.[155] In prison, the inmate has little responsibility, does not have to make decisions, does not have to engage in problem solving, does not have to plan for tomorrow. The institution meets all the inmate's basic needs. The institution dictates the inmate's schedule. Institutional rules are made without any input from the inmate. The envi-

deinstitutionalization Moving mentally ill people from long-term hospitalization to community-based care.

total institutions Institutions that meet all of the inmate's basic needs, discourage individuality, punish dissent, and segregate those who do not follow the rules.

ronment is rigid, and inmates are expected to conform to the values and expectations of the institution. Individuality is discouraged, dissent is punished, and failure to follow the rules can result in segregation from the prison population. As a consequence, the environment (1) does not promote effective treatment of the mentally ill offender—even people without mental health problems become depressed and mentally ill when exposed to this environment; and (2) encourages the development of **prisonization**—socialization into a distinct prison subculture with its own values, mores, norms, and sanctions.

Prisonization results in a subculture for inmates in which the rules of conduct are distinctly different from the official rules of the institution and from society in general. Prisoners learn to adapt to this prison code and conduct their life in prison by it. However, the mentally ill prisoner, who has difficulty adapting to society in general, often is unable to relate to fellow prisoners and conform to the prison code while, at the same time, maintaining the appearance of obedience to the institutional rules and norms. Often, the result of this failure to adapt to the prison code is dangerous ostracism by both inmates and administrators.

All prisoners are affected by prisonization, which is why most prisoners demonstrate maladaptive behaviors when they are returned to the community. Accustomed to being told what to do, when to do it, and how to do it, released inmates often demonstrate few of the job skills desired by employers. Prisoners who have been incarcerated for long terms may have lost the ability to plan for the future, to take responsibility for their actions, and exhibit proactive behaviors. They have become passive, dependent, and fixated on the rules.

THE MENTALLY ILL IN THE COMMUNITY The criminal justice system has been described as a revolving door for a person with mental illness, as the mentally ill go from the street to jail and back without treatment.[156] Mentally ill inmates tend to have more previous incarcerations than other prisoners. Among repeat offenders, 53 percent of mentally ill state inmates had a current or past sentence for a violent offense, compared with 45 percent of other inmates. Among federal prisoners with a prior sentence, the mentally ill (44%) were twice as likely as other inmates (22%) to have a current or prior sentence for a violent offense.[157] These statistics indicate that the mentally ill move back and forth between incarceration and the community without effective interventions and treatment.

Mentally ill offenders report high rates of homelessness, unemployment, alcohol and drug use, and physical and sexual abuse while in the community. About 4 percent of mentally ill state and federal prison inmates and 7 percent of jail inmates report that they were living on the street or in a shelter when arrested. These rates were at least double those for inmates who were not mentally ill.[158] Once released, the mentally ill offender continues to be a financial liability to society, as an estimated 30 percent of mentally ill and 13 percent of other inmates in state prison receive some type of financial support from government agencies. More than 15 percent of the mentally ill received welfare prior to their arrest, and another 20 percent received some type of supplemental income payments, such as unemployment or worker's compensation.[159]

About 60 to 65 percent of mentally ill inmates reported that they were under the influence of alcohol or drugs at the time they committed their offense.[160] Mentally ill inmates are more commonly alcohol dependent, and this has a significant impact on their ability to reenter the community successfully. For example, such tasks as holding down a job are complicated by alcohol abuse. About 17 percent of mentally ill offenders reported that they had lost a job due to drinking. Getting along with others is influenced by drinking, as 46 percent reported that they had gotten into a fight while drinking. The extent of drinking problems of the mentally ill is reflected in the fact that about half said they had consumed as many as 20 alcoholic drinks in a day.[161]

When released back into the community, the mentally ill offender is seldom cured as a result of the treatment received while incarcerated. Even if treatment and medication

prisonization Socialization into a distinct prison subculture with its own values, mores, norms, and sanctions.

in prison had made a significant impact on their behavior, it is doubtful that released mentally ill offenders would continue treatment or medication. For example, a Bureau of Justice Statistics survey reported that while an estimated 13 percent of probationers were required to seek mental health treatment as a condition of their sentence, fewer than half fulfilled this requirement.[162]

Mentally ill offenders live a chaotic life that does not promote successful reintegration into the community. Homeless, unemployed, drunk, and belligerent—it is little wonder that the public is alarmed by their presence on the streets, fearful of their approaches for handouts, and unsympathetic to their plight when arrested. Citizens are alarmed by their presence in the subways, fear being attacked by them, and are frustrated by the inability of the police to "do something" about the problem. Many see them as a danger and would prefer to leave the problem to the criminal justice system rather than develop effective treatment programs.

Neither police nor correctional institutions have been able to make a significant impact on the problem of the mentally ill offender. Providing medications in prison is a temporary approach to a much more serious community problem. In addition to the public-order crimes they commit, mentally ill offenders commit serious offenses. For example, about 13 percent of mentally ill inmates in prisons were convicted of murder, and about 12 percent were convicted of sexual assault. Andrea Yates, for example, was mentally ill when she murdered her five young children by drowning them one by one in the bathtub of her home. Mental health professionals posit that a significant percentage of youth involved in the juvenile justice system have unmet needs for mental health and substance abuse services.[163]

JUST THE FACTS 15.3

What reasons are given for the increasing elderly prison population? In what ways do gangs increase violence in prisons? What problems do privacy laws pose for dealing with inmates with HIV? In what ways do prison environments contribute to mental health problems? What is prisonization, and what are its consequences? Why are problems of prison populations important to the wider society?

Technology and the Criminal Justice System: New Weapons, New Crimes

THE MAIN IDEA

Technology has transformed criminal justice, creating new ways to solve old problems, creating new types of crime, and raising new constitutional issues.

Computer technology is causing dramatic changes in and to the criminal justice system. When a Massachusetts court released its decision acquitting British au pair Louise Woodward, it was the first electronically released decision in the state court's history.[164] Larry Froistad Jr. confessed to murder to an Internet chat group.[165] He was sentenced to 40 years in prison for the murder of his 5-year-old daughter. Froistad confessed "to getting wickedly drunk and killing his daughter by torching their house and then pretending that it was an accident." In March 2001, the Internal Affairs Unit of the Washington, D.C. police investigated complaints that the police used inappropriate profanity and racist remarks. The objectionable messages were found among about 4 million computer communications sent over a 1-year period by D.C. police officers on their patrol car computers.[166] During a routine stop, New York City Housing officers confronted Adrian Bowman for drinking beer on a Harlem stoop. They entered his name into a small Palm Pilot–style, handheld computer worn on an officer's gun belt. This small computer can run checks on stolen vehicles, license suspensions, warrants, gun registrations, and the like. When Bowman's name was entered into the computer, the officers were alerted to the fact that he was wanted for a triple homicide in St. Louis.[167]

Advances in computer technology have transformed criminal justice in numerous ways, beginning with improved communication abilities. Many police departments have placed computers in patrol cars so that officers can communicate with each other and have access to computerized data (see Table 15.6). As a result, some communities struggle to find qualified applicants for dispatching jobs, due in part to the changing technology required to perform the job. Computer programs help police identify crime and criminals. For example, police use license plate readers that automatically scan the license plates of passing vehicles in a fraction of a second and check for stolen cars. Citizens of New Orleans can track crime in their own neighborhoods by logging onto the police department's Comstat crime maps on the department's web site.[168] Citizens can be alerted to potential crime in their community by using "reverse 911," a computerized program that can phone citizens in a particular geographical area of the city to warn them of potential danger, such as a suspect on the loose or other crime threat.[169] And, in St. Louis, police use "auto mug shots," a computerized mug shot book of automobiles, to help crime victims and witnesses identify vehicles involved in crimes.[170]

Not all technology used by criminal justice agencies is well received by the public. Citizens were enraged when the City and County of Honolulu, Hawaii, started using digital cameras operated from unmarked vans and mounted near intersections to catch drivers who speed and run red lights. The program resulted in a record number of citations, but citizens resented being accused by a machine and the program was discontinued.[171] In 1998, the West Hartford, Connecticut, Police Department listed the names of drivers charged with traffic infractions on its Internet web site, another unpopular application.[172]

table 15.6 **Types of In-Field Computers or Terminals Used by Local Police Departments, by Size of Population Served, 1999**

	Percentage of Agencies Using In-Field Computers or Terminal							
			Car-Mounted			Handheld		
Population Served	Any Type	Laptop Computer	Either Type	Computer	Terminal	Either Type	Computer	Terminal
All sizes	31	22	17	6	12	1	—	1
1,000,000 or more	87	62	81	25	75	37	12	31
500,000–999,999	88	62	83	33	71	17	17	8
250,000–499,999	89	69	65	20	50	13	9	4
100,000–249,999	86	57	65	28	41	14	4	12
50,000–99,999	72	51	53	20	38	6	2	4
25,000–49,999	66	43	46	20	29	4	1	3
10,000–24,999	51	35	31	13	20	1	0	1
2,500–9,999	33	24	17	5	12	1	—	1
Under 2,500	15	11	6	1	5	—	0	—

Source: Matthew Hickman and Brian Reaves, *Local Police Departments 1999* (Washington, DC: U.S. Department of Justice, May 2001).

—Less than 0.5%.

Cybercrime

Computers and the Internet have given the criminal justice system new tools, but at the same time, information technology has created new ways to commit crimes and even new crimes. Responding to the challenge of computer-related crime and **cybercrime**—crimes against computers and the use of computers to commit crimes—is changing the way the criminal justice system operates. For example, Internet crime is increasing so rapidly that the criminal justice system cannot keep up with it. Many law enforcement problems in computer-related crime and cybercrime are a result of (1) a chronic lack of talented people qualified to investigate and prosecute cybercrimes and (2) legislation that has not kept up with the various criminal acts that are possible using the computer and the Internet.

Trained law enforcement experts are needed because traditional investigative techniques often are ineffective in investigating cybercrime. Few forensic agents have been trained to find and understand incriminating data on hard drives, and the complexity of evidence gathering makes computer crimes complicated to prosecute.[173] Computers are routinely seized in cases involving crimes such as fraud, embezzlement, child pornography, cybertheft, and malicious hacking, but there are not enough forensics experts qualified to examine the hard drives of these computers for the evidence that will allow the police to prosecute offenders. In some departments, the backlog of hard drives that need to be examined is so great that police are running out of room to store seized computers.[174] This backlog can be detrimental to innocent owners of seized computers, which police can retain as evidence until the statute of limitations runs out on the crime. One Texas business owner took a federal agency to court and won a $300,000 damage suit for the business losses he suffered after his computers were seized and not returned in a timely manner.[175]

The prosecution of computer and cybercrimes is hampered by the lack of legislation defining them. For example, "piggybacking," "page jacking," and "denial of service" are new technocrimes that are not clearly understood and defined in the criminal justice system. **Piggybacking** is a form of cybertrespass. However, the definition of *cybertrespassing* is not clear because there are search engines that routinely search computer sites, and computer sites that legitimately search and compile information from other web sites.[176] In **page jacking**, a program captures a user's computer and directs the computer to a web site that the user did not want to go to and cannot exit from except by turning off the computer. Often, page jackers direct the user to pornographic web sites, and the concern of the public is that juveniles could be unwillingly exposed to obscene material as they use the Internet. The page jacker's motivation is financial gain through sales of web site advertising to pornography companies. By forcing Internet users to the sites, they increase their profit margins from both advertising and possible sales to new consumers of porn.[177] **Denial of service** is considered a prank by hackers and is becoming one of the most common problems on the Internet. In a denial of service attack, the hacker attempts to crash or clog the targeted Internet site by overloading the web site with too many requests for information for the web site to respond.[178] A glossary of the language of cybercrime is presented in Table 15.7.

Other new cyberproblems include everything from illegal kidney auctions on Ebay to computer waste poisoning people in developing countries. While one can find just about anything for sale on Ebay and other Internet auction companies, under federal law it is illegal to trade or sell human organs. However, that did not stop one seller from posting his kidney for sale on Ebay. The posting announced:

> Human kidney. Fully functional. You can choose either kidney. Buyer pays all transplant and medical costs. Of course, only one for sale, as I need the other one to live. Serious bids only. Minimum offer $25,000."[179]

Other items that cannot be sold on Internet auctions include firearms, military weapons, and drugs.

cybercrime Crimes against computers, or the use of computers to commit crimes.

piggybacking A form of cybertrespassing.

page jacking A program that captures a user's computer and directs the computer to a web site that the user did not want to go to and cannot exit from except by turning off the computer.

denial of service An attack in which the hacker attempts to crash or clog the targeted Internet site by overloading the web site with too many requests for information for the web site to respond.

table 15.7 The Language of Cybercrime

The Weapons	
Back doors	Unauthorized, hidden way to gain access to a program. Usually placed in the software by the person who wrote the program or had access to it. Difficult to detect if written by the software engineer and embedded in the original program. These allow the person unauthorized access to the program virtually at will.
Buffer overflow	A technique for crashing or gaining control of a computer by sending too much data to the buffer in a computer's memory. Usually, this attack does not cause permanent damage but can cause the computer network to go down.
Denial of service (DOS)	One of the most common attacks on a computer network, primarily because it is so easy to execute. The attacker sends more requests for information to a network than the network can handle. This causes the computer system to overload and slow down or crash. In more sophisticated attacks, the hacker gains unauthorized control of many other computers and uses these computers to send bogus requests for information. No harm is done to the computer database, but the system cannot process requests from legitimate users. DOS can be used to cover up another more serious attack.
Dumpster diving	Sifting through a company's garbage to find information to help break into their computers. Sometimes, the information is used to make a stab at social engineering more credible. (See section on social engineering later in table.)
Logic bombs	An instruction in a computer program that triggers a malicious act. Logic bombs can be programmed to activate on certain dates, such as Christmas or Friday the 13th, and are named after this characteristic.
Malicious applets	Tiny programs, sometimes written in the popular Java computer language, that misuse your computer's resources, modify files on the hard disk, send fake e-mail, or steal passwords. The damage can very destructive, as it destroys or corrupts files. Because malicious applets can use the host computer's e-mail to attack other computers, which in turn can attack other computers, the damage can be extensive.
Password crackers	Software that can guess passwords by repeatedly trying different passwords until the correct one is found. The software is basically a dictionary that simply tries every word in the dictionary. Nonsense words, uncommon foreign words, or passwords with a combination of letters and numbers make it more difficult for this software to discover the correct password.
Scans	Widespread probes of the Internet to determine types of computers, services, and connections. In this way, the bad guys can take advantage of weaknesses in a particular make of computer or software program.
Sniffers	Programs that covertly search individual packets of data as they pass through the Internet, capturing passwords or the entire contents. Often, the user is unaware of the action of the sniffer, as the purpose is to gain data that can be used later as opposed to the data that the sniffer examines.
Social engineering	A tactic used to gain access to computer systems by talking unsuspecting company employees out of valuable information, such as passwords. Because many users use passwords based on family members' names, birthdays, and anniversary dates, even seemingly innocent information such as the names of the children in the user's family, may allow the hacker to guess the password.
Spoofing	Faking an e-mail address or web page to trick users into passing along critical information like passwords or credit card numbers.
Trojan horse	A program that, unknown to the user, contains instructions that exploit a known vulnerability in some software. The program is hidden in another "innocent" program so the user is unaware of the threat.

(continues)

table 15.7 The Language of Cybercrime (Continued)

The Weapons	
Virus	A virus is a malicious program used by hackers that spreads by attaching itself to another program. When the user runs that program, the virus attaches itself to more programs. The virus program itself remains hidden, so the user will not be aware of the actions of the virus. If any programs are transferred from the infected computer to a "healthy" computer, the healthy computer may become infected.
Worm	A worm is a piece of software that takes over the resources of a computer and uses them for its own purposes. A worm is self-contained in that it does not infect other programs. A common worm program is one that duplicates itself every time it is run. As the size of the worm program grows, all room on the disk for other programs is taken over by the worm. And as the worm program grows, other programs run slower, and eventually the user's hard disk is full.
War dialing	Programs that automatically dial thousands of telephone numbers in search of a way through a modem connection. A common attack is to use war dialing to obtain access to the long-distance telephone lines of a company's computer and then place unauthorized long-distance telephone calls.
The Players	
White-hat hackers	Good guys often employed by companies to find the weaknesses of a system or software. White-hat hackers can also be freelancers who attempt to find the vulnerabilities of the Internet, network, or software but are not hired by a company to do so. Law enforcement often is critical of these freelance white-hat hackers, because finding the weakness of a computer system or the Internet requires the hacker to attempt unauthorized access.
Black-hat hackers	The bad guys. They crash systems, steal passwords, look at confidential data, and send malicious e-mail. Often, their only motive is the thrill of being able to beat the system. Black-hat hackers can be juveniles as well as adults.
Crackers	The really bad guys. Hackers for hire, who break into computer systems to steal valuable information for their own financial gain, not for the kicks of it. These are the professional criminals who have found that they can make more money in cybercrime than old-fashioned robbery.
Script bunnies	Wannabe bad guys. Hackers with little technical expertise or ability who download "point and click" programs—scripts—that automate the job of breaking into computers. Often, these programs are downloaded from chat rooms on the Internet. They require little knowledge to operate, and there are many computer systems that lack even the most elementary protection against such novice attacks. Script bunnies can be pre-teen hackers who simply "want to be cool."
Insiders	"The Benedict Arnolds" of cybercrime. Bad guys with a grudge. Employees, disgruntled or otherwise, working solo or in concert with outsiders to compromise corporate systems. The damage done by these cybercriminals can be extensive, due of their inside knowledge of the system. Some attacks by insiders have gone undetected for years.

Source: "Storming the Fortress" reprinted from the February 21, 2000 issue of *Business Week*, by special permission, copyright © 2000 by the McGraw-Hill Companies, Inc.

Computer waste poisoning is primarily a problem in developing nations, which receive obsolete computer equipment mainly from the United States. Workers dismantle this equipment and scavenge it for the small amounts of silver, gold, copper, and other precious metals inside. Unfortunately, these workers, often poor children, also expose themselves to heavy metals and toxic hazards. In some high-tech dumps, the toxic hazards have polluted the groundwater.[180] While computer dumping is a serious public health problem, there are virtually no legal restrictions or provisions for safe recycling.

Computers also are used by criminals in the course of committing traditional crimes better and faster. For example, nearly 50 percent of all counterfeit money is printed using personal computers.[181] The Internet also has provided a new and better way to commit many frauds. One cybercriminal used Internet chat rooms and fraudulent "news web pages" to drive up the price of the stock he held.[182] Fraud on the Internet is so common and serious that the Department of Justice and the Federal Bureau of Investigation have a web site to address fraud committed over the Internet—the **Internet Fraud Complaint Center (IFCC)**. For fiscal year 2000, the IFCC received over 30,000 complaints, with auction fraud being the most common complaint.[183]

Go to the Internet Fraud Complaint Center at http://www.ifccfbi.gov to examine the scope and nature of Internet fraud or to report suspected terrorist activity. ■

Identity theft was the leading consumer fraud complaint reported in 2001, with over 100,000 complaints.[184] A common way to commit identity theft is to hack into big corporations' databases and download credit card numbers and other data on employees. The hacker victimizes these people by using their identities and credentials to make purchases. The Internet is one of the most common sources of fake ID documents necessary for the crime of identity theft. About 30 percent of all fake ID documents are obtained from the Internet.[185] Fake ID documents that can be obtained from the Internet often contain holograms, bar codes, magnetic stripes, and other security features found on genuine documents. Fake state driver's licenses and green cards can be obtained for as little as $200. While false identification is most commonly used for identity theft and underage purchases of alcohol, new concerns have been raised about the use of fake IDs by terrorists.

Internet pornography, or **cyberporn**, particularly child pornography, is a serious challenge to the criminal justice system. The Internet has become the tool of choice for child pornographers, pedophiles, and predators. The Internet is used to transmit images and even live video of child pornography and child molestation. Using secret passwords, users can meet in private chat rooms where they can trade child pornography. Law enforcement officers sometimes find thousands of sexually explicit images of children stored on the offenders' computers.[186] Because the Internet knows no national boundary, Internet pornography rings can be based in any country, making it difficult for U.S. officials to discover and convict the offenders.[187] Even more alarming are pedophiles who use the Internet to lure young victims. In an effort to catch these offenders, law enforcement agents often pose as child computer users and set up sting operations by agreeing to meet the pedophiles.[188]

Cybercrimes can be committed by juveniles as well as by adults. In fact, many juveniles are attracted to various cybercrimes, such as hacking, software fraud, and other forms of Internet mischief. Children have access to computers and frequently feel that trading copyrighted material such as movies, video games, and music is not a crime. Others engage in hacking and fraud. The extent of juvenile Internet crime is shocking. One child engaged in Internet stock manipulation fraud and made over $1 million.[189] Juveniles who get caught often get light sentences or only civil fines. One U.S. Department of Justice official suggested that the extent of juvenile Internet crime is so pervasive that it is beyond law enforcement. He lamented that juvenile cybercriminals have no sense of ethics that what they are doing is wrong.[190]

Technology and Constitutional Rights

Computers and the Internet have raised serious debates concerning constitutional issues and the threat posed by **cyberterrorism**—the use of the Internet to facilitate terrorism-related crimes. Three major issues about Internet use are freedom of speech, right to privacy, and enforcement jurisdiction. Many people champion the Internet as the ultimate instrument for freedom of speech. However, there are restrictions on freedom of speech even for great instruments. Hate groups, antiabortion groups, violent

identity theft Use of the computer to find and steal victims' identities and credentials, usually to make purchases.

cyberporn Internet-based pornography.

cyberterrorism The use of the Internet to facilitate terrorism-related crimes.

ethics in the system

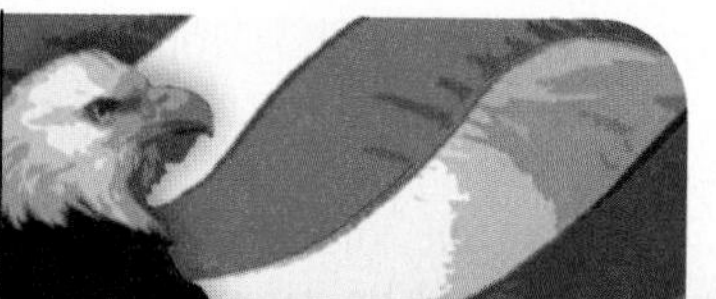

Corporate Crime: The Enron Case

Computers often take center stage in **corporate crime**—crimes committed by corporate executives. So-called white-collar crimes potentially have more harmful and far-reaching effects than traditional crimes against individuals and property. Large-scale corporate fraud can impact the entire national economy. Polluted water, hazardous industrial byproducts and waste, and destruction of nonrenewable natural resources have the potential to harm and even kill many citizens. Yet the criminal justice system often is poorly prepared to investigate, prosecute, or punish corporate offenders who would poison the air, water, and land.

The Enron Case is a good example of new challenges facing the criminal justice system in response to nontraditional crimes. The federal and state governments are investigating the collapse of this corporate giant, revelations about its unethical and criminal activities, and questions about its links to government officials. In 2002, the president of Enron's accounting agency, Arthur Anderson, was arrested in connection with the case. When Enron went bankrupt in 2001, many thousands of employees lost their retirement savings, and states suffered financial losses through the collapse of Enron stock. At the same time, Enron executives continued to make millions of dollars, even as the company headed for destruction.

In the wake of the Enron scandal, Congress is looking at new legislation that would prevent another similar situation. This is a difficult task, however. It is not clear if Enron accounting and reporting practices were illegal or unethical. It is also not clear who should be held responsible for the financial ruin. Federal, state, and local law enforcement have little role in policing corporate giants like Enron. These corporations answer to other government agencies that regulate security exchanges and stock fraud. Despite the fact that Enron's fall may have an even greater impact on society than the September 11 terrorist attacks, society and the criminal justice system seem ill-prepared to deal with such a disaster.[191] One of the greatest lessons of Enron is that effective interagency cooperation is necessary to properly regulate corporate giants.

Enron is one of the largest cases of corporate fraud, but there are numerous other white-collar crimes. The Tri-State Crematory scandal in Noble, Georgia, is a good example of small white-collar fraud crimes that can have a tremendous impact on people and the system. The owners of Tri-Sate Crematory failed to cremate the bodies of about 300 deceased persons in their charge.[192] Each offense is a misdemeanor, a relatively minor offense. The crime is a misdemeanor fraud, and the punishment for a single offense is often only a fine. However, the scope of the Tri-State Crematory fraud was so shocking, the owner was held without bail.[193] A review of the case reveals that there is very little that the criminal justice system could have done to prevent this grief to so many people. There is also little assurance that the criminal justice system could prevent a similar incident from occurring in the future,[194] although new legislation will no doubt make improper disposal of dead bodies a more serious crime.

Critics of the criminal justice system point out that a person may receive years in prison for possessing a small amount of crack cocaine but that corporate heads may steal millions of dollars, destroy the financial security of thousands, call into question the integrity of the political system, and yet escape punishment. Not only do they often escape punishment, but sometimes they get to keep the millions they made from illegal activities. Perhaps after the Enron case, this will change.

■ **Do you agree that corporate crime is more serious than traditional crime? If so, in what ways? If not, why not? How might computer-based technologies and the Internet make Americans more vulnerable to corporate crime as well as to cybercriminals? Do you think corporations should be held criminally liable for mismanagement of employee savings and pensions or for negligence in reporting business failure?**

corporate crime Crimes committed by corporate executives.

environmentalists, and other groups often come in conflict with the criminal justice system over the right to use the Internet to spread their messages. Hate groups have been held liable for civil damages as a result of posting hate messages urging violence toward minorities. A suit against an antiabortion web site resulted in a $107 million verdict for the violence that they advocated against doctors who performed abortions.[195]

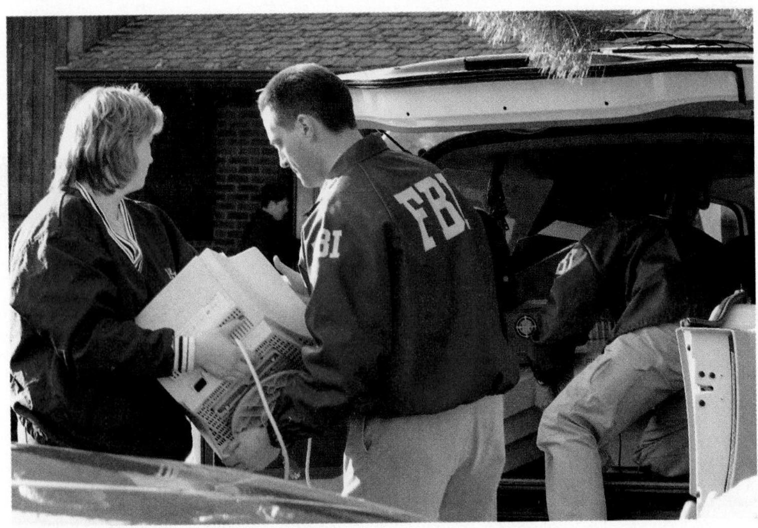

What new skills will these criminal justice professionals need to conduct investigations and gather evidence in the future? What computer- and Internet-related crimes will they investigate? What issues of constitutionality and national security will affect these investigations?

In an effort to regulate Internet communication and images, the government proposed two major pieces of legislation, but both have been unsuccessful. The U.S. Supreme Court has ruled that while these regulations ban hate speech, child pornography, and violence toward individuals, they also interfere with legitimate web sites. Thus, the **Communications Decency Act** of 1996 was struck down as unconstitutional, and challenges that the **Child Online Protection Act** was too broad were successful.

Pornography on the Internet involves both the right of free speech and jurisdiction. The U.S. Supreme Court has ruled that the definition of *pornographic* is determined by local community standards. This criterion raises several issues in the attempt to prosecute operators of web sites that are alleged to have pornographic images. If a web site is located in New York City, can a prosecutor in Des Moines, Iowa, claim that the community standards of Des Moines should be applied to judge whether the content of the web site is indecent? There is no nationwide legal standard for determining what constitutes pornographic images. To complicate the issue, it is possible for the web site to originate in a foreign country. What standard should be used to determine if the content of the web site is pornographic? As a result of this lack of agreement on the legal definition of *pornographic,* it has been difficult to regulate explicitly sexual images on the Internet.

Privacy also has been a major cyber issue. What is the balance between citizens' rights to privacy in communicating on the Internet and the government's right to monitor Internet communication. The extent of the public's sensitivity to this issue was evidenced by allegations in 1999 that the government had installed a "Big Brother" feature in Microsoft software. A cryptographer for a Canadian software firm, dissecting a piece of Microsoft security software, made an unexpected find: an element in the Windows operating system labeled "NSAKey."[196] This discovery set off a firestorm of Orwellian visions that the software was a Trojan horse that gave the National Security Agency (NSA) hidden entry into the world's computers.[197] Microsoft and the NSA, which gathers electronic signal intelligence worldwide and is responsible for the security of the government's computers, denied that the software program allows NSA unfettered access to any computer. Microsoft attributed the name to an unfortunate choice of words and a nonissue promoted by conspiracy theorists.[198] The controversy is fueled by the fact that the government has indeed repeatedly attempted to get legislation passed that would give the government such access. The FBI and the NSA have lobbied for bans on cryptography and for building trap doors into cryptography that would allow government agencies to have access to any cyber communication.[199]

careers in the system

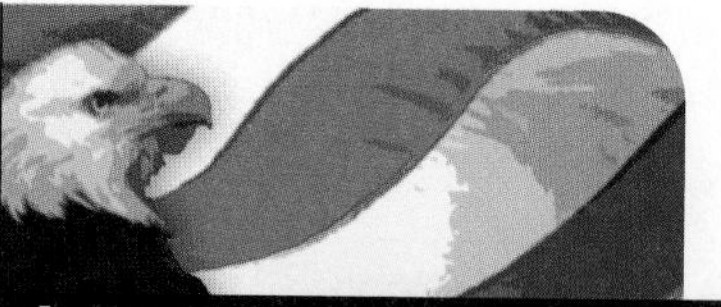

Computer Security and Cyberpolice

If you want to chase computer hackers, bring online child pedophiles to justice, and defend the nation's computers against attacks by foreign countries and terrorists, which criminal justice agency do you apply for and what will they teach you in the police academy? Do you apply for Net Force, headed by Alex Michaels, and join the elite group of government law enforcement agencies that uses sophisticated virtual reality supercomputers to chase bad guys across the Internet? No! Net Force is like Hawaii Five-0. It is a fictional law enforcement agency that has no counterpart in reality. There is no criminal justice agency in the real world like Net Force, a fictional law enforcement agency created by author Tom Clancy.[200]

There are very few full-time law enforcement agents whose job is to surf the web to catch cybercriminals. Local police do not recruit or hire people as police officers who are dedicated to fighting cybercrime. The FBI is the federal criminal justice agency that has official responsibility for responding to Internet crime, but there are only about 200 agents assigned to National Infrastructure Protection Center squads nationwide.[201] Local police departments do not recruit for officers with computer skills or have the ability to train officers in this area. Furthermore, departments cannot pay the competitive salaries demanded by civilian computer experts. Thus, the departments often have to rely on officers who have educated themselves in computer skills, perhaps working with computers as a hobby or personal interest. These officers, sometimes known as "byteheads," are assigned to white-collar crime details and computer crime because no one else in the department is qualified for the assignment. Most police officers are unaccustomed to using digital evidence and cyber evidence and find it difficult to investigate such crimes.[202] An additional challenge to the bytehead is getting others in the criminal justice system to understand the complexity of digital evidence, especially at trials. Jurors and judges often have difficulty comprehending evidence presented in computer and cybercrime cases.[203]

Police academies offer no training in digital evidence or how to fight cybercrime. Students interested in careers in fighting cybercrime will have to obtain a college degree in **computer security**. Most computer security degrees are at the master's level. The student must first complete an undergraduate degree in computer science and then specialize in computer security, much the same as a medical doctor first obtains his or her medical degree and then goes for additional schooling to become a surgeon, heart specialist, psychiatrist, or other medical specialist. One of the few, and the first, undergraduate degrees in computer security in the United States is offered by East Stroudsburg University of Pennsylvania.

■ **Why might the need for people with degrees in computer security continue to grow? Who might employ people with such a degree? How do you think state and local law enforcement agencies should address problems of investigating cybercrime and gathering and analyzing digital evidence? Do you think you might ever be interested in becoming a bytehead?**

The FBI and the NSA have argued that unbreakable cryptography allows criminals and terrorists to communicate without fear of the government being able to intercept and decode the communication. Privacy advocates argue that the advantages to be gained by allowing government access would not be worth the damage that such legislation would do to traditional constitutional protections.[204] Critics of the FBI and the NSA argue that people need to be able to protect their privacy and data and that government access would violate First Amendment rights and potentially damage businesses. They argue that (1) the government has not demonstrated a trustworthy track record for incorruptibility and for keeping secrets. If such a trapdoor existed, it would just be a matter of time before it became public information. (2) If the government did manage to kept the code secret, then hackers would find a way to access this key, enabling them to break into any databank or computer in the world.[205]

computer security An area of criminal justice aimed at fighting cybercrime.

If a state prohibits gambling, can Internet users go to virtual casinos with computer servers located outside the state or outside U.S. borders? If the laws prohibit certain citizens in certain states from gambling on the Internet, what is the responsibility of the virtual casino to screen out these unauthorized users? These are important questions that the criminal justice system must answer, as they have far-reaching impact on other forms of electronic commerce as well as Internet gambling. A 1999 New York case (*People v. World Interactive Gaming Corp.*) ruled that the state of New York could freeze the assets of a virtual casino located in Antigua, a Caribbean island nation where casino gambling is legal.[206] Defining the extent of state criminal jurisdiction over various Internet activities will be an evolving challenge in the twenty-first century.

Technology and Terrorism

On January 24, 2000, nearly half of the computing power in the world went dead. The top-secret NSA's massive array of supercomputers—which crunch information from America's spy satellites and global eavesdropping network—mysteriously shut down for 3 days. Government officials immediately feared hackers might have caused the shutdown.[207] In the end, the shutdown was attributed to human and computer error, but the fear that it was deliberate is justified. Previously, hackers have been successful in shutting down emergency 911 service, severing NASA uplinks to the *Atlantis* shuttle,[208] shutting down state governments' web pages,[209] infiltrating the U.S. Senate's main web site and defacing the web page (www.senate.gov),[210] defacing the U.S. Army's main web site,[211] and penetrating Defense Department national defense databases and stealing sensitive information.[212] Computer networks used by government and business are increasingly at risk of severe disruption. Critics argue that the government's response is "inefficient and ineffective." Statistics seem to support this claim, as the FBI has had little luck in catching hackers who break into government computers. The FBI catches only about 10 percent of those who probe or penetrate government computers.[213]

Attacks on the Internet have resulted in millions of dollars of damage worldwide, for example, through destructive software programs such as Melissa, VBS.freelink, Worm.Explore.Zip, Killer Resume, Code Red, W32/Kriz.3862, Christmas, and I Love You. Following the September 11, 2001, terrorist attacks, new concerns have been raised about the security of the nation's computers and the Internet. Despite building multimillion-dollar high-tech crime labs to fight Internet hackers, the government does not seem to be gaining ground on preventing hacking of sensitive computer systems.[214]

Investigation has indicated that the September 11 terrorists used the Internet to coordinate and communicate their attacks and the materials used in the attacks. In light of these findings, and fearing that the next terrorist attack may be aimed at the nation's Internet, the FBI is putting more emphasis on intelligence gathering and investigation of threats from computer hackers. This emphasis is at the expense of other traditional duties performed by the FBI, such as civil rights investigations, drug investigations, interstate auto theft, and bank robberies.[215] Furthermore, the FBI does not have the ability to respond to the huge volume of e-mailed tips it receives. In the first 3 months following the terrorist attacks, the FBI received 11,000 e-mails and had to turn to the private sector for assistance.[216]

As a result of concern over security, many government agencies are scrutinizing the security of their computer systems and databases. Unfortunately, when problems are found, sometimes there are no easy fixes. When it was revealed that the Department of the Interior's computer system could not safeguard the accounting system that manages money for Native Americans and could not fix the problem, a federal district judge ordered the department to shut down its entire computer system for 10 weeks until the security threat could be fixed.[217] The shutdown stopped Interior Department trust payments to over 40,000 Native Americans for the 10-week period and shut down e-mail to thousands of Interior Department employees. Many Native Americans complained that the 10-week suspension of government royalty checks caused extreme hardship and even caused some to fear that they would lose their homes, because they depended on the government royalty checks to pay their mortgages.[218]

Many are concerned that the nation's vulnerability to disruption of the entire society by attacks on the Internet may pose a greater danger than the attack on the World Trade Towers and the Pentagon. The extent of this fear is evidenced by the warning of White House technology advisor Richard Clarke, who told a judicial subcommittee hearing on cyberterrorism that the government would take charge in the event of a cyberattack sponsored by a foreign country: "We reserve the right to respond in any way appropriate: through covert action, through military action, any one of the tools available to the president."[219] A subcommittee member pointed out that a well-planned and well-executed cyberattack on America would result in terrorists gaining "the digital controls for the nation's utilities, power grids, air traffic control systems, and nuclear power plants."[220] Clarke said, "So far, the United States has not caught any foreign governments or terrorist groups using Internet warfare, although that does not mean it has not been attempted.... There are lots of cases where there have been unauthorized intrusions, but we have never been able to prove to our particular satisfaction that a particular government did it."[221]

JUST THE FACTS 15.4

What technological advances have helped criminal justice? What are some examples of cybercrimes? What other problems have been created by technology? What are the constitutional issues arising from the use of technology?

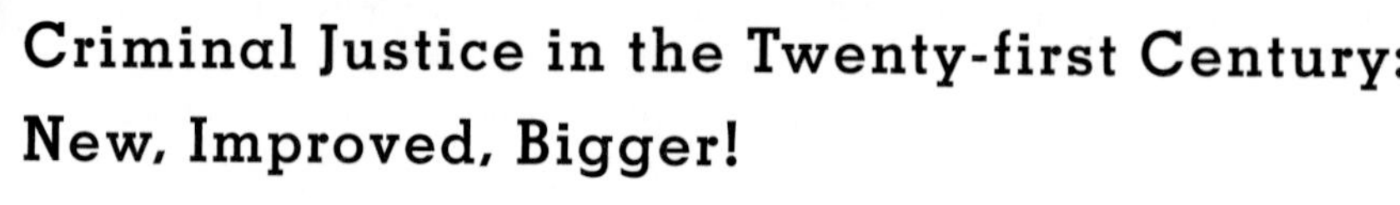

conclusion:

Criminal Justice in the Twenty-first Century: New, Improved, Bigger!

What new challenges will confront the criminal justice system in the twenty-first century? What threats will challenge personal and national security? What constitutional rights will be challenged? Who will respond to the new challenges? There are numerous questions that cannot be answered as we look toward the future. The criminal justice system is constantly changing and will continue to change, a point emphasized throughout this textbook. The criminal justice system is not a static system to be memorized, but a dynamic system to be understood and applied. Nevertheless, some predictions can be made about the immediate future of the criminal justice system.

Criminal justice agencies and personnel will be required to perform new roles and responsibilities. As mentioned in the discussion of the changing role of the FBI in responding to terrorism, some police agencies will abandon tradition roles and responsibilities and assume new ones. Police personnel will need new skills to be successful in their occupations. Corrections will continue to experiment with new tools to promote successful reintegration of offenders into society and to monitor them in the community. Legislative bills defining new crimes and new police powers will be passed. Often, the new crimes and powers will focus on entirely new concerns, such as Internet use, terrorism, DNA evidence, and privacy rights. New laws, such as for mandatory national identification cards, antiterrorist security measures, and drug abuse, could cause large-scale and unintended results. The criminal justice system and society will need to resolve the drug abuse problem in America. Scientific evidence about addiction will need to be integrated into the criminal law and criminal justice systems.

The criminal justice system certainly will become more intrusive into the lives of citizens. Whether justified on grounds of national security, the War on Drugs, or just because advances in technology make it possible, citizens will have more contact with the criminal justice system in their everyday lives. Surveillance of public places such as streets, stadiums, parking lots, buildings, and airports will become more common as cameras that can identify terrorists, wanted persons, and illegal aliens will routinely scan public places. New police powers will allow law enforcement agents to stop and question citizens. New laws will allow police to detain some people with less evidence than was previously necessary.

Computers will become nearly universal in the criminal justice system, and all personnel will be expected to be competent in their use. Police officers will have to know more criminal law than ever before, and police officers in the field will be required to make decisions that previously have been made only by supervisors. All criminal justice personnel will be held to a higher standard of professional behavior, and misbehavior will be discovered and punished. Video cameras in the hands of citizens, mounted in police cars, and nearly everywhere will provide powerful evidence of a police officer's misdeeds.

The criminal justice system will grow. Unable to keep pace with the required professional, technological advances and legal changes, small police departments will combine to form larger regional or metro police agencies. More courts will be created to process defendants, and more correctional facilities will receive defendants processed by the courts. The role of federal criminal justice agencies, once a very small part of the criminal justice system, will expand. Some will advocate that a national police agency is needed. Finally, the threat of terrorism will continue to result in an expansion of police powers, challenges to constitutional rights, and the creation of new criminal justice and antiterrorism agencies.

Chapter Summary

- People fear becoming victims of violent crime, largely because of sensational workplace crimes, media violence and coverage of violent crime, school homicides, and random violence perpetrated by youths. Causes of youth violence are unclear.
- Violent juvenile crime has increased dramatically. One response has been to try juveniles as adults and impose harsher and longer sentences. Preventing youth violence and rehabilitating violent juvenile offenders are challenges to the system.

- Stricter drug law enforcement has not reduced illegal drug use and has tended to discriminate against minorities. Critics of the War on Drugs call for some legalization or for treating drug abuse as addictive behavior rather than criminal behavior.
- The costs to society of drug use and drug law enforcement are enormous and relate to street crime as well as to international drug trafficking, money laundering, and narcoterrorism through organized crime.
- Two aggressive new strategies for the War on Drugs focus on reducing the supply and reducing the demand. Solutions to the drug problem often are hampered by opposition to public health measures.
- Prison inmates become elderly, critically ill, and seriously injured, burdening the system and society. Health care problems include prison gang violence, HIV/AIDS and communicable diseases such as TB, and mental illness. Each of these problems reaches into the communities from which inmates come and to which they return.
- Inmates join gangs for protection and access to contraband, and gang membership extends beyond prison walls. Innovative new programs for combating prison gangs, such as those initiated by New York's Gang Intelligence Unit, are achieving some success.
- AIDS-related deaths account for 17 to 18 percent of deaths in state and federal prisons. Infected prisoners can be dangerous to other inmates and to staff, especially as the health status of prisoners typically is not made known. The spread of drug-resistant TB from prison populations to their communities represents a public health disaster.
- White female inmates have the highest rates of mental illness. Mentally ill inmates do not do well in conditions of incarceration. At the same time, the indigent mentally ill do not do well in communities and end up in jails and prisons. All inmates typically undergo a prisonization process that adapts them to prison culture but does not promote good mental health and independent living.
- Advances in technology—from Comstat crime maps to DNA testing—have revolutionized law enforcement and the criminal justice system. Computer-based technologies also have contributed to new and more efficient crimes, corporate crime, and Internet crime.
- Cybercrime, identify theft, cyberporn, and cyberterrorism have led to new laws and a reexamination of constitutional matters relating to the Fourth and Fifth Amendments. Federal oversight of computer security is being increased in the interests of national security.

Vocabulary Review

computer security, 498
contraband, 484
corporate crime, 496
cybercrime, 492
cyberporn, 495
cyberterrorism, 495
deinstitutionalization, 488
demand reduction programs, 477
denial of service, 492
identity theft, 495
media violence, 466
money laundering, 476
narcoterrorism, 476
page jacking, 492
piggybacking, 492
prisonization, 489
school violence, 468
security risk groups, 484
supply reduction programs, 477
total institutions, 488
trafficking, 476
workplace violence, 463

Names and Events to Remember

Abraham case, 466
Anti-Drug Abuse Act, 472
Boggs Act, 472
Child Online Protection Act, 487
Communications Decency Act, 487
Comprehensive Drug Abuse Prevention and Control Act, 472
Drug Abuse Resistance Education (DARE), 481
Drug Enforcement Agency (DEA), 477
Gang Intelligence Unit (GIU), 485

Harrison Narcotics Act, 472
Internet Fraud Complaint Center (IFCC), 495
Marijuana Tax Act, 472
National Institute on Drug Abuse (NIDA), 473
Office of National Drug Control Policy (ONDCP), 472
Organized Crime Drug Enforcement Task Force (OCDETF), 477
War on Drugs, 471

Think about This

1. Imagine that you have been asked to address Congress on one of the "current challenges in the criminal justice system." Which challenge presented in this chapter would you choose, and why? Which aspect of this challenge would you choose to address, and what would you say about it?
2. At all levels of the criminal justice system, a major task is staying within an allotted budget—a decision process that requires tradeoffs. For each challenge discussed in this chapter, where would you increase or decrease the budget, and why? For instance, what priorities would you give to preventing youth violence, funding drug abuse prevention programs for juveniles, treating drug addicts, eliminating prison gangs, providing psychological counseling for inmates, and training cyberpolice?
3. How could you view the criminal justice system as a circle? What would be the elements that make up the circle, and how would they interrelate? Does this circle need to be broken? What is most important for making the operation of the criminal justice system effective and efficient?
4. After reading about the many aspects of the criminal justice system in this text, what would be your "dream job"? What level of education would such a job require? Are there any specialized courses or minor degrees that would help prepare you for such a career?

ContentSelect

Go to the ContentSelect web site and key in the search words "mental illness." Read "Persons with Serious Mental Illness in the Criminal Justice System: Background, Prevalence, and Principles of Care," from the December 2000 issue of *Criminal Justice Policy Review*. This article discusses how people with serious mental illnesses (PSMIs) come into the criminal justice system and how they are cared for. Sample the article to answer the following questions.

1. One problem in caring for PSMIs is defining *serious mental illness*. In your opinion, what would constitute a serious mental illness? Given that about half of the U.S. population will be diagnosed with some form of mental disorder during their lifetimes, what criteria could be used to differentiate "serious" from "not serious"?
2. A previous chapter of your text described how drug courts are used to divert nonviolent defendants out of the traditional criminal justice system. Consider the pros and cons of having a separate court system for PSMIs. What problems might arise (e.g., cost, rights of defendants, and so on)? Would there be a way for the court to enforce treatment?
3. The article states that police may choose "to arrest PSMIs because it was the best option at hand for persons who failed to meet inpatient commitment criteria." Should police arrest PSMIs in an effort to get them treatment? If the criminal justice system is not the appropriate placement for PSMIs, what is?
4. According to your text, "Prison environments contribute to mental health problems." What could be done in prisons to reduce the effects of mental illness?

The Constitution of the United States of America

We the People of the United States, in Order to form a more perfect Union, establish Justice, insure domestic Tranquility, provide for the common defence, promote the general Welfare, and secure the Blessings of Liberty to ourselves and our Posterity, do ordain and establish this Constitution for the United States of America.

Article I

SECTION 1 All legislative Powers herein granted shall be vested in a Congress of the United States, which shall consist of a Senate and House of Representatives.

SECTION 2 The House of Representatives shall be composed of Members chosen every second Year by the People of the several States, and the Electors in each State shall have the Qualifications requisite for Electors of the most numerous Branch of the State Legislature.

No person shall be a Representative who shall not have attained to the Age of twenty five Years, and been seven Years a Citizen of the United States, and who shall not, when elected, be an Inhabitant of that State in which he shall be chosen.

Representatives and direct Taxes shall be apportioned among the several States which may be included within this Union, according to their respective Numbers which shall be determined by adding to the whole Number of free Persons, including those bound to Service for a Term of Years, and excluding Indians not taxed, three fifths of all other Persons. The actual Enumeration shall be made within three Years after the first Meeting of the Congress of the United States, and within every subsequent Term ten Years, in such Manner as they shall by Law direct. The Number of Representatives shall not exceed one for every thirty Thousand, but each State shall have at Least one Representative; and until such enumeration shall be made, the State of New Hampshire shall be entitled to chuse three, Massachusetts eight, Rhode-Island and Providence Plantations one, Connecticut five, New York six, New Jersey four, Pennsylvania eight, Delaware one, Maryland six, Virginia ten, North Carolina five, South Carolina five, and Georgia three.

When vacancies happen in the Representation from any State, the Executive Authority thereof shall issue Writs of Election to fill such Vacancies.

The House of Representatives shall chuse their speaker and other Officers; and shall have the sole Power of Impeachment.

SECTION 3 The Senate of the United States shall be composed of two Senators from each State chosen by the Legislature thereof, for six Years; and each Senator shall have one Vote.

Immediately after they shall be assembled in Consequence of the first Election, they shall be divided as equally as may be into three Classes. The Seats of the Senators of the first Class shall be vacated at the Expiration of the second year, of the second Class at the Expiration of the fourth Year, and of the third Class at the Expiration of the sixth Year, so that one third may be chosen every second Year and if Vacancies happen by Resignation, or otherwise, during the Recess of the Legislature of any State, the Executive thereof may make temporary Appointments until the next Meeting of the Legislature, which shall then fill such Vacancies.

No Person shall be a Senator who shall not have attained to the Age of thirty Years, and been nine Years a Citizen of the United States, and who shall not, when elected, be an Inhabitant of that State for which he shall be chosen.

The Vice President of the United States shall be President of the Senate, but shall have no Vote, unless they be equally divided.

The Senate shall chuse their other Officers, and also a President pro tempore, in the Absence of the Vice President, or when he shall exercise the Office of President of the United States.

The Senate shall have the sole Power to try all Impeachments. When sitting for that Purpose, they shall be on Oath or Affirmation. When the President of the United States is tried, the

Chief Justice shall preside: And no Person shall be convicted without the Concurrence of two thirds of the Members present.

Judgment in Cases of Impeachment shall not extend further than to removal from Office, and disqualification to hold and enjoy any Office of honor, Trust or Profit under the United States; but the Party convicted shall nevertheless be liable and subject to Indictment, Trial, Judgment and Punishment, according to Law.

SECTION 4 The Times, Places and Manner of holding Elections for Senators and Representatives, shall be prescribed in each State by the Legislature thereof; but the Congress may at any time by law make or alter such Regulations, except as to the Places of chusing Senators.

The Congress shall assemble at least once in every Year, and such Meeting shall be on the first Monday in December, unless they shall by Law appoint a different Day.

SECTION 5 Each House shall be the Judge of the Elections, Returns and Qualifications of its own Members, and a Majority of each shall constitute a Quorum to do Business; but a smaller Number may adjourn from day to day, and may be authorized to compel the Attendance of absent Members, in such Manner, and under such Penalties as each House may provide.

Each House may determine the Rules of its Proceedings, punish its Members for disorderly Behaviour, and with the Concurrence of two thirds, expel a Member.

Each House shall keep a journal of its Proceedings, and from time to time publish the same, excepting such Parts as may in their judgment require Secrecy; and the Yeas and Nays of the Members of either House on any question shall, at the Desire of one fifth of those present, be entered on the Journal.

Neither House, during the Session of Congress, shall, without the Consent of the other, adjourn for more than three days, nor to any other Place than that in which the two Houses shall be sitting.

SECTION 6 The Senators and Representatives shall receive a Compensation for their Services, to be ascertained by Law, and paid out of the Treasury of the United States. They shall in all Cases, except Treason, Felony and Breach of the Peace, be privileged from Arrest during their Attendance at the Session of their respective Houses, and in going to and returning from the same; and for any Speech or Debate in either House, they shall not be questioned in any other Place.

No Senator or Representative shall, during the Time for which he was elected, be appointed to any civil Office under the Authority of the United States, which shall have been created, or the Emoluments whereof shall have been encreased during such time; and no Person holding any Office under the United States, shall be a Member of either House during his Continuance in Office.

SECTION 7 All Bills for raising Revenue shall originate in the House of Representatives; but the Senate may propose or concur with Amendments as on other Bills.

Every Bill which shall have passed the House of Representatives and the Senate, shall, before it become a Law, be presented to the President of the United States; If he approves he shall sign it, but if not he shall return it, with his Objections to that House in which it shall have originated, who shall enter the Objections at large on their journal, and proceed to reconsider it. If after such Reconsideration two thirds of that House shall agree to pass the Bill, it shall be sent, together with the Objections, to the other House, by which it shall likewise be reconsidered, and if approved by two thirds of that House, it shall become a Law. But in all such Cases the Votes of both Houses shall be determined by Yeas and Nays, and the Names of the Persons voting for and against the Bill shall be entered on the Journal of each House respectively. If any Bill shall not be returned by the President within ten Days (Sundays excepted) after it shall have been presented to him, the Same shall be a Law, in like Manner as if he had signed it, unless the Congress by their Adjournment prevent its Return, in which Case it shall not be a Law.

Every Order, Resolution, or Vote to which the Concurrence of the Senate and House of Representatives may be necessary (except on a question of Adjournment) shall be presented to the President of the United States; and before the Same shall take Effect, shall be approved by him, or being disapproved by him, shall be repassed by two thirds of the Senate and House of Representatives, according to the Rules and Limitations prescribed in the Case of a Bill.

SECTION 8 The Congress shall have Power To lay and collect Taxes, Duties, Imposts and Excises, to pay the Debts and provide for the common Defence and general Welfare of the United States; but all Duties, Imposts and Excises shall be uniform throughout the United States;

To borrow Money on the credit of the United States;

To regulate Commerce with foreign Nations, and among the several States, and with the Indian Tribes;

To establish a uniform Rule of Naturalization, and uniform Laws on the subject of Bankruptcies throughout the United States;

To coin Money, regulate the Value thereof, and of foreign Coin, and fix the Standard of Weights and Measures;

To provide for the Punishment of counterfeiting the Securities and current Coin of the United States;

To establish Post Offices and post Roads;

To promote the Progress of Science and useful Arts, by securing for limited Times to Authors and Inventors the exclusive Right to their respective Writings and Discoveries;

To constitute Tribunals inferior to the supreme Court;

To define and punish Piracies and Felonies committed on the high Seas, and Offences against the Law of Nations;

To declare War, grant Letters of Marque and Reprisal, and make Rules concerning Captures on Land and Water;

To raise and support Armies, but no Appropriation of Money to that Use shall be for a longer Term than two Years;

To provide and maintain a Navy;

To make Rules for the Government and Regulation of the land and naval Forces;

To provide for calling forth the Militia to execute the Laws of the Union, suppress Insurrections and repel Invasions;

To provide for organizing, arming, and disciplining, the Militia, and for governing such Part of them as may be employed in the Service of the United States, reserving to the States respectively, the Appointment of the Officers, and the Authority of training the Militia according to the discipline prescribed by Congress;

To exercise exclusive Legislation in all Cases whatsoever, over such District (not exceeding ten Miles square) as may, by Cession of particular States, and the Acceptance of Congress, become the Seat of the Government of the United States, and to exercise like Authority over all Places purchased by the Consent of the Legislature of the State in which the Same shall be for the Erection of Forts, Magazines, Arsenals, dock-Yards, and other needful Buildings;—And

To make all Laws which shall be necessary and proper for carrying into Execution the foregoing Powers, and all other Powers vested by this Constitution in the Government of the United States, or in any Department or Officer thereof.

SECTION 9 The Migration or Importation of such Persons as any of the States now existing shall think proper to admit, shall not be prohibited by the Congress prior to the Year one thousand eight hundred and eight, but a Tax or duty may be imposed on such Importation, not exceeding ten dollars for each Person.

The Privilege of the Writ of Habeas Corpus shall not be suspended, unless when in Cases of Rebellion or Invasion the public Safety may require it.

No Bill of Attainder or ex post facto Law shall be passed.

No Capitation, or other direct, Tax shall be laid, unless in Proportion to the Census or Enumeration herein before directed to be taken.

No Tax or Duty shall be laid on Articles exported from any State.

No Preference shall be given by any Regulation of Commerce or Revenue to the Ports of one State over those of another; nor shall Vessels bound to, or from, one State, be obliged to enter, clear, or pay Duties in another.

No Money shall be drawn from the Treasury, but in Consequence of Appropriations made by Law; and a regular Statement and Account of the Receipts and Expenditures of all public Money shall be published from time to time.

No Title of Nobility shall be granted by the United States: And no Person holding any Office of Profit or Trust under them, shall, without the Consent of the Congress, accept of any present, Emolument, Office, or Title, of any kind whatever, from any King, Prince, or foreign State.

SECTION 10 No state shall enter into any Treaty, Alliance, or Confederation; grant Letters of Marque and Reprisal; coin Money; emit Bills of Credit; make any Thing but gold and silver Coin a Tender in Payment of Debts; pass any Bill of Attainder, ex post facto Law, or Law impairing the Obligation of Contracts, or grant any Title of Nobility.

No State shall, without the Consent of the Congress, lay any Imposts or Duties on Imports or Exports, except what may be absolutely necessary for executing its inspection Laws: and the net Produce of all Duties and Imposts, laid by any State on Imports or Exports, shall be for the Use of the Treasury of the United States, and all such Laws shall be subject to the Revision and Controul of the Congress.

No State shall, without the Consent of Congress, lay any Duty of Tonnage, keep Troops, or Ships of War in time of Peace, enter into any Agreement or Compact with another State, or with a foreign Power, or engage in War, unless actually invaded, or in such imminent Danger as will not admit of delay.

Article II

SECTION 1 The executive Power shall be vested in a President of the United States of America. He shall hold his Office during the Term of four Years, and, together with the Vice President, chosen for the same Term, be elected as follows.

Each State shall appoint, in such Manner as the Legislature thereof may direct, a Number of Electors, equal to the whole Number of Senators and Representatives to which the State may be entitled in the Congress; but no Senator or Representative, or Person holding an Office of Trust of Profit under the United States, shall be appointed an Elector.

The Electors shall meet in their respective States, and vote by Ballot for two Persons, of whom one at least shall not be an Inhabitant of the same State with themselves. And they shall make a List of all the Persons voted for, and, of the Number of Votes for each; which List they shall sign and certify, and transmit sealed to the Seat of the Government of the United States, directed to the President of the Senate. The President of the Senate shall, in the Presence of the Senate and House of Representatives, open all the Certificates, and the Votes shall then be counted. The Person having the greatest Number of Votes shall be the President, if such Number be a Majority of the whole Number of Electors appointed; and if there be more than one who have such Majority, and have an equal Number of Votes, then the House of Representatives shall immediately chuse by Ballot one of them for President; and if no Person have a Majority, then from the five highest on the List the said House shall in like Manner chuse the President. But in chusing the President, the Votes shall be taken by States, the Representation from each State having one Vote; A quorum for this Purpose shall consist of a Member or Members from two thirds of the States, and a Majority of all the States shall be necessary to a Choice. In every Case, after the Choice of the President, the Person having the greatest Number of Votes of the Electors shall be the Vice President. But if there should remain two or more who have equal Votes, the Senate shall chuse from them by Ballot the Vice President.

The Congress may determine the Time of chusing the Electors, and the Day on which they shall give their Votes; which Day shall be the same throughout the United States.

No Person except a natural born Citizen, or a Citizen of the United States, at the time of the Adoption of this Constitution, shall be eligible to the Office of President; neither shall any Person be eligible to that Office who shall not have attained to the Age of thirty five Years, and been fourteen Years a Resident within the United States.

In Case of the Removal of the President from Office, or of his Death, Resignation, or Inability to discharge the Powers and Duties of the said Office, the Same shall devolve on the Vice President, and the Congress may by Law provide for the Case of Removal, Death, Resignation or Inability, both of the President and Vice President, declaring what Officer shall then act as President, and such Officer shall act accordingly, until the Disability be removed, or a President shall be elected.

The President shall, at stated Times, receive for his Services, a Compensation, which shall neither be encreased nor diminished during the Period for which he shall have been elected, and he shall not receive within that Period any other Emolument from the United States, or any of them.

Before he enter on the Execution of his Office, he shall take the following Oath or Affirmation—"I do solemnly swear (or affirm) that I will faithfully execute the Office of President of the United States, and will to the best of my Ability, preserve, protect and defend the Constitution of the United States."

SECTION 2 The President shall be Commander in Chief of the Army, and Navy of the United States, and of the Militia of the several States, when called into the actual Service of the United States; he may require the Opinion, in writing, of the principal Officer in each of the executive Departments, upon any Subject relating to the Duties of their respective Offices, and he shall have Power to grant Reprieves and Pardons for Offences against the United States, except in Cases of Impeachment.

He shall have Power, by and with the Advice and Consent of the Senate, to make Treaties, provided two thirds of the Senators present concur; and he shall nominate, and by and with the Advice and Consent of the Senate, shall appoint Ambassadors, other public Ministers and Consuls, Judges of the supreme Court, and all other Officers of the United States, whose Appointments are not herein otherwise provided for, and which shall be established by Law: but the Congress may by Law vest the Appointment of such inferior Officers, as they think proper, in the President alone, in the Courts of Law, or in the Heads of Departments.

The President shall have Power to fill up all Vacancies that may happen during the Recess of the Senate, by granting Commissions which shall expire at the end of their next Session.

SECTION 3 He shall from time to time give to the Congress Information of the State of the Union, and recommend to their Consideration such Measures as he shall judge necessary and expedient; he may, on extraordinary Occasions, convene both Houses, or either of them, and in Case of Disagreement between them, with Respect to the Time of Adjournment, he may adjourn them to such Time as he shall think proper; he shall receive Ambassadors and other public Ministers; he shall take Care that the Laws be faithfully executed, and shall Commission all the Officers of the United States.

SECTION 4 The President, Vice President and all civil Officers of the United States, shall be removed from Office on Impeachment for, and Conviction of, Treason, Bribery, or other high Crimes and Misdemeanors.

Article III

SECTION 1 The judicial Power of the United States, shall be vested in one supreme Court, and in such inferior Courts as the Congress may from time to time ordain and establish. The Judges, both of the supreme and inferior Courts, shall hold their Offices during good Behaviour, and shall, at stated Times, receive for their Services, a Compensation, which shall not be diminished during their Continuance in Office.

SECTION 2 The judicial Power shall extend to all Cases, in Law and Equity, arising under this Constitution, the Laws of the United States, and Treaties made, or which shall be made, under their Authority;—to all Cases affecting Ambassadors, other public Ministers and Consuls;—to all Cases of admiralty and maritime Jurisdiction;—to Controversies to which the United States shall be a Party;—to Controversies between two or more States;—between a State and Citizens of another State;—between Citizens of different States,—between Citizens of the same State claiming Lands under Grants of different States,—and between a State, or the Citizens thereof, and foreign States, Citizens of Subjects.

In all Cases affecting Ambassadors, other public Ministers and Consuls, and those in which a State shall be Party, the supreme Court shall have original Jurisdiction. In all the other Cases before mentioned, the supreme Court shall have appellate Jurisdiction, both as to Law and Fact, with such Exceptions, and under such Regulations as the Congress shall make.

The Trial of all Crimes, except in Cases of Impeachment, shall be by Jury; and such Trial shall be held in the State where the said Crimes shall have been committed; but when not committed within any State, the Trial shall be at such Place or Places as the Congress may by Law have directed.

SECTION 3 Treason against the United States, shall consist only in levying War against them, or in adhering to their Enemies, giving them Aid and Comfort. No Person shall be convicted of Treason unless on the Testimony of two Witnesses to the same overt Act, or on Confession in open Court.

The Congress shall have Power to declare the Punishment of Treason, but no Attainder of Treason shall work Corruption of Blood, or Forfeiture except during the Life of the Person attainted.

Article IV

SECTION 1 Full Faith and Credit shall be given in each State to the public Acts, Records, and judicial Proceedings of every other State. And the Congress may by general Laws prescribe the Manner in which such Acts, Records and Proceedings shall be proved, and the Effect thereof.

SECTION 2 The Citizens of each State shall be entitled to all Privileges and Immunities of Citizens in the several States.

A Person charged in any State with Treason, Felony, or other Crime, who shall flee from Justice, and be found in another State, shall on Demand of the executive Authority of the State from which he fled, be delivered up, to be removed to the State having Jurisdiction of the Crime.

No Person held to Service or Labour in one State under the Laws thereof, escaping into another, shall, in Consequence of any Law or Regulation therein, be discharged from such Service or Labour, but shall be delivered up on Claim of the Party to whom such Service or Labour may be due.

SECTION 3 New States may be admitted by the Congress into this Union; but no new State shall be formed or erected within the Jurisdiction of any other State; nor any State be formed by the Junction of two or more States, or Parts of States, without the Consent of the Legislatures of the States concerned as well as of the Congress.

The Congress shall have Power to dispose of and make all needful Rules and Regulations respecting the Territory or other Property belonging to the United States; and nothing in this Constitution shall be so construed as to Prejudice any Claims of the United States, or of any particular State.

SECTION 4 The United States shall guarantee to every State in this Union a Republican Form of Government, and shall protect each of them against Invasion, and on Application of the Legislature, or of the Executive (when the Legislature cannot be convened) against domestic Violence.

Article V

The Congress, whenever two thirds of both Houses shall deem it necessary, shall propose Amendments to this Constitution, or, on the Application of the Legislatures of two thirds of the several States, shall call a Convention for proposing Amendments, which, in either Case, shall be valid to all Intents and Purposes, as Part of this Constitution, when ratified by the Legislatures of three fourths of the several States, or by Conventions in three fourths thereof, as the one or the other Mode of Ratification may be proposed by the Congress; Provided that no Amendment which may be made prior to the Year One thousand eight hundred and eight shall in any Manner affect the first and fourth Clauses in the Ninth Section of the first Article; and that no State, without its Consent, shall be deprived of its equal Suffrage in the Senate.

Article VI

All Debts contracted and Engagements entered into, before the Adoption of this Constitution, shall be as valid against the United States under this Constitution, as under the Confederation.

This Constitution, and the laws of the United States which shall be made in Pursuance thereof; and all Treaties made, or which shall be made, under the Authority of the United States, shall be the supreme Law of the Land; and the Judges in every State shall be bound thereby, any Thing in the Constitution or Laws of any State to the Contrary notwithstanding.

The Senators and Representatives before mentioned, and the Members of the several State Legislatures, and all executive and judicial Officers, both of the United States and of the several States, shall be bound by Oath or Affirmation, to support this Constitution; but no religious Test shall ever be required as a Qualification to any Office or public Trust under the United States.

Article VII

The Ratification of the Conventions of nine States, shall be sufficient for the Establishment of this Constitution between the States so ratifying the Same.

Done in Convention by the Unanimous Consent of the States present the Seventeenth Day of September in the Year of our Lord one thousand seven hundred and Eighty seven and of the Independence of the United States of America the Twelfth. In witness whereof we have hereunto subscribed our Names,

Go. WASHINGTON
Presid't. and deputy from Virginia

Attest
WILLIAM JACKSON
Secretary

DELAWARE
Geo. Read
Gunning Bedford jun
John Dickinson
Richard Basset
Jaco. Broom

MASSACHUSETTS
Nathaniel Gorham
Rufus King

CONNECTICUT
Wm. Saml. Johnson
Roger Sherman

NEW YORK
Alexander Hamilton

NEW JERSEY
Wh. Livingston
David Brearley
Wm. Paterson
Jona. Dayton

PENNSYLVANIA
B. Franklin
Thomas Mifflin
Robt. Morris
Geo. Clymer
Thos. FitzSimons
Jared Ingersoll
James Wilson
Gouv. Morris

NEW HAMPSHIRE
John Langdon
Nicholas Gilman

MARYLAND
James McHenry
Dan of St. Thos. Jenifer
Danl. Carroll

VIRGINIA
John Blair
James Madison, Jr.

NORTH CAROLINA
Wm. Blount
Richd. Dobbs Spaight
Hu. Williamson

SOUTH CAROLINA
J. Rutledge
Charles Cotesworth Pinckney
Charles Pinckney
Pierce Butler

GEORGIA
William Few
Abr. Baldwin

Articles in addition to, and amendment of the Constitution of the United tates of America, proposed by Congress and ratified by the Legislatures of the several states, pursuant to the Fifth Article of the original Constitution.

(*The first ten amendments were passed by Congress on September 25, 1789, and were ratified on December 15, 1791.*)

Amendment I

Congress shall make no law respecting an establishment of religion, or prohibiting the free exercise thereof; or abridging the freedom of speech, or of the press; or the right of the people peaceably to assemble, and to petition the Government for a redress of grievances.

Amendment II

A well regulated Militia, being necessary to the security of a free State, the right of the people to keep and bear Arms, shall not be infringed.

Amendment III

No Soldier shall, in time of peace be quartered in any house, without the consent of the Owner, nor in time of war, but in a manner to be prescribed by law.

Amendment IV

The right of the people to be secure in their persons, houses, papers, and effects, against unreasonable searches and seizures, shall not be violated, and no warrants shall issue, but upon probable cause, supported by Oath or affirmation, and particularly describing the place to be searched, and the persons or things to be seized.

Amendment V

No person shall be held to answer for a capital, or otherwise infamous crime, unless on a presentment or indictment of a Grand Jury, except in cases arising in the land or naval forces, or in the Militia, when in actual service in time of War or public danger; nor shall any person be subject for the same offence to be twice put in jeopardy of life or limb; nor shall be compelled in any criminal case to be a witness against himself, nor be deprived of life, liberty, or property, without due process of law; nor shall private property be taken for public use, without just compensation.

Amendment VI

In all criminal prosecutions, the accused shall enjoy the right to a speedy and public trial, by an impartial jury of the State and district wherein the crime shall have been committed, which district shall have been previously ascertained by law, and to be informed of the nature and cause of the accusation; to be confronted with the witnesses against him; to have compulsory process for obtaining witnesses in his favor, and to have the assistance of counsel for his defence.

Amendment VII

In Suits at common law, where the value in controversy shall exceed twenty dollars, the right of trial by jury shall be preserved, and no fact tried by a jury, shall be otherwise re-examined in any Court of the United States, than according to the rules of the common law.

Amendment VIII

Excessive bail shall not be required, nor excessive fines imposed, nor cruel and unusual punishments inflicted.

Amendment IX

The enumeration in the Constitution, of certain rights, shall not be construed to deny or disparage others retained by the people.

Amendment X

The powers not delegated to the United States by the Constitution, nor prohibited by it to the States, are reserved to the States respectively, or to the people.

Amendment XI

(*Ratified on February 7, 1795*)

The Judicial power of the United States shall not be construed to extend to any suit in law or equity, commenced or prosecuted against one of the United States by Citizens of another State, or by Citizens or Subjects of any Foreign State.

Amendment XII

(*Ratified on June 15, 1804*)

The Electors shall meet in their respective states, and vote by ballot for President and Vice-President, one of whom, at least, shall not be an inhabitant of the same state with themselves; they shall name in their ballots the person voted for as President, and in distinct ballots the person voted for as Vice-President, and they shall make distinct lists of all persons voted for as President, and of all persons voted for as Vice-President, and of the number of votes for each, which lists they shall sign and certify, and transmit sealed to the seat of the government of the United States, directed to the President of the Senate;—The President of the Senate shall, in the presence of the Senate and House of Representatives, open all the certificates and the votes shall then be counted;—The person having the greatest number of votes for President, shall be the President, if such number be a majority of the whole number of Electors appointed; and if no person have such majority; then from the persons having the highest numbers not exceeding three on the list of those voted for as President, the House of Representatives shall choose immediately, by ballot, the President. But in choosing the President, the votes shall be taken by states, the representation from each state having one vote; a quorum for this purpose shall consist of a member or members from two-thirds of the states, and a majority of all the states shall be necessary to a choice. And if the House of Representatives shall not choose a President whenever the right of choice shall devolve upon them, before the fourth day of March next following, then the Vice-President shall act as President, as in the case of the death or other constitutional disability of the President.—The person having the greatest number of votes as Vice-President, shall be the Vice-President, if such number be a majority of the whole number of Electors appointed, and if no person have a majority, then from the two highest numbers on the list, the Senate shall choose the Vice-President; a quorum for the purpose shall consist of two-thirds of the whole number of Senators, and a majority of the whole number shall be necessary to a choice. But no person constitutionally ineligible to the office of President shall be eligible to that of Vice-President of the United States.

Amendment XIII

(Ratified on December 6, 1865)

SECTION 1 Neither slavery nor involuntary servitude, except as a punishment for crime whereof the party shall have been duly convicted, shall exist within the United States, or any place subject to their jurisdiction.

SECTION 2 Congress shall have power to enforce this article by appropriate legislation.

Amendment XIV

(Ratified on July 9, 1868)

SECTION 1 All persons born or naturalized in the United States, and subject to the jurisdiction thereof, are citizens of the United States and of the State wherein they reside. No State shall make or enforce any law which shall abridge the privileges or immunities of citizens of the United States; nor shall any State deprive any person of life, liberty, or property, without due process of law; nor deny to any person within its jurisdiction the equal protection of the laws.

SECTION 2 Representatives shall be apportioned among the several States according to their respective numbers, counting the whole number of persons in each State, excluding Indians not taxed. But when the right to vote at any election for the choice of electors for President and Vice President of the United States, Representatives in Congress, the Executive and Judicial officers of a State, or the members of the Legislature thereof, is denied to any of the male inhabitants of such State, being twenty-one years of age, and citizens of the United States, or in any way abridged, except for participation in rebellion, or other crime, the basis of representation therein shall be reduced in the proportion which the number of such male citizens shall bear to the whole number of male citizens twenty-one years of age in such State.

SECTION 3 No person shall be a Senator or Representative in Congress, or elector of President and Vice President, or hold any office, civil or military, under the United States, or under any State, who, having previously taken an oath, as a member of Congress, or as an officer of the United States, or as a member of any State legislature, or as an executive or judicial officer of any State, to support the Constitution of the United States, shall have engaged in insurrection or rebellion against the same, or given aid or comfort to the enemies thereof. But Congress may by a vote of two-thirds of each House, remove such diability.

SECTION 4 The validity of the public debt of the United States, authorized by law, including debts incurred for payment of pensions and bounties for services in suppressing insurrection or rebellion, shall not be questioned. But neither the United States nor any State shall assume or pay any debt or obligation incurred in aid of insurrection or rebellion against the United States, or any claim for the loss or emancipation of any slave, but all such debts, obligations and claims shall be held illegal and void.

SECTION 5 The Congress shall have power to enforce, by appropriate legislation, the provisions of this article.

Amendment XV

(Ratified on February 3, 1870)

SECTION 1 The right of citizens of the United States to vote shall not be denied or abridged by the United States or by any State on account of race, color, or previous condition of servitude.

SECTION 2 The Congress shall have power to enforce this article by appropriate legislation.

Amendment XVI

(Ratified on February 3, 1913)

The Congress shall have power to lay and collect taxes on incomes, from whatever source derived, without apportionment among the several States, and without regard to any census or enumeration.

Amendment XVII

(*Ratified on April 8, 1913*)

The Senate of the United States shall be composed of two Senators from each State, elected by the people thereof, for six years; and each Senator shall have one vote. The electors in each State shall have the qualifications requisite for electors of the most numerous branch of the State legislatures.

When vacancies happen in the representation of any State in the Senate, the executive authority of such State shall issue writs of election to fill such vacancies: Provided, That the legislature of any State may empower the executive thereof to make temporary appointments until the people fill the vacancies by election as the legislature may direct.

This amendment shall not be so construed as to affect the election or term of any Senator chosen before it becomes valid as part of the Constitution.

Amendment XVIII

(*Ratified on January 16, 1919*)

SECTION 1 After one year from the ratification of this article the manufacture, sale, or transportation of intoxicating liquors within, the importation thereof into, or the exportation thereof from the United States and all territory subject to the jurisdiction thereof for beverage purposes is hereby prohibited.

SECTION 2 The Congress and the several States shall have concurrent power to enforce this article by appropriate legislation.

SECTION 3 This article shall be inoperative unless it shall have been ratified as an amendment to the Constitution by the legislatures of the several States, as provided in the Constitution, within seven years from the date of the submission hereof to the States by the Congress.

Amendment XIX

(*Ratified on August 18, 1920*)

The right of citizens of the United States to vote shall not be denied or abridged by the United States or by any State on account of sex.

Congress shall have power to enforce this article by appropriate legislation.

Amendment XX

(*Ratified on February 6, 1933*)

SECTION 1 The terms of the President and Vice President shall end at noon on the 20th day of January, and the terms of Senators and Representatives at noon on the 3d day of January, of the years in which such terms would have ended if this article had not been ratified; and the terms of their successors shall then begin.

SECTION 2 The Congress shall assemble at least once in every year, and such meeting shall begin at noon on the 3d day of January, unless they shall by law appoint a different day.

SECTION 3 If, at the time fixed for the beginning of the term of the President, the President elect shall have died, the Vice President elect shall become President. If a President shall not have been chosen before the time fixed for the beginning of his term, or if the President elect shall have failed to qualify, then the Vice President elect shall act as President until a President shall have qualified; and the Congress may by law provide for the case wherein neither a President elect nor a Vice President elect shall have qualified, declaring who shall then act as President, or the manner in which one who is to act shall be selected, and such person shall act accordingly until a President or Vice President shall have qualified.

SECTION 4 The Congress may by law provide for the case of the death of any of the persons from whom the House of Representatives may choose a President whenever the rights of choice shall have devolved upon them, and for the case of the death of any of the persons from whom the Senate may choose a Vice President whenever the right of choice shall have devolved upon them.

SECTION 5 Sections 1 and 2 shall take effect on the 15th day of October following the ratification of this article.

SECTION 6 This article shall be inoperative unless it shall have been ratified as an amendment to the Constitution by the legislatures of three-fourths of the several States within seven years from the date of its submission.

Amendment XXI

(*Ratified on December 5, 1933*)

SECTION 1 The eighteenth article of amendment to the Constitution of the United States is hereby repealed.

SECTION 2 The transportation or importation into any State, Territory, or possession of the United States for delivery or use therein of intoxicating liquors, in violation of the laws thereof, is hereby prohibited.

SECTION 3 This article shall be inoperative unless it shall have been ratified as an amendment to the Constitution by conventions in the several States, as provided in the Constitution, within seven years from the date of the submission hereof to the States by the Congress.

Amendment XXII

(*Ratified on February 27, 1951*)

No person shall be elected to the office of the President more than twice, and no person who has held the office of President, or acted as President, for more than two years of a term to which some other person was elected President shall be elected to the office of the President more than once. But this Article shall not apply to any person holding the office of President when this Article was proposed by the Congress, and shall not prevent any person who may be holding the office of President, or acting as President, during the term within which this Article becomes operative from holding the office of President or acting as President during the remainder of such term.

Amendment XXIII

(Ratified on March 29, 1961)

SECTION 1 The District constituting the seat of Government of the United States shall appoint in such manner as the Congress may direct:

A number of electors of President and Vice President equal to the whole number of Senators and Representatives in Congress to which the District would be entitled if it were a State, but in no event more than the least populous State; they shall be in addition to those appointed by the States, but they shall be considered, for the purposes of the election of President and Vice President, to be electors appointed by a State; and they shall meet in the District and perform such duties as provided by the twelfth article of amendment.

SECTION 2 The Congress shall have power to enforce this article by appropriate legislation.

Amendment XXIV

(Ratified on January 23, 1964)

SECTION 1 The right of citizens of the United States to vote in any primary or other election for President or Vice President, for electors for President or Vice President, or for Senator or Representative in Congress, shall not be denied or abridged by the United States or any State by reason of failure to pay any poll tax or other tax.

SECTION 2 The Congress shall have power to enforce this article by appropriate legislation.

Amendment XXV

(Ratified on February 10, 1967)

SECTION 1 In case of the removal of the President from office or of his death or resignation, the Vice President shall become President.

SECTION 2 Whenever there is a vacancy in the office of the Vice President, the President shall nominate a Vice President who shall take office upon confirmation by a majority vote of both Houses of Congress.

SECTION 3 Whenever the President transmits to the President pro tempore of the Senate and the Speaker of the House of Representatives his written declaration that he is unable to discharge the powers and duties of his office, and until he transmits to them a written declaration to the contrary, such powers and duties shall be discharged by the Vice President as Acting President.

SECTION 4 Whenever the Vice President and a majority of either the principal officers of the executive departments or of such other body as Congress may by law provide, transmit to the President pro tempore of the Senate and the Speaker of the House of Representatives their written declaration that the President is unable to discharge the powers and duties of his office, the Vice President shall immediately assume the powers and duties of the office as Acting President.

Thereafter, when the President transmits to the President pro tempore of the Senate and the Speaker of the House of Representatives his written declaration that no inability exists, he shall resume the powers and duties of his office unless the Vice President and a majority of either the principal officers of the executive department or of such other body as Congress may by law provide, transmit within four days to the President pro tempore of the Senate and the Speaker of the House of Representatives their written declaration that the President is unable to discharge the powers and duties of his office. Thereupon Congress shall decide the issue, assembling within forty-eight hours for that purpose if not in session. If the Congress, within twenty-one days after receipt of the latter written declaration, or, if Congress is not in session, within twenty-one days after Congress is required to assemble, determines by two-thirds vote of both Houses that the President is unable to discharge the powers and duties of his office, the Vice President shall continue to discharge the same as Acting President; otherwise, the President shall resume the powers and duties of his office.

Amendment XXVI

(Ratified on July 1, 1971)

SECTION 1 The right of citizens of the United States, who are eighteen years of age or older, to vote shall not be denied or abridged by the United States or by any State on account of age.

SECTION 2 The Congress shall have power to enforce this article by appropriate legislation.

Amendment XXVII

(Ratified on May 7, 1992)

No law varying the compensation for the services of Senators and Representatives shall take effect until an election of Representatives shall have intervened.

Endnotes

CHAPTER 1

Criminal Justice

1. Roscoe Pound, *Social Control through Law* (New Haven, CT: Yale University Press, 1968), pp. 82,113.
2. Fletcher Martin, "We Don't Want Your Kind," *Atlantic Monthly*, October 1958, pp. 84–85.
3. James Q. Wilson, *Thinking about Crime* (New York: Basic Books, 1975), p. 65.
4. J. J. Preiss and H. J. Ehrlich, *An Examination of Role Theory: The Case of the State Police* (Lincoln: University of Nebraska Press, 1966), p. 137.
5. L. Zeitz, "A New Approach to Solving the Police Dilemma," *Police*, September-October 1970, pp. 58–61.
6. Robert Fogelson, "Reform at a Standstill," in Carl Klockars and Stephen Mastrofski (eds), *Thinking about Police* (New York: McGraw-Hill, 1991), p. 117.
7. American Bar Association, *New Perspectives on Urban Crime* (Washington, DC: ABA Special Committee on Crime Prevention and Control, 1972), p. 1.
8. *The Challenge of Crime in a Free Society: A Report by the President's Commission on Law Enforcement and Administration of Justice* (Washington, DC: U.S. Government Printing Office, 1967), pp. v–xi.
9. Fogelson, "Reform at a Standstill," p. 119.
10. Dae H. Chang and Richard J. Terrill, "An Introduction to the Study of Criminal Justice," in Dae H. Chang and James A. Fagin (eds.), *Introduction to Criminal Justice: Theory and Application*, 2nd ed. (Lake Geneva, WI: Paladin House of the Farley Court of Publishers, 1985), p. 9.
11. Larry Gaines, "Criminal Justice Education Marches On!" in Roslyn Muraskin (ed.), *The Future of Criminal Justice Education* (New York: Criminal Justice Institute, Long Island University, C.W. Post Campus, 1987).
12. Alexander MacLeod, "Britain and Ireland Tag-Team against Terrorism," *The Christian Science Monitor*, September 4, 1998, p. 5.
13. Clifford Krauss, "How to Save Democracy: Throw Away Liberty," *The New York Times on the Web*, September 12, 1999.
14. Ibid.
15. Associated Press, "Terrorist Fear Ends Tours at Underground Defense Site," *Honolulu Advertiser*, January 31, 1999, p. 13.
16. Associated Press, "Free Speech Backed in U.S.—to a Point," *Honolulu Advertiser*, December 16, 1997.
17. "Driver's License Will Mark Sex Offenders," *Honolulu Advertiser*, April 21, 1998, p. A3.
18. Randall E. Stross, "Counterfeit Freedom," *U.S. News & World Report*, October 8, 2001, p. 43.
19. Associated Press, "Web Sites Pulling Some Materials, Citing Attacks-Related Concerns," *Pocono Record*, October 4, 2001, p. A8.
20. Jerry Schwartz, "Ridge Becomes Point Man for U.S. Security," *Pocono Record*, October 7, 2001, p. A1.
21. Robert B. Swift, "Ridge Prepares for Homeland Security Post in Washington," *Pocono Record*, October 4, 2001, p. A4.
22. Ibid.
23. *USA Today*, "Clinton Selects Anti-Terrorism Chief," *Honolulu Advertiser*, May 22, 1998, p. A22.
24. Aristotle, *Politics*, translated by Benjamin Jowett, (Cambridge, MA: MIT Press, 1994–2000) p. 1118.
25. Ron Fournier, "Americans Face World of Sudden Terror," *Pocono Record*, October 8, 2001, p. A1.
26. Peter McWilliams, *Ain't Nobody's Business If You Do* (Los Angeles: Prelude Press, 1993), p. 43.
27. James Davidson and John Batchelor, *The American Nation* (Englewood Cliffs, NJ: Prentice-Hall, 1991), p. 799.
28. Ibid., p. 815.
29. McWilliams, p. 2.
30. Ibid.
31. Clarence Page, "Don't Trash Our Liberty to Save It," *Pocono Record*, October 5, 2001, p. A7.
32. Ibid.
33. Douglas Lederman, "Reno Orders Release of Former Professor Held on Suspicion of Terrorist Involvement," *Chronicle of Higher Education*, December 18, 2000.
34. Aristotle, *Republic*, in Richard McKee (ed.), *The Basic Works of Aristotle* (New York: Random House, 1970).
35. A. Coffey, E. Elderfonso, and W. Hartinger, *Human Relations: Law Enforcement in a Changing Community* (Englewood Cliffs, NJ: Prentice-Hall, 1971), p. 69.
36. Ron Fournier, "Americans Face World of Sudden Terror," *Pocono Record*, October 8, 2001, p. A1.
37. Samuel T. Francis, "The Terrorist: International and Western Europe," *The Heritage Foundation Backgrounder*, April, 1978, p. 2.
38. David Fromkin, "The Strategy of Terrorism," in John D. Elliott and Leslie K. Gibson (eds.) *Contemporary Terrorism* (Gaithersburg, MD: International Association of Chiefs of Police, 1978), pp. 11–24.
39. Albert Parry, *Terrorism: From Robespierre to Arafat* (New York: Vanguard, 1976), p. 39.
40. John Broder, "12 Puerto Ricans in Prison Accept Offer of Clemency," *The New York Times on the Web*, September 8, 1999.
41. Ibid.

42. Dirk Johnson, "Puerto Ricans Clinton Freed Leave Prisons," *The New York Times on the Web*, September 11, 1999.
43. The Associated Press, "Pardoned Militants Return as Heroes," *The New York Times on the Web*, September 11, 1999.
44. Associated Press, "Hundreds Gather to Welcome Pardoned Militants in Puerto Rico," *The New York Times on the Web*, September 12, 1999.
45. National Advisory Commission on Criminal Justice Standards and Goals, *Report of the Task Force on Disorder and Terrorism* (Washington, DC: U.S. Government Printing Office, 1976).
46. *Washington Post*, "Clinton Urges Unity Against Terrorism," *Honolulu Advertiser*, September 22, 1998, p. A7.
47. *Washington Post*, "Study Finds U.S. Lax in Terrorism Defense," *Honolulu Advertiser*, April 24, 1998, p. A12.
48. Associated Press, "More Armed Terrorism to Come, FBI Says," *Honolulu Advertiser*, October 3, 1998, p. A2.
49. Christine Haughney, "Teenagers' Activism Takes a Violent Turn," *Washington Post*, March 27, 2001, p. A3.
50. Sara Hebel, "Earth Liberation Front Takes Credit for Fire at U. of Washington Horticulture Center," *Chronicle of Higher Education*, June 4, 2001.
51. Scott Carlson, "Radical Environmentalists Destroy Genetically Altered Crops at U. of Minnesota," *Chronicle of Higher Education*, February 14, 2000.
52. Robin Wilson, "Extremist Environmental Group Claims Credit for Arson at Michigan State U.," *Chronicle of Higher Education*, January 25, 2000.
53. Associated Press, "Eco-Terrorist Group Takes Credit for Fires at Ski Resort," *Honolulu Advertiser*, October 22, 1998, p. A12.
54. Alex P. Kellogg, "Animal-Rights Group Takes Hundreds of Ducklings from Cornell University Lab," *Chronicle of Higher Education*, May 2, 2001.
55. Bruce Auster, "An Inside Look at Terror Inc.," *U.S. News & World Report*, October 19, 1998.
56. Associated Press, "Alleged Terrorist Leader Calls for Holy War on U.S.," *Honolulu Advertiser*, June 11, 1999, p. 2.
57. Evan Thomas, et al. "The Road to September 11," *Newsweek*, October 1, 2001, p. 40.
58. Ibid., p. 41.
59. Scott Peterson, "Terrorism's Trend Lines," *The Christian Science Monitor*, August 10, 1998, pp. 1, 10.
60. Jonathan S. Landay, "As Radicalism Declines, Terrorism Surges," *The Christian Science Monitor*, August 20, 1998, pp., 1,10.
61. Peter Grier and James N. Thurman, "Age of Anonymous Terrorism," *The Christian Science Monitor*, August 12, 1998, p. 10.
62. *Washington Post*, "FBI Planning Huge Computer Upgrade," *Honolulu Advertiser*, April 6, 2000, p. A6.
63. Douglas Pasternak, "A Welcome Mat for Terrorists," *U.S. News & World Report*, October 8, 2001, p. 31.
64. Reuters, "New York Woman, in Peru, Asks to Switch Jails," *The New York Times on the Web*, June 12, 1999.
65. Associated Press, "Sea Marauders Go for Higher Stakes in Violent Game," *Honolulu Advertiser*, May 24, 1998, p. A23.
66. "Some U.S. Cops on Duty in Bosnia Are Putting Their Worst Foot Forward," *Law Enforcement News*, May 31, 2001, p. 1.
67. Fogelson, "Reform at a Standstill," p. 116.
68. Robert Tanner, "U.S. Security Beefed up as Officials Expect Retaliation," *Pocono Record*, October 8, 2001, p. A3.

CHAPTER 2

An Overview of the Criminal Justice Process

1. Josiah Stamp, *Some Economic Factors in Modern Life* (London: P.S. King & Sons, 1929), p. 258.
2. Thomas Reppetto, *The Blue Parade* (New York: Free Press, 1978), p. viii.
3. The Cleveland Foundation Survey of the Administration of Justice in Cleveland, Ohio, *Criminal Justice in Cleveland* (Cleveland: Cleveland Foundation, 1922).
4. Illinois Association for Criminal Justice, *The Illinois Crime Survey* (Chicago: Illinois Association for Criminal Justice, 1929).
5. Robert Tannehill, "The History of American Law Enforcement," in Dae Chang and James Fagin (eds.), *Introduction to Criminal Justice: Theory and Application*, 2nd ed. (Lake Geneva, WI: Paladin House of the Farley Court of Publishers, 1985), p. 159.
6. Ibid.
7. The UCR also reports data for "all other offenses" and "suspicion." All other offenses include all violations of state or local laws except those listed in Part I and Part II and traffic offenses. Suspicion includes all offenses in which suspects are released without formal charges being filed against them.
8. H.R. 4797, 102nd Cong. 2d Sess. (1992).
9. Jan M. Chaiken and Marcia R. Chaiken, "Drugs and Predatory Crime," in Michael Tonry and James Q. Wilson (eds.), *Drugs and Crime* (Chicago: University of Chicago Press, 1990), pp. 203–204.
10. Elizabeth Shepard, "America's No. 1 Youth Drug Problem... Alcohol," *DRIVEN Magazine*, Fall 2000, http://www.madd.org/news/0,1056,1159,00.html.
11. National Center for Health Statistics, *Annual Report 1994* (Washington, DC: U.S. Government Printing Office, 1995).
12. Ibid.
13. U.S. Department of Justice, Bureau of Justice, *Sourcebook of Criminal Justice Statistics*. Justice system employment and payroll, March 1997, table 1.15.
14. The youngest person executed in the twentieth century was a 13-year-old, electrocuted in Florida in 1927. *National Law Journal* (August 8, 1983): 4.
15. David H. Bayley, *Democratizing the Police Abroad: What to Do and How to Do It*. (Washington, DC: U.S. Department of Justice Office of Justice Programs, 2001), pp. v, 33–50.
16. Thomas F. Adams, *Police Field Operations* (Upper Saddle River, NJ: Prentice Hall, 1998), p. 374.
17. Ibid., pp. 373–376.
18. Bureau of Justice Statistics, *Federal Criminal Cases Proceedings, 1999 with Trends 1982–1999* (Washington, DC: Department of Justice, February 2001), p. 11.
19. Ira J. Silverman and Manuel Vegg, *Corrections: A Comprehensive View* (Minneapolis, MN: West, 1996), pp. 515–518.
20. Bureau of Justice Statistics, *Federal Criminal Cases Proceedings*, p. 12.

CHAPTER 3

Criminal Behavior: Definitions and Causes

1. Tim Dowley (ed.), *Introduction to the History of Christianity* (Minneapolis: Fortress Press, 1995), p. 142.

2. Richard Trask, *The Devil Hath Been Raised* (Danvers: Yeoman Press, 1972).
3. George Burr (ed.), *Narratives of Witchcraft Cases 1648–1706* (New York: Barnes and Noble, 1959).
4. Cesare Lombroso, *Crime: Its Causes and Remedies* (Montclair, NJ: Patterson Smith, 1968).
5. Edwin Sutherland, *Principles of Criminology* (Philadelphia: Lippincott, 1966).
6. Frank Tannenbaum, *Crime and the Community* (Boston: Ginn, 1938).
7. Emile Durkheim, *Suicide* (New York: Free Press, 1951).
8. Kathleen Daly and Meda Chesney-Lind, "Feminism and Criminology," *Justice Quarterly* 5 (December 1988): 497–535.
9. Cesare Bonesana, Marchese Beccaria, *Of Crimes and Punishments* (Philadelphia: Philip H. Nicklin, 1819).
10. Jeremy Bentham, "An Introduction to the Principles of Morals and Legislation," in J. E. Jacoby (ed.), *Classics of Criminology* (Oak Park, IL: Moore, 1979).
11. Orson Squire Fowler and Lorenzo Niles Fowler, *Phrenology: A Practical Guide to Your Head* (New York: Chelsea House, 1980).
12. Richard Louis Dugdale, *The Jukes: A Study in Crime, Pauperism, Disease and Heredity,* 3rd ed. (New York: G. P. Putnam's Sons, 1985).
13. Henry Herbert Goddard, *The Kallikak Family: A Study in the Heredity of Feeblemindedness* (New York: Macmillan, 1912).
14. Lombroso, *Crime.*
15. Ibid.
16. Karl Christiansen, "A Preliminary Study of Criminality Among Twins," in Sarnoff Mednick and Karl O. Christiansen (eds.), *Biosocial Bases of Criminal Behavior* (New York: Simon and Schuster, 1985).
17. Patricia Jacobs, et al. "Aggressive Behavior, Mental Subnormality, and the XYY Male," *Nature* 208 (1965): 1351–1352.
18. Robin Marantz Heing, "Dispelling Menstrual Myths, *New York Times Magazine,* March 7, 1982.
19. C. Halwy and R. E. Buckley, "Food Dyes and Hyperkinetic Children," *Academy Therapy* 10 (1974): 27–32.
20. Sigmund Freud, *A General Introduction to Psychoanalysis* (New York: Boni and Liveright, 1920); Sigmund Freud, *An Outline of Psychoanalysis* (New York: Norton Press, 1963).
21. Adrian Raine, *The Psychopathology of Crime: Criminal Behavior as a Clinical Disorder* (Orlando: Academic Press, 1993).
22. Samuel Yochelson and Stanton E. Samenow, *The Criminal Personality,* 3 vols. (New York: Jason Aronson, 1976).
23. Robert E. Park and Ernest Burgess, *Introduction to the Science of Sociology,* 2nd ed. (Chicago: University of Chicago Press, 1942).
24. Robert E. Park (ed.), *The City* (Chicago: University of Chicago Press, 1925).
25. Clifford R. Shaw, *Juvenile Delinquency in Urban Areas* (Chicago: University of Chicago Press, 1942).
26. Clifford R. Shaw and Henry D. McKay, "Social Factors in Juvenile Delinquency," in Volume II of the *Report of the Causes of Crime, National Commission on Law Observance and Enforcement.* Report no. 13 (Washington, DC: U.S. Government Printing Office, 1931).
27. Oscar Neuman, *Defensible Space* (New York: Macmillan, 1972).
28. Mark H. Moore, Robert C. Trojanowicz, and George L. Kelling, *Crime and Policing* (Washington, DC: U.S. Department of Justice, June 1988).
29. Edwin H. Sutherland, *Principles of Criminology,* 6th ed. (Philadelphia: Lippincott, 1966).
30. Robert L. Burgess and Ronald L. Akers, "A Differential Association-Reinforcement Theory of Criminal Behavior," *Social Problems* 14 (Fall 1996): 128–147.
31. Travis Hirschi, *Causes of Delinquency* (Berkeley: University of California Press, 1969).
32. Francis T. Cullen, *Rethinking Crime and Deviance Theory* (Totowa, NJ: Rowman and Allenheld, 1969).
33. L. Craig Parker, "Rising Crime Rates in the Czech Republic," in Robert Heiner (ed.), *Criminology: A Cross-Cultural Perspective* (Minneapolis: West, 1996), pp. 15–20.
34. Cullen, *Rethinking Crime,* pp. 137–142.
35. Walter C. Reckless, *The Crime Problem,* 4th ed. (New York: Appleton-Century-Crofts, 1961).
36. Gresham Sykes and David Matza, "Techniques of Neutralization: A Theory of Delinquency," *American Sociological Review* 22 (1957): 664–670.
37. Hirschi, *Causes of Delinquency.*
38. Tannenbaum, *Crime and the Community.*
39. Howard Becker, *Outsiders: Studies in the Sociology of Deviance* (New York: Free Press, 1963).
40. Ibid., pp. 8–9.
41. Robert Merton, "Social Structure and Anomie," *American Sociological Review* 3 (1938): 672–682.
42. Robert Merton, *Social Theory and Social Structure* (New York: Free Press, 1968).
43. Richard Cloward and Lloyd Ohlin, *Delinquency and Opportunity: A Theory of Delinquent Gangs* (New York: Free Press, 1960).
44. Marvin Wolfgang and Franco Ferracuti, *The Subculture of Violence: Toward an Integrated Theory in Criminology* (London: Tavistock, 1967).
45. Albert K. Cohen, *Delinquent Boys: The Culture of the Gang* (Glencoe, IL: Free Press, 1958).
46. Ibid.
47. Walter B. Miller, "Lower Class Culture as a Generating Milieu of Gang Delinquency," *Journal of Social Issues* 14 (1958): 5–19.
48. Gary Becker, "Crime and Punishment: An Economic Approach," *Journal of Political Economy* 76 (1968): 169–217.
49. Michael J. Lynch and W. Byron Graves, *A Primer in Radical Criminology,* 2nd ed. (Albany, NY: Harrow and Heston, 1989).
50. Richard Quinney, *The Social Reality of Crime* (Boston: Little, Brown, 1970).
51. Ivan Taylor, Paul Walton, and Jock Young, *The New Criminology* (New York: Harper and Row, 1973).
52. Richard Quinney, *The Crime Problem* (New York: Dodd, Mead, 1970).
53. Austin Turk, *Criminality and the Legal Order* (Chicago: Rand McNally, 1969).
54. Freda Adler, *Sisters in Crime: The Rise of the New Female Criminal* (New York: McGraw-Hill, 1975).
55. Daly and Chesney-Lind, *Feminism and Criminology.*
56. Sally S. Simpson, "Feminist Theory, Crime and Justice," *Criminology* 27 (1989).
57. Gwynn Nettler, *Explaining Crime,* 2nd ed. (New York: McGraw-Hill, 1978).
58. William J. Chambliss, "Toward a Radical Criminology," in D. Kairys (ed.), *The Politics of Law: A Progressive Critique* (New York: Pantheon Books, 1982).

CHAPTER 4

Criminal Law: Control versus Liberty

1. Robert G. Clouse, "Flowering: The Western Church," in Tim Powley (ed.), *Introduction to the History of Christianity* (Minneapolis: Fortress Press, 1977), p. 264.
2. Joel Samaha, *Criminal Law* (Belmont, CA: West/Wadsworth, 1999), p. 3.
3. Arthur J. Crowns Jr., "The Law," in Dae H. Chang and James A. Fagin, *Introduction to Criminal Justice* (Lake Geneva, WI: Paladin House of the Farley Court of Publishers, 1985), pp. 110–111.
4. Jill Knueger, "With Blue Laws Gone, ABC Rethinks City Limits," *Orlando Business Journal,* May 1, 2000.
5. American Law Institute, *Model Penal Code and Commentaries,* vol. 1 (Philadelphia: American Law Institute, 1985) pp. 1–30.
6. U.S. Constitution, Article X, Section 10. Based upon the 17th century philosophy expressed by Lord Edward Coke, "no crime without law; no punishment without law." Jerome Hall, *General Principle of Criminal Law,* 2nd ed. (Indianapolis: Bobbs-Merril, 1960).
7. People ex rel. Lonschein v. Warden, 43 Misc. 2d 109, 250 N.Y. S. 2d 15 (1964).
8. Lonzetta v. New Jersey, 306 U.S. 451, 453 (1939).
9. State v. Metzger, 319 N.W. 2d 459 (Neb. 1982).
10. Ravin v. State, 537 P. 2d 494 (Alaska 1975).
11. Griswold v. Connecticut, 381 U.S. 479 (1965).
12. Stanley v. Georgia, 394 U.S. 557 (1969).
13. Bowers v. Hardwicke, 478 U.S. 186 (1986).
14. Texas v. Johnson, 491 U.S. 397, 109 S.Ct. 2533, 105 L.Ed. 2d 342 (1989).
15. The court has ruled that begging can be regulated in subways. See Young v. New York City Transit Authority, 903 F. 2d 146 (2d Cir. 1990). However, a general prohibition on all forms of begging may be declared too broad when extended to streets. See Loper v. NYPD, 999 F 2d 699 (2d Circ., 1993).
16. Barnes v. Glen Theatre, Inc., et al. 501 U.S. 560, 111 S.Ct. 2456, 115 L.Ed. 2d 504 (1991).
17. Weems v. United States, 217 U.S. 349, 30 S. Ct. 544, 54 L.Ed. 793 (1910).
18. Ibid.
19. Wilkerson v. Utah, 99 U.S. 130 (1878); in re Kemmler, 136 U.S. 436 (1890); Furman v. Georgia, 408 U.S. 238 (1972); Gregg v. Georgia, 428 U.S. 153 (1976).
20. State v. Kraft, N.W. 2d 840 (Minn. 1982).
21. Harmelin v. Michigan, 50 1 U.S. 957, 111 S.Ct. 2680, 115 L.Ed. 2d 836 (1991); Robinson v. California, 370 U.S. 660, 82 S.Ct. 1417, 8 L.Ed. 2d 758 (1962).
22. People v. Decina, 138 N.E. 2d 799 (N.Y. 1956).
23. George v. State, 681 S.W. 2d 43 (Tex. Crim. App. 1984).
24. People v. Oliver, 258 Cal. Rptr. 138 (1989).
25. Michael v. State, 767 P. 2d 193 (Alaska App. 1988).
26. Commonwealth v. Konz, 498 Pa. 639, 450 A 2d 638 (1982).
27. Samaha, *Criminal Law,* p. 104.
28. However, mere constructive possession of a controlled substance in one's home may be sufficient *actus reus* to constitute criminal intent. State v. Cleppe, 96 Wash. 2d 373, 635 P. 2d 435 (1981).
29. Samaha, *Criminal Law,* p. 111.
30. Ibid.
31. State v. Marks, 92 Idaho 368, 442 P. 2d 778 (1968).
32. People v. Hernandez, 61 Cal. 2d 529, 39 Cal. Rptr. 361, 393 P. 2d 673 (1964); People v. Navarette, 221, Neb. 171, 376 N.W. 2d 8 (1985).
33. State v. Furr, 292 N.C. 711, 235 S.E.2d 193 (1977).
34. People v. Lauria, 251 Cal.App.2d 471, 59 Cal.Rptr. 628 (1967).
35. Nos. 94-0978-CR and 94-1980-Cr, Court of Appeals, Wisconsin, 1995.
36. Young v. State, Md. 298, 493 A. 2d 352 (1985).
37. Le Barron v. State, 32 Wis.2d 294, 145 N.W.2d 79 (1966).
38. "The Roush-Sex Defense," *Time,* May 23, 1988, p. 55.
39. Hampton v. United States, 425 U.S. 484 (1976).
40. Sherman v. United States, 356 U.S. 369 (1958).
41. United States v. Calley, 46 C.M.R. 1131 (1973).
42. Montana v. Egelhoff, 116 S. Ct. 2013 (1996).
43. People v. Alderson and Others, 144 Misc. 2d 133, 540 N.Y. S. 2d 948 (N.Y. 1989).
44. The Crown v. Dudley and Stephens, 14 Q. B.D. 273, 286, 15 Cox C. C. 624, 636 (1884).
45. People v. Goetz, 68 N.Y. 2d 96, 506 N.Y. S. 2d 18, 497 N.E. 2d 41 (1986).
46. Lenore E. Walker, *The Battered Woman* (New York: HarperCollins, 1980).
47. Alan Dershowitz, *The Abuse Excuse and Other Cop-Outs, Sob Stories and Evasions of Responsibility* (Boston: Little, Brown, 1994).
48. State v. Mitcheson, 560 P. 2d 1120 (1977).
49. State v. Valentine, 935 P. 2d 1294 (Wash. 1977).
50. Thomas A. Johnson, *Introduction to the Juvenile Justice System* (St. Paul, MN: West, 1975), pp. 1, 3.
51. Samaha, *Criminal Law,* p. 317.
52. M'Naghten's Case, 8 Eng. Rep. 718 (1843).
53. State v. Merrill, 450 N.W. 2d 318 (Minn. 1990).
54. People v. Eulo, 63 N.Y. 2d 34, 482 N.Y. S. 2d 436, 472 N.E. 2d 286 (1984).
55. State v. Minister, 303 Md. 240, 486 A. 2d 1197 (1985).
56. Samaha, *Criminal Law,* pp. 406–410.
57. Casico v. State, 147 Neb. 1075, 25 N.W. 2d 897, 900 (1947); State v. Ely, 114 Wash. 185 (1921)
58. Commonwealth v. Mlinarich, 345 Pa. Super. 269, 498 A.2d 395, 397 (1985).
59. Frank Schmalleger, *Criminal Law Today* (Upper Saddle River, NJ: Prentice-Hall, 1999), pp. 301–302.
60. American Law Institute, *Model Penal Code and Commentaries,* Section 221.1.
61. Samaha, *Criminal Law,* p. 358.
62. Ibid., pp. 335–337

CHAPTER 5

Due Process and Police Procedure

1. Associated Press, "Compromise Proposed to Allow Local Police to Use Radar Guns," *Pocono Record,* September 3, 2001, p. C3
2. Weeks v. United States, 232 U.S. 383 (1914).
3. Mapp v. Ohio, 367 U.S. 643 (1961).
4. Silverthorne Lumber Co. v. United States, 251 U.S. 385 (1920).
5. Wolf v. Colorado, 338 U.S. 25 (1949).
6. Mapp v. Ohio.
7. Chimel v. California, 395 U.S. 752 (1969).
8. Harris v. United States, 390 U.S. 234 (1968).
9. Horton v. California, 110 S.Ct. 2301 47 CrL. 2135 (1990).

10. Arizona v. Hicks, 107 S.Ct. 1149 (1987).
11. Horten v. California, 1990.
12. Florida v. Jimeno, 111 S.Ct.1801 (1991).
13. Carroll v. United States, 267 U.S. 132 (1925).
14. Ormelas v. United States, 116 S.Ct. 1657 L.Ed. 2d 911 (1996).
15. Colorado v. Bertive, 479 U.S. 367, 107 S.Ct. 741 (1987).
16. Terry v. Ohio, 3129 U.S. 1 (1968).
17. Minnesota v. Dickerson, 113 S.Ct. 2130, 124 L.Ed. 2d 334 (1993).
18. "New Jersey: Ground-zero in Racial Profiling Uproar," *Law Enforcement News,* December 15/31, 2000, p. 11.
19. Marcia Davis, "Traffic Violation," *Emerge,* June 1999, p. 42.
20. *Washington Post,* "Police Abuse of Belt Law Feared," *Honolulu Advertiser,* December 12, 1998, p. A9.
21. Associated Press, "Searches of Blacks Racial, Suit Claims," *Honolulu Advertiser,* June 6, 1998, p. A19.
22. Davis, "Traffic Violation."
23. Mark Hosenball, "It Is Not the Act of a Few Bad Apples," *Newsweek,* May 17, 1999, p. 34.
24. Although a search warrant is required to conduct such a search, the court has ruled that a suspect may be x-rayed and detained until the subject passes the swallowed objects. See United States v. Montoya de Hernandez, 473 U.S. 531, 105 S.Ct. 3304 (1985).
25. "New Jersey: Ground-zero in Racial Profiling Uproar."
26. Ibid.
27. Hosenball, "It's Not the Act."
28. Ibid.
29. New Jersey: Ground-zero in Racial Profiling Uproar."
30. Associated Press, "Bias Claims Real in New Jersey Traffic Stops," *Honolulu Advertiser,* April 21, 1999, p. A3.
31. Ibid.
32. "Lawsuit Filed for Traffic Stop," *Honolulu Advertiser,* May 19, 1999, p. A3.
33. "Facing Up to an Unflattering Profile," *Law Enforcement News,* December 15/31, 2000, pp. 10–11.
34. Aguilar v. Texas, 378 U.S. 108 (1964).
35. New York v. Quarles, 104 S.Ct. 2626, 81 L.Ed. 2d 550 (1984).
36. Florida v. Bostick, 111 S.Ct. 2382 (1991).
37. United States v. Martinez-Fuerte, 428 U.S. 543 (1976).
38. Tennessee v. Garner, 471 U.S. 1 (1985).
39. Terry R. Sparher and David J. Goacopassi, "Memphis Revisited: A Reexamination of Police Shootings after the Garner Decision," *Justice Quarterly,* 9 (1992): 211–225.
40. Graham v. Connor, 490 U.S. 386, 396–397 (1989).
41. Illinois v. Gates, 416 U.S. 318 (1982).
42. United States v. Leon, 468 U.S. 897, 104 S.Ct. 3405, 82 L.Ed. 2d 677, 52 U.S.L.W. 5515 (1984); Massachusetts v. Sheppard, 104 S.Ct. 3424 (1984).
43. Olmstead v. United States, 277 U.S. 438 (1928).
44. Katz v. United States, 389 U.S. 347 (1967).
45. Brown v. Mississippi, 297 U.S. 278 (1936).
46. Kenneth J. Peak, *Policing in America* (Saddle River, NJ: Prentice-Hall, 1993), p. 283.
47. Ashcraft v. Tennessee, 322, U.S. 143 (1944).
48. Donald A. Dripps, "Forward: Against Police Interrogation and the Priviledge against Self-Incrimination," *Journal of Criminal Law and Criminology,* 78 (1988): 701.
49. Leyra v. Denno, 347 U.S. 556 (1954).
50. Kevin Johnson and Gary Fields, "Jewell Investigation Unmasks FBI 'Tricks'," *USA Today,* April 9, 1997, p. 13A
51. United States v. Karo, 468 U.S. 705 (1984).
52. United States v. Dionisio, 410 U.S. 1 (1973).
53. United States v. Wade, 388 U.S. 218 (1067); Kirby v. Illinois, 406 U.S. 682 (1972); Foster v. California, 394 U.S. 1 (1973).
54. Gideon v. Wainwright, 372 U.S. 335 (1963).
55. Argersinger v. Hamlin, 407 U.S. 25 (1972).
56. In re Gault, 387 U.S. 1 (1967).
57. Escobedo v. Illinois, 378 U.S. 478 (1964).
58. Miranda v. Arizona, 384 U.S. 436 (1966).
59. Jacobsen v. United States, 112 S.Ct. 1535 (1992).
60. Michael Kinsley, "When Is Racial Profiling Okay?" *Law Enforcement News,* October 15, 2001, p. 9.
61. Thomas A. Reppetto, *The Blue Parade* (New York: Free Press, 1978), p. 252.
62. Robert M. Fogelson, *Big City Police* (Cambridge, MA: Harvard University Press, 1977), pp. 179, 283–284.
63. James A. Fagin, "Police Review Boards," in Jay M. Shafritz (ed.), *International Encyclopedia of Public Policy and Administration* (Boulder, CO: Westview Press, 1998), p. 1683.
64. Ibid., p. 1683.
65. Wayne A. Kerstetter, "Who Disciplines the Police? Who Should?" in W. A. Geller (ed.), *Police Leadership in America* (Chicago: American Bar Association, 1985), pp. 149–182.
66. Fagin, "Police Review Boards," p. 1683.
67. Ibid., p. 1682.
68. Peak, "Policing in America," p. 325.
69. Ibid., p. 326.
70. Bivens v. Six Unknown Federal Agents, 403 U.S. 388 (1971).
71. F.D.I.C. v. Meyer, 510 U.S. 471 (1994).
72. Fagin, "Police Review Boards," p. 1682.

CHAPTER 6

Historical Development of American Policing

1. Thomas A. Reppetto, *The Blue Parade* (New York: Free Press, 1978), p. 17.
2. Ibid., p. 300.
3. James Q. Wilson, *Varieties of Police Behavior* (Cambridge, MA: Harvard University Press, 1968), pp. 16–17.
4. James Hernandez Jr., *The Custer Syndrome* (Salem, WI: Sheffield, 1989) p. 133.
5. Ronald L. Tannehill, "The History of American Law Enforcement," in Dae H. Chang and James A. Fagin (eds.), *Introduction to Criminal Justice: Theory and Application,* 2nd ed. (Lake Geneva, WI: Paladin House of the Farley Court of Publishers, 1985), pp. 151–168.
6. David Ascoli, *The Queen's Peace: The Origins and Development of the Metropolitan Police 1829–1979* (London: Hamish Hamilton, 1979), p. 1.
7. Ibid.
8. Ibid., pp. 12–13.
9. Ibid., p. 11.
10. W. Ward Gasque, "The Challenge to Faith," in Tim Dowley (ed.), *Introduction to the History of Christianity* (Minneapolis: Fortress Press, 1995), p. 82.
11. Graham Webster, *The Roman Imperial Army of the First and Second Centuries A.D.,* 3rd ed. (Norman: University of Oklahoma Press, 1998).
12. Ibid.
13. Ibid.

14. Barbara A. Hanawalt, *The Ties That Bound: Peasant Families in Medieval England* (London: Oxford University Press, 1986).
15. Susan Reynolds, *Fiefs and Vassals: The Medieval Evidence Reinterpreted* (London: Oxford University Press, 1994).
16. Ascoli, *The Queen's Peace,* pp. 12–13.
17. Ibid., pp. 13–14.
18. P. Aries and G. Daby (eds.), *A History of Private Lives II: Revelations of the Medieval World* (Cambridge, MA: Harvard University Press, 1988); J. T. Rosenthal, *Patriarchy and Families of Privilege in Fifteenth Century England* (Philadelphia: University of Pennsylvania Press, 1991).
19. M. M. Sheehan, *Marriage, Family and Law in Medieval Europe: Collected Studies* (North York, ONT: University of Toronto Press, 1995).
20. Ascoli, *The Queen's Peace,* p. 14.
21. Bernal D. Cantwell, *One Hundred Twenty-Five Years of Service: A History of the United States Marshal in the District of Kansas* (Unpublished thesis, Wichita State University, 1976), pp. 19, 41–42.
22. Tannehill, *The History of American Law Enforcement,* p. 155.
23. Albert Loan, "Institutional Bases of the Spontaneous Order: Surety and Assurance," *Humane Studies Review,* 7 (Winter 1991/1992).
24. Ibid.
25. Helena Chew and Mardin Weinbaum (eds.), "The London Eyre of 1244," *London Record Society,* 6 (1970): 24.
26. Ibid.
27. Ibid.
28. Ibid.
29. Ibid.
30. Ascoli, *The Queen's Peace,* p. 30. In 1735, the population of London was about 650,000 and the consumption of gin was 5,500,000 gallons. The Gin Act of 1736 resulted in widespread riots under the slogan, "No gin, no King!"
31. J. J. Tobias, *Crime and Police in England, 1700–1900* (Dublin: McMillan, 1979), p. 43.
32. Ibid., p. 41.
33. Ascoli, *The Queen's Peace,* pp. 16–17.
34. Ibid., p. 48.
35. Ibid., p. 55.
36. Ibid., p. 46.
37. Ibid., p. 66.
38. Ibid., p. 75.
39. Ibid., pp. 82, 87.
40. Ibid., p. 89.
41. Ibid., p. 86.
42. Ibid., p. 93.
43. David Taylor, *The New Police in Nineteenth-century England: Crime, Conflict and Control* (Manchester: Manchester University Press, 1997), pp. 44–55.
44. Dale's law required Jamestown settlers to work or they would not receive food and required strict observance of the rules of the community. Violators could be put to death.
45. The Plymouth Compact, also known as the Mayflower Compact, was a document signed by the Pilgrim settlers, promising to abide by the rules of the community and to work for the common good of the community.
46. Reppetto, *The Blue Parade,* p. 41.
47. Ibid.
48. Ibid., p. 45.
49. Ibid., p. 4.
50. The Chicago School claimed that crime was associated with neighborhoods in which the poor lived. Merton's theory focused on the desire to achieve economic rewards and stated that crime was a way to achieve economic gain.
51. Samuel Walker, *A Critical History of Police Reform* (Lexington, MA: Lexington Books, 1997), p. 9.
52. Hernandez, *The Custer Syndrome,* p. 31.
53. Larry D. Ball, *The United States Marshals of New Mexico and Arizona Territories, 1846–1912* (Albuquerque: University of New Mexico Press, 1978), pp. 108–118; Herbert A. Johnson, *History of Criminal Justice* (Cincinnati: Anderson, 1988), p. 92.
54. William C. Cunningham, John J. Strauchs, and Clifford W. Van Meter, *The Hallcrest Report II: Private Security Trends 1970–2000* (McLean, VA: Hallcrest System, 1990).
55. Hubert Williams and Patrick V. Murphy, "The Evolving Strategies of Police: A Minority View," (Washington, DC: National Institute of Justice, January 1990), p. 3.
56. Ibid., p. 5.
57. Ibid., p. 4.
58. Ibid.
59. Ibid., p. 3.
60. Ibid., p. 7.
61. Ibid., p. 5.
62. Ibid., p. 7.
63. State laws in southern states prohibiting interracial marriages remained on the books and were enforced by some states well into the twentieth century.
64. Williams and Murphy, "The Evolving Strategies of Police," p. 2.
65. Ibid.
66. Ibid.
67. Ibid., p. 9.
68. Following the Civil War, southern states sought to limit the right of freed slaves to vote by instituting poll taxes (voters were required to pay a fee each time they voted), literacy tests, grandfather clauses (exempted voters from fees and requirements if their grandfather voted), and Jim Crow laws. Jim Crow laws separated blacks and whites in schools, churches, restaurants, theaters, trains, street cars, hospitals, beaches, and cemeteries. When blacks challenged segregation, the Supreme Court declared in *Plessy v. Ferguson* that segregation was permitted as long as separate facilities for blacks and whites were equal. Despite obvious inequalities in facilities, *Plessy v. Ferguson* legally sanctioned the practice of segregation.
69. Williams and Murphy, "The Evolving Strategies of Police," p. 9.
70. Walker, *A Critical History of Police Reform,* pp. 139–166.
71. Hernandez, *The Custer Syndrome,* p. 33.
72. Ibid.
73. Reppetto, *The Blue Parade,* pp. 55–57.
74. Ibid., p. 243.
75. Ibid., p. 245.
76. Ibid., p. 247.
77. Ibid., pp. 244, 248.
78. Kenneth J. Peak, *Policing America: Methods, Issues, Challenges* (Upper Saddle River, NJ: Prentice-Hall, 1997), pp. 26–27.
79. Ibid.
80. Cantwell, *One Hundred Twenty-Five Years of Service,* p. 3.
81. Ibid., pp. 19, 41–42.
82. James Fagin, "Contemporary Law Enforcement," in Chang and Fagin, *Introduction to Criminal Justice,* p. 175.

CHAPTER 7

Roles and Functions of the Police

1. Bureau of Justice Statistics, *Police Departments, 1999* (Washington, DC: U.S. Department of Justice, May 2001), p. iii.
2. Bureau of Justice Statistics, *Census of State Law Enforcement Agencies, 1996* (Washington, DC: U.S. Department of Justice, June 1998).
3. Bureau of Justice Statistics, *Federal Law Enforcement Officers, 2000* (Washington, DC: U.S. Department of Justice, July 2001).
4. Bureau of Justice Statistics, *Sheriffs' Offices, 1999* (Washington, DC: U.S. Department of Justice, May 2001).
5. James Fagin, "Authority," in Jay M. Shafritz (ed.), *International Encyclopedia of Public Policy and Administration* (Boulder, CO: Westview Press, 1998), p. 163.
6. Bureau of Justice Statistics, *Sheriffs' Offices, 1999.*
7. Bureau of Justice Statistics, *Law Enforcement Management and Administrative Statistics, 1997: Data for Individual State and Local Agencies with 100 or More Officers* (Washington, DC: U.S. Department of Justice, April 1999).
8. Vincent T. Bugliosi, in *Helter Skelter* (New York: Doubleday Dell, 1995), describes how lack of interagency cooperation between the Los Angeles Police Department and the Los Angeles Sheriff's Department hindered the investigation of the murders committed by the followers of Charles Manson.
9. Bureau of Justice Statistics, *Local Police Departments, 1999.*
10. Ibid.
11. Charles R. Swanson, Leonard Territo, and Robert W. Taylor, *Police Administration: Structures, Processes, and Behavior* (Upper Saddle River, NJ: Prentice-Hall, 1998), pp. 290–293.
12. Fagin, "Authority," p. 163.
13. Bureau of Justice Statistics, *Law Enforcement Management and Administrative Statistics, 1997,* pp. 91–120.
14. Jack Greene and Carl B. Klockars, "What Police Do," in Carl B. Klockars and Stephen D. Mastrofski (eds.), *Thinking about Police: Contemporary Readings* (New York: McGraw-Hill, 1991), p. 297.
15. Swanson, Territo, and Taylor, pp. 160–161.
16. For a description of campus police and their responsibilities, see Bureau of Justice Statistics, *Campus Law Enforcement Agencies, 1995* (Washington, DC: U.S. Department of Justice, December 1996).
17. Kenneth Peak, *Policing America: Methods, Issues, Challenges* (Upper Saddle River, NJ: Prentice-Hall, 1997), pp. 64–65.
18. *Report of the Executive Committee for Indian County Law Enforcement Improvements: Final Report to the Attorney General and the Secretary of the Interior* (Washington, DC: U.S. Department of Justice, 1997), pp. 2–3. The primary agencies having jurisdiction on Indian reservations are the Bureau of Indian Affairs Office of Law Enforcement Services and the Federal Bureau of Investigation. The U.S. government has a unique relationship with Indian reservations. Indian reservations were created by treaties, and the U.S. government has a trust responsibility to ensure the sovereignty of each tribal government (25 U.S.C Section 3601).
19. Ibid., p. v.
20. Bureau of Justice Statistics, *American Indians and Crime* (Washington, DC: U.S. Department of Justice, February 1999), p. v.
21. Ibid., p. 2.
22. "Tribal, Municipal Police Haggle over Arrest Power," *Law Enforcement News* (John Jay College of Criminal Justice, vol. XXV, no. 522), November 30, 1999, p. 6. The authority of the Indian tribal police is defined by 18 U.S.C. Section 1152-1153, 18 U.S.C. Section 1162 (P.L. 280) and the Major Crimes Act of 1994.
23. C. Reith, *A Short History of the Police* (Oxford: Oxford University Press, 1948).
24. Richard J. Terrill, *World Criminal Justice Systems: A Survey* (Cincinnati, OH: Anderson, 1987), pp. 103–169.
25. "Feds Pour in Millions to Aid Tribal Justice," *Law Enforcement News* (John Jay College of Criminal Justice, vol. XXV, no. 522), November 30, 1999, p. 6.
26. See http://www.usdoj.gov/otj/otjmiss.htm for further information about the Office of Tribal Justice.
27. *Report of the Executive Committee for Indian County Law Enforcement Improvements,* p. 2.
28. See http://www.albany.edu/sourcebook/1995/pdf/t171.pdf.
29. Samuel Walker, *Popular Justice: A History of American Criminal Justice* (New York: Oxford University Press, 1980), p. 191.
30. Ibid., p. 192.
31. Ibid.
32. "Cyber Crime," *Business Week,* February 21, 2000, p. 39; "FBI Will Supervise High-Tech Crime Staff," *Honolulu Advertiser,* February 29, 1988, p. A3.
33. Neil A. Lewis, "Ashcroft Permits F.B.I. to Monitor Internet and Public Activities," *New York Times on the Web,* http://www.nytimes.com. June 5, 2002.
34. Don Van Natta Jr. and David Johnson, "Wary of Risk, Slow to Adapt, F.B.I. Stumbles in Terror War," *New York Times on the Web,* http://www.nytimes.com. June 2, 2002.
35. Ibid.
36. Associated Press, "F.B.I. Chief Tells Congress His Agency Needs More Resources," *New York Times on the Web,* http://www.nytimes.com. June 6, 2002.
37. Robert S. Mueller III, "Remarks prepared for delivery by Robert S. Mueller III, Director, Federal Bureau of Investigation at a Press Availability on the FBI's Reorganization May 29, 2002. http://www.fbi.gov. June 8, 2002.
38. FBI Jobs, http://www.fbi.gov. June 10, 2002.
39. See http://www.atf.treas.gov/about/hist.htm for a history of the Bureau of Alcohol, Tobacco and Firearms.
40. See http://www.usdoj.gov/dea/pubs/briefing/1_2.htm for a discussion of the history of the Drug Enforcement Agency.

CHAPTER 8

Police Professionalism and the Community

1. From 1987 to 1997, minority representation among local police officers increased from 14.5% to 21.5%. In sheriffs' offices, minorities accounted for 19% of sworn personnel in 1997 compared with 13.4% 10 years earlier. In 1987, 7.6% of local law enforcement officers were women. In 1997, 15% of sheriff officers, 11% of county officers, and 9% of municipal officers were women. See Brian Reaves, *Profile of State and Local Law Enforcement Agencies, 1987* (Washington, DC: U.S. Department of Justice, March 1989), and Brian Reaves, *Law Enforcement Management and Administrative Statistics, 1997* (Washington, DC: U.S. Department of Justice, April 1999), p. xiii.
2. Title VII of the Civil Rights Act of 1964 as amended in 1972 required that employment screening be based on bona fide occupational requirements (BFOQ). This requirement was further

defined in Griggs v. Duke Power Company (1971), 401 U.S. 424; Albemark Paper Company v. Moody (1975), 422 U.S. 405; and Washington v. Davis (1979), 426 U.S. 299.

3. Brian A. Reaves and Andrew L. Goldberg, *Law Enforcement Management and Administrative Statistics, 1997: Data for Individual State and Local Agencies with 100 or More Officers* (Washington, DC: U.S. Department of Justice, April 1999), pp. 31–40.
4. Bureau of Justice Statistics (BJS), *State and Local Law Enforcement Statistics,* http://www.ojp.usdoj.gov/bjs/sandle.htm/ December 18, 2001.
5. Reaves and Goldberg, *Law Enforcement Management,* pp. 31–40.
6. Ibid., pp. 41–50.
7. Herman Goldstein, *Policing a Free Society* (Cambridge, MA: Ballinger, 1977), pp. 283–284.
8. Robert E. Worden, "A Badge and a Baccalaureate: Policies, Hypotheses and Further Evidence," *Justice Quarterly,* 7 (September 1990): 565–592.
9. Reaves and Goldberg, *Law Enforcement Management,* pp. 41–50.
10. National Advisory Commission on Criminal Justice Standards and Goals, *Police* (Washington, DC: Government Printing Office, 1973), p. 369.
11. As of June 1997, local and state law enforcement agencies required the following minimum level of education to apply for a position as a police agent: 78% require a minimum of a high school diploma, 13% require some college, 7% require a 2-year college degree, and 2% require a 4-year college degree. See Reaves and Goldberg, *Law Enforcement Management,* p. xiv.
12. Kenneth J. Peak, *Policing America* (Upper Saddle River, NJ: Prentice-Hall, 1997), p. 86.
13. Matthew J. Hickman and Brian A. Reaves, *Local Police Departments, 1999* (Washington, DC: U.S. Department of Justice, May 2001), pp. 17–18.
14. Reaves and Goldberg, *Law Enforcement Management,* pp. 61–70.
15. Robert M. Fogelson, "Reform at a Standstill," in Carl B. Klockars and Stephen D. Mastrofski (eds.), *Thinking about Police: Contemporary Reading* (New York: McGraw-Hill, 1991), p. 116.
16. Robert Trojanowicz and T. Nicholson, "A Comparison of Behavioral Styles of College Graduate Police Officers and Non-college Going Police Officers," *The Police Chief,* 43 (August 1976): 56–59; BJS, *State and Local Law Enforcement Statistics.*
17. Judith A. Lewis, Michael D. Lewis, Federico Souflée, Jr., and Thomas Packard, *Management of Human Services Programs,* 3rd ed. (Pacific Grove, CA: Brooks/Cole, 2001).
18. Charles R. Swanson, Leonard Territo, and Robert W. Taylor, *Police Administration: Structures, Processes, and Behavior* (Upper Saddle River, NJ: Prentice-Hall, 1998), p. 270.
19. Peak, *Policing America,* p. 75.
20. PL 104-208. An amendment to Section 921(a) of Title 18 U.S.C. Also known as the Lautenberg Amendment.
21. Jacob R. Clark, "Police Careers May Take a Beating from Fed Domestic-Violence Law," *Law Enforcement News,* 23 (February 14, 1997): 1.
22. Reaves and Goldberg, *Law Enforcement Management,* p. xiii.
23. Ibid.
24. George E. Hargrave and Deirdre Hiatt, "Law Enforcement Selection with the Interview, MMPI, and CPI: A Study of Reliability and Validity," *Journal of Police Science and Administration, 15* (1987): 110–117.
25. Reaves and Goldberg, *Law Enforcement Management,* pp. xiv, 41–50.
26. Ibid.
27. John J. Broderick, *Police in a Time of Change* (Prospect Heights, IL: Waveland Press, 1987), p. 215.
28. Peak, *Policing America,* pp. 78–84.
29. Reaves and Goldberg, *Law Enforcement Management,* pp. 41–50.
30. *Post Administration Manual* (Sacramento, CA: State of California Department of Justice, July 1995).
31. Thomas E. Mahoney, *Organizational Socialization and Police Cadet Attitudes in Authoritarian-Based Police Academy Environment,* Unpublished dissertation, School of Organizational Management, Department of Public Administration, University of La Verne, CA, 1996.
32. Reaves and Goldberg, *Law Enforcement Management,* pp. 41–50.
33. Peak, *Policing America,* pp. 84–85.
34. Egon Bittner, "Popular Conceptions about the Character of Police Work," in Carl B. Klockars and Stephen D. Mastrofski (eds.), *Thinking about Police: Contemporary Readings* (New York: McGraw-Hill, 1991), pp. 35–51.
35. James Q. Wilson, *Varieties of Police Behavior: The Management of Law and Order in Eight Communities* (Cambridge, MA: Harvard University Press, 1968).
36. Ibid.
37. Ibid.
38. Ibid.
39. James Hernandez, *The Custer Syndrome* (Salem, WI: Sheffield, 1989), p. 134.
40. Ibid.
41. Ibid., p. 165.
42. Ibid., pp. 132–133.
43. Ibid., p. 165.
44. George Kelling and Mark H. Moore, "The Evolving Strategy of Policing," *Perspectives on Policing,* No. 4 (Washington, DC: National Institute of Justice and Harvard University, November 1988), p. 2.
45. Ibid.
46. Ibid.
47. Ibid., p. 8.
48. Ibid., p. 6.
49. Ibid.
50. Ibid., p. 7.
51. Ibid., p. 5.
52. Fogelson, "Reform at a Standstill," pp. 117–119.
53. Ibid.
54. Mark H. Moore and Robert C. Trojanowicz, "Corporate Strategies for Policing," *Perspectives on Policing,* No. 6 (Washington, DC: National Institute of Justice, November 1988).
55. George Kelling, "Police and Communities: The Quiet Revolution," *Perspectives on Policing,* No. 1 (Washington, DC: National Institute of Justice and Harvard University, June 1988).
56. Swanson et al., *Police Administration,* p. 13.
57. Kelling and Moore, "The Evolving Strategy of Policing," p. 14.
58. As of June 1997, 68% of local police agencies reported they had a community policing unit with personnel assigned full time, and 76% reported they had full-time community policing officers. See Reaves and Goldberg, *Law Enforcement Management,* p. 41–50.
59. Herman Goldstein, *The New Policing: Confronting Complexity* (Washington, DC: National Institute of Justice, December 1993), p. 1.
60. Kelling and Moore, "The Evolving Strategy of Policing," p. 1

61. George L. Kelling and William J. Bratton, "Implementing Community Policing: The Administrative Problem," *Perspectives on Policing,* No. 17 (Washington, DC: National Institute of Justice and Harvard University, July 1993), p. 2.
62. Goldstein, *The New Policing,* p. 4.
63. Lee P. Brown, "Community Policing: A Practical Guide for Police Officials," *Perspectives on Policing,* No. 12 (Washington, DC: National Institute of Justice and Harvard University, September 1989).
64. Kelling and Bratton, "Implementing Community Policing," p. 2.
65. "Jaywalking Ban," *Honolulu Advertiser,* August 8, 1998, p. E1.
66. Ibid.
67. Ibid.
68. Edwin Meese III, "Community Policing and the Police Officer," *Perspectives on Policing,* No. 15 (Washington, DC: National Institute of Justice and Harvard University, January 1993).
69. Ibid., p. 2.
70. William Spelman and John E. Eck, *Problem-Oriented Policing* (Washington, DC: National Institute of Justice, January 1987), p. 2.
71. Ibid., p. 3.
72. Ibid., p. 4.
73. Ibid., pp. 6–7.
74. Ibid.
75. William Spelman and John E. Eck, *Newport News Tests Problem-Oriented Policing* (Washington, DC: National Institute of Justice, February 1987).
76. David M. Kennedy, "The Strategic Management of Police Resources," *Perspectives on Policing,* No. 14 (Washington, DC: National Institute of Justice and Harvard University, January 1993).
77. Ibid., p. 5.
78. Hernandez, *The Custer Syndrome,* p. 184.
79. Peak, *Policing America,* pp. 402–403.
80. Kennedy, "The Strategic Management of Police Resources."
81. Meese, "Community Policing and the Police Officer," p. 5.
82. A 1995 survey of 2,214 state and local police agencies indicated that 48% of police chiefs and sheriffs agreed that implementation of community policing would require major changes in organizational policies, and 56% anticipated that rank-and-file employees would resist such a change. National Institute of Justice, *Community Policing Strategies* (Washington, DC: National Institute of Justice, November 1995), p. 1.
83. Hernandez, *The Custer Syndrome,* p. 184.
84. Ibid., p. 185.
85. National Institute of Justice, *Community Policing Strategies,* p. 1.
86. Hubert William and Patrick V. Murphy, "The Evolving Strategy of Police: A Minority View," *Perspectives on Policing,* No. 13 (Washington, DC: National Institute of Justice and Harvard University, January 1990), pp. 2, 12.
87. Ibid., p. 12.
88. George L. Kelling and James K. Stewart, "Neighborhoods and Police: The Maintenance of Civil Authority," *Perspectives on Policing,* No. 10 (Washington, DC: National Institute of Justice and Harvard University, May 1989), p. 7.
89. George L. Kelling, *What Works—Research and the Public* (Washington, DC: National Institute of Justice, 1988), p. 2.
90. Robert Wasserman and Mark H. Moore, "Values in Policing," *Perspectives on Policing,* No. 8 (Washington, DC: National Institute of Justice and Harvard University, November 1988), p. 1.
91. Ibid., p. 3.
92. Swanson et al., *Police Administration,* p. 204.
93. The following percentages of departments have policies and procedures addressing deadly force (100%), employee conduct and appearance (99%), less-than-lethal force (97%), juveniles (97%), citizen complaints (96%), domestic disputes (96%), and off-duty employment (95%). See Reaves and Goldberg, *Law Enforcement Management,* p. xiv.
94. Swanson et al., *Police Administration,* pp. 394–430.
95. Ibid., p. 38.
96. Samuel Walker, *Popular Justice: A History of American Criminal Justice* (New York: Oxford University Press, 1980), pp. 166–169.
97. Ronald L. Miller and James Fagin, "Police Unionism," *Michigan Police Officer,* 4 (Autumn 1976): 9–15.
98. Ibid.
99. Reaves and Goldberg, *Law Enforcement Management,* pp. 61–70.
100. Swanson et al., *Police Administration,* pp. 336–340.

CHAPTER 9
The Court System

1. George Strawley, "Race Tests Limits of Rules against Candidates Debating Issues," *Pocono Record,* October 28, 2001, pp. 1, 3A.
2. Marbury v. Madison, 1 Cranch 137 (1803).
3. Law Day speech to the San Antonio Bar Association, May 1, 1998.
4. *Sourcebook of Criminal Justice Statistics Online,* http://www.albany.edu/sourcebook/1995/pdf/t532.pdf, Table 5.32, Defendants Disposed of in U.S. District Courts.
5. Ibid.
6. *Sourcebook of Criminal Justice Statistics Online,* http://www.albany.edu/sourcebook/1995/pdf/t575.pdf, Table 5.75, Petitions for Review on Writ of Certiorari to the U.S. Supreme Court Filed, Terminated, and Pending, 2000.
7. Ibid.
8. *Sourcebook of Criminal Justice Statistics Online,* http://www.albany.edu/sourcebook/1995/pdf/t573.pdf, Table 5.73, Activities of the U.S. Supreme Court.
9. *Sourcebook of Criminal Justice Statistics Online,* http://www.albany.edu/sourcebook/1995/pdf/t576.pdf, Table 5.76, U.S. Supreme Court Cases Argued and Decided on Merits, 1982–1999.
10. Matthew R. Durose et al., *Felony Sentences in State Courts, 1998* (Washington, DC: U.S. Department of Justice Office of Justice Programs, 2001), p. 2.
11. *Sourcebook of Criminal Justice Statistics Online,* http://www.albany.edu/sourcebook/1995/pdf/t227.pdf, Table 2.27, Respondents' Ratings of the Honesty and Ethical Standards of Judges, 2000.
12. *Sourcebook of Criminal Justice Statistics Online,* http://www.albany.edu/sourcebook/1995/pdf/t223.pdf, Table 2.23, Respondents' Ratings of the Honesty and Ethical Standards of Lawyers, 1976–2000.
13. *Sourcebook of Criminal Justice Statistics Online,* http://www.albany.edu/sourcebook/1995/pdf/t224.pdf, Table 2.24, Respondents' Ratings of the Honesty and Ethical Standards of Lawyers, 2000.
14. Arthur Crowns Jr., "The Law: A Catalyst Holding Together Many Systems of Criminal Justice," in Dae H. Chang and James Fagin (eds.), *Introduction to Criminal Justice: Theory and*

Application, 2nd ed. (Lake Geneva, WI: Paladin House of the Farley Court of Publishers, 1985), p. 108.

15. Ken Kobayashi, "Few Clients Drop Arrested Lawyer," *Honolulu Advertiser,* January 6, 1998; Advertiser Staff, "Lawyer Who Faces Charges Taken Off Case," *Honolulu Advertiser,* January 10, 1998, p. 3.
16. There are some exceptions to this practice. Some state law schools teach the laws of that state rather than the model penal code, and students who graduate in good standing from law school are qualified to be licensed to practice law without taking the state bar examination. Some adjoining states have reciprocal agreements whereby a person licensed to practice law in one state can qualify to practice law in the adjoining state by means other than passing the state's bar examination.
17. Richard J. Terrill, *World Criminal Justice Systems: A Survey* (Cincinnati, OH: Anderson, 1984), pp. 24–38.
18. *Sourcebook of Criminal Justice Statistics Online,* http://www.albany.edu/sourcebook/1995/pdf/t166.pdf, Table 1.66, Annual Salaries of Federal Judges, 2001.
19. David Rottman et al., *State Court Organization 1998* (Washington, DC: U.S. Department of Justice Office of Justice Programs, Bureau of Justice Statistics, 2000), p. ix.
20. Ibid.
21. Ibid.
22. Turney v. Ohio, 480, 485n103; Turney v. Ohio, 308, 331n8.
23. The Cleveland Foundation, *Criminal Justice in Cleveland* (Cleveland, OH: The Cleveland Foundation, 1922), pp. 627–641; H. Ted Rubin, *The Felony Processing System, Cuyahaga County, Ohio* (Denver: Institute for Court Management, 1971), pp. 16–17.
24. *Sourcebook of Criminal Justice Statistics Online,* http://www.albany.edu/sourcebook/1995/pdf/t2103.pdf, Table 2.103, College Freshmen Reporting There Is Too Much Concern in the Courts for the Rights of Criminals, 1969–2000.

CHAPTER 10

Courtroom Participants and the Trial

1. Bail is not required in a civil trial, as the court has no jurisdiction to incarcerate either party of a civil suit prior to trial.
2. Hudson v. Parker, 156 U.S. 277 (1895).
3. McKane v. Durston, 153 U.S. 684 (1894).
4. Stack v. Boyle, 342 U.S. 1 (1951).
5. Carlson v. Landon, 342 U.S. 524 (1952); U.S. v. Salerno, 55 U.S.L.W. 4663 (1987).
6. Bail Reform Act of 1984, 18 U.S.C. 4142(e).
7. U.S. v. Hazzard, 35 CrL. 2217 (1984); U.S. v. Motamedi, 37 CrL. 2394, CA 9 (1985).
8. C. Ares, A. Rankin, and H. Sturz, "The Manhattan Bail Project: An Interim Report on the Use of Pre-Trial Parole," *New York University Law Review,* 38 (January 1963): 68–95.
9. Wayne R. LaFave and Jerald H. Israel, *Criminal Procedure* (St. Paul, MN: West, 1984), p. 626.
10. United States v. Werker, 535 F.2d 198 (2d Cir. 1976), certiorari denied 429 U.S. 926.
11. Klopfer v. North Carolina, 386 U.S. 213 (1967).
12. Beavers v. Haubert, 1998 U.S. 77 (1905).
13. Klopfer v. North Carolina, 386 U.S. 213 (1967).
14. Barker v. Wingo, 407 US. 514 (1972).
15. A 30-day extension is granted for indictment if the grand jury is not in session, and a 110-day extension can be granted between indictment and trial in cases in which the delay is due to problems associated with calling witnesses.
16. National Advisory Commission on Criminal Justice Standards and Goals, *Courts* (Washington, DC: U.S. Government Printing Office, 1973), standard 9.3.
17. Brady v. Maryland, 363 U.S. 83 (1963).
18. Moore v. Illinois, 408 U.S. 786 (1972).
19. Mapp v. Ohio, 367 U.S. 634 (1961); Escobedo v. Illinois, 368 U.S. 478 (1964); Miranda v. Arizona, 384 U.S. 436 (1966).
20. Kenneth S. Bordens and Irwin A. Horowitz, "Joinder or Criminal Offenses," *Law and Human Behavior,* 9 (1985): 339–353.
21. One of the strategies used against organized crime figures is to grant them immunity so that they cannot take the Fifth Amendment, and then ask them questions regarding their organized crime activities and partners. If they refuse to answer, they can be held in prison for contempt of court.
22. Ann Fagan Ginger, *Minimizing Racism in Jury Trials* (Berkeley, CA: National Lawyers Guild, 1969).
23. Taylor v. Louisiana, 419 U.S. 522 (1975).
24. Bureau of Justice Statistics, *Report to the Nation on Crime and Justice* (Washington, DC: U.S. Department of Justice, 1988), p. 86.
25. Baldwin v. New York, 399 U.S. 66 (1970); Gideon v. Wainwright, 372 U.S. 335 (1963).
26. Bureau of Justice Statistics, *Indigent Defendants* (Washington, DC: Bureau of Justice Statistics, February 1996).
27. Bureau of Justice Statistics, *Indigent Defense Services in Large Counties, 1999* (Washington, DC: Bureau of Justice Statistics, November 2000), p. 1.
28. Ibid., p. 4.
29. Ibid.
30. Ibid.
31. Bureau of Justice Statistics, *Felony Defendants in Large Urban Counties, 1998* (Washington, DC: U.S Department of Justice, November 2001), p. iv.
33. Swain v. Alabama, 380 U.S. 202 (1965).
34. Batson v. Kentucky, 106 S.Ct. 1712 (1986); J.E.B. v. Alabama ex rel. T.B., 55 CrL. 2003 (1994).
34. Richard J. Terrill, *World Criminal Justice Systems: A Survey* (Cincinnati, Ohio: Anderson Publishing Company, 1987), pp. 103–137.

CHAPTER 11

Sentencing and Sanctions

1. Associated Press, "Confession Linked to Killing of 140 Children," *Honolulu Advertiser,* October 30, 1999, p. A3.
2. Associated Press, "Woman Jailed for Leaving Children in Trunk," *Pocono Record,* August 1, 2000, p. A5.
3. "Teenager to Prison for Throwing Elbow," *Honolulu Advertiser,* February 9, 2000, p. C4.
4. "Britain Toughens Punishment Laws," *Honolulu Advertiser,* January 19, 2000, p. A3.
5. Associated Press, "Woman Sentenced to 100 Lashes for Extramarital Sex," *Pocono Record,* August 13, 2001, p. A5.
6. Associated Press, "Fourteen Men Lashed in Public in Iran for Drinking," *Pocono Record,* August 15, 2001, p. A5.
7. Associated Press, "Saudi Gov't Flogs 55 Youths, Including 12 Foreigners," *Pocono Record,* November 9, 2001, p. A5.
8. Los Angeles Times, "Sweden Pays 200 Who Were Forcibly Sterilized," *Honolulu Advertiser,* November 14, 1999, p. A17.

9. Associated Press, "Japanese Sterilized in Eugenics Program Demand Apology, Money," *Honolulu Advertiser,* December 21, 1997, p. G12.
10. Associated Press, "Australian Woman Gets Life for Murder, Cooking Body," *Pocono Record,* November 9, 2001, p. A5.
11. Associated Press, "Banishment Now Alternative to Jail," *Pocono Record,* October 24, 2001, p. A6.
12. Ira J. Silverman and Manuel Vega, *Corrections: A Comprehensive View* (Minneapolis: West, 1996), p. 63.
13. "Boy, 10, Executes Killer of Father," *Honolulu Advertiser,* February 14, 2000, p. 2A.
14. Associated Press, "That Man Needs to Be Dragged Himself," *Honolulu Advertiser,* February 24, 2000, p. A6.
15. William F. Buckley Jr., "Word Games: You Say Assassination, I Say Targeted Killing," *Pocono Record,* October 19, 2001, p. A8.
16. "President Bush's Order on the Trial of Terrorists by Military Commission," *New York Times,* November 14, 2001, p. B8.
17. Ibid.
18. Elisabeth Bumiller and David Johnston, "Bush May Subject Terror Suspects to Military Trials," *New York Times,* November 14, 2001, p. B8.
19. Ibid.
20. David E. Sanger, "President Defends Secret Tribunals in Terrorist Cases," *New York Times on the Web,* http://www.nytimes.com, November 30, 2001.
21. Datharine Q. Seelye, "Draft Rules for Tribunals Ease Worries, but Not All," *New York Times on the Web,* http://www.nytimes.com, December 29, 2001.
22. William Glaberson, "Critics' Attack on Tribunals Turns to Law Among Nations," *New York Times on the Web,* http://www.nytimes.com, December 26, 2001.
23. Seelye, "Draft Rules for Tribunals Ease Worries."
24. Bureau of Justice Statistics, *Federal Criminal Case Processing, 1999* (Washington DC: Department of Justice, February 2001), p. 12.
25. Bureau of Justice Statistics, *Felony Sentences in State Courts, 1998* (Washington, DC: Department of Justice, October 2001), p. 9.
26. Ibid., p. 8.
27. Even the U.S. Supreme Court has argued both sides of the argument on the constitutionality of victim impact statements. In Booth v. Maryland, 197 S.Ct. 2529 (1987), the U.S. Supreme Court ruled that victim impact statements in capital murder cases could lead to the risk that the death penalty might be imposed in an arbitrary and capricious manner. In Payne v. Tennessee, 501 U.S. 808 (1991), the U.S. Supreme Court reversed itself and ruled that, in imposing sentence, victim impact statements were a legitimate method of presenting the harm done by the defendant.
28. Joel Samaha, *Criminal Law* (Belmont, CA: West/Wadsworth, 1999), p. 317.
29. 18 U.S.C. Section 17.
30. United States v. Cameron, 907 F.2d 1051, 1065 (11th Cir., 1990).
31. Ira Mickenberg, "A Pleasant Surprise: The Guilty but Mentally Ill Verdict Has Both Succeeded in Its Own Right and Successfully Preserved the Traditional Role of the Insanity Defense," *University of Cincinnati Law Review,* 55 (1987): 943, 987–991.
32. Samaha, *Criminal Law,* p. 315.
33. Ibid.
34. G. Kleck, "Racial Discrimination in Criminal Sentencing: A Critical Evaluation of the Evidence with Additional Evidence on the Death Penalty," *American Sociological Review,* 46 (1981): 783–805.
35. National Council on Crime and Delinquency, *National Assessment of Structured Sentencing* (Washington, DC: Bureau of Justice Administration, 1996).
36. Associated Press, "Judge Says Cookie Thief Must Face Life Sentence," *Honolulu Advertiser,* March 15, 1998, p. 18.
37. Ibid.
38. Associated Press, "Courts Concentrate on Domestic Violence," *Honolulu Advertiser,* November 23, 1997, p. A16.
39. U.S. Sentencing Commission, *Federal Sentencing Guidelines Manual* (Washington, DC: Government Printing Office, 1987).
40. Mistretta v. the United States, 488 U.S. 361 (1989).
41. Melendez v. the United States, 117 S.Ct. 383, 136 L.Ed. 2d 301 (1996).
42. George Ryley Scott, *The History of Capital Punishment* (London: Torchstream, 1950), p. 179.
43. Harry Elmer Barnes, *The Repression of Crime* (New York: George H. Doran, 1926), p. 220.
44. "Pakistan Criminal to Be Strangled," *Honolulu Advertiser,* March 17, 2000, p. A2.
45. Bureau of Justice Statistics, *Capital Punishment 2000* (Washington, DC: U.S. Department of Justice, December 2001).
46. An October 2000, poll reported that 43 percent of medical doctors said it is all right for doctors to inject condemned inmates with lethal drugs, and 74 percent said it is all right for doctors to pronounce an inmate dead. See Associated Press, "Study Finds That Many Doctors Back Participation in Executions," *St. Louis Post Dispatch,* October 23, 2000, p. A5.
47. Plato, "Crito," in Benjamin Jowett, trans., *The Apology, Phædo and Crito of Plato* (New York: P. F. Collier & Son, 1937), p. 40.
48. Richard Cohen, "Despite Data, Politicians Continue to Support Death Penalty," *Pocono Record,* October 1, 2000, p. A7.
49. Southern Center for Human Rights, http:www/schr.org/January 1, 2002.
50. Witherspoon v. Illinois, 391 U.S. 510 (1968).
51. Wilkerson v. Utah, 99 U.S. 130 (1878).
52. In re Kemmler, 136 U.S. 436 (1890).
53. Louisiana ex. Rel. Francis v. Resweber, 329 U.S. 459 (1947).
54. Furman v. Georgia, 408 U.S. 238 (1972).
55. Woodson v. North Carolina, 428 U.S. 280 (1976).
56. Coker v. Georgia, 433 U.S. 584 (1977).
57. Gregg v. Georgia, 428 U.S. 153 (1976).
58. Used in Arizona, Idaho, Montana, and Nebraska.
59. Used in Alabama, Delaware, Florida, and Indiana.
60. Associated Press, "Several States Reconsider Death Penalty Laws," *Honolulu Advertiser,* February 13, 2000, p. A10.
61. Ibid.
62. "Georgia's Electric Chair Found Cruel and Unusual," Southern Center for Human Rights, http://www.schr.org, December 28, 2001; Associated Press, "Judge Clears Florida to Use Injection for Execution," *Honolulu Advertiser,* February 13, 2000, p. A10; "Gory Death on Florida Electric Chair Creates Furor," *Honolulu Advertiser,* July 9, 1989, p. A9.
63. "Texas Passes Ban on Executing Mentally Retarded Murderers," *Pocono Record,* May 27, 2001; Charles Lane, "High Court to Review Executing Retarded," *Washington Post,* March 27, 2001, p. 1; Charles Lane, "Court Hears Death Penalty Case: Justices to Rule if Jury Got Proper Instruction on Retardation," *Washington Post,* March 28, 2001, p. A8.

64. Reuters, "Court Finds Death Penalty Is Misused in Kansas," *New York Times on the Web,* http://www.nytimes.com, December 30, 2001.
65. Michael L. Radelet and Hugo Adam Bedau, "Fallibility and Finality: Type II Errors and Capital Punishment," in Kenneth C. Hass and James A. Inciardi (eds.), *Challenging Capital Punishment: Legal and Social Science Approaches* (Newbury Park, CA: Sage, 1988), pp. 91–112.
66. Associated Press, "Texas Executes Inmate Whose File Was Lost," *Honolulu Advertiser,* December 16, 1998, p. A10.
67. Deborah Hastings, "Police Say Evidence That Led to Execution Doesn't Actually Exist," *Pocono Record,* August, 30, 2001, p. A5; "Reasonable Doubts: Work under the Microscope," *Law Enforcement News,* May 31, 2001.
68. "Condemned Man Exonerated," *Honolulu Advertiser,* May 19, 1999, p. 3.
69. Associated Press, "Prosecutors on Trial in False Charge of Murder," *Honolulu Advertiser,* March 21, 1999, p. A10.
70. Todd S. Purdum, "Los Angeles Police Officer Sets Off Corruption Scandal," *New York Times on the Web,* http://www.nytimes.com, September 18, 1999.
71. Associated Press, "30 Freed from Death Row Support Reform," *Honolulu Advertiser,* November 8, 1998, p. A10.
72. "Center Director Presents Wrongfully Convicted Client to U.S. Senate Judiciary Committee in Calling for Competent Counsel," Southern Center for Human Rights, http://www.schr.org, January 2, 2002.
73. Associated Press, "Judge Overturns Murder Conviction," *New York Times on the Web,* http://www.nytimes.com, December 28, 2001.
74. Larry McShane, "62,000 Letters and 13 Years Later, Innocent Man Goes Free," *Pocono Record,* September 23, 2001, p. A4.
75. Associated Press, "Charges Dismissed for 17-Year Death Row Inmate," *Honolulu Advertiser,* March 12, 1999, p. A11.
76. Isidore Zimmerman, *Punishment without Crime* (New York: Manor, 1973).
77. "Justice System Abuses Minorities at All Levels, Study Finds," *Honolulu Advertiser,* May 4, 2000, p. A3.
78. C. Spear, *Essays on the Punishment of Death* (London: John Green, 1844), pp. 227–232.
79. David A. Jones, *The Law of Criminal Procedure* (Boston: Little, Brown, 1981), p. 543.
80. President's Commission on Law Enforcement and Administration of Justice, *The Courts* (Washington, DC: U.S. Government Printing Office, 1967), p. 28.
81. Marvin E. Wolfgang and Marc Riedel, "Race Judicial Discretion, and the Death Penalty," *Annals of the American Academy of Political and Social Science,* 407 (May 1973): 129.
82. Thomas J. Keil and Gennaro F. Vito, "Race and the Death Penalty in Kentucky Murder Trials: 1976–1991, *American Journal of Criminal Justice,* 20 (1995): 17–36.
83. Bureau of Justice Statistics, *Capital Punishment 2000.*
84. Ibid.
85. Ibid.
86. Ibid.
87. "Judge Overturns Death Sentence for Abu-Jamal," *Pocono Record,* December 19, 2001, p. A8.
88. "Judge Asks Prosecutors to Address Race Question in Death Penalty Case," *Pocono Record,* December 6, 2001, p. A4.
89. McCleskey v. Kemp, 41 CrL 4107 (1987).
90. Ibid.
91. "Justice System Abuses Minorities at All Levels, Study Finds."
92. Ibid.
93. "DNA Tests Clear 3,000 Suspects," *Honolulu Advertiser,* November 30, 1997, p. G2.
94. Associated Press, "Two Inmates Freed after New DNA Tests," *Honolulu Advertiser,* December 7, 1997, p. G10; Associated Press, "DNA Testing Frees Two Inmates Imprisoned 12 Years for Murder," *Honolulu Advertiser,* April 16, 1999, p. A6; Associated Press, "DNA Test Frees 60-Year-Old Inmate," *Honolulu Advertiser,* September 2, 1999, p. 3A; Helen O'Neil, "False Conviction," *Pocono Record,* October 1, 2000, p. A5; Associated Press, "Convicted Killer Freed on New DNA Evidence," *Pocono Record,* March 16, 2001, p. B6; Associated Press, "Convicted Murderer Finally Acquitted," *Pocono Record,* April 5, 2001, p. A4; Associated Press, "DNA Clears Man Jailed for 13 years for Rape," *Pocono Record,* October 19, 2001, p. C10.
95. R. H. Melton, "Gilmore Sets Limit on DNA Evidence: Window Would Close 3 Years after Trial," *Washington Post,* March 28, 2001, p. 1.
96. Brooke A. Masters, "New DNA Testing Urged in Case of Executed Man," *Washington Post,* March 28, 2001, p. B1.
97. F. Carter Smith and Corbis Sygma, "A Life or Death Gamble," *Newsweek,* May 29, 2000, pp. 22–27.
98. Ibid.
99. Ibid.
100. National Institute of Justice, *Effects of Judges' Sentencing Decisions on Criminal Careers* (Washington, DC: U.S. Department of Justice, November 1999).
101. Ibid.
102. Ibid.

CHAPTER 12
Jails and Prisons

1. Harry B. Weiss and Grace M. Weiss, *An Introduction to Crime and Punishment in Colonial New Jersey* (Trenton, NJ: Past Times Press, 1960), p. 91.
2. Ibid.
3. Law Enforcement Assistance Administration (LEAA), *Two Hundred Years of American Criminal Justice: An LEAA Bicentennial Study* (Washington, DC: U.S. Department of Justice, 1976), p. 7.
4. Ira J. Silverman and Manuel Vega, *Corrections: A Comprehensive View* (Minneapolis/Saint Paul: West, 1996), p. 51.
5. Weiss and Weiss, *An Introduction to Crime and Punishment,* p. 11.
6. Ibid.
7. Ibid., p. 36.
8. Silverman and Vega, *Corrections.*
9. Ibid., pp. 56–57.
10. Weiss and Weiss, *An Introduction to Crime and Punishment,* p. 36.
11. Silverman and Vega, *Corrections,* p. 52.
12. Ibid., p. 54.
13. Ibid.
14. Ibid., p. 52.
15. Weiss and Weiss, *An Introduction to Crime and Punishment,* p. 13.
16. Silverman and Vega, *Corrections,* p. 53.

17. Joseph M. Hawes, "Prisons in Early Nineteenth-Century America: The Process of Convict Reformation," in Joseph M. Hawes (ed.), *Law and Order in American History* (Port Washington, NY: National University Publications, 1979), pp. 37–52.
18. Weiss and Weiss, *An Introduction to Crime and Punishment*, p. 93.
19. Norman Johnston, *The Human Cage: A Brief History of Prison Architecture* (New York: Walker and Company, 1973), p. 10.
20. Silverman and Vega, *Corrections*, p. 476.
21. Johnston, *The Human Cage*.
22. Raymond A. Mohl, "Poverty, Pauperism, and Social Order in the Preindustrial American City, 1780–1840," in Joseph M. Hawes (ed.), *Law and Order in American History* (Port Washington, NY: National University Publications, 1979), pp. 25–26, 31.
23. Ibid.
24. Ibid.
25. Johnston, *The Human Cage*, p. 5.
26. Weiss and Weiss, *An Introduction to Crime and Punishment*, p. 10.
27. Silverman and Vega, *Corrections*, p. 59.
28. Ibid.
29. LEAA, *Two Hundred Years*, p. 46.
30. Weiss and Weiss, *An Introduction to Crime and Punishment*, pp. 17–18.
31. Ibid., p. 18.
32. Ibid., p. 64.
33. Ibid., p. 10.
34. Ibid., p. 47.
35. Ibid.
36. Johnston, *The Human Cage*, pp. 13–14.
37. The society still operates under the name of the Philadelphia Prison Society.
38. Hawes, "Prisons in Early Nineteenth-Century America," p. 39.
39. LEAA, *Two Hundred Years*, p. 47.
40. Hawes, "Prisons in Early Nineteenth-Century America."
41. Ibid., p. 40.
42. Ibid., p. 39.
43. LEAA, *Two Hundred Years*, p. 49.
44. O. L. Lewis, *The Development of American Prisons and Prison Customs, 1776–1845* (Montclair, NJ: Patterson Smith, 1996/1922).
45. D. J. Rothman, *The Discovery of the Asylum: Social Order and Disorder in the New Republic* (Boston: Little, Brown, 1971), p. 106.
46. Silverman and Vega, *Corrections*, p. 78.
47. Ibid.
48. LEAA, *Two Hundred Years*, p. 49.
49. Lewis, *The Development of American Prisons*.
50. John W. Fountain, "Time Winds Down at a Storied Prison," *New York Times on the Web*, http://www.nytimes.com, December 26, 2001.
51. E. Ayers, *Vengeance and Justice: Crime and Punishment in the 19th-Century American South* (New York: Oxford University Press, 1984).
52. M. C. Moos, *State Penal Administration in Alabama* (Tuscaloosa, AL: Bureau of Public Administration, University of Alabama, 1942), p. 18.
53. B. McKelvey, *American Prisons: A History of Good Intentions* (Montclair, NJ: Patterson Smith, 1977).
54. Thomas Murton and J. Hyams, *Accomplices to the Crime: The Arkansas Prison Scandal* (New York: Grove Press, 1969).
55. Holt v. Sarver, 300 F. Supp. 825 (1969); Holt v. Sarver, 309 F. Supp. 362 (E.D. Ark. 1970); Jackson v. Bishop, 404 F. 2d 571 (8th Cir., 1968).
56. Holt v. Sarver, 309 F. Supp. 362 (E.D. Ark. 1970).
57. Sam Vincent Meddis, "U.S. Incarceration Rate Is Highest in the World," *Honolulu Star Bulletin*, January 8, 1991, p. A16.
58. Associated Press, "State Prisons' Growth Rate Slows," *Washington Post*, March 26, 2001, p. A4.
59. Ibid.
60. U.S. Department of Justice, Bureau of Justice Statistics, *1999 Justice Expenditure and Employment*. http://www.ojp.usdoj.gov/bjs/pub/shets/cjee99.zip.
61. Bureau of Justice Statistics, *State Prison Expenditures, 1996* (Washington, DC: U.S. Department of Justice, August 1999), p. iv.
62. David Jones, *History of Criminology: A Philosophical Perspective* (New York: Greenwood Press, 1986), p. 123.
63. American Correctional Association, *The American Prison: From the Beginning* (Lanham, MD: American Correctional Association, 1983), p. 220.
64. Ibid., p. 158.
65. Ibid., pp. 163, 208, 222.
66. Ruiz v. Estelle, 666 F. 2d 854 (1982).
67. Thomas Bonczar and Allen Beck, *Lifetime Likelihood of Going to State or Federal Prison* (Washington, DC: U.S. Department of Justice, March 1997), p. 1
68. Ibid.
69. Bureau of Justice Statistics, *Prisoners in 2000* (Washington, DC: U.S. Department of Justice, August 2001), pp. 10, 11.
70. Bureau of Justice Statistics, *Profile of State Prisoners under Age 18, 1985–97* (Washington, DC: U.S. Department of Justice, August 2001), p. 1.
71. Gannett News Service, "13% of US. Black Men Barred from Voting," *Honolulu Advertiser*, October 23, 1998, p. A3.
72. Ibid.
73. Ibid.
74. Ibid.
75. Bureau of Justice Statistics, *Census of Jails, 1999* (Washington, DC: U.S. Department of Justice, August 2001), pp. 1, 7.
76. Military prisoners are primarily military personnel who have been convicted by court martial of violating the Uniform Code of Military Conduct, the body of law that defines crime and punishment for military personnel. In 1997, there were 2,466 military prisoners from all branches of the service (*Sourcebook of Criminal Justice Statistics 2000*, p. 533). The oldest military prison still in operation in the United States is the U.S. Disciplinary Barracks at Fort Leavenworth, Kansas, the only military prison for the long-term incarceration of military personnel.
77. Thirty-three states contain around 300 Native American areas or reservations. Generally, the local government authority on Native American lands is a tribal government or council. Jurisdiction over crimes in these areas depends on several factors, including the identity of the victim and the offender, the severity of the crime, and where the crime was committed. In 2000, there were 69 facilities operating in tribal lands, holding 1,700 persons in custody. From: Bureau of Justice Statistics, *Jails in Indian Country, 2000* (Washington, DC: U.S. Department of Justice, July 2001), p. 1.
78. Bureau of Justice Statistics, *Census of Jails*, p. 3.

79. Bureau of Justice Statistics, *Law Enforcement Management and Administrative Statistics, Sheriffs' Offices, 1999* (Washington, DC: U.S. Department of Justice, May 2001), p. 7.
80. Ibid., p. 3.
81. Bureau of Justice Statistics, *Census of Jails*, p. 4.
82. Ibid., p. 5.
83. American Correctional Association, *The American Prison*, p. 172.
84. Ibid., p. 164.
85. Allen Beck and Jennifer C. Karberg, *Prison and Jail Inmates at Midyear 2000* (Washington, DC: U.S. Department of Justice, March 2001), p. 5.
86. Ibid., p. 7.
87. Ibid., p. 5.
88. Ibid.
89. John Scalia, *Federal Drug Offenders, 1999, with Trends 1984–99* (Washington, DC: U.S. Department of Justice, August 2001), p. 6.
90. Anne L. Stahl, *Drug Offense Cases in Juvenile Courts, 1989–1998* (Washington, DC: U.S. Department of Justice, September 2001), p. 1.
91. Chen, "Number of Women."
92. Ibid.
93. Laura Maruschak, *HIV in Prisons and Jails, 1999* (Washington, DC: U.S. Department of Justice, July 2001), p. 4.
94. Chen, "Number of Women."
95. Caroline Wolf Harlow, *Prior Abuse Reported by Inmates and Probationers* (Washington, DC: U.S. Department of Justice, April 1999), p. 2.
96. Lennie Magida, "Doing Hard Time," *Honolulu Weekly*, July 14, 1993, p. 4.
97. Joan Petersilia, *When Prisoners Return to the Community* (Washington, DC: U.S. Department of Justice, November 2000), p. 4
98. Marilyn C. Moses, *Keeping Incarcerated Mothers and Their Daughters Together: Girl Scouts beyond Bars* (Washington, DC: U.S. Department of Justice, October 1995), p. 1.
99. Petersilia, *When Prisoners Return.*
100. Chen, "Number of Women."
101. Moses, *Keeping Incarcerated Mothers.*
102. Bureau of Justice Statistics, *Capital Punishment 2000* (Washington, DC: U.S. Department of Justice, December 2001), p. 7.
103. Victor L. Streib, "Death Penalty for Female Offenders January 1, 1973, to December 31, 2000. See http://www.law.onu.edu/faculty/steib/femdeath.htm, February 14, 2002.
104. Kevin Johnson, "Inmate Swap Worked—Until Impostor Fled," *USA Today*, October 25, 2000, p. 2.
105. Ibid.
106. Nearly all jails, state prisons, and federal prisons have abandoned the use of the term *guard* to describe security personnel. In the federal prisons, these employees are called "correctional officers." Correctional institutions do not consider the job title "guard" as appropriately describing the duties of the employee, and use of the term is considered rather derogatory and demeaning of the professionalism required for the position.
107. The actual responsibility for transferring prisoners from one federal facility to another is that of the U.S. Marshal Service. Also, the U.S. Marshal Service is responsible for locating and arresting escaped federal prisoners.
108. Allen J. Beck and Paige M. Harrison, *Prisoners in 2000* (Washington, DC: U.S. Department of Justice, August 2001), p. 2.
109. Bureau of Justice Statistics, *Census of Jails*, p. 6.
110. Beck and Harrison, *Prisoners in 2000*, p. 6.
111. Ibid.
112. Associated Press, "Private Prisons Said to Do Little for Communities," *Pocono Record*, October 22, 2001, p. A5.
113. Ibid.
114. Ibid.
115. Richardson et al. v. McKnight, No. 96-318.
116. Bureau of Justice Statistics, *Challenging the Conditions of Prisons and Jails: A Report on Section 1983 Litigation* (Washington, DC: U.S. Department of Justice, December 1994).
117. David T. Johnson and Meda Chesney-Lind, "Does Hawaii Really Need Another Prison?" *Honolulu Advertiser*, March 29, 1998, p. B1.
118. William D. Nueske, "Four Prisoners Who Killed Themselves Did Us a Favor," *Honolulu Star-Bulletin*, January 13, 1992.
119. Associated Press, "Official Resists Plan of Computers for Jail," *Pocono Record*, January 17, 2002, p. A4.
120. Ibid.

CHAPTER 13
Probation and Parole

1. Fox Butterfield, "Tight Budgets Force States to Reconsider Crime and Penalties," *New York Times Online*, http://www.nytimes.com, January 21, 2002.
2. Ibid.
3. Ibid.
4. Ken Kobayashi, "Second Chance Starts with Death, New Life," *Honolulu Advertiser*, December 29, 1997, p. A1.
5. Associated Press, "Clinton Pardons 33 Convicted Criminals," *Honolulu Advertiser*, December 25, 1998, p. A6.
6. Ira Silverman and Manuel Vega, *Corrections: A Comprehensive View* (Minneapolis/Saint Paul: West, 1996), p. 495.
7. Bureau of Justice Statistics, *Probation and Parole Statistics*, http://www.ojp.usdoj.gov/bjs/pandp.htm, January 29, 2002.
8. Silverman and Vega, *Corrections*, p. 499.
9. Bureau of Justice Statistics, *Probation and Parole Statistics.*
10. Patrick A. Langan and Mark A. Cunniff, *Recidivism of Felons on Probation 1986–1989* (Washington, DC: Bureau of Justice Statistics, 1992).
11. Bureau of Justice Statistics, *Probation and Parole Statistics.*
12. Ibid.
13. James M. Byrne, *Probation: A National Institute of Justice Crime File Series Study Guide* (Washington, DC: U.S. Department of Justice, 1988), p. 1.
14. In Escoe v. Zerbst, 295 U.S. 490 (135), the Court ruled that probation was an act of grace, and thus the probationer was without due process rights. In Mempa v. Rhay, 389 U.S. 128 (1967), the Court reversed the ruling of *Escoe v. Zerbst* and ruled that probationers were entitled to due process rights.
15. Gagnon v. Scarpelli, 411 U.S. 778 (1973).
16. Griffin v. Wisconsin, 483 U.S. 868, 107 S.Ct. 3164 (1987).
17. Minnesota v. Murphy, 465 U.S. 420, 104 S.Ct. 1136, 79 L. Ed. 2d 409 (1984).
18. *Gagon v. Scarpelli* (1973); *Mempa v. Rhay* (1967).
19. Kelly v. Robinson, 479 U.S. 36, 107 S.Ct. 353, 93 L. Ed. 2d 216 (1986).

20. Silverman and Vega, *Corrections*, p. 501.
21. H. Burns, *Corrections Organization and Administration* (St. Paul, MN: West, 1975).
22. G. I. Giardini, *The Parole Process* (Springfield, IL: Charles C. Thomas, 1959), p. 9.
23. David Dresser, *Practice and Theory of Probation and Parole* (New York: Columbia University Press, 1969), pp. 56–76.
24. Marjorie Bell (ed.), *Parole in Principle and Practice* (New York: National Probation and Parole Association, 1957).
25. A. W. Pisciotta, "Scientific Reform: The 'New Penology' at Elmira, 1876–1900," *Crime and Delinquency*, 29 (1983): 613–630.
26. Bureau of Justice Statistics, *Probation and Parole Statistics.*
27. Ibid.
28. Bureau of Justice Statistics, *Likelihood of Going to State or Federal Prison* (Washington, DC: U.S. Department of Justice, March 1997), p. 5.
29. Bureau of Justice Statistics, *Probation and Parole Statistics.*
30. "Federal Funds at Stake for 14 States with Megan's Law Problems," *Law Enforcement News*, November 30, 2001, p. 7.
31. Task Force on Corrections, *Task Force Report: Corrections* (Washington, DC: President's Commission on Law Enforcement and the Administration of Justice, U.S. Government Printing Office, 1967).
32. William Parker, *Parole: Origins, Development, Current Practices and Statutes* (College Park, MD: American Correctional Association, 1975).
33. See http://www.usdoj.gov/uspc/history.htm, February 4, 2002.
34. Menechino v. Oswald, 430 F. 2d 403 (2d Cir., 1970); Greenholtz v. Inmates of Nebraska Penal and Correctional Complex, 422 U.S. 1 (1979).
35. Johnson, U.S. ex. Rel. v. Chairman, New York State Board of Parole, 363 F. Supp. 416, aff'd, 500 F. 2d 925 (2d Cir., 1971).
36. Don M. Gottfredson, Peter B. Hoffman, Maurice H. Sigler, and Leslie T. Wilkins, "Making Paroling Policy Explicit," *Crime and Delinquency*, 21 (January 1975): 36.
37. Southern Center for Human Rights, "Federal Judge Finds Alabama Jail Like a Slave Ship, Orders Immediate Reduction in Population, Other Reforms, http://www.schr.org/news/news_slaveshipstory.htm, December 28, 2001.
38. James Austin, "The Consequences of Escalating the Use of Imprisonment," *Corrections Compendium*, September 1991: 1, 4–8.
39. Ibid.
40. See http://www.usdoj.gov/uspc/release.htm, February 4, 2002.
41. Bureau of Justice Statistics, *Trends in State Parole, 1990–2000* (Washington, DC: U.S. Department of Justice, October 2001), p. 11.
42. Silverman and Vega, *Corrections*, p. 506.
43. Bureau of Justice Statistics, *Trends in State Parole*, p. 14.
44. Ibid., p. 13.
45. Ibid.
46. Bureau of Justice Statistics, *Probation and Parole Violators in State Prison, 1991* (Washington, DC: U.S. Department of Justice, August 1995), p. 1.
47. Morrissey v. Brewer, 408 U.S. 471 (1972).
48. See http://www.usdoj.gov/uspc/questions.htm, February 4, 2002.
49. Bureau of Justice Statistics, *Trends in State Parole*, p. 11.
50. See http://www.usdoj.gov/uspc/questions.htm, February 4, 2002.
51. http://www.usdoj.gov/uspc, February 4, 2002.
52. Silverman and Vega, *Corrections*, p. 495.
53. J. V. Barry, *Alexander Maconochie of Norfolk Island: A Study of Prison Reform* (London: Oxford University Press, 1958).
54. E. E. Dooley, "Sir Walter Crofton and the Irish or Intermediate System of Prison Discipline," *New England Journal on Prison Law*, 72 (Winter 1981).
55. Bureau of Justice Statistics, *Probation and Parole Violators in State Prison.*

CHAPTER 14

Prevention and Corrections in the Community

1. Associated Press, "Prison Lifer Charged with 1997 Murder of Fellow Inmate," *Pocono Record*, September 1, 2001, p. B3.
2. Michael Janofsky, "A Rare Legal Quest: From Murderer to Lawyer," *New York Times on the Web*, http://nytimes.com, December 27, 2001.
3. Jeremy Travis, *But They All Come Back: Rethinking Prisoner Reentry* (Washington, DC: U.S. Department of Justice, May 2000), p. 10.
4. Joan Petersilia, "Challenges of Prisoner Reentry and Parole in California," California Policy Research *Brief Series*, June 2000, http://www.ucop.educ/cprc/parole.html.
5. Joan Petersilia, *When Prisoners Return to the Community: Political, Economic, and Social Consequences* (Washington, DC: U.S. Department of Justice, November 2000), p. 1.
6. Travis, *But They All Come Back*, p. 1.
7. Petersilia, "Challenges of Prisoner Reentry."
8. Ibid.
9. Petersilia, *When Prisoners Return*, p. 3.
10. Ibid., p. 2.
11. Ibid., p. 3.
12. Ibid.
13. Travis, *But They All Come Back*, p. 1.
14. Petersilia, *When Prisoners Return*, p. 3.
15. Ibid., p. 1.
16. Ibid.
17. Travis, *But They All Come Back*, p. 3.
18. Office of Justice programs, *Rethinking Probation: Community Supervision, Community Safety* (Washington, DC: U.S. Department of Justice, December 1998), p. 26.
19. *Time*, November 14, 1988, p. 20.
20. *New York Times*, April 6, 1994, p. A16.
21. Ibid.
22. Bureau of Justice Statistics, *Profile of State Prisoners under Age 18, 1985–1997* (Washington, DC: U.S. Department of Justice, February 2000), p. 1.
23. Travis, *But They All Come Back*, p. 3.
24. Mark S. Umbreit, "Community Service Sentencing: Last Alternative or Added Sanction? *Federal Probation*, 45 (1981): 3–14.
25. Ira J. Silverman and Manuel Vega, *Corrections: A Comprehensive View* (St. Paul, MN: West, 1996), p. 515.
26. Ibid., 516.
27. Travis, *But They All Come Back*, p. 3.
28. Petersilia, *When Prisoners Return*, p. 3.
29. Elijah Anderson, *Streetwise: Race, Class, and Change in an Urban Community* (Chicago: University of Chicago Press, 1990), p. 4.
30. Petersilia, "Challenges of Prisoner Reentry," p. 3.
31. Joan Moore, "Bearing the Burden: How Incarceration Weakens Inner-City Communities." Paper read at the Unintended Con-

sequences of Incarceration Conference at the Vera Institute of Justice, New York City, 1996.

32. Office of Justice Programs, *Rethinking Probation: Community Supervision, Community Safety* (Washington, DC: U.S. Department of Justice, December 1998), p. 1.
33. Ibid.
34. Petersilia, *When Prisoners Return*, p. 3.
35. T. Clear and P. Hardyman, "The New Intensive Supervision Movement," *Crime and Delinquency*, 35 (1990): 42–60.
36. R. Carter and L. Wilkins, "Caseloads: Some Conceptual Models," in R. Carter and L. Wilkins (eds.), *Probation, Parole and Community Corrections* (New York: John Wiley and Sons, 1976).
37. Office of Justice Programs, Rethinking Probation, p. 2.
38. Petersilia, *Challenges of Prisoner Reentry*, p. 2.
39. Ibid.
40. Marta Nelson and Jennifer Trone, *Why Planning for Release Matters* (New York: Vera Institute of Justice, 2000), p. 2.
41. Ibid.
42. James P. Levine et al., *Criminal Justice in America: Law in Action* (New York: John Wiley, 1986), p. 549.
43. Administrative Office of the Courts, New Jersey Intensive Supervision Program, Progress Report 12, No. 1 (Trenton, NJ: State of New Jersey, 1995), p. 3.
44. Ibid.
45. Joan Petersilia, "Georgia's Intensive Probation: Will the Model Work Elsewhere?" in Belinda McCarthy (ed.), *Intermediate Punishments: Intensive Supervision, Home Confinement and Electronic Surveillance* (Monsey, NY: Criminal Justice Press, 1987), p. 21.
46. Susan B. Noonan and Edward J. Latessa, "Intensive Probation: An Examination of Recidivism and Social Adjustment for an Intensive Supervision Program," *American Journal of Criminal Justice*, 12 (1987): 45–61.
47. *Going Home: Serious and Violent Offender Reentry Initiative.* See Communities in Action, http://www.ojp.usdoj.gov/reentry/communities.htm, February 16, 2002.
48. Joan Petersilia, *Expanding Options for Criminal Sentencing* (Santa Monica, CA: The Rand Corporation, 1987).
49. Ibid.
50. Cherie L. Clark, David W. Aziz, and Doris L. MacKenzie, *Shock Incarceration in New York: Focus on Treatment* (Washington, DC: U.S. Department of Justice, August 1994), p. 2.
51. Silverman and Vega, *Corrections*, p. 529.
52. Doris Layton MacKenzie and Deanna Bellew Ballow, "Shock Incarceration Programs in State Correctional Jurisdictions—An Update," *NIJ Report: Shock Incarceration*, (May/June 1989): 9–10; D. G. Parent, *Shock Incarceration: An Overview of Existing Programs* (Washington, DC: U.S. Department of Justice, 1989).
53. Cherie Clark, David Aziz, and Doris Mackenzie, *Shock Incarceration in New York*, p. 5.
54. Ibid., p. 4.
55. Ibid., p. 3.
56. Ibid., p. 9.
57. Ibid., p. 10.
58. Ibid., p. 6.
59. Doris MacKenzie and Claire Souryal, *Multisite Evaluation of Shock Incarceration* (Washington, DC: National Institute of Justice, September 1994), p. 1.
60. Clark et al., *Shock Incarceration in New York*, p. 4.
61. Doris MacKenzie, Angela Gover, Gaylene Armstrong, and Ojmarr Mitchell, *A National Study Comparing the Environment of Boot Camps with Traditional Facilities for Juvenile Offenders* (Washington, DC: U.S. Department of Justice, August 2001), p. 1.
62. Ibid., pp. 3–4.
63. Doris Layton MacKenzie et al., *A National Study Comparing the Environments of Boot Camps*, pp. 1–2.
64. Ibid., p. 2.
65. Ibid., p. 11.
66. Michael Janofsky, "States Pressed as 3 Boys Die at Boot Camps," *New York Times on the Web*, http://www.nytimes.com, July 15, 2001.
67. Ibid.
68. Ibid.
69. Michael Janofsky, "Arizona Boot Camp Where Boy Died Reopens," *New York Times on the Web*, http://www.nytimes.com, September 7, 2001.
70. Michael Janofsky, "Boot Camp Proponent Becomes Focus of Critics," *New York Times on the Web*, http://www.nytimes.com, August 9, 2001.
71. James Sterngold, "Head of Camp in Arizona Is Arrested in Boy's Death," *New York Times on the Web*, http://www.nytimes.com, February 16, 2002.
72. Joan Petersilia, "House Arrest," National Institute of Justice, *Crime File Study Guide* (Washington, DC: U.S. Department of Justice, 1988), p. 1.
73. Silverman and Vega, *Corrections*, p. 523.
74. Ibid., p. 524.
75. M. Renzema and D. Skelton, *Final Report: The Use of Electronic Monitoring by Criminal Justice Agencies* (Washington, DC: U.S. Department of Justice 1990), pp. 1–3.
76. Bureau of Justice Statistics, *Correctional Populations in the United States, 1995* (Washington, DC: Bureau of Justice Statistics, 1997), pp. 22, 34, 41.
77. Michael Tonry, *Intermediate Sanctions in Sentencing Guidelines* (Washington, DC: U.S. Department of Justice, 1997), p. 10.
78. Joan Petersilia, "House Arrest," p. 1.
79. David C. Anderson, *Sensible Justice: Alternatives to Prison* (New York: The New Press, 1998), p. 44.
80. Ibid.
81. John Schwartz, "Internet Leash Can Monitor Sex Offenders," *New York Times on the Web*, http://www.nytimes.com, December 31, 2001.
82. Christopher Baird and Dennis Wagner, *Evaluation of the Florida Community Control Program* (Madison, WI: National Council on Crime and Delinquency, 1990).
83. J. Muncie, "A Prisoner in My Home: The Politics and Practice of Electronic Monitoring," *Probation Journal*, 37 (1990): 72–77.
84. Federal Government Information Technology, *Electronic Surveillance and Civil Liberties* (Washington, DC: Congress of the United States, Office of Technology Assessment, 1985); R. Ball, R. C. Huff, and J. P. Lilly, *House Arrest and Correctional Policy: Doing Time at Home* (Newbury Park, CA: Sage, 1988).
85. Reginald A. Wilkinson, "Offender Reentry: A Storm Overdue," http://www.drc.state.oh.us/Articles/article66.htm, January 16, 2002.
86. Ibid.
87. "History of the Office of Community Corrections," http://www.michigan.gov, February 16, 2002.

88. National Criminal Justice Reference Service, "Prisoner Reentry Resources—Legislation," http://www.ncjrs.org/reentry/legislation.htm, February 17, 2002.
89. Ibid.
90. Serious and Violent Offender Reentry Initiative, "See Communities in Action," http://www.ojp.usdoj.gov/reentry/communities.htm, February 18, 2002.
91. Dan Nakaso, "Inmates Pay Debt in Sweat, while Learning Lure of 'Aina," *Honolulu Advertiser*, March 11, 1999, pp. A1, A7.
92. Nelson and Trone, *Why Planning for Release Matters*, p. 2.
93. Elmer H. Johnson and Kenneth E. Kotch, "Two Factors in Development of Work Release: Size and Location of Prisons," *Journal of Criminal Justice*, 1 (March 1973): 44–45.
94. Silverman and Vega, *Corrections*, p. 520.
95. Harry Holzer, *What Employers Want: Job Prospects for Less-educated Workers* (New York: Russell Sage, 1996).
96. Petersilia, *When Prisoners Return*, p. 4.
97. U.S. Department of Labor, *From Hard Time to Full Time: Strategies to Move Ex-Offenders from Welfare to Work* (Washington, DC: U.S. Department of Labor, June 2001), p. 7.
98. "Woman Files Lawsuit against Company for Using Inmate Telemarketers," *Pocono Record*, November 15, 2001, p. A5.
99. Nelson and Trone, *Why Planning for Release Matters*, pp. 4–5.
100. Ibid.
101. Ibid., p. 3.
102. Rhonda Cook, "State Prison-to-Work Program Falls Short," *Atlanta Journal-Constitution*, June 1, 2000.
103. Nelson and Trone, *Why Planning for Release Matters*, p. 2.
104. U.S. Department of Labor, *From Hard Time to Full Time: Strategies to Help Move Ex-Offenders from Welfare to Work* (U.S. Department of Labor, Washington, DC: June 2001), p. 10.
105. Ibid., p. 11.
106. Susan Kreifels, "New Rules Add Teeth to Convict-Hiring Law," *Honolulu Star-Bulletin*, January 9, 1998, pp. A1, A8.
107. U.S. Department of Labor, *From Hard Time to Full Time*, pp. 9–10.
108. David Koeppel, "Job Fairs Give Ex-Convicts Hope in Down Market," *New York Times on the Web*, http://www.nytimes.com, December 26, 2001.
109. George E. Sexton, *Work in American Prisons: Joint Ventures with the Private Sector* (Washington, DC: U.S. Department of Justice, November 1995), pp. 2, 10.
110. Ibid., p. 3.
111. Ronald D. Stephens and June Lane Arnette, *From the Courthouse to the Schoolhouse: Making Successful Transitions* (Washington, DC: U.S. Department of Justice, February 2000), p. 1.
112. Ibid., p. 3.
113. Thomas Barlett, "Prime Numbers," *Chronicle of Higher Education*, January 19, 2002, p. A7.
114. Ibid.
115. O. I. Keller and B. S. Alper, *Halfway Houses: Community-Centered Correction and Treatment* (Lexington, MA: Heath Lexington Books, 1970).
116. Task Force on Corrections, *Task Force Report: Corrections* (Washington, DC: President's Commission on Law Enforcement and the Administration of Justice, U.S. Government Printing Office, 1967); Task Force on Corrections, *Task Force Report: Corrections* (Washington, DC: National Advisory Commission on Criminal Justice Standards and Goals, 1973).
117. Office of Justice Programs, *Rethinking Probation*, pp. 19–21.
118. Dale G. Parent, *Day Reporting Centers for Criminal Offenders: A Descriptive Analysis of Existing Programs* (Washington, DC: U.S. Department of Justice, 1990), p. 1.
119. Dale G. Parent, "Day Reporting Centers," in Michael Tonry and Kate Hamilton (eds.), *Intermediate Sanctions in Overcrowded Times* (Boston: Northeastern University Press, 1995), p. 15.
120. *Criminal Justice Abstracts* (Monsey, NY: Willow Tree Press, 1998), pp. 105–106.
121. Drug Court Clearinghouse and Technical Assistance Project, "Looking at a Decade of Drug Courts," http://www.ojp.usdoj.gov/, November 16, 2001.
122. Adele Harrell, Shannon Cavanagh, and John Roman, *Evaluation of the D.C. Superior Court Drug Intervention Programs* (Washington, DC: National Institute of Justice, April 2000), pp. 1–2.
123. John Scalia, *Federal Drug Offenders, 1999 with Trends 1984–1999* (Washington, DC: U.S. Department of Justice, August 2001), p. 10.
124. Ibid., p. 1.
125. Elizabeth A. Peyton and Robert Gossweiler, *Treatment Services in Adult Drug Courts: Report on the 1999 National Drug Court Treatment Survey Executive Summary* (Washington, DC: U.S. Department of Justice, May 2001), p. 5.
126. Allen J. Beck, "State and Federal Prisoners Returning to the Community: Finding from the Bureau of Justice Statistics," Paper presented at the First Reentry Courts Initiative Cluster Meeting, Washington, DC, April 13, 2000.
127. Drug Court Clearinghouse and Technical Assistance Project, "Looking at a Decade."
128. Ibid.
129. Ibid.
130. Ibid.
131. Adele Harrell, Shannon Cavanagh, and John Roman, *Evaluation of the D.C. Superior Court Drug Intervention Programs* (Washington, DC: U.S. Department of Justice, April 2000), p. 2.
132. Ibid.
133. Caroline S. Cooper, *Juvenile Drug Court Programs* (Washington, DC: U.S. Department of Justice, May 2001), p. 1.
134. Ibid., p. 3.
135. Ibid., p. 6.
136. Ibid., p. 9.
137. Ibid., p. 13.
138. Ibid., p. 11.
139. Ibid., p. 13.
140. Tribal Law and Policy Institute, *Healing to Wellness Courts: A Preliminary Overview of Tribal Drug Courts* (Washington DC: U.S. Department of Justice, July 1999), p. 14.
141. Ibid., p. 9.
142. Ibid., p. 2.
143. Ibid., p. 4.
144. Ibid., pp. 9–10.
145. Ibid., p. 12.
146. Ibid., p. 13.
147. Ibid., p. 14.
148. National Institute of Justice, *Reducing Offender Drug Use*, p. 21; Bureau of Justice Assistance, *Treatment Accountability for Safer Communities* (Washington, DC: U.S. Department of Justice, November 1995), pp. 1–2.

149. Bureau of Justice Assistance, *Treatment Accountability for Safer Communities* (Washington, DC: U.S. Department of Justice, November 1995), p. 1.
150. National Institute of Justice, *Reducing Offender Drug Use*, p. 21.
151. Joan Petersilia and Elizabeth Piper Deschenes, "What Punishes? Inmates Rank the Severity of Prison versus Intermediate Sanctions," in Joan Petersilia (ed.), *Community Corrections: Probation, Parole and Intermediate Sanctions* (New York: Oxford University Press, 1998), pp. 149–159.
152. Joan Petersilia, "When Probation Becomes More Dreaded Than Prison," *Federal Probation*, 54 (1990): 23–27.

CHAPTER 15

Challenges in the Criminal Justice System

1. Knight-Ridder Service, "Accused Slayer Is Also a Vampire, Prosecutor Claims," *Honolulu Advertiser*, June 4, 1992, p. 6.
2. Associated Press, "Teenagers Kill Girl over Threat to Tell Plans," *Honolulu Advertiser*, May 22, 1998, p. 3.
3. Detis T. Duhart, *Violence in the Workplace, 1993–99* (Washington, DC: U.S. Department of Justice, December 2001), pp. 1–2.
4. Ken Kobayashi, "Uyesugi Indicted on Nine Counts," *Honolulu Advertiser*, November 10, 1999, p. A1.
5. "Gunman Kills Three People, Dies in California Shootout," *Los Angeles Times*, December 19, 1997, p. 3.
6. Associated Press, "Evicted Apartment Dweller Kills 2 in Shooting Rampage," *Honolulu Advertiser*, January 14, 1998, p. 4.
7. Kevin Sack, "Gunman Slays 9 at Brokerages in Atlanta," *New York Times on the Web*, http://www.nytimes.com, August 1, 1999.
8. Associated Press, "Pennsylvania Gunman Kills 5 in Suspected Hate-Crime Spree," *Honolulu Advertiser*, April 29, 2000, p. 1A.
9. Daniel J. Wakin, "Gunfire Wounds 2 Students Inside a Manhattan High School," *New York Times on the Web*, http://www.nytimes.com, January 16, 2002.
10. Fox Butterfield, "Killings Increase in Many Big Cities," *New York Times on the Web*, http://www.nytimes.com, December 21, 2001.
11. Eric Hoover, "A Deadly Shooting Pierces 2 Small Colleges," *Chronicle of Higher Education*, February 8, 2002, p. A37.
12. Associated Press, "Churches Increase Security Efforts," *New York Times on the Web*, http://www.nytimes.com, September 17, 2001; Jim Yardley, "An Angry Mystery Man Who Brought Death," *New York Times on the Web*, http://www.nytimes.com, September 17, 1999.
13. Hilary Hylton, "Death Rides the Rails," *Time*, June 28, 1999, p. 45; Associated Press, "Latest Homicides Leave Denver Homeless Wary," *Honolulu Advertiser*, November 19, 1999, p. A10.
14. *Office of Juvenile Justice and Delinquency Prevention Statistical Briefing Book*, http://ojjdp.ncjrs.org/ojstatbb/html/qa251.html, January 20, 2002.
15. *Office of Juvenile Justice and Delinquency Prevention Statistical Briefing Book*, http://ojjdp.ncjrs.org/ojstatbb/html/qa136.html, September 30, 1999.
16. Ibid.
17. H. Synder, *Juvenile Arrests 2000* (Washington, DC: Office of Juvenile Justice and Delinquency Prevention, 2000).
18. Associated Press, "Boy, 4, Fatally Shoots 18-Month-Old," *New York Times on the Web*, http://www.nytimes.com, March 4, 2002.
19. Associated Press, "7-Year-Old Boy Is Arrested for Stabbing Death," *Honolulu Advertiser*, December 4, 1991, p. A13.
20. Associated Press, "Boy, 8, Charged in Stabbing Death of 4-Year-Old." *Pocono Record*, September 8, 2001, p. A5.
21. Associated Press, "Girl, 8, Charged with Poisoning Grandmother," *Honolulu Advertiser*, February 22, 1998, p. 15.
22. "11-year-old Boy to Be Tried as Adult," *Honolulu Advertiser*, December 15, 1997, p. A3.
23. "Boy Found Guilty of Murder," *Honolulu Advertiser*, November 17, 1999, p. A3.
24. Associated Press, "13-Year-Old Killer Spared Life Term," *Honolulu Advertiser*, January 14, 2000.
25. Lawrie Mifflin, "Pediatricians Give TV Thumbs Down for Kids," *Star Bulletin*, August 4, 1999, p. 1A.
26. Ibid.
27. Thom Geier, "Eye on the '90s," *U.S. News and World Report*, July 8, 1996, p. 21.
28. David E. Rosenbaum, "Politicians Speak Out but Are Wary of Restricting Film Violence," *New York Times on the Web*, http://www.nytimes.com, October 13, 1999.
29. Ibid.
30. Stephen Braun, "Film Linked to School Shootings," *Honolulu Advertiser*, December 5, 1997, p. A8.
31. Caryn James, "TV Diet of Torture Games and Gross-Out Stunts," *New York Times on the Web*, http://www.nytimes.com, February 4, 2002.
32. Associated Press, "Texas Convicts Boy of Murder," *Honolulu Advertiser*, October 19, 1997, p. A7.
33. Associated Press, "13-Year-Old Killer Spared Life Term."
34. "Congress Threatens to Regulate Violence in Movies, Games," *Honolulu Advertiser*, May 5, 1999, p. A3.
35. Rosenbaum, "Politicians Speak Out."
36. Associated Press, "Chicago Aldermen Throw Questions at Special Guest, TV's Jerry Springer," *Star Bulletin*, June 5, 1999, p. 2.
37. "Controversial Lyrics Prompt Wal-Mart, Kmart to Pull Album," *Honolulu Advertiser*, December 7, 1997, p. A22; Associated Press, "Women Activists Protest Time Warner Role in Rock Song," *Honolulu Advertiser*, December 19, 1997, p. 7; Associated Press, "MTV Pulls Video after Women Protest," *Honolulu Advertiser*, December 20, 1997, p. 3.
38. Associated Press, "Thousands See Suicide on TV," *Honolulu Advertiser*, May 1, 1998, p. A 16.
39. "Police Slay Freeway-Case Driver," *Honolulu Advertiser*, November 27, 1999, p. A3.
40. James, "TV Diet of Torture Games."
41. Dean E. Murphy, "Teenager Held in Killings of Six People," *New York Times on the Web*, http://www.nytimes.com, February 23, 2002.
42. Associated Press, "Teen Arraigned in Deaths of Five," *Honolulu Advertiser*, December 4, 1998, p. A19.
43. Associated Press, "6 Classmates Watched Rape, Prosecutor Says," *Honolulu Advertiser*, October 12, 1996, p. A15.
44. Associated Press, "Fla. Youngsters Admit Killing," *New York Times on the Web*, http://www.nytimes.com, December 28, 2001.
45. Associated Press, "16-year-old Arrested in Zoo Shooting," *Honolulu Advertiser*, April 2, 2000, p. A3.
46. Jim Yardley, "U. of Texas Seeks to Close Wound of Mass Killing and Suicides," *New York Times on the Web*, http://www.nytimes.com, September 16, 1999.
47. Gannett News Service, "School Violence Report Finds Campuses Generally Safe," *Honolulu Advertiser*, July 29, 1998, p. 3.

48. "Schools Singling Out Threatening Students," *Honolulu Advertiser*, September 23, 1988, p. 3.
49. Associated Press, "Mayors Seek School Violence Remedy," *Honolulu Advertiser*, September 23, 1988, p. A3.
50. Robert McFadden, "Violence, Real and Imagined, Sweeps through Schools after the Shootings," *New York Times on the Web*, http://www.nytimes.com, April 30, 1999.
51. Associated Press, "Schoolmate Held in Shooting Death of Girl, 13," *Honolulu Advertiser*, November 21, 1999, p. A22.
52. Jon Nordheimer, "Seventh-Grade Boy Held in Killing of Teacher," *New York Times on the Web*, http://www.nytimes.com, May 26, 2000
53. "12-year-old Pulls Gun on Classmates," *Honolulu Advertiser*, March 24, 2000, p. A5.
54. Associated Press, "Expert: Suspects Spurred by Dares," *New York Times on the Web*, http://www.nytimes.com, February 24, 2002.
55. "Teenagers Indicted in Satanic Murders," *Honolulu Advertiser*, October 17, 1997, p. A3.
56. Tom Kisken, "No Matter What, Boys will be Boys," *Star-Bulletin*, August 4, 1999, p. A3.
57. Barbara Tatem Kelley, David Huizinga, Terence P. Thornberry, and Rolf Loeber, *Epidemiology of Serious Violence* (Washington, DC: U.S. Department of Justice, June 1997), p. 9.
58. Tamara Henry, "School Shooters Defy Profiling, Secret Service Study Reports," *Honolulu Advertiser*, April 7, 2000, p. 3.
59. Office of Juvenile Justice and Delinquency Prevention, *The 8% Solution* (Washington, DC: U.S. Department of Justice, November 2001), p. 1.
60. Ibid.
61. Roger Rosenblatt, "The Killing of Kayla," *Time*, March 13, 2000, pp. 26–29.
62. *National Drug Control Strategy* (Washington, DC: The White House, February 2002), p. 1.
63. Ibid.
64. Ibid.
65. Associated Press, "2 Amish Admit Drug Dealing," *Honolulu Advertiser*, October 6, 1998, p. A2.
66. Rufus King, "It's Time to Open the Doors of Our Prisons," *Newsweek*, April 19, 1999, p. 10.
67. Ellis Cose, "Locked Away and Forgotten," *Newsweek*, February 28, 2000, p. 54; "Race Said to Be Factor in Arrests," *Honolulu Advertiser*, June 8, 2000, p. A3.
68. "CIA Investigation Clears Agency of Ties to Crack Cocaine Dealers," *Honolulu Advertiser*, December 18, 1997, p. A16.
69. Timothy Egan, "A Drug Ran Its Course, Then Hid with Its Users," *New York Times on the Web*, http://www.nytimes.com, September 20, 1999.
70. Peggy Orenstein, "Staying Clean," *New York Times on the Web*, http://www.nytimes.com, February 10, 2002.
71. Webb v. United States, 249 U.S. 96.
72. Knight Ridder News Service, "War on Drugs Attacked by Lawmaker on Far Right," *Honolulu Advertiser*, October 11, 1999, p. A7.
73. Ibid.
74. *The Economic Costs of Drug Abuse in the United States, 1992–1998* (Washington, DC: Office of National Drug Control Policy, September 2001), p. 34.
75. Ibid., p. 30.
76. Ibid., p. 57.
77. Ibid., p. 25.
78. Ibid., p. 82.
79. *National Drug Control Strategy*, p. 95.
80. *Economic Costs of Drug Abuse*, p. 9.
81. "Marijuana Growers Ravage U.S. Forests." *LATimes.com*, http://www.latimes.com, March 26, 2000.
82. Jodi Wilgoren, "Babies Used in Drug Ring, Officials Say." *New York Times on the Web*, http://www.nytimes.com, December 15, 2001.
83. David Waite, "Drugs, Child Abuse Interrelated," *Honolulu Advertiser*, May 27, 1999, p. A12.
84. Fox Butterfield, "As Drug Use Drops in Big Cities, Small Towns Confront Upsurge." *New York Times on the Web*, http://www.nytimes.com, February 11, 2002.
85. Alan I. Leshner, "Addiction Is a Brain Disease—and It Matters," *National Institute of Justice Journal*, October 1998: 2.
86. Ibid., p. 3.
87. Ibid., pp. 3–5.
88. *National Drug Control Strategy*, Foreword.
89. Ibid., p. 22.
90. Ibid.
91. Ibid., p. 23.
92. Ibid.
93. Ibid., p. 3.
94. Michael Jonofsky, "Border Agents on Lookout for Terrorists Are Finding Drugs," *New York Times on the Web*, http://www.nytimes.com, March 6, 2002.
95. "Afghan Farmers Heavily Cultivating Opium Poppies Again," *Pocono Record*, March 1, 2002, p. 3.
96. "Drug Traffic Rolls on Despite Terror," *Law Enforcement News*, December 15/31, 2001, p. 7.
97. "Pay Phones to Reject Coins in Drug War," *Star Bulletin*, July 16, 1991, p. 1.
98. "Matters of Opinion," *Law Enforcement Bulletin*, December 15/31, 2001, p. 21.
99. "ABC Refused to Submit Scripts to White House Drug Office," *Honolulu Advertiser*, January 16, 2000, p. A5.
100. Associated Press, "43,000 Students with Drug Convictions Face Denial of Aid," *New York Times on the Web*, http://www.nytimes.com, December 29, 2001.
101. Ibid.
102. Associated Press, "HUD's 'One-Strike' Drug Policy Upheld," *Honolulu Advertiser*, February 15, 2000, p. A7.
103. "Needle Exchange Endorsed," *Honolulu Advertiser*, April 21, 1998, p. A3.
104. Pam Belluck, "Program Offers Women Addicts $200 in Exchange for Sterilization," *New York Times on the Web*, http://www.nytimes.com, August 24, 1999.
105. "Has the DARE Curriculum Gone to Pot?" *Law Enforcement News*, December 15/31, 2001, p. 6.
106. *National Drug Control Strategy*, p. 4.
107. Kevin Dayton, "Release Foreseen for Comatose Halawa Inmate," *Star-Bulletin & Advertiser*, December 8, 1991, p. A3.
108. Joan Petersilia, *When Prisoners Return to the Community: Political, Economic, and Social Consequences* (Washington, DC: U.S. Department of Justice, November 2000), p. 4.
109. Laura M. Maruschak and Allen J. Beck, *Medical Problems of Inmates, 1997* (Washington, DC: U.S. Department of Justice, January 2001), p. 1.
110. "Unintended Consequences of Sentencing Policy: The Creation of Long-Term Healthcare Obligations," in *Research in*

Review (Washington, DC: U.S. Department of Justice, November 2001), p. 1.
111. Bureau of Justice Statistics, *Challenging the Conditions of Prisons and Jails: A Report on Section 1983 Litigation* (Washington, DC: U.S. Department of Justice, December 1994), p. 8.
112. Tammerlin Drummond, "Cellblock Seniors," *Time*, June 21, 1999, p. 60.
113. Ibid.
114. Maruschak and Beck, *Medical Problems of Inmates, 1997.*
115. Ibid., p. 1.
116. Ibid., p. 4
117. Ibid., p. 6.
118. "Guards Allegedly Shot Inmate for Sport," *Honolulu Advertiser*, February 27, 1998, p. A11; "Panel Finds Prison Misused Deadly Force," *Honolulu Advertiser*, November 27, 1998, p. A 17.
119. Ira J. Silverman and Manuel Vega, *Corrections: A Comprehensive View* (Minneapolis/Saint Paul, MN: West, 1996), p. 313.
120. Southern Center for Human Rights, "US Penitentiary Officials to Pay $99K Settlement in Prison Torture Case Brought by Center's Attorneys." Southern Center for Human Rights, http://www.schr.org/news/news_uspenitentiary.htm, December 28, 2001.
121. Silverman and Vega, *Corrections*, p. 235.
122. "Deputies Investigated in Prison Beatings," *Honolulu Advertiser*, February 27, 1998, p. B10.
123. Joan Petersilia, *When Prisoners Return to the Community*, p. 2.
124. William J. Fraser, "Getting the Drop on Street Gangs and Terrorists," *Law Enforcement News*, November 30, 2001, p 11.
125. Silverman and Vega, *Corrections*, p. 208.
126. Fraser, "Getting the Drop."
127. Ibid.
128. Ibid.
129. Ibid.
130. Rebecca Widom and Theodore M. Hammett, *HIV/AIDS and STDs in Juvenile Facilities* (Washington, DC: U.S. Department of Justice, April 1996), p. 1.
131. Laura M. Maruschak, *HIV in Prisons and Jails, 1999* (Washington, DC: U.S. Department of Justice, July 2001), p. 1.
132. Ibid.
133. Ibid.
134. Ibid.
135. Ibid.
136. Ibid.
137. Lawrence K. Altman, "Much More AIDS in Prisons Than in General Populations," *New York Times on the Web*, http://www.nytimes.com, September 2, 1999.
138. Ibid.
139. Karen Wilcock, Theodore M. Hammett, Rebecca Widom, and Joel Epstein, *Tuberculosis in Correctional Facilities 1994–1995* (Washington, DC: U.S. Department of Justice, July 1996), p. 1.
140. Ibid.
141. Joan Petersilia, *Challenges of Prisoner Reentry and Parole in California*, California Policy Research Center Brief Series, June 2000, http://www.ucop.edu/cprc/parole.html, February 11, 2002.
142. Fox Butterfield, "Experts Say Study Confirms Prison's New Role as Mental Hospital," *New York Times on the Web*, http://www.nytimes.com, July 12, 1999.
143. Ibid.
144. Ibid.
145. ACLU News Wire, "Jails No Place for the Mentally Ill, ACLU of Mississippi Says," http://www.aclu.org/news, January 16, 2002.
146. Paula M. Ditton, *Mental Health and Treatment of Inmates and Probationers* (Washington, DC: U.S. Department of Justice, July 1999), p. 1.
147. Allen J. Beck and Laura M. Maruschak, *Mental Health Treatment in State Prisons, 2000* (Washington, DC: U.S. Department of Justice, July 2001), p. 1.
148. Ibid.
149. Joan Petersilia, *When Prisoners Return to the Community*, p. 2.
150. ACLU News Wire, "Jails No Place."
151. Butterfield, "Experts Say Study Confirms."
152. Ditton, *Mental Health and Treatment*, p. 3.
153. Ibid.
154. Butterfield, "Experts Say Study Confirms."
155. Erving Goffman, *Asylums: Essays on the Social Situation of Mental Patients and Other Inmates* (Garden City, NY: Anchor Books, 1961).
156. Butterfield, "Experts Say Study Confirms."
157. Ditton, *Mental Health and Treatment*, p. 5.
158. Ibid.
159. Ibid.
160. Ibid.
161. Ibid.
162. Ibid., p. 9.
163. Linda A. Teplin, *Assessing Alcohol, Drug, and Mental Disorders in Juvenile Detainees* (Washington, DC: U.S. Department of Justice, January 2001), p. 1.
164. Associated Press, "Au Pair Ruling Coming via E-Mail," *Honolulu Advertiser*, April 15, 1998, p. 11.
165. "Man Who Confessed on Internet to Killing Daughter Sentenced to 40 years," CNN Custom News, http://www.customnews.cnn.com, October 9, 1998.
166. Arthur Santana and Allan Lengel, "D.C. Police Probe Blue E-Mail," *Washington Post*, March 28, 2001, p. 1.
167. "Giant Techno Leaps in Small Packages," *Law Enforcement News*, December 15/31, 2001, p. 22.
168. "NOPD to Make Crime Maps Interactive," *Law Enforcement News*, November 30, 1998, p 5.
169. Associated Press, "Reverse 911 Helps Nabs Thief," *Honolulu Advertiser*, January 24, 2000, p. 3A.
170. "Auto Mug Shots Show Their Worth in St. Louis Area," *Law Enforcement News*, November 30, 2001, p. 5.
171. "Camera Rage Strikes Hawaii Drivers," *New York Times on the Web*, http:/www.nytimes.com, January 27, 2002.
172. "On-line Humiliation for Traffic Violators," *Law Enforcement News*, November 30, 1998, p. 10.
173. Matt Richtel, "Investigators Face a Glut of Confiscated Computers," *New York Times on the Web*, http://www.nytimes.com, August 27, 1999.
174. Ibid.
175. Ibid.
176. Carl Kaplan, "A Search Site for Search Sites Is Accused of Trespassing," *New York Times on the Web*, http://www.nytimes.com, September 27, 1999.
177. Stephen Lagbaton, "Net Sites Co-Opted by Pornographers," *New York Times on the Web*, http://www.nytimes.com, September 27, 1999.
178. "Storming the Fortress," *Business Week*, February 21, 2000, p. 40.

179. Amy Harmon, "Illegal Kidney Auction Pops Up on Ebay's Site," *New York Times on the Web*, http://www.nytimes.com, September 3, 1999.
180. "Computer Waste Poisoning People in Third World," *Pocono Record*, March 1, 2002, p. A6; Associated Press, "Computer Waste Exposing Many to Numerous Hazards," *Pocono Record*, February 25, 2002, p. 5.
181. Gannett News Service, "Computers Helping Counterfeiters Cash In," *Honolulu Advertiser*, March 31, 1998, p. 1.
182. Michael White, "Man Ordered to Repay $93,000 for Stock Hoax on Internet," *Honolulu Advertiser*, August 31, 1999, p. C4.
183. National White Collar Crime Center and the Federal Bureau of Investigation, "IFCC Annual Internet Fraud Report," http://www.ifccfbi.gov, March 15, 2002.
184. Associated Press, "Identity Theft Is Top Consumer Fraud Complaint," *Pocono Record*, January 24, 2002, p. A8.
185. Marcy Gordon, "U.S. to Combat Fake IDs from Internet," *Milwaukee Journal Sentinel*, May 20, 2000, p. 8A.
186. "14 Countries Strike at Net Child Pornography Ring," *Honolulu Advertiser*, September 3, 1998, p. A3.
187. "Child Porn Ring on Internet Broken Up, Agency Says," *Washington Post*, March 18, 2001, p. A5.
188. "Online Sting Suspect Says It Was Just Fantasy," *Honolulu Advertiser*, December 10, 1999, p. A16; Associated Press, "Missing Teen-ager Found Restrained," *New York Times on the Web*, http://www.nytimes.com, January 5, 2002.
189. Associated Press, "Teen Internet Fraud on the Rise," *New York Times on the Web*, http://www.nytimes.com, February 14, 2002.
190. Ibid.
191. "The Ripple Effect," *Newsweek*, February 18, 2002, p. 29.
192. David Firestone and Michael Moss, "More Corpses Are Discovered Near Crematory," *New York Times on the Web*, http://www.nytimes.com, February 18, 2002.
193. Associated Press, "No Bail for Crematory Operator," *New York Times on the Web*, http://www.nytimes.com, February 23, 2002.
194. Pam Belluck and Greg Winter, "Crematory Case Highlights Gaps in Oversight of Funeral Business," *New York Times on the Web*, http://www.nytimes.com, February 23, 2002.
195. Adam Cohen, "Cyberspeech on Trial," *Time*, February 15, 2000, p. 52.
196. John Markoff, "A Mysterious Component Roils Microsoft," *New York Times on the Web*, http://www.nytimes.com, September 5, 1999.
197. Ibid.
198. Ibid.
199. Jeri Clausing, "New Fight over Encryption Rules," *New York Times on the Web*, http://www.nytimes.com, September 27, 1999.
200. Tom Clancy, *Net Force: Point of Impact* (New York: Berkley Books, 2001).
201. "Net Crime Does Pay for Cops," http://www.cnn.com, March 4, 2000.
202. Vicki Viotti, "High-Tech Crimes and Misdemeanors," *Honolulu Advertiser*, January 22, 1999, p. C1.
203. William Doolittle, "Man Pleads Guilty to Selling Porn on Net," *Pocono Record*, March 4, 2002, p. A3.
204. Ibid.
205. Steven Levy, "Courting a Cryptro Win," *Newsweek*, May 17, 1999, p. 85; John Markoff, "U.S. Drafting Plan for Computer Monitoring System," *New York Times on the Web*, http://www.nytimes.com, August 1, 1999.
206. Anthony Ramirez, "Judge Rules Internet Gambling Is Not Beyond Reach of State Authorities," *New York Times on the Web*, http://www.nytimes.com, July 27, 1999.
207. Gregory Vistica, "Inside the Secret Cyberwar," *Newsweek*, February 21, 2000, p. 48.
208. Ibid.
209. "Hacking Shuts Down State Site," *Honolulu Advertiser*, July 6, 1999, p. B3.
210. Associated Press, "Hackers Infiltrate Again at Senate," *Honolulu Advertiser*, June 12, 1999, p. A9.
211. "Hackers Attack Army Web Site," *Honolulu Advertiser*, June 29, 1999.
212. Jeri Clausing, "Computer Intruders Apparently from Russia, Senate Panel Is Told," *New York Times on the Web*, http://www.nytimes.com, October 7, 1999.
213. Vistica, "Inside the Secret Cyberwar."
214. Associated Press, "New Center Will Combat Computer Crime Security Threats," *New York Times on the Web*, http://www.nytimes.com, October 1, 1999; Associated Press, "High-Tech Crime-Fight Lab Unveiled," *New York Times on the Web*, http://www.nytimes.com, September 27, 1999.
215. "Traditional FBI Roles Are History as A-G Redefines Bureau's Mission," *Law Enforcement News*, November 30, 2001, p. 1.
216. "Justice by the Numbers," *Law Enforcement News*, December 15/31, 2001, p. 23.
217. Timothy Egan, "A Computer Shutdown Plays Havoc at Interior," *New York Times on the Web*, http://www.nytimes.com, February 14, 2002.
218. Ibid.
219. "Expert Says U.S. May Retaliate with Force if Countries Try Cyberterrorsim," *Pocono Record*, February 14, 2002, p. A2.
220. Ibid.
221. Ibid.

Glossary

abolitionists People opposed to the use of capital punishment.

accreditation Voluntary rating of police departments according to standards set by the Commission on Accreditation for Law Enforcement Agencies (CALEA), designed to promote police professionalism.

actus reus The actions of the person committing a crime as defined by law, one of the key elements of a crime.

adjudicated A court case is decided without determination of guilt or innocence, especially in juvenile court, when a judge places a juvenile in the custody of the state for treatment or confinement.

alibi A witness or evidence in court establishing that the defendant could not have committed the crime.

anomie Emile Durkheim's concept of normlessness and social isolation as symptoms of a dysfunctional society and causes of deviant behavior.

appellate courts Appellate courts have the authority to review the proceedings and verdicts of general trial courts for judicial errors.

arraignment Short hearing before a judge in which the charges against the defendant are announced and the defendant is asked if he or she is guilty or not guilty.

arrest Official taking into police custody of a lawbreaker or suspect with a warrant or probable cause.

arson The malicious burning of a structure.

Article X Article X of the United States Constitution proscribes that all powers not explicitly granted to the federal government are reserved as state powers.

assault The crime of willfully inflicting injury on another.

atavistic stigmata Physical characteristics, representing earlier or prehuman stages of evolution, that were believed to distinguish criminals from others.

attempt An incomplete criminal act, the closest act to the completion of the crime.

bagnes Private French seaport prisons of the 1700s housing former galley slaves.

bail Release of a defendant from custody on the promise by the accused—not a custodian—often secured with a monetary bond, that the defendant will return to court at the necessary times to address the charges.

bail bondsperson An agent of a private commercial business that has contracted with the court to act as a guarantor of a defendant's return to court.

bailiff A county deputy sheriff or U.S. deputy marshall responsible for providing security and maintaining order in a courtroom.

banishment Removal of the offender from the community.

bar examination A rigorous test of the laws and procedures of a state that must be passed in order to practice law in that state.

bench trial Judicial process to determine the guilt or innocence of a defendant in which the determination is made by a judge, not a jury.

benevolent associations Local or municipal collective bargaining units.

bifurcated trial Two-part trial structure in which the jury first determines guilt or innocence and then considers new evidence relating to the appropriate punishment.

biocriminology A new field in criminology encompassing modern biological approaches (such as neurochemistry and neuroendocrinology) to explaining criminal behavior.

bioterrorism Use of biological or biochemical weapons in terrorist acts.

Bivens actions Civil suits against federal law enforcement agents for denial of constitutional rights.

Black Codes Laws passed by southern states after the Civil War to disenfranchise freed slaves.

blue-collar policing Style of policing emphasizing physical expression and interaction between police and public and reflecting the values of lower middle class and urban communities.

booking Police activity that establishes the identification of an arrested person and formally charges that person with a crime.

branding Burning a mark or letter on an offender's body.

Bridewell A workhouse in London in the 1500s, in which basic necessities and skills to be productive were taught to the incarcerated poor and mentally ill.

brief A concise statement of the main points of a law case.

broken window theory Belief that ignoring public order violations and disruptive behavior leads to community neglect, which fosters further disorder and crime.

burglary A combination of tresspass and the intent to perform a crime.

capital punishment The sentence of death.

Carroll Doctrine Terms defining the admissibility of evidence obtained in a warrantless search of an automobile, established in *Carroll v. United States* (1925).

causation The legal requirement for a crime that the harm is the result of the union of *actus reus* and *mens rea*.

certiorari power If four members of the Supreme Court believe a case meets its criteria for review, a writ of certiorari is issued, ordering the lower court to forward the record of the case to the Supreme Court.

chain gang In the southern penal system, convicts chained together during outside labor.

charge to the jury Written instructions about the application of the law to a case that the judge gives to the jury to help them achieve a verdict.

chief law enforcement officer Title applied to the sheriff of the county because his or her jurisdiction is greater than that of the local police agencies within the county.

chief of police Title of the chief administrative officer of a municipal police agency. The chief obtains his or her position by appointment of the mayor, city council, or other designated city agency, such as the police commission.

circuit court Any court that holds sessions in various locations within its jurisdiction.

circumstantial evidence Evidence that *implies* that the defendant is connected to the crime but does not *prove* the defendant is connected to the crime.

citizen input model Moderate oversight of police by non-sworn personnel who investigate complaints independently of the police department.

citizen monitor model Minimum oversight of police by civilian employees of the police department who monitor complaints.

citizen review board Permanent oversight body comprised of civilians with the power to inquire into alleged police misconduct.

citizen review model Maximum oversight of police by civilians appointed by a governmental agency that does not answer to the police department.

civil commitment process Process by which a person found not guilty by reason of insanity can be either released or confined in a mental institution.

civil law (private law) Civil law (private law) covers the law concerned with the definition, regulation, and enforcement of rights in cases in which both the person who has the right and the person who has the obligation are private individuals.

classical school Theories of crime causation based on Cesare Beccaria's assumption that criminal behavior is a matter of free-will choice.

clear and present danger Condition relating to public safety that may justify police use of deadly force against a fleeing suspect.

clearance rate Percentage of reported crimes determined to be solved.

Clerk of Court Government employee who works directly with the trial judge and is responsible for court paperwork and records before and during a trial.

Code of Hammurabi Earliest example of legal codes defining crimes and civil offenses.

common law Unwritten, simply stated laws from the English common laws, based on traditions and common understandings in a time when most people were illiterate.

community-based corrections Prevention and treatment programs to promote the successful transition of the offender from prison to the community.

community policing Decentralized policing programs that focus on crime prevention, quality of life in the community, public order, and alternatives to arrest.

commutation of sentence Reduction in the severity or length of an inmate's sentence, issued by a state governor or the president of the United States.

competent to stand trial The concept that defendants comprehend the charges against them and are able to assist their attorney in their defense.

computer security An area of criminal justice aimed at fighting cybercrime.

concurrence The legal requirement for a crime that there is a union of *actus reus* and *mens rea*.

conditional release A bail alternative in which the defendant is released from custody if he or she agrees to a number of court-ordered terms and restrictions.

conflict theories Theories of crime causation based on Marxian theory or the assumption that the sources of criminal behavior are class conflict and social inequality.

congregate work system The practice of moving inmates from sleeping cells to other areas of the prison for work and meals.

consent A defense in criminal law in which the defendant claims the action that caused the injury or death occurred during normal, acceptable standards of conduct.

consolidated model Organization of decision making about parole as a function of a state department of corrections.

conspiracy Criminal act requiring no *actus rea* other than communication.

constructive intent When an actor did not intend to harm anyone but should have known that his or her behavior created a high risk of injury.

containment theory Walter Reckless's theory that people are deterred from deviant behavior because of the influence on individuals of both internal and external social control factors.

contempt of court A charge against any violator of the judge's courtroom rules, authorizing the judge to impose a fine or term of imprisonment.

contraband Smuggled goods, such as drugs, cigarettes, money, or pornography.

convict lease system In southern penal systems, leasing prisoners to work for private contractors.

corporal punishment The administration of bodily pain, based on the premise that a painful experience suffered as the result of criminal activity will deter future crime.

corporate crime Crimes committed by corporate executives.

corpus delicti Reasonable evidence that a crime has actually occurred.

correctional case managers Social work caseworkers who specialize in helping offenders adjust to life in prison, release from prison, and successful reentry into the community.

correctional officer Uniformed jail or prison employee whose primary job is the security and movement of inmates.

counterterrorism The response to terrorism and efforts to stop it.

court docket The calendar on which court cases are scheduled for trial.

court of last resort A state court that reviews lower court decisions and whose decisions can be appealed to the U.S. Supreme Court.

court recorder (court reporter) Stenographer who transcribes every word spoken by the judge, attorneys, and witnesses during a trial.

courtroom work group Adversarial and neutral parties, usually the prosecutor, defense attorney, judge, and other court personnel, who get together and cooperate to settle cases with the least effort and conflict.

courts of limited jurisdiction State courts of original jurisdiction that are not courts of record (e.g., traffic courts, municipal courts, or county courts).

courts of record Courts in which trial proceedings are transcribed.

Crime Clock Data presentation strategy used by the FBI to report crime rates in terms of how often a crime occurs.

crime control model Model of the criminal justice system in which emphasis is placed on fighting crime and protecting potential victims.

crime prevention through environmental design (CPTED) Theory that crime can be prevented through environmental design, particularly urban housing design.

crimes of omission Crimes resulting from the failure to act or the lack of action rather than the commission of illegal acts.

criminal justice The study of the processes and people involved in a system of justice and the public policies, laws, and procedures that shape the administration and outcomes of those processes.

criminal justice system The enforcement, by the police, the courts, and correctional institutions, of obedience to laws.

criminal personality Theories from psychology that identify personality traits and habits of mind believed to be associated with criminality.

criminology The body of knowledge regarding crime as a social phenomenon and as a behavior.

cruel and unusual punishment Punishment that violates the principle of proportionality and is considered too harsh for the crime committed; prohibited by the Eighth Amendment.

cultural deviance theory Theories of crime causation based on the assumption that criminal behavior is learned through participation in deviant subcultures or countercultures within a society.

cybercrime Crimes against computers, or the use of computers to commit crimes.

cyberporn Internet-based pornography.

cyberterrorism The use of the Internet to facilitate terrorism-related crimes.

day reporting centers An intermediate sanction to provide a gradual adjustment to reentry under closely supervised conditions.

deadly force Police power to incapacitate or kill in the line of duty.

defenses Justifications or excuses defined by law by which a defendant may be released from prosecution or punishment for a crime.

deinstitutionalization Moving mentally ill people from long-term hospitalization to community-based care.

demand reduction programs Programs aimed at reducing the demand for drugs by users through educational programs and persuasion.

denial of service An attack in which the hacker attempts to crash or clog the targeted Internet site by overloading the web site with too many requests for information for the web site to respond.

deputy chief Title of the second in command of a municipal police agency. This is an appointed position by the chief of police.

deputy sheriffs Law enforcement officers working for the Office of the Sheriff. All law enforcement officers in the sheriff's office, regardless of rank, are deputy sheriffs.

determinate sentencing A sentencing model in which the offender is sentenced to a fixed term of incarceration.

deterrence Philosophy and practices that emphasize making criminal behavior less appealing.

deviance Behavior that violates social norms; deviance becomes crime when the behavior violates social norms that are expressed as criminal laws.

differential association theory Edwin Sutherland's theory that criminal behavior is learned through association with a peer group that engages in criminal behavior.

differential opportunity theory Richard Cloward and Lloyd Ohlin's theory that criminality stems from blocked opportunities based on where one lives, who one knows, and what skills, talents, and resources one has.

direct evidence Evidence that connects the defendant with the crime.

Dirty Harry syndrome Form of police corruption in which police officers take the law into their own hands in the belief that they are achieving justice.

diversion Sentencing option in which the defendant is diverted from the correctional system through alternatives such as community service, drug courts, boot camps, and treatment programs.

domestic terrorism Acts of terrorism committed by citizens of the country being terrorized.

double jeopardy The defendant can be charged only once and punished only once for a crime. If tried and found innocent, the defendant cannot be retried if new evidence of his or her guilt is discovered.

drug court An approach for dealing with drug offenders that is aimed at breaking the cycle of drug use and crime.

dual court system The political division of jurisdiction into two systems of courts, federal and state. Under this system, federal courts are separate from but have limited jurisdiction over state courts.

ducking stool In colonial America, forced immersion in water as punishment, through pain and public humiliation.

due process Rules and procedures for protecting individuals accused of crimes from arbitrary and excessive abuse of power by the government.

due process model Model of the criminal justice system in which emphasis is placed on protecting the rights of the accused.

duress A legal defense in which the accused acted involuntarily under threat of immediate and serious harm by another person.

ecoterrorism Violent destruction of the environment or natural resources on which people depend.

electronic monitoring An approach in home confinement programs that assures compliance through electronic means.

elements of a crime The illegal actions (*actus reus*) and criminal intentions (*mens rea*) of the actor along with the circumstances that link the two, especially causation.

entrapment Illegal arrest based on criminal behavior for which the police provided both the motivation and the means, tested in *Jacobson v. United States* (1992). Also, a legal defense in criminal court.

exclusionary rule Prohibits the use of evidence or testimony obtained in violation of the Fourth and Fifth Amendments of the U.S. Constitution, established in *Weeks v. United States* (1914) and extended to the states in *Mapp v. Ohio* (1961).

executive pardon An act by a governor or the president that forgives the prisoner and rescinds the sentence.

ex post facto law A law related to the principle that persons cannot be punished for actions committed before the law prohibiting the behavior was passed.

federal law enforcement Law enforcement agency under the control of the executive branch of the federal government.

felicitic calculus In classical and neoclassical theory, such as Jeremy Bentham's, the pain-pleasure principle by which people decide whether or not to commit a crime.

felony Serious criminal conduct punishable by incarceration for more than one year.

feminist criminology Field based on the assumption that gender inequality lies at the heart of crimes in which women are the victims or the perpetrators.

field-training program Probationary period during which police academy graduates train in the community under the direct supervision of experienced officers.

first appearance Judicial hearing before a magistrate, following booking. The magistrate judge reviews the charges, advises defendants of their rights, and sets bail.

fleeing felon doctrine Police practice of using deadly force against a fleeing suspect, made illegal in *Tennessee v.*

Garner (1985), except when there is clear and present danger to the public.

formal sanctions Social norms enforced through the laws of the criminal justice system.

frankpledge System of policing by use of kinship associations common in the Middle Ages in England.

Fruit of the Poisoned Tree Doctrine Extends the exclusionary rule to secondary evidence obtained indirectly in an unconstitutional search, established in *Silverthorne Lumber Co. v. United States* (1918) and in *Wolf v. Colorado* (1949).

furlough A reentry program for offenders, allowing them a chance to live in the community for a short period of time, in an effort to promote successful reentry into the community.

gag order A judge's order to participants and observers at a trial that the evidence or proceedings of the court may not be published, aired, or discussed publicly.

general deterrence Deterrence based on the logic that people who witness the pain suffered by those who commit crimes will desire to avoid that pain and will refrain from criminal activity.

general trial courts State courts of original jurisdiction; often called circuit courts, superior courts, district courts, courts of common pleas, and courts of first instance.

good faith exception Admissibility of evidence obtained in an illegal search when the police are found to have acted in good faith on the belief that their search was legal, established in *United States v. Leon* (1984) and *Massachusetts v. Sheppard* (1984) in contradiction to an earlier ruling in *Illinois v. Gates* (1982).

good-time credit A strategy of crediting inmates with extra days served toward early release, in an effort to encourage the prisoner to obey rules and participate in programs.

grand jury Panel of citizens similar to a trial jury that decides whether there is probable cause to indict a defendant on the charges alleged.

guilty but mentally ill An alternative verdict in capital cases based on the standard that the defendant was mentally ill but also was sufficiently aware (had sufficient *mens rea*) to be held "morally blameworthy" for the crime.

habitual offender laws Tough sentencing laws, such as "three strikes" laws, to punish repeat offenders more harshly.

halfway houses Transition programs that allow inmates to move from prison to the community in steps.

hearsay evidence Information about a crime obtained second-hand from another rather than directly observed.

hierarchy rule Practice in data collection for the FBI's *Uniform Crime Reports* of counting only the most serious crime in incidents involving multiple crimes or with multiple victims of the same crime.

home confinement A court-imposed sentence requiring offenders to remain confined in their own residences.

homicide Murder and manslaughter.

identity theft Use of the computer to find and steal victims' identities and credentials, usually to make purchases.

immunity A legal defense that the accused is exempt from prosecution because of diplomatic immunity, legislative immunity, witness immunity, or professional privilege.

incapacitation Deterrence based on the premise that the only way to prevent criminals from reoffending is to remove them from society.

incarceration The bodily confinement of a person in a jail or prison.

inchoate offenses Incomplete crimes such as solicitation, conspiracy, and attempt.

incomplete crimes Crimes that go beyond thought, but the *actus reus* and *mens rea* do not coincide because the plans were not carried out for any reason.

independent model Decision making about parole is under the authority of an autonomous parole board.

indeterminate sentence The defendant is sentenced to a prison term with a minimum and a maximum number of years to serve.

indeterminate sentencing A model of sentencing in which judges have nearly complete discretion in sentencing an offender.

Index Crimes The eight crimes in Part I of the *Uniform Crime Reports:* murder, forcible rape, robbery, aggravated assault, burglary, larceny, motor vehicle theft, and arson.

indictment The formal verdict of the grand jury that there is sufficient evidence to bring a person to trial.

indigent defense (1) Right to have an attorney provided free of charge by the state if a defendant cannot afford one, established in *Gideon v. Wainwright* (1963) and extended in *Argersinger v. Hamlin* (1972), *In re Gault* (1967), and *Escobedo v. Illinois* (1964). (2) Defense counsel for a defendant who cannot afford a private attorney.

informal sanctions Social norms that are enforced through the social forces of the family, school, government, and religion.

insanity A legal claim by a defendant that he or she did not understand the difference between right and wrong or was suffering from a disease or mental defect that made the defendant unable to appreciate the criminality of his or her action.

inside cell block Prison construction in which individual cells are stacked back to back in tiers in the center of a secure building.

intensive probation supervision (IPS) Probation supervised by probation and parole officers with smaller case loads, placing a greater emphasis on compliance with the conditions of supervision.

intent Criminal intentions or the state of "guilty mind" in *mens rea,* including general, specific, transferred, and constructive intent.

intermediate sanctions A term for punishments that restrict offenders' freedom without imprisoning them; community-based prevention and treatment programs to promote the successful transition of the offender from prison to the community.

internal affairs units Detective units within police departments that investigate alleged violations of department rules, citizens' complaints of police conduct, and criminal wrongdoing by police officers.

international terrorism Acts of terrorism committed by citizens of another nation.

investigative commission Municipal, state, or national body appointed as needed to investigate specific complaints about police behavior, such as the Wickersham, Knapp, and Mollen crime commissions.

Irish system Early form of parole invented by Sir Walter Crofton on the basis of the mark system, in which prisoners were released conditionally on good behavior and were supervised in the community.

jails Short term, multipurpose holding facilities that serve as the gateway for the criminal justice system.

judicial misconduct Unprofessional or illegal behavior by a judge that is considered inappropriate for his or her position or prejudicial to the persons involved in a trial.

jurisdiction Geographical area of responsibility and legitimate duties of an agency, court, or law enforcement officer.

jurisprudence The science or philosophy of law.

jury trial Judicial process to determine the guilt or innocence of a defendant in which the determination is made by a jury, not a judge.

labeling theory Frank Tannenbaum and Howard Becker's theory that people are strongly influenced by society's expectations of them, such that juveniles labeled as criminals are more likely to become criminals.

landmark cases U.S. Supreme Court cases that mark significant changes in interpretations of constitutionality.

larceny Wrongfully taking and carrying away of another's property with the intent to permanently deprive the property's owner of its possession.

legalistic style Style of policing emphasizing the role of the police officer as crime fighter and rule enforcer.

legal standard of evidence Evidence and the testimony of witnesses must be competent, material and relevant.

Legis Henrici Laws of England issued by King Henry I that established judicial districts and gave the government new powers in regard to the criminal justice system.

local law enforcement Municipal or county law enforcement officer; also includes certain special police agencies with limited jurisdiction, such as campus police.

Magna Carta Secured civil and criminal rights for English noblemen and similar to America's Bill of Rights in establishing due process for citizens of Great Britain.

mala in se Acts that are crimes because they are inherently evil or harmful to society.

mala prohibita Acts that are prohibited because they are defined as crimes by law.

mandatory release After prisoners serve the entire length of their maximum sentence, it is required by law that they be released.

mandatory sentencing The strict application of full sentences in the determinate sentencing model.

manslaughter The killing of another without malice, without the specific intent to kill.

mark system Early form of parole invented by Alexander Maconochie in which prisoners demonstrated their rehabilitation by earning points for good behavior.

maximum-security prisons Prisons for inmates at high risk of escape or who are dangerously violent to other inmates or staff.

media violence The portrayal of violence in the media.

medium-security prisons Fortress-like, walled, self-contained institutions that offer inmates educational, vocational, and rehabilitation programs.

memorandum of agreements (MOA) Union contract negotiated between the bargaining unit and the police department.

mens rea The state of mind and intent of the person committing the *actus reus,* one of the key elements of a crime.

metro police Local police agency that spans several geographical jurisdictions, such as cities or city and county.

military police Military personnel with special training and jurisdiction to provide law enforcement services on military installations.

minimal brain dysfunction (MBD) A biological explanation of crime, suggesting that small disruptions of normal brain functioning are responsible for violent behavior.

minimum-security prisons Prisons with few physical barriers to escape and many programs for inmates.

Miranda rights Five rights protecting, for example, the right to avoid self-incrimination and the right to an attorney, of which citizens are informed during police arrest and interrogation, established in *Miranda v. Arizona* (1966).

misdemeanor Less serious criminal conduct punishable by incarceration for less than a year.

mistake or ignorance of fact or law An affirmative legal defense claiming that the defendant made a mistake or acted out of ignorance and therefore did not meet the requirement for *mens rea*.

Model Penal Code Guidelines for U.S. criminal codes published in 1962 by the American Law Institute that define and classify crimes into categories according to victim, including crimes against the state, persons, habitations, property, public order, and public morals.

money laundering Concealment of the source of money.

motion Formal request by the prosecution or defense for the court to rule on any relevant matter in a case, such as the competency of the defendant to stand trial, the location of the trial, the jurisdiction of the court, or objections to evidence gathered by police.

motion for a bill of particulars Allows the defense to receive more details as to exactly what items the prosecution considers illegal if a defendant is charged with possession of burglary tools, illegal weapons, drug paraphernalia, or illegal gambling paraphernalia.

motion for change of venue A pretrial request, either by the prosecutor or the defense, to move the trial to another courtroom.

motion for continuance A pretrial request to delay the start of the trial.

motion for discovery A pretrial motion filed by the defense counsel, requesting that the prosecutor turn over all relevant evidence, including the list of witnesses, that the prosecution may use at the trial.

motion for dismissal A pretrial defense motion that the charges against the defendant be dismissed.

motion for severance of charges or defendants A pretrial request that the defendant be tried for each charge separately or that multiple defendants charged with the same crime be tried separately.

motion for suppression A pretrial motion made by the defense to exclude certain evidence from being introduced in the trial.

murder All intentional killings and deaths that occur in the course of aggrevated felonies.

mutilation Cutting off of body parts as punishment for criminal offenses.

narcoterrorism The redefinement of drug trafficking as terrorism, used to emphasize its significance.

necessity An affirmative legal defense claiming the defendant committed the act as a result of forces of nature and therefore did not meet the requirement for *mens rea*.

negligent practices Negligent hiring, training, supervision, or retention of personnel as grounds for civil suits against the police.

neoclassical school A later version of classical theory in which children under the age of seven and offenders suffering mental disease should be exempt from criminal liability because their conditions interfere with the exercise of free will.

neutralization theory Gresham Sykes and David Matza's theory that criminals learn techniques that allow them to rationalize their behavior, deny responsibility for harm, and avoid being guilt ridden.

not guilty by reason of insanity A verdict in which the defense has proven to the jury's satisfaction that the defendant was guilty but legally insane.

officer of the court Law enforcement officer that is used by the court to serve papers, provide courtroom security, and transport defendants.

official misconduct and error A label for abuses of power and mistakes by people in the criminal justice system that can lead to wrongful convictions and wrongful incarceration.

order maintenance (1) A system of maintaining the day-to-day life of ordinary citizens, a primary goal of the criminal justice system. (2) Non-crime-fighting services performed by the police, such as mediation, providing for the welfare of vulnerable persons, and crowd control.

original jurisdiction The first court to hear and render a verdict regarding the charges against the defendant.

page jacking A program that captures a user's computer and directs the computer to a web site that the user did not want to go to and cannot exit from except by turning off the computer.

parens patriae Philosophy of the juvenile court that the court is acting in the best interests of a juvenile, as if it were the juvenile's parent.

parole Early release from prison before the maximum sentence is served, based on evidence of rehabilitation and the good behavior of the inmate.

parole board Individuals appointed to a body that meets in prisons to make decisions about granting parole release to inmates.

parole d'honneur Origin of parole based on the concept of releasing prisoners "on their honor" after serving a portion of their sentence but before the maximum term.

parole hearings Meetings with inmates, attorneys, and others in which the parole board decides whether to grant, deny, or revoke parole.

pat-down search Right to search a person for a concealed weapon on the basis of reasonable suspicion, established in *Terry v. Ohio* (1968).

penitentiary Correctional institution based on the concept that inmates could change their criminality through reflection and penitence.

per curiam opinion A case that is disposed of by the U.S. Supreme Court that is not accompanied by a full opinion.

peremptory challenge The subjective evaluation of the attorney that is used to exclude jurors.

phrenology Franz Joseph Gall's science of reading bumps on the skull to identify character traits such as criminality.

picket fence model Model of the criminal justice system, with the local, state, and federal criminal justice systems depicted as three horizontal levels connected vertically by the roles, functions, and activities of the agencies that comprise them.

piggybacking A form of cybertrespassing.

pillory (stocks) In colonial America, a torturous restraining device in which offenders were forced to endure pain and public ridicule.

plaintiff The party that brings suit in court.

plain-view search Right to gather evidence in plain sight without a warrant, established in *Harris v. United States* (1968) and redefined in *United States v. Irizarry* (1982), *Arizona v. Hicks* (1987), and *Horton v. California* (1990).

plea Defendant's statement that he or she is guilty, not guilty, or offers "no contest."

plea bargaining Negotiations between the prosecution and the defense for a plea of guilty in exchange for reduced charges or a lighter sentence.

Plessy v. Ferguson (1896) U.S. Supreme Court landmark case that established the "separate but equal" doctrine that allowed racial segregation.

police academy Facility or programs for the education and training of police recruits.

police commission Board of civilians appointed by the mayor or city council to act in an oversight role.

police lineups Opportunities for victims to identify a criminal from among a number of suspects.

police unions Labor unions of diverse types that represent the interests law enforcement personnel.

polygraph Lie-detector test given to help screen law enforcement applicants.

positive school School of thought that emphasizes the importance of the scientific method to determine the factors that contribute to criminal behavior.

posse comitatus The power of a law enforcement officer to utilize civilians or military troops to assist in law enforcement work.

possession Knowingly having, holding, carrying, or knowing the location of an illegal or prohibited item; can constitute the *mens rea* of a crime.

praetors Roman Empire era officials who assisted in the investigation of charges against a person.

preliminary hearing Hearing before a magistrate judge in which the prosecution presents evidence to convince the judge that there is probable cause to bring the defendant to trial.

presentence investigation report Report on the background of the convicted defendant, the circumstances of the crime, and any other information relevant for determining the most appropriate sentence.

presentence investigator The person appointed by the court to investigate the offender's life, previous crimes and punishments, and present attitudes, as well as the impact of the crime on victims and the community.

presumption of innocence Most important principle of the due process model, requiring that all accused persons are treated as innocent until proven guilty in a court of law.

presumptive sentencing A structured sentencing model that attempts to balance sentencing guidelines with mandatory sentencing and at the same time provide discretion to the judge.

principle of legality The belief that specific laws defining crimes and penalties for crimes must exist and be made public before the government can punish citizens for violating them.

principle of proportionality The belief that less serious harms should carry lesser punishments than more serious harms.

prisoner classification The reception and diagnosis of an inmate to decide the appropriate security level in which to place the prisoner and services of placement.

prison farm system In southern penal systems, using inmate labor to maintain large profit-making prison farms or plantations.

prisonization Socialization into a distinct prison subculture with its own values, mores, norms, and sanctions.

privatization Trend toward the use of for-profit jails and prisons run by private companies.

probable cause (1) Determination from evidence and arguments that there are valid reasons for believing that the accused has committed a crime. (2) Strong likelihood of a direct link between a suspect and a crime.

probation and parole officers State and federal professional employees who report to the courts and supervise defendants released on probation and offenders released from prison on parole.

probation (1) Disposition in which a convicted defendant is offered an opportunity to avoid serving any time in prison by agreeing to fulfill conditions set forth by the court. (2) Conditional release of a convicted offender prior to his or her serving any prison time.

problem-oriented policing Proactive type of community policing that focuses on solving the underlying problems of delinquency and crime.

pro bono Free counsel offered to indigent defendants.

procedural due process The requirement that the government must follow established procedures and treat defendants equally.

procedural law Body of laws for how things should be done at each stage of the criminal justice process.

prosecutorial discretion The power of prosecutors to decide whether or not to charge the defendant and what the charge will be and to gather the evidence necessary to prosecute the defendant in a court of law.

psychoanalytic theory Sigmund Freud's theory that behavior is not a free-will choice but is controlled by subconscious desires.

public defenders Attorneys who are employees of the state, hired to provide defense counsel to indigent defendants as an alternative to the assigned-counsel and contract attorney systems.

public safety exception Right to search without probable cause for the public good.

quaestore Roman Empire era judicial official whose responsibilities were similar to those of a magistrate judge.

rape (sexual assault) Non-consensual sexual relations.

reaction formation Albert Cohen's term for his cultural deviance theory in which lower-class youths reject middle-class values that they cannot attain and instead join countercultures that express the opposite values.

real evidence Physical evidence such a gun, a fingerprint, a photograph, or DNA matching.

rehabilitation Deterrence based on the premise that criminals can be "cured" of their problems and criminality and returned to society.

release on recognizance (ROR) Provides for the pretrial release of the accused, based merely on the defendant's unsecured promise of return for trial.

remanded The reversal of a decision by a higher court and the return of the case to the court of original jurisdiction with instructions to correct the judicial error.

restorative justice Model of deterrence that uses restitution programs, community work programs, victim-offender mediation, and other strategies to not only rehabilitate the offender but also address the damage done to the community and the victim.

retribution Deterrence based on the premise that criminals should be punished because they deserve it.

robbery The taking and carrying away of property from a person by force or threat of immediate use of force.

RSAT Residential Substance Abuse Treatment, a federal assistance program to help states provide for treatment instead of prison for substance abusers.

rule of law Principle that standards of behavior and privilege are established by laws and not by monarchs or religious leaders.

rules of evidence Requirements for introducing evidence and testimony in court.

school violence Violence that takes place at schools.

search incident to lawful arrest Right to search an arrestee without a warrant, established in *Chimel v. California* (1969).

Section 1983 lawsuits Civil suits based on a federal law making it illegal for anyone "acting under color of state law" to deny a citizen's constitutional rights.

security risk groups Groups that raise special threats, such as prison gangs.

self-defense An affirmative legal defense in which a defendant claims he or she committed the crime in defense of self and lacked criminal intent.

self-incrimination Involuntary confession or forced testimony of the accused, prohibited by the Fifth Amendment, as in the inadmissibility of evidence obtained by force in *Brown v. Mississippi* (1936) and extended in *Ashcraft v. Tennessee* (1944) and *Leyra v. Denno* (1954).

sentence Disposition of a case by determining the punishment for a defendant convicted of a crime.

sentencing The punishment for a crime as determined by a judge.

sentencing guidelines A sentencing model in which crimes are classified according to their seriousness, and a range of time to be served is mandated for crimes within each category.

sentencing hearing A gathering before a judge that hears appeals, in which the prosecution and the defense argue the accuracy of the presentence report and the appropriateness of the sentence.

service style Style of policing emphasizing community service and social service over crime-fighting activities.

sex offender registries Open-access online databases identifying known sex offenders on parole, maintained to protect communities and potential victims.

sheriff (1) County-level law enforcement official whose origin is from medieval England. (2) Chief administrative officer of the Office of Sheriff. The only elected position in law enforcement.

shire-reeve Early English Middle Ages name for "sheriff."

shock incarceration Programs (boot camps) that adapt military-style physical fitness and discipline training to the correctional environment.

shock probation Sentence for a first-time, nonviolent offender who was not expecting a sentence, intended to impress on the offender the possible consequences of his or her behavior by exposure to a brief period of imprisonment before probation.

signature bond Release based on the defendant's signature on a promise to return for trial.

silent system Correctional practice of prohibiting inmates from talking to other inmates.

slave patrols Civilian groups in the southern states whose primary role was to protect against rioting and revolts by slaves.

social bond theory Travis Hirschi's theory that strong social and emotional ties to social values and norms lessen the likelihood of deviant behavior.

social control theory Theories of crime causation based on the assumptions that people's belief in and identification with the values of their society and culture influence their behavior.

social determinism The assumption that criminal behavior is caused by social factors and social forces rather than by moral, environmental, psychological, or biological causes.

social disorganization theory Theories of crime causation based on the assumption that social conditions such as poverty, unemployment, poor schools, and substandard housing are significant factors contributing to delinquency and crime.

social injustice The state in which citizens of a legitimate government are powerless and oppressed.

social norms The expected normative behavior in a society.

solicitation The incomplete crime of urging, requesting, or commanding another person to commit a crime.

solitary confinement Practice of confining an inmate such that there is no contact with other people.

somatotype school Theories of crime causation based on the assumption that there is a link between the mind and the body and that this link is expressed in body types, and based on Cesare Lombroso's theory that a criminal can be identified by physical appearance.

sovereign immunity The historic claim of local, state, and federal governments that they were "above the law" and thus could not be sued in civil court.

special police Police with limited jurisdiction. Special police have very narrowly defined duties and sometimes extremely limited geographical jurisdiction.

specific deterrence Deterrence based on the premise that an individual is best deterred from committing future crimes by the specific nature of the punishment.

split sentencing After a brief period of imprisonment, the judge brings the offender back to court and offers the option of probation.

standard conditions of release Federal and state guidelines with rules with which parolees must comply to meet their conditions of release.

standard operating procedures (SOP) Standard departmental rules, regulations, and punishments for infringements, designed to promote police professionalism.

stare decisis The American system of developing and applying case law on the basis of precedents established in previous cases.

state law enforcement Law enforcement agencies under the command of the executive branch of the state government, such as the highway patrol and state police.

state prisons Correctional facilities for prisoners convicted of state crimes.

state-sponsored terrorism International terrorist threats instigated and sponsored by certain nations, such as Afghanistan under the Taliban-led government.

status offenses Offenses committed by a juvenile that are prohibited (declared illegal) only because of the offender's age.

statute of limitations Legal limits regarding the length of time between the discovery of the crime and the arrest of the defendant.

strain theory Robert Merton's theory that people are naturally law abiding but resort to crime when frustrated in finding legitimate means to economic success.

strict liability crimes Actions that do not require criminal intent to be defined as crimes, such as parking violations.

structured sentencing A sentencing model—including determinate sentencing, sentencing guidelines, and presumptive sentencing—that defines punishments rather than allowing indeterminate sentencing.

substantive due process Limits on the power of governments to create crimes unless there is compelling, substantial public interest in regulating or prohibiting the conduct.

supermax prisons Controversial, extreme forms of maximum-security prisons.

supply reduction programs Programs attempting to stop illegal drugs from entering the United States, disrupt distribution networks in the United States, put drug dealers out of business, destroy illegal drug crops, control chemicals needed to make illegal drugs, and arrest sellers and buyers.

suspended sentence Another term for *probation*, based on the fact that convicted offenders must serve their full sentence if they violate the terms of release.

system of social control A social system designed to maintain order and regulate interactions.

TASC Treatment Accountability for Safer Communities, a federal assistance program to help states break the addiction-crime cycle.

team policing Decentralizing development during the 1960s and 1970s in which small units of police personnel took responsibility for a particular geographical area.

technical violation Grounds for imprisonment of a probationer or parolee based on his or her violation of a condition of release.

terrorism The organized use of violence, the aim of which is the promotion of political or social change.

terrorists People who use violence and fear in an effort to panic or punish groups, institutions, or countries that they perceive as perpetrating social injustice.

testimonial evidence The testimony of a witness.

theories Statements of relationship or of cause and effect that attempt to explain or predict behavior or events; theories are macro, middle range, or micro depending on the number of cases and level of generalization.

thin blue line A metaphor for the police as lonely heroes forming a barrier between criminals and law-abiding citizens.

three strikes law The application of mandatory sentencing to give repeat offenders longer prison terms.

ticket of leave In the mark system, unconditional release from prison purchased with marks earned for good behavior.

tithing system System based on kinship and civilian responsibility and used to maintain social order and provide criminal justice for medieval England.

torts Private wrongs that cause physical harm to another.

total institutions Institutions that meet all of the inmate's basic needs, discourage individuality, punish dissent, and segregate those who do not follow the rules.

trafficking Movement of illegal drugs across borders.

transportation Eighteenth century practice by Great Britain of sending offenders to the American colonies and later Australia.

tribal police Police agency that provides police services on Indian reservations. Tribal police operate independently of local, state, and federal police due to a special relationship between the United States and Native Americans living on reservations.

truth in sentencing In the application of presumptive sentencing in states that cannot eliminate parole, the legal requirement that courts disclose the actual prison time the offender is likely to serve.

unsecured bond Release based on the defendant's promise to pay the court an amount similar to a cash bail bond if the defendant fails to fulfill a promise to return for trial.

Urban Cohort Roman Empire era military unit used to maintain law and order in the cities.

U.S. courts of appeals The panel of federal judges that hears appeals from the U.S. district courts and determines if a judicial error was made that could have substantially affected the court's decision.

U.S. district courts Trial courts of the federal system.

U.S. magistrate courts Federal lower courts with powers limited to trying lesser misdemeanors, setting bail, and assisting district courts in various legal matters.

U.S. Supreme Court The highest court in the American judiciary system, whose rulings on the constitutionality of a law, due process rights, and rules of evidence are binding on all federal and state courts.

victim impact statements Statements that the victims of a crime make at the sentencing hearing for the convicted offender.

vigilantism The system by which citizens assume the role and responsibility of official law enforcement agencies and act independently, often without observation of due process and rights, to take justice into their own hands.

violation An illegal action that is less serious than a misdemeanor and may carry the punishment of only a fine or suspension of privilege.

void for overbreadth Laws that are illegal because they are stated so broadly as to prohibit legal activities as well as illegal activities.

void for vagueness Laws that are illegal because they do not provide clear and reasonable definitions of the specific behaviors that are prohibited.

voir dire The process through which a jury is selected from the members of the jury pool who have been determined eligible for service.

warden The chief administrator of a prison.

warrant Legal permission to conduct a search, signed by a judge.

watchman style Style of policing emphasizing order maintenance, police discretion, and diversion.

Weed and Seed Nationwide federally supported crime prevention program that helps states reduce their crime rates by weeding out offenders and restoring neighborhoods.

white-collar policing Style of policing emphasizing education and upper middle class values, often found in college towns and suburbs.

wiretapping A form of search and seizure in which citizens' rights to privacy on the telephone are protected by the Fourth Amendment, first established in *Olmstead v.*

United States (1928) and extended to e-mail in *Katz v. United States* (1967).

workplace violence The use of violence in the workplace.

work release Program allowing facilities to release inmates for paid work in the community.

writ of certiorari The power of the U.S. Supreme Court to choose what cases it will hear.

XYY chromosome theory Biological theory of crime causation that an extra Y chromosome may lead to criminal behavior in males.

zero tolerance Strict enforcement of the laws, even for minor violations.

zone theory Environmental theory of crime causation based on the belief that structural elements of society such as poverty, illiteracy, lack of schooling, unemployment, and illegitimacy are powerful forces that influenced human interaction.

Name Index

Subject Index

Italic *t* denotes table; italic *f* denotes figure.

Photo credits:

Continued from the copyright page.

74, North Wind Picture Archives; 76, © Chris Hondros/Newmakers/Getty Images; 79, The Granger Collection; 81, University College London Library; 85 L, Library of Congress; 85 M, Brown Brothers; 85 R, National Library of Medicine; 92, © Underwood & Underwood/Corbis; 96, © Bob Daemmrich/The Image Works; 105, Drawn by Paddy Ferriter, Copyright held by Jeff Koon and Andy Powell; 110, © Jim Shaffer; 112, © B.W. Hoffmann/Unicorn Stock Photos; 115, Granger Collection; 119, © Photo by John Chiasson/Liaison/Getty Images; 127, ©1995 Raymond/Contact Press Images; 131, © Richard T. Nowitz/Corbis; 141, © Michael Karlsson/911 Pictures; 145, AP/Wide World Photos; 152, © Spencer Grant/PhotoEdit; 155, © John Kuntz/Reuters/Getty Images; 164, © *New York Post*; 167, Photo by POOL/Philip Kamrass/Getty Images; 174 TL, © Bettmann/Corbis; 174 TR, © Shaun Stanley/*The Denver Post*; 174 ML, © 1998 Robin Nelson/Stockphoto.com; 174 MR, © Susan Goldman/The Image Works; 174 BL, © Mark Richards/PhotoEdit; 174 BR, © Syracuse Newspapers/Dick Blume/The Image Works; 177, AP/Wide World Photos; 180, © Erich Lessing/Art Resource, NY; 185, © Snark/Art Resource, NY; 187, Hulton/Archive by Getty Images; 191, Culver Pictures; 194, Berkeley Police Department, Historical Preservation Society; 203, Photofest; 206, © Michael Newman/PhotoEdit; 211, AP/Wide World Photos; 216, © 1998 Robin Nelson/Stockphoto.com; 217, © Mark Richards/PhotoEdit; 221, © Susan Goldman/The Image Works; 227, AP/Wide World Photos; 228, © Bettmann/Corbis; 235, © Michael Heller/911 Pictures; 238, © Jim Shaffer; 248, © Syracuse Newspapers/Dick Blume/The Image Works; 258, © Syracuse Newspapers/The Image Works; 262 TL, AP/Wide World Photos; 262 TR, Photo by Kenderson Studios/Courtesy of The Superior Court of Pennsylvania; 262 ML, AP/ Wide World Photos; 262 MR, © Jim Pickerell/Stock Boston; 262 BL, © Reuters NewMedia Inc./Corbis; 262 BR, © David Leeson/*Dallas Morning News*/The Image Works; 265, © Reuters NewMedia Inc./Corbis; 269, © Bettmann/Corbis; 275, AP/Wide World Photos; 277, North Wind Picture Archives; 280, Photo by Kenderson Studios/Courtesy of The Superior Court of Pennsylvania; 288, © TOPHAM/The Image Works; 297, "Stand Up and Speak Out," 7′ × 5′ × 10′ Bonded Bronze Installed at the Nassau University Medical Center on Long Island, NY. Sculptor Michael Alfano, Photo by Bob Zucker; 303, 311, AP/Wide World Photos; 317, © Jim Pickerell/Stock Boston; 322, AP/Wide World Photos; 333 BOTH, "True North" TV; 336, © Reuters NewMedia Inc./Corbis; 338, © Tony Savino/The Image Works; 348, AP/Wide World Photos; 355, © David Leeson/*Dallas Morning News*/The Image Works; 366 TL, The State Penitentiary for the Eastern District of Pennsylvania, 1855. Lithograph by P.S. Duval and Co., $8\frac{3}{4} \times 10\frac{7}{16}$. The Library Company of Philadelphia. Engraved by Samuel Cowperthwaite. Courtesy of Eastern State Penitentiary; 366 R, AP/Wide World Photos; 366 ML, © Michael Greenlar/Black Star Publishing/ PictureQuest; 366 MR, © Mikael Karlsson; 366 BL, © Jack Kurtz/The Image Works; 366 BR, AP/Wide World Photos; 369, © Jim O'Connell; 372, © Historical Picture Archive/Corbis; 377, The State Penitentiary for the Eastern District of Pennsylvania, 1855. Lithograph by P.S. Duval and Co., $8\frac{3}{4} \times 10\frac{7}{16}$. The Library Company of Philadelphia. Engraved by Samuel Cowperthwaite. Courtesy of Eastern State Penitentiary; 380, 390, AP/Wide World Photos; 391, © Stephen Ferry/Liaison/Getty Images; 395, © Michael Greenlar/Black Star Publishing/PictureQuest; 403, Freedom of Information/SCPD; 407, AP/Wide World Photos; 410, © Bill Aron/PhotoEdit; 418, 424, © Mikael Karlsson; 429, © AFP/Corbis; 431, © Ron Haviv/Corbis SABA; 438, © Jack Kurtz/The Image Works; 442, 448, AP/Wide World Photos; 458 TL, Photofest; 458 TR, AP/Wide World Photos; 458 ML, © Kevin Moloney/Liaison Agency/Getty Images; 458 MR, © 2000 Joseph Rodrigues/Stockphoto.com; 458 BL, © Sean Sayton/The Image Works; 458 BR, © Alex Wong/ Newsmakers/Getty Images; 461, Photofest; 465, AP/Wide World Photos; 468. © Kevin Moloney/Liaison Agency/Getty Images; 473, © 2000 Joseph Rodrigues/Stockphoto.com; 486, © Sean Sayton/The Image Works; 497, © Alex Wong/Newsmakers/Getty Images.